W9-DHU-406

Cities in World Perspective

Cities

in World Perspective

Ivan Light

Department of Sociology
University of California,
Los Angeles

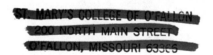
Macmillan Publishing Co., Inc.
NEW YORK

Collier Macmillan Publishers
LONDON

Macmillan Publishing Co., Inc.
866 Third Avenue, New York, New York 10022

Collier Macmillan Canada, Inc.

Library of Congress Cataloging in Publication Data

Light, Ivan Hubert.
  Cities in world perspective.

  Lectures accompanied by slides to further explain
and elaborate points in the book are available from
the author.
  Includes bibliographies and index.
  1. Sociology, Urban. 2. Cities and towns.
3. Urbanization. I. Title.
HT111.L53   307.7'64   82-15288
ISBN 0-02-370680-5   AACR2

Printing: 1 2 3 4 5 6 7 8   Year: 3 4 5 6 7 8 9 0

ISBN   02-370680-5

To Matthew and Nathaniel
in hope of a peaceful future
for all the world's children

Preface

Urbanization is the process of city-making and peopling. Urbanism is the way of life of city people. Taken together, urbanization and urbanism are the subject matter of urban sociology. *Cities in World Perspectives* provides an introduction to this interesting and international subject.

Just what belongs in a basic introduction is, to some extent, a matter of judgment, but the center of gravity of informed opinion has changed more rapidly in the last decade than in the previous four (Walton 1976: 302). In general, changes in the field of urban studies have favored historical, internationally comparative, institutional, and Marxist approaches, and these trends are reflected in this book (Zukin, 1980). These new research directions have produced illuminations compelling thoughtful and informed students of the subject to rethink basic problems. On the good side, this obtrusive critique has prompted a "resurgence of intense and challenging theoretical debate" in the field of urban sociology (Saunders, 1980: 13). In marked contrast to the somnolent orthodoxy that prevailed a decade ago, urban sociology currently struggles to restrain the fragmentation that arises from too much new thinking. The problem of integrating new materials is the raw aspect of intellectual breakthrough. In a historical sense, integration is impossible now, and must wait for solution upon the passage of time.

On the other hand, the effort to integrate, however halting, is the process by which urban sociology moves toward a new synthesis. People must have a big picture, but as Bendix has observed (1978: 15), there is a basic tension between the advance of knowledge—which depends upon specialization—and the integration of specialized results. The hazards and challenges of integration are so great

vii

that specialists shy away from the task. Under this circumstance, "the burden of integrating knowledge" falls upon the unfortunate student who, even if willing, has little assistance in or preparation for this immense task. "One must not expect of students what one is unwilling to undertake oneself," Bendix (1978: 15) justly concludes.

The outline of this book developed from lectures I have presented in twelve years of teaching urban sociology at the University of California, Los Angeles. In Parts One and Two urbanization is the dependent variable to be explained. In Parts Three, Four and Five, urbanization is basically treated as the cause of urbanism, the dependent variable. My students convinced me that this subject was much more interesting than the tedious textbooks I was compelled to assign. I hope this book will satisfy the tension between the requirements of professional objectivity on the one hand and timely, interesting, persuasive argumentation on the other. Naturally, this book has a point of view, and tends to endorse and encourage the new trends in urban sociology. However, the difficult problem is to rescue and retain the valuable insights of the old urban sociology while bringing together the best of the new. In both cases, wheat and chaff must be sifted. My intention is to provide a balanced treatment, reasoned in approach, that any professionally fluent person would agree was a fair effort to reduce a complex and immense subject to dimensions appropriate for an undergraduate course. Where I have failed, I am prepared to revise my thinking, and I welcome critical response.

Those who have helped most in preparing this book are the numerous graduate and undergraduate students who have debated and discussed these issues with me over more than one decade. I am especially indebted to Leslie Cohen, Terry Chang and Lina Chatterji. The workers at Central Word Processing slogged through drafts and revisions of these long chapters. The staff at the Honnold Library of the Claremont Colleges generously extended access to their library's resources. Nuffield College of Oxford University offered hospitality during a sabbatical leave.

The people of California most deserve recognition. When this book was being written over a period of several years, the people of California supported a public university in which *what* is taught was deemed as important as how it is taught. After all, there is no point in ably teaching falsehoods, but the discrimination of true and false requires much freedom for faculty to pursue research interests. This freedom is expensive, and the people of California picked up the bill. In my opinion, it is in the long-range best interest of the people that the state's university pursue truth with vigor, and I devoutly hope that the people will not listen to those who contend the state should cut truth out of the university's budget.

Writing a book of this length imposes a great strain on one's family life because the temptation is always to cut back on what is owed the family. My lovely wife, Leah, never let me forget that such chiseling is unfair, unpleasant, and unproductive. Nathaniel and Matthew ably seconded her view, thus helping me to pursue the kind of balanced existence that reconciles the claims of working, living, and loving.

Los Angeles, California   I. L.

REFERENCES

Bendix, Reinhard. 1978. *Kings and People*. Berkeley and Los Angeles: University of California.

Saunders, Peter. 1980. *Urban Politics*. London: Hutchinson University.

Walton, John. 1976. "Political Economy of World Urban Systems," pp. 301–313 in John Walton and Louis H. Masotti, eds. *The City in Comparative Perspective*. New York: Wiley.

Zukin, Sharon. 1980. "A Decade of the New Urban Sociology." *Theory and Society* 9: 575–601.

Illustrated Slide Lectures

The author has compiled slide-acquainted lectures corresponding to some chapters in this book. Each slide lecture contains spoken text and about 40 numbered slides corresponding to text. The one-hour slide lectures illustrate, explain, and elaborate basic points made in each chapter.

For current availability and price list, please write to: Professor Ivan Light, Department of Sociology, University of California, 405 Hilgard Avenue, Los Angeles, Cal. 90024 USA.

Contents

WORLD URBANISM

Part Four   Communities

Part Five   Political Economy

PART ONE

Preindustrial Cities

World
Urbanization

CHAPTER 1

Origins of City Life

The world's urban history falls into three epochs of unequal length: preurban, preindustrial urban, and industrial urban. In the lengthy preurban period, no one was urban and there were no cities. In the preindustrial urban epoch, less than 3 percent of the world's population was urban. In the industrial urban epoch, the percentage of people living in cities increased rapidly and so did the number of cities. Figure 1-1 compares estimates of the world's total population since 10,000 B.C. with estimates of the urban component of total population. The longest epoch of world history was the preurban. This epoch began when humankind was evolutionarily complete, around 50,000 B.C. It ended in approximately 4000 B.C., when the first cities appeared in southern Mesopotamia, a riverine region in modern Iraq. The preurban period, therefore, encompassed the first 46,000 years of human history.

The next epoch is the preindustrial urban. This epoch begins in 4000 B.C. with the creation of the world's first cities. It ends in A.D. 1750 with the Industrial Revolution in Europe. In this 5,700-year epoch cities existed, a few were even large, but only a tiny minority of the world's population resided in them. In 4000 B.C., of course, no one resided in cities because cities were just on the brink of appearing. By 1800, Durand (1967: 137) has estimated, only 3 percent of the world's people were urban. The world's total population increased from about 60 to 978 million in this period, and the urban population increased from nothing to approximately 29 million. Although the absolute growth of the world's population was much larger than the absolute growth of cities, the rate of growth of cities was much more rapid than the rate of growth of world population. Nonetheless, the rate of change was leisurely.

3

WORLD POPULATION GROWTH

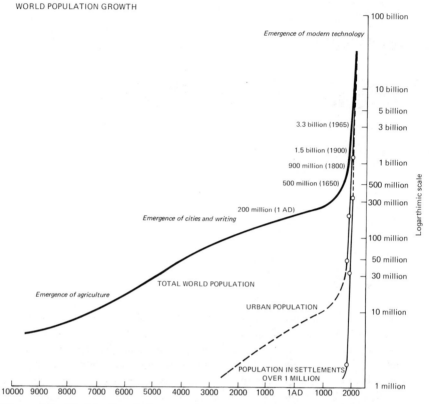

Figure 1-1. World Populations and Urban Component since 10,000 B.C. (Source: The Regional Plan Association. *The Region's Growth.* New York: The Regional Plan Association, 1967, p. 13. Reproduced by permission.)

This period of leisurely change ended around A.D. 1750. Thereafter, both world population and urban population displayed wildly accelerated rates of growth. Figure 1-1 shows graphically how rapid was this acceleration after 1750. This rapid acceleration of growth rate indicates that something occurred around 1750 to liberate a potential for growth that had been suppressed in the previous 5,700 years. What occurred was, of course, the Industrial Revolution. As Figure 1-1 makes clear, there was ten times more growth in world population and its urban component in the 180 years between 1800 and 1980 than in the preceding 5,700-year period. Because its consequences were so massive and abrupt, Finley (1977: 308) discerns an "unbridgeable divide in the history of cities created by the Industrial Revolution." This divide justifies a firm distinction between the very short industrial urban epoch and the 5,700-year-old preindustrial urban epoch that preceded it.

There are points of continuity between epochs as well as abrupt contrasts. One is continuation of the earlier tendency for the world's urban population to close the gap with total population. From 1800 to 1970 the urban component of world population had risen from 3 percent to 37 percent, even though the world's population was growing wildly in this period. Obviously, the gap between world population and its urban component could only be narrowed because, rapid as was the growth of world population, the world's urban population was growing even more rapidly. This point underscores a result of the Industrial Revolution. It caused world population to explode but caused an even wilder explosion of the urban component. The age of mass urbanism that the world is still entering began with and was made possible by the Industrial Revolution.

LIMITATIONS OF THE EVIDENCE

Some skepticism about these estimates (Figure 1-1) is in order. After all, these dates, numbers, and percentages depend upon fragmented evidence that yields estimates only when simplifying assumptions are made. To overcome this uncertainty, Durand (1974: 12) calculated "indifference ranges," boundaries within which there is no valid basis for choosing between high and low estimates of world population. The indifference ranges (Figure 1-2) narrow and disappear as we move from antiquity to modernity, reflecting improved record-keeping. In principle, indifference ranges could be calculated for the urban component of world population too. However, this subject has received less scholarly attention than has world population. As a result, present data do not permit indifference ranges. This shortcoming matters little in the modern period when indifference ranges are narrow because reliable statistics exist. But in antiquity urban data are weak. All that can be asserted with confidence is that no cities existed prior to about 4000 B.C. and that approximately 29 million persons were urban in A.D. 1800. The line between 4000 B.C. and A.D. 1800 is conjectural.

Figure 1-3 shows the percentage of total world population residing in the world's forty largest cities between 1 B.C. and A.D. 1900. This chart understates world urbanization because it counts only the forty largest cities. Still, the shape of the visible figure presumably reflects the true curve of world urbanization. The figure shows that the percentage of world population residing in the forty largest cities increased hardly at all between 1 B.C. and A.D. 1000. Then the percentage declined and regained the level of 1 B.C. only in A.D. 1550. The level of A.D. 1000 (1.4 percent) was regained only in 1750, a gap of 750 years. After A.D. 1750 the percentage abruptly increased, gaining more in the period 1750-

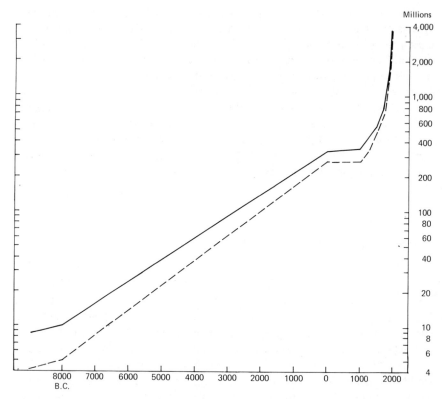

Figure 1-2. Indifferences Ranges of World Population Estimates since 8,000 B.C. (Source: John D. Durand. *Historical Estimates of World Population: An Evaluation.* Philadelphia: Population Studies Center of the University of Pennsylvania, 1974, p. 62. Reproduced by permission.)

1800 than in the entire preceding 1,750-year period. By 1900 nearly 3 percent of the world's population resided in the forty largest cities.

Another difficulty is deciding who is urban. In the modern world, this problem arises because statistical definitions of who is urban vary widely from country to country. According to the United States Bureau of the Census, anyone who resides in a place of 2,500 or more inhabitants is urban. All others are rural. Yugoslavia's criterion is 15,000; India uses 5,000 (United Nations 1980: xix). It is not obvious which criterion is preferable, but the choice affects the number of urban people who will be counted. If the United States employed India's criterion, fewer Americans would be classified as urban, and fewer places would qualify as cities. But even if statistical standardization were achieved, many difficulties would remain because of international discrepancies in economic activity. In India most people are peasant farmers who reside in agricultural villages from which they journey daily to their fields. In the United States farm-

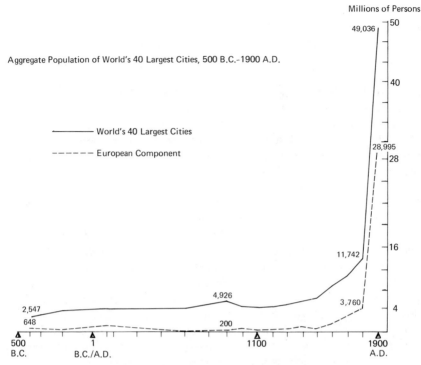

Figure 1-3. Aggregate Population of World's 40 Largest Cities, 1 B.C. to 1900 A.D. as Percentage of World Population with European Component. (Source: Tertius Chandler letter to author.)

ers are few and live in detached houses amid their fields, not in agricultural villages. Therefore, if the United States Census definition of a city were applied to India, agricultural villages would be classified as cities, exaggerating the number of city people in India. But if India's high criterion were applied to the United States, the number of urban people in the United States would be unjustifiably reduced because of the exclusion of nonagricultural workers residing in small towns.

In the ancient world statistical disparities are not an issue. Instead, scholars estimate the urban population of each place on the basis of fragmentary evidence. For example, archaeologists measure the area of a ruin and, by estimating density of settlement, estimate the probable population of the site (Chandler and Fox 1974: 3-4) [1]. Since true cities were few and agricultural villages many, determining how many people were urban in some ancient society requires the imposition of tests to distinguish villages from cities. Moreover, agricultural villages appeared in every world region long before true cities. Therefore, to date the first city in a region one must exclude agricultural villages. The more liberal the test, the earlier one can find evidence of city life.

What is a city? Sjoberg (1965: 56) called it "a community of substantial size and population density that shelters a variety of nonagricultural specialists, including a literate elite." No single test yields an unambiguous determination of whether an archaeological site was a village or a city. Therefore, scholars have long employed what Wheatley (1972) calls "trait complexes" to make the determination. These are criteria all or some of which must be met before a place can be accepted as a city and its inhabitants as urban. Hammond (1972: 7–8) has provided a three-trait list [2]. First, he defines a city as "a community whose members live in close proximity under a single government and in a unified complex of buildings often surrounded by a wall." Archaeological and historical evidence can indicate whether a site met this criterion, but this criterion alone would not exclude large villages, military camps, and monasteries. Therefore, Hammond imposes a second test. A city is also a community wherein "a considerable number" of inhabitants pursue "nonrural occupations" within the built-up area. This second test excludes large villages whose people engage in agriculture, which they conduct outside the built-up area. However, the second test does not exclude a monastery or small factory so Hammond declares a city is also a community that extends its religious, political, and economic influence over a territory much wider than that required for mere self-sufficiency. When historical or archaeological evidence indicates an ancient community satisfied each of these three tests, we may reliably declare that a city existed there.

As these remarks suggest, the measurement of world city population is rough. Even in the modern period, it is possible to argue that estimates of world or regional urbanization are too high or too low, depending upon one's definition of urbanization and methodological assessments of research. In the premodern world, problems are tougher. The estimated date and size of ancient cities and villages has, therefore, slid back and forth, depending upon the state of evidence and prevailing interpretations of that evidence (Mellaart 1979). The origin of cities in Mesopotamia may have been as early as 5000 B.C. or as late as 3500 B.C., and 4000 B.C. is only a likelihood. The population of Rome in the first century A.D. may have been as large as two million or as small as 300,000 (Anderson 1978: 78).

These uncertainties do not shake the distinction between preurban, preindustrial urban, and industrial urban epochs. When and where the preurban period ended is uncertain, but end it did, and it ended first in southern Mesopotamia [3]. Similarly, the dates and profile of the preindustrial urban epoch are vague. Nonetheless, there is firm ground for believing a preindustrial urban epoch of several millennia did intervene between the development of cities and the Industrial Revolution. The Industrial Revolution did cause a tremendous acceleration in urban population growth and may for this reason be regarded as a watershed separating the preindustrial urban epoch from what occurred since then. In this sense, the tripartite division of world urban history is clear even though details are blurred.

THE COURSE OF WORLD URBANIZATION

Urbanization is measured by the percentage of people who are urban in a society, a region, or the world. Urbanization, therefore, summarizes the relationship between total population and its urban component, as illustrated in Figure 1-1. This figure gives the impression that the course of world urbanization has been unreversed, unilinear, and continuous since 4000 B.C. [4]. Every year the proportion that is urban appears to have increased slightly over the previous year, and the rate of increase accelerated after the Industrial Revolution. Broadly speaking, this impression is correct, but this generalization conceals the roller-coaster manner in which this basically upward trend proceeded in the preindustrial epoch (4000 B.C.-A.D. 1750).

In the preindustrial epoch, the fortunes of world and regional urbanization rose and fell in response to political conditions. When empires grew, cities within them grew in number, population, and opulence. [5]. When empires crumbled, the number, size, and opulence of their cities also declined (Davis 1973: 17). A familiar illustration is the abrupt recession of urbanization in the territories of the western Roman Empire after the barbarian invasions of the fourth through sixth centuries A.D. Taagepera (1979) has charted the land area of the world's great empires of antiquity (Figure 1-4). His results visually display the political roller coaster to which urbanization was hitched in the preindustrial epoch.

The case histories of Alexandria, Mexico City, Baghdad, and Peking illustrate the roller-coaster effect (Table 1-1). The close connection of urbanization and political power produced a roller-coaster effect on regional urbanization in antiquity, and ancient historians were fully aware of the effect and its causes (Sjoberg 1963; Schaedel 1978: 33).

Of course, recession of urbanization in a region did not require recession of world urbanization. However, the basis of world urbanization was sufficiently slender that the abrupt recession of urbanization in any region could reduce the world's level. The roller-coaster rhythm was by no means missing at the world level, although a gentler ride probably prevailed. On the other hand, there was an overall gentle increase in world urbanization over the course of this 5,700-year epoch. The trends and reversals are apparent in Table 1-2, which shows the absolute population of the world's biggest city and the median population of the world's twenty largest cities for a sequence of dates between 1360 B.C. and A.D. 1975. Reversals occurred when population sizes decreased between successive dates. Thus, the population of Rome, the world's largest city in A.D. 100, was not matched again until A.D. 622 when Constantinople reported as large a population. Similarly, the median population of the world's twenty largest cities

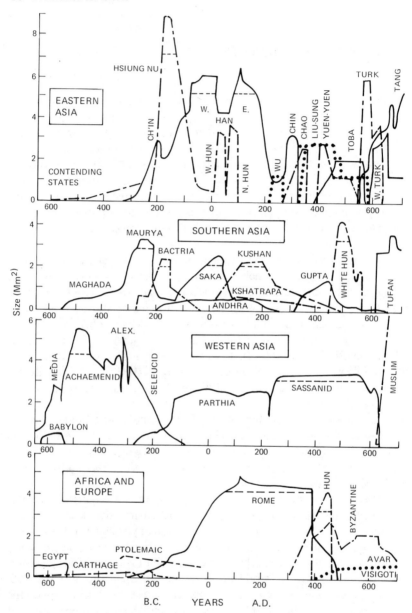

Figure 1-4. Growth/Decline Curves of Empires, 600 B.C. to 700 A.D. The curves measure the physical area of political empires in millions of square kilometers. (Source: Rein Taagepera. "Size and Duration of Empires: Systematics of Size." *Social Science Research* 7 (1978): 118. Reproduced by permission.)

Table 1-1. Population History of Selected Capitals of Preindustrial Epoch

Location	Population	Comment
Rome		
A.D. 100	650,000	World's largest city
600–800	50,000	Barbarian invasions
900	40,000	
1000	35,000	
1377	17,000	Pope returned from exile
1400	33,000	
1500	35,000	
1600	109,000	
Alexandria		
730	216,000	Sixth largest in world
860	100,000	After several sieges
1365		plundered by Cypriotes
1400	40,000	
1634		"Heap of ruins"
Mexico City		
1500	80,000	Spanish conquest begins
1524	30,000	After destruction by Spaniards
1600	75,000	Rebuilt
Baghdad		
765	480,000	Caliphate established A.D. 750
932	1,100,000	World's largest city
		Declining power of Caliphate
1000	125,000	Tenth largest in world
1258		Sacked by Mongols
c. 1400	90,000	Tamerlane attacks; city sacked in 1401
1638	30,000	
Peking		
1200	150,000	
1264		Capital of China
1270	401,000	
1368		Capital moved
1400	320,000	
1409		Capital returned
1492	669,000	World's largest city

Source: Tertius Chandler and Gerald Fox, *Three Thousand Years of Urban Growth* (New York: Academic Press, 1974), pp. 83–299. Reproduced by permission.

declined between A.D. 1200 and A.D. 1400, and between A.D. 100 and A.D. 800. These two periods are, however, the only reversals of the overall upward movement of median population between A.D. 100 and A.D. 1975. In 1750, the median size of the world's twenty largest cities was ten times greater than the median population size in 1360 B.C. This substantial difference signals a gradual increase with but few reverses.

Table 1-2.   World's Largest Cities, 1360 B.C. to A.D. 2000

	City	Present-day Location	Estimated Population	Median Population Largest 20 Cities
1360 B.C.	Thebes	Egypt	100,000	30,000
1200 B.C.	Memphis	Egypt	50,000+	25,000
650 B.C.	Nineveh	Iraq	120,000	45,000
430 B.C.	Babylon	Iran	200,000	75,000
200 B.C.	Patna	India	400,000	80,000
A.D. 100	Rome	Italy	500,000	85,000
A.D. 361	Constantinople	Turkey	300,000	80,000
A.D. 622	Constantinople	Turkey	500,000	72,000
A.D. 800	Changan	China	700,000	100,000
A.D. 900	Baghdad	Iraq	900,000	100,000
A.D. 1000	Cordova	Spain	450,000	100,000
A.D. 1100	Kaifeng	China	442,000	125,000
A.D. 1200	Hangchow	China	255,000	150,000
A.D. 1300	Hangchow	China	432,000	110,000
A.D. 1400	Nanking	China	487,000	150,000
A.D. 1500	Peking	China	672,000	153,000
A.D. 1600	Peking	China	706,000	224,000
A.D. 1750	Peking	China	900,000	310,000
A.D. 1800	Peking	China	1,100,000	373,000
A.D. 1850	London	Great Britain	2,320,000	446,000
A.D. 1875	London	Great Britain	4,241,000	718,000
A.D. 1900	London	Great Britain	6,480,000	1,418,000
A.D. 1925	New York	United States	7,774,000	2,085,000
A.D. 1950	New York	United States	12,300,000	4,800,000
A.D. 1975	New York	United States	19,800,000	8,498,000
A.D. 2000	Mexico City	Mexico	23,400,000	16,600,000

Source: Tertius Chandler, March 1980 (personal communication with author); and United Nations, Department of Economic and Social Affairs, Population Studies, No. 68. *Patterns of Urban and Rural Population Growth.* [Sales No. E.79.xiii.9] (New York: United Nations, 1980), Table 23, p. 58.

THE PREURBAN EPOCH, 50,000 B.C.–4000 B.C.

The preurban epoch has two natural boundaries. The earlier (ca. 50,000 B.C.) marks the appearance of "the modern physical type of man," the culmination of evolutionary descent (Braidwood 1972b: 71–73). The later boundary is the world's first city, whose appearance brings to an end the preurban period. This first city grew up in Mesopotamia near the confluence of the Tigris and Euphrates rivers. Other regions followed (Table 1-3). Egypt, the Indus Valley, the Near East, Greece, and Italy were in communication with one another, so the probability of cultural diffusion exists. Urban life in China and Central America apparently developed independently of foreign influences (Sjoberg 1960: 26). Urbanization in these two isolated regions suggests that "emergence of the city is a natural stage in the development of any human society, given the proper conditions of environment, economy, and culture" (Hammond 1972: 9). Where urban diffusion was possible, in the other cases, the issue of cultural borrowing or independent invention is harder to resolve. Recent excavations at Mehrgarh on the Bolan River of North Pakistan have, however, undermined the diffusionist argument. Previous research had failed to find evidence of settled agriculture in the region, thus strengthening the belief that Indus urbanization developed by cultural diffusion from earlier centers. However, Merhgarh excavations have now offered "proof of the existence" of agriculture settlements in the vicinity of Indus approximately 3,000 years before the founding of Mohenjo-Daro and Harappa, oldest cities of the Indus (Jarrige and Meadow 1980: 130).

In the long preurban period we distinguish two subperiods. In the first (50,000 B.C. until 7000 B.C.), the human population of the world engaged exclusively in hunting and gathering for subsistence. This period ended in the Neolithic or Agricultural Revolution. The Agricultural Revolution began in southwest Asia. The major archaeological sites were located in Turkey, Iraq, and Israel. Braidwood (1972a) declares that the evidence that food production and village life began here is "overwhelming." The most fully explored agricultural village of the early period is Jarmo, Iraq, which probably dates from the first half of the seventh millennium B.C. This site consists of about twenty-five small houses of packed mud that had been sun-dried. The farmers continued to hunt, and animal bones indicate hunting contributed about 5 percent of their diet. For the rest of their food, Jarmo villagers depended upon cereal grain cultivation and herding goats and sheep.

The Agricultural Revolution in Mesopotamia refers to a sedentary culture of cereal grains (Clark 1977: 46). Cereal grains were capable of protracted storage

Table 1-3. World's Earliest Cities, by Region and Approximate Date

Region	Location	Approximate Date of Earliest City
Mesopotamia	Tigris and Euphrates rivers	3500 B.C.
Egypt	Nile River	3200 B.C.
Pakistan	Indus River	2400 B.C.
Aegean	Crete	1600 B.C.
China	Yellow River	1600 B.C.
Mexico	Yucatan Peninsula	200 B.C.

Source: Adapted from Gideon Sjoberg, "The Origin and Evolution of Cities," in Kinglsey Davis, ed., *Cities: Their Origin, Growth, and Human Impact* (San Francisco: W. H. Freeman, 1973), pp. 20–21.

and were what Pharaoh loaded into the storehouses of Egypt when Joseph's interpretation of his dream indicated a time of famine to come (*Genesis* 41: 2–36). Prior to about the seventh millennium B.C. no peoples of the world were engaged in sedentary culture of cereal grains (Clark 1977: 19). After this date, increasing numbers of people adopted agriculture for their principal livelihood and abandoned hunting and gathering, their previous livelihood (Lenski 1974: 100). Today a majority of the world's people still engage in agriculture for their principal livelihood, but in inaccessible jungles dwindling tribes still depend upon hunting, fishing, and gathering wild berries and roots.

What did people do for subsistence before the Agricultural Revolution? Most were hunters and gatherers, but some were horticulturalists (Lenski 1976: 559). Horticulture involves maintaining a garden, chiefly root crops, to supplement a food supply derived partially from hunting and gathering (Ho 1975: 43). Horticulture precedes sedentary agriculture in human history. It represents a mixture of food production and hunting/gathering and is semi-nomadic. True hunters and gatherers, the bulk of the world's population in the seventh millennium B.C., lived in caves or mobile shelters and were "obliged to spend almost all their time in the quest for food; they hunted, fished, and gathered a few edible wild plants" (Braidwood 1972a: 70). The aboriginal inhabitants of North America were chiefly hunters and gatherers, although some were fishing specialists and others horticulturalists (Clark 1977: 40). The Indians' economic activities were hunting game, fishing, gathering natural materials (nuts, plants, fibers), and herding. When game moved away, tribes had to move after it. Aboriginal dependence upon nature's bounty necessitated a migratory existence.

Migratory tribes did not create cities. One reason was the migratory life-style that hunting and gathering demanded (Clark 1977: 19). Another reason was the incompatibility between the massing of population and hunting/gathering. Hunting and gathering require low population density to reduce the burden of population on natural resources. Whenever human populations increased relative to available game (or whenever game declined), hunting grounds became overcrowded and hunting parties returned empty-handed. Migration from the territory then restored a lower population density, relieving the pressure on resources. A disastrous dislocation of precisely this sort occurred during the settlement of the Great Plains of North America. Europeans killed the buffalo, thereby depriving the Plains Indians of their food and compelling them to turn to new economic activities such as pottery and tourism. These ecological issues still affect people. Any resident of New York City is free to hunt and gather for a living, but the effort to do so will convince skeptics that settlement at high population density is incompatible with hunting and gathering.

Similar objections govern the incompatibility of settled agriculture and hunting/gathering. True, primitive agricultural peoples have supplemented their diet with game (Flannery 1972: 24). Domestication of plants and animals actually began as early as 12,000 B.C. in Mesopotamia. However, horticulturalists "merely supplemented" hunting and gathering, "the main activity" (Davis 1973: 12). Nomadic hunters and gatherers cannot coexist in the same territory with wholly agricultural people. For one thing, agriculturalists fence the land. Additionally, they clear the land of timber and vegetation, thus driving away the game and eliminating easily gathered vegetable resources. Finally, agriculture permits a much higher density of human settlement than is desirable for hunters and gatherers. For example, African pygmies require eight square kilometers of jungle per individual to subsist by hunting and gathering. Australian bushmen need thirty square kilometers. Eskimo must have 300 square kilometers of frozen land per individual. Augmented population creates a scarcity of resources within which it is no longer possible to live only by hunting or gathering. Therefore, the initiation of agriculture in a region compels nomadic peoples to migrate or change their life-style. Agriculture is capable of supporting much larger populations than can survive on the basis of hunting and gathering (Childe 1950: 4-8). In the territory of France, no more than 50,000 humans lived by hunting and gathering in the Paleolithic era. Agriculture permitted France to support 5 million, a one-hundredfold increase in density of population (Reinhard et al. 1968: 15). Industrial France now supports 55 million people.

Why did hunting and gathering societies become agricultural? The answer is controversial (Meyers 1971). Childe's (1957: 15-26) explanation emphasized climatic changes in the Near East at the end of the Pleistocene era. According to this view, desiccation reduced the supply of game and wild grasses, thus compelling ancient people to develop a "food-processing economy." Subsequent research has indicated that Childe's environmental explanation was too simple. First, equally dramatic climatic changes had occurred before without triggering a food-producing revolution. Second, "climate did not change radically where farming began in the hills that flank the fertile crescent" (Braidwood 1972b: 74). Finally, the Agricultural Revolution was, in Braidwood's view, a predictable culmination of "cultural differentiation and specialization of human communities." Therefore, no external climatic change is necessary to explain it.

Archaeologists agree population increase could have compelled early hunters and gatherers to farm. Indeed, an abrupt population increase would have had the same disastrous impact on the adequacy of food supply as had climatic desiccation. By 10,000 B.C., humans had occupied "virtually every major land mass in the world," so migration no longer served, as previously, to keep human densities low (Flannery, 1972: 283). Human life expectancies were increasing throughout prehistory (Table 1-4). Coupled with the equalization of population densities on the world's land masses, gradual population increase suggests mounting pressure on the food supply available by hunting and gathering. Flannery (1972) finds evidence in the ancient Near East of food shortages resulting from changes in the physical environment as well as increasing density of population.

Table 1-4. Mortality in Prehistory and Antiquity (age at death percentages)

	0-14	14-20	21-40	41-60	60 or older	Total
Neanderthal Man (20 skeletons)	40	15	40	5	0	100
Paleolithic (102 skeletons)	24.5	9.8	53.9	11.8	0	100
Mesolithic (65 skeletons)	30.8	6.2	58.5	3	1.5	100
Austrian Bronze Age (273 skeletons)	7.9	17.2	39.9	28.6	7.3	100
Egypt, Roman Epoch (141 skeletons)	17	17	39.7	16.3	13.4	100

Source: Henri V. Vallois, "La Durée de la Vie Chez L'Homme Fossile." *L'Anthropologie* 47(1937): 529. On this subject, see also Reinhard, et al. 1968: 18 ff.

Population density and climatic change affected the ancient Near East, but they do not explain the change from hunting and gathering to agriculture. Population density was high, but it was not the highest in the world; the climate was favorable, but not the most favorable in the world (Flannery 1972: 283). Why, then, should the Near East have been the site of earliest agriculture? Cultural attitudes of the people might explain the transition as Braidwood has argued, but these are most difficult to assess because religious beliefs of preurban peoples remain unknown. El Juyo Cave in Northern Spain contains the world's oldest religious artifacts: half man—half animal statuettes left in the cave 14,000 years ago. The statuettes were placed in the cave long before agriculture was practiced in Spain, but anthropologists do not know what were the rites or beliefs of those ancient people who sealed the cave (Dembart 1981). However, we know contemporary hunting and gathering societies have religious beliefs and cultural attitudes unfavorable toward settled agriculture. For example, the religions and cultural attitudes of North American Indians stress their dependence upon the natural environment. One may properly interpret this religion as a protoscientific understanding of ecological relationships, as well as an evaluational preference for their hunting and gathering way of life. Presumably ancient peoples also preferred hunting and gathering to agriculture and resisted agriculture for this reason.

Even so, many archaeologists suppose that agriculture was an undesired alternative toward which early societies needed to be driven by adverse circumstances. Hunters and gatherers had modest needs. To satisfy them, they did not have to work hard (Sahlins 1968: 79). Indeed, the life of primitives was, in many respects, a soft one by contemporary standards (Wilkinson 1973). Renfrew (1973: 114) concludes that only the pressure of the population on food resources could have generated the "incentive to work harder" to produce food. Flannery (1972: 307) also points out that farming is harder work than hunting and gathering. Moreover, farmers eat less meat and more cereals and grains. Why should ancient humans wish to work harder for cereal foods if tasty game was easily acquired? Presumably, "people did it because they felt they *had* to, not because they *wanted* to" (Flannery, 1972: 308).

THE URBAN REVOLUTION, 4000 B.C.

The Ubaid culture in southern Mesopotamia introduced the first farming settlements, but this culture never advanced beyond the village level to full cityhood. Approximately one thousand years after the initial development of Ubaid agricultural settlements, the first cities appeared one hundred miles northward in the early Uruk culture, ca 3950 B.C. (Childe 1957: 122). Childe (1950) called this event the Urban Revolution and rated it equal in importance to the earlier Agricultural Revolution. A generation later, Childe's view persists: "Childe seems fully justified in speaking of an urban revolution" (Hammond 1972: 31). The revolutionary innovation consisted in the scale, area, and social complexity of Uruk settlements. All three were appreciably bigger than Ubaid farming settlements. Ur occupied 220 acres and housed a population of 5,000. Erech covered two square miles on which resided 25,000 persons (Davis 1955: 430-431). The Uruk cities also contained a temple, their central building, and temple priests were numerous. The cities also contained "specialist craftsmen" such as smiths, carpenters, sculptors, leather workers, and potters. These workers and priests were "supported by the products of fishing, farming, and hunting" but did not themselves engage in these activities (Childe 1957: 128). Some inhabitants of Uruk cities continued to engage wholly or partially in agriculture or hunting. However, wholly nonagricultural occupations are a distinguishing feature of true cityhood and were first attained in the Uruk period in Sumer.

Why did an Urban Revolution occur at all, and why in Sumer? Surplus theory has offered the orthodox solution to both questions (Mosley and Wallerstein 1978). According to this theory, the initial creation of any cities depended upon prior availability of an agricultural surplus. This surplus was a necessary prerequisite of urbanization because only an agricultural surplus permitted a society to support nonagricultural workers, that is, city people. Sumer was the first place to have an agricultural surplus (Braidwood 1972b: 79).

Agricultural surplus arises when agricultural workers produce enough food (and raw materials) to support more people than themselves and their dependents. Table 1-5 distinguishes between society's food producers and food con-

Table 1-5. The Agricultural Surplus

Type of Society	Agricultural Workers	Agricultural Product Feeds	Surplus	Cities
No-surplus society	100	100	0	None
Small-surplus society	99	100	1	A few small ones
Big-surplus society	5	100	95	Many big ones

sumers at three levels of technical efficiency in agriculture. At the no-surplus level, the full-time work of 100 agricultural producers is necessary to support the 100 producers and their dependents. When a small but reliable surplus exists, the labor of 99 agricultural producers creates enough food to support 100 consumers. A small agricultural surplus now exists. This small surplus opens the possibility for one person in every 100 to find employment outside of agriculture. Most people must still work in agriculture, but a minority need not. Since nonagricultural employment is closely related to urban residence, a small-surplus society has the technical ability to support an urban minority whereas the no-surplus society does not. For example, a small-surplus society of 1,000,000 agricultural workers would have the capability to support 10,000 city people at this level of agricultural efficiency. Of course a bigger surplus makes possible a higher proportion of city people. In the United States today, agriculture is so efficient that less than 5 percent of the national work force is engaged in this industry. Yet this minority produces more than enough food to support the remaining 95 percent, of whom roughly three quarters are urban.

Surplus theory emphasizes the importance of technical improvements during the preurban period. Early agricultural workers, it is argued, lacked the knowledge and tools (technology) to produce a food surplus. With the passage of time, agricultural technology improved and therewith a food surplus first appeared, then grew in size. Among the technical prerequisites of urban civilization, Davis (1955: 430) lists the ox-drawn plow, the wheeled cart, sailboats, metallurgy, irrigation, and domestication of plants and animals. Childe (1950) includes writing and accounting among the technological prerequisites of urbanism. Sumer was able to satisfy all these technological prerequisites of urban life. "By about 4000 B.C., the people of southern Mesopotamia achieved such increases in [agricultural] productivity that their farms were beginning to support an urban civilization" (Braidwood 1972b: 79). As other world regions passed this threshold of technological efficiency in agriculture, they too developed cities. Therefore, the Agricultural Revolution of 7000 B.C. was a necessary prerequisite for the Urban Revolution of 4000 B.C.

COLLECTING, TRANSPORTING, AND
DISTRIBUTING THE SURPLUS

Even given the technical means for reliably producing a food surplus, urbanization could not proceed without an agency to collect the surplus and distribute it to city people. After all, the food surplus waits on the scattered landholdings that produced each tiny portion. Only the collection of these scattered small surpluses made it possible to support city people. The necessity for collecting, transporting, and redistributing the food surplus implies the prior existence of regional social organization capable of making these coordinated arrangements.

The collector and distributor of the food surplus was the ancient state, usually a monarchy. However, the earliest cities of Mesopotamia were city-states ruled by priests; only later were they consolidated into a monarchy. The existence of a collector state still leaves unanswered the issue of why this collection should have been deemed desirable at all. True, the food surplus had to be collected to support urbanization, but why urbanize? Answer: the city was the seat of the ancient state. Hence, collection, transport, and distribution of the food surplus supported the state's personnel: monarch, priests, warriors, employees, and slaves. The existence of the state, therefore, required cities, and cities required the food surplus.

The origin of the state is a basic problem that remains controversial (Wright 1977). Service (1978: 21) has distinguished conflict and integrative theories. Conflict theories explain the origin of the state from the need of privileged groups to repress the unprivileged. The state performs this coercive service. In older Marxist formulations, the privileged group was thought to be an indigenous ruling class or alien conquerors. More recently, Fried (1978; see also Adams 1966: Ch. 3) has stressed a stratification of kinship groups with privileged clans obtaining control of the state. In any conflict formulation, however, social inequality precedes the formation of the state and the state, in turn, precedes the creation of cities. The temporal priority of social stratification or state remains controversial (Cohen 1978: 7), but the temporal priority of the state to cities is universal. Some ancient civilizations lacked cities and others (notably Egypt; see Kemp 1977) had states long before cities, but cities never existed prior to agriculture or political states.

Integrative theories of state formation stress the benefits that the state conferred. Military security is the most obvious. Barbarians lurked on the borders of agricultural societies, forming a continuous military threat (Service 1978: 29). As late as 550 B.C., Aristotle (1946: Ch. 7) divided peoples into pastoral nomads (barbarians), agriculturalists, and those who combined the two. Aristotle described the nomads as inhabiting territories bordering Greece and also constituting a military threat to Greece. The Roman Empire also represented a civilized, urbanized core of agricultural peoples confronting nomadic barbarians at their borders. This was also true of the Chinese empire that erected the Great Wall (ca. 250 B.C.) to protect itself against barbarian nomads. A startling illustration of the same situation is the invasion of Palestine by nomadic Hebrews in the twelfth century B.C. (Turner 1941: 3321–3332). Under the command of Joshua, Hebrews captured the cities of Palestine, notably Jericho, and slew or enslaved the inhabitants. But the Bible records that the war was hard to win because the defenders fought from "chariots of iron" and the invaders did not have such sophisticated weapons.

Carneiro (1970, 1978) has proposed that ancient states arose in regions whose fertile lands were surrounded by infertile ones. Under this circumstance, the growth of population in the fertile zone increased intergroup competition for access to arable lands, ultimately precipitating warfare and defeat of one party. Since the losers could not move away, the vanquished remained in place as a lower class. To retain supremacy, the winners needed a state to repress the vanquished. This explanation resembles a conflict explanation in its emphasis upon stratification and repression. However, in Carneiro's formulation the state is really rationing access to limited resources, and those who endure slavery do so because their alternative (starving in the desert) is even worse.

Another integrative theory is Wittfogel's (1957) explanation of Asiatic despotism [6]. According to Wittfogel, agriculture in Asia required irrigation. This necessity compelled agricultural people to finance a powerful, despotic state capable of carrying out irrigation projects. Wittfogel's theory is plausible, but evidence does not support it. Ho (1975: 46) has shown that cereal grains cultivation in China antedated irrigation by many centuries. Growing rice "does not depend on irrigation." Therefore, Ho (1975: 48) concludes, "the theory of the 'hydraulic' genesis of culture or of 'despotism' is completely groundless." In Mesopotamia Adams (1966: 76) finds irrigation requirements did not create the state. Reviewing these issues, Bailey and Llobera (1979: 557) concede that "comparative results of empirical research" indicate large-scale irrigation was not necessarily prior to a centralized state as Wittfogel had supposed. Nonetheless, Adams (1966: 139) agrees that in Mesopotamia irrigation encouraged city growth by "engendering inequalities in access to productive land" and thus promoting a "warlike atmosphere" conducive to state centralization. Childe (1957: 140) also supposes that the social function of Sumerian religion was to assure "the cooperation of 'large bodies of men' in flood control and irrigation projects." These views indicate that the state was supporting and encouraging irrigation even though the comparative evidence does not support Wittfogel's view that the state came into existence for this purpose.

Integrative and conflict theories of the state are "not mutually exclusive" (Service 1978: 31). In the present state of knowledge evidence is not "yet sufficient for decisive conclusions" about how states first came into existence. There is room for speculative recombination of the elements of various theories. Mumford (1974) has proposed that military harassment by nomads compelled settled agriculturalists to establish a state for military protection. A barbarian chief and warriors accepted the task. They derived their wealth and exalted social position from continuing military ability to protect the agricultural region from other warrior bands on the outside, and on the inside, their ability to collect taxes. The conqueror's state needed cities for military garrisons, strongholds, transportation links, storehouses, and administration. The support of state personnel engaged in these tasks, therefore, provided the sovereign's motive for collecting an agricultural surplus, transporting it, and redistributing it among his urban retinue.

Mumford's speculation has some basis in Sumerian evidence. Childe (1957: 130) acknowledges that "the first direct evidence" of organized warfare is coincident with the Urban Revolution in Mesopotamia. "Disputes about water rights" were endemic and "permanent war leaders" indispensable. Sumerian city-states also engaged in warfare to produce slaves and raw materials and to forestall "raids by still barbarous mountaineers or desert tribes." The sanguinary reign of Sargon I (2350-2300 B.C.) consolidated the warring city-states into a unitary empire capable of mobilizing a professional military class in the service of a settled agricultural population (Adams 1966: 153-158).

Central Place Explanations

Why was the state the only possible agency for collecting and distributing the surplus? This task might have been left to owners of the agricultural surplus whose self-interest would induce them to bring the surplus to town markets. This assumption is compatible with *central place theory* (Mayer 1965: 90 ff.), an approach that many archaeologists currently endorse (Ucko et al. 1972). According to this view, the origin of cities was their utility as places of exchange for locally produced goods and services, and as nodes for distribution of goods imported over long distances. Cities came into existence because dispersed agricultural people needed a central place in which to exchange goods. The central place explanation depends upon commerce for confirmation, because absence of commerce would indicate that people were not using cities as central places. Evidence of local and long-distance commerce in antiquity is incontrovertible (Childe 1957: 170), and research continually pushes back the temporal frontier (Oates et al. 1977). This evidence has rendered the central place explanation increasingly attractive (Price 1978: 175). However, decisive evidence is still adverse to central place explanations of urban origins. After all, the first problem is to explain why cities came into existence at all, not how they functioned once created. "Many primitive societies manage entirely without a market, or exchange rates, or commercial trade at all" (Renfrew 1973: 116). The earliest period is accordingly crucial, and available evidence indicates that commerce arose only *after* cities had been established for noncommercial reasons. "It would be forcing the evidence," writes Kemp (1977: 199) to suggest that the origins of cities in Egypt were "significantly dependent" on commerce. In Mesopotamia too, "the earliest communities in the south clearly developed a connection with the exploitation of agriculture. Commerce came only at a later stage. . . . " (Hammond 1972: 25). Moreover, the existence of a propertied merchant class in Mesopotamia cannot be proven by the time of Hammurabi, whose reign was much after the first cities arose. Without merchants, commerce must have been negligible, and because the central place explanation of city origins depends upon commerce, the absence of merchants is disconfirmatory (Polanyi: 1957: 16–17) [7].

"The Economy Has No Surplus"

The discussion of surplus theory has thus far proceeded on the assumption that a surplus "exists" when food production exceeds the physiological minimum of the agricultural population. Then the state takes away the surplus and uses it to support a city population. This technological version is too simple. At present, "there is general agreement that an agricultural surplus product" was a prerequisite to urban life, but important controversy "surrounds the manner" in which the surplus should be conceived and "the way in which surpluses arise, are acquired, and put to use" (Harvey 1973: 216). First, a surplus is a psychological rather than a physiological standard. A generation or more ago, American farmers got along without indoor toilets, hot water, electricity, or television. But a level of taxation that deprived them of these "necessities" they would now regard as excessive. A level of taxation that returned farmers to a survival diet would encounter stubborn resistance, based upon farmers' conception of what constitutes a decent standard of living. Knowing some baseline subsistence minimun (say, in calories per day) is, therefore, of limited value. True, this conception does yield an insight into the dim origins of urbanization in antiquity, but beyond this rude beginning, the psychological issues of relative deprivation begin to obtrude, then quickly catch up with and surpass the physiological issue.

A second objection is the role of the state in the creation as well as the collection of the surplus. In the early pharaonic period (ca. 3200 B.C.), a single farming family already had the technology to "extract from the fertile soil of Egypt . . .

three times as much food as was needed for domestic consumption" (Childe 1957: 88–89; see also Ho 1975: 59). But why should they? Coercion. Apparently, the pharaohs "made the peasants produce the potential surplus." Their method was taxation. Peasants produced a surplus in order to pay taxes. The size of the surplus and its existence was, therefore, dependent upon coercion. "There are always and everywhere potential surpluses available" but cities and urbanization are only variably present. Therefore, Pearson (1957: 339) concludes, "what counts is the institutional means for bringing [surpluses] to life." Social stratification of ancient society and the attitude of the ancient state thus emerge as immediate determinants of how much surplus was collected and how unequal was its distribution.

Who controls the state, and what is the rulers' attitude toward the rural population? The simple technological version of surplus theory ignores these questions, yet the political sociology of the state is crucial to urbanization. Weak states cannot collect harsh taxes, so the societal surplus "available" for urbanization is small. Strong states can compel the agricultural population to reduce their living standard in order to collect heavy taxes that support high levels of urbanization. Here the issue is not the psychological sense of the population, but the *effectiveness* of the state in collecting taxes from farmers who have a motive to resist.

SURPLUS THEORY IN PERSPECTIVE

The state's role in the collection and distribution of the surplus was complex. First, the seat of the ancient state was the capital city and its administrative satellites. From the capital city, ancient states extended their jurisdiction over tributary populations of agricultural producers (Schaedel 1978: 32, 33, 44). The functions of the state in an agricultural society of antiquity were mixed. On the one hand, the military power of the state assured peace and therewith prosperity. The state also supported irrigation and flood control projects, which enhanced agricultural output. On the other hand, the ancient state was exploitative in internal policy and predatory in foreign policy. States warred with one another for water rights, slaves, and territory. God-kings pressed captives into slavery and exploited their own agricultural population for selfish gain. For the useful services they performed, god-kings, warriors, and priests exacted more than a fair compensation. Thus, in the fifth century B.C., Egyptian priests told the Greek historian Herodotus that building the great pyramid of Cheops had consumed the labor of 100,000 men for thirty years. Egyptians remembered this labor as an oppressive burden. This is not surprising. If the president of the

United States required equivalent labor service as partial compensation for his services, taxpayers would feel the price too high, whatever irrigation benefits the United States might have conferred in his reign.

The ancient state was simultaneously service-producing and predatory. Hence, Mumford (1974: 65) declares the function of the ancient city was "containment and control of a large population . . . for the benefit of a ruling class *and* [my italics] for the ultimate benefit of a whole community whose capital resources and creative potential had been raised to a higher level by this ruling minority." Agricultural society needed the state's protection and public works, and the state needed the city as the organizational capsule for these services. But there is much evidence that the emergence of cities was synonymous with the invention of war, refinement of exploitation, mass enslavement, and enhancement of social class differences in consumption and life-style (Sjoberg 1960: 53-54, 108-144; 1965: 216-217). Naturally, agrarian people resented and struggled against exploitation by urban interests. This scenario produced the recurrent city-country conflicts, Braudel (1973: 373) has described as the first and longest class struggles "known to history."

SUMMARY

The creation and collection of an agricultural surplus was the crucial prerequisite of urbanization in antiquity. For this reason, technological improvement in agriculture had to precede urbanization, and the pace of technological improvement was slow. However, a narrowly technological interpretation of surplus theory overlooks the interaction between technology and society. Religious beliefs, political power, and social class relations also affected the state's ability to create, collect, and distribute any technologically available surplus as well as the pace of technological change, the size of the surplus surrendered, and the capacity of the state to exact a larger surplus from unwilling producers.

NOTES

1. Davis (1955: 430-431) supplies the following dimensions of early cities: Babylon, 3.2 square miles; Ur, 220 acres and 5,000 population; Erech, 2 square miles and 245,000 population; Mohenjo-Daro, 1 square mile; Harappa, 2.5 miles in perimeter; Thebes, 14 miles in circumference, and 225,000 population in 1600 B.C.
2. Childe (1950) offered a more complex list, superior in detail to Hammond's

but serving the same purpose: discriminating between villages and cities in antiquity. Childe mentions the following city characteristics that never appear in villages: extensive, dense population; full-time specialists not engaged in agriculture; a concentration point of extracted surplus; the presence of monumental public buildings; a resident ruling class of warriors, priests, and officials; a seat of predictive sciences; a literate class in residence; full-time artists in residence; luxury traffic in imported goods; specialist craftsmen with citizenship.

3. For a complete review of archaeology, see Klein (1977).
4. An important controversy concerns the interpretation of catastrophic events like the fall of Rome. Lenski (1976) has argued that unique catastrophes are statistical deviations from the unilinear main line of evolutionary development. This interpretation is compatible with a "ramp" analogy (Adams 1966: 17-18) of urbanization rather than the "step" analogy stressed here. Becker (1979) criticizes Lenski.
5. A forceful statement appears in the collected works of Ibn Khaldun, a North African historian of the thirteenth century. "Dynasties are prior to towns and cities. Towns and cities are secondary products of royal authority." "Cities that are the seats of royal authority fall into ruins when the ruling dynasty falls into ruins and crumbles." Ibn Khaldun, *The Muqaddimah: An Introduction to History*, trans. Franz Rosenthal, Vol. II. London: Routledge and Kegan Paul, 1958, pp. 235, 297.
6. Wittfogel's (1957) typology derived from Karl Marx's passing reference to Asiatic Despotism, a precapitalist social system. Marx distinguished three branches of Oriental government: war or plunder of the exterior; finance or plunder of the interior; and public works. The necessity of irrigation "devolved upon all Asiatic governments" the responsibility for providing it. See Karl Marx, "The British rule in India," pp. 345-351 in Karl Marx and Frederick Engels, *Selected Works*, Vol. I. Moscow: Foreign Languages Publishing House, 1962a.
7. "In ancient civilizations the urban centers were usually political-religious or political-intellectual; in the modern world they are economic." (Redfield and Singer, 1954-1955: 54). For a treatment of preindustrial urbanization favorable to central place theory, see Rozman (1976: 13-14, 33-85).

REFERENCES

Adams, Robert McC. 1960. "The Origin of Cities." *Scientific American* 9: 3-10. Reprinted in V. V. Lamberg-Karlovsky, ed., *Old World Archeology*. San Francisco: W. H. Freeman, 1972.
———. 1966. *The Evolution of Urban Society: Early Mesopotamia and Prehispanic Mexico*. Chicago: Aldine.
Anderson, Perry. 1978. "Bourgeois Revolutions." Paper presented, First Annual

Irvine Seminar on Social History. University of California, Irvine, April 1, 1978.

Aristotle. 1946. *The Politics of Aristotle.* Trans. Ernest Barker. Oxford: Clarendon Press.

Bailey, Anne M. and Joseph R. Llobera. 1979. "Karl A. Wittfogel and the Asiatic Mode of Production: A Reappraisal." *The Sociological Review* 27: 541–559.

Becker, George. 1979. "Comment on Lenski's 'History and Social Change.'" *American Journal of Sociology* 84: 1238–1242.

Braidwood, Robert. 1972a. "From Cave to Village," pp. 67–70 in V. V. Lamberg-Karlovsky, ed. *Old World Archeology.* San Francisco: W. H. Freeman.

———. 1972b. "The Agricultural Revolution," pp. 71–79, in V. V. Lamberg-Karlovsky, ed. *Old World Archeology.* San Francisco: W. H. Freeman.

Braudel, Fernand. 1973. *Capitalism and Material Life, 1400–1800.* Translated by Miriam Kochan. New York: Harper and Row.

Carneiro, Robert L. 1970. "A Theory of the Origin of the State." *Science* 169: 733–738.

———. 1978. "Political Expansion as an Expression of the Principal of Competitive Exclusion," pp. 205–223, in Ronald Cohen and Elman R. Service, eds. *Origins of the State.* Philadelphia: Institute for the Study of Human Issues.

Chandler, Tertius, and Gerald Fox. 1974. *3000 Years of Urban Growth.* New York: Academic Press.

Childe, V. Gordon. 1950. "The Urban Revolution." *Town Planning Review* 21: 3–17.

———. 1957. *New Light on the Most Ancient East,* 4th ed. New York: Grove Press.

Clark, Grahame. 1977. *World Prehistory,* 3rd ed. Cambridge: Cambridge University Press.

Cohen, Ronald. 1978. "Introduction," pp. 1–20, in Ronald Cohen and Elman R. Service, eds. *Origins of the State.* Philadelphia: Institute for the Study of Human Issues.

Davis, Kingsley. 1955. "The Origin and Growth of Urbanization in the World." *American Journal of Sociology 60:* 429–437.

———, ed. 1973. *Cities: Their Origin, Growth, and Human Impact.* San Francisco: W. H. Freeman.

Dembart, Lee. 1981. "Stone Age Discovery Sheds Light on Earliest Religion." *Los Angeles Times* November 28: I, 1.

Durand, John D. 1967. "The Modern Expansion of World Population." *Proceedings of the American Philosophical Society* 3: 136–159.

———. 1974. *Historical Estimates of World Population: An Evaluation.* Philadelphia: Population Studies Center of the University of Pennsylvania.

Finley, John. 1977. "The Ancient City: From Fustel de Coulanges to Max Weber and Beyond." *Comparative Studies in Society and History* 19: 305–327.

Flannery, Kent J. 1972. "The Origins of the Village as a Settlement Type in Mesoamerica and the Near East: A Comparative Study," pp. 23–53, in Peter J. Ucko et al., eds. *Man, Settlement, and Urbanism.* N.P.: Duckworth.

———. 1973. "The Origins of Agriculture." *Annual Review of Anthropology* 2: 271–310.

Fried, Morton H. 1978. "Toward an Explanation of the Origin of the State," pp. 35–48, in Ronald Cohen and Elman R. Service, eds. *Origins of the State.* Philadelphia: Institute for the Study of Human Issues.

Hammond, Mason. 1972. *The City in the Ancient World.* Cambridge: Harvard University Press.

Harvey, David. 1973. *Social Justice and the City.* Baltimore: Johns Hopkins University Press.

Heider, Karl G. 1972. "Environment, Subsistence, and Society." *Annual Review of Anthropology* 1: 207–226.

Ho, Ping-Ti. 1975. *The Cradle of the East.* Hong Kong: Chinese University of Hong Kong.

Jarrige, Jean, and Richard H. Meadow. 1980. "The Antecedents of Civilization in the Indus Valley." *Scientific American* 243: 122–133.

Kemp, Barry J. 1977. "The Early Development of Towns in Egypt." *Antiquity* 5: 185–200.

Keyfitz, Nathan. 1965. "Political-Economic Aspects of Urbanization in South and Southeast Asia," pp. 265–309, in Philip M. Hauser and Leo F. Schnore, eds. *The Study of Urbanization.* New York: Wiley.

Klein, Leo. 1977. "A Panorama of Theoretical Archeology." *Current Anthropology* 18: 1–42.

Lenski, Gerhand, and Jean Lenski. 1974. *Human Societies,* 2nd ed. New York: McGraw-Hill.

——. 1976. "History and Social Change." *American Journal of Sociology* 82: 548–564.

Mayer, Harold M. 1965. "A Survey of Urban Geography," pp. 81–113, in Philip M. Hauser and Leo F. Schnore, eds. *The Study of Urbanization.* New York: Wiley.

Mellaart, James. 1979. "Egyptian and Near Eastern Chronology: A Dilemma?" *Antiquity* 53: 6–18.

Meyers, J. Thomas. 1971. "The Origin of Agriculture: An Evaluation of Three Hypotheses," pp. 101–121, in Stuart Stoeuver, ed. *Prehistoric Agriculture.* Garden City, N.Y.: American Museum of Natural History.

Moseley, K. D., and Immanual Wallerstein. 1978. "Pre-Capitalist Social Structures." *Annual Review of Sociology* 4: 259–290.

Mumford, Lewis. 1974. "City Invincible," pp. 54–68, in Charles Tilly, ed. *An Urban World.* Boston: Little, Brown.

Oates, J., T. E. Davidson, D. Kamilli, and H. McKerrell. 1977. "Seafaring Merchants of Ur?" *Antiquity* 51: 221–234.

Pearson, H. W. 1957. "The Economy Has No Surplus," pp. 320–341, in Karl Polanyi, C. M. Arensberg, and H. W. Pearson, eds., *Trade and Markets in the Early Empires.* New York: Free Press.

Polanyi, Karl. 1957. "Marketless Trading in Hammurabi's Time," pp. 12–26, in Karl Polanyi, Conrad M. Arensberg, and Harry W. Pearson, eds. *Trade and Markets in the Early Empires.* Glencoe: Free Press.

Price, Barbara J. 1978. "Secondary State Formation: An Explanatory Model," pp. 61–186, in Ronald Cohen and Elman R. Service, eds. *Origins of the State.* Philadelphia: Institute for the Study of Human Issues.

Redfield, Robert, and Milton B. Singer. 1954-1955. "The Cultural Role of Cities." *Economic Development and Cultural Change* 3: 53-73.

Reinhard, Marcel, et al. 1968. *Histoire Générale de la Population Mondiale.* Paris: Editions Montcrestien.

Renfrew, Colin. 1973. *Before Civilization: The Radiocarbon Revolution and Prehistoric Europe.* New York: Knopf.

Rozman, Gilbert. 1976. *Urban Networks in Russia, 1750-1800.* Princeton: Princeton University Press.

Sahlins, Marshall. 1968. *Tribesmen.* Englewood Cliffs, N.J.: Prentice-Hall.

Schaedel, Richard P. 1978. "The City and the Origin of the State in America," pp. 31-45, in Richard Schaedel, Jorge E. Hardoy, and Nora Scott Kinzer, eds. *Urbanization in the Americas from its Beginnings to the Present.* The Hague: Mouton.

Service, Elman R. 1978. "Classical and Modern Theories of the Origins of Government," pp. 21-34, in Ronald Cohen and Elman R. Service, eds. *Origins of the State.* Philadelphia: Institute for the Study of Human Issues.

Sjoberg, Gideon. 1960. *The Preindustrial City.* New York: Free Press.

———. 1963. "The Rise and Fall of Cities: A Theoretical Perspective." *International Journal of Comparative Sociology* 4: 107-120.

———. 1965. "Theory and Research in Urban Sociology," pp. 157-190 in Philip M. Hauser and Leo F. Schnore, eds. *The Study of Urbanization.* New York: Wiley.

Taagepera, Rein. 1979. "Size and Duration of Empires: Growth-Decline Curves, 600 B.C. to 600 A.D." *Social Science History* 3: 115-138.

Turner, Ralph. 1941. *The Great Cultural Traditions,* Vol. I, The Ancient Cities. New York: McGraw-Hill.

Ucko, Peter J., Ruth Tringham, and G. W. Dimbley, eds. 1972. *Man, Settlement and Urbanism.* London: Duckworth.

United Nations, Department of International Economic and Social Affairs, Population Division Working Paper No. 66, 1980. "Urban, Rural and City Population, 1950-2000 as Assessed in 1978." New York: United Nations.

Wheatley, Paul. 1972. "The Concept of Urbanism" pp. 601-637, in Peter J. Ucko, et al., eds. *Man, Settlement and Urbanism.* London: Duckworth.

Wiley, Gordon R. 1982. "Maya Archeology." *Science* 214: 260-267.

Wilkinson, Richard G. 1973. *Poverty and Progress.* New York: Praeger.

Wittfogel, Karl A. 1957. *Oriental Despotism.* New Haven: Yale University Press.

Wright, H. T. 1977. "Recent Research on the Origin of the State." *Annual Review of Anthropology* 6: 379-397.

CHAPTER 2 _____

Basic Industries of Preindustrial Cities

Cities must earn a living to survive. The livelihood of any city depends upon its industries. When its industries prosper, a city grows; when its industries wither, a city declines too. Industries are groupings of economic activity. Goods-producing industries produce tangible commodities, such as automobiles or washing machines. Service industries produce helpful interventions such as those of legislators, priests, or professors.

Although all cities have industries, the industries they have are not identical. The industrial composition of a city is the industries carried on in it and their relative importance. Many cities have distinctive industries that stand out in importance above others. For example, Detroit's major industry is the automotive, and Detroit's employment profile reflects the importance of this industry. Washington, D.C., employs many government workers and government is its major industry. Miami is a tourist resort city, where services, transportation, and retail trade bulk very large. New York City is a financial center. Cities whose industrial composition is evenly distributed among numerous industries are balanced-industries cities. Marked dependence upon one or a few industries produces dominant-industry cities such as those mentioned above. A basic industry need not be a dominant one, but whenever it is, that industry is crucially important to the economic life of its city. New York City represents a balanced-industry city despite its strength in finance. Detroit, Miami, and Washington are imbalanced because a single industry dominates the economic life of each.

Basic industries enable a city to acquire goods or services originating elsewhere. In the modern world, basic industries bring revenue into the city from without

29

(Mayer 1965: 84). An example is the sale of automobiles by manufacturers in Detroit. When automobiles are bought by purchasers living outside Detroit, revenues flow back to Detroit where they are dispersed to workers in the automotive industry. Wages received permit residents to buy goods and services (Hill, 1978). *Nonbasic industries* are local industries that do not generate revenue from beyond the city's limits because all or most customers are local. Grocery stores in Detroit are nonbasic. Forty percent of Detroit's consumers work in the automotive industry, a basic industry. Wages earned in this basic industry permit workers to buy groceries; therefore, local grocery stores depend indirectly upon the automotive industry (Mayer 1965: 83).

BASIC INDUSTRIES OF PREINDUSTRIAL CITIES

Preindustrial cities depended upon the extraction of surplus food from the adjacent countryside [1]. Any industries accomplishing this extraction were basic industries. Religion and government were the two industries that everywhere extracted the needed surplus. As a basic industry, slave exploitation was variable, effective only when owners of slave-worked agricultural lands made their residence in cities. This situation prevailed, for example, in Greco-Roman antiquity but not during the European Middle Ages (Weber 1976: 343-344). Although religion, government, and slave exploitation were not the only basic industries, they were the only basic industries that were routinely dominant. Other basic industries of preindustrial cities (notably manufacturing and trade) were of secondary importance in terms of the employment they created and the urban population they supported.

Controversy continues about the fairness of exchanges between ancient cities and their agricultural tributaries (Moseley and Wallerstein 1978: 272-274). As basic industries, religion and government performed services to benefit agricultural producers and received in return a share of the producers' food surplus. Some urban services were of obvious benefit to agricultural producers. For example, a stable, strong state provided military protection and public works for the agricultural people it taxed. Protection and irrigation were state services; taxes were state revenue. As for public works, the irrigation projects of ancient states assured the productivity of agriculture (N. Smith 1978). Even the priests of the state cult contributed to agricultural prosperity by propitiating the gods, thus assuring rainfall and sunlight. Priests studied nature and planned the calendar. The early development of mathematics in Greece, Mesopotamia, and Egypt wholly depended upon the temple priesthoods whose monopoly of this craft did not end until the European Middle Ages (Hogben 1937: 40-41). Surely these urban services were worth their purchase price?

On the other hand, aggressive warfare was a state service of no utility to agricultural workers. But ancient elites took a favorable view of warfare and slave hunting. First, enemies captured in boundary wars then provided slave labor for agriculture. Second, boundary wars added new territories to the conqueror's domains, and the unfree agricultural workers in these territories now shipped their surplus food to their conqueror's administrative cities. Either way, subdued peoples supported their conqueror's elites in luxury with surplus agricultural products and also provided the agricultural labor to support new armies of enslaving aggression. This abuse of military power is repugnant to contemporary ethics, but ancient sages repeatedly justified aggressive warfare and enslavement of captives (Gouldner 1965: 139, 145). Aristotle (1946: 21) called war a "natural mode of acquisition" and slave-hunting "naturally just" [2]. Anderson (1974: 28) claims slave exploitation and military predation were specialties of Greco-Roman civilization, but no ancient society was free of either. Because captives provided the labor to enrich their enslavers, military predation upon neighboring societies paid for itself with a surplus left over to divide among the warriors. Slaves acquired in one war thereafter supported production at home when warriors set out to gain more booty and slaves in the next war.

Other ambiguous areas are justice, high culture, and religion. Preindustrial cities also exported these to the conquered countryside and extracted the taxes to pay for them. Some of these services arguably benefited the agricultural populations who paid the bill. For example, some administration of justice was desirable anywhere; gods obviously needed propitiation; and high culture improved the crudity of rural life. Any analysis must acknowledge the compensatory benefits that the political domination of cities accorded agricultural people. But suppose conquered agricultural people did not wish to honor the laws, speak the language, or revere the gods of their conquerors. Were law, religion, and culture then urban services worthy of their price, or exactions forced out of conquered people?

The preponderant opinion is preindustrial cities were exploitative and parasitic of the countryside even though some urban services were valuable (Bendix 1978: 7; Finley 1973: 125). First, ancient cities depended on unfree labor and aggressive warfare, the whole burden of which was born by victimized workers. Second, victims had to purchase conquerors' services whether they wanted them or not. Third, the cost of the services cities provided was high in that the services did not cost as much to provide as the cities extracted in taxes to pay for them. The cause was prodigious governmental waste. For example, pharaohs of Egypt did not need numerous palaces, gold plates, retinues of servants, and immense pyramids as compensation for their administrative, religious, and military services; a modest salary and old-age pension would have been adequate for that. The actual level of monarchical opulence in Egypt and elsewhere testifies to splendors far in excess of what the agricultural hinterland needed to pay in order to support a minimal state [3]. Finally, the income of urban slave owners rested wholly upon the exploitative appropriation of the surplus product created by the labor of unfree agricultural workers.

Exploitation begets social unrest, and the relations between ancient city and countryside were uneasy in consequence. Therefore, military coercion was indispensable to tax collection. However, the cities of the preindustrial epoch could not rely wholly upon coercion to extract the agricultural surplus from dependent populations. Urban powers always sought legitimation of authority from the governed. *Legitimation* is public acknowledgment of the ruler's right to command and the people's obligation to obey (Sjoberg 1960: 224-231). Legitimation of authority made tax collection possible without military coercion. Obviously, a city's services to the rural population were a necessary prerequisite of legitimation; a city could not collect taxes for protection and public works unless these services were actually provided. But cities of the preindustrial epoch did not justify their taxation on the basis of cost-benefit analysis. Instead, political capitals depended upon the imposition of official culture in tributary provinces to legitimate their rule. Cities played a crucial role in this process of state legitimation.

Cities were conduits through which official culture diffused into the conquered territories (Sjoberg 1963: 115). Religion was the most reliable and significant (but not the only) cultural agency of political legitimation. In fact, temples are the oldest sites yet excavated in Sumer. Apparently the priests of the temple owned the surrounding land and appropriated its surplus in the name of the city-state's pantheon (Childe 1957: 119). Political kingship thereafter imposed the problem of how to legitimate taxation among conquered nonbelievers. Methods of legitimation were direct. Every state proclaimed its official cult, and the temples of the cult proclaimed the legitimacy of the ruler. In Mediterranean antiquity, state cults were mostly polytheistic [4]. Polytheism encouraged flexible accommodations with local pantheons, as well as the partial or entire deification of the ruler. Priests of the state cult proclaimed the divinity of the ruler to the populations of the conquered territories. The gods ruled the universe and, the priests claimed, the monarch was one of the gods, an associate of the gods, or the voice of the gods. Pharaohs of Egypt were regarded as gods or demigods deserving not only obedience but also worship. Indeed, the pharaonic name Ramses means "son of God." During the imperial period (30 B.C.-A.D. 750), Roman authorities also encouraged the worship of emperors whose progenitors were inscribed among the Olympian deities for this purpose (Carcopino 1940: 61, 143-46). Even where, as in Assyria, deification of the head of state did not proceed, the state cult always proclaimed an intimate relationship between the ruler and deities whom the ruler was understood to consult about state policy (Rostovzeff I, 1930: 144). In China, the ruler lost his authority when calamities (war, earthquake, famine) proved that heaven had withdrawn its mandate.

Temples of the state cult were located in cities of tributary regions. Sometimes local temples received disbursements from the state and were, therefore, free of the necessity for deriving a livelihood from users. Hence, the payment of taxes was as much a religious as a political obligation. Indeed, the merger of state and religion in the person of the ruler blurred any clear distinction between religion and politics throughout the preindustrial epoch. Naturally the faithful made voluntary donations to local temples of the state cult, and these increased the flow of surplus from countryside to city, thus augmenting the city population. Most important, religious legitimation of the state encouraged agricultural workers to pay more willingly the product of their labors (Davis 1973: 14).

JUDEA UNDER ROMAN RULE

The New Testament's account of the birth of Jesus is a familiar story offering a convenient medium for illustrating the process of taxation and legitimation in antiquity. The Roman province of Judea was a tax-paying tributary of Rome, the empire's political capital. Rome extracted from Judea—as from its other provinces—the taxes that supported the great capital city itself, as well as its hierarchy of administrative and military centers around the Mediterranean. The Bible (Luke, 2: 1-3) records that

there went out a decree from Ceasar Augustus that all the world should be taxed. . . . And all went to be taxed, every one into his own city.

Taxation was what brought Mary and Joseph away from home on the night of Jesus' birth. The payment of these taxes was unpopular in Judea because Hebrews rejected Roman law, Latin culture, the imperial cult, and Olympian deities and, as a result, questioned the legitimacy of Roman rule in Judea.

Romans could justify the taxes by reference to the political-military services they performed, and Roman aqueducts survive today as mute witnesses to massive public works conducted under Roman authority. Indeed, North Africa has never been so fruitful as it was under Roman rule because subsequent rulers permitted the Roman irrigation system to deteriorate (N. Smith 1978: 158). Nonetheless, these justifications never sufficed. To further support its legitimacy, Rome encouraged the Latinization of local culture in dress, language, and life-style. Additionally, Rome desired subjects to acknowledge the divinity of Augustus Caesar, the emperor (Kautsky 1972: 127-128). Admittedly, Rome only desired that conquered people add Caesar to their local pantheon; this done, the Romans permitted complete religious freedom (Rostovtzeff II, 1930: 340). This religious formula was generally successful among polytheistic peoples who had no difficulty in adding another god to their pantheon [5]. Indeed, the

Romans regularly added the gods of conquered peoples to their own, thus returning the religious acknowledgment (Carcopino 1940: 143-146). However, the monotheistic Jews declined to acknowledge the Olympian deities, much less the divinity of Augustus Caesar. An extremist Jewish sect, the Zealots, repudiated the legitimacy of Roman tax collection. Their slogan was "No God but Yahweh; No law but the Torah; No tax but to the Temple." In effect, the Zealots declined by pay for the administrative and religious services the Roman Empire was compelling Jews and other colonial peoples to buy. The military revolt of the Zealots began in A.D. 67 and ended in disaster when the Roman Tenth Legion besieged and destroyed the Zealot garrison at Masada in A.D. 73.

Why was Roman rule in Judea so precarious that military coercion was necessary to collect taxes there? Clearly, the strict monotheism of the Jews was the first, quite unusual difficulty. This monotheism prevented Roman emperors from obtaining religious legitimation of their state. Second, pious Jews refused to acknowledge the legitimacy of Roman law on religious grounds ("No law but the Torah"). Finally, Jewish nationalists resisted Latinization of Hebrew culture on ethnic grounds. These reservations undermined Roman rule in Judea and hinted at unwillingness to pay the taxes that rule imposed. Roman suspicions of Jesus on this account even compelled him to advise his followers to "render unto Caesar" what was Caesar's; but as events proved, this answer did not convince the Roman authorities that Jesus was not subversive.

In a sense, Roman suspicions were well founded. The subsequent spread of monotheistic Christianity throughout the empire taught conquered peoples everywhere to repudiate Rome's pagan deities as well as the divinity of Roman emperors and thus to dispute the religious legitimacy of Roman imperialism (Bloch 1961: 32). Persecution of Christians was contrary to the religious toleration that had prevailed in Roman antiquity, and Rostovtzeff (II, 1930: 345) supposes the persecution resulted from the unwillingness of Christians to worship Roman emperors. Christianity first shivered, then destoryed the foundation of Roman imperialism in the Western empire. In the Eastern empire, the timely conversion of Emperor Constantine to Christianity propped up the legitimacy of Roman rule for an additional millennium.

CITIES AND EMPIRE

Cities flourished when the Roman Empire was at its height, then declined in size and number when the boundaries of the empire receded as a result of barbarian invasions. The premier city was, of course, Rome. "From the time that Rome became an imperial city until today she has been a parasite-city, living on gifts, rents, taxes, tribute" (Finley 1973: 125). This imperial capital reached its zenith in area and population in the reign of Trajan during the second century

A.D. Greater Rome's population may have numbered as many as one million or more, a size the city did not reach again until 1900 (Carcopino 1940: 24). The ability of the imperial capital to support this immense population depended upon the vast expansion of its tributary areas. From these tributaries were sucked up the taxes that Rome's wealthy classes consumed (Hauser 1965: 2).

To administer the tributary provinces, Rome established a hierarchy of cities throughout the empire. Each Roman province had its capital, and each capital its administrative subsidiaries. Smaller cities collected local taxes, which they passed up to higher-ranking cities—after first deducting their own share. Each higher level took its share of what it received from below, then passed the balance upward, ultimately to Rome, the final beneficiary. Thus lower-ranking cities shared with Rome, their mistress, the spoils of empire. The power of Rome permitted city people to obtain a bigger share of the surplus, and the *pax romana* guaranteed prosperity. The upshot was urbanization wherever Roman rule firmly established itself. When the Romans invaded Britain, the island's cities were few, rude, and small. While Roman rule in Britain was firm, the existing cities grew and numerous cities came into existence. When the Romans left, Britain's cities declined in size and number.

This relationship between imperialism and urbanization is characteristic of preindustrial societies everywhere (Sjoberg 1963). Indeed, it is among the oldest sociological generalizations. Moorish scholar Ibn Khaldun (1332-1406) commented upon the propensity of cities to flourish when the state flourished, then decline when state power declined. What Ibn Khaldun described was cyclical urbanization. The most basic cause of the urbanization cycle was the industrial dependence of cities upon religion and public administration. These were never the only urban industries, and their relative importance tended to decline whenever public order was protected over long periods of time. Moreover, the expenditure of absentee landlords who resided in cities enabled some townsmen to obtain access to the agricultural surplus by serving the gentry who owned it. How much to weight the contributors is a controversial problem. On balance, however, taxation and religious obligation appear to have been the original and most basic means whereby city people obtained the surplus product of agricultural hinterlands. When these bases expanded, as imperial boundaries and power expanded, the available surplus increased and therewith the size and number of cities (Anderson 1974: 68). Reversals of state power correspondingly reduced the available surplus and thus compelled reductions in city size and number.

MODERN ILLUSTRATIONS

Political and religious capitals still exist, although they are no longer the only great cities or the largest. Nonetheless, like their ancient predecessors, modern political and religious capitals still depend for their basic industry upon taxes and donations by nonresidents. Washington, D.C., is a political capital whose basic industry is the federal government, a tax-supported institution. Taxes flow to Washington from the states of the American union, and most of the tax monies return to the states in the form of government services. These reciprocated benefits make tax paying advantageous to the governed, although the issue of government waste is still a lively one.

However, some portion of taxes paid provides a livelihood for 314,000 federal workers in Washington who spend their income locally, thus generating nonbasic occupations and industries. Although Washington exports some nongovernment goods and services to other localities, the bulk of the city's income—and its basic industry—is government. If the nation's capital were moved, Washington would lose its basic industry. The predictable result would be an abrupt economic decline and sequential loss of population through emigration.

Many religious capitals still exist: Jerusalem, Mecca, Rome, Canterbury. Sometimes religious centers have ancillary industries that are independently important. Jerusalem is the political capital of Israel as well as the site of Muslim, Jewish, and Christian holy places. Similarly, Salt Lake City, Utah, is the world capital of Mormonism as well as the state capital of Utah. When religion is a city's basic industry, the city's size still depends on the number and fervor of the faithful as well as on their ability to pay. Being relatively few, Mormons are required to tithe so their church receives a lot of money. As the ultimate repository of church income, Salt Lake City has grown up around disbursements of the Mormon Church as has Washington, D.C., around government. Were Mormons to lose their fervor tomorrow, the income of the Mormon Church would drop. This decline would lead to reductions in the population of Salt Lake City through emigration of the unemployed. This kind of constraint also affects every other world religious center, but the generalization illustrates the continued dependence of religious capitals upon religious currents in society.

THE CONTRIBUTION OF TRADE AND MANUFACTURING

The preceding analysis argued that religion, public administration, and absentee land ownership were the basic industries of ancient cities. A plausible objection to this analysis centers on trade. *Trade* is exchange of comodities. In principle this exchange confers the ability to support city people because profits from trade can buy the agricultural surplus of the countryside for urban dwellers. Therefore, urban merchants can support themselves and their dependents in trade, and the more flourishing the trade, the more city people can be supported by it. Numerous trading cities have also been identified in the historical record. In Arabia Felix, for example, the basic, dominant industry of this desert city was commerce (Van Beek 1973; see also Lamberg-Karlovsky 1972: 37). Even in political or religious centers, trade was always of at least subsidiary importance in economic life. Childe (1957: 170) reported "concrete evidence" of trade networks linking the Tigris-Euphrates, the Indus, and the Nile as early as 2500 B.C.

The existence of urban-based trade and manufacturing in even remote antiquity is indisputable. Some authorities (Davis 1973: 15) complain that too little attention has been paid to the city-forming capacity of ancient commerce. However, the prevailing tendency of authorities is to belittle the city-forming importance of commerce in pre-Christian antiquity (Anderson 1974: 19-25). First, trade's contribution was small because its volume was small and customers few. Long-distance trade was mostly in luxury products, whose ultimate consumers were the religious, political, and landed elites residing in the cities (Chapman 1957: 115). Only elites could afford imported luxuries. Owners of slave plantations were able to buy imported luxuries, exchanging for them some portion of the producers' surplus they owned. In Roman times, plantation owners resided in cities so their purchases of imported luxuries actually represented a mechanism whereby the city population came into possession of a portion of the agricultural surplus. First, field hands produced the agricultural surplus. Then the slave owner appropriated his legal share of their surplus. The more lands and slaves owned, the greater was the personal income of the owner. This exploitation permitted owners of the surplus to buy imported luxuries from urban traders. Finally, these traders supported their dependents and, in so doing, created nonbasic industries based upon local artisanship and so forth. The upshot of trade was therefore a swelling of urban populations beyond the limit otherwise imposed by public administration, religion, or slave exploitation as basic industries. But trade's contribution was slight. To illustrate the relative economic importance of trade and agriculture in antiquity, Anderson (1974: 20) calls attention to the Emperor Constantine's *collatio lustralis,* an imperial levy of the fourth century B.C. This legislation subjected town commerce and agricultural land alike to taxation. Duty from town commerce never amounted to more than 5 percent of what was collected in the countryside.

Manufacturing

Manufacturing is the process of transforming raw materials into finished products. A shoe is a finished product, leather its raw material. Manufacturing is the process whereby the leather is made into a shoe. Manufacturing in preindustrial cities was the province of craftsmen using hand tools and muscle power. Their economic contribution to ancient urbanization requires attention. However, one must distinguish ancient craft manufacturing from contemporary industrial manufacturing (Weber 1976: 45). The technology of ancient production depended wholly upon skilled workers using hand tools. Heavy power-driven machinery did not exist. There is "no evidence of factories" or "cottage industry."

The profit motive and free, price-making markets led a precarious existence at best (Polanyi 1977: 57–96) [6].

Urban craftsmen had few customers in the agricultural hinterland (Keyfitz 1965: 269). The agricultural household of antiquity was self-sufficient in most manufactured goods. In a technical sense, the city did not possess a comparative advantage in manufactured goods, which could be produced as well and as cheaply in villages or in the household of the final consumer. The only exceptions were estate owners or feudatories. Because rich people were able to purchase specialized products of urban craftsmen, urban craftsmen could produce luxury products for consumption by the very rich. This production did permit the craftsmen to acquire a share of the agricultural surplus and thus to earn a living in the city. The craftsmen and their dependents swelled the city's population, but when they satisfied the luxury demand of elites residing in the city, they merely appropriated a portion of the agricultural surplus already obtained by their elite customer. The nonluxury production of manufactured goods for municipal nonelites also had this quality because nonelite customers were dependents of the religious or political elite. Most urban craftsmanship was, in fact, directed toward such people and was, like retail trade, a nonbasic industry. For this reason, urban craftsmanship was of secondary importance in the political economy of preindustrial cities [7].

These conclusions are startling because they are so contradictory to the preponderant importance of trade and manufacturing in contemporary urbanization. However, one must guard against the naïve presumption that cities of antiquity were just like modern cities only smaller. Evidence contradicts this presumption. In pharaonic Egypt, export trade and industry existed but "the market for industrial products and craftsmanship was limited to the state and dependent nobility" (Childe 1964: 131). Weber (1976: 356) also observes that in antiquity people had "so little disposable income" after securing life's necessities that they provided "little demand for industrial products." Athens in the fourth century B.C. offers a "test case" because documentation is so rich and the city's economy was extraordinarily well developed. Finley's analysis shows Athens's prosperity depended upon local agricultural production, special vegetable and mineral resources, shipping and tourism, and, above all, "the income from land ownership and empire, rents, taxes, tribute, gifts from clients and subjects" (Finley 1973: 139). Manufacturing's contribution to Athenian prosperity was "negligible."

APPROPRIATION OF THE SURPLUS

Figures 2-1 and 2-2 are flowcharts illustrating two ways in which urban elites appropriated the agricultural surplus. The charts explain the process in terms of exchanges between cities and agricultural areas. These areas are always called *hinterlands*. Figure 2-1 shows how city-hinterland exchanges occurred in kind. First, workers (slaves, serfs, peasants) produced an agricultural surplus in response to the city's taxation policy. This surplus was collected and passed along to the capital where king, warriors, priests, and resident owners of slave plantations appropriated their shares. An example is fourteenth-century Russia, where warriors, priests, and princes residing in towns owned agricultural estates (*votchiny*) that wholly supported them in kind (Rozman 1976: 52). With the surplus they owned, these elites were able to feed their household dependents and barter or sell any unused portion. In partial exchange for the agricultural surplus received, urban elites ordered their followers to provide military, governmental, and public works services benefiting tributary hinterlands. These urban services supported social conditions that permitted field workers to produce a surplus for another year.

A money model of the same process of appropriation appears in Figure 2-2 [8]. Again, field hands created a surplus, then took it to the city marketplace and exchanged it for cash. The cash earned in this manner was turned over to tax collectors, who passed it up to the urban elite of warriors, priests, and officials. The elite now bought the food and raw materials necessary to support their household dependents. The elite also hired servants and purchased imported services and locally manufactured goods [9]. By serving the elite in this manner, artisans, merchants, and workers obtained entitlement to a portion of the agricultural surplus already appropriated by the elite. The money they earned was proof of entitlement, and they exchanged it for goods in town marketplaces. Rural food sellers used the money earned to pay taxes or rents to the urban elite, thus completing the cycle. A special case involved the access of slave plantation owners to the surplus. When these owners resided in cities, they appropriated the surplus of their slaves in the form of cash. That cash was obtained by the sale of the uncompensated agricultural produce of agricultural slaves in town markets. Town-dwelling renters of agricultural land received their

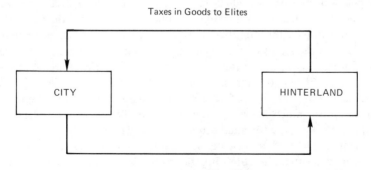

Figure 2-1. City-Hinterland Exchanges in Kind

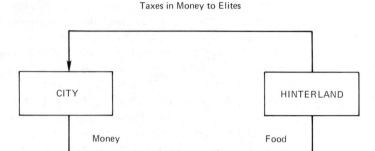

Figure 2-2. City-Hinterland Exchanges in Money

share of the surplus in money by means of the same circuitous process. Payments in cash and in kind were not mutually exclusive. Town elites normally received the surplus in part as goods and in part as cash. Food they consumed or bartered; cash they spent. In so doing, they supported independent workers whose numbers increased the city's population. However, the workers engaged in these derivative industries depended upon the prior appropriation of the agricultural surplus by the landed, bureaucratic, religious, or political elite.

SOCIAL STRATIFICATION AND CITIES

Migratory societies were relatively unstratified and their leaders were usually elective. Their claim to leadership rested upon demonstrated ability and war service, and these capacities they continued to exercise every day. The bulk of the population consisted of equal-status freemen. Everyone lived a simple existence under the close moral scrutiny of tribesmen. However, the development of cities undermined the primitive equality of nomadic life. On the one hand, cities enhanced the status of the urban elite in relation to freemen. The exalted status of urban kings, bureaucrats, warriors, priests, and landlords soared high above the level of the common man. On the other hand, the city-state perfected and expanded the institution of slavery. The enslaved inhabitants of conquered territories ranked much below the common man. Slavery therefore lengthened the distance between the top and bottom of the social hierarchy.

The exalted status of urban elites violated nomadic norms of social equality at the same time that the elite's luxurious life-style violated the old-fashioned morality of the tribal camp. Tribesmen everywhere regarded cities as centers of immorality. In the opinion of Ibn Khaldun (1958), city people first acquired a taste for luxury, then for immorality, especially sexual promiscuity. "The city . . . teems with low people of blameworthy character" (Khaldun 1958: 294). Catering to the jaded taste of the urban rich, merchants reflected and contributed to the deterioration of the "sedentary culture." Cunning, disputatious, quarrelsome, persistent, merchants developed character qualities "remote from virtue and manliness" that tended to undermine nomadic simplicity. For this reason, Ibn Khaldun supposed the sedentary culture of cities undermined the warriors' toughness that had founded the state. The life cycle of a great city began with foreign conquests, continued to luxury, and ended in depravity, military defeat, and obliteration.

The Hebrew prophets of the Old Testament reflect the same belief. As nomadic invaders, the Hebrews had occupied the towns of Canaan, even adopting the idolatrous religion of the conquered. However, the newly urbanized Hebrews retained in their religious tradition the equalitarian values of the nomadic encampment. Monarchy and class distinction were alien to this religious tradition. "Men were brothers, equal persons, and bound to the service of their tribe by an intense in-group loyalty" (Turner 1941: 334). In the ninth century B.C. the prophets Elijah and Elisha protested against the worship of Baal, the greed of the rich, the misery of the poor, royal misdeeds, and the sensuality of the cities (Turner 1941: 349). As a result of their protest, Phoenician Baalism was overthrown in Israel but urban civilization persisted (Weber, 1952: 154-155). Eighth-century prophets (Amos, Hosea, Micah, Isaiah) returned to the evils of the urban class system, interpreting the rise of neighboring Assyria as God's judgment upon the wickedness of Israel's kings and plutocrats.

This critique of the urban social order depended upon the juxtaposition of the strict moral values of the Hebrew tribesmen with the depravity that urban civilization had precipitated. In actuality, Hebrews were not the world's worst offenders. Hebrews never deified their rulers and never fully legitimated slavery, whose practice was less extensive than in neighboring countries. The religious tradition of the Hebrews apparently prevented the extremes of social inequality that urban civilization produced elsewhere. Nonetheless, the prophets' furious reaction to the social inequality, depravity, and luxury of urban civilization in Israel is proof of the underlying direction of social change. The prophetic lament was exceptionally powerful, but their critical reaction to urban civilization was rather typical of the transition from nomadic to urban existence in antiquity.

URBAN TRADE GUILDS

Most people residing in preindustrial cities were nonelite. Trade guilds were "the most obvious" social institutions of nonelite people (Sjoberg 1960: 187). *Trade guilds* were involuntary membership organizations for people engaged in trades. Every trade had its guild, even marginal trades such as begging or thieving. Therefore, most free workers belonged to a trade guild. Notable exceptions were the religious, political, and military bureaucracies whose access to the agricultural surplus provided the basic industry. Slaves too were usually excluded from guild membership. Nonetheless, the "overwhelming number" of urban workers were guild members.

Guilds had eight functions (Burrage and Corry 1981: 375-376). First, every guild wanted a monopoly over its trade: to this end, guilds everywhere tried to obtain legal authority to exclude nonmembers from trade in their product or service [10]. A modern heritage of this practice are laws preventing unlicensed persons from serving as medical doctors or attorneys. Second, guilds wanted exclusive authority to admit people to membership. Because guild membership was a prerequisite to practicing an occupation, the right to admit members was tantamount to determining the size and composition of the trade's work force. Among the various qualifications required for guild membership, "kinship ranks paramount" (Sjoberg 1960: 191). Guilds were resoundingly nepotistic, admitting to full membership the kin of members while excluding outsiders.

Guilds also monopolized the training of personnel for practice of the occupation. Craft "mysteries" were closely guarded from outsiders, thus protecting the guildsmen's monopoly. Guilds also made binding rules about how members could practice the occupation. Guild rules prescribed tools, sequence of work, product quality, wages, prices, and hours. Political control was a fifth function of trade guilds. Ancient guilds were "nearly always" a state organization of social control (Weber 1976: 47). Here the ancient guilds differed from medieval guilds in Europe, which began for the first time to serve as representatives of the membership against the warrior or priestly elite (Weber 1976: 337-365; Finley 1973: 138). The sixth function of guilds was to assist members in business life. There were no commercial banks so guildsmen pooled their money and lent capital to members who wished to engage in trade. In the same sense, guildsmen undertook mutual assistance for social welfare, there being no public welfare to fall back upon in distress. Guilds assured members of a proper burial and assisted widows and children of deceased members. Finally, guilds performed religious services on behalf of their membership. Each guild normally had patron dieties to whom members looked for divine protection and assistance. Placating these dieties was both pious and prudent (Sjoberg 1960: 187-196).

A common error equates ancient trade guilds with modern chambers of commerce, associations of manufacturers, or trade unions. Admittedly, there are some parallels, but the differences are more important than the similarities. First, the ancient guilds united employers and employees in the same organization rather than, as in industrial capitalist societies, separating the two. Second, guilds usually functioned as agencies of the government rather than as independent representatives of the common man to the government. Third, the mentality of guildsmen was "acquisitive but not productive" (Finley 1973: 144). The religious, social, and benevolent activities of ancient guilds were their central activities. "Technical progress, economic growth, productivity, even efficiency have not been significant goals since the beginning of time" (Finley 1973: 144). Custom still regulated the economic life of ancient towns. The ancients knew about price-making markets and rejected them because they were repugnant to their moral values. In this climate of opinion, guilds put principal emphasis upon the sacred and fraternal aspect of the occupational community and denigrated technological improvement. Merchants occupied an inferior social status in every preindustrial city [11].

NETWORK DEVELOPMENT IN PREINDUSTRIAL SOCIETY

Because ancient cities depended upon imperialism, religion, and slave-owning, the long-prevailing tradition in sociological analysis has emphasized their abrupt contrast with modern cities. Weber called the cities of antiquity and the Middle Ages "consumer cities" because they depended for basic industry upon the extraction of rent and taxes from the agricultural hinterland. He contrasted these cities with "producer cities" more characteristic of industrial modernity (Hoselitz 1954-1955). Producer cities obtain their food by exchanging efficiently manufactured goods produced in the city for food grown in the countryside (Keyfitz 1965: 275-275). This contrast has strong basis in fact, and it makes a useful point about the abrupt emergence of industrial society in Europe during the Middle Ages.

On the other hand, the abrupt contrast between preindustrial and industrial, or consumer and producer city presumes that nothing of importance happened to urban life during the entire preindustrial period from 4000 B.C. until A.D. 1750. Then cataclysmic changes began (Cahnman 1966). That interpretation suggests revolution rather than evolution. Moreover, the abrupt contrast assumes there were no differences among preindustrial societies, whereas "premodern societies differ a great deal" in complexity of urban network (Rozman 1976). Functionalists (Hauser 1965; Davis 1973) have complained that the consumer-producer contrast exaggerates the abruptness of change, thus overlooking evolutionary continuities. Rozman's research in urban networks has supported their evolutionary view. Preindustrial cities were not static; their societies underwent continuous evolutionary change in urban network for at least a thousand years before the Industrial Revolution. These evolutionary changes paved the way for the more abrupt changes that followed.

Rozman (1976: 33) defines *urban network* as a "hierarchy of settlements" that specialize in commerce or administration. These settlements form a hierarchy because they contain many small settlements, some middle-sized ones, and a few big ones. Settlements in the urban "network" are called *central places,* distinguished from ordinary agricultural villages by the presence of an administrative seat or a recurrent marketplace. A recurrent marketplace is one held regularly, say, every month. These central places form a functional hierarchy reflected in population size. Rozman (1976: 149) charted the distribution of central places in the Russian Empire in 1782, a half century before industrialization began there. The highest-ranking central place was Moscow, population 300,000. Russia also contained five major administrative centers and 538 intermediate cities as well as 1,100 villages. Thus the central places of Russia formed a pyramidal hierarchy on the basis of population.

When assured political continuity, preindustrial urban networks matured. Comparative research in preindustrial Russia, Japan, and China has indicated the presence of urban networks long before the Industrial Revolution. In the pre-urban period, only villages existed. There was no regional or national political center to tax agriculture. The urban period began when, at last, regional and national political centers developed. In Russia, Kiev and Moscow were such centers; in Japan, Edo (later Tokyo). Rozman (1973, 1976) found that these capitals directed smaller cities to administer their rule in outlying territories. This political process filled the urban hierarchy from the top level to the bottom. Big cities spawned smaller ones. As states matured and political stability persisted, commercial centers began to take hold at the bottom, usually initiated on the periphery of administrative settlements.

The downward construction of an administrative hierarchy preceded the development of commercial cities. Rozman distinguishes three preliminary stages of urban development: tribute city, state city, and imperial city. "Marketing settlements" appeared only at the conclusion of the imperial phase. In Japan, the three political stages lasted from the seventh century until the thirteenth. In Russia, the strictly political stages lasted from the eighth century until the fifteenth (Rozman 1976: 8, 74, 76). Thereafter, mercantile settlements developed; so a mixed political-commercial urban network existed. However, mercantile settlements started as numerous small trading centers from which larger trading centers eventually emerged. Smaller cities now spawned bigger ones. Thus commerce constructed its urban network from the bottom up, whereas the political order constructed a network from the top down. The fruition of both processes was a multicity network with numerous large and small administrative, commercial, and mixed central places.

SUMMARY

Basic industries of preindustrial cities were the state, religion, and absentee ownership of agricultural estates. High-ranking persons in each sector constituted the urban elite: priests, warriors, public officials, and estate owners. The king was supreme and united in his person the realms of religion and state (Bendix 1978: 7). Commerce and manufacturing existed, but these were for the most part nonbasic and otherwise secondary in importance to the first three. The households of elite urban families received the agricultural surplus in money, in kind, or in some combination of the two. The elite supported merchants and artisans out of the surplus received from the agricultural hinterland. Therefore these nonelite persons obtained entitlement to a share of the agricultural surplus by performing services of value to the ruling elite. The urban nonelite was organized into trade guilds that performed religious, fraternal, and commercial services for their membership. In return for the agricultural surplus received, the urban elite organized and directed the religious, protective, administrative, and public works services that supported agricultural productivity in the hinterland.

NOTES

1. "The inhabitants of a city . . . must always ultimately derive their subsistence, and the whole materials and means of their industry, from the country." Adam Smith, *The Wealth of Nations.* New York: Modern Library, 1937, p. 380.
2. " . . . the art of war is in some sense a natural mode of acquisition. Hunting is part of that art; and hunting ought to be practiced—not only against wild animals, but also against human beings who are intended by nature to be ruled by others and refuse to obey that intention—because war of this order is naturally just."
3. In fact, pharaohs could not consume it all despite their lavish way of life. "Quite a lot was redistributed to support a whole new population of non-farmers, from laborers to clerks, and some was used . . . to pay for imported raw materials" (Childe, 1957: 89).
4. For a review of Far Eastern kingship, see Melford Spiro, "Ancient Buddhist Conception of Kingship," *Journal of Asian Studies* 36 (1977): 789-791; see also Spiro's exchange with J. S. Tambiah, pp. 801-812.
5. Pagan syncretism did not end abruptly when people became Christians. The vehement opposition of the ancient Church to astrology reflected the difficulty that Christian priests experienced in compelling adherents to disavow their old-fashioned belief in the ability of pagan deities to affect personal destiny. See St. Augustine, *The City of God.* New York: Modern Library, 1950, p. 143. Even in the Middle Ages, most Christians continued to believe in pagan gods. "When Christians refused to pray to the gods of the various pagan cults, it was not as a rule for any want of belief in their existence; on the contrary, they regarded them as evil demons, dangerous indeed, but weaker than the sole Creator." Marc Bloch, *Feudal Society,* trans. L. A. Manyon. London: Routledge and Kegan Paul, 1961, p. 32.

6. "Many primitive societies manage entirely without a market, or exchange rates, or commercial trade at all." Colin Renfrew, *Before Civilization*. New York: Knopf, 1973, p. 116.

7. "The Graeco-Roman towns were never predominantly communities of manufacturers, traders, or craftsmen: they were, in origin and principle, urban congeries of land owners" (Anderson 1974: 19).

8. One classic view links the decline of European feudalism to the growing use of money in towns. See Maurice Dobb, *Studies in the Development of Capitalism*. New York: International, 1947, pp. 34-57.

9. Ibn Khaldun called this appropriation process the typical form of a "sedentary culture." "The dynasty collects the property of the subjects, and spends it on its inner circle . . . The money comes from the subjects, and is spent among the people of the dynasty and then among those inhabitants of the city who are connected with them." Ibn Khaldun, *The Muqaddimah: An Introduction to History*, trans. Franz Rosenthal, Vol. II. London: Routledge and Kegan Paul, 1958, pp. 286-287.

10. "A guild is an organization of craft workers specialized in accordance with the type of occupation. It functions through undertaking two things, namely, internal regulation of work, and monopolization against outsiders. It achieves its object if everyone joins the guild in the location in question." (Max Weber 1961: 136).

11. Regarding the inferior social status of merchants, see also Jospeh P. L. Jiang, "Towards a Theory of Pariah Entrepreneurship," pp. 147-162, in Gehan Wijeyewardene, ed., *Leadership and Authority*. Singapore: Centre for Southeast Asian Studies in the Social Sciences, University of Singapore, 1968; F. Stambouli and A. Zghal, "Urban Life in Pre-Colonial North Africa," *British Journal of Sociology* 27 (1976): 16-17.

REFERENCES

Anderson, Perry. 1974. *Passages From Antiquity to Feudalism*. London: Verso.

Aristotle. 1946. *The Politics of Aristotle*. Trans. Ernest Barker. Oxford: Clarendon.

Bendix, Reinhard. 1978. *Kings or People*. Berkeley and Los Angeles: University of California Press.

Bloch, Marc. 1961. *Feudal Society*. Trans. L. A. Manyon. London: Routledge and Kegan Paul.

Burrage, Michael C., and David Corry. 1981. "At Sixes and Sevens: Occupational Status in the City of London from the Fourteenth to the Seventeenth Century." *American Sociological Review* 46: 375-393.

Cahnman, Werner J. 1966. "Historical Sociology of Cities: A Critical Review." *Social Forces* 45: 155-161.

Carcopino, Jerome. 1940. *Daily Life in Ancient Rome*. New Haven: Yale University Press.

Chapman, Ann M. 1957. "Port of Trade Enclaves in Aztec and Maya Civilizations," pp. 114–153, in Karl Polanyi, Conrad M. Arensberg, and Harry W. Pearson, eds. *Trade and Market in the Early Empires.* Glencoe, Illinois: Free Press.

Childe, V. Gordon. 1957. *New Light on the Most Ancient East,* 4th ed. New York: Grove Press.

——. 1964. *What Happened in History.* New York: Penguin.

Davis, Kingsley, ed. 1973. *Cities: Their Origin, Growth, and Human Impact.* San Francisco: W. H. Freeman.

Finley, M. I. 1973. *The Ancient Economy.* Berkeley and Los Angeles: University of California Press.

Gouldner, Alvin. 1965. *Enter Plato.* New York: Basic Books.

Hauser, Philip M. 1965. "Urbanization: An Overview," pp. 1–47, in Philip M. Hauser and Leo Schnore, eds. *The Study of Urbanization.* New York: Wiley.

Hill, Richard Childe. 1978. "At The Cross Roads: The Political Economy of Postwar Detroit." *Urbanism Past and Present* No. 6: 1–21.

Hogben, Lancelot. 1937. *Mathematics for the Million.* New York: Norton.

Hoselitz, Bert F. 1954–1955. "Generative and Parasitic Cities." *Economic Development and Cultural Change* 3: 278–294.

Kautsky, Karl. 1972 [1909]. *Foundations of Christianity.* New York: Monthly Review.

Keyfitz, Nathan. 1965. "Political-Economic Aspects of Urbanization in South and Southeast Asia," pp. 265–309, in Philip Hauser and Leo Schnore, eds. *The Study of Urbanization.* New York: Wiley.

Khaldun, Ibn. 1958 [1284]. *The Muqaddimah: An Introduction to History.* London: Routledge and Kegan Paul.

Lamberg-Karlovsky, V. V., ed. 1972. *Old World Archeology.* San Francisco: W. H. Freeman.

Mayer, Harold M. 1965. "A Survey of Urban Geography," pp. 81–113, in Philip Hauser and Leo Schnore, eds. *The Study of Urbanization.* New York: Wiley.

Moseley, K. D., and Immanuel Wallerstein. 1978. "Precapitalist Social Structures." *Annual Review of Sociology* 4: 259–290.

Polanyi, Karl. 1977. *The Livelihood of Man.* New York: Academic Press.

Rostovzeff, Michael. 1930. *A History of the Ancient World,* 2 vols. Oxford: Clarendon Press.

Rozman, Gilbert. 1973. *Urban Networks in Ch'ing China and Tokugawa Japan.* Princeton: Princeton University Press.

——. 1976. *Urban Networks in Russia, 1750–1800.* Princeton: Princeton University Press.

Sjoberg, Gideon. 1960. *The Preindustrial City.* New York: Free Press.

——. 1963. "The Rise and Fall of Cities: A Theoretical Perspective." *International Journal of Comparative Sociology* 4: 107–120.

Skinner, G. William. 1977. *The City in Late Imperial China.* Stanford: Stanford University Press.

Smith, Adam. 1937 [1776]. *The Wealth of Nations.* New York: Modern Library.

Smith, Norman. 1978. "Roman Hydraulic Technology." *Scientific American* 238: 154–161.

Turner, Ralph. 1941. *The Great Cultural Traditions,* Vol. I, *The Ancient Cities.* New York: McGraw-Hill.

Van Beek, Gus. 1973. "The Rise and Fall of Arabia Felix," ch. 3, in Kingsley Davis, ed. *Cities: Their Origin, Growth and Human Impact.* San Francisco: W. H. Freeman.

Weber, Max. 1952. *Ancient Judaism.* New York: Free Press.

———. 1961 [1927]. *General Economic History.* New York: Collier Books.

———. 1968 *Economy and Society.* Vol. III New York: Bedminster Press.

———. 1976 [1909]. *The Agrarian Sociology of Ancient Civilizations.* Trans. by R. I. Frank. London: NLB.

CHAPTER 3 _____

Reorganization of Europe, 1150–1750

It is convenient to treat 1750 as the year in which the long epoch of preindustrial urbanism finally ended. But how did this transition occur? Obviously, not all at once on December 31, 1749! The initial transition was regional, not international. Industrial urbanization first appeared in western Europe. Later, industrial urbanization spread to the rest of the world and has by now incorporated or at least affected every world region. However, in the eighteenth century, industrial urbanization existed only in Europe; the rest of the world was preindustrial. The year 1750 only marks the fruition of industrial urbanization in Europe and the beginning of its worldwide diffusion. Figure 1-3 shows Europe's share of the aggregate population of the world's forty largest cities since 500 B.C. In Greco-Roman antiquity, Europe's proportion of the total was generous, but this share decreased virtually to nothing after the fall of Rome. Thereafter, Europe's rate of urban recovery was gradual until approximately A.D. 1500, when its share of the world's total began to soar. In 1550 the absolute population of Europe's cities finally regained the level of A.D. 100. Europe's share of big forty population peaked around 1900 and since then has declined.

Although industrial urbanization in Europe came to fruition in 1750, the underpinnings of change began six centuries earlier. These underpinnings preceded maturity, and industrial urbanization must therefore be understood as a developmental process extending across six centuries (Ashton 1948: 2). In 1750 the union of capitalism and industrial technology was completed, producing an acceleration in the rate of urbanization and justifying the significance of the year. However, between 1150 and 1750, the economic reorganization of Europe proceeded without industrial technology. Europe's cities began the twelfth century as isolated military fortresses ruled by warriors and priests. The basic industry of these cities was government and religion, and city growth depended upon extending a city's hinterland. By the end of the sixteenth century, the economic function of western Europe's cities had eclipsed their political-religious functions. Warriors and priests had lost their control; capitalists had achieved social and political prominence. Europe's cities were now organized in regional hierarchies with each bigger city serving as a center for a cluster of smaller ones. These regional hierarchies were linked to one another through free, price-making markets within national states. The economies of national states were linked together in a capitalist world system. Therefore the fortunes of urbanization in any nation or region of Europe now rode upon changing world markets—not political empire.

The modernization of Europe is a case study in how preindustrial urbanism ground to a halt, giving rise to industrial urbanization, its successor. This lengthy transition (1150-1750) is called the reorganization of Europe. Reorganization proceeded in two waves. The first occurred in the period 1150-1450. These changes lowered the barriers that feudalism has posed to capitalist reorganization. By the end of this period, capitalism was at last preponderant in Britain, France, the Low Countries, Scandinavia, Germany, Switzerland, and northern Italy. The second wave of change occurred between 1450 and 1750. In this period, the capitalist reorganization of European society progressed while the Scientific Revolution consolidated the foundation for industrial technology (Ashton 1948: 16). After 1750 capitalism and industrial technology came together as the Industrial Revolution (Table 3-1).

EUROPEAN FEUDALISM, 1150-1450

Town life had been moderately developed in Europe under Roman rule, but Roman withdrawal exposed Europe to invasions incompatible with preindustrial urbanization. In the bleak aftermath of Roman collapse, Muslim, Hungarian, and Scandinavian raiders laid waste the poorly defended European countryside

Table 3-1. Origins of Industrial Urbanization in Europe

	Society	Science	Technology
1150-1450	Capitalist cities in feudal societies	Aristotelian	Preindustrial
1450-1750	Capitalist societies	Scientific Revolution	Preindustrial
1750-present	Capitalist societies	Experimental	Industrial

(Bloch 1961). Towns were deserted, commerce ceased, population declined, and European regions reverted to rudimentary economies based on subsistence agriculture, barter, and domestic self-sufficiency. Unable to rely on defended frontiers, the European countryside sprouted military fortresses to which the surrounding population repaired when invaders appeared. The armor-clad warriors who commanded these castles depended for subsistence upon the agriculture of the people they ruled. The tracts of agricultural land were called *feuds*. The overlords of every *feud* received a share of the agricultural surplus in goods (not money) and lived in the fortress. Most overlords were secular nobles: knights, barons, margraves, and so forth. Some were ecclesiastical. However, all commanded a military garrison, exercised high and low justice, and made political decisions in the locality. In the strict economic sense, therefore, feudalism was an exchange of protection for a share of the agricultural surplus, but the protector lived in the countryside rather than in the city, and the protection was the shelter of a local fortress rather than a defended frontier.

Pirenne (1947: 41-43) has described the urban revival in Europe after the Dark Ages. The cities of Europe began around A.D. 1100 as "suburbs" of warrior-controlled fortresses, and merchant colonies developed under the shadow of the fortress. The cities were called *bourgs* and their inhabitants *bourgeois*. Warriors encouraged the merchant colonies because the latters' long-distance trade in luxury products permitted the elite classes of warriors and priests to acquire fancy goods (Pirenne 1947: 142). In origin, therefore, the trading suburb of early medieval Europe was a derivative of and a tributary to the military fortress. This arrangement was typical of preindustrial urbanism everywhere. However, subsequent events in the medieval Occident departed from the usual scenario of preindustrial societies, and, by creating enclaves of capitalism in feudal society, set the stage for the Industrial Revolution of the eighteenth century.

Before the Industrial Revolution could happen, townspeople had to overcome the political and social repression of feudal lords. This social conflict had three principal sources. First, the humble social origins of tradesmen exposed them to contempt. Medieval craftsmen and merchants were at first serfs whose masters "allowed them" to move to the city in return for a fee. Only gradually "did the serfs in medieval cities gain full personal freedom" (Weber 1976: 338). Feudal lords "despised" the bourgeoisie, whom they considered, as Adam Smith (1937: 376) recounted, "a parcel of emancipated slaves." The second cause of social conflict was political and social rivalry. Warriors and priests had no desire to share political authority or social prestige with tradesmen. However, reviving commerce continually gave rise to wealthy plebeians. Wealth conferred economic power on the basis of which merchants and artisans could seek political power and social prestige. The third cause was ideological hostility to the commercial way of life (Hirschman 1977). The Church was hostile to commerce, regarding profit "as a danger to salvation" repugnant to its "ascetic ideal" (Pirenne 1947: 28-29). The prosperity and power of the urban bourgeoisie contradicted "the interests and ideas of a society dominated materially by the Church whose aversion to trade was unconquerable" (Pirenne 1947: 50-51).

Under the leadership of the mercantile classes of artisans, traders, and financiers, medieval cities successfully challenged the right of priests and warriors to rule. They demanded and obtained full or limited self-rule (Pirenne 1947: 150). This challenge involved an inversion of power and status relations in cities whose very origins reflected the priority of political-religious authority. In many cases, feudal authorities granted cities charters of self-rule in exchange for money (Smith 1937: 376). These payments often revived the flagging fortunes of warrior families, which as chivalry waned shifted their investments into commercial farming. Some cities employed mercenary soldiers to drive out feudal lords. Others mustered a civic militia to overcome the armed resistance of feudal elites and proclaim a city-state (Tigar 1977: 3-4). Rich urban merchants also allied themselves with monarchs against the feudatories. Loans of money by city financiers enabled princes to suppress independent nobles or clerics; and cities received as a reward limited grants of self-rule from triumphant monarchs (Pirenne 1947: 218). The consequence was creation of a continental network of commercial cities in which the bourgeoisie was politically, economically, and socially supreme within the city walls (Pirenne 1947: 201). The freedom of action this supremacy accorded laid the basis for capitalist industrialization later.

Municipal self-rule in the medieval Occident was a historically unique event (Abrams 1978: 29-30). All preindustrial societies had experienced the tension between warriors and priests, on the one hand, and merchants, on the other. But only in the medieval Occident were merchants able to unsurp political power in the cities, and then develop the cities as capitalist enclaves in feudal societies. Equivalent usurpations never occurred, for example, in Greco-Roman antiquity (Finley 1973: 138), even though the great cities of antiquity were larger in population than the early medieval cities (Anderson 1974: 150; Weber 1976: 339). The world of Islam also produced numerous trading cities that were centers of science and enlightenment, but Islamic cities never obtained political independence from the warrior-priest elite. China, Russia, and India offer further examples of imperial societies whose great cities never achieved municipal autonomy under the political control of a bourgeoisie. In China, for example, the imperial cities were ruled by appointive mandarins responsible to the emperor. Mandarins commanded detachments of imperial troops. Local commercial classes never overpowered the imperial troops, and never obtained self-rule in cities. "No Chinese cities ever established themselves as municipalities possessing defined powers of independent jurisdiction" (Van der Sprenkel 1977: 609; see also Daunton 1978: 259). As a result, mandarins imposed their law, science, religion, status ethic, and values upon China's cities. Mandarins stifled capitalism and thus obstructed China's economic development.

Trade guilds were fraternal organizations of merchants, artisans, and journeymen. As with other associations in the preindustrial world, these guilds had economic, political, social, and religious responsibilities. However, Occidental trade guilds in the Middle Ages became politically independent of the warrior-priest elite and organized the struggle of the bourgeoisie against this traditional elite. This revolutionary employment of guild affiliations was historically unique. In Greco-Roman antiquity (Finley 1973: 138) and other preindustrial eras, elites used guilds to organize their power, but in medieval Europe guilds organized the resistance of nonelites. The guilds were successful in this struggle, and after ousting the warriors and priests, the richer guildsmen established themselves as the new rulers of Europe's flourishing cities.

The victory of the European bourgeoisie in the Middle Ages was an indispensable prerequisite to the Industrial Revolution in the eighteenth century. What permitted the townsmen to win this victory? Max Weber (1968: III, 1236-1265; Murvar 1967; Hoselitz 1969) argued that townsmen won because they were united (Abrams 1978: 30-32). Their unity reflected the townsmen's sense of being members of the city. Membership in a city depended upon joining it, and this was accomplished by taking an oath of allegiance and satisfying the residence requirement. Medieval cities thus acquired the form of "oath-bound communes" whose residents pledged allegiance to the city that conferred citizenship upon them in return [1]. Each urbanite obtained this citizenship as an individual, independent of any ethnic, regional, or locality origins.

The source of urban citizenship was the oppressed countryside. In the countryside, city folk had been unfree; each belonged to the land, and every tract of land had its feudal overlord. To escape unfree status, agricultural workers fled to cities. Escaped serfs could be captured in the city and returned in chains to the countryside, where their feudal overlord would decide what punishment they deserved [2]. However, municipal law bestowed personal freedom upon serfs who had lived a year and a day in the city without recapture by their feudal *seigneur* (Wallerstein 1974: 19-20). "City air breathes free" was the maxim. As a result, European cities became refuges for escaped serfs. These refugees could never return to the countryside because their feudal overlords waited there to punish them. Therefore city people had to band together for mutual protection, and those thus associated nourished a collective animosity toward the feudal social structure still very much alive in the rural countryside (Anderson 1974: 150).

The significance of this civic bond in Europe emerges in contrast to the vast preponderance of preindustrial societies in which municipal self-rule did not eventuate (Hoselitz 1969). In China, for example, the populations of cities were recruited from the countryside. But the people thus recruited viewed themselves as rural people temporarily sojourning in the city (Skinner 1977: 538). The consequence of this identity was the multilateral formation of ethnic groups. These exclusive groupings fragmented the city's population and also militated against the formation of an urban citizenship capable of uniting people of diverse background.

Each trade tended to recruit people from the same rural locality. These "same place people" were coethnics. The result was "an ethnic division of labor" in urban occupations (Skinner 1977: 544). The spirit of trade guilds was fraternal because the members were coethnics [3]. Their ethnic spirit reinforced the natural propensity of trade guilds to combat innovation in technique, impersonal labor-management relations, and a price system of production. Chinese guilds were too strong for capitalism. In contrast, Occidental trade guilds consisted of rural refugees whose only basis of solidarity was voluntary adherence. The social relations within the guilds and Occidental cities were, as a result, impersonal, individualistic, and competitive compared with social relations in Chinese cities and trades [4]. This spirit of impersonality decisively weakened the solidarity of guilds in the Occident and permitted price-cutting capitalists to emerge. As events proved, this victory was crucial for capitalist industrialization in the Occident—which could not occur in China.

The growth of towns in medieval Europe encouraged the capitalist reorganization of agriculture. The shortage of serfs caused by the plague epidemic (1347-1350) and urban runaways more or less compelled feudal lords to put the remaining tenantry on a cash rather than enserfed status (Brenner 1976: 54). Next, the landowners began to enclose their agricultural estates. *Enclosure* was a process by which, from 1100 on, agricultural land that had been unoccupied or shared among enserfed villagers and landlord "passed into individual use and enjoyment" (Heaton 1931: 523). On the continent of Europe, enclosure proceeded in spurts, but in Britain the process was continuous after 1200. By 1500 the manorial system in Europe was entirely dissolved (van Bath 1977: 113-114). Early enclosers were urban merchants who purchased agricultural land from feudal overlords, then evicted the resident population, substituting hired labor to work the land. Later, feudal overlords began to enclose land on their own account (Pirenne 1947: 64, 82; Smith 1937: 389; Ashton 1948: 24). Either way, enclosure was associated with concentration of land ownership into fewer hands, "improvement" of agricultural technique, and eviction of peasantry. Evicted peasants had then to find some other livelihood, and seeking this, wandered into medieval towns. Enclosure continued into the early modern period. In Britain, Tudor (1485-1603) and early Stuart (1603-1649) monarchs attempted to slow the enclosure movement by protecting the peasants' traditional rights to till the soil and punishing rural-urban migration (Polanyi 1944). The punishments were bloody. Tudor legislation delayed but could not reverse the deterioration of feudal society and the growth of cities.

Reviving commerce, municipal self-rule, and enclosures combined to produce a revival of urban life in Europe between 1100 and 1300. Pirenne (1947: 58-59) reported Europe's urbanization approached 10 percent from the twelfth century, and this level was slightly exceeded in the Low Countries, Lombardy, and Tuscany. However, this urbanization peaked around 1350, then declined until about 1450. Historians call this recession the crisis of feudalism. The first blow was the Black Death, or bubonic plague, which carried away one third of Europe's population between 1347 and 1350. At about this time, peasant revolts broke out and "social hatred" raged like "madness" (Pirenne 1947: 192, 201). Wallerstein (1974: 37) explains the crisis of feudalism as a "conjuncture" of unfavorable but unrelated events. Whatever the causes, the hundred years' crisis of feudalism was a period in which the boundaries of Europe contracted, trade and population declined, cultivated land returned to wilderness, villages were deserted, and the size and number of cities were reduced. This decline of European urbanization in the fourteenth century suggests cyclical urbanization characteristic of antiquity. Therefore the crisis of feudalism indicates that the preceding period of modernization, although fruitful and unprecedented, had not yet created societies capable of surmounting the limitations of preindustrial urbanization.

EARLY MODERN PERIOD, 1450-1750

From roughly 1450, the flagging fortunes of European urbanization reversed themselves. Commerce revived, population grew, science flourished, and cities increased in number and size. A technical regression in the level of urbanization occurred between 1600 and 1700 (see Table 3-2) because population growth outstripped urban growth, with a consequent reduction in the percentage of urban population (Tilly 1974: 39). This regression distinguishes the early modern period from industrial urbanization in the eighteenth century and thereafter. Yet the continuous growth of European population in the early modern period also distinguishes this phase from the crisis of feudalism during which European population declined—for the last time. Polanyi (1944: 68) defines *capitalism* as

Table 3-2. European Population in Cities of 100,000 and More, 1500-1950

Date	European Population (millions)	Number of Cities of 100,000+	Percent of Total Population in Cities of 100,000+
1500	50–60	4	1.2–1.7
1600	80–90	13–14	2.1–3.6
1700	115–125	14	2.1–2.7
1800	187	23	2.9
1850	401	143	12.3
1950	548	374	21.8

Source: Charles Tilly, "Urbanization," in Charles Tilly, ed., *An Urban World* (Boston: Little, Brown, 1974), p. 39. Reprinted by permission.

an economic system wholly dependent upon free markets in the factors of production: land, labor, and capital [5]. Markets are free when goods and services exchange at prices governed only by the interplay of supply and demand. According to this view, capitalism is a three-stage, self-correcting system. First, people produce goods and services for sale; these are commodities. Second, commodities are purchased at whatever price clears the market; high prices lead to unsold goods; low prices lead to shortages. Third, producers make a rational-instrumental evaluation of profitability in various lines of trade and enter those in which profits are highest. Under these circumstances, the price-making market governs how many people will engage in each trade and thus allocates labor among the various industries. When prices, interest rates, wages, or technology are administered by government or private monopolies, the autonomy of the price-making market is reduced in direct proportion to their interference. The more they interfere, the narrower the autonomy of the price-making market, and the less capitalistic the economic system.

Capitalism does not require industrial technology, and it can exist in a preindustrial society. Early modern Europe was such a society; capitalism had already emerged, but the technology of production and transportation was still preindustrial in character (Wallerstein 1974: 51, 58). Thus capitalism arrived 250 years before the Industrial Revolution, and the capitalist economic system was itself instrumental in creating the science and technology required to produce the Industrial Revolution.

The capitalist reorganization of European society was a unique historical event (Collins 1980: 935). A similar societal reorganization had never transpired in antiquity, nor did it transpire in any contemporaneous non-European society (Wallerstein 1974: 47). True, typically capitalist economic behavior and institutions are identifiable in antiquity and in non-European societies at various times. An important and continuing debate among scholars has focused on the existence of capitalism in Greco-Roman antiquity. This "oikos controversy" is complex (Harvey: 1973). Weber (1961: 275) defined capitalism as the "method of enterprise" applied to the satisfaction of human needs. In this sense much commercial activity of the middle ages and antiquity was capitalistic so capitalism is exceedingly ancient. Recognizing this objection, Weber (1961: 276) nevertheless insisted that "a whole epoch" could be described as "typically capitalistic" only when the contribution of private enterprise to want satisfaction had become so preponderant that if abruptly halted "the whole economic system must collapse." In other words, a *capitalist society* is one in which want satisfaction preponderantly depends upon private enterprise rather than state enterprise, householding, reciprocity, or redistribution—the principal economic alternatives (Polanyi, 1977: 35–43). Weber (1961: 276) argued that early modern Europe was the first capitalist society in this sense, and contemporary scholars (Wallerstein, 1974: 24) agree. Prior to this moment in history, capitalism had been restricted to enclaves in basically non capitalistic economies. In early modern Europe

(1500-1750) capitalism became preponderant in society, and then shaped the world to suit itself.

The capitalist reorganization of European society depended upon political, economic, and cultural changes (see Table 3-3) that involved social conflicts. The central political drama was the formation of national states ruled by monarchs. In the medieval period, kingdoms had been only figures of speech because real political power was in the hands of warrior dukes, margraves, and barons scattered over the countryside. A partial exception was England, in which, as a result of the Norman conquest, a national government in London continuously existed (Bendix 1978: Ch. 6). In the early modern period, kings gained authority and reduced the military-political power of the feudal nobility. The titled nobility resisted the growth of centralized monarchical power, but monarchs prevailed, always with the support of the urban bourgeoisie who lent money and soldiers to the royal cause. Centralization of political power finally produced the "age of absolutism" in which seventeenth-century monarchs, notably Louis XIV of France, obtained power against whose capricious exercise subjects had later to revolt.

Centralization of political power in the early modern period produced urbanization in two ways. Most important, national societies were much larger than the petty principalities they consolidated. Therefore free markets were vastly enhanced. Nations tried to protect their own industries against foreign competitors by means of import quotas, export incentives, tariffs, and legal restrictions on foreigners' commerce. This protectionist policy was called *mercantilism* (Weber 1961: 347). Its objective was to enhance national power by creating a

Table 3-3. Capitalist Reorganization of European Society, 1450-1750

Type of Change	Nature of Change	Associated Social Conflict
Political	Formation of national societies	Kings and bourgeoisie vs. feudal nobility
	Monarchical absolutism	Kings vs. people
	Colonialism	Nation vs. nation
Economic	Breakup of trade guilds	City vs. countryside Guilds vs. capitalists Cheap labor vs. guild labor
	Technological improvement in communication and transportation	International warfare and imperialist rivalries: nation vs. nation, capitalist vs. capitalist
Cultural	Reformation	Protestants vs. Catholics
	Scientific Revolution	Clergy vs. scientists

hoard of gold through a favorable balance of trade. This policy fell short of international free trade, which is the extension of the domestic free market across national boundaries. Nonetheless, mercantilist nations of Europe created large free trade zones within each new nation state [6]. In these zones, the capitalist reorganization of society progressed to the limit of technology and market size (Weber 1961: 337). This meant that the amount of trade passing through cities hugely increased, thus enhancing this basic industry. At the same time, cities began to export manufactured goods to distant markets, some urban but most rural. This export trade created a new industry capable of supporting city workers and thus encouraged the growth in population of European cities.

The formation of national markets was associated with the breakup of medieval trade guilds in cities (Unwin 1904: 19). These guilds had earlier been instrumental in freeing commercial cities from political rule by feudal authorities. This political objective gained, trade guilds began to experience conflicts of interest between wealthy and nonwealthy members. Wealthy members hoped to profit from the opening of distant markets, and they resented the trade guilds' protectionist and restrictive economic posture. On the one hand, poor guildsmen were afraid of outside competition and tried to restrain it by law. On the other, their restrictive policies interfered with adjustments required to surpass foreign competitors. For example, trade guilds specified the tools, methods, prices, and wages permissible in any trade to protect the livelihood of guild members by preventing cheap labor, innovative techniques, or price competition. Wealthy members had a financial motive to violate these restrictions. They wished to employ new production techniques involving the employment of cheap rural labor. These techniques comprised the "putting out" system whereby an urban merchant (a "factor") provided impoverished rural workers with raw materials and later with tools as well. The woolen industry was the most significant site of this technique. The cheap textiles competed with higher-priced products manufactured by urban craftsmen. Municipal guilds resented the competition of cheap rural labor, and they exerted their political influence to frustrate the "factors" who conducted it. One method was to regulate by law selling prices in the city market, thus preventing factors from underselling guildsmen. Another was to outlaw the sale of nonlocal manufactured goods in city markets, or to insist that all goods brought to market for sale be first approved by the relevant trade guild (Pirenne 1947: 212; Weber 1961: 327).

Medieval trade guilds opposed the factory system of production. Instead, guildsmen tried to perpetuate the fraternity of skilled workers, social equals who conducted trade in small shops using hand tools [7]. This romantic ideal was attractive but inefficient. Factories substituted a capitalist owner for the fraternity of guildsmen. The capitalist made all decisions and relied upon bureaucracy to pass these down to a work force of hired hands. Capitalists divided complex craft jobs into simple routines capable of mastery by unskilled workers. Capitalists also owned the means of production. In effect, guild policies precluded the expensive, power-driven factories that capitalists provided because workers could afford to provide only hand gools for themselves.

Medieval trade guilds were anticapitalist (Clark 1976: 7). They opposed competition, price-cutting, and profit maximization in the interest of "fair prices." They always attempted to exclude outside merchants from trading in their town (Hibbert 1963: 162, 165-172, 216), yet innovative techniques and relations of production could penetrate town markets only by competitive price-cutting and profiteering. Had the anticapitalist guilds prevailed, the craft organization of production would have excluded capitalism, thereby forestalling the Industrial Revolution in Europe. The Industrial Revolution of the eighteenth century depended upon the factory system of production as well as free markets. Therefore urban trade guilds were barriers to capitalist industrialization. The conflict between guildsmen and factors was a conflict of class interests. The wealthy desired the freedom to rearrange production for their own profit and the guildsmen defended their vested interest in the craft organization of manufacturing. The actual course of events in Europe involved the defeat and liquidation of trade guilds, and therewith a new freedom of action for manufacturing capitalists.

The further progress of the enclosure movement supported the capitalist reorganization of manufacturing in two ways. First, wealthy enclosers were efficient producers of agricultural commodities. Their efficient production guaranteed a big surplus of agricultural goods for nonagricultural workers. Second, enclosure prevented peasants from working the soil for subsistence and thus compelled them to look for nonagricultural livelihoods. Underemployed agricultural families provided a cheap labor reserve for urban factors in the textile and woolen industries. The factors took raw materials such as wool to the cottages where families spun and wove it. Wages of cottage industry workers were very low (Weber, 1961: Ch. 11). Had this cheap labor pool been unavailable, factors would not have been able to circumvent guild control of urban manufacturing. As it was, underemployed agricultural families took work away from high-priced guild labor in the cities (Hibbert 1963: 213). Underemployed agricultural workers tilted the balance in favor of urban capitalists and against urban labor. In this manner, the capitalist reorganization of agriculture supported the capitalist reorganization of manufacturing (Marx 1965: Vol. I, 134).

THE PROTESTANT REFORMATION

The Protestant Reformation in Europe, which began in 1517, introduced cultural changes supportive of capitalist modernization [8]. These cultural changes flourished in the process of capitalist reorganization already underway, but the Reformation also forwarded the process of change. Puritan support for modern-

ization came in two ways: legitimation of the social role of the capitalist entre-
preneur and endorsement of scientific research [9]. The first of these was the
earlier and more consistent. Catholic doctrine had always viewed merchants
with suspicion. The Church taught that virtuous conduct consisted in asceticism
and charity. Neither of these qualities particularly exalted the ordinary businessman (Weber 1961: 366-368). Moreover, the Church specifically condemned
high interest on loans and also demanded a "just price" in business transactions;
frugality was at best a minor virtue, shading into sin when developed at the
expense of charity. None of these ideas favored capitalism. Free markets required the taking of interest on money, a factor of production. They also
operated on the presumption that sellers charged "what the traffic would bear"
rather than some just price reflecting moral self-restraint. Finally, cost-cutting
frugality was a preoccupation of capitalist rationality. This preoccupation overrode old-fashioned charity.

In preindustrial societies everywhere, priests had claimed a monopoly of
natural scientific knowledge that they subsumed within their metaphysic. The
"inevitable confusion between theology and science" had been evident as early
as the fourth millennium B.C. (Childe 1964: 145). In early modern Europe this
priestly monopoly was successfully overturned, but the change required a social
conflict. The name of this conflict was the *Scientific Revolution.* The implicit
roots of this conflict reach back into the Judeo-Christian tradition on the one
hand, and the feudal separation of church and secular authorities on the other.
But the immediate source of the conflict was the emergence of a status group
of natural scientists who advanced interpretations of nature at variance with
the Bible. The conflict between science and religion began in astronomy, but it
quickly moved into medicine, biology, geography, geology, archaeology, anthropology, meteorology, chemistry, physics, philology, comparative mythology, and
political economy as well (White 1955: 168).

Household names of the Scientific Revolution are Copernicus (1473-1543),
Galileo (1564-1642), Kepler (1571-1630), and Newton (1642-1727). In the sixteenth century, both Protestant and Catholic theologians condemned their findings. Martin Luther "execrated the cosmology of Copernicus" and John Calvin
"frowned" upon scientific research (Merton 1957: 580). In the seventeenth
century, Catholics became the principal opponents of science. In 1616 the
Jesuits declared the Copernican system heretical. The Catholic Church then
turned over to the Holy Inquisition the task of combatting Copernican astronomy. Accused heretics were tried before Inquisition tribunals and if convicted,
they were offered the choice of recantation or death. This fate befell Galileo,
who was denounced, tried, and convicted of Copernican heresy in 1633. First
shown the instruments of torture, Galileo was advised to recant his belief in a
heliocentric universe. This recantation Galileo prudently made [10]. Others had
refused. The Copernican publicist Giordano Bruno, himself a Dominican friar,
was burned at the stake on February 2, 1600, because he refused to recant

heliocentric heresy. As events proved, clerical opposition was unsuccessful. There ultimately emerged a realm of natural science in which free inquiry was tolerated and truth judged on the basis of evidence rather than conformity to scripture. Nonetheless, the effort to prevent this outcome convulsed European society for three hundred years.

In the seventeenth century, the initial resistance of Reformation theologians to natural science ended. Puritan divines of the seventeenth century maintained instead that the true worship of God demanded "the systematic, rational, and empirical study of Nature. . . . " (Merton 1957: 575). To this end, Puritans founded many universities at which natural science was taught (Merton 1957: 588). Puritans were also heavily represented among professional scientists in the seventeenth through the nineteenth centuries (Merton 1957: 594). The Puritans' endorsement of natural science eliminated the antagonism between religion and natural science. Indeed, the Puritans' theological revision conferred upon natural science the prestige of religion and thus encouraged science and technology wherever Puritan pulpits prevailed.

"The knowledge gained through the application of the scientific method is the one factor above all others that made the modern city possible" (Sjoberg 1965: 62). The Scientific Revolution accompanied and, to some extent, caused technological innovation in manufacturing, transportation, communications, and agriculture (Ashton 1948: 16). In agriculture, the Middle Ages had been undynamic (Postan 1972: 44). Toward the end of the Middle Ages, however, important crop substitutions improved output and diet. Wheat substituted for rye as the principal winter crop, and the planting of legumes as soil improvers became standard practice (Hawley 1981: 42-43; Wallerstein 1974: 32). The invention of the printing press in the fifteenth century reduced the cost of books and thus increased their accessibility. Books communicated the results and spirit of the Scientific Revolution. Manufacturing benefited from harnessing wind and water as sources of power. These sources had never been tapped in Greco-Roman antiquity. Armaments industries flourished in the context of international conflict and exploration of the New World. Responding to military need, mines and quarries provided raw materials for cannon foundaries.

Transportation illustrates the close relationship between warfare, science, and technology. Ships grew larger, faster, more seaworthy, and capable of undertaking longer voyages than ever before. In the age of Elizabeth I (1558-1603), there were only four merchant ships of 400 tons each in England. But nearly a hundred ships of 40,000 tons were constructed in the single decade 1649-1659 (Merton 1957: 611). Most were warships. Technical problems of navigation attracted the finest scientific minds, including Newton. Practical navigation problems stimulated science and vice versa. For example, improving the compass led to research in magnetism. The finding of longitude gave rise to the theory of logarithms; tides tables provided verification data for Newton's law of attraction (Merton 1957: 619-620). In the periods 1661-1662 and 1686-1687,

41 percent of scientific investigations in Britain were "pure science" and 59 percent applied.

EUROPE AND CHINA

The capitalist reorganization of European society between 1450 and 1750 is, on its face, puzzling because many other world regions offered conditions that ought to have been superior for capitalism to those in Europe. Above all, China offered a continental empire of unrivaled political extent and size (Levinson 1967). China's capital was also the world's largest city (see Table 1-2). Chinese civilization was technologically advanced and superior in this respect to Europe's until 1450. A unitary coinage and boundary created an internal market of vast size. In contrast, Europe's polities were weak, divided, quarrelsome, and protectionist. The proliferation of independent and semi-independent principalities created barriers to trade. Yet the beginnings of capitalist urbanization took place in Europe rather than in China [11].

Explaining why requires a comparison of China and Europe: one point of comparison is religion. China had two religions. The elite religion was Confucian ethics; the popular religion a combination of ancestor worship and Taoism. Confucian ethics emphasized the right ordering of hierarchical social relationships. Its objective was a harmonious family in a harmonious society. Popular religion was riddled with superstition. Weber (1951) claimed that both Chinese traditions discouraged "rational bourgeois capitalism." Confucian ethics spurned commerce altogether and advanced the scholar-poet (not the capitalist) as most praiseworthy [12]. The Tao substitued superstitition for rational-instrumental mastery of the world. Therefore the life ethic of neither religious tradition supported the individualism, thrift, and technological innovation that bourgeois capitalism demanded. In contrast, Calvinism interpreted business prosperity as a manifestation of divine favor, thus sanctifying the life of the businessman rather than the humanist. Harmonious relationships were not sanctified. There is no contrast in this intersocietal comparison of supernatural China with secular Europe. On the contrary, in common with China and every other world society, Europe permitted religious ideas to regulate economic conduct. Weber concluded that the crucial difference among societies was in the ideas (Moulder 1977: 17). Europe's religious ideas produced capitalistic behavior, and this behavior, whatever of value it may have destroyed, was productive of capitalist reorganization of society (Weber 1961: 313).

Another reflection of this cultural contrast is the realm of science. China was superior to the West in science and technology throughout the Middle Ages. When Marco Polo visited China in 1215, he was unquestionably the representative of a technologically underdeveloped society (Wallerstein 1974: 39-47). Scholars disagree about the date when Europe at last pulled ahead of China in scientific technology. Joseph Needham (1963: 53) used 1450, a date sixty-six years in advance of the Reformation. There is, however, general agreement that no scientific revolution occurred in China, and that the stagnation of science in China supported the stagnation of China's economic development. Needham's (1969) research offers emphatic support for an intellectual explanation. On the other hand, Wallerstein (1974: 38-47) claims that imperial China did not want and did not need colonial expansion, whereas Europe, seeking escape from the crisis of feudalism, both needed and wanted it. If so, China had no practical motive for supporting natural science, and religious or cultural grounds might not be necessary to explain Chinese uninterest.

Chinese cities were supremely mercantile, and their inhabitants ruthlessly acquisitive. But Chinese cities, as noted earlier never developed oath-bound communes, remaining instead internally differentiated into mutually suspicious ethnic groups [13]. Workers organized their livelihood into trade guilds that hindered the development of free markets in labor and capital. The collapse of trade guilds supported the capitalist reorganization of European society, and this collapse did not occur in China (Golas 1977).

China's bureaucratic monarchy and traditional legal system "kept it from realizing the full implications of feudalism," unlike Europe (Levinson and Schurmann 1969: 99). Confucian law stigmatized merchants and made weak provision for property rights, contracts, or corporations—all legal fundamentals of capitalism. Furthermore, the Chinese bureaucracy turned into a traffic in offices whose holders milked them for personal profit. This is quite different from engaging in business for profit. In effect, China created a mandarin elite of official humanists whereas Europe invented the bourgeoisie.

DISCOVERY OF THE NEW WORLD

The capitalist reorganization of Europe in the sixteenth century has thus far been presented as a strictly European process involving changes in the state, the economy, and the culture of Europe. This is the orthodox view. But what about the discovery of the New World and its exploitation? Here were events outside of Europe whose consequences dramatically affected European society. Wallerstein has stressed this issue in a far-reaching but still unsettled revision of the orthodox view. In Wallerstein's (1974: 47) view, sixteenth-century northwestern Europe became the core of an emerging "capitalist world-economy." The periphery of the system was the New World and parts of Asia and Eastern Europe. The economic basis of the capitalist world-system was the shipment of manufactured goods produced in the core to the periphery where they were exchanged for raw materials. Producers in the core were free laborers working for wages. In the periphery, slavery and semislavery was the customary status of labor. In Wallerstein's view, the raw materials and gold of the New World were indispensable to the consolidation of capitalism in the European core. The riches of the New World lowered the real cost of supporting nonagricultural workers in Europe and the cost of producing manufactured goods. European powers were also able to exert political control in their colonies, thus pressing down the cost of necessary imports of raw materials.

Bluntly stated, Wallerstein (1974) holds that capitalism could not have triumphed in Europe without the exploitation of Europe's colonies. This view is quite different from the older Eurocentric one according to which capitalism came to fruition in Europe, then spread into the rest of the world. Wallerstein does not dispute the uniqueness of Europe's economic development: "As of 1450, the stage was set in Europe but not elsewhere for the creation of a capitalist world-economy" (Wallerstein 1974: 47). But the uniqueness of Europe was the combination of an integrated world economy on the one hand, and a proliferation of sovereign states on the other. In this situation the exigencies of the world economy were more powerful than the sovereign nations it encompassed. Therefore the world economy dominated weak, individual states. Wallerstein repeatedly contrasts this capitalist world system with old-fashioned empire. In an empire, the core derives its profit from exploitative taxation of and tribute from the periphery. The capital city is the principal beneficiary. In a capitalist world economy, the core's profit depends upon economic linkages that, once formed, are more efficient and more powerful than armed forces (Wallerstein 1974: 15).

The world-system interpretation of European modernization compels a recognition of Europe's debt to its exploited colonies. This view also reaches forward to develop the historical sources of twentieth-century neoimperialism based upon economic interdependence rather than political control. Yet Wallerstein's view has been criticized (Brenner 1977) for displacing class relations within societies as the focus of principal interest. Instead, the world-system theory has emphasized the world division of labor as though this world property could explain historical development in every region. The problem is to balance purely local causes for economic stagnation or development, freedom or slavery, against the externally imposed pressures of the newly formed world economy. For example, is the retarded economic development of Africa or Latin America the result of European colonialism or of the resistance of indigenous priests and warriors to economic change? Was Europe's economic development caused by exploitation of its colonies or by unique, Eurocentric upheavals in culture, economy, and polity? Obviously, the polarities need not exclude one another. However, ideological implications often guide arguments into the all or none extreme, and social science has thus far been unable to offer a fully satisfactory reconciliation.

SUMMARY

Between 1150 and 1450 commercial cities in Europe emerged as capitalist enclaves in feudal societies. Between 1450 and 1750 capitalism escaped from its urban enclaves and reorganized European and, later, world society. The Europe of 1500 was capitalist but preindustrial. The capitalist reorganization of Europe involved the formation of national states, the destruction of urban trade guilds, agricultural enclosure, cottage industry, and the formation of a capitalist world economy. On the cultural side, reorganization produced and was stimulated by the Protestant Reformation and the Scientific Revolution. All these social changes involved shifts of political, economic, and social power from warriors and priests, the traditional elite, to the urban bourgeoisie and agricultural capitalists. Such people controlled capital and capital had become the key to prosperity and political power.

Urban growth in the early modern period reflected the capitalist reorganization of European and world society. But urban growth fell short of urbanization! This was because European population grew even faster than urban population. Hence, urbanization actually declined between 1600 and 1700. In this period, the underemployed rural population began to engage in cottage industry, a capitalist precursor of the Industrial Revolution. This type of manufacturing did not require big cities or urbanization.

Europe's example shows that capitalism and urbanization need not accompany each other. The capitalism of commercial towns produced urbanization between 1150 and 1350. Indeed, capitalism then advanced by sealing itself up in urban enclaves. However, between 1450 and 1700, capitalism proceeded by building up the nation state and the rural countryside at the expense of protectionist towns. The formation of national economies in a capitalist world system brought economic pressure to bear upon the parochialism of Europe's towns. This parochialism collapsed, and towns ceased to have economic frontiers of their own or high-wage work forces enrolled in restrictive trade guilds. Thus the capitalism created in towns in the first period turned against the towns in the second.

Without medieval towns, there would have been no capitalist societies; without capitalist societies, no Scientific Revolution; without science, no industrial technology; without capitalism, science, and technology, no Industrial Revolution; without Industrial Revolution, no industrial urbanization in Europe. In this sense, medieval towns, capitalism, and the Scientific Revolution caused industrial urbanization in Europe.

NOTES

1. "The burgher joined the citizenry as an individual, and as an individual he swore the oath of citizenship. His personal membership in the local association of the city guaranteed his legal status as a burgher, not his tribe or sib." Max Weber, *Economy and Society,* Vol. II. New York: Bedminster Press, 1968, p. 1246.

2. "The flight of the serfs into the town went on without interruption right through the Middle Ages. These serfs, persecuted by their lords in the country, came separately into the towns, where they found an organized community . . . in which they had to subject themselves to the station assigned to them by the demand for their labor and the interest of their organized urban competitors." Karl Marx, *Capital,* Vol. I. Moscow: Foreign Languages Publishing House, 1965, p. 165.

3. "The free market, that is, the market which is not bound by ethical norms . . . is an abomination to every system of fraternal ethics." Max Weber, *Economy and Society,* Vol. II. New York: Bedminster Press, 1968, p. 637.

4. On the weakness and ineffectiveness of late medieval gilds in Europe, see Thrupp 1963: especially 264, 275.

5. Wallerstein (1979: 15) defines *capitalism* as "production for sale in a market in which the object is to realize the maximum profit." For still other definitions of capitalism, see Maurice Dobb, *Studies in the Development of Capitalism.* New York: International, 1947, pp. 1–9.

6. Economic historians have argued that mercantilism and state-building were related, a view accepted here. But Holland poses a challenging exception to this generalization because the Dutch built mercantilism without a national state. See Jelle C. Riemersma, "Economic Enterprise and Political Power After the Reformation," *Economic Development and Cultural Change* 3 (1954–1955): 297–308.

7. "The rules of the guilds . . . by limiting most strictly the number of apprentices and journeymen that a single master could employ, prevented him from becoming a capitalist. . . . The guilds zealously repelled every encroachment by the capital of merchants. . . . A merchant could buy every kind of commodity, but labour as a commodity he could not buy." Karl Marx, *Capital,* Vol. I. Moscow: Foreign Languages Publishing House, 1965, pp. 358–359.

8. Cohen (1980: 340) disputes Weber's view, claiming that "rational capitalism was born in pre-Reformation Italy, where Catholicism, not Protestantism, predominated. His observations about Renaissance Italy's commercial development before 1500 are correct. However, he acknowledges that guilds were more powerful in Renaissance Italy than in medieval cities of Protestant Europe. Moreover, the economic development of Renaissance Italy reflected a laxity of Catholic practice in a period of institutional decay; good Catholics could not have been capitalists in this historical

epoch. Cohen acknowledges that Protestantism completed the emancipation of capitalism, but he claims Weber overlooked the "long gradual historical period of development that produced" Reformation capitalism. This is a matter of textual interpretation because Weber's *General Economic History* contains many references to Italian banking (1961: 259–261). Weber always claimed that Catholicism was the feature of post-Roman civilization that basically distinguished Europe from the rest of the world's historical development.

9. Some clarifications are necessary. Protestantism refers to the whole reform movement emerging after Luther. Calvinism was one powerful sect of Protestantism, and Calvinist doctrine reached out to affect all Protestants (except Lutherans) in the Puritan movement. Important tenets of Puritanism included the sanctification of diligence and industry as means of glorifying God; the choice of vocation should depend upon social utility; the blessedness of reason, God's gift to man; the desirability of utilitarian education (Merton 1970: 57). For a historian's critique of Weber's Protestantism thesis, see Roland Bainton, *The Reformation of the Sixteenth Century* (Boston: Beacon, 1952).

10. Louis B. Fleming, "Vatican Opens Study on Clearing Galileo," *Los Angeles Times,* October 24, 1980, pt. I, p. 5.

11. Reviewing this large issue, Siu-Lun Wong distinguishes three approaches purporting to explain the lateness of Chinese industrialization: the cultural conservatism of Chinese society, the high-level equilibrium trap of Chinese population and agriculture, and the repressiveness of the Chinese state. See Siu-Lun Wong, "Industrial Entrepreneurship and Ethnicity," Ph.D. dissertation, Wolfson College of the University of Oxford, 1979, pp. 22–23. See also Anthony M. Tang, "China's Agricultural Legacy," *Economic Development and Cultural Change* 28 (1979): 1–22.

12. Wong (sup., p. 152) points out that merchants were not always disdained in traditional China. The Chinese state was prepared to alter its attitude "quite drastically" when necessary. The mercantile city of Shanghai also offered a regional exception to the prevailing contempt for merchants in traditional China.

13. This was still true in the early twentieth century: "Guilds usually sought to draw their membership from the people engaged in a single economic activity . . . The requirement in many guilds that members be natives of a single area other than the city in which the guild was located provides one of the most striking contrasts between European and Chinese guilds." Peter J. Golas, "Early Ch'ing Guilds," in William Skinner, ed., *The City in Late Imperial China.* Stanford: Stanford University Press, 1977, p. 563.

REFERENCES

Abrams, Philip. 1978. "Towns and Economic Growth: Some Theories and Problems," pp. 9–34, in Philip Abrams and E. A. Wrigley, eds. *Towns in Societies.* Cambridge: Cambridge University Press.

Anderson, Perry. 1974. *Passages from Antiquity to Feudalism*. London: Verso.

Ashton, T. S. 1948. *The Industrial Revolution, 1760-1830*. London: Oxford University Press.

Bendix, Reinhard. 1978. *Kings or People*. Berkeley and Los Angeles: University of California Press.

Bloch, Marc. 1961. *Feudal Society*. Trans. by L. A. Manyon. London: Routledge and Kegan Paul.

Brenner, Robert. 1976. "Agrarian Class Structure and Economic Development in Pre-Industrial Europe." *Past and Present* 70: 30-75.

———. 1977. "The Origins of Capitalist Development: A Critique of Neo-Smithian Marxism." *New Left Review* 104: 25-90.

Childe, Vere Gordon. 1964. *What Happened in History*. New York: Penguin.

Clark, Peter, ed. 1976. *The Early Modern Town*. London: Longman.

Cohen, Jere. 1980. "Rational Capitalism in Renaissance Italy." *American Journal of Sociology* 85: 1340-1355.

Collins, Randall. 1980. "Weber's Last Theory of Capitalism: A Systematization." *American Sociological Review* 45: 925-942.

Dalton, George. 1974. *Economic Systems and Society*. Harmondsworth: Penguin.

Daunton, M. J. 1978. "Towns and Economic Growth in Eighteenth Century England," pp. 245-277, in Philip Abrams and E. A. Wrigley, eds. *Towns in Societies*. Cambridge: Cambridge University Press.

Dobb, Maurice. 1947. *Studies in the Development of Capitalism*. New York: International.

Finley, M. I. 1973. *The Ancient Economy*. Berkeley and Los Angeles: University of California Press.

Golas, Peter J. 1977. "Early Ch'ing Guilds," pp. 555-580, in William Skinner, ed. *The City in Late Imperial China*. Stanford: Stanford University Press.

Harvey, David. 1973. *Social Justice and the City*. Baltimore: Johns Hopkins University Press.

Hawley, Amos H. 1981. *Urban Society*. 2d Ed. New York: Ronald.

Heaton, Herbert. 1931. "Enclosures." *Encyclopedia of the Social Sciences* 5: 523-527.

Hibbert, A. B. 1963. "The Economic Policies of Towns," pp. 157-229, in M. M. Postan, E. E. Rich, and Edward Miller, eds. *The Cambridge Economic History of Europe*, Vol. II. Cambridge: Cambridge University Press.

Hirschman, Albert O. 1977. *The Passions and the Interests: Political Arguments for Capitalism before its Triumph*. Princeton: Princeton University Press.

Hoselitz, Bert F. 1969. "The City, the Factory, and Economic Growth," pp. 72-90, in William A. Faunce and William H. Form. *Comparative Perspectives on Industrial Society*. Boston: Little, Brown.

Levinson, Joseph R. 1967. *European Expansion and the Counter-Expansion of Asia*. Englewood Cliffs N.J.: Prentice-Hall.

———, and Franz, Schurmann. 1969. *China: An Interpretive History*. Berkeley and Los Angeles: University of California Press.

Marx, Karl. 1965. [1887]. *Capital*. 3 vols. Moscow: Foreign Languages Press.

Merton, Robert K. 1957. *Social Theory and Social Structure*. Rev. Ed. New York: Free Press.

Moulder, Frances V. 1977. *Japan, China and The Modern World Economy.* Cambridge: Cambridge University Press.

Murvar, Vatro. 1967. "Max Weber's Urban Typology and Russia." *Sociological Quarterly* 8: 481–494.

Needham, Joseph. 1969. *The Great Titration: Science and Society in East and West.* London: George Allen and Unwin.

——. "Poverties and Triumphs of Chinese Scientific Tradition," pp. 117–153, in A. C. Crombie, ed. *Scientific Change.* New York: Basic Books.

Ozment, Steven E. 1975. *The Reformation in the Cities: The Appeal of Protestantism to Sixteenth Century Germany and Switzerland.* New Haven: Yale University Press.

Pirenne, Henri. 1947. *Economic and Social History of Medieval Europe.* New York: Harcourt.

Polanyi, Karl. 1944. *The Great Transformation.* New York: Holt, and Winston.

Postan, M. M. 1972. *The Medieval Economy and Society.* Berkeley and Los Angeles: University of California Press.

Sjoberg, Gideon. 1965. "The Origin and Evolution of Cities." *Scientific American* 213: 55–63.

Skinner, G. William. 1977. "Introduction of Urban Social Structure in Ch'ing China," pp. 521–553 in G. William Skinner, ed. *The City in Late Imperial China.* Stanford: Stanford University Press.

Smith, Adam. 1937. [1776] *The Wealth of Nations.* New York: Modern Library.

Thrupp, Sylvia. 1963. "The Gilds," pp. 230–280, in M. M. Postan, E. E. Rich, and Edward Miller, eds. *The Cambridge Economic History of Europe,* Vol. III. Cambridge: at the University Press.

Tigar, Michael E. with Madelein R. Levy. 1977. *Law the the Rise of Capitalism.* New York: Monthly Review.

Tilly, Charles, ed. 1974. *An Urban World.* Boston: Little, Brown.

Unwin, George. 1904. *Industrial Organization in the Sixteenth and Seventeenth Centuries.* Oxford: Clarendon Press.

van Bath, Slicher. 1977. "Agriculture in the Vital Revolution," ch. 2, in E. E. Rich, and C. H. Wilson, eds. *The Cambridge Economic History of Europe,* Vol. V. Cambridge: Cambridge University Press.

Van der Sprenkel, Sybille. 1977. "Urban Social Control," pp. 609–632, in William Skinner, ed. *The City in Late Imperial China.* Stanford: Stanford University Press.

Wallerstein, Immanuel. 1974. *The Modern World-System.* New York: Academic.

——. 1979. *The Capitalist World Economy.* Cambridge: Cambridge University Press.

Weber, Max. 1951. *The Religion of China.* New York: Free Press.

——. 1961. *General Economic History.* New York: Collier Books.

——. 1968. *Economy and Society.* New York Bedminster Press.

——. 1976 [1909]. *The Agrarian Sociology of Ancient Civilizations.* Trans. R. I. Frank London: NLB.

White, Andrew D. 1955. *History of the Warfare of Science with Theology in Christendom.* New York: George Braziller.

PART TWO

Industrial Urbanization

CHAPTER 4

Industrial Urbanization in Britain

The modern tendency is to treat urbanization as a continuous, unidirectional process in the course of which an ever higher proportion of societal, regional, and world population becomes urban. The beginning point is a rural society in which cities are few, small in size, and most of the population is agricultural. The terminus is a society in which cities are large, numerous, and most people urban. This conception of urbanization accurately reflects the direction of change in the world since 1750. Table 4-1 shows that between 1800 and 1970 the world's rural population increased 235 percent, whereas the world's total population increased 371 percent. This imbalance indicates that the rural share of world population declined and the urban share increased. Urban population increased 4,570 percent in this period, twelve times faster than world population increased. Moreover, big cities (100,000 or more in population) increased 5,204 percent. Thus the bigger cities increased their share of world population even faster than smaller and medium cities did.

World urbanization has always been uneven in rate and extent. Of the five continents, Africa had the lowest level of urbanization in 1950 and Oceania the highest (Table 4-2). This is inequality in extent of urbanization. On the other hand, the rate of urbanization in the period 1800 to 1950 was highest in Africa and lowest in Europe. This is inequality in rate of urbanization. Taken together these differences have tended to reduce the regional imbalance of world urbanization. The best measure of this is the ratio of urbanization in Europe to urbanization in the world. Around A.D. 100 Europe's urbanization was no greater than that of other regions of the world, so this ratio was 1.0 or less. Nineteenth-century urbanization in Europe provided Europe with a lead over the rest of the

Table 4-1. Growth of the World's Total, Rural, Urban and Big City Populations, 1800–1970 (millions)

Date	World Population	Rural	Urban	Cities 100,000 or More
1800	978	948.7	29.3	16.6
1850	1,262	1,181.2	80.8	29.0
1900	1,650	1,425	224.4	90.8
1950	2,502	1,795.5	706.4	406.0
1970	3,628	2,229.0	1,339.0	863.9
Index of change, 1800–1970	371	235	4,570	5,204

Source: John D. Durand, "The Modern Expansion of World Population," *Proceedings of the American Philosophical Society* 3 (1967), p. 137. Reproduced by permission.

world. This Europe-centered imbalance peaked in 1850 when the Europe/world ratio reached 2.0 (Table 4-2). Thereafter the difference in level of urbanization between Europe and the rest of the world declined, indicating that the rest of the world was catching up with Europe. In 1950, the Europe/world ratio was 1.6 and Europe was no longer the most heavily urbanized continent.

These continuous changes were accomplished without protracted backsliding anywhere but there have been brief interruptions in the generally upward trend in the wake of wars and natural disasters. An example is the reduction of urbanization in Japan between 1943 and 1945 as a result of bombing. Presumably the level of world urbanization would decline yet more abruptly in the aftermath of thermonuclear war because any wretched survivors would be compelled to till the soil to live.

Unidirectional urbanization is new. In the long preindustrial epoch (4000 B.C.

Table 4-2. Population in Large Cities (100,000 and More) by Major Continental Regions, 1800–1950

Continent	1800 Millions %		1850 Millions %		1900 Millions %		1950 Millions %	
Asia	9.8	1.6	12.2	1.7	19.4	2.1	105.6	7.5
Europe*	5.4	2.9	13.2	4.9	48.0	11.9	118.2	19.9
Africa	0.3	0.3	0.25	0.2	1.4	1.1	10.2	5.2
America	0.1	0.4	1.8	3.0	18.6	12.8	74.6	22.6
Oceania					1.3	21.7	5.1	39.2

Source: Leonard Reissman, *The Urban Process* (New York: Free Press, 1964), p. 159. Reproduced by permission.
   *Includes the USSR.

to A.D. 1750), urbanization was neither continuous nor unidirectional. Although urbanization generally progressed, regional backslidings were frequent, giving a roller-coaster effect to regional urbanization. Moreover, such urbanization as occurred had only a slow rate of population growth to overcome. In the modern world, population growth has been more rapid than ever before, and accelerated urbanization has occurred despite this growth. Table 4-3 shows that population grew only at a rate of 0.2 percent yearly in 4000 B.C.; 0.4 percent yearly in 1650, and 2 percent yearly in 1962. Another way to measure the change is to count the years required to double the world's population. The first doubling (A.D. 1-1650) required 1,650 years; the second, 200; the third, 75; the fourth, 52; and the fifth, only 38 years. Accelerated population growth posed a barrier to industrial urbanization because city populations had to grow ever faster in order to increase the proportion of people who were urban. This raises another point of difference between preindustrial urbanization and what the world has experienced since 1750: an acceleration of the rate of city formation, as well as vast augmentation in city size. The triadic formula is more cities, bigger cities, and relatively more people in cities.

These distinctions indicate that urbanization in the modern world is a sudden, frantic acceleration in what used to be a slow, faltering process. This frantic acceleration is industrial urbanization. *Industrial urbanization* is urbanization resulting from industrial development of nations, regions, and the world. Industrial urbanization is therefore a special type of urbanization that builds upon and supersedes preindustrial urbanization (4000 B.C. to A.D. 1750). In contrast to preindustrial urbanization, industrial urbanization is unidirectional, cumulative, massive, and rapid. Industrial urbanization is a worldwide phenomenon affecting every region of the globe.

Industrial urbanization began first in Britain because the Industrial Revolution began there. In the first decades of the nineteenth century Britain produced

Table 4-3. Estimated World Population, 4000 B.C. to A.D. 2000

Date	Estimated World Population	Years Required to Double Population
2000	6,000,000,000	38
1977	4,000,000,000	52
1962	3,000,000,000	
1925	2,000,000,000	75
1850	1,000,000,000	200
1650	500,000,000	1,650
A.D. 1	250,000,000	
4000 B.C.	10,000,000	

Source: Adapted from Philip Hauser, "Urbanization: An Overview," in Philip Hauser and Leo F. Schnore, eds., *The Study of Urbanization* (New York: Wiley, 1965), p. 6.

"more than half of the world's industrial output" even though Britain contained only 2 percent of the world's population (Briggs 1974: 93). Authorities no longer believe that world urbanization must follow trajectories outlined for all time by the British experience. Still, Britain remains the classic illustration of industrial urbanization, and its case is vital to any informed comparison with other regions now or in the past.

PREMODERN URBANIZATION IN BRITAIN, 1500-1700

Between 1500 and 1700 the population of England roughly doubled. The proportion of population living in towns rose considerably faster, possibly twice as fast. The result was urbanization of this capitalist but still preindustrial society (Clark and Slack 1976: 83). The growth of towns "created in the English countryside a market for agricultural products," thus encouraging further enclosure of agricultural lands (Moore 1966: 12).

However, the Stuart monarchs opposed enclosure of commons. By breaking the power of the monarchs, the English Civil War (1642-1646) swept away this barrier to the enclosing landlord (Moore 1966: 19). By 1700 English landlords controlled (as a result of enclosures) fully three quarters of all arable land. These enclosing landlords took a strictly commercial attitude toward farming, and when demand increased, they were prepared to utilize the most effective technology in order to increase agricultural yield. This augmentation of agricultural production, Brenner (1976: 66) observes, permitted sixteenth- and seventeenth-century English towns to increase in population. In the medieval period, spurts of urban demand had petered out because agriculture had been insufficiently productive to generate the food that growing town populations required. Capitalist agriculture "was the key to England's uniquely successful overall development" (Brenner 1976: 63).

Sixteenth- and seventeenth-century urbanization was uneven. At least half of total urbanization was attributable to the "extraordinary growth of London," the political capital [1]. Moreover, there were "chronological fluctuations" in urbanization (Clark and Slack 1976: 85). These were roller-coaster fluctuations indicative of preindustrial urbanization. Table 4-4 shows the population of selected English towns in 1520, 1603, and 1695. London's growth in this period was almost tenfold. The second-ranking city, Norwich, was much smaller than London throughout and grew less than threefold altogether. Salisbury actually declined in population and Coventry grew hardly at all. In 1600 London was so much larger than other cities that its population exceeded the combined population of the next six cities.

These figures treat only the largest towns in England. The bottom rows suggest

Table 4-4. Population of Selected English Towns, 1520-1695

	ca. 1520	ca. 1603	ca. 1695	Index of Change 1695/1520 ($\times$ 100)
London (metropolitan)	60,000	200,000	575,000	958
Norwich	12,000	15,000	29,332	244
Bristol	10,000	12,000	19,403	194
York	8,000	11,000		
Exeter	8,000	9,000		
Salisbury	8,000	7,000	6,976	87
Coventry	6,601	6,500	6,710	102

Source: Peter Clark and Paul Slack, *English Towns in Transition, 1500-1700* (London: Oxford University Press, 1976), p. 83. Reproduced by permission.

but do not fully express the amount of real distress that smaller towns were undergoing. In fact, the period 1500-1695 was one of "considerable difficulty for most town economies." This difficulty arose from several causes. The pre-eminent cause was the tendency of investors to switch their money from town crafts to commercial farming and cottage industry, both rural (Phythian-Adams 1978: 185). Rural cloth manufacture was the principal beneficiary of capital flights from towns to suburban countryside. Another precipitant of capital flight was urban poverty and social unrest caused by the influx of rural beggars. Supporting indigent migrants necessitated high taxes for social welfare. To avoid these taxes rich people began to abandon Elizabethan cities (Clark and Slack 1976: 102-107). Furthermore, foreign trade reversals and a series of bad harvests combined to reduce the profitability of town industries while increasing the return to agriculture. The response of the declining towns was protectionism. The craft guilds strode to the forefront of urban protectionism and demanded restrictions and regulation on production and marketing (Weber, 1961: Ch. 11). The objective of restrictionism was to prevent capital flight to the suburbs by preventing the sale of rural products. Additionally, the craft guilds hoped to prevent capitalist owners from reorganizing urban manufacturing in factories (Hibbert 1963: 172).

Distressed cities were mostly small- or medium-sized places that formed, however, "the vast majority of urban settlements" in England (Clark and Slack 1976: 17). But distress was not universal. London prospered throughout this period, industrial new towns also grew rapidly, and provincial capitals experienced moderate growth. The upshot was a complex rearrangement of England's urban hierarchy. This rearrangement was especially important at the top, among the larger cities and towns. The changing array of cities at the top of the urban hierarchy is evidence of what political and economic processes were transforming British society.

Between 1600 and 1801 London retained its place as the largest city in Britain. Pawson (1979: 204) has shown that London was much larger than geographers normally expect on the basis of rank and size of smaller cities. However, London's rate of growth dropped from first place in this period; London's growth was 384 percent whereas the second-ranking city, Norwich-Manchester, grew 560 percent. The rate of growth of Manchester was even higher because that industrial city was not among the top-ranking cities in 1600. London's "spectacular development" in this period was the result of political and commercial supremacy (Daunton 1978: 247). One source of London's prosperity was its international trade, especially commercial exploitation of New World colonies (Fisher 1976: 209). The East India, Hudson's Bay, and Royal African companies all had headquarters in London. However, London's domestic commercial role was as important as its international role in money volume of transactions (Clark and Slack 1976: 77). London was also a center of shipbuilding, much of it military. Absentee owners of vast agricultural estates built townhouses in London and spent the proceeds of their estates on religion, education, professional services, entertainment, and "conspicuous consumption" of luxuries (Clark and Slack 1976: 77). Finally, London was the political capital of an expanding colonial empire. Government business was a basic industry of the city, and the volume of government business was growing with the expansion of British possessions abroad.

The basic industries enumerated in London are those of preindustrial capitals of political empires. Hence, Clark and Slack (1976: 77) conclude that prior to 1640 "London's exceptional growth was mainly parasitical." This was also true of provincial capitals in Britain, but these did not fully share in London's growth so their population growth was modest but steady. Five towns were provincial capitals: Bristol, York, Exeter, Newcastle, and Norwich. All of these towns were political foci of regions larger than counties and transportation nodes on navigable rivers. Therefore "marketing and inland trade" complemented their political basic industry (Clark and Slack 1976: 48). In 1600 these five provincial towns followed London in the urban hierarchy (Table 4-5). By 1750, York and Exeter had been displaced from the top six by Liverpool and Birmingham, the latter industrial cities of the north and midlands, respectively. By 1801, only Bristol was still in the top six. The remaining provincial capitals had been displaced in the urban hierarchy. Yet the population of every provincial capital had increased between 1600 and 1801. They were displaced from the top six because their growth rate was not fast enough—not because they declined in size.

The towns that displaced the provincial capitals in the urban hierarchy were Manchester, Liverpool, Birmingham, and Leeds. All were industrial "new towns" that had been scarcely villages in 1600. These industrial towns had several growth advantages. First, they were located near sources of raw materials for industry. Second, their very smallness had protected them against the guild-oriented ossification of urban economy that had so adversely affected the country towns of England. "The absence of effective municipal controls" on

Table 4-5. Changing Urban Hierarchy of England, 1600–1801

1600			1801	
Rank	Population		Rank	Population
1. London	250,000		1. London	960,000
2. Norwich	15,000		2. Manchester	84,000
3. York	12,000		3. Liverpool	78,000
4. Bristol	12,000		4. Birmingham	74,000
5. Newcastle	10,000		5. Bristol	64,000
6. Exeter	9,000		6. Leeds	53,000
			8. Norwich	37,000
1750			14. Newcastle	28,000
			15. Exeter	17,000
Rank	Population		17. York	16,000
1. London	675,000			
2. Bristol	50,000			
3. Norwich	36,000			
4. Newcastle	29,000			
5. Birmingham	23,700			
6. Liverpool	22,000			
7. Exeter	16,000			
16. York	11,400			

Source: Daunton 1978: 247. World Copyright: The Past and Present Society, Corpus Christi College, Oxford, England. This Table is reprinted with the permission of the Society and the author from Philip Abrams and E. A. Wrigley (eds.) *Town in Societies: Essays in Economic History and Historical Sociology* (Past and Present Publications, Cambridge, 1978), p. 247.

capitalist industry was a "striking feature" of new towns (Clark and Slack 1976: 43, Daunton 1978: 246-247). Because controls were few, industrial new towns attracted capital and thus became centers for the Industrial Revolution of the eighteenth century.

However, the growth of new industrial cities was not the principal industrial development of the eighteenth century. In fact, throughout this century "rural industry increased relative to urban" in Britain (Daunton 1978: 249). The workers in cottage industries were distressed agricultural laborers, underemployed as a result of enclosures. They were content to work long hours for low wages on raw materials supplied by urban factors. The relations between factors and cottage workers were capitalistic but preindustrial. Still, the cottage industry produced more and cheaper goods, especially textiles and woolens, than had been produced by urban tradesmen in the late Middle Ages. In this sense, improvements in industrial technique were already well underway. However, these industrial improvements occurred in the deprived countryside rather than in cities so Daunton (1978: 249) concludes that "industrialization led urbanization in eighteenth-century England."

THE INDUSTRIAL REVOLUTION IN BRITAIN, 1750

The Industrial Revolution involved the substitution of steam power for animal and wind power. It substituted complex machines for simple hand tools. The agents of the Industrial Revolution were the coal mine, the factory, the railroad, and the steamboat (Weber, 1961: Ch. 27). As it happened, factories were built in the industrial towns of the North and Midlands whose growth had already been discernible in the seventeenth century. This location of factory production reversed the trend toward rural industry that had prevailed since the sixteenth century. The growth of manufacturing industry encouraged town growth and rural enclosures. The result was massive urbanization of Britain's North and Midlands and population loss or stagnation in the agricultural South and Southeast.

These connections are observable in the British census (Table 4-6). One trend is continuous reduction in agriculture, forestry, and fishing. It is true that these

Table 4-6. Economically Active Population by Major Industrial Groups and Sex for the United Kingdom, 1841, 1901, 1961 (thousands)

	1841	1901	1961
Males			
Agriculture, forestry, and fishing	1,458	1,390	777
Mining	218	1,202	728
Manufacturing	1,816	4,062	6,308
Construction	376	1,216	1,597
Commerce, finance, and the like	94	597	2,066
Transportation and communications	196	1,409	1,486
Services	459	1,056	3,136
Other	474	887	135
Total	5,091	11,819	16,233
Females			
Agriculture, forestry, and fishing	81	86	97
Mining	7	6	21
Manufacturing	639	2,123	2,666
Construction	1	3	69
Commerce, finance, and the like	1	76	1,773
Transportation and communications	4	27	230
Services	1,041	2,358	2,861
Other	41	75	64
Total	1,815	4,754	7,781

Source: B. R. Mitchell, *Abstract of British Historical Statistics* (Cambridge: at the University Press), p. 163. Reproduced by permission.

reductions had begun as early as the thirteenth century, but the rate of decline accelerated during the eighteenth and nineteenth centuries. Table 4-6 shows the continuity of decline from 1841 until 1961. Declining employment in agriculture was matched by increased employment in nonagricultural industries: construction, commerce, transportation and communications, and manufacturing. These are typical urban industries. In many cases, redundant agricultural workers migrated to British cities and took jobs in these expanding industries (Weber, 1961: 306-307). Others emigrated to the New World and were replaced by rural-urban migrants from Ireland (Ashton 1948: 124). Either way, British cities grew in absolute and relative population. However, the biggest gainers were industrial centers such as Manchester, Liverpool, Glasgow, and Birmingham. These cities increased ten- to twentyfold between 1801 and 1951, whereas the political and mercantile capital, London, increased only threefold in the same period (Table 4-7).

The decline in number of agricultural workers did not occasion any reduction in agricultural product. On the contrary, production increased. In the eighteenth century, land under cultivation increased by one third and the yield per acre increased by one tenth, even though the work force in agriculture decreased (Ashton 1948: 146). But the population of Britain increased more rapidly in the eighteenth century than did food production. In 1700 the population of England and Wales was 5.5 million. This had become 9 million in 1801 and 14 million in 1831. The result of population increase was a food deficit. This deficit might have compelled Britain to slow the pace of industrial urbanization had the island nation depended wholly upon its own agriculture to feed a growing population of nonagricultural workers. Instead, the improvement of long-haul transportation by canal, railroad, and ship permitted Britain to import food for city workers. Table 4-8 shows the change. In 1700 and 1750 Britain exported wheat. By 1800 Britain had begun to import wheat, and the amount imported doubled during the next forty years.

The supplier of this wheat was at first Prussia. Later, Canada, the United

Table 4-7. Population of the Principal Towns of the United Kingdom, 1801–1951 (thousands)

	1801	1851	1901	1951
Birmingham	71	233	522	1,113
Glasgow	77	345	762	1,090
Liverpool	82	376	704	789
London*	1,088	2,491	4,563	3,353
Manchester	75	303	544	703

Source: B. R. Mitchell, *Abstract of British Historical Statistics* (Cambridge: at the University Press, 1962), p. 24. Reproduced by permission.
*County of London.

Table 4-8. Overseas Wheat Trade of Great Britain, 1700–1840 (thousands of quarters)

	Imports	Exports
1700		49
1750		950
1800	1,266	22
1840	2,698	87

Source: B. R. Mitchell, *Abstract of British Historical Statistics* (Cambridge: at the University Press, 1962), p. 94. Reproduced by permission.

States, and Australia became suppliers. Foreign wheat traveled by canal and railroad from grain-exporting regions to seaports, and by sea to Britain. The construction of railroads in Europe and the New World made it possible for the first time in the world's history to carry this grain overland, and the improvement of sea transport made it possible to move the grain across oceans to final consumers in British cities. The transportation lines that carried foreign wheat to Britain carried back British manufactured goods to pay for the wheat. In the process British industrial cities gained access to the agricultural surplus of foreign nations by exchanging manufactured goods. This new method of surplus extraction obviated the old-fashioned recourse to political conquest and taxation. Moreover, exchange enhanced the wealth of nations whereas war and conquest depleted it.

Between 1838 and 1938, the population of England and Wales increased nearly threefold. Feeding all these people required food imports, but that solution would not have been sufficient without the demographic transition. The *demographic transition* was a lagged reduction in the birthrate to match reductions in the death rate (Table 4-9). In one hundred years the crude birthrate declined by one half and infant mortality by two thirds. Declining infant mortality was attributable to improved diet, sanitary conditions, and medical knowledge (Tilly 1974: 39–40). These were the results of the Scientific Revolution of two centuries earlier. Taken by itself, however, the reduction in infant mortality meant an abrupt increase in population because infants who would otherwise have died in their first year now lived to the age of reproduction. Therefore, the reduction in the birthrate (Table 4-9) was timely. This reduction prevented population growth from proceeding even more rapidly than it did. "In eighteenth century England, the growth of population was low enough to be absorbed fairly easily by the growing industrial employment, whether in country or town" (Daunton 1978: 276). Had the birthrate remained in 1938 what it was in 1838, Britain's economy would not have been able to increase fast enough to maintain the standard of living. The result would have been a deterioration of living standards as population growth outstripped the capacity of the British economy to produce goods and services. As it was, the output of industry increased faster than population growth so that real income of people in Britain (measured in goods and services) increased over the whole course of the century 1838-1938.

Most of the urbanization in Britain resulted from the rural-urban migration of displaced agricultural workers. This migration, in turn, was attributable to industrial growth in big cities (Thomis 1974: 48). "Urbanization increased in almost direct proportion to industrialization" (Mumford 1938: 146). But why did factories locate in cities rather than in towns or even in villages? The old orthodoxy found a solution in the technology of factory production: the steam engine "made it possible to set up factories in the towns where labour was more plentiful. . . . " (Ashton 1948: 115-116). According to this view, the new technology of production required factories because of fixed capital investments, the great size of the new machines, and the need for a centralized power source to run the machinery. Factories, it was further argued, had to locate in cities because only cities provided adequate labor, and cities conferred upon factories convenient access to sea and railroad transportation radii (Mumford 1938: 157-160).

Correct as far as they go, these conventional views have been challenged on several grounds. First, the coming of the factory system did not depend only on the availability of technology. Factory technology was ready a generation before factories appeared. Smelser (1959: 100) has "explicitly rejected" the old view that technology alone caused the factory system of production, arguing instead that technology only set the stage. In reality, the factory system in Britain waited on a readjustment of family roles to legitimate the full-time employment of men in spinning jobs once reserved for women and children. Some time had to elapse before English households were prepared to contribute labor to a factory system they once viewed as demeaning and scandalous [2]. This was a social rather than a technological condition of factory production.

Second, the location of factories in big cities reflected employers' need to discipline and motivate workers. Proximity to work-age population was never the real issue. Motivating rural workers was difficult because they produced some of their own food and had few material wants beyond food. These wants satisfied, they stopped working and began to enjoy leisure for gardening, gossip, dancing, fighting, sports, and drinking. Many were home owners. Urban workers had to buy all their food and shelter with wages earned in factories. Additionally, urban residence induced "new patterns of consumption" among dislocated peasants. Urban migrants had learned to want what money could buy. Their insatiable appetite for consumer goods encouraged urban workers to log long hours in low wage jobs (Daunton 1978: 250).

Table 4-9. Population and Birthrate in England and Wales, 1838-1938

	Population (000)	Births per 1,000 Population	Births per 1,000 Women Aged 15-44	Infant Mortality: Deaths of Infants Under 1 Year per 10,000 Live Births
1838	15,288	30.3		151
1850	17,773	33.4	141	162
1875	24,045	36.3	156.7	158
1900	32,349	28.7	115.9	154
1925	38,935	18.3	73.5	75
1938	41,215	15.1	62.4	53
1838⎫ 1938⎭	270	50	44	35

Source: B. R. Mitchell, *Abstract of British Historical Statistics* (Cambridge: at the University Press, 1962), pp. 29, 30, 37. Reproduced by permission.

Another reason factories located in big cities was proximity to slums. Slums contained unemployed workers desperate for a job (Engels 1958). Proximity to slums permitted factory owners to fire refractory or undisciplined workers in the confident expectation of finding a ready replacement. For example, a worker who came drunk to the job or talked back to a supervisor could be fired at 8:00 A.M. and fully replaced by nine. This threat also encouraged workers to accept the authority of supervisors and bend willing backs to the tasks they imposed (Bendix 1956: Ch. 2). In case of a work stoppage, employers could replace striking workers with strike-breakers recruited among the unemployed. This threat was a deterrent to unionization of the employed. Thus what employers sought in the city was surplus labor—not merely labor. The benefit of the surplus was improved discipline on the job. Towns offered sufficient labor for a single factory but they did not offer surplus labor, so factory owners preferred cities.

Finally, a city location permitted employers to evade financial or moral responsibility for unemployed hands laid off in slack seasons or during downswings of the business cycle. Until 1832, England's Poor Law required the indigent to return to their parishes of origin for welfare relief [3]. Displaced peasants who had traveled to the cities for factory jobs in boom times came flooding home again when unemployed. Thus urban employers laid upon the rural countryside the cost of supporting their unemployed work force. Moreover, workers who traveled to cities for factory jobs often left their families behind in rural villages in this early period. The parish poor authorities paid the cost of subsistence for these families, thus relieving urban employers of this expense. Relief expenses were substantial: in many villages and towns of the Midlands and the South, one half of the resident families were relief recipients by 1832 (Moore 1966: 28).

The New Poor Law of 1832 abolished all relief for the able-bodied indigent and instituted a system of public workhouses for the disabled. Dickens's Oliver Twist was born in one of these public workhouses. Poor Law reform (Polanyi 1944: 88) created a national labor market in which cities could no longer shift to the countryside the cost of supporting unemployed factory hands and their families. If industrial cities had promptly accepted the responsibility for housing, educating, policing, and maintaining these people, the tax cost to employers would have been great. However, in the laissez-faire climate then prevailing, cities refused to accept any welfare responsibilities and did not tax employers to meet them (Cherry 1972: 30-33). In effect, no public agency accepted any responsibility for alleviating the wretchedness of the urban working class, who were permitted to die when incapable of providing food, shelter, and medical care from their wages [4]. Industrial cities provided no public services, no public education, no public health, no sanitation, no housing code, and no public welfare relief (Thomis 1974: 51-55). Horrifying slums emerged (Hammond and Hammond 1920: 40-42) and living standards deteriorated (Thomis 1974: 57). Contagious diseases raged unchecked, thousands died, but new thousands of displaced countryfolk continually arrived to take their place. In the squalid industrial slums of Britain the world first read the horrors of capitalist urbanization. Some humanitarian voices were raised in protest, and the causal connections between living conditions and death rates were also well understood (Thomis 1974: 55), but individual cities were powerless to remedy local conditions because levying taxes for welfare relief reduced local attractiveness to capital, thus worsening the plight of already wretched slum dwellers. Environmental standards legislation merely drove the polluting factories to places without environmental protection, leaving behind newly unemployed workers [5]. Only national legislation could impose uniform standards of social welfare, but this legislation did not emerge until late in the nineteenth century. In the meantime, cities offered factory owners access to cheap labor on the most favorable terms.

These financial considerations do not contradict the purely technological advantages of factory location in the nineteenth century; those are indisputable. However, the technology of transportation was not the *only* attraction that impelled factories to locate in cities. Cities also offered surplus labor to discipline a work force, a motivational stimulus for acquisitive appetites, and the means of evading financial responsibility for the unemployed. In general, cities provided capitalists with access to cheap labor. This benefit was economic rather than technological. There was therefore no necessary connection between industrialization and urbanization in nineteenth-century Britain. One could imagine an industrializing Britain in which employers would have preferred to locate factories in villages, towns, and small cities—as indeed they later did [6].

REGIONAL INEQUALITIES IN BRITISH URBANIZATION

At the beginning of the eighteenth century, the population of Britain was, with the exception of London, spread rather evenly throughout the island. By 1800, however, this once even distribution of population had developed noticeable clusters around the major industrial towns of the English North and Midlands (Cherry 1972: 20). Durham and Lancashire were the leading industrial counties in 1787. Durham's industrial base was coal; Lancashire's cities depended upon their forty or more water-powered cotton mills. As heavy industry switched from water to coal, demand for coal increased, and coal mining spurred urbanization in south Wales as well as in Durham. The whole urbanization of Wales depended on coal mining, a fatally undiversified dependence. As diesel engines took over after about 1920, Welsh mining towns experienced an erosion of consumer demand for their coal. The diminished demand for the output of this basic industry caused a decrease in population through migration of unemployed Welsh miners to England and the British Commonwealth (Thomis 1974: 181). Scotland developed only one industrial city: Glasgow, which is the core of the Clydeside conurbation, the only conurbation in Britain located outside England. But Glasgow's dependence on shipbuilding exposed it to economic vulnerability too, and in the 1960s depression in this industry had left Glasgow the most distressed city in the United Kingdom.

Diversified industrial cities developed only in England. Beginning in England's North, urbanization spread progressively south after 1881 (Cairncross 1949). The London region served as an urbanization pole in the south. In approximately 1951 the northern and southern urbanized regions joined in a megalopolitan belt that extends across central England but excludes Scotland and Wales (Friedlander 1970: 430). Figure 4-1 shows this English megalopolitan belt. The peripheral parts of the British Isles (Wales, Scotland, Ireland) have served this urbanization of England in two ways. First, the Celtic periphery provided labor reserves for English urbanization. England utilized little foreign labor in its factories and transportation lines because the Celtic periphery provided the needed labor reservoir. Second, the growth of towns in England stimulated the demand for agricultural products, thus "giving the Celtic landowner a powerful incentive to clear his common fields" (Hechter 1975: 82). As the enclosure movement spread to Ireland, Scotland, and Wales, it dispossessed peasants whose desperate circumstances compelled them to migrate. Some went to the New World and the British Commonwealth (Handlin 1969: 38-50). Others resettled in English cities (Ashton 1948: 124).

Friedlander's (1970) data show that the unevenness of urbanization affected England itself—not merely the Celtic periphery. Between 1851 and 1951, urban-

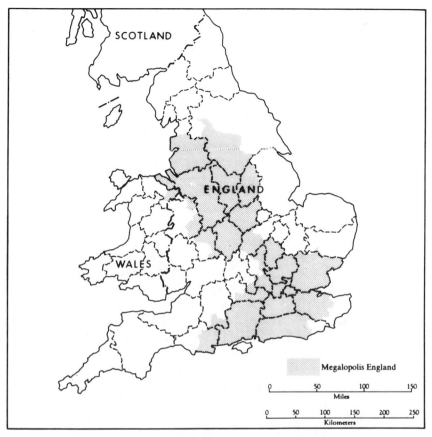

Figure 4-1. Megalopolis England. (Source: Marion Clawson and Peter Hall. *Planning and Urban Growth: An Anglo-American Comparison.* Baltimore: Resources for the Future published by the Johns Hopkins University Press, p. 64. Reproduced by permission.)

ization hardly disturbed England's eastern and south western regions, while urbanization of the North and the Midlands approached 100 percent. On the other hand, the urban and industrial retardation of the Celtic periphery has produced now manifest, now latent political tensions in British life because of the suggestion of ethnic domination that this regional imbalance implies. The Scots, Irish, and Welsh have been and, to some extent, still remain culturally distinct from the English. England conquered and annexed Wales in 1536. Cromwell's conquest of Ireland prepared for its annexation in 1801. England obtained union with Scotland by treaty in 1707. The expansion of the English state into these Celtic regions was "accompanied by measures designed to suppress Celtic culture" (Hechter 1975: 74). England's language replaced Welsh and Gaelic in official and educated speech. England's monarch and church crowded out the symbols of Celtic nationalism. Some indigenous people resented Anglicization, especially when it occurred in the wake of military conquest.

In an old-fashioned sense, England's imperialism obtained for London the tribute of Wales, Scotland, and Ireland. This tribute increased the size of London, the political capital of the empire, while reducing the centrality of the Irish, Welsh, and Scottish political capitals. In exchange for this tribute, London offered governmental services and England's language, religion, and culture as well. But the imperial expansion of England into the Celtic regions was not just a replay of preindustrial urbanization. The industrialization of northern England set in motion new economic forces that tended, according to Hechter, to integrate the English and Celtic economies on a footing of industrial inequality. England's northern cities produced manufactured goods and exported them to Celtic regions in exchange for food and coal. This economic integration arose chiefly because England could produce manufactured goods better and more cheaply than could the Celtic regions, and these regions lacked a state capable of extending tariff protection. Moreover, London bankers controlled investment decisions, and these bankers favored English cities for reasons that may have had some component of ethnic chauvinism (Hechter 1975: 88). As urbanization in England intensified, Celtic regions were depopulated by rural-urban migration to England. This depopulation increased local alarm about the survival of the indigenous culture and provoked Celtic nationalism in response. Hechter (1975: 265) claims that the failure of regional development in the Celtic periphery triggered the Scottish and Welsh nationalism that has buffeted Britain since the mid-1960s. Reviewing voting data by counties, Ragin (1977, 1979) disputes Hechter's interpretation, arguing that Labour votes in Scotland and Wales are class votes, not, as Hechter maintains, nationalist votes. This issue remains unresolved, but there is no doubt that regional cultures in the British Isles rendered industrial urbanization a more politically sensitive phenomenon than it need otherwise have been.

SUMMARY

Urbanization in Britain developed around two distinct poles: London and the North. The earlier pole centered on London. Between 1600 and 1750 London's remarkable growth depended on the enhancement of its administrative, cultural, maritime, military, and commercial role as linchpin of the British Empire. London's growth was affected by capitalist enclosure in British agriculture, the growth of Britain's population, and the stirrings of industrial power elsewhere. However, London's growth in this period was basically preindustrial in character and resembled Rome or Athens—cities that were also political centers of pre-industrial imperialism. London did not participate in the Industrial Revolution of the eighteenth and nineteenth centuries [7]. Her continued growth in this period did, however, reflect industrial change in central and northern England because the port of London served as an export outlet for manufactured goods from these regions as well as a domestic market. The addition of these export and consumptive roles made London's urban role more complex than it had been before the Industrial Revolution.

Industrial urbanization in Britain began in northern England around 1750. Thereafter the factory system spread southward into the Midlands. Lancaster, Birmingham, and Manchester were the largest centers of factory production. These and other industrial cities specialized in the manufacturing of consumer and producer goods, which could now for the first time be produced more cheaply and more soundly in city factories than in cottages or villages. British cities exchanged their manufactured goods for foreign food. Railroad and steamship transportation permitted this food to travel great distances to its point of final consumption. Therefore, British cities were able to feed British workers with imported food. This exchange of manufactured goods for food and other primary products was not imperialistic or predatory in the old-fashioned sense, for it did not require the subsumption of a trading partner into Britain's political empire. Manufacturing thus provided a basis for supporting a much higher proportion of British people in cities than had ever been so supported before. Even the massive population increases of the nineteenth century could not prevent the growth in number and size of cities in Britain, home of the Industrial Revolution.

The Industrial Revolution in Britain accelerated urbanization at every level but particularly at the top of the urban hierarchy. Big cities grew most rapidly. The reason was that factories preferred big cities. Big cities separated workers from gardens and taught them to want material goods. These changes improved worker motivation. Big cities also provided surplus labor to discipline the employed. Big cities permitted employers to evade financial responsibility for the unemployed. These benefits to employers were social and economic rather than technological. They indicate that capitalism made use of big cities, but they do not indicate a necessary technological connection between industrialization and big cities.

In nineteenth-century Britain, urbanization shot up chiefly because of rural-urban migration. However, rural people might produce urbanization by moving to small towns rather than big cities. An urban society composed of a plurality of small towns would be quite different from an urban society composed of a few big cities. Yet both may be equally "urbanized" in terms of proportion of people who reside in urban (nonrural) areas. In eighteenth- and nineteenth-century Britain, industrialization arguably required urbanization in a technological sense. After all, factories and steam engines could not operate efficiently in rural settings. However, the technology of industrialization did not require big city growth. Big city growth was also produced by the social and economic conflicts associated with the rise of wage labor in factories.

NOTES

1. "From Roman days and perhaps earlier times, London has been the largest city of the British Isles." Josiah Cox Russell, *Medieval Regions and Their Cities.* NP: Indiana University Press, 1972, p. 121. London's supremacy was the result of its maritime and road centrality as well as England's "strong central government." "If York had been free," Russell (1972: 127) adds, it would have conquered nearby cities in northern England. These conquests would have drawn away from London the governmental functions it actually exercised and thus have reduced the size of London.
2. "What is clear is that there was no strong desire on the part of the workers themselves to congregate in large establishments" (Ashton 1948: 109).
3. "The proletariat created by the breaking up of the bands of feudal retainers and by forcible expropriation of the people from the soil, this 'free' proletariat could not possibly be absorbed by the nascent manufactures as fast as it was thrown upon the world." Karl Marx, *Capital.* Vol. I. Moscow: Foreign Languages Publishing House, 1965, p. 734. The result was the invasion of towns by rural vagabonds. To prevent this vagabondage, Elizabethan poor laws had required rural parishes to make welfare provision for their own needy. "Sturdy beggars" were also whipped, then sent back to their rural place of origin. Sup., chs. 27–31.
4. Polanyi (1944: 117) describes the prevailing philosophy as abolition of the Elizabethan right to live. "No assessment of wages, no relief for the able-bodied unemployed, but no minimum wages either, nor a safeguarding of the right to live. Labor should be dealt with as . . . a commodity which must find its price in the market. The laws of commerce were the laws of nature and consequently the laws of God." Poverty is untamed nature challenging society; hunger, nature's physical sanction; death, nature's remedy for poverty.
5. Regulations arose, Friedrick Engels noted, when the "pestilential air and poisoned water" of working-class slums threatened to infect the bourgeoisie. In self-protection, factory owners made some efforts to suppress pathogenic conditions, and when these efforts were insufficient, they moved their residences to suburbs at a safe distance from the noise, stink, and disease of the slums. Friedrick Engles, "The Housing Question," in Karl Marx and Friedrick Engels, *Selected Works,* Vol. I. Moscow: Foreign Languages Publishing House, 1962, p. 578.
6. "It is probably safe to affirm the centralization of manufacturing industry has reached its limit." Adna F. Weber, *The Growth of Cities in the Nineteenth Century.* New York: Columbia University Press, 1899, p. 202. "A

reaction toward decentralization began when manufacturers located their mills in the suburbs of large cities in order to escape the high city rents and still avail themselves of the city's superior shipping facilities." Ibid., p. 212. Weber acknowledged that technology was "but one factor" in the "triumph of the factory system" (Ibid., 104), but when seeking to explain factory location he paid no attention to cost of labor and municipal infrastructure, thus contributing to the long-prevailing impression that only technology and rent affected industrial location.

7. Braudel (1973: 440) notes that all European capitals participated in the Industrial Revolution "in the role of spectators." The capital cities were too big, too luxurious, and too parasitic to become industrial centers.

REFERENCES

Abrams, Philip, and E. A. Wrigley, eds. 1978. *Towns in Societies*. Cambridge: Cambridge University Press.

Ashton, T. S. 1948. *The Industrial Revolution, 1760-1830*. London: Oxford University Press.

Bendix, Reinhard. 1956. *Work and Authority in Industry*. New York: Wiley.

Braudel, Fernand. 1973. *Capitalism and Material Life, 1400-1800*. Trans. by Miriam Kochan. New York: Harper Colophon Books.

Brenner, Robert. 1976. "Agrarian Class Structure and Economic Development in Pre-Industrial Europe." Past and Present 70: 30-75.

Briggs, Asa. 1974. "Technology and Economic Development," ch. 8, in Gene I. Rochlin, ed. *Scientific Technology and Social Change*. San Francisco: W. H. Freeman.

Cairncross, A. K. 1949. "Internal Migration in Victorian England." *The Manchester School of Economic and Social Studies* 17: 67-87.

Cherry, Gordon, E. 1972. *Urban Change and Planning*. Henley-on-Thames: G. T. Foulis.

Clark, Peter, and Paul Slack. 1976. *English Towns in Transition, 1500-1700*. London: Oxford University Press.

Daunton, M. J. 1978. "Towns and Economic Growth in Eighteenth Century England," pp. 245-277 in Abrams and Wrigley, eds. *Towns in Societies*. Cambridge: Cambridge University Press.

Durand, John. 1967. "The Modern Expansion of World Population." *Proceedings of the American Philosophical Society* 3: 136-159.

Engels, Frederick. 1958 [1844]. *The Condition of the Working Class in England*. Trans. and ed. by W. O. Henderson and W. H. Chaloner. Oxford: Basil Blackwell.

Fisher, F. J. 1976. "London as an 'Engine' of Economic Growth," pp. 205-215, in Peter Clark, ed. *The Early Modern Town*. London: Longman.

Friedlander, Dov. 1970. "The Spread of Urbanization in England and Wales, 1851-1950." *Population Studies* 24: 423-443.

Hammond, J. L., and Barbara Hammond. 1920. *The Town Labourer, 1760–1832.* London: Longmans Green.

Handlin, Oscar. 1969. *Boston's Immigrants,* 2nd ed. Cambridge: Harvard University Press.

Hauser, Philip. 1965. "Urbanization: An Overview," pp. 1–47, in Philip Hauser, Philip and Leo F. Schnore, eds. *The Study of Urbanization.* New York: Wiley.

Hechter, Michael. 1975. *Internal Colonialism.* Berkeley and Los Angeles: University of California Press.

Hibbert, A. B. 1963. "The Economic Policies of Towns," pp. 157–229, in M. M. Postan, E. E. Rich, and Edward Miller, eds. *The Cambridge Economic History of Europe,* vol. III. Cambridge: Cambridge University Press.

Mitchell, B. R. 1962. *Abstract of British Historical Statistics.* Cambridge: Cambridge University Press.

——. 1975. *European Historical Statistics, 1750–1970.* New York: Columbia University Press.

Moore, Barrington, Jr. 1966. *Social Origins of Dictatorship and Democracy.* Boston: Beacon Press.

Mumford, Lewis. 1938. *The Culture of Cities.* New York: Harcourt.

Pawson, Eric. 1979. *The Early Industrial Revolution: Britain in the Eighteenth Century.* London: Batsford.

Pythian-Adams, Charles. 1978. "Urban Decay in Late Medieval England," pp. 159–185, in Philip Abrams and E. A. Wrigley, eds. *Town in Societies.* Cambridge: Cambridge University Press.

Polanyi, Karl. 1944. *The Great Transformation.* New York. Holt, Rinehart and Winston.

Ragin, Charles. 1977. "Class, Status, and 'Reactive Ethnic Cleavages': The Social Bases of Political Regionalism." *American Sociological Review* 42: 438–450.

——. 1979. "Ethnic Political Mobilization: The Welsh Case." *American Sociological Review* 44: 619–635.

Reissman, Leonard. 1964. *The Urban Process.* New York: Free Press.

Smelser, Neil. 1959. *Social Change in the Industrial Revolution: An Application of Theory to the Lancashire Cotton Industry, 1770–1840.* London: Routledge and Kegan Paul.

Thomis, Malcolm I. 1974. *The Town Labourer and the Industrial Revolution.* New York: Barnes and Noble Books.

Tilly, Charles. 1974. "Urbanization," ch. 2, in Charles Tilly, ed. *An Urban World.* Boston: Little, Brown, 1974.

Weber, Max. 1961 [1927]. *General Economic History.* New York: Collier Books.

CHAPTER 5 ─────────────────

Urbanization of the United States

The urbanization of North America began two centuries before the Industrial Revolution. In this period (roughly 1640-1840) European societies were undergoing the tumultuous changes in science, culture, business, and class structure that prepared and made possible the Industrial Revolution. The principal colonizers of North America—England, Holland, and France—were themselves in the forefront of European modernization, and North America received as a result a very powerful impetus toward capitalist modernization. Indeed, North American colonies were nearly free of the residues of feudalism that obstructed Latin America as well as the colonizing mother countries. The initial urbanization of North America resembled in some respects the classic scenarios of preindustrial urbanism. European mother countries struggled for colonies and the winner sucked up the surplus produce of the conquered lands. From a European perspective, North American cities were political appendages of Paris, The Hague, or London (Chudacoff 1975: 22). Their function was to maintain the mother country's political authority; to absorb her people and exports; to transship the surplus primary products of the colonies as taxes, rents, and fees; and, more difficult of fulfillment, to consume the mother country's cultural products, especially her religion. When cities changed ownership, these functions persisted; only the beneficiary changed. Thus the English conquest of New Amsterdam in 1664 did not alter the functions of the thriving city at all. But London rather than The Hague now became the recipient of the city's export product, and in recognition of its new cultural orbit, the city took the name New York.

Urbanization in colonial North America was capitalist but preindustrial. The cities of the North American colonies were limited to four major functions:

political centers, commercial centers, ports or transportation nodes, craft manufacturing. Heavy industry was lacking. Urbanization was neither continuous nor
unidirectional. In 1690 North America was 9 percent urban; by 1790, only 5.1
percent of its colonists were urban (Gordon 1978: 29-31). In part, this recession of urbanization resulted from the penetration of the interior from early
coastal settlements, but the mercantilist policies of Britain were also important.
The Navigation Acts of 1660 and 1663 declared Britain's intention to monopolize the whole "trade of the plantations" (Lovejoy 1972: 3). London authorities regulated the issuance of town charters in North America in the interest of
British commerce. North American cities were assumed to produce commercial
competition with British interests so London authorities restricted their establishment [1].

The spirit animating North American cities was inharmonious with feudalism.
Guilds failed to develop, and newcomers could take up any craft or business
they wished. The crucial strata in feudal Europe, aristocrats and priests, played a
negligible role in North America. The founders of the United States were aware
of this beneficial difference and desirous of perpetuating their nonaristocratic
society. Therefore, they wrote into the U.S. Constitution (Art. I, Sec. 9:8) a
prohibition upon granting any "Title of Nobility" or receipt of same by any
officeholder of the United States. Instead of nobility, private business owners
were the predominant class. Virginia was settled by the Virginia Company;
Massachusetts by the Massachusetts Bay Company, and so forth. These were
profit-making corporations to whom the British crown had by charter ceded
limited rights or self-government in its colonial territories (Diamond 1958).
North American commerce was also in the hands of urban merchants imbued
with "modern" values. Even where religion was most prominent—in the New
England colonies—the dominant ethos was Puritan (Rostow 1978: 384). Puritanism sanctified the life ethic of the urban businessman rather than the warrior or
great landholder. The businessman made a profit in honest commerce and lived
a sober life. In contrast, Puritans maintained, the soldier earned his living by
pillage of the weak and lived a life of conspicuous waste, parasitic luxury, and
aristocratic pretension. This view reversed the traditional equation of soldiering
with honor and commerce with dishonor, the basis on which the class system of
European feudalism rested.

The seeming exception to this generalization is the contrast between the New
England and the Middle Atlantic colonies on the one hand and the Southern
colonies on the other. Puritan "roundheads" settled in the North and "cavaliers," supporters of Charles I, in the South and in the Caribbean [2]. Southern
elites emulated the aristocratic life-style and cultivated, as its twin reflections,
agriculture and warfare. From very early, the Southern colonies depended
chiefly upon government and agriculture rather than commerce for subsistence.
Agriculture permitted great plantations on which the landed gentry lived amid
slaves. The relationships of plantation owners and slaves were patriarchal and

authoritarian, thus recalling the patriarchal relationships of warriors and serfs in the European Middle Ages (Moore 1966: 121). Plantation aristocrats regarded with disdain the calculating merchants of the North, who measured out their lives in countinghouses and treated their human relationships as mere ciphers in a profit-and-loss statement (Bellah 1974: 36; Hartz 1955: 4).

Regional contrast between life-styles and values set the stage for regional contrasts of urbanization. From the beginning the Northern colonies had larger and more numerous cities than the Southern colonies. In 1700 the Southern colonies contained 40 percent of the population of what later became the United States but only one city of prominence, Charleston, S.C. A century later (Table 5-1), Baltimore had edged ahead of Charleston, whose urban fortunes never revived. Between 1720 and 1790, New York, Philadelphia, Boston, and Baltimore alone accounted for 67 percent of urban population and 48 percent of urban growth (Gordon 1978: 31-32). By 1790, the urban population of the South was 2.3 percent of the South's total population, whereas in the Middle Atlantic and New England states, urban population constituted 8.7 percent and 7.5 percent of total population, respectively (Gordon 1978: 59, n. 7).

Geography contributed to regional differences in urbanization. The South provided riverine access to the interior so coastal ports were "not required at all" (Gordon: 59, n. 7). For example, planter-merchants of Virginia loaded tobacco for export at scattered landings along tributaries of Chesapeake Bay. Because ocean-going vessels docked at these landings, planters avoided overland transshipment of crops to the coast, and Virginia developed no seaports in consequence (Earl and Hoffman 1977: 32). In this manner, geography inhibited Southern urbanization. But it is unlikely geography explains all regional differ-

Table 5-1. U.S. Population of Regions by Urban Residence, 1790-1920

	1790	1820	1860	1890	1920
Northeast					
Population (000)	1,968	4,360	10,594	17,407	29,662
Percentage urban	8.13	11.0	35.74	58.98	75.53
North Central					
Population (000)		859	9,097	22,410	34,020
Percentage urban		1.16	13.88	33.10	52.25
South					
Population (000)	1,961	4,419	11,133	20,028	33,126
Percentage urban	2.14	4.62	9.58	16.28	28.07
West					
Population (000)			619	3,134	9,214
Percentage urban			15.99	37.04	51.8

Source: U.S. Bureau of the Census, *Historical Statistics of the United States, Colonial Times to 1970, Bicentennial Edition* (Washington, D.C.: U.S. Government Printing Office, 1975). Part I, p. 22.

ences in urbanization. The South might have been commercial and seafaring as well as agricultural in the colonial period. Yet only slave-worked agriculture took hold, and Northern colonies acquired commercial and shipping hegemony. Table 5-2 shows that Northern colonies depended on shipping earnings to pay for imports whereas the South depended on agricultural exports to pay for imported slaves and manufactured goods. For commerce and shipping—both capitalistic growth industries of the nineteenth century—the colonial South depended upon Northern seaports.

Because Northern cities were commercial and seafaring in the eighteenth century, they were ready to industrialize in the nineteenth. Their urban merchants possessed the vision, science, technology, business acumen, and capital upon which industrialization depended. Because Southern cities were undeveloped in the colonial period, the South did not develop these resources and was unprepared to break through to modernization after 1840. Many telling evidences of regional disparities were apparent quite early. One was the growth of factory production in the Northeast. Between 1840 and 1860, the number of factory workers in the United States increased from 500,000 to 1,530,000. Of these, 75 percent were located in the Northeast (Bruchey 1975: 44). Another piece of evidence is the virtual absence of canal construction in the Southeast in the whole period 1818-1860, when this construction was massively underway in the Northern states (Table 5-3). Canal investment in the Northeastern states was $103.5 million in this period but only $23.9 in the South. Canal technology was preindustrial: tow paths alongside the canals permitted draft animals to haul unpowered barges. Nonetheless, canal technology permitted a 90 percent reduction in overland freight charges by wagon (Warner 1972: 67).

Canals stimulated commerce and manufacturing in the regions they served. Constructed in 1817-1825, the Erie Canal, longest and most successful of all, accelerated the industrial development of western New York State and the Great Lakes ports and engendered a string of middle-sized cities along the canal route

Table 5-2. Value of Commodity Exports and Imports, Shipping Earnings, and Value of Slaves Imported into British North American Colonies, 1772 (thousands of pounds sterling)

	Exports	Imports	Shipping Earnings	Slaves Imported
Northern Colonies (Canada)	229	417	12	
New England	509	1,335	354	
Middle Colonies	688	1,332	181	
Southern Colonies	2,019	1,971	95	389

Source: U.S. Bureau of the Census, *Historical Statistics of the United States, Colonial Times to 1970, Bicentennial Edition* (Washington, D.C.: U.S. Government Printing Office, 1975), Part II, p. 1182.

"from Albany to Buffalo." These canals were constructed in the Northeast because commercial traffic there was sufficient to support them. Once constructed, the canals accentuated and reinforced the industrial urbanization of the Northeast, thus perpetuating and increasing the regional contrast with the South (Table 5-3).

Canals rearranged geography to suit commerce, reducing the significance of river access. Chicago and Buffalo grew rapidly after the Erie Canal gave them access to the Hudson River, and thus to the port of New York. Southern ports continued to depend upon unimproved nature for access to the sea. The key Southern linkage was the New Orleans-St. Louis section of the Mississippi River. River traffic along this linkage favored the commercial development of the South whereas traffic along the New York-Albany-Chicago circuit favored urbanization of the North. Competition between these transport linkages was intense for decades, but there would have been no competitition had not the Erie Canal created a manmade link that nature overlooked. The Chicago-New York transit link was later strengthened by railroad construction, another manmade device that reduced the riverine advantage of the South. Even so, Chicago and St. Louis engaged in an epic commercial rivalry during the nineteenth century. After the Civil War, Chicago displaced St. Louis in the nation's urban hierarchy (Table 5-4).

Another indication of regional differences before the Industrial Revolution is the flow of immigrants to the United States in the period 1790-1860. Nearly all foreign immigrants entered the United States in Northern ports, and few subsequently moved South (Bruchey 1975: 39). The agricultural economy of the South offered few jobs and the competition of slaves was unattractive to free labor. Immigrants settled in Northern cities, where they found employment in commerce and industry. In 1860 the foreign-born constituted 19 percent of the population of the Northeast but only 3.5 percent of the population of the

Table 5-3. Investment in Canals by Region and Agency, 1818-1860 (millions of dollars)

	United States Total	Percentage of Which State Funds	Northeast	South
1818-1830	46.8	51.5	31.7	5.2
1831-1840	74.3	62.3	18.4	11.1
1841-1850	34.5	65.2	23.2	3.9
1851-1860	35.5	76.8	30.2	3.7
Total	191.1	62.6	103.5	23.9

Source: U.S. Bureau of the Census, *Historical Statistics of the United States, Colonial Times to 1970, Bicentennial Edition* (Washington, D.C.: U.S. Government Printing Office, 1975), Part 2, p. 766.

Table 5–4. Ten Largest U.S. Cities, 1800–1975

Rank	1800	1860	1930	1975
1.	Philadelphia	New York	New York	New York
2.	New York	Philadelphia	Chicago	Chicago
3.	Baltimore	Baltimore	Philadelphia	Los Angeles
4.	Boston	Boston	Detroit	Philadelphia
5.	Charleston	New Orleans	Los Angeles	Detroit
6.	Salem	Cincinnati	Cleveland	San Francisco
7.	Providence	St. Louis	St. Louis	Washington D.C.
8.	New Haven	Chicago	Baltimore	Boston
9.	Richmond	Buffalo	Boston	Dallas-Ft. Worth
10.	Portsmouth	Newark	Pittsburgh	St. Louis

Source: Lance E. Davis, Jonathan R. T. Hughes, and Duncan M. McDonald, *American Economic History* (Homewood, Illinois: Richard Irwin, 1961), p. 287; and U.S. Bureau of the Census, *County and City Data Book, 1977* (Washington, D.C.: U.S. Government Printing Office, 1978), p. xxv. Appropriate portions reproduced by permission of authors and publisher.

South. The channeling of immigrants to the Northeast continuously increased regional disparities in population. By the time of the Civil War (1861-1865) the South's share of U.S. population had declined to 22 percent from 40 percent in 1700.

Regional differences in social and economic development became starkly apparent during the Civil War. The South's cavalier tradition provided the Confederacy with a preponderance of military professionals, but generalship and martial ardor were the South's only advantage. In the end, the Union armies prevailed because of the logistical support of Northern industry, the naval monopoly of Northern ports, and the population preponderance of the Northern states. Indeed, the Irish and German troops who clinched the war for Abraham Lincoln were in origin immigrant workers attracted to the United States by urban jobs that the South could not offer.

INDUSTRIAL URBANIZATION OF THE UNITED STATES: A STATISTICAL PROFILE

The Industrial Revolution reached the United States from Europe around 1840 and touched off a process of urbanization that has not yet run its course. Industrial urbanization in the United States involved interconnected changes in population, number of cities, and urban hierarchy. Population changes were most obvious: population increased, and the percentage of the nation's population residing in cities also increased. Table 5-5 documents this trend. In 1840, there were roughly fifteen rural Americans for every urban dweller. The increasing proportion of urban residents occurred despite an absolute increase in the

Table 5-5. Urban and Rural Population, 1840-1970 (thousands)

Size	1840	1860	1900	1940	1970	1970/1840
Cities of 1,000,000 or more			6,429	15,911	18,769	
Cities of 50,000 or more	705	3,091	16,916	45,333	73,188	103.8
Cities of 2,500 to 49,999	1,145	3,126	13,244	29,097	76,138	66.5
All Urban	1,845	6,217	30,160	74,424	149,325	80 9
All Rural	15,224	25,227	45,835	57,246	53,887	3.5

Source: U.S. Bureau of the Census, *Historical Statistics of the United States, Colonial Times to 1970, Bicentennial Edition* (Washington, D.C.: U.S. Government Printing Office, 1975), Part 1, p. 11.

number of rural people until 1940. In that year rural population peaked at fifty-seven million, then began to decline. Between 1940 and 1970 America's rural population experienced absolute as well as relative decline. Another view of this population process (Table 5.6) shows that rural population increased only 3.5 fold over the whole period 1840-1970, whereas urban population increased 66.5 fold—nineteen times more.

The urbanization of America's population might have occurred with no increase in the number of cities. In this case, cities existing in 1840 would simply have grown in population. Conversely the urbanization of America's population was also compatible with *no* increase in size of cities—provided the number of cities increased sufficiently to accommodate all the new city dwellers. In other words, 100 small towns of 10,000 population could substitute for one big city of 1,000,000 population. Strictly speaking, a country with one big city of 1,000,000 is as urbanized as a country with 100 towns of 10,000 each: both have the same percentage of urban population. This illustration shows that talking about urbanization leaves unresolved the important question of whether

Table 5-6. Number of U.S. Urban Places by Size, 1840-1970

	1840	1860	1900	1940	1970
Cities of 1,000,000 or more			3	5	6
Cities of 50,000 or more	5	16	78	199	396
Cities of 2,500 to 49,999	126	376	1,659	3,265	6,666
Total urban	131	392	1,737	3,464	7,062

Source: U.S. Bureau of the Census, *Historical Statistics of the United States, Colonial Times to 1970, Bicentennial Edition* (Washington, D.C.: U.S. Government Printing Office, 1975), Part 1, p. 11.

urban people are living in big cities, medium cities or in towns. What actually occurred in the United States was a balance between the extremes of growth in number of cities and growth of urban population. The number of urban places increased, but urban population increased even faster.

The U.S. Bureau of the Census defines urban places as settlements with a population of 2,500 or more. The number of urban places in the United States was 131 in 1840, 1,737 in 1900, and 7,062 in 1970 (Table 5-6). Table 5-7 expresses this growth as a percentage change for the intervals 1840-1900, 1900-1970, and 1840-1970. In every interval the number of cities increased more rapidly than did rural population but fell behind the rate of increase in urban population. For example, in the period 1840-1970 the number of cities of size 2,500 to 49,999 increased forty-one fold, whereas the population of cities of this size class increased sixty-six fold. This discrepancy indicates city-making was proceeding less rapidly than the growth of urban population, thus placing upward pressure on city size.

Table 5-7 also shows that this overall trend conceals two phases. In the first period, 1840-1900, the trend toward big cities was overpowering. The population of big cities increased 2,399 percent whereas the population of cities of 2,500 to 49,999 increased less than half as rapidly. Similarly, the number of cities of 50,000 or more population increased 1,560 percent, whereas smaller cities increased only 1,317 percent. Both measures show that the bigger cities were growing faster than the smaller in the nineteenth century. These trends were reversed in the twentieth century. Since 1900 the population of cities of 50,000 or more has increased *less* rapidly than the population of smaller cities. The number of bigger cities has also increased slightly less rapidly than the number of smaller cities. This reversal in relative growth did not end urbanization, but it did affect the kind of cities in which Americans live.

Table 5-7. Growth of U.S. Cities, 1840-1900, 1900-1970, and 1840-1970 (percentage change)

	1840-1900	1900-1970	1840-1970
Population by city size			
50,000 or more	2,399	433	10,381
2,500 to 49,999	1,157	575	6,649
Number of places by city size			
50,000 or more	1,560	402	4,198
2,500 to 49,999	2,317	407	4,115
Rural	301	118	354

Source: U.S. Bureau of the Census, *Historical Statistics of the United States, Colonial Times to 1970, Bicentennial Edition* (Washington, D.C.: U.S. Government Printing Office, 1975), Part 1, p. 11.

MILL TOWNS AND CITIES

A statistical description of U.S. urbanization does not explain how urbanization worked. Between 1860 and 1910, the growth of manufacturing industry was "fundamental" to the country's urbanization (Glaab and Brown 1976: 102). Here there were both contrasts and similarities with industrial urbanization in Britain. As in Europe, the earliest sites of the Industrial Revolution in North America were towns, not major cities. The first factories located in New England towns like Lowell, Lawrence, Waltham, and Lynn. Dependent on water power, these factories located along riverbanks, then built canals to divert the river's waters past their machinery. Industrial towns continued to attract workers until the first decade of the twentieth century, but their heyday was the period 1840-1880. After the Civil War, steam engines and railroads increasingly shifted the new manufacturing sites to the larger cities. Most of these cities had been commercial centers prior to 1860, and the addition of manufacturing only spurred their growth. Manufacturing was "seldom responsible" for the creation of large cities, but only for the additional growth of already founded cities (Glaab and Brown 1976: 102).

The technology of transportation and production is still the basic explanation of the shift of manufacturing industry from town to city. Railroads ended the factories' dependence on riverine transportation and increased the advantages of centrality that big cities already conferred. Moreover, steam-powered machinery eliminated factories' dependence on water-driven mill wheels. Yet Gordon (1978: 39) has criticized as "too indeterminate" the "conventional arguments" about this transition. As in Europe, labor discipline was an important influence on industrial relocation in the United States. In the mill towns of New England, labor unrest had been modest before the Civil War. Most factory workers were farm girls who returned to their family homesteads during the slack season and lived in dormitories under the avuncular supervision of their employer. After 1848, Irish immigrants replaced native-born women. Immigrant laborers did not have a family farm to visit during their factory's slack season (Ware 1959: 149). Therefore unemployment and low wages were life-threatening hardships they were compelled to resist. This situation rendered the labor force of industrial towns increasingly fractious [3]. On the other hand, when the business cycle deteriorated in big cities, factories closed and employees were left to shift for themselves until trade revived. There were no expectations of paternalism in big cities. Additionally, the slums of big industrial cities contained many unemployed workers whose hungry presence at the factory gate moderated the labor militance of the employed. In all, big cities offered a more favorable climate for industrial discipline in the post-Civil War era than did the mill towns (Gordon 1978: 41).

CIVIC BOOSTERISM: THE URBAN GROWTH COALITION

Unlike North America, Europe was fully settled before the Industrial Revolution. North American urbanization had to be more complex than Europe's because the process involved the peopling of wilderness as well as the growth and relocation of population. The incorporation of the western frontier necessitated continuous city-making. But the old-fashioned idea of a frontier edging westward in advance of city-making has been proven wrong. Cities "accompanied and even preceded" the western frontier (Chudacoff 1975: 31). For example, Pittsburgh, Cincinnati, Louisville, and St. Louis preceded the frontier in their localities. In every case, the earlier city residents included businessmen who sensed the coming growth of the surrounding region and the centrality of their new city's site. Getting there first gave them an opportunity to get rich in city-building. City-building was itself a speculative business activity, and during the nineteenth century interest in this business approached a "virtual mania" (Chudacoff 1975: 31).

The westward expansion of the frontier created another regional gap in urbanization: the West lagged behind the East. At the same time, the South lagged behind both (Table 5-1). Therefore the characteristic structure of this phase of urbanization was regional inequality in urbanization. For quite different reasons, the South and the West remained agricultural and extractive, and the cities that grew up in these regions served chiefly administrative, military, transshipment, and retail functions. The Northeast and the North Central regions were more urban and their cities contained more heavy industry. The erosion of this regional imbalance since 1920 is a reversal of the historic preponderances.

Even during the colonial period, filling wilderness with cities was strictly in the hands of private enterprise. Colonial municipalities erected only the slenderest public works, and those they did sponsor, private enterprise constructed under contract. However, the visibility of private enterprise in the construction phase must not conceal the role of government. European crowns made grants of land to private individuals and corporations. These land grants usually included limited rights of self-government as well. In fact, every North American colony began its existence under a separate land grant from some European monarch. These grants were political acts that set the stage for the economic development of the continent by private enterprise. The grants preceded urbanization because no settler could develop any land without the permission of European sovereigns. Of course, European states were unable to administer the colonies at close hand, and the terms of their grants conceded various rights to settlers, including the freedom to plan their own municipalities. Nonetheless, the political grant of land was always the original source of colonial urbanization, and the terms of these grants were, in principle, susceptible to variation as it pleased a sovereign to vary them.

The United States early adopted a policy of public generosity toward private enterprise (Geruson and McGrath 1977: 70-71). Under the terms of the Northwest Ordinances of 1784-1787, lands west of the Allegheny Mountains were held and divided in simple ownership. This law wiped out feudal restraints upon the sale of land or its capitalistic management (Warner 1972: 17-19). Moreover, the federal government accepted the responsibility for surveying the frontier and dividing the wilderness into tracts for sale. Speculators purchased tracts of land, advertised them for resale, and introduced improvements. Typically, developments were laid out in a gridiron pattern for convenient sale. Minimal space was set aside for public purposes: parks yielded no profit (McKelvey 1963: 11). As settlers were enticed, speculators resold federal land at a profit.

The long-range value of lots thus purchased depended on the commercial future of a city. This was always problematic because no one could say for certain which of numerous villages would grow into metropolises and which would remain villages (Glaab and Brown 1976: 27). Cleveland's growth is illustrative. Founded in 1796, the city grew little in the first twenty years of its existence. In 1815 the population was only 150. By 1818 the first Great Lakes steamboat called. In 1828 the city's harbor was improved at federal expense, a local improvement attributable to the boosterism of Cleveland speculators. The effects of the Erie Canal had become clear by 1830, when Cleveland's population reached 1,000. A decade later the city's population had experienced a sixfold increase. Cleveland's businessmen and property owners profited from the city's growth, but success had not resulted wholly from natural advantages of site. New York State's investment in the Erie Canal stimulated Cleveland's growth, and local business owners had taken advantage of this stimulus to expand their city's harbors at federal expense (Glaab and Brown 1976: 103). This story was typical of successful cities. Riverine or lake access, good harbors, a central location, and attractive climate always encouraged commerce and manufacturing, and thus city growth. However, the competition of localities for growth was rarely a purely natural competition of position and topography. Cities also competed in terms of the enterprise, political influence, and financial resources of their region's investors (Warner 1972: 20-21). Speculators touted the attractiveness of their investment, the village, because settlement would fulfill the growth prophecy. The more people who settled in a village, the greater its commercial role and the more valuable its lots. Everyone who bought land in a city acquired an economic interest in its commercial growth because growth meant higher land prices.

In this manner, every American city acquired a municipal growth bloc [4]. Its membership consisted of persons who stood to profit from local growth. A minority of city population, the growth bloc was politically and socially preponderant. The largest class of members consisted of residential property owners. These were a smaller proportion of city population in the nineteenth century than currently. In 1870, only 37 percent of skilled workers in Boston were owners of property, mostly taxable real estate. Only in the upper salaried stratum was a majority owners of taxable property (Thernstrom 1973: 299). U.S. Census (1975, Part II: 646) reports indicate that nonfarm home owners were 37 percent of nonfarm population in 1890. When city populations grew this group profited because land bought cheap could be resold dear. Municipal growth often brought neighborhood deterioration and overcrowding. Therefore, residential property owners had some ambivalence about growth. But offsetting this conflict was the opportunity to sell property for a profit and then purchase a bigger, nicer home in a better neighborhood, usually on the urban periphery.

Although residential property owners made up the rank and file of the municipal growth bloc, a city's business community was normally its activist vanguard. Real estate speculators, construction companies, retail tradesmen, professionals, banks, newspapers, insurance agents, and some clergymen shared financial interest in municipal growth to increase the value of their real property, or to create more demand for their product or service. These people came together in local chambers of commerce to "boost" their city's future. The ideology of the municipal growth bloc thus acquired the name "civic boosterism" (Glaab 1967).

One expression of civic boosterism was the frequent affirmation of the rosy future awaiting one's city and region. Many municipal seals evidence civic boosterism in the city motto. An example is Chicago's echoing "I will." Transportation machinery was a favorite advertising medium. Steamboats and railroad specials were named "spirt of . . . " in testimony of the indomitable growth energy of the place. The Fourth of July and other patriotic occasions also brought to public platforms speakers who bragged about their growing city. A "rah-rah" spirit animated these spectacles, and the analogy with sports enthusiasm is close.

There was, however, more to boosterism than public displays of rah-rah spirit. Chambers of commerce competed with one another to attract industry, transportation, and population. The first and most crucial determinant of civic growth was transportation accessibility. In the colonial period, only waterborne transportation access mattered, so entrepreneurship was of limited value (Geruson and McGrath 1977: 56). Transportation was a matter of natural endowment, and the competition of cities for commerce in this early period was a test of comparative natural advantage. However, the canal era produced a new form of intercity competition. Sites along canal routes were enhanced in value, so speculators bought up cheap land and then used political influence to bring the canal past it. Once the canals were constructed, alternative and competing transportation networks existed. Cities abutting each network employed their political and economic influence to entice trade along their route, thus causing urbanization to occur in their region faster than elsewhere. Cities along successful canal routes grew much, and the owners of lots in them made big profits. Cities along lesser canal routes grew less, and owners of property there made less profit. In part, the construction of canals was responsive to market incentives and thus nonpolitical in character. However, the funding of canals always depended upon public money, thus introducing a political consideration at the stage of appropriation, and the location of publicly financed canals—a crucial decision for competing localities—was always susceptible to political influence in state legislatures (Table 5-3).

In the period 1850-1900 railroad construction continued the intercity and interregional competition of the canal era. The federal government gave immense tracts of public land to railroad companies. These gifts amounted to one tenth of the land area of the United States. As soon as the track was laid, land acquired value for farming, and the railroads were able to resell the land for huge profits, thus recouping their original investment. Towns that had attracted canals now attracted railroads (Hoyt 1933: 54). Hence, they became cities; cities that became hubs of railroad networks became big cities; and regions in which track was extensive became urbanized (Warner 1972: 88). Since railroad lines could be laid anywhere, cities tried to attract the railroads by offers of free rights-of-way, free railroad station sites, or outright bribes to railroad officials.

The Illinois Central Railroad's operations in the 1850s are illustrative. Railroad owners forced communities to offer concessions to obtain service, and when the offers were not rich enough, railroad "associates" established the cities of Centralia, Kankakee, Champaign, and LaSalle through which track was subsequently laid. When property values rose in response, the railroad associates sold for a profit (Glaab and Brown 1976: 103). Many scandals resulted from bribery of railroad and public officials by cities and towns eager to influence routing decisions. Indeed, crookedness was rampant in the railroad construction era and surely accounts for a significant amount of decision-making. The local history of large western cities in the nineteenth century always involved complex machinations among politicians, property and business interests, and railroad tycoons. Oakland, Calif., offers a colorful illustration. A lucky gold strike in 1849 permitted Andrew Moon and several mining cronies to buy a municipal charter from the California legislature in 1850. This charter bestowed self-government on Oakland and acknowledged the property right of Moon and his associates, whose gunmen had already driven away the Spanish grantee, Senõr Peralta. Moon and his gang were elected to public office in the newly chartered city. The city council hired Moon to build a one-room schoolhouse in exchange for a ninety-nine-year lease of the city's waterfront. As Bay Area population increased, the value of Moon's property increased. Additionally, the only transportation between San Francisco and Oakland was via the ferry line nicknamed "Minturn's monopoly," owned by a Moon associate. The city of Oakland made many legal challenges to Moon's waterfront lease but was never able to regain the land for the public. Ultimately, Moon negotiated a secret deal with Leland Stanford, owner of the Southern Pacific Railroad. Moon sold his land to Southern Pacific for an undisclosed sum and retired. This deal brought the railroad to Oakland (Hinkel and McCann 1939: Vol. 2).

Railroad construction was complete by the turn of the century. Railroad service was superior in the Northeast and Midwest, but overland trucking developed as a competitor in the motor age, thus challenging the transportation centrality of these regions and stimulating industrial growth in the South and West. Since 1920 trucking has attracted an increasing proportion of intercity freight haulage and currently accounts for more of the total than does railroad transport. Trucks have economic advantages over railroad transport, the chief of which is reduction of loading costs. Trucks load at the beginning of their run and unload at its end. In contrast, railroad transport requires shippers to load their goods for delivery to the railroad terminal, where they are unloaded and reloaded in railroad cars. At the other end, the goods must once more be unloaded, then reloaded, and finally unloaded at their final destination. Trucking eliminates four of the six loadings and thus lowers the cost of shipping. In this sense, trucking has economic advantages.

On the other hand, trucks also depend on interstate highways for rapid delivery. These highways depended on legislative decisions because the polity has the authority to exercise eminent domain for the acquisition of land for highways (Warner 1972: 90). Moreover, the state's taxation authority maintains highways for the benefit of users and determines highway specifications, including width, straightness, gross weight limitations, and maintenance standards. The trucking industry could not prevail in competition with railroads so long as the nation's highway system consisted of two-lane roads maintained by states with varying standards. The Federal Roads Act of 1916 brought the federal government into the business of building and maintaining an automotive highway system capable of supporting the trucking industry (Warner 1972: 37, 50). At this juncture, the issue of intercity haulage became federal because the direction and extent of highway building were federal decisions. On these decisions hinged the value of property along the route and the profitability of railroads. That is, the interstate highway system greatly increased the value of locations along its route so existing towns, cities, and regions competed with one another to bring the interstate highway into their area or to increase its local extent. The process of local and regional competition did not singly account for the actual course of the existing highway system because strictly economic determinants (profit incentives, natural endowment, and so on) also contributed. Nonetheless, the highway system was in origin a federal political act, and the existing highway system represents in substantial measure the outcome of a half century of political competition among various localities. As in the eras of railroad and canal construction, the reward for political success was the enhanced value of real property in fully served localities.

REGIONAL URBANIZATION SINCE 1920

The urban predominance of the Northeast reached its peak in 1920 when that region alone contained 55 percent of the U.S. urban population. Since 1920, the rest of the nation has tended to catch up with the Northeast. The trend toward equalization of urban population among regions is not, therefore, of strictly postwar origin. On the other hand, urbanization of the so-called Sunbelt states of the South and West has greatly accelerated since World War II. Table 5-8 documents the changes in regional population and percentage urban. Both measures show that the Northeast and North Central regions grew less than the South and West in the period 1940-1970. Another indicator is the changing urban hierarchy (Table 5-4). In 1860 St. Louis was the only one of the ten largest U.S. cities west of the Mississippi River. By 1930, Los Angeles had joined the top ten, but the Northeast and North Central regions were unambiguously predominant (Table 5-4). This predominance was still apparent in 1975 but much reduced. Between 1930 and 1975, Los Angeles advanced its rank from

Table 5-8. Population of U.S. Regions, Percentage Urban, and Percentage Change, 1940-1970

	1940	1970	Percentage Change (1970/1940 × 100)
Northeast			
Population (000)	35,977	49,041	136.3
% urban	76.66	80.44	143.1
North Central			
Population (000)	40,143	56,572	140.9
% urban	58.38	71.55	172.7
South			
Population (000)	41,666	62,795	150.7
% urban	36.69	64.55	265.1
West			
Population (000)	14,379	34,804	242.0
% urban	58.48	82.90	343.1

Source: U.S. Bureau of the Census, *Historical Statistics of the United States, Colonial Times to 1970, Bicentennial Edition* (Washington, D.C.: U.S. Government Printing Office, 1975), Part 1, p. 22.

fifth to third while both San Francisco and Dallas-Ft. Worth entered the top-ranking ten. Two North Central cities, Cleveland and Pittsburgh, were displaced from the top ten between 1930 and 1975.

In the past, America's cities and regions competed for growth, and some grew faster than others. Fortunately there were no losers because every city gained population, albeit at different rates. What is novel about the postwar rise of the Sunbelt is the absolute decline of jobs and population registered by some Northern and Eastern major cities. Table 5-9 compares the ten biggest gainers and losers of population among U.S. metropolitan areas in the period 1970 to 1980. Gainers still outnumber losers, and average gains are bigger than average losses. In the period 1970-1974 only one sixth of U.S. metropolitan areas registered population loss; the rest were gainers (Alonso 1978: 71). Nonetheless, the evidence proves that absolute population losses are occurring, and this occurrence is historically eccentric in the United States. Small- and medium-sized cities of the South and West have generally displayed the greatest growth, whereas reduced population concentrates in metropolitan areas of the North Atlantic coast, the lower Great Lakes, and to a lesser extent the Pacific coast. Declining population accompanies declining jobs. For example, between 1969 and 1976, New York City lost 452,000 jobs, and New York was "not alone" in terms of job loss (Tabb 1978: 247). By 1972 most "major cities of the Northeast" had lost between 14 and 18 percent of their jobs whereas Sunbelt cities had "average employment gains of between 60 and 100 percent" (Perry and Watkins 1977: 292). The sharp contrast between Northeast loss and Sunbelt gain (Table 5-9) exacerbated the normal tensions surrounding interregional urbanization because of the growing conviction that Sunblet cities grew at the expense of the Northeast.

What produced the postwar shift of urbanization toward Sunbelt states? Five causes stand out: climate and natural advantages, annexation, resource competition, political influence, and the world economy. Mild climates have attracted certain industries to Sunbelt cities, and employees have followed. A familiar example is the Hollywood film industry that developed in southern California because the climate permitted year-round filmmaking. Another illustration is Lockhead Aircraft, which chose Burbank, Calif., for its aircraft construction plants largely because the climate never interfered with production. Oil and natural gas have attracted industry to Texas and Louisiana, causing high rates of growth in cities like Ft. Worth and Baton Rouge. The increasing dependence of the U.S. economy on coal, a result of the world energy crisis, has also resurrected mining in West Virginia and Nevada, producing population gain and urbanization there.

Annexation causes growth when central cities expand their boundaries to encompass formerly independent suburban municipalities. Thus Sunbelt cities appear to be growing rapidly, but one study found that only two of the nation's forty-five largest cities actually grew in population during the 1950s as a result

Table 5-9. U.S. Metropolitan Areas: 10 Biggest Gainers and Losers of Population, 1970–1980 (percentages)

	Percentage Change, 1970-1980	
	Increase	Decrease
Ten Biggest Gainers		
Fort Myers–Cape Coral, Fla.	+ 95.1	
Ocala, Fla.	77.4	
Las Vegas, Nev.	69.0	
Sarasota, Fla.	68.0	
Fort Colins, Colo.	65.9	
West Palm Beach–Boca Raton, Fla.	64.2	
Fort Lauderdale–Hollywood, Fla.	63.5	
Olympia, Wash.	61.6	
Bryan-College Station, Tex.	61.4	
Reno, Nev.	59.9	
Ten Biggest Losers		
Elmira, N.Y.		– 3.8
Newark, N.J.		4.5
Boston, Mass.		4.7
Pittsburgh, Pa.		5.7
Utica-Rome, N.Y.		6.0
Pittsfield, Mass.		6.5
Buffalo, N.Y.		7.9
Cleveland, Oh.		8.0
Jersey City, N.J.		8.4
New York, N.Y.–N.J.		8.6

Source: U.S. Department of Commerce, Bureau of the Census. 1980 Census of Population. Supplementary Reports, PC80–S1–5. *Standard Metropolitan Statistical Areas and Standard Consolidated Statistical Areas: 1980.* (Washington, D.C.: U.S. Government Printing Office, 1981), Table C and Table 4.

of net in-migration. These two were Los Angeles and San Diego. "All the other Sunbelt cities expanded their cores by annexation" (Geruson and McGrath 1977: 132). Sunbelt chambers of commerce have pursued annexationist policies as "integral and consistent parts" of civic boosterism (Fleischmann 1977: 167). First, suburban lands have been annexed *after* development by free market forces. Second, annexation headed off political competition centered in outlying areas [5]. Finally, annexation created an image of irresistible growth, thus "boosting" the annexer and augmenting property values. Aggressive entrepreneurship is the cause of annexationist policies in Sunbelt cities. This view of the matter suggests that Sunblet urbanization cannot be explained away as statistical artifacts produced by annexations.

A great attraction of Sunbelt states has been cheap, nonunion labor (Tabb 1978: 249). To obtain access to this cheap labor, some low-wage industries, notably textiles, closed Northeastern and North Central plants, then reopened in the Sunbelt [6]. The causes of interregional wage differentials are complex, but the effects are visible to employers. For example, about 90 percent of garment workers in New York City are union members. As a result, employers must offer high wages and excellent working conditions in New York City. But the garment workers' union in Los Angeles has enrolled about 10 percent of the area's workers. Garment firms in Los Angeles routinely pay much lower wages than those prevailing in New York City, and working conditions are also inferior. Eighty percent of workers in Los Angeles garment plants are recent immigrants from Mexico. According to contractors, the garment industry in Los Angeles could not survive without the cheap labor of Mexicans illegally working in the United States (Bonacich and Light in press). The interregional contrasts in industrial working conditions are dramatic, but so is the shift of garment work away from New York City, which has lost 50 percent of its garment industry jobs since 1950.

To stem the job less, New York City formed committees of business people and politicians to "boost" the Big Apple. American Airlines was a charter member of this booster effort, so its decision to move its corporate headquarters to Dallas came as a shock to the New York public in 1978. Airline spokespersons explained that workers in Texas put in more hours for the same pay. Therefore the New York airline shifted its corporate headquarters to Dallas. The example illustrates how powerful are the economic incentives arising from cut-rate labor in the Sunbelt and the extent to which these incentives affect even high-wage industries with many white-collar employees.

By 1977 the South contained 60 to 70 percent of the low-wage manufacturing industries in the United States [7]. However, low-wage industries have not been the most rapid growers in the South. Between 1940 and 1960, 90 percent of growth in Southern manufacturing was centered in "above average growth, high wage" industries (Watkins and Perry 1977: 42-43). Thus Southern urbanization did not result principally from attracting low-wage industries formerly located in other regions, although this attraction has been real. Rather, the low wages and relaxed working standards in the South have provided lower-wage sites for traditionally high-wage occupations. Sometimes Southern urbanization occurred because of industrial relocation. More commonly, growth involved a decision to open a new plant in the Sunbelt rather than elsewhere. For example, computer technology chose to locate in the Sunbelt where land and labor costs were cheaper, but this decision did not remove anything from other regions nor introduce a below-average-wage industry into the economy of the South.

Civic boosterism has also contributed to Sunbelt growth. Sunbelt cities boast aggressive chambers of commerce that have widely advertised the amenities of climate, cheap land, low wages, and low taxes that their city affords industry. Additionally, the political influence of the chamber of commerce in Sunbelt municipalities has been predominant. Reflecting this is the probusiness ideological stance of Sunbelt politicians. Therefore these places have offered tax incentives to industries considering relocation or new plant construction. There is, of course, nothing new in chamber of commerce civic boosterism and alliances to elect probusiness politicians. Indeed, interlocal and inter-regional competition to attract business has been the mechanism of urbanization in the United States since independence [8].

Stagnating cities of the Northeast and North Central regions have complained that Sunbelt regions benefited from disproportionate and "unfair" spending by the federal government in their region (Moynihan 1978; Markusen and Fastrup 1978); that is, Sunbelt states have received more in federal spending, especially for aerospace and defense, than they have contributed in taxes (Tabb 1978: 248–49). Thus federal spending has contributed to Sunbelt urbanization but to stagnation in the Northeast. This analysis is valid, but the interpretation may be disputed. First, the federal government has been influenced in locational decisions by the same environmental and resource-availability considerations that have channeled private industry to the Sunbelt. An example is the Manned Spacecraft Center locational contest in 1961. Cities under consideration were Tampa, Houston, Dallas, and Corpus Christi. All were located in the Sunbelt because space launches required a mild climate. This requirement excluded Frostbelt cities. Houston's proposal apparently won out over its Sunbelt competitors because Vice President Lyndon B. Johnson favored this city. In an inter-city test of political influence, Houston's chamber of commerce was proven to have the most. Therefore the Manned Spacecraft Center located in Houston, and federal spending produced a "major economic growth spurt" in Houston during the next decade (Angel 1977: 125). Second, as an employer, the federal government wants value for its wage dollar and has found labor cheaper in the Sunbelt. The federal government's recurrent preference for the Sunbelt is not merely a reflection of the institutional power of Dixie Congressmen, although that power exists, because the nonpolitical influences affecting private industry also affect federal locational decisions.

Moreover, political influence has always channeled growth among U.S. regions (Sjoberg 1963: 119-120). "Entrepreneurship in the Sunbelt is . . . the type of entrepreneurship practiced during the penetration of the frontier" (Angel 1977: 116). Interregional competition for urbanization is the game played in the United States since independence and today's losers cannot claim that foul play tilted the balance against them. However, there is more to this complex issue than merely history repeating itself. The role of the federal government has expanded so vastly that its funding decisions have shifted power away from states. Bell (1973: 130-131) shows that government employment expanded 16,800 percent in the period 1870-1980, whereas total employment expanded only 772 percent in this 110-year period. As federal budgets have increased, regional urbanization has tended to depend on how much power boosters can exert in Congress rather than on what happens in the state capitol or city hall. Since the federal government spends tax money collected in every region, the politics of its spending decisions now bring regions into collision. Therefore, the growth of federal budgets has made a problem in political science out of what was earlier seen as a problem of regional economics.

The changing world economy has also encouraged urbanization of the United States Sunbelt. As Sternleib and Hughes (1980: 51) have observed, arguments about regional shares of manufacturing industry obscure the fact that the United States is losing manufacturing jobs to cheap-labor countries overseas. Until approximately 1965 most overseas investments of United States corporations were in Canada or Western Europe. However, in the 1970s multinational corporations began to open manufacturing plants in Taiwan, South Korea, Singapore, Mexico, and Brazil. By 1975, 30 percent of U.S. corporate profits were derived from overseas investments. United States trade unions refer to this overseas movement of multinational corporations as "runaway shops." The runaway shops are leaving the United States for the Far East in order to exploit the cheap labor in these countries (International Labour 1976: 11). Since this overseas movement did not begin until the 1970s but the growth of the Sunbelt began decades earlier, the runaway shops clearly do not explain Sunbelt urbanization. On the other hand, cheap labor in the Sunbelt has permitted the United States to hang onto some manufacturing plants that would otherwise have left the country altogether for the Far East. In this sense the availability of Sunbelt cheap labor has buffered the declining fortunes of U.S. manufacturing industries on world markets.

POPULATION CHANGES IN U.S. URBANIZATION

Urbanization in North America needed massive immigration. The fortyfold increase in population (1800 to 1970) occurred *despite* a continuous decline in birthrate (Table 5-10). It is true that life expectancies increased as a result of lowered death rates. Nonetheless, natural increase was a strictly secondary factor in American population gain. Far more important was international migration. Urbanization of America's growing population also depended on the migration of rural people into cities. Sometimes this rural-urban migration involved the settlement of rural aliens in America's cities. Sometimes rural-urban migration involved resettlement of rural Americans in American cities. Either way, cities grew because people moved into them from the countryside. The nation grew because foreigners moved in. These international and national relocations were important turning points in the lives of the people who made them.

Urbanization of the United States is the result of three successive waves of rural-urban migration: Anglo-Irish (1820–1880), southern and eastern Europe (1880–1924), and blacks from the South (1917–1970). The first wave was an

Table 5-10. Total and Urban Population of the United States, 1800-1970, Percentage Urban, and Age-Specific Birthrate

	Total Population (000)	Percentage Urban	Live Births per 1,000 Women 15-44	Deaths per 1,000 Population
1800	5,308	6.07	55.0*	
1850	23,192	15.28	43.3*	18.7†
1900	75,995	39.69	32.3	16.5
1950	150,697	64.01	24.1	8.2
1970	203,235	73.47	18.4	8.1

Source: U.S. Bureau of the Census, *Historical Statistics of the United States, Colonial Times to 1970, Bicentennial Edition* (Washington, D.C.: U.S. Government Printing Office, 1975), pp. 22, 49, 57, 58.
   *White only.
   †Massachusetts, 1860.

international migration of northern and western European people, notably English and Irish. In 1820 these two nations alone provided 72 percent of total immigration to the United States. But Anglo-Irish sources were inadequate to provide as much labor as employers needed. Their proportion of total immigration had declined to 41 percent in 1880. New sources of immigrants were being tapped. This "new" immigration came principally from central, eastern, and southern Europe. In 1900 people from these regions accounted for 71 percent of total immigration to the United States (Table 5-11). As were their Anglo-Irish predecessors, these new European immigrants were overwhelmingly rural in origin, poor, and unskilled. The dependence of foreign whites on industrial jobs

Table 5-11. Immigrants to the United States by European Regions of Origin, 1860-1919

Time Priod	Northwestern Europe and Germany		Central, Eastern, and Southern Europe		All Areas*
	Number*	Percent	Number*	Percent	
1860-1869	1,852	89	26	1	2,081
1870-1879	2,079	76	173	6	2,742
1880-1889	3,803	72	837	16	5,249
1890-1899	1,826	49	1,754	47	3,694
1900-1909	1,812	22	5,823	71	8,202
1910-1919	1,113	18	3,944	62	6,347

Source: U.S. Bureau of the Census, *Historical Statistics of the United States, Colonial Times to 1970, Bicentennial Edition, Part 1* (Washington, D.C.: U.S. Government Printing Office, 1975), Series C-89-119.
   *All numbers in thousands.

channeled the newcomers into the industrial cities of the Northeast and North Central regions.

The massive increase in urban population required increased agricultural product. As a result, the farm population of America continued to increase until 1940, although its relative decline began earlier. Even so, successive generations of American farmers facing the choice of farm or city chose the city. The upshot was rural-urban internal migration. In this case the rural migrants were internal migrants rather than, as among foreign whites, international migrants. However, the rural migrants shared many characteristics with the foreign whites. Mainly, they were poor. Successful farmers did not, in general, choose to give up farming for city life. The people who did were the unsuccessful farmers for whom a factory job or even urban life on welfare were more satisfactory than what they enjoyed in the country.

Both "push" and "pull" factors affected the rate and timing of internal migration from farm to city. Push factors arose from adverse conditions on farms such as low prices for crops, mechanization, or drought. Where adverse conditions prevailed, rural people migrated to cities because they had no choice. Pull factors reflected attractive conditions in cities, especially the availablity of high wage employment. When cities had many good jobs to offer, rural people chose to migrate there in hope of economic improvement. Two familiar illustrations are helpful. Dust-bowl refugees were rural whites who fled from the South and Southwest in the 1930s. Stigmatized as "Oakies," "Arkies," and "hillbillies," these rural whites were displaced from their land by the conjoint influence of drought and depression. The cities to which they fled were also suffering from depression, and there were no jobs for uprooted farmers. These rural migrants did not enter cities because urban conditions were appealing; rather, displaced from agriculture, they were compelled to look for survival in cities. On the other hand, rural blacks in 1917-1918 and again in 1942-1945 moved in great numbers to industrial cities. The immediate cause of their rural-urban migration was abrupt labor shortages produced by World Wars I and II. In this case, the attractions of the city absorbed rural people who had no urgent reason to quit agriculture. Hence, the wartime migration of blacks illustrates the process of urban pull and the rural-urban migration of poor whites the push of circumstances.

The distinction between push and pull migrations is useful but, in most cases, strictly analytical because pure types of one or the other are exceptional. In most cases, the rural poor of America and Europe were encountering deteriorating conditions ("push") in agriculture at the same time that the lure of cities ("pull") was also increasing. The lure did not need to be a high-paying job, effective as that lure has always proved. As standards of living in cities generally improved, the agricultural minimum standard had always to keep pace, and where it did not, migration resulted. For example, generations of American farmers had been content to use unheated redolent privies, and abrasive corn

Table 5-12. Regional Population of the United States by Nativity and Color, 1920 and 1970 (millions)

	1880	1920	1970	Percentage Change	
				1880–1920	1920–1970
Northeast					
Native white	11,465	22,175	40,624	193	183
Foreign-born white	2,808	6,783	3,778	242	56
Black	233	704	4,642	302	659
Total	14,506	29,662	49,044	204	165
Northcentral					
Native white	14,049	28,569	49,919	203	175
Foreign-born white	2,912	4,585	1,780	158	39
Black	403	856	4,866	212	568
Total	17,364	34,020	56,565	196	166
South					
Native white	10,113	23,285	49,282	226	212
Foreign-born white	442	847	1,220	192	144
Black	5,961	8,993	12,291	151	137
Total	16,516	33,125	62,793	205	190
West					
Native white	1,215	7,080	25,461	583	360
Foreign-born white	397	1,487	1,955	375	131
Black	155	336	3,291	218	979
Total	1,767	8,903	30,707	504	345

Source: U.S. Bureau of the Census, *Historical Statistics of the United States, Colonial Times to 1970, Bicentennial Edition* (Washington, D.C.: U.S. Government Printing Office, 1975), pt. 1, p. 23.

cobs but American farmers today demand indoor plumbing, and when farms are not profitable enough to buy flushing toilets, they migrate to cities.

Conventional treatments have understood urban pull and rural push as linked reflections of industrial urbanization, the master process. On the one hand, industrial urbanization creates job in cities, thus developing an urban pull. On the other hand, mechanization eliminates jobs in agriculture, thus developing a rural push. According to this view, small farm abandonment and rural-urban migration are inevitable results of basic and irreversible economic processes. Broadly speaking, that view is correct, but it has become increasingly apparent that in the twentieth century government policy became a major influence upon the rate of agricultural modernization and, therefore, upon the rate and timing of rural push. Under the Agricultural Adjustment Act of 1933 the federal government paid Southern farmers to reduce cotton acreage while lending them money for mechanization. As a result, cotton production decreased 26 percent between 1932 and 1934 at the same time that tractor use increased. According to Fligstein (1981), these linked developments reduced planter demand for agricultural workers, thus depriving many rural blacks of employment. In this situation many unemployed blacks migrated to Northern cities. A result of mechanization, the rural-urban migration of blacks thus reflected a governmentally contrived push—not merely the autonomous operation of the private economy.

World War I and the restrictive U.S. Immigration Act of 1924 reduced the flow of immigrants from Europe. Employers wanted more workers than they could obtain in Europe so they turned to the American South and sought to attract agricultural blacks. These employers actually sent labor agents to scour the South for workers, and wherever the agents went blacks threw up their hoes and left for Chicago on the next train. Thus began the rural-urban migration of Southern blacks to Northern and Western cities. Between 1920 and 1970, the black population of the Northeast, North Central, and Western states doubled or tripled its already high rate as a result of migration from the South (Table 5-12). At the same time the foreign white population of Northeast and North Central states declined. By 1970 blacks were more numerous than foreign whites in every region, but not more numerous in Northeast and North Central states than foreign whites had been in 1920. Between 1970 and 1980, the exodus of blacks from the South ended. Sunbelt urbanization encouraged a return flow of urban blacks from the North and West to the South, so the South actually gained more blacks from in-migration in this decade than it lost from out-migration.

Population Changes In Postindustrial Urbanization

Industrial urbanization depended upon the growth of manufacturing to provide livelihoods for displaced rural people. In the early phases of industrialization manufacturing did greatly expand. However, the experience of all developed nations (Bell 1973: 16-17) also shows that industrialization based on manufacturing reaches an early plateau, then recedes in terms of total employment. Yet cities continue to grow even after manufacturing industries cease to expand their proportion of the national labor force. The basis of this urban expansion is the so-called service sector of the economy, also urban-based. Government, leisure, education, health care, research, high technology, and managerial coordination are the preeminent services in modern societies.

In "postindustrial" America the service sector has become the largest source of employment, and its rate of growth continues to outdistance the others (Bell 1973: 130-131). Between 1870 and 1980 goods-producing industries increased their employment 297 percent, whereas service-producing industries increased employment 2,273 percent (Bell 1973: 130-131). Agriculture's share of employment dropped, but manufacturing outdistanced other goods-producing industries in percentage growth. However, manufacturing employment grew less than half as fast as employment in service industries and only one sixteenth as rapidly as government employment. Government employment increased 16,800 percent between 1870 and 1980. Most of this increase was in state and local rather than federal employment.

Service industries do not have so many jobs for unskilled rural migrants as do manufacturing industries. To a substantial extent, expanding service industries attract workers who are already urban. These workers move in response to economic incentives too, but they are interurban rather than rural-urban migrants. Interurban migration is, accordingly, the typical form of migration in societies and regions that emphasize service industries, and it has become the predominant form of internal migration in the United States today.

The timing of regional urbanization dramatically affects industrial competition. The belated industrialization of the South and West encouraged these regions to emphasize service functions rather than manufacturing. The overall result is an industrial mix in these regions heavily oriented toward the service sector (Warner 1972: 63). Indeed, the population growth of these regions has largely resulted from the internal migration of well-educated native whites previously residing in the Northeast and North Central regions. Unlike the earlier streams of poor Europeans and blacks to the industrial cities of the North, and postwar postindustrial migration to the Sunbelt selected the most educated and culturally advanced for intercity migration.

A possible exception to this generalization is the post-1965 immigration of undocumented Mexican aliens to cities of the Southwest. These illegal migrants are poor, unskilled in urban trades, and uneducated. In these respects they resemble nineteenth-century European immigrants and represent a fourth wave of rural-urban migration. These undocumented workers have provided limitless labor for low-wage manufacturing industries in the Southwest. This sector is an important but subordinate support of the regional urbanization in the Sunbelt since World War II.

SUMMARY

Urbanization of the United States proceeded as interlocal and interregional competition for growth. Growth depended on natural advantages, technology, entrepreneurship, political influence, and transportation access. Transportation access was a heavily political issue because success depended on what government decided to do. The growth bloc in every city centered around an activist core of business owners who advanced an ideology of "civic boosterism" to enlist home owners and the general public to the cause of local industrial and population growth. Civic boosterism has been a persistent influence on the direction, speed, and quality of American urbanization [9].

The regions of the United States urbanized at unequal rates and in series. The Northeast and North Central regions developed earliest on the basis of commerce in the colonial era and heavy manufacturing since 1840. They recruited labor for heavy industry among distressed agricultural people in Europe and among poor whites and blacks of the South. Rural-urban migration from South to North and from foreign countries to America was the basic cause of industrial urbanization in the United States until 1945.

Since World War II, the South and West have urbanized more rapidly than the Northeast and North Central regions. The growth of the Sunbelt has been especially rapid because Sunbelt cities are attractive industrial sites offering low wages, cheap land, low taxes, non-union workers, business-oriented local government, and aggressive boosterism. In addition, the South has benefited from federal spending for defense and aerospace and the general turning of the U.S. economy toward service-producing industries. Urbanization of the Sunbelt since 1945 has reversed the earlier flow of black migration that is now shifting southward in response to job availability. The Sunbelt has also attracted educated, largely white manpower for high-level jobs from other regions. In the Southwest illegal Mexican migrants provide low-wage workers who have attracted some manufacturing from the unionized Northeast.

NOTES

1. As the Industrial Revolution spread in Britain, American business naturally wanted to develop an independent manufacturing capacity too. However, London's mercantilism stifled the development of manufacturing in colonial cities. Not surprisingly, resistance to British mercantilism began in the Northeastern cities most adversely affected by it. Independence won, James Madison led a protective tariff through Congress in the interest of "promoting domestic industries." According to Dawley (1976: 14) the protective tariff had "a significant effect in reducing existing import competition and in preserving the future American market for domestic firms." With the development of a heavy manufacturing sector, the capitalist economy of the United States became an industrial economy as well.
2. The issue of Cavlier vs. Roundhead is historically controversial. Taylor (1979: 15–16) acknowledges that Americans of the Civil War era attributed regional differences in character to the heritage of Roundheads and Cavaliers. However, he dismisses the belief as a "legendary past" based on "fictional sociology." He concludes that "no such absolute division" ever characterized North and South. After all, Southerners engaged in business, lived in towns,

voted for the same national parties, and believed in "many of the same" ideals and beliefs as did other Americans (1979: 335). Taylor dismisses the contrast of Northern and Southern character on the grounds that some overlap existed. Surely, his position is as absurd as disputing the distinction between night and day on the ground that twilight is common to both. One need not insist on a literal derivation of Cavaliers and Roundheads to suppose that modal character in North and South was quite different before 1860. Abrahamson's factor analysis indicates it is still quite different. William R. Taylor, *Cavalier and Yankee*, 2nd ed. Cambridge: Harvard University Press, 1979. See also Mark Abrahamson, "The Social Dimensions of Urbanism" *Social Forces* 52 (1974): 376–383.

3. In 1855, a former agent of a Lowell mill visited the new, immigrant-employing mills at Fall River, Mass. He was shocked by the abrupt hardening of the employers' attitude toward workers.

> I enquired of the agent of a principal factory whether it was the custom of the manufacturers to do anything for the physical, intellectual, and moral welfare of their people . . . "We never do," he said. "As for myself, I regard my work people just as I regard my machinery. So long as they can do my work for what I choose to pay them, I keep them, getting out of them all I can."

Quoted from Norman Ware, *The Industrial Worker: 1840-1860*. Gloucester, Mass.: Peter Smith, 1959, p. 77.

4. "The political and economic essence of virtually any given locality, in the present American context, is growth." The "growth machine" is a booster coalition of businessmen and professionals who benefit from local population growth. Harvey Molotch, "The City As a Growth Machine: Toward a Political Economy of Place." *American Journal of Sociology* 82 (1976): 309, 315. Molotch's article is correct, but too modest in scope: the growth machine has always directed the policy of American cities, and urbanization in the United States is largely the result of successive interplace competitions. John Logan ("Suburban Industrialization and Stratification") makes a similar point in this issue of the *American Journal of Sociology*. See also his exchange with Molotch.

5. Sometimes suburban cities annex one another. A freakish intersuburban battle broke out in California when a loophole in California's Municipal Reorganization Act of 1977 permitted cities legally to detach part of a neighboring city without the neighbor's permission. Until this loophole was eliminated, suburban cities were grabbing away one another's territories in a frantic round of annexations and counterannexations. See Bob Baker, "Cities Fighting Over Annexation Claims," *Los Angeles Times,* August 20, 1978, p. S-1.

6. "'Corporations are relocating at a pace unparalleled in history. And too many are moving simply to get away from the union. They are moving to get away from unions. They are moving South and Southwest to get away from unions.'" Richard Bommarito, President, United Rubber Workers, AFL–CIO. Quoted in *U.S. News and World Report*, May 21, 1979, p. 95.

7. In October 1980, J. P. Stevens and Co. signed a union contract with the Amalgamated Clothing and Textile Workers Union of America recognizing Amalgamated as the sole bargaining agent for 3,500 of Stevens and Co.'s 40,000 workers in Southern states. Still, the agreement ended a decade-long strike and boycott of Stevens and Co., and was widely hailed as an opening wedge in unionization of the South. Hollywood's *Norma Rae* was based on Amalgamated's long organizational struggle with Stevens and Co. See Harry Bernstein, "The Fall of J. P. Stevens and Co.: A Triumph for Labor's Southern Strategy," *Los Angeles Times,* October 26, 1980, pt. VIII, p. 1.
8. "The notion of competition of places is applicable to systems of places at any geopolitical level." John R. Logan, "Growth, Politics, and the Stratification of Places," *American Journal of Sociology* 84 (1978): 412.
9. "The unparalleled growth of cities has been accompanied by uncontrolled subdivision and speculative practices and by the most fantastic real estate booms . . . " U.S. National Resources Committee, *Our Cities.* Washington, D.C.: U.S. Government Printing Office, 1937, p. 14.

REFERENCES

Alonso, William. 1978. "Metropolis Without Growth." *The Public Interest* 53: 68–86.

Angel, William D. 1977. "To Make a City; Entrepreneurship on the Sunbelt Frontier," pp. 109–128, in David C. Perry and Alfred J. Watkins, eds. *The Rise of the Sunbelt Cities.* Beverly Hills: Sage.

Bell, Daniel. 1973. *The Coming of Post-Industrial Society.* New York: Basic Books.

Bellah, Robert N. 1974. "Civil Religion in America." pp. 21–44 in Russell E. Richey and Donald G. Jones, eds. *American Civil Religion.* New York: Harper and Row.

Bonacich, Edna, and Ivan H. Light. In Press. *Immigrant Entrepreneurs.* Berkeley and Los Angeles: University of California Press.

Bruchey, Stuart W. 1975. *Growth in the Modern American Economy.* New York: Dodd, Mead & Co.

Chudacoff, Howard P. 1975. *The Evolution of American Urban Society.* Englewood Cliffs, N.J.: Prentice-Hall.

Clark, Peter. 1976. "Introduction: The Early Modern Town in the West," pp. 1–42, in Peter Clark, ed. *The Early Modern Town.* London: Longman.

Dawley, Alan. 1976. *Class and Community: The Industrial Revolution in Lynn.* Cambridge: Harvard University Press.

Diamond, Sigmund. 1958. "From Organization to Society: Virginia in the Seventeenth Century." *American Journal of Sociology* 63: 457–475.

Earl, Carville, and Ronald Hoffman. 1977. "The Urban South: The First Two Centuries," pp. 23–51, in Blaine A. Brownell and David R. Goldfield, eds. *The City in Southern History.* Pt. Washington, N.Y.: Kennikat Press.

Fleishchman, Arnold. 1977. "Sunbelt Boosterism: The Politics of Postwar

Growth and Annexation in San Antonio," pp. 151–168, in David C. Perry and Alfred J. Watkins, eds. *The Rise of the Sunbelt Cities.* Beverly Hills: Sage.

Fligstein, Neil. 1981. "The Transformation of Southern Agriculture and the Migration of Blacks and Whites, 1930–1950." Paper presented, Center for International Studies, Conference on New Directions in Theory and Method of Immigration and Ethnicity Research, May 16.

Friedland, Roger. 1981. *Power and Crisis in the Central City.* London: Macmillan.

Geruson, Richard T., and Dennis McGrath. 1977. *Cities and Urbanization.* New York: Praeger.

Glaab, Charles N. 1967. "Historical Perspective on Urban Development Schemes," pp. 197–219, in Leo F. Schnore, ed., *Social Science and the City.* New York: Praeger.

——. and A. Theodore Brown. 1976. *A History of Urban America,* 2nd ed. New York: Macmillan.

Gordon, David M. 1978. "Capitalist Development and the History of American Cities," pp. 25–63, in William Tabb and Larry Sawers, ed. *Marxism and the Metropolis.* New York: Oxford University Press.

Hartz, Louis. 1955. *The Liberal Tradition in America.* New York: Harcourt.

Hinkel, Edgar J., and William E. McCann. 1939. *Oakland, 1852–1938.* Oakland: Oakland Public Library and Works Progress Administration, mimeographed.

Hoyt, Homer. 1933. *One Hundred Years of Land Values in Chicago.* Chicago: University of Chicago Press.

International Labour Organization. 1976. *The Impact of Multinational Enterprises on Employment and Training.* Geneva: International Labour Office.

Lovejoy, David S. 1972. *The Glorious Revolution in America.* New York: Harper & Row.

McKelvey, Blake. 1963. *The Urbanization of America, 1860–1915.* New Brunswick N.J.: Rutgers University Press.

Markusen, Ann R., and Jerry Fastrup. 1978. "The Regional War for Federal Aid." *The Public Interest* 53: 87–99.

Moore, Barrington, Jr. 1966. *Social Origins of Dictatorship and Democracy.* Boston: Beacon Press.

Moynihan, Daniel P. 1978. "The Politics and Economics of Regional Growth." *The Public Interest* 51: 3–21.

Perry, David C., and Alfred J. Watkins. 1977. "People, Profit, and the Rise of the Sunbelt Cities," pp. 277–305, in David C. Perry and Alfred J. Watkins, eds. *The Rise of the Sunbelt Cities.* Beverly Hills: Sage.

Roberts, Bryan R. 1978. "Comparative Perspectives on Urbanization," pp. 592, in David Street, ed. *Handbook of Contemporary Urban Life.* San Francisco: Jossey-Bass.

Rostow, Walt W. 1978. *The World Economy.* Austin: University of Texas.

Sjoberg, Gideon. 1963. "The Rise and Fall of Cities: A Theoretical Perspective." *International Journal of Comparative Sociology 4:* 107–120.

Sternlieb, George, and James W. Hughes. 1980. "The Changing Demography of the Central City." *Scientific American* 243: 48–53.

Tabb, William K. 1978. "The New York City Fiscal Crisis," pp. 241–266, in

William Tabb and Larry Sawers, eds. *Marxism and the Metropolis*. New York: Oxford University Press.

Thernstrom, Stephan. 1973. *The Other Bostonians*. Cambridge: Harvard University Press.

U.S. Bureau of the Census. 1975. *Historical Statistics of the United States, Colonial Times to 1970*, Bicentennial Edition. Washington, D.C.: U.S. Government Printing Office.

——. 1977. *City and County Data Book*. Washington, D.C.: U.S. Government Printing Office.

Ware, Norman. 1959. *The Industrial Worker: 1840-1860*. Gloucester, Mass.: Peter Smith.

Warner, Sam Bass, Jr. 1972. *The Urban Wilderness*. New York: Harper & Row.

Watkins, Alfred J., and David C. Perry. 1977. "Regional Change and the Impact of Uneven Urban Development," pp. 19-54, in David C. Perry and Alfred J. Watkins, eds. *The Rise of the Sunbelt Cities*. Beverly Hills: Sage.

CHAPTER 6

Third World Urbanization

The Third World consists of less developed countries in Africa, Latin America, the Middle East, and Asia. According to Saffire (1978: 723) the term "Third World" originally denoted nonaligned countries in the Cold War. "Third World" has now become synonymous with "less developed" regardless of politics. Less developed countries (LDCs) are usually contrasted with more developed countries. The development in question is strictly economic—not cultural. Developed economies have vastly reduced the proportion of population engaged in agriculture. They have strong independent manufacturing industries that export finished goods. The most developed economies also have rapidly growing service sectors that emphasize technology, health, education, and research. Even "developed" countries are still developing. The crucial criteria are the existence of heavy industrial sectors and the reduction of the agricultural population—characteristics, it is true, only of the first stage of industrial development. The world's developed regions include North America, Western and Eastern Europe, the Soviet Union, Oceania, and Japan.

The contrast appears in Table 6-1, which displays the sectoral shares of the working population in the United States, Argentina, Mexico, and Brazil. The United States has a smaller proportion of workers engaged in agriculture, forestry, and fishing than do the other countries. This is the preindustrial sector. On the other hand, the United States has a higher percentage of workers engaged in goods-producing industries in general, especially manufacturing, than do the other countries. This is the industrial sector. The United States also has the largest service sector. This is the postindustrial sector. In sum, the economy of the United States is the most developed of the four and is obviously capable of turning out more goods and services per capita than are the others. However, there are big differences among the three "less developed" Latin American nations. Argentina has a more developed economy than Mexico, and Mexico is slightly more developed than Brazil. The rank order of these nations in per capita income follows the rank order of industrial development.

Developed countries are rich countries. Their per capita gross national product (GNP) measures the average money value of goods and services that people of these nations consumed. Table 6-2 shows the rank order of world regions in 1977. The highest-ranking region was North America, with a per capita GNP of US$8,710 per capita. The next highest was Japan, followed by Oceania, Western Europe, the USSR, and so forth. The per capita income of the lowest-ranking region, Asia, was only 4 percent of the North American figure. In these money terms, North America, Japan, Oceania, Western Europe, and the USSR are developed; all the others are less developed. However, these gross generalizations conceal great variation within regions. For example, Europe's highest-ranking nation, Switzerland, had a gross national product of $11,080—in excess of North America's on the upper side. On the lower side, Europe also included Albania, whose per capita GNP ($660) was much lower than that of Venezuela ($2,630) or Libya ($6,520), even though these countries are in less developed regions. Similarly, Japan's per capita income exceeded the average for Europe, but Japan belongs in "less developed" Asia. The highest per capita money income in the world was in the United Arab Emirates ($14,800)—a Third World nation.

World disparities in standard of living are very slowly declining (Elliott 1978). Between 1950 and 1970 the percentage of gross world product consumed by the 20 percent of world population residing in the wealthiest countries declined from 73.8 to 69.2 percent. The share of the middle 60 percent of countries increased slightly in the same period (Table 6-3) and the share of the bottom-

Table 6-1. Economically Active Population by Sector: Selected Countries, 1970 (percentages)

Sector	USA	Argentina	Mexico	Brazil
Agriculture, forestry, fishing	4.0	14.8	39.5	44.3
Mining	0.7	0.5	1.4	0.6
Goods-producing, total	59.6	50.0	33.5	29.2
manufacturing	24.0	19.7	16.7	11.0
Services	35.7	26.0	19.8	23.5
Unclassified	–	8.7	5.8	2.4
Total	100.0	100.0	100.0	100.0
Number (millions)	(91,040)	(9,011)	(12,955)	(29,557)

Source: James Wilkie, ed., *Statistical Abstract of Latin America*, Vol. 17. Los Angeles: UCLA Latin American Center Publications, University of California Press, 1976, p. 146.

Table 6-2. GNP* per Capita of Major Regions and Selected Countries

Region or Country	GNP per Capita, 1977 (US $)
North America	8,710
Japan	6,510
Oceania	5,490
Europe, except USSR	4,810
USSR	3,330
Middle East	2,950
South America	1,360
Central America	1,120
Africa	490
Asia, except Japan and Middle East	330
World	1920

Source: The 1979 World Bank Atlas, p. 10.
  *GNP = gross national product, a measure of monetarized economic activity.

20 percent of countries declined. In 1980 developed nations accounted for 28 percent of the world's population but consumed 89 percent of gross world product. Conversely, 72 percent of the world's population resided in LDCs but received only 11 percent of gross world product. Per capita incomes tell the same story. Third World income per capita was US$520 in 1978, whereas in the West and Japan per capita income was $6,114 in the same year. The developing world's income share has risen since 1950, but discrepancies are still so great and the rate of change so slow that Third World people are discouraged about catching up (Hermassi 1978: 249). The only really significant changes in world consumption since 1950 have been the declining share of the United States and the growing share of communist societies (Table 6-3).

Table 6-3. World Consumption Shares, 1950 and 1970

Proportion of Gross World Product Going to:	1950	1970
Highest GNP countries with 20% of world population	73.8	69.2
Middle GNP countries with 60% of world population	23.4	28.6
Lowest GNP countries with 20% of world population	2.8	2.2
United States	41.9	30.4
13 Communist Nations	12.4	23.2

Source: John W. Meyer, John Boli-Bennett, and Christopher Chase-Dunn, "Convergence and Divergence in Development," *Annual Review of Sociology,* Vol. 1 (Palo Alto, Calif.: Annual Reviews, Inc., 1975), p. 232. Reproduced with permission from the *Annual Review of Sociology,* Volume 1, © 1975 by Annual Reviews Inc.

The real meaning of money income is ambiguous because of local disparities in cost of living. A more basic measure of well-being is nutrition. On the
bright side, nutritional standards have been generally improving in the last generation. Table 6-4 shows that average daily kilocalories per capita increased in
every region of the world between 1961/63 and 1972/74. In the decade 1965-
1975 the number of undernourished persons in the world increased from 1.1 to
1.4 billion, but since this increase was smaller than world population growth, the
percentage of undernourished persons in the world declined. On the gloomy
side, averages conceal the deteriorating food situation in many countries. In the
1960s, 56 of 128 developing countries experienced population growth rates
higher than growth of food production. In the 1970s, 69 developing countries
were in this predicament, and the 69 included big countries like Egypt, India,
Mexico, and Pakistan. Table 6-4 also shows that, except in North America, the
percentage growth of agricultural production per capita dropped between 1961
and 1976, thus reducing the margin between survival and starvation.

World hunger has two aspects: production and distribution of food. Assessing
food production capability, the United Nations (1980: 207) concludes "available world supplies should be sufficient to provide everyone with an adequate
diet." But the distributional problem is intractable. In developed countries, obesity is an increasing health problem caused by excessive calorie consumption. In
developing regions between one fifth and one-third of people are malnourished.
Within the developing countries, members of the upper socio-economic classes
suffer the same obesity problem as do the citizens of the United States. Available data invariably demonstrate that poor people receive smaller amounts of
food than wealthy people, and the discrepancy is sufficiently great that it "must
lead to inadequate dietary intake for a large proportion" of the world's people

Table 6-4. World Food Production and Consumption by Regions

	Average Annual Percentage Growth of Agricultural Production per Capita		Average Daily Kilocalories per Capita	
	1961/65-1970	1970-1976	1961/63	1972/74
World	0.6	0.4	2410	2550
Developed Regions	1.2	1.2	3170	3380
North America	0.2	1.9	3320	3530
Developing Regions	0.7	0.2	2060	2210
Asian centrally planned economies	1.0	0.7	1960	2290

Source: United Nations, Department of International Economic and Social Affairs. Population Studies No. 70. *World Population Trends and Policies: 1979 Monitoring Report.* Vol.
I. *Population Trends.* (United Nations Publication Sales No. E.79.XIII.4), Tables 95 and
100. Reproduced by permission of the United Nations.

(United Nations, 1980: 207). Of the poor in developed nations, those most often undernourished are the urban unemployed, landless agricultural laborers, pregnant and lactating women, and especially children. "Young children are particularly vulnerable to nutritional deficiencies" (United Nations, 1980: 209).

Lack of income affects food production as well as distribution in LDCs. The United Nations (1980: 207) observes that many Third World countries do not produce more food because their malnourished population does not have "effective demand" to buy it. How fair is the unequal distribution of the world's wealth?

This question is highly political (Hermassi 1978: 246), but international comparisons clarify the stakes. In 1970, the richest 20 percent of American families consumed 41 percent of aggregate income in the United States; their percent of income was roughly twice their percent of population. In contrast, the world's most affluent 20 percent consume three times their share of world product. Thus the distribution of income in the world is more unequal than its distribution in the United States. Political pressure for equalization of income shares everywhere emanates from those who have less than their statistical share. The intensity of pressure for redistribution of income is more severe in the rest of the world than in the United States, given the world's more severe inequality. The ferment of other nations currently lacks a coercive political forum, but ferment cannot persist at high intensity without ultimately finding a channel for expression. Nuclear terrorism is a threat that some Third World political leaders already direct at the developed nations to back their demands for redistribution of world income [1].

URBANIZATION IN THIRD WORLD INDUSTRIAL DEVELOPMENT

In the Third World as in the developed, urbanization has accompanied economic development and cultural modernization. Indeed, urbanization is possibly the single best indicator of the extent of modernization in a Third World country because heavily rural populations simply cannot produce the goods and services that create high per capita income. Therefore scholars initially approached Third World urbanization with the assumption that more urbanization meant more wealth (Taeuber 1962: 13). "The growth and development of cities," wrote Hoselitz (1954-1955: 278) "is a necessary condition of economic development." This conclusion was in conformity with the experience of the developed nations in the early phases of industrial urbanization (1750-1900), and most scholars believed urbanization of the Third World would recapitulate the industrial urbanization of the West. Thus Reissman (1964: 153) believed that Third World urbanization offered an "opportunity to see the history of Western cities reiterated in the developing countries today." On this assumption, Third World cities would grow in response to industrialization, and urban factories would soak up rural unemployment. Rural-urban migration would move redundant peasants to factory jobs in middle-sized cities with only temporary dislocations caused by too many ex-peasants chasing too few factory jobs.

The evidence of the last quarter century has compelled most social scientists to reassess this early assumption (Moir 1977: 25; Hermassi 1978: 242). First, Third World urbanization is proceeding faster than did industrial urbanization of the West in the nineteenth century. In sixteen heavily industrialized Western nations the rate of urbanization in the nineteenth century was 15 percent a decade. In the 1960s, the rate of urbanization in forty Third World countries was 20 percent a decade (Davis 1974: 170). Table 6-5 compares indices of change for total and urban population of world regions in the nineteenth and twentieth centuries. Urban population has increased faster than total population everywhere in the world since 1800. However, between 1900 and 2000, the total population of less developed regions increased more than twice as fast as did the total population of the developed regions of the world a century earlier. The differences in interregional rates of urbanization are staggeringly bigger than this. In the twentieth century, the urban population of Third World countries is expected to increase seventy fold—nine times faster than did the urban population of the world's developed regions in the nineteenth century. The astounding magnitude of this difference expresses more forcefully than any other single statistic the

Table 6-5. World Urbanization: Indices of Change* for Regions, 1800-1900 and 1900-2000

	1800-1900	1900-2000
World		
Total population	169	379
Urban population	440	1458
More developed regions		
Total population	211	241
Urban population	750	728
Less developed regions†		
Total population	152	453
Urban population	233	7000

Source: Adapted from John V. Grauman, "Orders of Magnitude of the World's Urban Population in History," *United Nations Population Bulletin* No. 8, 1976 (United Nations Publication, Sales No. E.76.XIII.3); also United Nations Department of International Economic and Social Affairs Population Studies No. 68, *Patterns of Urban and Rural Population Growth* (United Nations Publication, Sales No. E.79.XIII.9), Tables 3, 4, 8. Reproduced by permission.

*Index of change = later year/earlier year × 100. Thus an index of 379 means an increase of 3.79 times the earlier year.

†Includes Cyprus, Israel, and Turkey.

stark contrast of urbanization in developing countries today with what occurred a century ago in the world's developed countries.

Second, some Third World LDCs are already perdominantly urban even though industrially less developed [2]. Most of these are in Latin America. Beier (1976) called these Type 1 LDCs. Other Third World countries are still predominantly rural in population, but they are already close to equality of rural and urban populations and by 2000 the urban component will exceed the rural. These are Type 2 LDCs. Most are in East Asia and North Africa. Type 3 and Type 4 LDCs are both predominantly rural societies that will still be predominantly rural in 2000, despite urban growth. Beier (1976) distinguishes Types 3 and 4 on the basis of the presumptive ability of agriculture to absorb population increase. In Type 3 LDCs agriculture can support an increased population. This capacity reduces the pressure on cities to find nonagricultural jobs for workers. Most Type 3 LDCs are in sub-Saharan Africa. In contract, Type 4 LDCs have superdense rural populations with cities already swollen beyond employment capacity. In these LDCs the rural-urban influx in response to population growth could produce social crises by 2000. Exemplary societies include India, Pakistan, Bangladesh, Indonesia, and the People's Republic of China.

Beier's typology usefully indicates how wide is the range of Third World nations. Moreover, none of the four types corresponds exactly to industrial urbanization in the nineteenth-century West. Their balance of population growth, urbanization, and industrial development are out of alignment with Western norms. What produced these imbalances? There are three immediate causes. First, the demographic transition accompanying industrial urbanization had a characteristic form in the developed countries of the West that it does not have in Third World countries today. Second, rural-urban migration in the developing West bore a closer resemblance to urban industrial growth than it currently does in the Third World. Third, the regional development of the industrializing West was more balanced than in currently developing nations of the Third World.

THE DEMOGRAPHIC TRANSITION

The demographic formula for Western modernization was simple: death rates declined and, after a lag, birthrates declined too. Death rates declined because human diets and sanitary conditions improved. The most remarkable reduction in death rates were in the first year of life. Infants survived to adulthood who a century earlier would have perished in childbirth or in the cradle. Partially offsetting declining mortality was a decline in the birthrate (Reissman 1964: 172). The causes of this decline are much harder to localize than the obvious technical causes for declining mortality. Nonetheless, the decline in birthrates was a big contributor to economic development in the West. Even given this decline, Western populations rose dramatically in the late eighteenth, the nineteenth, and the early twentieth centuries. However, the expanding industrial sector could employ the increased population and the agricultural sector could feed it. Urban manufacturing jobs appeared to employ the extra people who, thanks to improved sanitation, survived to adulthood. Food production increased sufficiently rapidly to feed them. Had the birthrate not declined, the rate of population growth in the developing West would have been higher than it actually was. This extra population would have placed a greater burden on the capacity of the industrial sector to employ the new people and on the agricultural sector to feed them. One imagines a worst case in which the population increased more rapidly than the food supply, creating a Malthusian nightmare. Something similar actually occurred in Europe, but the New World provided a vast reservoir of land to support the unabsorbed surplus of Europe's population. If those who fled to America in the eighteenth and nineteenth centuries had been required to find a living in Europe's cities, the Industrial Revolution in Europe would have been infinitely more terrible than what actually transpired, horrible as that was.

Ireland provides the most extreme example. The potato famine of 1846-1849 deprived millions of peasants of their staple crop. Ireland's population was reduced by 30 percent in the period 1845-1851 as a joint result of starvation and emigration. The immigrants fled to industrial cities of Britain, but Britain did not absorb all the hungry Irish. North America and Australia also received Irish immigrants. Harsh as life was for these impoverished immigrants, the new continents nonetheless offered them a subsistence that Britain was unable to provide. Similar if less dramatic emigrations occurred from continental Europe. Europe exported 34 million people to the United States during the period 1820-1955 (Taeuber 1962: 14; Mitchell 1975: 135). Had Europe been required to find jobs for these people, life conditions would have been worse than they actually were.

The world's population is increasing more rapidly than ever before. The time required to double population was seventy-five years between 1850 and 1925. This time was reduced to fifty-two years between 1925 and 1977, and thirty-eight years between 1962 and 2000 (Table 4-3). The most rapid population change is occurring in LDCs of the Third World, where 71 percent of the world's population already lives. Third World LDCs double their population every thirty years at rates presently prevailing, whereas more developed nations now require eighty years to double their population.

In Third World countries death rates have declined as a result of the dietary, sanitary, and medical advances that reduced infant mortality in the developing West (Reissman 1964: 172). Indeed, the pace of decline has been more rapid and its advent more abrupt in Third World countries because these countries inherited scientific technology that the West developed in a century and a half of gradual advance. In 1946-1947 public health authorities in Ceylon (present-day Sri Lanka) sprayed DDT and reduced the death rate 40 percent in one year (Taeuber 1962: 4). However, LDC death rates have not yet been counterbalanced by declining birthrates. More babies survive to maturity, and survivors have nearly as many babies as their parents had. The result has been abrupt increases in population. These increases pace increases in agricultural productivity and industrial output. Thus when population increases at the rate of 2 percent a year, agricultural output and manufacturing productivity must increase at this rate merely to maintain the population at a given standard of subsistence. Improvement in the well-being of population requires increases in output greater than increases in population. Most Third World nations today are increasing their agricultural productivity and industrial output as rapidly or more rapidly than did the industrial West in the nineteenth century. However, population increases resulting from high birthrates and low death rates absorb the increment in production [3]. Demographers believe birthrates will ultimately fall in the Third World, thus eliminating the temporary imbalance in birthrates and death rates (Abu Lughod 1974: 77). Table 6-6 compares crude birth- and death rates of more and less developed countries in 1950-1955, 1980-1985 with a projection to 1995-2000. This United Nations projection indicates that in 2000 the birthrate in LDCs will still be higher than it was in the more developed countries a half century earlier.

European urbanization in the nineteenth century benefited from a New World to soak up "surplus agricultural population," but there are no longer any new worlds to siphon off population growth from the less industrialized countries (Gibbs and Schnore 1960: 166). The density of population in the New World is

Table 6-6. Crude Birth- and Death Rates for Regions and Selected Countries of the World, 1950-2000

	1950-1955	1980-1985*	1995-2000*
World total			
Crude death rate†	18.8	11.0	8.9
Crude birthrate‡	35.6	30.1	25.1
More developed regions			
Crude death rate	10.1	9.6	9.9
Crude birthrate	22.9	17.4	15.6
Less developed regions			
Crude death rate	23.3	11.5	8.6
Crude birthrate	42.1	34.6	27.8

Source: United Nations Department of International Economic and Social Affairs, Population Studies, No. 62, *World Population Trend and Policies: 1977 Monitoring Report* (United Nations Publication, Sales No. E.78XIII.3), Tables 73 and 74. Reproduced by permission.
   *Estimated.
   †Deaths per 1,000 population.
   ‡Births per 1,000 population.

still less than in Europe or Asia, so there is room for North America to triple its population by immigration from abroad without achieving present world levels of population density. Australia has even greater land yet available for settlement at what are, by world standards, low densities. Moreover, technology makes possible the exploitation of lands that have been abandoned to wilderness a century or two ago. The Soviet Union is in the forefront of land reclamation for human settlement. In Siberia and the Gobi Desert, Soviet workers have built industrial cities where only nomads could previously live. To achieve this land reclamation, the Soviets deployed the latest technology, and their experience exposes the possibilities for population support that the less densely settled portions of the world still offer.

But political and technological restraints are nonetheless real. A key example is illegal immigration from Mexico to the United States. Counting illegal immigrants is obviously impossible and estimates are both discrepant and controversial. Arguing in favor of immigration restriction, Briggs (1975: 477) estimated the number of undocumented Mexicans in the United States at seven to twelve million in 1974. Since this estimate is higher than others and occurs in a restrictionist polemic, it is suspect. However, Hirschman (1978: 1197) estimated the number at between five and ten million in 1978. This range represents between 2.2 and 4.5 percent of the United States population, and, according to Hirschman, an additional 500,000 Mexicans sneak across the border every year, escape detection, and settle in the United States.

A generation ago it was already clear (Whetten 1962: 71) that rapid population increase in Mexico would continue into the twenty-first century. This population increase has produced extensive rural-urban migration within Mexico as elsewhere in the Third World (Davis 1979). Internal migration accounts for the spectacular growth of Mexico City, which the United Nations expects to become the world's biggest city by 2000. But internal migration does not relieve Mexico's distress. In 1980 Mexico had nearly one quarter of its work force unemployed and ten million peasants lived in poverty. But for the emigration of undocumented workers to the United States, the situation in Mexico would be even more desperate.

The illegal migration of Mexicans to the United States serves much the same function as did the migration of Europeans to the New World in the nineteenth and early twentieth centuries (Petersen 1978: 547-549). However, only Mexicans who evade legal controls enter the United States. Although evaders are numerous, they are presumably less numerous than would be unrestricted migrants from Mexico. The common border between the United States and Mexico makes the evasion of immigration controls uniquely possible. Lacking this common border with Mexico, other developed countries seal their border to Mexican immigration and make their exclusion completely effective [4].

The technological restraints on world population growth are also real. Abraham Lincoln's father made a living in central Illinois with only an ax and a Bible.

Settling on the Gobi Desert or in northern Siberia requires much more capital in both hardware and educational investment (Perevedentsev 1981). For this reason, the unabsorbed population of developing nations cannot simply be let loose to settle in the wasteland of central Australia. Settlers require money, sophisticated equipment, and the knowledge of how to handle and repair it. The illiterate, unassisted peasantry of the world cannot match this requirement so their relocational prospects today are gloomier than they would have been a century ago in North America or coastal Australia.

OVERURBANIZATION

In the nineteenth-century West, industrial development more or less kept up with urbanization. Taken together, cities of North America and Europe had a job to offer every rural-urban migrant. In Third World nations, cities still rely on rural migrants for labor to staff their manufacturing industries, but the supply of labor flowing into cities from the countryside greatly exceeds available jobs. Therefore "cities of the underdeveloped nations are the embarrassed recipients of a labor force they cannot fully employ" (Reissman 1964: 158; Davis 1974: 174). The predictable result has been unemployment (Ham 1976: 224-226). Commenting on this phenomenon of development, Davis and Golden (1954) labeled it "overurbanization" in recognition of the cities' inability to supply with jobs and housing the large population they now contain. Castells (1977: 41-43) has defined *overurbanization* as "a level of urbanization higher than that which can 'normally' be attained, given the level of industrialization."

Overurbanization arises when cities grow more rapidly than jobs and housing in them. Two scenarios can produce this imbalance. Gibbs and Schnore (1960) found that in the period 1940-1950 the more rapidly cities in a region were growing, the lower was the region's level of industrial growth. This is an inverse relationship. Moir (1977: 39) found no relationship between level of urbanization and level of economic development. Either conclusion is compatible with data in Table 6-7, which shows that cities in the Third World will increase almost three times more rapidly than population growth in the period However, this contrast understates the true extent of stress because larger cities have grown more rapidly than smaller ones. For example, between 1920 and 1980, Castells (1977: 17) has reported, big cities of the Third World grew more than threefold whereas the urban population increased only twofold. In Latin America, big cities increased twentyfold whereas the urban population increased only elevenfold. This imbalanced urban growth is hard to reconcile with Western experience in which cities grew in closer proportion to the jobs they created. Big cities of the Third World simply do not fit this expectation. One current view supposes that when urbanization of a society reaches about 30 percent, it ceases

Table 6-7. World Population and Urban Component, 1950-2000 (millions)

	1950	1980	2000	Index of Change*
World				
Total population	2507	4412	6200	247
Urban population	727	1809	3162	435
Percentage urban	28.9	41.0	51.0	
More developed regions				
Total population	833	1130	1272	153
Urban population	444	801	1010	227
Percentage urban	53.3	70.9	79.4	
Less developed regions				
Total population	1685	3283	4924	292
Urban population	283	1008	2152	760
Percentage urban	16.8	30.7	43.7	

Source: United Nations Department of International Economic and Social Affairs, Population Working Paper No. 66, "Urban, Rural, and City Population, 1950-2000 as Assessed in 1978," (June 1980), Tables 1, 2. Reproduced by permission.
*Index of Change = 2000/1950 × 100.

to depend on industrial growth. Urbanization over this threshold proceeds independently of job creation. (Ibrahim 1975: 31).

Why do peasants leave the countryside when there are no jobs or housing for them in cities? One possibility is that population growth in rural districts is so rapid that the overburdened land cannot support all the people. This is a "push" theory (Firebaugh 1979: 201). Table 6-8 shows that despite the heavy rural-urban migration in less developed regions, the population of rural districts is still increasing. The United Nations projection indicates that rural areas will continue to expand their population until 2000. The contrast is great with the more developed countries, where rural districts have been losing population while cities gained. The growth of rural population in Third World countries strains the capacity of agriculture to support people, thus encouraging redundant peasants to migrate to cities where they *hope* to find work. There are also pull factors operating (Shaw 1976: Ch. 1). These attractions are opportunities, real or imagined, for enhanced education, social welfare, and health services in cities. Third World cities have lower rates of infant mortality than rural countryside, for example; and they have more movies and daily excitement, not to mention the possibility that a job will sooner or later be found. Obviously the people who migrate to cities think they are better off in so doing—otherwise they would not migrate at all.

The phenomenon of overurbanization is unambiguous, but the word has been criticized on several grounds. First, it implies that Western history is the yardstick agains which LDCs ought to measure their present. This is ethnocentric (Moir 1977: 15). Second, "overurbanization" implies that fault lies in the size of population and its location rather than in the social system of the developing

Table 6-8. Average Annual Growth Rates of Urban Population and Rural Population of More and Less Developed Regions, 1950–2000

	1950–1960	1970–1975	1990–2000
More developed regions			
Urban	2.44	1.75	1.20
Rural	–0.08	–0.76	–0.99
Less developed regions			
Urban	4.68	3.95	3.76
Rural	1.36	1.69	0.83

Source: United Nations Department of International Economic and Social Affairs, Population Studies, No. 68, *Patterns of Urban and Rural Population Growth* (United Nations Publication, Sales No. E.79.XIII.9), pp. 13, 15. Reproduced by permission.

country or the world division of labor (Sovani 1964). The critique has some merit: when local industrial stagnation results principally from corruption, traditional elites, vested interests, or external political or economic pressure, the term "overurbanization" conceals an unpleasant reality [5]. Casual employment of the term "overurbanization" perpetuates this mystification and ought, on this ground, to be avoided.

Communist countries have experienced no overurbanization, no do they have teeming slums in which rural-urban migrants reside. Because this blight is characteristic of urbanization in the non-Communist world, one must inquire why Communist societies of the Third World do not display it (Whyte et al. 1977: 192-194). The People's Republic of China is an important illustration. Sidel (1974: 149) stresses the superior organization of education, work, housing, and health care in China's urban neighborhoods. These neighborhoods provide a setting in which the functioning of the entire person is a concern of the community in which he or she lives. The Chinese government encouraged neighborhood nonprofessionals to assume responsibility for and to organize a variety of health and welfare services. Apparently, the neighborhoods have been able to erect a crude but reliable floor of support for the people who live in them.

However, control of population growth has also helped China to restrict the visible appearance of urban unemployment. China's population growth has been lower than the rest of the world's since 1950 (Chen 1970). The government has employed a wide battery of social and economic control to achieve this objective. In 1980, Chinese law restricted each family to one child. Families with additional children must pay higher taxes and forego priority access to education, health care, and housing [6]. The much discussed antiurbanism of Chairman Mao may have played a contributory role too by reducing urban growth. During the Great Leap Forward (1957-1960), China adopted a policy favoring countryside and town over cities. Mao proposed to reduce the unwanted growth of cities by locating industry and towns in rural communities. However, evaluating the success of Mao's policy, Frolic (1978: 400) denies that antiurbanism had more than a "cosmetic" effect in China [7].

Political controls over residence have prevented or reduced urban growth in some countries. During the Great Leap Forward, China's government simply compelled about 20 million urban residents to relocate in the countryside, thus reducing China's urban population. The Cultural Revolution (1966-1969) also introduced a near compulsory policy of encouraging urban youths to sojourn several years on rural communes. Ostensibly to educate youths in the value of socialist labor, the policy also reduces youth unemployment in cities (Frolic 1978: 396-398). Finally, the Chinese government requires peasants to obtain permission to relocate in a city, and government policy is to deny permission (Cheng 1980: 110, 179). Instead, China's government seeks to utilize the surplus population in agricultural work, even in subsistence agriculture. This government policy naturally frustrates many peasants who would prefer to migrate to the great cities, abandoning their harsh routine in agriculture for what they regard as a chance to make an improvement in the city. Denying this human aspiration, Communist governments "solve" the problem of overurbanization by restricting rural-urban migration. This solution channels poverty away from visible centers, thus conferring the illusion of solution upon overurbanization.

Even this illusion now stands in jeopardy of exposure. In 1981 China's national government announced repeal of a long-standing constitutional provision that had guaranteed a job to all adult citizens. Additionally, China's government advised its citizens that each must now assume responsibility for finding a job. This remarkable policy change probably signals official toleration of open unemployment in Chinese cities. Such toleration does not prove that growth and migration restrictions had no effect, but it does suggest even vigorous and protracted efforts to prevent overurbanization in this manner at last proved inadequate to the Herculean task.

PRIMATE CITIES

When cities in the developed world are grouped by size of population, they form a pyramid. There are a few very big cities at the apex, numerous middle-sized cities in the center, and a multitude of small cities at the base. Geographers have developed a measure of this pyramid called the *rank-size rule*. This rule predicts a city's population from its rank in the urban hierarchy (and vice versa) according to a formula that states, "within a country or region there is a tendency for cities of any given rank . . . to have a population which is in inverse proportion to its rank" (Mayer 1965: 91). Thus the population of the second-ranking city should be one half the first; and the population of the third-ranking city, one third the first, and so forth. If the largest city has a population of 1,000,000, the second-ranking city's population ought to be 500,000 and the fourth-ranking city's population 250,000 (Duncan 1974: 206). The rank-size rule is a useful tool for comparing the size distribution of cities observed in a region or society with what would be expected for a region with the same population but located in the developed world.

The trend toward very big cities is apparent in Table 6-9, which displays the changes in size and composition of the world's thirty-five largest cities in 1950, 1980, and 2000. In 1950 only twelve Third World cities were on this list. This number will have doubled by 2000. Indeed, of the world's ten largest cities in 2000, eight will be in Third World countries. The average population of the Third World metropolises among the largest thirty-five already exceeds the average in the developed world, and by 2000 the difference will be still larger. Obviously Third World nations' cities will not overtake the developed world's in 2000 and will not have created industrial economies whose output exceeds that of the developed world. Remaining relatively underdeveloped, these Third World nations will nonetheless have bigger cities than developed nations. This imbalance is evidence that Third World big cities are too big for the economies that support them.

As a result of big city growth, many developing countries have one outsized big city towering over a myriad of villages (Brutkus 1975: 633). These outsized giants are called *primate cities*. Middle-ranking and small cities are relatively scarce in the developing world. The result is imbalanced urbanization in which people are either rural or inhabitants of excessively large cities. Some observers compare the primate cities of developing countries to immense heads swollen

Table 6-9. Mean Size of World's Thirty-five Largest Cities and Third World Participation, 1950–2000 (millions)

	1950	1980	2000
World's largest urban agglomeration	12.3	20.2	31.0
Mean population, world's ten largest urban agglomerations	6.76	13.7	21.5
Mean population, world's thirty-five largest urban agglomerations	3.65	8.54	13.3
Number of Third World agglomerations in largest thirty-five	12	20	25
Mean population, Third World agglomerations in largest thirty-five	3.04	8.58	14.0

Source: Adapted from United Nations, Department of International Economic and Social Affairs, Population Division Working Paper No. 66, "Urban, Rural and City population, 1950–2000 as assessed in 1978" (June 1980), Table 6.

out of proportion to their body. The analogy easily leads to a vocabulary of pathology according to which a diseased urbanization process has produced a monstrous offspring. The rhetoric is misleading because rank-size relationships deemed "normal" are derived from already developed societies. There is in principle no reason why LDCs of Asia, Africa, or Latin America must attain Western rank-size relationships nor any stigma against departing from Western norms. On the other hand, the fact of this discrepancy is proof that urbanization in the Third World is not the same as urbanization in the developed world.

Illustrations or urban primacy appear in Table 6-10, which compares the United States and three Latin American societies. In 1970 the largest city in Argentina was Buenos Aires, population 8,352,900. The second largest city was Rosario, population 810,840. Following the rank-size rule, Rosario "ought" to have had a population one half that of Buenos Aires, or 4,176,450. Therefore the observed population of Rosario was only 19 percent as large as predicted. Similarly, the population of Cordoba, third in rank, ought to have been one

Table 6-10. Selected Primate Cities of Latin America Compared with the United States

Urban Rank	Country/City	Observed Population	Predicted Population*	Observed/ Predicted [100 = Normal]
	Argentina, 1970			
1	Buenos Aires	8,352,900	4,231,580	197
2	Rosario	810,840	4,176,450	19
3	Cordoba	798,663	2,784,300	29
4	La Plata	506,287	2,088,225	24
	Chile, 1970			
1	Santiago	2,661,920	642,249	415
2	Valparaiso	292,847	1,330,960	22
3	Concepcion	196,317	887,307	22
4	Viña del Mar	153,085	665,480	23
	Mexico, 1973			
1	Mexico City	10,223,102	3,616,928	283
2	Guadalajara	1,700,000	5,111,551	33
3	Monterrey	1,459,893	3,407,700	43
4	Juarez	457,035	2,555,770	18
	United States, 1970			
1	New York	16,206,841	19,087,066	100
2	Los Angeles-Long Beach	8,351,266	8,103,421	103
3	Chicago	6,714,758	5,402,280	124
4	Philadelphia	4,021,042	4,051,710	99

Source: James Wilkie, ed., *Statistical Abstract of Latin America,* Vol. 17 (Los Angeles: UCLA Latin American Center Publications, University of California Press, 1976), pp. 78-79.
    *Rank-size rule.

third that of Buenos Aires (2,784,300) but was in reality only 798,663. Therefore the population of Cordoba was only 29 percent of the expected size. Similar results appear for Mexico and Chile, whose second-, third-, and fourth-ranking cities were "too small" for their first-ranking city. On the other hand, the second-, third-, and fourth-ranking cities of the United States corresponded fairly closely to what would be expected on the basis of the rank-size rule. Therefore Argentina, Chile, and Mexico evidence primacy in urban hierarchy whereas the United States does not. In general urban primacy is characteristic of Asian, African, and Latin American societies.

Worked in reverse, the rank-size rule permits an estimation of how large the first-ranking city "ought" to be given the population of the second-, third-, and fourth-ranking cities, that is, the sum of the second, third, and fourth gives a rough indicator of how large the first city "ought" to be (Davis 1972: 242). Thus the sum of the population of Rosario, Cordoba, and La Plata in Argentina was 4,231,580 in 1970. This "ought" to have been the size of Buenos Aires in 1970, but the real population was 8,352,900 so Buenos Aires was nearly twice (197 percent) its expected size. Using this procedure, we again find that Santiago, Chile, was 415 percent larger than predicted by the rank-size rule; Mexico City was 283 percent larger; but New York was just 100 percent of its predicted size. The computation indicates that first-ranking cities were "too big" for their hierarchies in the Latin American countries. (See also Portes and Walton 1976: 29–30). On the other hand, New York was just about the right size given the second-, third-, and fourth-ranking centers of the United States.

Primate cities are usually associated with regional imbalances in urbanization. First, primate cities cluster along seacoasts and most were political centers of colonialism before 1945 (Brutkus 1975; Waterbury 1972: 116). Figure 6-1 illustrates the coastal tendency in Latin America. Coastal cities also are predominant in Asia and Africa. Second, primate cities claim a huge share of a nation's population. The cartogram of Latin America (Figure 6-2) illustrates this point by shading the portion of a nation's land area that corresponds to the proportion of its big city population to total population. Because cities are coastal and too big, inland areas are sparsely settled and economically undeveloped. The characteristic result is extreme contrast of modernization in the seacoast metropolis and peasant agriculture in the interior.

Population growth, overurbanization, and primate cities—this trilogy describes contemporary Third World urbanization in contrast with earlier urbanization of developed societies. Scholars agree on the descriptive contrast but disagree about how the situation arose and how it perpetuates itself. The two leading explanations are modernization and dependence theories. Modernization and dependence theories developed as ideological competitors and because of divergent implications are often treated as mutually exclusive (Horowitz 1977). But here, as so frequently in social science, a synthesis is possible.

Figure 6-1. Costal Urbanization of Latin America. Latin American cities originated as import/export centers for the world economy. (Source: James W. Wilkie,
ed. *Statistical Abstract of Latin America.* Vol. 17 Los Angeles: UCLA Latin
American Center Publications, University of California, 1976, p. 38)

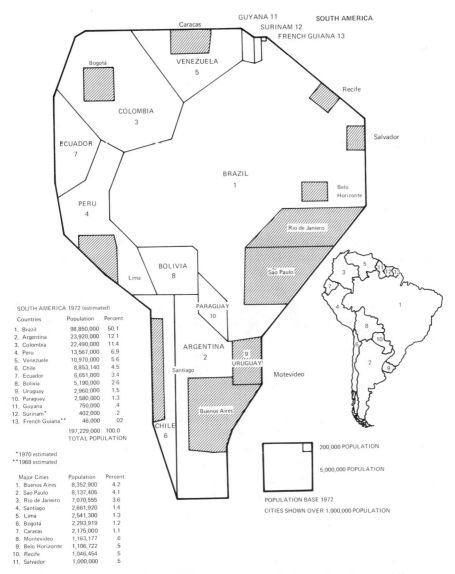

Figure 6-2. Latin America, 1972. Cartograph displays the disproportionate share of great cities in national populations. This is a symptom of dependent urbanization. (Source: James W. Wilkie, ed. *Statistical Abstract of Latin America.* Vol. 17. Los Angeles: UCLA Latin American Center Publications, University of California, p. 3.)

MODERNIZATION

Bendix has defined *modernization* as "all those social and political changes" that accompanied industrialization in Europe and North America (1964: 413). Among these are urbanization, social mobility, wage labor, mass education, representative government, and the welfare state. In the Third World context, modernization is dualistic because the social values supporting modernization are foreign in origin. As a result, modernization theorists argue, a modern sector and a traditional (or preindustrial) sector coexist in every developing society. These sectors do interpenetrate, thus forming fringe zones, but the geographical boundaries of the modern sector are basically the urbanized regions surrounding primate cities. Within these regions are people who are prevailingly modern in cultural style. One manifestation of modernity is low birthrates. Urban families in Third World countries have two or three children only—not ten or twelve as do rural families. These urban people are well educated too, and their occupations are in manufacturing and service industries, typical of advanced economies.

Modernization therorists view the modern sector as in conflict with the traditional sector (Hermassi 1978: 242-43). The modern sector exists at all, they maintain, because colonialists compelled the traditional social order to make room, often by means of military coercion (Boeke 1953: 3-4). In Asia and Africa, European colonialists intruded into traditional societies and set up within them "modern" sectors with cultural and economic ties to the motherland. The traditional society rejected and encapsulated the alien, whose secularism and profit-seeking undermined ancient ways of life. As matters stand, the modern sector can expand only at the expense of the traditional sector surrounding it. Therefore the traditional sector resists modernization. Economic development occurs when the modern sector expands into the traditional hinterland. Stagnation occurs when the balance of the sectors persists undisturbed. Regression arises when the traditional sector expands at the expense of a depleted modern sector.

In Latin America, Iberian colonizers were themselves feudal in outlook (Portes and Walton 1976: 7-18). Conquistadors "glorified the roles of soldier and priest" while denigrating commercial activity, often left to Muslims and Jews (Lipset 1967: 3). Their cities were originally political-religious seats from which landowners exercised neofeudal authority over peasants and slaves (Smith 1963: 239). On vast latifundia in the interior of the continent, large landowners long maintained a traditional society based on worker subservience and aristocratic paternalism. In Chile, for example, 10 percent of landowners held 90 percent of the arable land in 1965. The large landowners showed "little interest in efficient productivity," preferring to "sustain semi-feudal relations with their workers"

(Lipset 1967: 9). In this social climate even the urban bourgeoisie has preferred to invest in agriculture the profits of commerce, hoping to move from a despised mercantile way of life to aristrocratic leisure on vast estates (Portes and Walton 1978: 26-27).

Modernization theory stresses the resistance of Third World societies to industrial urbanization. The resistance has two sources. The first is indigenous cultural tradition. The values, attitudes, and norms of traditional societies are incompatible with industrial urbanization. For example, many Third World villagers value warm social relationships higher than money income. The preference in understandable, but industrial urbanization does involve economic calculations. Such calculations arise, for example, when peasants have to choose between continued poverty in a village or taking their chances in a big city. If villagers refuse to calculate the money value of community relationships, they obstruct the industrial urbanization of their country (Reissman 1964: 180ff). The enclave of capitalist urbanization around major seaports gathers up the peasants who chose money while those who preferred community stayed behind.

Second in importance are native elites. Their power, wealth, and prestige depend on the perpetuation of traditional society (Reissman 1964: 192). European competition deprived them of privileges. For instance, when Europeans appeared, native healers had to compete with European-trained physicians; native shamans had to compete with Christian clergy; native warriors had to face European cannon; and native chieftains had to treat with European states. Since native elites had cherished privileges to lose, they had a real interest in resisting modernization. The encapsulation of the modern sector proves that this resistance continues, for whenever the modern sector seeks to expand, as industrial urbanization requires, traditional elites in the hinterland organize resistance of culturally undisturbed native masses. Social revolutions can "remove those dominant strata which seek to maintain their position and traditional values" (Lipset 1967: 38), but the Iranian revolution of 1978–1979 shows that priests and peasants are still capable of combining to eject modernizers and return their country to theocratic traditionalism.

DEPENDENCY THEORY

Dependency theory is more recent than modernization theory. Its advocates more frequently reside in developing nations, and their writing conveys a pungent reaction to modernization, long the orthodox explanation of why developing nations have not made more rapid industrial progress. *Dependency* is an imbalanced economic relationship in which one side enjoys advantageous terms of trade or direct control over the other. In general, modernization theories blamed the traditional social system for resisting modernization, but dependency theorists blame the world capitalist system for causing underdevelopment. For example, André Frank, a Latin American *dependentista,* asks angrily why Latin America should be underdeveloped today "while North America is developed" even though both continents began as European colonies. Frank (1972) rejects the answer that "regressive institutions of Iberian feudalism" doomed Latin America to economic stagnation whereas North America benefited from British capitalism. He also rejects the claim the hard-working Protestants in North America developed their continent while "lazy Catholics" were taking afternoon siestas [8]. Instead Frank and other dependence theorists lay the blame for underdevelopment on the world capitalist system (Harvey 1973: 232). The world capitalist system locked the Third World into dependent inferiority that the "metropolitan" powers, chiefly European and North American, have an interest in perpetuating. "The central idea" of dependence theory is that "development of the industrial countries and the underdevelopment of poor countries are opposite phases of the same historical process" (Hermassi 1978: 2490). The key to this argument is massive rejection of the liberal doctrine of free trade and comparative advantage in international commerce (Frank 1972: 15).

Dependence theorists have developed a two-stage theory of colonialism and neocolonialism. In the period of colonialism (roughly 1600–1945) European powers imposed their political as well as economic predominance on colonial "possessions." The metropolitan powers developed colonial cities as centers of political-military administration, outlets for manufactured goods from the mother country, and centers for collection and then export of primary products. The political preponderance of the mother country prevented colonists from developing manufacturing industries that could process raw materials for export. These infant industries required protective tariffs, but the political predominance of colonial powers and the nineteenth-century ideology of "free trade" prevented colonial territories from protecting infant industries. Therefore European manufactured goods flooded the colonies, and people bought these in preference to more expensive domestic manufactures. On the other hand, "export agriculture" developed as a large-scale capitalist industry oriented to "metropolitan" demand. Plantations exported through port cities that accordingly developed as unitary hubs of transportation networks reaching into the interior (Frank 1972: 69-80). In this manner, seaports attracted all the nonagricultural business of the territory while interior points stagnated. Here then, claim dependence theorists, are the true origins of primate cities and regional imbalance in developing nations (Johnston 1977).

The era of colonialism is over, and now dependence theorists distinguish colonialism from neocolonialism, its postwar successor. Neocolonialism is basically economic, not political. Its principal agencies are multinational corporations with headquarters in one of the developed countries. Examples include General

Motors, I. G. Farben, Shell Petroleum, and so forth. These corporations invest in Third World countries and use their economic leverage in key sectors to influence the political and social life in the developing country. For example, U.S. copper mining interests persuaded the Nixon Administration covertly to undermine and overthrow Chile's Marxist government in 1974. This is a source of "nationalist outrage" in the developing societies (Chirot 1977: 176). In addition to obvious complaints about outside interference in national politics, Third World countries complain that the investments of the multinational corporations, though superficially advantageous, actually restrict their economic development in the long run. The debate is complex (Chirot 1977: 177-179), but Third World complaints reduce it to the claim that the investments and political meddling of multinational corporations have locked Third World countries into subordinate roles in the capitalist world system [9]. This capitalist world system still revolves about the exchange of high-priced manufactured goods (and technology) originating in the "metropolitan" countries for the cheap agricultural and mining exports of developing countries. LDCs want big manufacturing sectors of their own, but they are unable to produce manufactured goods as cheaply as Japan or the West. Hence they must export primary products to live, but this adjustment leaves no room for developing manufacturing industries of their own. Table 6-11 exposes the imbalance of world trade in 1975. Developed market economies (Europe, North America, Japan) exported more manufac-

Table 6-11. Structure of World Trade by Region, 1975, Value of Goods (percentages)

	Primary*	Manufactured	Total
West and Japan			
Exports	23.4	75.1	98.5
Imports	43.0	56.1	99.1
Third World			
Exports	82.7	16.9	99.6
Imports	31.1	65.6	96.7
Communist countries			
Exports	36.6	57.4	94
Imports	29.8	67.4	97.2
OPEC†			
Exports	98.8	1.1	99.9
Imports	16.1	80.6	96.7

Source: United Nations Department of International Economic and Social Affairs, *United Nations Statistical Yearbook,* 1976, pp. 464-469. Copyright, United Nations 1976. Reproduced by permission.

*Agricultural, mineral, and raw materials.

†Organization of Petroleum Exporting Countries. This organization includes Algeria, Ecuador, Gabon, Indonesia, Iran, Iraq, Kuwait, Libya, Nigeria, Qatar, Saudi Arabia, United Arab Emirates, Venezuela. See *Los Angeles Times,* May 4, 1979, pt. I, p. 1.

tured goods than primary products (agricultural, mineral). On the other hand, Third World market economies were exporters of primary goods and importers of manufactured goods, mostly Western (Snyder and Kick 1979). OPEC countries exported oil, a primary product, but imported manufactured goods. But this arrangement stifles the independent development of the manufacturing sector around which autonomous industrial urbanization of the Third World could develop. Worse, "mono-crop" agriculture pegs the economic welfare of the developing society to its chief export (bananas or cocoa, for example), and when prices of that crop fall on world markets, vast dislocations at home result (Frank 1972: 70).

A few Third World countries, notably Hong Kong, Taiwan, and South Korea, have recently developed some labor-intensive manufacturing industries (shoes, garments, toys) that export manufactured goods to developed nations. These cases prove that developing countries can manufacture and export because cheap labor makes their products competitive in world markets. Therefore, mono-crop agriculture is not an inexorable fate for LDCs. On the other hand, protectionist pressures in the United States and Europe reflect a desire by metropolitan countries to prevent developing nations from obtaining access to domestic markets for manufactured goods. The reactive protectionism in developed countries supports the world's unequal division of labor and thus sustains the political analysis of dependency theorists.

MODERNIZATION AND DEPENDENCY IN PERSPECTIVE

Modernization stresses the continuing resistance of traditional cultures and elites to economic development. Priests, landlords, big families, and archaic values are the central culprits that allegedly cause economic retardation of LDCs. These factors are indigenous to LDCs and most existed before Western colonialists ever appeared. Dependency theorists claim instead that the industrial urbanization of the West underdeveloped the Third World, and neocolonialism still locks LDCs into inferior roles in the world's division of labor (Allen 1976: 292). Dependency theory reverses the self-congratulatory message implicit in the older dualist explanation of international inequalities. There is also wide agreement that dependency analysis has given proper weight to "neglected" problems of world capitalism. This "cogent interpretation of backwardness and uneven development" is currently the starting place for any analysis of Third World urbanization (Hermassi 1978: 252).

On the other hand ". . . dependency theorizing has neglected the internal dynamics of Third World societies and in particular their political structures and cultural tradition"(Hermassi 1978: 252). Therefore sociologists are inclined to believe the time for a "vigorous criticism" of dependency theory has now come. "Not every regional balance has to do with internal colonialism. A central intellectual chore is to distinguish between what is imposed from without, and what is generated within" (Horowitz 1977: 764).

SUMMARY

Industrial urbanization of the Third World has not duplicated industrial urbanization in the West a century and a half earlier. Rapid population growth, over-urbanization, and primate cities are three evidences of the difference. As a result of these factors, cities in the developing world have more residents than they can supply with jobs and municipal services. The cities are also very big compared with Western norms of rank and size. Urbanization is regionally imbalanced so that abrupt contrasts of modern and traditional sectors result.

Accounting for these characteristics of Third World urbanization is still a matter of debate. Modernization theorists blame the resistance of traditional culture and elites. They often regard excessive population growth as the efficient source of all the other difficulties and recommend that Third World people adopt a modern two-child family.

Dependence theorists blame the political-economic legacies of Western colonialism for the overpopulation, overurbanization, and primacy of Third World countries. They also claim that the world's division of labor now frustrates the efforts of LDCs to improve the life chances of their population. They look to political action and cartels for redress of their grievances and redirection of the world's wealth to their region.

NOTES

1. *U.S. News and World Report,* July 31, 1978, pp. 61–62.
2. Although often used interchangeably, economic growth and economic development actually refer to different processes. *Economic growth* is an increase in measurable quantity of output, such as corn per acre or tons of steel. *Economic development* is a qualitative change in structure, and this change is usually (but not invariably) accompanied by economic growth. Thus the shift of labor force from agriculture into manufacturing is an aspect of economic development. See Robert A. Flammang, "Economic Growth and Economic Development: Counterparts or Competitors?" *Economic Development and Cultural Change* 28 (1978): 47–61.

3. Asked why economic development in the Third World is not progressing faster, Dr. Kingsley Davis, a world authority on urbanization, declared that neocolonialism is a "lame" explanation because imperialism has ended and there is "a net flow of international aid" to the Third World. Of the many contributors Davis did acknowledge, the one that, in his estimation, stood foremost was "the greater density of population and the more rapid rate of population growth in the developing world." The ultimate cause is the high value people in Third World countries still place on having many children. See the testimony of Kingsley Davis, in U.S. Congress, House of Representatives, 95th Congress 2nd Sess., Select Committee on Population, *World Population: A Global Perspective*. Washington, D.C.: U.S. Government Printing Office, 1978, p. 516.

4. Bach (1978: Ch. 2) argues that the underdevelopment of Mexico is the result of prior colonialist and neocolonialist interference in Mexico's affairs. The heritage of this interference is a Mexican economy that cannot provide jobs for all its people, thus compelling some surplus workers to emigrate to the United States. See Robert Bach, "Mexican Workers in the United States: A Study of Migration and Social Change." Ph.D. dissertation, Duke University, 1978.

5. Are there too many people or is there too little food? See the exchange between the Environmental Fund and Bread for the World in "World Hunger: Too Little Food? Or Too Many People?," pp. 358–365, in U.S. Congress, House of Representatives, 95th Congress, 2nd Sess., Select Committee on Population, No. 6 *Population and Development*. Washington, D.C.: U.S. Government Printing Office, 1978.

6. "The Two child family . . . is a luxury China can no longer afford, Hua said, for it would mean that population growth would wipe out the economic gains made possible through modernization. . . . In the past decade, China has slashed its population growth rate in half from 23.4 to 11.7 per thousand according to the New China News Agency." Linda Mathews, "Each Couple to Be Limited to One Child, China Announces," *Los Angeles Times*, September 8, 1980, pt. I, p. 5.

7. Other Third World countries have apparently been more successful than China in controlling urbanization by means of state planning. For instance, in Cuba a Central Planning Council "diverts investment" from big cities to towns and villages. "As a result, the growth of Havana levelled off, and its population actually decreased slightly as a proportion of the country's total." John Walton, "Urban Political Movements and Revolutionary Change in the Third World," *Urban Affairs Quartery* 15 (1979): 19. In Taiwan, decentralized industrialization has permitted rural nonfarm employment to grow, thus enabling many rural workers "to participate in industry without having to leave the countryside." Between 1962 and 1975, the share of rural households' income derived from nonfarm sources increased from 24 to 43 percent in reflection of industrial decentralization. See Samuel S. P. Ho, "Decentralized Industrialization and Rural Development: Evidence from Taiwan," *Economic Development and Cultural Change* 28 (1979): 78.

8. In Brazil, Catholic men drink, gamble, chase women, and compete for *ma-*

chismo. Men of the country's Protestant minority do not join this competition. Protestants work harder and are regarded generally as more honest and trustworthy. See Emilio Williams, "Protestantism As a Factor of Cultural Change in Brazil," *Economic Development and Cultural Change* 3 (1954–1955): 321–333. In a thorough historical review, James Lang shows that economic differences between Latin America and North America were present from the inception of colonization. Spain's purpose was conquest, Britain's commerce. James Lang, *Conquest and Commerce.* New York: Academic Press, 1975.

9. But multinational corporations have political and economic allies within the less developed world. In Kenya, for example, the government turned European-owned highland farms over to black Africans upon independence. These black Africans then acquired the material interests in export agriculture that had previously belonged to the Europeans. Big African landlords became a stratum "closely allied to" the multinational corporations. Colin Leys, *Underdevelopment in Kenya: The Political Economy of Neo-Colonialism.* Berkeley and Los Angeles: University of California Press, 1975, p. 26.

REFERENCES

Abu-Lughod, Janet. 1974. "Urban-Rural Differences as a Function of the Demographic Transition," pp. 68–86, in Charles Tilly, ed. *An Urban World.* Boston: Little, Brown.

Allen, Chris. 1976. "A Bibliographic Guide to the Study of the Political Economy of Africa," pp. 291–313, in Peter C. W. Gutkind and Immanuel Wallerstein, eds. *The Political Economy of Contemporary Africa.* Vol. I. Beverly Hills: Sage.

Beier, George J. 1976. "Can Third World Cities Cope?" *Population Bulletin* 31: 3–32.

Bendix, Reinhard. 1964. *Nation-Building and Citizenship.* Berkeley and Los Angeles: University of California Press.

Boeke, J. H. 1953. *Economics and Economic Policy of Dual Societies.* New York: Institute of Pacific Relations.

Briggs, Vernon M. 1975. "Illegal Aliens: The Need for a More Restrictive Border Policy." *Social Science Quarterly* 3: 477–484.

Brutkus, Eliezer. 1975. "Centralized vs. Decentralized Pattern of Urbanization in Developing Countries: An Attempt to Elucidate a Guideline Principle." *Economic Development and Cultural Change* 23: 633–652.

Castells, Manuel. 1977. *The Urban Question.* Trans. by Alan Sheridan. Cambridge: M.I.T. Press.

Chase-Dunn, C. 1975. "The Effects of International Economic Dependence on Development and Inequality: A Cross-National Study." *American Sociological Review* 40: 720–738.

Chen, Pi-Chao. 1970. "China's birth control action program, 1956–1964." *Population Studies* 24: 141–158.

Cheng, Man-Tsun. 1980. "An Exploratory Case study of the Management Systems and Work Attitudes in the Farm Machinery Manufacturing and Repairing Factory at the Huan-Cheng Commune." M.A. thesis, Chinese University of Hong Kong.

Chirot, Daniel. 1977. *Social Change in the Twentieth Century*. New York: Harcourt.

Davis, Diane. 1979. "Rank-Size Distribution, Migration, and Economic Development: The Case of Mexico." Paper presented, the 1979 Annual Meeting of the American Sociological Association, Boston.

Davis, Kingsley and Hilda Golden. 1954. "Urbanization and the Development of Preindustrial Areas." *Economic Development and Cultural Change* 3: 6–24.

Davis, Kingsley. 1972. *World Urbanization, 1950–1970*, Vol. II. Analysis of Trends, Relationships and Development. Berkeley: Institute of International Studies of the University of California.

——. 1974. "The Migrations of Human Populations." *Scientific American* 231: 93–105.

Duncan, Otis D. "Population Structure and Community Structure," pp. 190–216, in Charles Tilly, ed. *An Urban World*. Boston: Little, Brown.

Elliott, Joy. 1978. "Gap Between Rich, Poor Nations Less Than Believed." *Los Angeles Times* (Nov. 24): XI, 1.

El-Shakhs, Salah. 1972. "Development, Primacy, and Systems of Cities." *Journal of Developing Areas* 7: 11–35.

Epstein, David G. 1973. *Brasilia: Plan and Reality*. Berkeley and Los Angeles. University of California Press.

Firebaugh, Glenn. 1979. "Structural Determinants of Urbanization in Asia and Latin America." *American Sociological Review* 44: 199–215.

Frank, André Gunder. 1972. *Lumpen Bourgeoisie: Lumpen Development*. New York: Monthly Review.

Frolic, B. Michael. 1978. "Reflections on the Chinese Model of Development." *Social Forces* 57: 384–418.

Gibbs, Jack, and Leo F. Schnore. 1960. "Metropolitan growth: an International Study." *American Journal of Sociology* 66: 160–170.

Ham, Euiyoung. 1976. "Urbanization and Asian Lifestyles," pp. 222–233, in Paul Meadows and Ephraim Mizruchi, eds. *Urbanism, Urbanization and Change: Comparative Perspectives,* 2nd ed. Reading, Mass.: Addison-Wesley.

Harvey, David. 1973. *Social Justice and the City*. Baltimore: Johns Hopkins University Press.

Hermassi, Elbaki. 1978. "Changing Patterns in Research on the Third World." *Annual Review of Sociology* 4: 239–257.

Hirschmann, Charles. 1978. "Prior U.S. Residence among Mexican Immigrants." *Social Forces* 56: 1179–1202.

Horowitz, Irving L. 1977. "Review Essay: Coming of Age of Urban Research in Latin America." *American Journal of Sociology* 83: 761–765.

Hoselitz, Bert F. 1954–1955. "Generative and Parasitic Cities." *Economic Development and Cultural Change* 3: 278–294.

Ibrahim, Saad. 1975. "Over-Urbanization and Under-Urbanism: The Case of the Arab World." *International Journal of Middle East Studies* 6: 29-45.

Johnston, R. J. 1977. "On the Progression from Primacy to Rank-Size in an Urban System: The Deviant Case of New Zealand." *Area* 3: 180-184.

Lipset, Seymour Martin. 1967. "Values, Education, and Entrepreneurship," pp. 3-60, in Seymour Lipset and Aldo Solari, eds. *Elites in Latin America.* New York: Oxford University Press.

McDonald, Angus, Jr. 1979. "Wallerstein's World Economy: How Seriously Should We Take It?" *Journal of Asian Studies* 38: 535-540.

Mayer, Harold M. 1965. "A Survey of Urban Geography," pp. 81-113, in Philip M. Hauser and Leo F. Schnore, eds. *The Study of Urbanization.* New York: Wiley.

Meyer, John W., John Boli-Bennett, and Christopher Chase-Dunn. "Convergence and Divergence in Development." *Annual Review of Sociology* 1: 223-246.

Mills, Edwin S., and Byung-Nak Song. 1979. *Urbanization and Urban Problems: Studies in the Modernization of the Republic of Korea, 1945-1975.* Cambridge: Council on East Asian Studies of Harvard University.

Mingione, Enzo. 1977. "Theoretical Elements for a Marxist Analysis of Urban Development," pp. 89-109, in Michael Harloe, ed. *Captive Cities.* London: Wiley.

Mitchell, B. R. 1975. *European Historical Statistics, 1750-1970.* New York: Columbia University Press.

Moir, Hazel. 1977. "Dynamic Relationships Between Labor Force Structure, Urbanization, and Development." *Economic Development and Cultural Change* 26: 25-42.

Perevedentsev, Victor. 1981. "Siberia and Siberians." *Soviet Life* 293: 3-13.

Petersen, William. 1978. "International Migration." *Annual Review of Sociology* 4: 533-576.

Portes, Alejandro and John Walton. 1976. *Urban Latin America: The Political Condition from Above and Below.* Austin: University of Texas Press.

Reissman, Leonard. 1964. *The Urban Process.* New York: Free Press.

Richardson, Harry. 1973. *The Economics of Urban Size.* Westmead, England: Saxon House.

Saffire, William. 1978. *Saffire's Political Dictionary,* rev. ed. New York: Random House.

Shaw, R. Paul. 1976. *Land Tenure and Rural Exodus in Chile, Colombia, Costa Rica, and Peru.* Gainesville: University of Florida Press.

Sidel, Ruth. 1974. *Families of Fengsheng: Urban Life in China.* Harmondsworth: Penguin.

Smith, T. Lynn. 1963. "Urbanization in Latin America." *International Journal of Comparative Sociology* 4: 227-242.

Snyder, David and Edward L. Kick. 1979. "Structural Position in the World System and Economic Growth, 1955-1970: A Multiple-Network Analysis of Trans-National Interactions." *American Journal of Sociology* 84: 1096-1125.

Sovani, N. V. 1964. "The Analysis of Overurbanization." *Economic Development and Cultural Change* 12: 113-122.

Taeuber, Irene B. 1962. "Asian Populations: The Critical Decade," In U.S. Congress, House of Representatives, Committee on the Judiciary, Subcommittee No. 1, Special Series No. 4. *Study of Population and Immigration Problems.* Washington D.C.: U.S. Government Printing Office.

United Nations, Department of International Economic and Social Affairs, Population Studies No. 68. 1980. *Patterns of Urban and Rural Population Growth.* [United Nations Publication Sales No. E.79.XIII.79] New York: United Nations.

U.S. Bureau of the Census. 1977. *Statistical Abstract of the United States.* Washington, D.C.: U.S. Government Printing Office.

Waterbury, John. 1972. *North for the Trade.* Berkeley: University of California Press.

Whetten, Nathan. 1962. "Population Trends in Mexico," In U.S. Congress, House of Representatives, Committee on the Judiciary, Subcommittee No. 1, Special Series No. 5. *Study of Population and Immigration Problems.* Washington D.C.: U.S. Government Printing Office.

Whyte, Martin, et al. 1977. "Social Structure of World Regions: Mainland China." *Annual Review of Sociology* 3: 179–207.

Wilkie, James, ed. 1976. *Statistical Abstract of Latin America.* Los Angeles: Latin American Center of the University of California.

CHAPTER 7

Catch-up Urbanization: Japan and the Soviet Union

Sharp contrasts between developed and developing regions dominate contemporary writing on urbanization. Explanations of these regional contrasts convey a sense of inevitability as if social-economic forces condemned global regions to permanent membership in one bloc or the other. This impression is misleading. Notable cases exist in which once backward societies became industrial-urban leaders in the twentieth century. Of these Japan and the Soviet Union are the most prominent (Black 1975: 15). In the nineteenth century, both countries were agricultural and industrially underdeveloped. In less than a century, both moved into the forefront of industrial urbanization. To make matters more complex, Japan achieved this dynamic transition on the basis of private enterprise, whereas in the Soviet Union the same transition occurred in a comand economy.

How was catch-up urbanization possible in either society? The question raises obvious theoretical difficulties for both dependency and modernization theory. On the one hand, the industrial urbanization of both societies occurred despite the presumptive restraints imposed by the world's division of labor. These achievements imply that world system constraints must be less than fully restrictive. If Japan and the Soviet Union were able to break out of the vicious cycles of underdevelopment, then why do world system dependencies prevent other developing nations from achieving the same objective today? On the other hand, both Japan and the Soviet Union were traditional societies in the nineteenth century. Modernization theories claim that feudal residues obstruct industrial urbanization in developing nations today; but traditional residues were obviously insufficient to block the industrial urbanization of either Japan or the Soviet

Union. This anomaly proves that domestic traditionalism is no insurmountable barrier to urban industrialization in this century. Hence modernization theories of development presumably exaggerate the importance of this issue.

This chapter presents contrasting case studies of industrial urbanization in Japan and the Soviet Union. The case histories do place limits on the scope of both modernization and dependency theory and thus clarify just what each theory contributes. But the appropriate conclusion is not that one is simply right and the other wrong. In actuality, these competing theories are not in principle incompatible, and processes described by both were simultaneously at work in both Japan and the Soviet Union. Moreover, the restraints of dependency and feudalism, although overcome in both societies, were nonetheless real in both. Thus the case histories of both countries bring out the limitation of existing theories at the same time that they validate their basic premises.

Table 7-1. Chronology of Japanese History

A.D. 550	Recorded history of Japan begins.
1192–1868	Feudalism.
1500–1603	The era of "warring states."
	Consolidation of Tokugawa power restored domestic peace.
1543–1616	Reign of Tokugawa Ieyasu.
	This warlord defeated rival clans, located the capital at Edo, and established the Tokugawa dynasty.
1603–1868	Tokugawa (Edo) period.
	Rulers of the Tokugawa family consolidated and supervised the feudal system.
1868–1912	Meiji Period.
	Disaffected *samurai* overthrew Tokugawa and restored Meiji dynasty. This restoration marked the creation of a modern nation-state in Japan.
1912–1926	Taisho Period.
	Emperor Yoshihito continued policies of the Meiji period.
1921–1945	Showa Period.
	Army and navy became the dominant forces in the government, with the peasantry supporting the military against the bourgeoisie. Militarists undertook a daring program of imperialistic aggression culminating in World War II.
1945–	Reconstruction.
	May 3, 1947: New constitution providing for a bicameral legislature, supreme court, civil liberties, and local self-government. War renounced as an instrument of national policy. Japan concentrated on export of manufactured goods.

INDUSTRIAL URBANIZATION OF JAPAN

André Frank (1970: 11) asks why "resource-poor Japan" was able to industrialize at the end of the nineteenth century whereas "resource-rich Latin America" was not? According to Frank, Japan's escape into modernization entirely validates the dependency model of underdevelopment in Latin America: European colonialists never achieved economic-political domination of Japanese society and were therefore unable to incorporate the island as a satellite of their world system. Because Japan did not become a satellite it "did not have its development structurally limited as did the countries which were so satellitized" (Frank 1970: 11).

Frank's argument is sound as far as it goes. Japan did repel colonialist penetration at the same time that its hapless neighbor, imperial China, fell victim to open door policy and "unequal treaties." Moulder (1977: 199) concludes that Japan's political and economic autonomy in the world system permitted and encouraged its subsequent industrialization, whereas China's incorporation condemned it to satelitic stagnation. However, even conceding the objection, there reamins the prior question of why Japan resisted satellitization whereas China succumbed to it. Answering that question requires attention to the internal characteristics of Japanese and Chinese society before the appearance of Western navies in the Sea of Japan and even before the formation of a capitalist world economy.

When Admiral Perry "opened up" Japan in 1853, the island nation was still feudal in political structure and traditional in culture. These were the closing years of the Tokugawa shogunate (1603-1868), the patrimonial government of the Tokugawa family, which exerted direct military rule over one fifth of Japan. For the rest, the shogun's bureau (*bakufu*) evaluated agricultural land according to its rice yield and granted it as feudal benefices to 260 barons (*daimyos*) who regranted it to faithful warriors (*samurai*) (Weber 1961: 62). In these arrangements Japanese feudalism distinctly resembled European feudalism of the Middle Ages (Totman 1979: 547).

The consistent policy of Tokugawa rulers was to support traditional Japanese society. To this conservative end, they excluded missionaries, banned Christianity, closed their ports to foreign vessels, and generally sought to insulate Japan from foreign cultural influences. The Tokugawa also supported the status hierarchy of traditional Japan whose titular authority was the *shogun*, followed in descending order by his barons, warriors, farmers, artisans, and merchants [1]. Only outcasts and prostitutes ranked lower than merchants (Bellah 1957: 25). When merchants prospered and sought to emulate the prestigious life-style of warriors, sumptuary legislation compelled them to maintain the external trappings of inferior status [2]. Samurai even had legal authority to kill anyone who failed to offer them proper deference.

By 1700 urban life in Japan was already extraordinarily developed. Many towns had populations in excess of 50,000 and the capital city, Edo (now Tokyo), was the world's largest city (Kornhauser 1976: 63). Tokugawa rulers further encouraged the urbanization of Japan to an extent unparalleled in other preindustrial societies. By the end of the eighteenth century, more than 10 percent of the population of Japan resided in cities of 10,000 or more. Rozman (1973: 6) believes that this level was the highest ever achieved by any preindustrial society. Japan's urbanization under the Tokugawa differed from China's in volume and character. Prior to 1600, Japan and China had enjoyed similar levels of urbanization, but thereafter China's urbanization stayed at the level of 6 to 7 percent whereas Japan's "climbed above 16 percent" (Rozman 1973: 300). Japan's urban hierarchy was also much narrower at the base than China's, reflecting the Tokugawa's ability to extract oppressive taxes in support of urbanization (Rozman 1973: xv).

This Japan-China divergence is important because Moulder (1977: Pt I) has claimed that modernization theorists have exaggerated many supposed differences between Japan and China. She concludes that Japanese society under the Tokugawa was no more dynamic than Chinese society in the Ch'ing dynasty, roughly the same historical period (1977: 90), and both would have modernized had not Western imperialists captured and "underdeveloped" China. If true, a world system's analysis would be indicated since differences between China and Japan in the twentieth century would then depend only upon the historical events after 1700. However, Moulder overlooked Rozman's urban evidence, which shows that Japan and China were different kinds of society long before the Europeans consolidated their capitalist world system. Rozman's (1973) data show that in respect to urbanization, a crucial issue, Japan and China were already different by 1700, with Japan alone showing clear signs of modernization (see also Hanley and Yamamura 1977).

The purpose of Tokugawa urbanization was to strengthen civil administration and enhance military security (Hall 1968: 170). Taxes were high so peasant revolts were a persistent threat, and in the period 1599–1867, 1,240 revolts occurred (Yazaki 1968: 251). To solidify their rule, the shoguns created a network of "castle towns" linked by road. Every prefecture had its own castle town so the network of fortified cities evenly covered the entire realm (Yazaki 1968: 243). Castle towns centered around the fortress belonging to their feudal overlord, but as in Europe, castle towns acquired additional commercial functions. In the late Tokugawa period, the proportion of warriors to the total population began to decline as the commercial functions advanced in importance and warriors sank into poverty. Nonetheless, the proportion of warriors to the total population of these castle towns was usually in excess of 30 percent and often nearer 50 percent.

The basic industry of castle towns was tax collection. On this industry the warrior residents depended for their livelihood. Castle towns absorbed in taxes fully one half of the total rice yield of their districts (Yazaki 1968: 128). However, the shoguns also determined to support the economic viability of castle towns by awarding commercial monopolies to guild merchants. Wholesaler guilds of merchants in the towns had the exclusive right to distribute goods for sale to local retailers. Prices were high, and the monopolistic policy compelled retail dealers to channel purchases through the castle town, thus supporting the town's economy. Since Tokugawa policy raised prices to the final consumer, official monopolies really imposed additional financial burdens on the peasantry. Peasants paid high taxes to the castle town and then paid high prices for goods that only castle town merchants were permitted to sell.

Castle towns were deliberate political creations of the government, but these were naturally not the only towns in preindustrial Japan. Kornhauser (1976: 69) distinguishes five additional types of city in Tokugawa Japan: ports, post or stage towns, religious centers, market towns, and spas. None of these cities was industrial in the sense of heavy manufacturing industry. Market towns and ports were, of course, commercial rather than political-military, but market towns were ephemeral, "merely gathering places for a certain length of time" (Kornhauser, 1976: 69). Under the Tokugawa, the numerous ports of Japan were generally given over to domestic commerce, fishing, boat building, and piracy—all preindustrial industries. Nonetheless, some large seaports engaged in international or domestic commerce, and growing prosperous, were perceived as political threats to feudal society. Osaka and Sakai are outstanding examples of commercial cities in Tokugawa Japan. Osaka was not a castle town, and its warrior population was much smaller than usual as a result. Commerce, handicrafts, and cultural life flourished. Townsmen occupied all but the highest positions in city government and were subject few feudal restrictions, but the situation of Osaka was unusual. Most Japanese cities had more warriors in residence, less commerce, less merchant political power, and less freedom of cultural experimentation (Hauser 1977-1978: 36). Near Osaka, Sakai flourished in the China and Southeast Asia trade largely through the export of swords, a Japanese craft specialty. Sakai acquired "an unusual degree of local autonomy" including its own military force (Kornhauser, 1976: 57). Many foreigners lived there, and merchants were politically supreme.

Sensing a challenge, Tokugawa authorities intervened to divert the commerce of Sakai to other cities and in this manner to disarm the merchant class. The Tokugawa pursued a similar policy against other growing commercial cities. In this manner, feudal authorities guided the destinies of Japan's cities by political interventions into their commercial life. The general purpose of these interventions was always to bolster traditional social values wherever they appeared to crumble (Yazaki 1968: 124–125). There is an important contrast with medieval Europe here (Hall 1968: 173). In feudal Europe, commercial cities had become centers from which capitalism, spreading into the hinterlands, undermined feudalism. In feudal Japan, the authorities intended to prevent commercial activity from acquiring the capability of challenging traditional society. Therefore they observed a policy of continuous surveillance of rapid city growth and intervention to direct commercial activity away from independent centers.

These successes delayed but could neither halt nor reverse the commercialization of Japanese society. An historical overview tends rather to confirm the futility of Tokugawa efforts to prop up traditional social arrangements. First, the growth of domestic commerce tended constantly to increase the number and power of the merchant class. Second, patterns of commercial activity tended constantly to promote the growth of cities through which commerce flowed rather than only castle towns favored by Tokugawa authorities. In the period 1714–1834, the population of thirty-five castle towns actually declined 18 percent as a result of commercialization elsewhere (Smith 1973: 138). On the other hand, cities like Kagoshima, Kurume, Toyama, and Nagaoka managed to break out of the crippling embrace of the monopolizing guilds and therefore flourished in the same period (Yazaki 1968: 253). Third, prolonged peace reduced the influence of warriors. Low-ranking warriors fell into poverty and into debt to merchant creditors (Yazaki: 126). As a result, the population of warriors declined and distressed ex-warriors gravitated into artisan, commercial, and manufacturing pursuits (Hall 1968: 184). Finally, urban prosperity, land reclamation, technological improvement in agriculture, and taxation tended to depopulate the rural areas, drawing the distressed peasants into commercial cities. In these cities, former peasants mingled with former warriors in secular occupations coordinated as much by market forces as by feudalistic regulations. A class-based commercial society thus developed despite the efforts of Tokugawa leaders to maintain the preindustrial, status-oriented society of old Japan.

THE MEIJI, TAISHO, AND SHOWA PERIODS, 1868–1945

The decay of Japanese feudalism was well underway when Western colonialists began to pound at the doors of the closed society in the middle of the nineteenth century. The colonialist presence accelerated but did not cause the already visible self-liquidation of Japanese feudalism. However, the end of feudalism in Japan occurred in 1868 when a clique of impoverished samurai deposed the shogun and restored the Meiji dynasty. "The new Meiji government abolished Tokugawa restraints on commerce and industry and undertook many reforms that furthered industrialization" (Moulder 1977: 13). Rebellious warriors were convinced Japan needed to industrialize in order to maintain national independence. As Bellah has emphasized, political power was the utlimate objective of the rebels, and economic development only a means to that end. Under the slogan National Wealth and Military Strength, the modernizing elite of ex-warriors set out to industrialize Japan as rapidly as possible. This policy reversed the Tokugawa attempt to retain feudalism. Its success depended on the support of warriors, and to gain this support, the Japanese government paid a stipend to unemployed warriors as compensation for the abolition of their feudal salaries (Yazaki 1968: 307).

Prior to 1899, international treaties prevented Japan from raising tariffs to protect its infant industries from Western competition (Lockwood 1968: 326). Moulder (1977: 194) regards these tariff-restricting treaties as having imposed a "substantial handicap" upon Japan's early efforts to industrialize. But later Japanese governments did employ tariffs to exclude Western manufactured goods and to encourage infant industries. Of course, their ability to do so depended on political independence backed by military power. Tariff protection also imposed austerity on Japanese consumers, who were thereby prevented from purchasing cheap imports and thus compelled to pay high prices for inferior domestic goods. Naturally, tariff protection did not render Japan's manufactured goods competitive on world markets. Nineteenth-century Japan was inferior to Western Europe and North America in technology, capital, labor force, transportation, and city environment. Meiji governments intervened to promote industrial development, and their basic method was encouragement of capitalist monopolies (*zaibatsu*) with public funds. In many instances, government created whole industries with tax money, then sold them to private enterprise for less than cost. Tax money also supported the construction of railroads (later sold to private enterprise), highways, port facilities, public education, the banking system, and the acquisition of markets in Asia by military force.

Japan's development strategy had a peaceful and belligerent side in the Taisho era. On the peaceful side, Japan exphasized labor-intensive, light industries, of which the key one was textiles (Black 1975: 191). Japanese products were cheap but shoddy because Japan was unable to compete directly with more developed nations in the production of high-quality goods. The cheapness of Japanese goods reflected government suppression of labor unrest, but there was, more importantly, a transfer of feudal loyalty from preindustrial Japan to the industrial monopolies that could rely on worker diligence to a much greater extent than in the capitalist West (Vogel 1967: 91). Furthermore, the nationalism of the Japanese people, a heritage of feudalism and religious tradition, permitted Taisho authorities to call upon the spirit of sacrafice to promote national strength through industrialization.

Japanese governments used military force to expand markets for Japanese goods in Asia (Lockwood 1968: 306). When Japan conquered a territory, it excluded Western manufactured goods and compelled the inhabitants to purchase inferior Japanese products. In the period 1928-1937 approximately one third of the manufacturing output of Japan was sold abroad, a much larger share than any other manufacturing nation achieved at that time (Lockwood 1968: 387). The Japanese were not alone in the use of military power for commercial ends, but they were more aggressive, probably as a result of their initial economic retardation.

A series of naval and military victories expanded the access of Japanese goods to markets in Asia. First were naval victories over China (1894-1895) and Russia (1904-1905). Korea was annexed in 1910. These military successes produced war indemnities from the defeated powers that paid for the cost of subjugating them. Additionally, the victories produced "further economic stimulation, particularly of the armaments industry, of marine transport, and of industrial technology in general" (Kornhauser 1976: 107). When the military faction returned to power in 1936, Japan resumed military aggression (Yazaki 1968: 378). Declaring a Greater East Asian Co-Prosperity Sphere, Japan invaded Manchuria in 1937 and attacked British colonies in the Far east in 1939 and 1940. "By 1940 the Japanese had become heavily committed to an industrial empire based on war" (Kornhauser 1976: 112). Japan bombed U.S. naval forces at Pearl Harbor, Hawaii, in 1941. The great victory there permitted Japanese conquests in Indonesia and the Philippines until the battle at Midway Island in 1942 reversed the fortunes of war in the Pacific theater.

Military defeat in 1945 discredited militarism in Japanese society. Occupation-era reforms also weakened the monopolistic power of the zaibatsu, humanized the "divine" emperor and strengthened parliamentary institutions (Burks, 1981: 120-127). Japan's industry lay in ruins in 1946. Output in that year was only 30 percent of prewar production. Nonetheless, three subsequent decades of hard work, low wages, and high domestic prices have produced a peaceful industrialization in Japan that exceeded the accomplishments of the warlike Meiji leaders in 80 years of aggression. Japan still depends on the export of manufactured goods [3], but Japanese industry no longer depends on labor-intensive methods to produce cheap goods. On the contrary, Japanese manufactured goods are often superior in quality to European and North American goods and sell briskly at higher prices because of their superior quality. Japan no longer needs military aggression to penetrate foreign markets because the quality of its goods penetrates them peacefully [4].

JAPANESE URBANIZATION SINCE 1868

The urbanization of Japanese society since 1868 depended on the political, military, and industrial events just described. These events promoted industrialization, and industrialization was the cause and condition of Japanese urbanization. Therefore, the explanation of Japanese urbanization is Japanese industrialization. However, this kind of very general explanation does not specifically address the amount, timing, or quality of Japanese urbanization nor the specifically Japanese solutions to universal problems of urbanization that emerged in a century.

Japanese urbanization favored the growth of big cities to an extent unusual among even developed capitalist countries. Evidence of this tendency is the relative growth of cities (*shi*), towns (*cho*), and villages (*son*) in the period 1884 until 1969. These units form a hierarchy of big-, medium-, and small-sized settlements and correspond to the indicated Japanese classification. Between 1884 and 1969, the number of cities increased from 19 to 564, a thirtyfold gain. In the same period, the number of towns decreased by five sixths, and the number of villages by ninety-nine one hundredths. Of course, the urban population was increasing both absolutely and relatively in this period so the growth of cities signaled a major shift of Japanese population. United Nations projections (Table 7-3) indicate that the growth of big cities in Japan is still continuing. Between 1950 and 2000 United Nations statisticians expect the population of Tokyo, Japan's largest city, to grow 3.58 times the 1950 population. In the same half century, Japan's largest four cities will grow only 3.2 times their aggregated population in 1950 and Japan's urban population will grow only 2.17 times. Rural population will decline to less than one half the 1950 number.

Despite the presence of Tokyo, the world's biggest city, Japan does not exhibit urban primacy. Comparing the population of Tokyo with the aggregate of the second-, third-, and fourth-ranking cities provides a simple test. Using data for 1950 and 1975 and projections for 2000, this test indicates that Tokyo's immense population is only 8 percent larger in each year than what would be predicted from the rank-size rule. In other words, big as it is, Tokyo is not too big for Japan. The normality of gigantic Tokyo is really another measure of how much Japanese urbanization has favored big cities because only a country favoring big cities could support a first city of Tokyo's size without urban primacy.

How did big Japanese cities acquire the food for growing populations of non-

Table 7-2. Urbanization of Japan, 1883–1980

	1883	1910	1940	1980
Number of Cities	37	61	160	646
Number of Towns	12,194	1,144	1,754	1,993
Number of Villages	59,284	10,743	9,325	616
Percentage Urban			37.9	79.1
Japan Population (millions)	38.3	42.2	71.9	103.7

Source: Dr. Mitsuo Hoshino, Director, Tokyo Institute for Municipal Research. Letter to the author dated January 19, 1982. The author acknowledges this assistance with thanks.

Table 7-3. Japan and the Soviet Union: Urbanization, 1950 and 2000 (thousands)

	1950	2000	2000/1950
Japan			
Largest city	6,736	24,172	3.58
Top four cities	12,500	39,983	3.20
Urban population	41,977	114,128	2.71
Rural population	41,648	18,801	0.45
Soviet Union			
Largest city	4,841	9,087	1.88
Top four cities	8,917	19,634	2.20
Urban population	70,765	239,614	3.38
Rural population	109,310	75,413	0.69

Source: United Nations Department of International Economic and Social Affairs. Population Studies, No. 68 *Patterns of Urban and Rural Population Growth.* Sales No. E.79.XIII.9 (New York: United Nations, 1980), Tables 4, 6, 48. Reproduced by permission.

agricultural workers? The sale of manufactured goods abroad was one method. As noted, these sales depended upon protective tariffs at home, military aggression in Asia, and labor-intensive production using cheap labor. The hand of government in this formula is unmistakable. In addition, government encouraged land reclamation for agricultural products. Land reclamation enlarged the agricultural surplus and lowered food prices, thus encouraging urban residence. Finally, Japanese governments squeezed the farm population by taxation (Hagen 1975: 337). The method of taxation was a flat charge based on acreage cultivated, and only efficient producers could raise the required amount. Tax pressure compelled peasants to work harder, longer, and seek technological improvements. Peasants could not engage in subsistence or semisubsistence agriculture and still pay their taxes. Peasants who could not pay high taxes, the less successful agriculturists, were also compelled in this manner to abandon agriculture, migrate to cities, and accept employment at low wages in manufacturing industries.

As a result of severe taxation, the living standard of Japanese agricultural workers declined after 1868. Discontent among the peasantry might have compelled government authorities to reduce taxes, but Japan was not a democratic society, and the ruling class regarded peasant suffering as an acceptable sacrifice for industrialization. An ironic limit was the Japanese military, which championed the cause of the masses in the interest of the health and stamina of draftees (Dore 1967: 41). Yazaki (1968: 78) alleges that underpaid Japanese workers were unable to consume the product of Japanese industry, thus compelling the "bureaucratic and capitalist elite" to attack neighboring countries in order to enlarge markets. This is a standard Marxist explanation of imperialism, and Lockwood (1968: 308) acknowledges there is some truth in it, although he contends the exploitation-underconsumption-imperialism sequence does not fit Japan's history so well as widely supposed.

The industrial urbanization of Japan built upon an unusually extensive and balanced infrastructure carried over from the Tokugawa period. During that era, Japan's feudal government intervened to promote a national plan of urban settlement. The government's plan controlled the urbanization that followed the relentless commercialization of the country. In the postrestoration era, the government abandoned this policy of direct intervention in the urban environment. Instead, government adopted a laissez-faire policy of industrial development and permitted the monopolies to lay out any urban environment they pleased.

Most castle towns adapted successfully to post-Meiji conditions. They added manufacturing, services, and foreign trade to their existing administrative functions (Hall 1968: 186). One cause of successful transition was the foresight with which Tokugawa authorities had selected geographical sites as well as inherited advantages of highway termini. Since railroads generally followed the highway right-of-ways inherited from Tokugawa urban planning, castle towns of old Japan became railroad termini as well. Nonetheless, the abrupt transition to industrial urbanization was never easy. Even the ultimately successful cities experienced initial decades of population decline in the early years of the Meiji era. For example, the population of Tokyo dropped 50 percent between 1869 and 1872 because "depletion of the warrior sector" ruined the capital city's basic industry (Yazaki 1968: 317-318). Some castle towns never recovered and never adapted. Meiji reforms were more favorable to commercial towns that had been restrained by Tokugawa policy. Many of these experienced rapid population and industrial growth when business enterprise was at last permitted to reorganize the urban environment to suit itself.

The general result of laissez-faire in Japan was the uneven growth of regions and the extravagant growth of major cities (Tachi 1964: 202). Favored regions in central Honshu tended to increase in population rapidly, whereas peripheral regions grew less rapidly or even declined in population (Tachi 1964: 186). The changing regional balance reduced the more even settlement achieved under the Tokugawa, promoting instead dramatic contrasts of densely settled and rural districts. Nearly all of the change in regional population was attributable to rural-urban migration. The biggest cities also increased their relative share of total population. By 1940 four major industrial regions included 75 percent of the urban population. (Black 1975: 206). Indeed, the Tokyo metropolitan region became in the post-World War II era the largest urban concentration on earth, with a gross population in excess of 25 million.

The free enterprise policy initiated under the Meiji has continued into the postwar period under the sponsorship of the Liberal Democratic Party (Burks, 1981: 136). The policy has undeniably produced an immense national wealth. Japan's per capita income is second only to North America's (Table 6-2) and continues to move upward. Yet the Japanese people have become increasingly aware that unrestrained free enterprise has imposed real costs on the quality of their lives. The overall trend has, accordingly, been toward reluctant intervention by government in the urban and social environment to restrain or rechannel urban growth. Increasingly, interventions have restricted the freedom of decision of giant corporations.

An early instance of government intervention was the campaign for birth control in 1947–1960 (Taeuber 1962: 25). As elsewhere in the world, industrial urbanization in Japan had accelerated population growth by reducing death rates and infant mortality (Table 7–4). City birthrates were lower than rural, so rural-urban migration tended to reduce birthrates in crowded Japan throughout the Meiji era. Nevertheless, serious concern about high birthrates and unrestrained population growth became evident in 1947 (*Statistical Handbook of Japan* 1976: 25). The result was public and private campaigns in favor of birth restriction. The government intervened to promote birth control chiefly by means of abortion. Results were spectacular: "History offers no example of an equally radical revolution in birth rates . . . " (Reinhard *et al.* 1968: 640). Birthrates declined from 343 per 10,000 inhabitants in 1947 to 193 in 1955. The abrupt decline coincided with a shortage of labor that became noticeable around 1959 despite a massive outflow of farm population to urban industries (*Statistical Handbook of Japan* 1976: 111). Given the reduction in birthrates, the labor shortage could not be relieved by rural-urban migration, and this labor shortage has been a force for improved real wages of Japanese workers since 1960. Unlike the case in developing countries, Japan's rural counties do not possess enough reserve labor to supply the needs of its thriving urban industries. In fact, 88 percent of farming households in 1967 worked only part-time in agriculture. Japan's "farmers" actually derived 69 percent of their gross income from nonfarm employment (*Statistical Handbook of Japan* 1976: 30). Urban unemployment has been accordingly low in Japan, and the chronic overurbanization of the developing world has not afflicted urban Japan. Private enterprise may take

Table 7-4. Japan: Vital Statistics, 1933–1974

Year	Births	Deaths	Natural Increase	Infant Mortality*	Expectation of Life at Birth†
1933–1937 average	30.8	17.4	13.3	115.1	49.92
1955–1959 average	18.1	7.8	10.3	37.7	63.6
1974	18.6	6.5	12.1	10.8	71.16

Source: Statistical Handbook of Japan, 1976 (Tokyo: Bureau of Statistics, Office of the Prime Minister, 1976), p. 25. Reproduced by permission of the Bureau of Statistics.
   *Rate per 1,000 live births.
   †Males only.

credit for the urban prosperity that provides jobs, but government intervention in reducing births has been as responsible for the nation's healthy stortage of labor.

The government has also equalized distribution of population by shifting employment from densely populated districts to peripheral zones. This intervention responded to increased public concern about "excessive concentration of industry within larger cities." In 1962 the Liberal Democratic government introduced a National Multiple Purpose Development Program that sought to decentralize manufacturing production by creating fifteen industrial new towns in rural areas. Because the program was ineffective, the government introduced a successor scheme in 1969, but this plan also failed to effect the desired redistribution. Therefore the government introduced a third decentralization scheme in 1977. Its prospects seem no brighter than those of its predecessors "because of the financial difficulties of the government" (Taniguchi 1981: 5), yet individual projects have succeeded. Begun in 1966, the Tama New Town is a planned community 35 kilometers from downtown Tokyo. An intergovernmental consortium had constructed 18,000 housing units by 1980 with commercial and cultural facilities to serve the needs of 63,000 residents.

Pollution became a major government concern in Japan in the 1960s. Because of the premium placed on economic growth, Japan was long willing to overlook pollution to promote jobs (World Economic 1976: 74). The long-term result was the creation of air, water, noise, and chemical pollution much worse than those experienced by other capitalist countries (Kornhauser 1976: 135–138). ". . . Air pollution causes an unusually high incidence of respiratory disease in some areas of Japan, and . . . serious consequences to health can hardly be avoided at the pollution levels observed in Kawasaki and elsewhere" (Mills and Ohta, 1976: 736). Public protest, which was intense in the 1960s, compelled the Liberal Democratic government to pass the Pollution Prevention Fundamental Law of 1967 and more than twenty supplementary enactments in succeeding years. The regulations were only partially effective. Pollution of rivers was reduced by one half and atmospheric sulfur dioxides were reduced by three quarters in the 1970s. However, nitrogen dioxides in the atmosphere, mainly the product of automobile emissions, increased between 1969 and 1979. Pollution abatement legislation requires the government to conduct regular censuses of pollution-caused diseases. The number of officially confirmed cripples from pollution was 76,340 in 1979, but unofficial estimates claimed 200,000 persons incapacitated by pollution. "Japan, which was famous for her great natural beauty has turned into a country notorious for pollution such as Minimata disease" (Taniguchi 1981: 11). According to Kuroda (1977: 454, 461) big city pollution and crowding caused redirection of internal migration streams after 1965 such that small and medium towns have grown faster than the Tokaido megalopolis.

Government intervention to reduce population concentration, regional imbalances, and pollution has not proceeded as rapidly as metropolitan Japanese would prefer. The reason is the political preeminence of the Liberal Democratic Party (LDP), an "unabashed spokesman" for big business; in the interest of free enterprise, the LDP has resisted government intervention to protect the urban environment and has received in return generous subventions from big corporations (Awanohara and Nakamura 1975: 196–197). In 1974, the Liberal Democrats received only 42 percent of the total vote but continued in power because of support from rural voters, gerrymandering and fragmentation among the opposition (Awanohara and Nakamura 1975: 196). In 1980 the Liberal Democratic Party won 65 percent of rural seats but only 33 percent of metropolitan seats. Sixty percent of voters in the six biggest metropolitan regions (Tokaido megalopolis) preferred the Japan Socialist Party, which strongly criticized the reluctance of the Liberal Democrats to address the country's urban problems.

INDUSTRIAL URBANIZATION OF RUSSIA

During the Middle Ages, a series of Mongol invasions (1237–1241, 1273–1297, 1370–1390) overthrew the kingdom of Kiev and reduced the various Rus tribes to satrapies of the Golden Horde (Langer 1976: 14–15). Mongol invasions (Table 7-5) had a disastrous effect upon Russia's cities. Three walled cities emerged from the chaos of Mongolian invasion as centers of Russian civilization: Novgorod, Moscow, and Tver. A period of intercity rivalry for Russian leadership ensued. With political support of the Great Khan, the princes of Moscow were able to surpass rivals and assume Russian leadership. Under Ivan III, Moscow added Novgorod and Tver to its domain in 1478 and 1485, respectively, eliminating the rival city-states whose competition had blocked its hegemony. These acquisitions reflected the incipient centralization of the Russian state under the leadership of the princes of Moscow. The crucial reign was that of Ivan IV, ("the Terrible") who by defeating the Tatar Khans in the east assured the political autonomy of Moscow, whose tsar now rightly added "all of the Russias" to his territorial claim.

Moscow tsars built defensive cities on the perimeter of their dominions. The center of each city was a *kremlin* (fortress) in which were located the cathedrals, armories, and public buildings. Kremlins were also the residence of the warrior nobility and high clergy who ruled the city (Baranov 1970: 710). "The town was the principal center for extraction of all kinds of taxes and fixed payments" as well as the "focus of military organization of the class of feudal lords" (Sakharov 1979: 67). Common people lived outside the kremlin but normally within the walls of the city (gorod). The tsar's peace encouraged additional city formation in Russia between 1462 and 1689. In 1550, the Russian state in-

Table 7-5. Chronology of Russian History

300–1462	Feudal growth*
	Golden Horde domination: 1240–1480
1462–1689	Centralization of the Russian state
	Ivan IV: 1547–1584
1689–1861	Late feudalism
	Peter I: 1672–1725
	Catherine II: 1729–1796
1861–1917	Capitalist period
	Emancipation of serfs: 1861
	Abortive revolution: 1905
	Stolypin reforms: 1906
1917–	Soviet Communism
	October Revolution and Civil War: 1917–1922
	Stalin dies: 1953

*This is a Soviet periodization. The existence of true feudalism in Russia is disputed by many Western authorities. See Dobb (1947: 33–34), Langer (1979: 220–221, 232).

cluded 160 cities; this had risen to 226 in 1600 and 336 in 1708. The trend in all cases was, as in the West, from state and palace settlements toward the "merchant-artisan character" of city life (Pokshishevskii: 29ff.). The growth in number of preindustrial Russian cities did not reverse the preponderance of agricultural workers in the population. After three centuries of tsarist urbanization, the proportion of urban people in Russia was only 4.1 percent in 1800. By 1863, when capitalist urbanization had just begun, 10 percent of all Russians were urban. This percentage equaled the world's average but lagged far behind the developed nations of the West as well as Japan (Roland 1976: 117).

In the medieval West, city communes came into existence, cities acquired municipal self-rule, and merchant-artisan strata rose to political supremacy. These developments laid the basis for capitalist urbanization and the Industrial Revolution. Nothing similar happened in medieval Russian cities (Langer 1976: 30). Residence never superseded kinship ties or "bonds of servitude" to ruler and landlord. Serfs who lived in cities still belonged to the aristocratic landowner from whose village they hailed, and all city residents owed political allegiance to the tsar (Murvar 1967: 407). These dependent relationships prevented the development of municipal status groups independent of the feudal structure dominating the countryside. The tsar's rule was also very firm in the cities, which remained "political and economic centers" of the country's conservative government rather than enclaves of modernization in a feudal society (Murvar 1967: 402). Every city had its *veche,* a popular assemblage, and these did serve on occasion as vehicles for antifeudal uprisings by urban people, but the futility of these uprisings only underscores the general conclusion that Russian cities had no political basis for independence from the tsarist government in Moscow.

An independent bourgeoisie never came into existence in medieval Russian cities. On the contrary, the tsar himself was Russia's foremost merchant, and his agents were slaves rather than freemen. "Artisans, slaves and beggars" constituted the lowest class of municipal society in medieval Russia (Murvar 1967: 404). Under Peter I ("the Great"), Russian government studied Western technology, business, and culture in order to imitate it. But Russian society had no bourgeoisie to carry out capitalist industrialization, and the gentry were uninterested, so the imitation of the West ordered by the tsar took the form of slave-operated factories owned by the tsar himself. Russia in particular and eastern Europe in general had by Peter's reign already been sucked into the developing capitalist world economy centered in western Europe. Russian industry had come to depend on the export of raw materials (timber, grain, furs) and the importation of finished goods. Russia's late development had already condemned the country by the time of Peter the Great to peripheral status in the world economy. However, to claim that Western economies blocked Russia's access to independent development ignores the long-standing obstacles that Russia's feudal traditions themselves raised. These preceded the capitalist development of the West in time and were not caused by any world system effects. Moreover, the subsequent industrialization of Soviet Russia (and of Meiji Japan) conclusively demonstrates that internal changes in society and government were capable of reversing the admitted constraints that the deepening world system imposed on peripheral members.

RUSSIA'S CAPITALIST PERIOD, 1861-1917

In 1861 Tsar Alexander II decreed the abolition of serfdom. The tsar's decree bestowed personal freedom upon millions of peasants heretofore compelled to labor on the gentry's estates under severe conditions (Weber 1961: 20). As events proved, the tsar understood abolition as an economic as well as a humanitarian measure. Abolition promoted the commercialization of Russian agriculture. The tsar's decree simply turned over to large landlords tracts of land that had been used by peasants. The effect was, as in England, the enclosure of commons land. Moreover, the state paid compensation to the gentry for lands retained by the former serfs but laid upon the emancipated peasantry the obligation to redeem the bonds over a forty-nine-year period. The intention was to compel the peasants to raise cash crops, to work for wages on large estates, and to obtain the lands of the less successful peasants while compelling them to migrate to cities. Great inequalities of land ownership naturally resulted. By 1900 ten million peasant farms held as much land as 30,000 landlord farms. The Stolypin agrarian reforms in 1906 were also intended to encourage "the establishment of large consolidated, private farms" and to weaken the peasant commune, a heritage of the Middle Ages (Black 1975:180). As a result of these reforms, 25 percent of the peasants withdrew from communes and engaged in farming on their own, a form of capitalist agriculture. The tsar hoped that "rich productive farmers" would support his political regime, and he looked to these capitalist farmers for increased output from the agricultural sector. In reality, agricultural output increased only slightly, but grain exports increased fivefold between 1861 and 1900. The exports reflected the unrelenting pressure of the tsar's government, which desired to export grain in order to import foreign technology and machinery with the profit (Black 1975: 180). Tsarist development policy thus emphasized export agriculture and dispossession of landless peasants—classic themes of the world system's periphery.

Signs of industrial urbanization were also numerous in late tsarist Russia, but interpretation is controversial. Pokshishevskii (1970: 29) observes that the abolition of serfdom accelerated the growth of cities in Russia. Some old cities were transformed into "large industrial centers." Annual rates of industrial growth were higher in the later tsarist period than under Soviet power (Black 1975: 194-195).

Thiede (1976: 136) also claims that industrialization was actually strong in this period and offers as evidence the case of "new Russia," the southern steppe of Russia. Table 7-6 shows that urban growth in the period of 1859/1864-1910 actually outstripped population growth, and that manufacturing cities grew more rapidly than commercial cities. On the other hand, Roland (1976: 118) found only a weak correlation between rural-urban migration and the percentage of urban population engaged in manufacturing. Since rural-urban migration accounted for 79 percent of urban growth in the period 1885-1897, he concludes that "migrants moved out of desperation and took jobs in the personal services sector" in preference to life in rural areas. In Roland's account, the "push" of deteriorating rural conditions rather than the "pull" of manufacturing

Table 7-6. Urban Population in New Russia,* 1859/1864-1910

	Population (000)		Percentage of Total Urban Population		Percentage Increase 1859/1864-1910
	1859/1864	1910	1859/64	1910	
Trade cities	476	1843	77	69	287
Industrial cities	143	838	23	31	484
All cities	619	2681	100	100	333

Source: Roger L. Thiede, "Industry and Urbanization in New Russia from 1860 to 1910," in Michael F. Hamm, ed., *The City in Russian History* (Lexington: University Press of Kentucky, 1976), p. 133. Reproduced by permission.

*New Russia: "Southern steppe of Russia" including provinces of Kherson, Tavrida, Ekaterinoslav, and westernmost districts of Don Oblast.

employment actually accounts for the urbanization of Russia's population in the late nineteenth century. The actual urbanization of Russia in this period is, however, indisputable. In 1863 Russia's urban population was 10 percent; in 1897 it had grown to 12.9 percent; by 1917, when Bolsheviks seized power, there were 800 cities in the Russian Empire and 18 percent of the population lived in them (Poksishevskii 1970: 28–29).

Urbanization exceeded the capacity of tsarist cities to cope. Soviet authors stress the "substandard and often unsanitary housing conditions" under which urban workers were compelled to live in tsarist Russia (Klopotov 1970: 605). Western authorities agree that municipal conditions in late tsarist Russia were deplorable and contributed to the overthrow of the autocracy. Hamm (1976: 183) blames "inadequacies of municipal finance" for urban deterioration in this period. The cities were required by law to quarter troops without compensation. In addition, state and church property was untaxed. The tsarist government refused to make loans to bankrupt cities, which turned in desperation to foreign money markets for working capital. The high interest paid interfered with the cities' capacity to "cope with the needs of a rapidly growing urban population." Leagues of cities were formed to press urban problems on the tsar, but they received scant attention, and urban workers turned to revolution.

INTERNATIONAL TRADE, 1922–1950

When the Bolsheviks came to power, Russia bore many characteristics of a developing country. Its cities contained more people than industrial jobs, and the surplus urban population resided in slums reminiscent of favillas and barrios in Third World countries today. In foreign trade too, tsarist Russia "manifested all the characteristics typical of an underdeveloped economy" (Black 1975: 180, 192). Its exports were grain, oil, and lumber; imports were machinery, equipment, rubber, and nonferrous metals. To reverse these dependencies and encourage indigenous development, Soviet governments employed techniques sometimes similar and sometimes contrary to those of Japanese governments.

One source of sharp contrast was the Soviet decision to reduce rather than to expand Russia's international trade. This sector had accounted for 10.4 percent of national income in 1913, but this proportion dropped to 3.1 percent in 1929. Thereafter trade involvements continued to decrease by policy choice as much as by necessity during the Great Depression. Unlike Japan, whose course of modernization led through intensified international commerce, Soviet Russia withdrew from international trade in order to become increasingly self-sufficient. The Soviets made this decision in the conscious desire to avoid entanglement in the capitalist world system. As Stalin (1932: 383) declared, "We must devote all our energies to making our country remain an independent entity based upon the home market. . . We emphatically reject the policy of transforming our country into an appendage of the capitalist world system."

The key to Stalin's decision was the vast and untapped natural resources of the Soviet Union, which enabled Soviet governments to withdraw from international commerce and rely instead on the capacity of their subcontinent to produce raw materials needed for rapid industrialization. This course of action involved a decision to expand the frontier of industrial urbanization ever eastward into unsettled terrain. This policy has characterized Soviet urbanization for the last half century. Even in 1965, 80 percent of the Soviet Union's "power potential" lay east of the Ural Mountains, thus encouraging the formation of non-European industrial centers for processing raw materials (Osborn 1970: 197).

Autarkic development permitted the Soviet Union to evade the pressures for specialization in raw materials exports that derive from the capitalist world system. Access to raw materials and a vast internal market also obviated the necessity for invading neighboring lands as the Japanese had done. Since World War II, of course, the formation of fraternal communist regimes in the nations of Eastern Europe accompanied the formation of trading relationships. The COMECON Nations form a trading bloc analogous to the European Economic Community. By international standards, COMECON trade is not extensive (Black 1975: 300), but there is evidence (Nove 1968: 155) that the Soviet Union has profited more from it than have its junior partners. Reviewing the evidence, Szymanski (1979: Ch. 7) agrees that the Soviet Union exploited its East European trading partners in the period 1945-1953. Since then, however, he finds no evidence of unfair trading relationships. In fact, the Soviet Union is an exporter of raw materials to its communist trading partners and a net importer of manufactured goods from them. As Szymanski notes, this pattern is "exactly the reverse" of trade relationships linking the capitalist core and the Third World periphery. In Czechoslovakia, for example, the Soviet Union has been a "monopoly supplier of raw materials" and the "almost exclusive purchaser" of Czechoslovak manufactured goods (Kansky 1976: 9-10). COMECON prices are always "well below" the world market, but Czechs believe COMECON schedules charge more for things the Soviets sell than for things the Soviets buy, thus cheating the Soviet Union's communist trading partners, who have an economic motive to rebel. Political threats to the status quo in East Germany (1953), Hungary (1956), and Czechoslovakia (1968) produced military intervention by the Soviet Union. In this sense, the Soviet Union employs military force to prop up political relationships that have advantageous economic consequences. This is imperialism. However, the basic industrialization of the Soviet Union actually occurred before 1950, when the first of these political relationships arose, so it would be incorrect to explain the basic industrialization of the Soviet Union on the basis of later trading relationships.

THE COLLECTIVIZATION OF AGRICULTURE, 1929–1940

To industrialize the nation, Soviet authorities needed to support a large and growing body of urban workers engaged in manufacturing heavy industrial goods [5]. The nation also needed to build an urban infrastructure for these workers (housing, roads, facilities) as well as an educational system capable of producing technical leadership. To pay for these vast expenditures, Stalin's strategy was the collectivization of agriculture. This policy amounted to the compulsory relocation of peasants into state or collective farms where they were expected to produce bigger yields [6]. The state then purchased the harvest at prices much below free market prices. The intention was to deprive peasants of their harvest in order to support an urban population heavily engaged in basic industrialization. In effect, the collectivized peasant was to pay for industrial urbanization by gifts of labor to the Soviet state. Dalton (1974: 121) therefore describes the collectivization of agriculture as "a technique to acquire from the peasants the food and raw materials necessary to industrialize without making commensurate return payments to the peasants of manufactured goods" [7].

Peasants resisted collectivization because they were unwilling to sell food and raw materials to the cities unless the money they earned could be spent on services and goods. At this juncture Stalin employed police terror to compel the peasantry to grow free food for the cities or, if they objected, to provide convict labor brigades on Siberian construction projects. Chirot (1977: 112) estimates five million peasants were shot or deported to Siberia between 1929 and 1940. Stalin also ordered "the liquidation of the *kulaks* [rich peasants] as a class," a policy that produced another large force of convict labor [8]. Stalin's purges of the army, bureaucracy, and Communist Party uncovered about five million enemies of the state. In all, about ten million Soviet citizens were sentenced or shot. Peasant and political convicts provided labor brigades who laid railroad track and planted cities in the Soviet north and Asia. Convicts worked fifteen hour days, seven days a week under extraordinarily harsh climatic conditions, receiving inadequate food, clothing, medical care, and housing on the job. As a result, the life expectancy of a new *zek* (convict) in Siberia was only three months in 1940 (Begin 1977). At the end of that period, the average zek had died, but his place was taken by another condemned unfortunate. Inhuman as was this treatment, convict labor did provide, Horowitz (1972: 182) notes, a ready source of cheap labor whose value to Soviet industrialization is unquestionable. In a sense, the zek army played the same constructive role in Soviet industrialization as did immigrant laborers of the nineteenth century in the United States, except that the latter were cheap labor employed by capitalists rather than convict labor owned by the state.

The level of hardship in the countryside was also severe under Stalin. Peasants had to work harder for less money, and the money they received could purchase no consumer goods because few were produced and none imported. To make matters worse, planning authorities skimped on housing and welfare benefits in the countryside, intending therby to encourage rural-urban migration. In this last policy, they succeeded sensationally (Harris, 1970: 299-304). Rural-urban migration in the Soviet Union between 1926 and 1940 was "one of the largest movements of people within such a short time span in world history" (Black 1975: 210). In the decade 1928-1939 alone, the urban population increased from 27.6 to 60.4 million; the percentage of population increased from 18 to 32 (cf Table 7-7). What is more remarkable, food consumption per capita in cities declined by more than 20 percent in the same decade (Black 1975: 181). The decline was the unsurprising result of abrupt increases in grain exports on top of the inability of agriculture to feed so many urban people. Yet undesirable as conditions apparently were in cities, conditions in the countryside were worse because people in the best position to comment, the peasants, left the country-side in unprecedented numbers.

Agriculture is still an obstacle to development in the Soviet Union. In 1968 Soviet agriculture utilized 45 percent of total labor power and produced 25 percent of the Soviet gross national product (Willett, 1968: 140). The tiny private sector is embarrassingly productive compared with the huge state and collective sector. This disparity results in part from the continued unwillingness of Soviet authorities to pay collective farmers realistic prices for their output; as a result, the private sector receives more attention from the workers because it is so lucrative. Living conditions in rural areas are still much inferior to city living. People wish to quit agriculture and are prevented from doing so only by regulation (Frolic 1976: 151). Also low productivity compels Soviet authorities to employ much labor power in agriculture, thus reducing the labor available for manufacturing or service work in the "developed" sector of the economy.

Table 7-7. Population of the Soviet Union, 1870-1977

	Total (millions)	Urban (millions)	Urban as Percent of Total Population
1870	86.3	9.5	11
1897	124.6	18.4	15
1913	159.2	28.5	18
1940	194.1	63.1	33
1959	208.8	100.0	48
1978	260.0	162.5	62

Source: Central Statistical Board of the Council of Ministers of the USSR, *The USSR in Figures for 1977* (Moscow: Statistika, 1978), p. 7.

PLANNING CITY SIZE IN THE SOVIET UNION

Russia has never been so urbanized as Japan. Even in 1800, the Russian Empire was only 8 to 9 percent urban whereas Japan was 16 to 17 percent urban. Since 1867, the rate of urbanization in Russia has exceeded Japan's, so the distance between the two nations has declined. However, a decade's disparity in level of overall urbanization continued to distinguish the nations in 1970. In that year Soviet urbanization was 56 percent and Japanese urbanization was 72 percent.

Another, more significant convergence has been bringing together the proportion of total population residing in the largest cities. In 1800, Japan's largest cities (100,000 or more) contained three times the proportion of total population found in the same size class in Russia. Japan's urban hierarchy was already top-heavy whereas Russia's favored middle- and small-sized cities. This difference persisted although the cities of both societies greatly increased in size. For example, in 1939-1940, Japan's cities of 100,000 or more contained only 1.8 times as large a proportion of population as did Russia's (Table 7-8). But intersocietal differences were still quite apparent in bigger cities of 500,000 or more and cities of 2.5 million or more. In these Japan had in proportion to population twice and three times as many persons as did the Soviet Union in 1930 (Black 1975: 205-206).

Japan still houses a much higher proportion of its total population in very large cities than does the Soviet Union. The densely populated area extending from Tokyo to Osaka has 45 percent of Japan's inhabitants, and Tokyo metropolitan area contains nearly 25 percent (Baranov 1970: 714). The Soviet Union has no comparable metropolitan concentrations of population, "and its annual

Table 7-8. Urbanization of Japan and Russia, 1867-1940

Size of Cities (000)	Percentage of Population in Cities			
Japan	1867-1878	1897-1898	1920-1926	1939-1940
10+	11	9	32	44-48
20+	9	14-15	24	38
100+	6	8	18	30
Russia				
10+	9	12	13-14	26-27
20+	5	9-10	12	24-25
100+	2	4	6-7	16

Source: Cyril E. Black, et al., *The Modernization of Japan and Russia* (New York: Free Press, 1975), p. 206. Reproduced by permission.

rate of metropolitan growth is lower than would be expected on the basis of energy consumption . . . " (Gibbs and Schnore 1960: 165). The Moscow metropolitan region contains only 3 percent of the nation's population. Table 7-3 compares the big city and urban growth of Japan and the Soviet Union between 1950 and 2000. United Nations projections show that in Japan the bigger cities will grow faster than the urban population in general. However, the opposite situation prevails in the Soviet Union. The largest city, Moscow, will not even double its 1950 population by 2000, and the aggregated population of the Soviet Union's four largest cities will increase only 2.2 times the 1950 total. But in the same half century, United Nations statisticians expect the urban population to increase 3.38 times. In other words, most urban growth in the Soviet Union will occur in the smaller- and medium-sized towns—not in the big cities.

Why has the Soviet Union generally lagged behind Japan and other developed capitalist societies in the movement of population to very big cities? Government policy was a principal restraint (Frolic 1970: 684). In the Soviet Union, central and regional planning authorities had the responsibility for deciding where to locate industry, a decision that capitalist societies assign to the market. "In the unrestrained pursuit for profits lies the meaning of the philosophy of unchecked growth of oversized cities under capitalism" (Khorev and Moiseenko, 1977: 709). Until relatively recently, Soviet planners argued that very big cities were both uneconomical and unhealthful (Osborn 1970: 200). They were uneconomical because small- and middle-sized cities generally contained underemployed populations who already had housing whereas big cities required new housing for new workers. Additionally, Soviet planners felt that long-distance commutation was a waste of time and money that small- and middle-sized cities could avoid. Therefore they criticized the "extraordinarily concentrated" cities of Japan where residential suburbs were constructed forty to seventy kilometers from workplaces (Baranov 1970: 714). Instead, Soviet planners adhered to the notion of "optimal size" of cities, which they defined as much smaller than the biggest cities of the rest of the world (Sawers 1978: 339). Planners took upon themselves "the regulation of the growth of small and medium-sized cities" in the expectation that restraints on city growth would have "substantial national economic importance" (Baranov 1970: 714).

This consistent policy of growth restraint was hard to implement (Frolic 1976: 154). Soviet cities continually bumped up against the topmost limits that planners had decreed, thus necessitating belated changes in master plans or rearguard efforts to reduce population. Target population figures for the largest cities—usually twenty years in projection—have repeatedly been surpassed before half the targeted period elapsed. Thus for Sverdlovsk, the 1954 Gosplan (national 5-year plan) projected a target population of 800,000 in 1975, but this level was reached in 1960. For the Siberian city of Angarsk, planners projected a population of 80,000 in 1975, but the real population was already 179,000 in 1966 (Osborn 1970: 206-207).

An important technique for restraining growth was political control over population movement to high-growth centers. Fifteen Soviet cities had "closed" populations in 1970. These included Moscow, Leningrad, and Kiev. "These cities are closed to all immigration from other parts of the Soviet Union" (Frolic 1970: 684). The police have the task of registering new residents and issuing or denying a resident permit (*propiska*) for municipal residence. But the enforcement of the propiska system depends ultimately on the control of housing. Only people bearing a propiska are permitted to rent housing in population-controlled cities; hence people without a propiska are compelled to return to their original home town.

After decades of attempting to restrain the growth of the largest cities, Soviet planners have begun to revise their thinking about optimal city size (Sawers 1978: 341). To an increasing extent, planners in the Soviet Union now argue that the very biggest cities are actually more economical than small- or middle-sized cities. Some say that big cities are also more interesting to inhabit than smaller ones and ought on this account to be preferred. More commonly, planners simply conclude that the issue of population size is secondary to how an urban region is structured. These planners feel that population size is a matter of indifference so long as the urban whole is articulated into multifunctional districts, each of which is largely autonomous in housing, employment, transportation, recreation, and other functions (Osborn 1970: 208).

REGIONAL GROWTH IN THE SOVIET UNION

The Soviet Union is basically a federation of fifteen union republics. Each union republic is the official homeland for the ethnic group whose name it bears. Thus the Russian Federative Soviet Socialist Republic is the ethnic homeland of Russians, and the Ukrainian SSR is the ethnic homeland of Ukrainians. Russians are the largest ethnic group in the Soviet Union and made up 53 percent of the national population in 1970. The remaining 47 percent are ethnic minorities whose native language is not Russian. There are 100 ethnic minorities in the Soviet Union. Some minorities (Poles, Germans, Jews) do not have a union republic bearing their name. About one quarter of the Soviet population is non-Slavic, and among these Mongolians are the largest subgroup.

Since the October Revolution of 1917, the Communist Party has endorsed a program of equality of development for the various regions of the nation. In 1976 General Secretary Leonid Brezhnev (1976: 55), addressing the 25th Congress of the Communist Party, publicly reaffirmed the "programme of industrial development for all republics, nations, and nationalities." To a substantial extent, the program has committed the Soviet Union to compensatory urbanization of the non-Russian republics east of the Urals. These areas were the most backward in 1917, lagging well behind the Russian-speaking regions of the west in every index of social development. Khorev and Moiseenko (1977: 700) also maintain that "pre-revolutionary Russia was notorious for its high level of industrial and spatial concentration and its highly uneven territorial concentration." Industrial urbanization of the eastern regions coincided with the long-range plan for bringing labor power to natural resource sites rather than shipping eastern resources to western cities for processing. Conceivably, Soviet industrial urbanization would have clustered more heavily in the Russian republic had it not been for central planning and the policy of regional decentralization. Were this arrangement to have been tolerated, the Baltic and European republics would export manufactured goods to the eastern republics and import raw materials, an arrangement replicating internally the core-periphery arrangement of the capitalist world system.

The evenness of regional development in the Soviet Union is controversial. East of the Ural Mountains the urban population has grown and continues to grow more rapidly than in the western portion of the Soviet Union (Harris 1970: 305–306). Khorev and Moiseenko (1977: 702) have presented statistics showing that between 1940 and 1971 growth of USSR total national output was 1282 (1940 = 100) whereas in regions east of the Urals Mountains output growth was 1582. However, Bennigsen and Wimbush (1978: 175) find evidence as well as "strong feeling among Central Asians themselves" that Soviet resource allocation has favored Russian cities and slighted the Asian ones. On the other hand, the "relative comparative standing" of ethnic groups remains unchanged since 1917 (Raskowa-Harmstone 1977: 79). The economic and social development of the nation is most advanced in the Baltic northwest and in the other European republics. The central Asian southeast remains at the lowest level of economic development, urbanization, and wealth. Table 7-9 displays the coefficient of development of various Soviet ethnic groups in 1965. The coefficient is the ratio of a republic's share of Soviet gross domestic product to the republic's total population. This measure shows that the Latvian republic produced 117 percent of expected output in that year whereas, at the other extreme, the Tadzhik republic produced only 69 percent of expected output.

The ethnicity of the republics has made regional urbanization a politically complex task. Ethnic republics compete with one another for social investment capital, the basis of economic development and urbanization. There is some evidence that leaders in power favor their regions of origin; hence, republics try to push their people into positions of authority in the government and Communist Party. Georgia, for example, has long enjoyed exceptional local autonomy, and Rakowska-Harmstone (1977: 81) attributes the Georgian republic's privileged status to the patronage of Josef Stalin, a native son of that republic.

The political competition of republics for union development capital resembles the competition of American regions for federal contracts, military installations,

Table 7-9. Major Ethnic Groups in the USSR, 1970

| Ethnic Groups | Numbers | | Urbanization in Percent | | Coefficient Development 1965* |
	Millions	Percent of Total	By Group	By Republic	
Russians	129.0	53.3	68	64	1.05
Ukrainians	40.8	16.9	49	56	1.04
Uzbeks	9.2	3.8	25	37	0.71
Belorussians	9.1	3.7	44	46	1.01
Tatars	5.9	2.4	55	N.A.	N.A.
Kazakhs	5.3	2.2	27	52	0.88
Azerbaijani	4.4	1.8	40	51	0.71
Armenians	3.6	1.5	65	61	0.84
Georgians	3.2	1.2	44	48	0.87
Moldavians	2.7	1.1	20	33	0.97
Lithuanians	2.7	1.1	47	53	1.02
Jews	2.2	0.9	98	N.A.	N.A.
Tadzhiks	2.1	0.9	26	38	0.69
Germans	1.8	0.8	46	N.A.	N.A.
Turkmen	1.5	0.6	31	48	0.77
Kirghiz	1.5	0.6	15	38	0.76
Latvians	1.4	0.6	53	64	1.17
Poles	1.2	0.5	45	N.A.	N.A.
Estonians	1.0	0.4	55	66	1.14
USSR, Total	242	100	56		100

Source: Reprinted from "Ethnicity in the Soviet Union," by Teresa Rakowska-Harmstone in Vol. 433 of *The Annals of American Academy of Political and Social Science.* © 1977 by the American Academy of Political and Social Science. All Rights Reserved. Reproduced by permission.

*Ratio of republic's share of USSR gross domestic product to republic's total population in 1965.

and public works projects. As in the United States, the rate of industrial urbanization in a Soviet region depends heavily on how much public money the national government invests in the region. Therefore residents want their region to receive at least its share of investment. However, the basis of competition is probably more severe in the Soviet Union than in the United States. First, the regions of the United States are linguistically homogeneous, so federal investment decisions do not spell patronage for one language group over another—only for one geographical region or another. This impersonality reduces interarea tension surrounding federal investment decisions. Second, the federal government's share of American gross national product is 20 percent or less. The process of regional urbanization in the United States, Japan, and other capitalist "mixed" economies still has its center of gravity in the private sector. Were the

U.S. federal government to assume direct responsibility for all regional urbanization, the political pressure on decision making would vastly increase. Because the Soviet Union is a centrally planned economy and virtually no private sector exists, Moscow's investment decisions are the sole source of regional urbanization. For this reason, the various ethnic republics scrutinize allocations very carefully, and each one employs its political resources to obtain at least its fair share of national investment capital (Rakowska-Harmstone 1977: 84).

Rendering the political balance more complex are interregional differentials in birthrates, family size, and population growth (DiMaio 1980). Overall figures for the Soviet Union (Table 7-10) show the continuous declines in birthrates, improvement in infant mortality, and reduction in family size that have accompanied the demographic transition to modernity in every developed society. Moreover, the vastness of the Soviet Union has tended to render the issue of population growth less critical than in resource-poor, densely populated Japan. However, rural areas of the Soviet Union have been depopulated as a result of rural-urban migration and low birthrates. Since the Soviet Union is industrially developed, this demographic situation had produced a labor power shortage, yet in Islamic central Asia, the poorest region of the Soviet Union, birthrates are among the highest in the world, families are large, and population growth is rapid (Bennigsen and Wimbush 1978: 185). Given the general retardation of industrial urbanization in central Asia, the result has been a build-up of underemployed rural labor power in central Asia. These Islamic peasants could, in principle, migrate to the unsettled Soviet north for work—but they prefer not to, and they also resent the out-migration of educated Slavs to their republics. For their part, Russians are unsure why high birthrates should entitle backward republics to a bigger share of social investment capital at the expense of low birthrate republics. The resulting interethnic tensions are polite but severe, and one authority calls ethnic tension the "major force for change in the Soviet Union" today (Rakowska-Harmstone 1977: 81, 75).

Table 7-10. Vital Statistics of the Soviet Union: Rates per 1,000 Population, 1913-1977

	Births	**Deaths**	**Natural Increase**
1913	45.5	29.1	16.4
1940	31.2	18.0	13.2
1965	18.4	7.43	11.1
1977	18.2	9.7	8.5

Source: Central Statistical Board of the Council of Ministers of the USSR, *The USSR in Figures for 1977* (Moscow: Statistika, 1978), p. 17.

SUMMARY

The contrasting paths of industrial urbanization in the Soviet Union and Japan are case histories that reflect and explain theoretical debates. First, feudalism obstructed the passage of both societies toward indigenous capitalism. In neither Japan nor Russia did there appear full analogies to the municipal autonomy, religious individualism, or mercantile bourgeoisie whose confluence permitted capitalism to break apart the traditional social order in western Europe. In Russia, residual feudalism remained an obstacle until removed by the October 1917 revolution. In Japan, the warrior class embraced the cause of industrial urbanization in the interest of national power in 1868, and this decision permitted warriors to guide the nation's industrial urbanization in a free enterprise society.

Second, both Russian and Japan faced an underdog's struggle in their efforts to industrialize. This struggle each successfully surmounted in its own manner, but in both cases the center of the latecomers' development problem was the preemption by industrial Europe and North America of the technology, the infrastructure, and the capital for industrial development. Japan employed military aggression and cheap products to circumvent this obstacle. Russia concentrated on forced industrialization based on exploitation of resources east of the Urals. Both countries resisted the international division of labor, and their success proves that the world's division of labor does not simply impose itself upon helpless victims. On the other hand, only popular suffering, authoritarian government and social dislocation permitted these two latecomer nations to overcome the international obstacles they encountered.

Third, Japan assigned urban decision making to private enterprise and restricted the government's role to guidance and support of private enterprise. This method yielded a capitalist urbanization characterized by interregional inequalities of development, formation of immense metropolitan regions containing most of the population, and very high levels of overall urbanization. In the Soviet Union, government preempted urban decision making altogether, leaving no role whatsoever for private enterprise. As a result, Soviet urbanization was from the beginning a political process directed from Moscow in response to political imperatives rather than market pressures. A further result was the development of national and regional planning staffs whose business was urban decision making on behalf of the Soviet government. Regional urbanization in the Soviet Union has been remarkably equal, thus indicating the authorities' attempt consciously to bring peripheral regions to the standard of the core. On the other hand, the Soviet method has exposed planners to ethnic pressures and conflicts that a market economy can evade. Additionally, Soviet planners did not always make as sagacious choices as did free markets in Japan. On the specific issue of city size, Soviet planners attempted for four decades to prevent the growth of great cities and only belatedly acknowledged what Japanese markets had all along understood: the economic superiority of metropolitan regions.

NOTES

1. "For Buddhists greed was one of the cardinal sins, and greed has been closely linked to the merchants' quest for profit" (Bellah 1957: p. 119).
2. "Class distinctions were defined in such detail that one's clothes and hair style were regulated. . . . Only the *samurai* warriors could have a family name, carry a sword, and wear the distinctive hairstyle." Speech also differed. Katsuhiko Abe, "Educational Norms in Japanese Immigrant Communities," M.A. research paper, University of California, Santa Barbara 1981.
3. "Foreign trade is the foundation of the economy of this resource-poor country with abundant population" (*Statistical Handbook:* 84).
4. "It would be completely mistaken either to hope that Japan will play a military role in the international community or to feel anxiety that Japan might once again emerge as a military giant." Zenko Suzuki, Prime Minister of Japan, January 18, 1981. See *Los Angeles Times,* February 1, 1981, pt. IA, p. 3.
5. Stalin claimed that the Soviet Union had to postpone consumer consumption in order to build heavy industry—otherwise the country would have become a peripheral dependent of the capitalist world system. Stalin acknowledged that citizens who objected were "handled roughly." See Josef Stalin, "Address to the Graduates from the Red Army Academy," in Emile Burns, ed., *A Handbook of Marxism.* New York: International,1935, pp. 958–959. "If socialists come to power in an underdeveloped country, they have no choice but to play the role of a nationalist bourgeoisie and that entails . . . keeping consumption levels at a minimum so as to provide the maximum for investment" (Horowitz 1972: 163).
6. "Instead of patiently explaining the government's policy to the hesitating middle peasants, the latter were forced to join the collective farms and some were even dispossessed" (Academy of Sciences of the USSR: 169). Stalin is blamed for this abuse, but no quantitative estimate of its volume is offered.
7. Stalin's collective farms "operated essentially as collection agencies to extract grain from the peasants at low prices." In this manner, much of the "burden of accumulating an industrialization fund was transferred to the countryside." Merle Fainsod, "Soviet Communism," *International Encyclopaedia of the Social Sciences,* Vol. 3, p. 107.
8. "The small peasant farms were unable to meet the grain requirements which had increased on account of the growth of the urban population, while the kulaks who had considerable grain surpluses refused to sell them to the state,

thus threatening to leave the towns and the army without food and to hold up industrialization" (Academy of Sciences of the USSR 1965: 162). According to the Soviet Academy, the "liquidation of the kulaks" amounted to no more than compulsory relocation of 240,757 families, most of them to towns. The Academy of Sciences also insists the kulaks were engaged in anti-Soviet plotting.

REFERENCES

Academy of Sciences of the USSR, Institute of History. 1965. *A Short History of the USSR*. Moscow: Progress Publishers.

Awanohara, Susumu, and Koji Nakamura. 1975. "Japan," pp. 196–205, in Lewis Christopher, ed. *Asia 1975 Yearbook*. Hong Kong: Far Eastern Economic Review.

Baerwald, Diane, and Chizuko Saeki. 1970. *The Urban Way: Guide to Research on Japanese Cities*. Monticello, Ill. Council of Planning Librarians.

Baranov, N. V. 1970. "Urban Planning." *Great Soviet Encyclopedia*. 3rd ed. 7: 710–715. New York: Macmillan.

Begin, Menachem. 1977. *White Nights: Memoirs of a Prisoner in Russia*. New York: Harper & Row.

Bellah, Robert N. 1957. Tokugawa Religion. New York: Free Press.

Bennigsen, Alexandre A., and S. Enders Wimbush. 1978. "Migration and Political Control: Soviet Europeans in Soviet Central Asia," pp. 173-187, in William H. McNeill and Ruth S. Adams, eds. *Human Migration*. Bloomington, Indiana: Indiana University Press.

Black, Cyril, et al. 1975. *The Modernization of Japan and Russia*. New York: Free Press.

Blair, Thomas L. 1974. *The International Urban Crisis*. London: Hart-Davis, MacGibbon.

Brezhnev, L. I. 1976. *Report of the CPSU Central Committee and the Immediate Tasks of the Party in Home and Foreign Policy*. Moscow: Novosti Press.

Burks, Ardath W. 1981. *Japan: Profile of a Postindustrial Power*. Boulder, Colo.: Westview Press.

Chirot, Daniel, 1977. *Social Change in the Twentieth Century*. New York: Harcourt.

Clarke, Roger A. 1972. *Soviet Economic Facts, 1917–1970*. New York: Wiley.

Dalton, George. 1974. *Economic Systems and Society*. Harmondsworth, England: Penguin.

Davis, Kingsley. 1972. *World Urbanization, 1950–1970*, Vol. II: *Analysis of Trends, Relationships, and Development*. Berkeley: Institute of International Studies of the University of California.

DiMaio, Alfred J., Jr. 1980. "The Soviet Union and Population: Theory, Problems and Population Policy." *Comparative Political Studies* 13: 97-136.

Dobb, Maurice, 1947. *Studies in the Development of Capitalism.* New York: International.

Dore, R. P. 1967. *City Life in Japan.* Berkeley and Los Angeles: University of California Press.

Frank, André Gunder. 1970. *"The Development of Underdevelopment,"* pp. 3–17, in James D. Cockcroft, et al., eds. *Dependence and Underdevelopment.* Garden City, N.Y.: Anchor Press Doubleday.

Frolic, B. Michael. 1970. "The Soviet Study of Soviet Cities." *Journal of Politics* 32: 675–695.

———. 1976. "Noncomparative Communism: Chinese and Soviet Urbanization," pp. 149–161, in Mark G. Field, ed. *Social Consequences of Modernization in Communist Societies.* Baltimore: Johns Hopkins University Press.

Gibbs, Jack, and Leo F. Schnore. 1960. "Metropolitan Growth: An International Study." *American Journal of Sociology* 66: 160–170.

Hagen, Everett E. 1975. *The Economics of Development.* Homewood, Ill.: Richard D. Irwin.

Hall, John W. 1968. "The Castle Town and Japan's Modern Urbanization," pp. 169–188, in John W. Hall and Marius B. Jansen, eds. *Studies in the Institutional History of Early Modern Japan.* Princeton: Princeton University Press.

Hamm, Michael F. 1977. "The Modern Russian City: An Historiographical Analysis." *Journal of Urban History* 4: 39–76.

Hanley, Susan, and Kozo Yamamura. 1977. *Economic and Demographic Change in Preindustrial Japan, 1600–1868.* Princeton: Princeton University Press.

Harris, Chauncey D. 1970. *Cities of the Soviet Union.* Chicago: Rand McNally.

Hauser, William B. 1977–1978. "Osaka: A Commercial City in Tokugawa Japan." *Urbanism Past and Present* 5: 23–32.

Horowitz, Irving Louis. 1972. *Three Worlds of Development.* 2nd ed. New York: Oxford University Press.

Kansky, Karel Joseph. 1976. *Urbanization under Socialism: The Case of Czechoslovakia.* New York: Praeger.

Khorev, B. S. and V. M. Moiseenko. 1977. "Urbanization and Redistribution of the Population of the U.S.S.R," pp. 643–720, in Sidney Goldstein and David F. Sly, eds. *Patterns of Urbanization: Comparative Country Studies,* vol. II. Douhain, Belgium: Ordina Editions for the International Union for the Scientific Study of Population.

Klopotov, K. K. 1970. "Municipal Economy." *Great Soviet Encyclopedia,* 3rd ed. 7: 605–1606. New York: Macmillan.

Kornhauser, David, 1976. *Urban Japan: Its Foundations and Growth.* London: Longman.

Kuroda, Toshio. 1977. "Urbanization and Population Redistribution in Japan," pp. 433–463, in Sidney Goldstein and David F. Sly, eds. *Patterns of Urbanization: Comparative Country Studies,* Vol. II. Douhain, Belgium: Ordina Editions for the International Union for the Scientific Study of Population.

Langer, Lawrence N. 1976. "The Medieval Russian Town," pp. 11–33, in Michael F. Hamm, ed., *The City in Russian History.* Lexington: University of Kentucky Press.

——. 1979. "The Historiography of the Preindustrial Russian City." *Journal of Urban History* 5: 209–240.

Lockwood, William W. 1968. *The Economic Development of Japan,* 2nd ed. Princeton: Princeton University Press.

Mills, Edwin S., and Katsutoshi Ohta. 1976. "Urbanization and Urban Problems," pp. 673–751 in Hugh Patrick and H. Rosofsky, eds. *Asia's New Giant: How the Japanese Economy Works.* Washington, D.C.: Brookings Institution.

Moore, Wilbert E. 1979. *World Modernization.* New York: Elsevier.

Moulder, Frances V. 1977. *Japan, China and the Modern World Economy.* Cambridge: Cambridge University Press.

Murvar, Vatro. 1967. "Max Weber's Urban Typology and Russia." *Sociological Quarterly* 8: 481–494.

Nove, A. 1968. "Communism, Economic Organization of: Internal Trade." *International Encyclopedia of the Social Sciences* 3: 151–155.

Osborn, Robert J. 1970. *Soviet Social Policies: Welfare, Equality, and Community.* Homewood, Ill.: Dorsey Press.

Pokshishevskii, V. V., et al. 1970. "City." Great Soviet Encyclopedia, 3rd ed. 7: 22–34. New York: Macmillan.

Rakowska-Harmstone, Teresa. 1977. "Ethnicity in the Soviet Union." *Annals of the American Academy of Political and Social Science* 433: 73–87.

Reinhard, Marcel, et al. 1968. *Histoire Générale de la Population Mondiale.* Paris: Editions Montchrestien.

Roland, Richard H. 1976. "Urban In-Migration in Late Nineteenth Century Russia," pp. 115–124. In Michael F. Hamm, *The City in Russian History.* Lexington: University Press of Kentucky.

Rozman, Gilbert. 1973. *Urban Networks in Ch'ing China and Tokugawa Japan.* Princeton: Princeton University Press.

Sakharov, A. M. 1979. "The Town—Center of Feudal Dominance." *Soviet Studies in History* 18: 53–71.

Sawers, Larry. 1978. "Cities and Countryside in the Soviet Union and China," pp. 338–364, in William K. Tabb and Larry Sawers, ed. *Marxism and the Metropolis.* New York: Oxford University Press.

Smith, Thomas C. 1973. "Premodern Economic Growth: Japan and the West." *Past and Present* 60: 127–160.

Stalin, Joseph, 1932. *Leninism.* Vol. I. Trans. by Eden and Cedar Paul. London: George Allen and Unwin.

Statistical Handbook of Japan. 1976. Tokyo: Bureau of Statistics, Office of the Prime Minister.

Szymanski, Albert. 1979. *Is the Red Flag Flying?* London: Zed Press.

Tachi, Minoru. 1964. "Regional Income Disparity and Internal Migration of Population in Japan." *Economic Development and Cultural Change* 12: 186–204.

Taniguchi, Shigeru. 1981. "Urbanization and Urban Problems in Japan After World War 2." NP: Nagoya Institute of Technology.

Thiede, Roger L. 1976. "Industry and Urbanization in New Russia from 1860 to 1910," pp. 125–137. In Michael F. Hamm, ed. *The City in Russian History.* Lexington: University Press of Kentucky.

Totman, Conrad. 1979. "English-Language Studies of Medieval Japan: An Assessment." *Journal of Asian Studies* 38: 541–551.

Vogel, Ezra F. 1967. "Kinship Structure, Migration to City, and Modernization." pp. 91–111, in R. P. Dore, ed. *Aspects of Social Change in Modern Japan,* Princeton: Princeton University Press.

Wallerstein, Immanuel. 1974. *The Modern World System.* New York: Academic Press.

Willett, Joseph. 1968. "Communism, Economic Organization of Agriculture," pp. 139–146, in *International Encyclopedia of the Social Sciences,* vol. 3. New York: Macmillan.

World Economic Information Services. 1976. *Economic Information File: Japan,* 1974–75 Edition. Tokyo: World Economic Information Services.

Yazaki, Takeo. 1968. *Social Change and The City in Japan.* San Francisco: Japan Publications.

PART THREE

Urban Spatial Arrangement

CHAPTER 8 ───────────────────────

Urban Morphology of the United States

Urban morphology is the physical arrangement of cities, their buildings, streets, and neighborhoods. Urban morphology has a dynamic and a static aspect. In its static aspect, the subject describes the physical plan of cities at a moment in time, relating this plan to current social life. In its dynamic aspect, urban morphology addresses the changing form of cities. In the modern world, this issue unavoidably means urbanization, the matrix process that organizes urban form everywhere. Static depictions of urban morphology freeze a fluid reality whose process of change is the ultimate concern. On the other hand, the dynamics of urban morphology always require the juxtaposition of static depictions in sequence. As in a movie, the dynamics of change emerge from sequential, accurate portrayals of stopped action. Static depictions of urban morphology are necessary, but they achieve their scientific value when juxtaposed to display a dynamic process (Castells 1977: 61).

Unfortunately, static images are easier to construct and less controversial than dynamic processes. Therefore there is agreement about the morphology of American cities at various moments in time but less agreement about how the separate moments should be linked together to form a whole. One issue is how to divide the historic process. Some writers divide urban history into three and others into two growth periods. Terminologies also differ. Hawley (1981: 86, 149) distinguishes an early cellular city and a later metropolitan community. McKelvey (1963, 1968) treats city, metropolitan region, and, by implication, colonial types. Gordon advances a different tripartite classification of urban morphology: commercial, competitive, and monopoly capitalist. Another problem is how to conceive of change from one phase to another. Functionalist writers treat change as irreversible and continuous (Hawley 1981: 340-342). The system tendency toward rest is disturbed by "intrusion from the outside" of disruptive influences from the natural or social environment [1]. Marxists have approached the history of urban morphology as a succession of discrete types. Each type tends toward self-destruction because of internal contradictions (Gordon 1978: 26-28).

Issues are complex, and there is presently no universally acceptable solution. Yet the description of North American city structure since 1600 is uncontroversial. The gist is radial expansion of city perimeters in response to increasing size. Colonial cities small in size and compact in shape, gave way in the middle of the nineteenth century to manufacturing cities whose dense populations were greatly in excess of what had been possible earlier. A consequence was the radial expansion of city limits. Radial expansion accelerated in the twentieth century to such an extent that the largest cities absorbed whole regions, including much territory outside of city limits. The fourth development, often labeled "megalopolitan," is the interpenetration of metropolitan regions.

The process is easy to depict in successive maps showing the growth of Philadelphia since 1770. The first map (Figure 8-1) shows the town of 1770-1780. In this decade Philadelphia's population was 25,000 and the city ranked behind only New York in size (Chudacoff 1975: 4). Colonial Philadelphia was about one mile in length and one-half mile in width. An able-bodied person could walk across the city in thirty minutes. An overland journey from Philadelphia to New York required three days of travel through rural countryside. During the early Industrial Revolution, Philadelphia grew rapidly. The second map (Figure 8-2) depicts the industrial city's structure. In 1860 the population was 565,529, a twentyfold increase of ninety years earlier. The land area of the city had increased too. The area from Sixth Street to the Schuylkill River had filled with population in the interim so the city's width was two miles. Additionally, Philadelphia's north-south expansion had produced a densely settled strip four miles in length. Downtown Philadelphia now amounted to eight square miles compared with one-half square mile in 1770. A railroad trip to New York City was only a day's travel, but the journey still passed through an agricultural region between the two cities.

In the early automobile age metropolitan Philadelphia (Figure 8-3) had expanded to cover the whole western shore of the Delaware River. From the Navy Yard on the south to Winsohocking Avenue on the north, the densely settled core of downtown Philadelphia now stretched eight miles in length. Suburban areas of the west, northwest, and northeast were each as large as the more densely settled core. To the east of the Delaware River, Camden, N.J., could now be easily reached via the Benjamin Franklin Bridge. Bridge access permitted Philadelphia's growth to spill over the river so the whole urbanized region

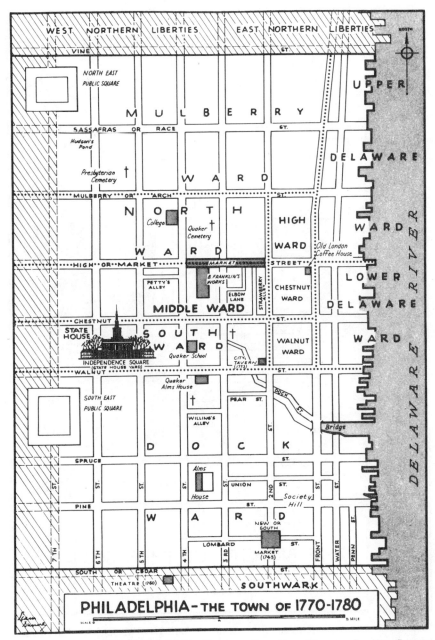

Figure 8-1. Colonial Philadelphia. (Source: Sam Bass Warner, Jr. *The Private City.* Philadelphia: University of Pennsylvania, 1968, p. 2. Reproduced by permission.)

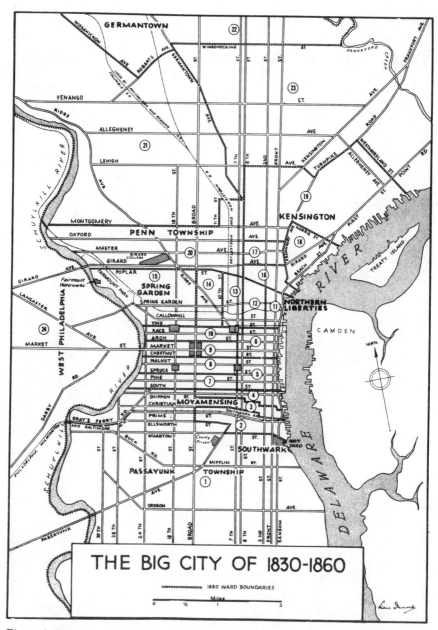

THE BIG CITY OF 1830-1860

1860 WARD BOUNDARIES

Miles

0   ½   1   2

Figure 8-2. Industrial Philadelphia. (Source: Sam Bass Warner, Jr. *The Private City*. Philadelphia: University of Pennsylvania, 1968, p. 48. Reproduced by permission.)

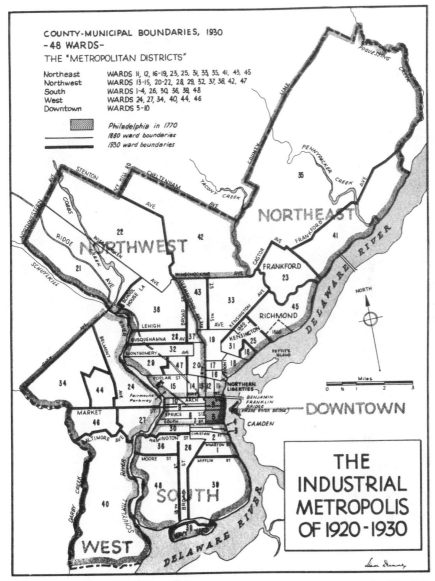

Figure 8–3. Metropolitan Philadelphia. (Source: Sam Bass Warner, Jr. *The Private City*. Philadelphia: University of Pennsylvania, 1968, p. 160. Reproduced by permission.)

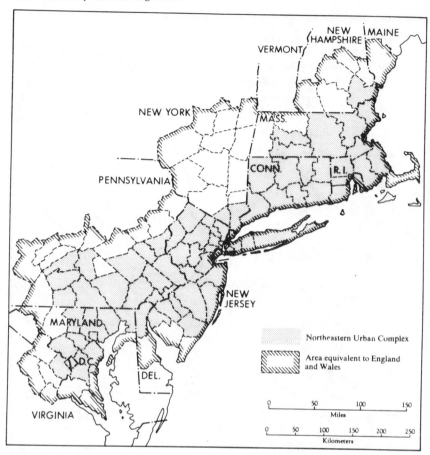

Figure 8-4. Northeastern Megalopolis. (Source: Marion Clawson and Peter Hall. *Planning and Urban Growth: An Anglo-American Comparison.* Baltimore: Resources for the Future published by the Johns Hopkins University Press, 1973, p. 65. Reproduced by permission.)

around Philadelphia now encompassed part of New Jersey too. In 1920 the population of Philadelphia was 1,823,779, and the population of Camden was 116,309. But these statistics actually understate the population of the metropolitan region. Beyond the municipal limits of Philadelphia were suburban cities whose residents made frequent trips from their home to downtown Philadelphia for shopping, business, and recreation. Nonetheless, the Philadelphia metropolitan region still had a boundary in 1920-1930 beyond which rural countryside set in.

The fourth map (Figure 8-4) displays the urbanized region of the Northeastern seaboard in 1970. In the preceding half century Philadelphia had grown in population and area, especially the latter, but so had neighboring cities. As a result, sharp boundaries between Philadelphia and other cities had disappeared. Philadelphia still existed as a municipality, but the radial expansion of Philadelphia and neighboring cities had finally interpenetrated, forming a megalopolitan corridor 500 miles long and 200 miles wide. This corridor contained crowded central cities and residential suburbs contrasting more and less densely settled places, but it contained no rural countryside. Therefore a traveler from Philadelphia to New York no longer passed through such countryside. Indeed, a traveler could proceed as far north as Providence, R.I., without ever leaving an urbanized environment.

Philadelphia's pattern of growth is not unique. This four-stage sequence also offers a general description of urban morphology in North America since 1600. Bearing in mind the controversies surrounding the number and naming of morphological stages, we may identify them as *colonial, industrial, metropolitan,* and *megalopolitan.* Each cell is a static depiction of a type. Together and in sequence, the cells present a dynamic account of how the shape of cities has changed.

This is an empirically accurate though simplified account, but it does not explain why this sequence developed rather than another. Obviously urbanization offers part of the answer as the urbanization of population implied (but did not necessitate) more cities. Population growth also contributed because, holding urbanization constant, bigger populations meant more people living in cities. For example, the United States population in 1790 was 3,930,000, of whom roughly 5 percent (202,000) were urban. By 1890, America's population was 62,947,000, and 5 percent was 3,147,350. Because of urbanization, 35 percent of Americans actually lived in cities in 1890, thus yielding a true urban population of 22,106,000. The difference between 5 percent of the 1790 population and 5 percent of the 1890 population is 2,945,350. This increase in urban population is attributable to population growth, not urbanization. The difference between 35 percent of the 1890 population and 5 percent of the 1890 population is 18,959,650. Urbanization produced this increase in urban population. Therefore, the whole change in urban population between 1790 and 1890 is actually the result of joint increases in population and urbanization.

Neither urbanization, nor population increase, nor the two in tandem are fully capable of accounting for what actually transpired. Urbanization would have been compatible with a proliferation of colonial-type cities. Instead of one big city whose population is one million, there might have emerged a network of 333 villages of 3,000 each. In either case a million people would be urban, but morphology would be different. In actuality, urbanization took the form depicted in Figures 8-1 through 8-4; growth in scale of cities, elongation of urban hierarchies, and radial expansion of big cities into surrounding territory. The problem is why this form, rather than some other, developed.

COLONIAL CITIES, 1600–1840

Colonial cities were typically coastal, few in number, small in population size, and compact in shape. In 1776 New York was the largest city in the United States, and its population was only 40,000 (Warner 1968: 14). The center of town was typically the harbor in which incoming cargoes were transferred from seagoing vessels for riverine or overland transportation to inland points, or vice versa. The commercial function of the North American city was to arrange these transfers. Merchants were in charge of this activity and supervised laborers. Cities also employed craftsmen in manufacturing, officials in government, and service professionals for law, religion, medicine, and so forth. The various groups were differentiated in terms of political power, social prestige, and wealth. Still, residential segregation of social classes was minimal (Warner 1968: 11). Rich and poor, master and worker, all city people lived in residential propinquity (Warner 1972: 82–84) and residential and commercial districts were only rudimentarily separated. In many cases, workers lived over or behind their work place. Transportation in the city depended on walking, and communication was in person. These conditions created an intense public life that all the residents of the city shared (Geruson and McGrath 1977: 80). The exceptions were shanty dwellers— unemployed workers and transients—who maintained a precarious existence on the periphery of the town.

Why did colonial cities have this shape? First, they were preindustrial and therefore depended on animate sources of energy in manufacturing and transportation. Manufacturing was the province of solitary craftsmen using muscle power and hand tools. Transportation was by sailship, canal boat, animal, or foot. These preindustrial technologies set a topside limit on the size of population that colonial cities could support. Moreover, reliance on pedestrian transportation within the city obviously precluded the radial expansion of city boundaries beyond the perimeter that a person could conveniently walk.

Population and natural environment must also be considered. Given the pre-industrial technology of production and transportation, an urban population of 202,000 in twenty-four cities set obvious limits to city formation and shape. For example, mean city size had to be 8,416 given these parameters. This is small by current standards. Nature also imposed limits: natural harbors and inland waterways were the sites of most colonial cities, whose shape and location depended on terrain, climate, and population, and could not have been much different.

Therefore the ecological view explains the morphology of colonial cities on the basis of technology, population, and natural environment. This explanation over-looks internal dynamics of class and culture and is for this reason, it is increasingly argued, correct as far as it goes but incomplete. The differences between cities of North and South America illustrate the point (Lang 1975). Cities of colonial North America were merchant capitalist settlements whose basic industry was profitable exploitation of natural resources by settlers. South American cities had their origins in feudal conquest of Indian civilizations (Weber, 1961: 61). The conquistadores occupied the continent of South America in forty years, massacred Indian populations, and employed their fortress settlements as agencies of military control of the interior. The Spanish purpose was to plunder the riches of the Indians rather than, as in North America, to bring natural resources into profitable development. Spanish conquerors also laid their cities out in conformity with Spain's Laws of the Indies, which decreed a central plaza on which faced the goverer's palace, a Roman Catholic church, and mansions of prominent families. The laws also called for broad avenues and plazas. No such laws governed the North American colonies, whose cities tended to develop meandering, narrow lanes in response to sale and purchases of land in free markets. In New England merchants were the urban elite; in New Spain warriors, priests, and plantation owners were the urban elite.

These differences between colonial cities of North and South America were profound, but they are impossible to explain on the basis of population, natural environment, or technology, which account for the otherwise numerous points of similarity between North American and South American cities. That is, cities of colonial North America were preindustrial and, as such, identical to preindustrial cities in South America. On the other hand, North American cities were predominantly capitalistic in law, social structure, and culture. Therefore, they nourished a technical and economic dynamism that overcame the limitations of preindustrial technology. Ecological variables ignore class structure and culture, and therefore do not fully explain morphological change, even though these variables are indispensable in a complete explanation.

INDUSTRIAL CITIES, 1840-1920

The Industrial Revolution accelerated urbanization in North America. More and bigger cities arose. Formerly commercial cities now added heavy manufacturing to their basic industries. They exchanged manufactured goods for raw materials, and in this manner supported vastly increased populations (Glaab and Brown 1976: 102). Whole cities devoted to manufacturing came into existence; for example, Pittsburgh and Detroit depended on the manufacture of steel in factory settings using power-driven machinery. The growth of manufacturing swelled the number of urban Americans. Factory workers obtained entitlement to a share of the agricultural surplus by exchange of their manufactured goods for food. On the other hand, the existence of manufacturing does not explain why industrial cities took the exact form they did. In principle, a proliferation of small or medium cities would have been compatible with industrial production. Indeed, in the earlier years of the Industrial Revolution, manufacturing growth did not occur in the largest, commercial cities. Instead, mill towns sprang up to serve this function. The towns of Lowell and Lynn in Massachusetts are representative examples of early manufacturing centers. Obviously the trend toward the concentration of manufacturing in small- or middle-sized cities did not continue. Instead, manufacturing after the Civil War began increasingly to leave these early centers. Gordon (1978: 49–50) argues that this massive relocation of industrial plants occurred because employers faced increased labor turbulence in the mill towns. The immigrant Irish were more strike-prone than had been the New England farm girls who constituted the original labor force in the mill towns. Employers concluded that big cities contained unemployed workers whose reserve would restrain the wage demands of the employed. Naturally, the congregation of manufacturing in the biggest cities augmented their size, and as a result, big industrial-era cities attained population sizes unheard of in the colonial period.

Industrial city manufacturing districts were in or adjacent to the city core. Around the manufacturing district arose slums to accommodate the working class. Workers walked to factory jobs and could easily change employers without changing residence. Because of the living arrangements, factories could depend on the mill whistle to rouse slumbering hands from their beds and pace them through their early morning routine into the factory on time. Unlike colonial cities, the residential slums of the industrial cities contained only workers. They were not public areas in which persons of diverse social levels freely mixed on the streets. Instead, the employers and the small but growing class of salaried workers occupied higher status apartments and single-family dwellings in more attractive neighborhoods. This was class segregation. Nonetheless, nineteenth-century industrial cities tended to include the entire population within the common municipal boundary. The city was a bounded political unit in which people of diverse social origins resided at high density.

As industrial cities grew in population, their diameters increased too. However, cities of the nineteenth century added population faster than surface area of settlement. The inevitable result was augmented population density. Population density is the number of persons per square measure. Density of settlements in industrial cities of the nineteenth century exceeded colonial standards by large margins. Teeming industrial slums consisted of closely build tenements. Sanitation and health conditions deteriorated. In the shadows of the sprawling slums, sunlight did not penetrate, and children of the working class developed rickets (Loomis 1973). The alarming growth of high-density slums became a central urban issue of nineteenth-century reformers and humanitarians (Engels 1958).

In the last decades of the nineteenth century, however, signs of change became evidence. Rich people began to move toward suburban housing on the periphery of the city, leaving behind the "gold coast" neighborhoods in which they had previously resided (Zorbaugh 1929). With the appearance of horse-drawn and then electric trolley cars, the process of residential dispersion toward the periphery accelerated (Warner 1968: 171). By the 1890s, salaried workers had begun to move away from the city's core toward lower-density communities located on the periphery. This movement accentuated the class segregation of residential neighborhoods. The working class resided in the city core at high density, the next ring contained the middle class, and in "streetcar suburbs" the wealthy resided in single-family dwellings. The trend toward radial expansion did not, however, eventuate in independent suburbs in this period. Instead, central cities expanded their political boundaries to reabsorb those who had moved to the suburbs. For example, in 1854 the Pennsylvania State Assembly voted to increase the size of Philadelphia from 2 to 129 square miles, annexing at a stroke twenty-eight bouroughs and towns (Ashton 1978: 66-67). The last major example is the annexation of Brooklyn by New York City in 1911. This annexation brought into the political jurisdiction of New York City what had been until then a thriving, independent suburban municipality.

Late in the nineteenth century, another decentralizing trend became apparent: the dispersion of manufacturing from central city districts (Weber 1904: 36-37). One sign of this trend was the formation of separately incorporated manufacturing suburbs. Thus East St. Louis, Ill., became a manufacturing suburb of St. Louis. Another symptom was the formation of one-employer factory towns such as Pullman, Ind., or Hershey, Pa. (Warner 1972: 104). In most cases, decentralization of manufacturing industry involved nonreplacement of closed plants rather than actual relocation of functioning mills. Nonetheless, the outcome was the same: a relative decline of heavy manufacturing employment in central cities. On the other hand, retail trade and office work in central cities increased their prominence.

METROPOLITAN REGIONS, 1920 TO THE PRESENT

Suburbanization of residence and industry has been the master trend in the twentieth century. Suburbs are "politically independent municipalities located outside the corporate boundaries of large central cities but within an economically interdependent metropolitan area" (Ashton 1978: 64). Heavy manufacturing plants are now preponderantly suburban. The chief residue of manufacturing industry in central cities is now light industry, such as garment factories. The trend toward suburbanization of residence has also continued, but what began as a movement of the wealthy has absorbed the middle and stable working class. Suburbs no longer contain only the rich, although their average economic level is appreciably above the central cities (Westcott 1979: 5). Reflecting relocation of metropolitan populations, shopping centers have sprung up in the suburbs to provide convenient retail and service outlets. The suburban shopping centers compete with downtown stores, and as a result, the share of downtown retail business has declined.

Kasarda's data (Tables 8-1 and 8-2) illustrate trends in city and suburban employment for the period 1947-1972. Central cities of 500,000 or less gained a few retail jobs in this period, but their suburbs gained six to ten times more jobs. Central cities of 500,000 or more actually lost retail jobs while their suburbs were gaining jobs. Loss of retail jobs also occurred in older cities (established before 1900) and in the Northeast and North Central regions. Overall, central cities lost 576,498 retail jobs and suburbs gained 3,911,739 jobs (Table 8-1). Similar patterns turned up in manufacturing: central cities lost jobs and suburbs gained them. But job loss was heaviest in big, old, central cities of the Northeast and North Central regions (Table 8-2).

The key to urban morphology in this century is still the balance between population growth and areal expansion of the city. In the nineteenth century, population expanded faster than area so density increased. In this century, areas have expanded faster than population; the inevitable result has been reduction of population density. Admittedly, central city apartment and slum districts still

Table 8-1. Changes in Retail Employment of Central Cities and Suburban Rings (adjusted for annexation), 1947-1972

Metropolitan Characteristics	Number of Cities	Change in Central City Employment	Change in Suburban Employment
Size			
Under 250,000	115	63,250	361,560
250,000-500,000	63	5,481	543,312
500,000-1 million	36	-80,100	646,596
Over 1 million	33	-565,125	2,360,424
Inception date (age)			
Before 1900	49	-757,491	2,211,419
1900-1920	63	28,287	744,219
1930-1950	53	52,142	480,922
After 1950	82	100,614	475,272
Region			
Northeast	42	-382,116	735,924
South	99	61,974	1,189,386
North Central	68	-320,824	1,196,188
West	38	64,524	790,324
Total	247	-576,498	3,911,739

Source: John D. Kasarda, "Urbanization, Community, and the Metropolitan Problem," in David Street, ed., *Handbook of Contemporary Urban Life*. (San Francisco: Jossey-Bass, 1978), p. 48. Reproduced by permission.

Table 8-2. Changes in Manufacturing Employment of Central Cities and Suburban Rings (adjusted for annexation), 1947–1972

Metropolitan Characteristics	Number of Cities	Change in Central City Employment	Change in Suburban Employment
Size			
Under 250,000	113	27,572	402,958
250,000–500,000	63	-67,977	572,922
500,000–1 million	36	-226,404	679,392
over 1 million	33	-880,077	2,522,850
Inception date (age)			
Before 1900	49	-1,370,873	2,308,096
1900–1920	63	35,469	771,246
1930–1950	53	109,074	591,586
After 1950	80	79,360	507,280
Region			
Northeast	42	-770,532	682,584
South	98	315,658	1,165,808
North Central	68	-906,236	1,431,876
West	37	214,193	897,916
Total	245	1,146,845	4,178,230

Source: John D. Kasarda, "Urbanization, Community, and the Metropolitan Problem," in David Street, ed., *Handbook of Contemporary Urban Life* (San Francisco: Jossey-Bass, 1978), p. 46. Reproduced by permission.

persist, and in these older districts density of settlement is still high, but much lower than the peaks attained in working-class slums around the turn of this century. However, expanding suburbs on the metropolitan periphery typically house their populations in single-family dwellings. Hence suburban neighborhoods are low-density settlements, and their proliferation has depressed the average density of settlement in metropolitan regions. The morphology of the New York City metropolitan region in 1965 illustrates this point (Table 8-3). On Manhattan island, the core town, density of population was still 77,200 per square mile in 1965, but within the metropolitan region of 1922 an overall density of 2,960 per square mile prevailed. With the somewhat wider 1947 definition of the metropolitan region, the overall density of population was reduced to 2,340 per square mile. According to the 1965 definition including thirty-one counties, the metropolitan region's overall density fell to 1,381. The contrasts show that population densities have become successively lower in the New York region but still remain high in the core.

As metropolitan regions expanded, Census Bureau statisticians found old-fashioned methods of measuring city size increasingly unrealistic. The old-fashioned technique was simply to list every city in a state and write against it the population residing within the city limits. This method had been adequate for dispersed colonial or early industrial cities, but it concealed the intermingling of city limits in the metropolitan period. Metropolitan regions now consisted of

Table 8-3. New York City Population Density, 1965

	Population (000)	Square Miles	Density*
Manhattan†	1,698	22	77,200
1922 definition of region	15,822	5,528	2,960
1947 definition of region (22 counties)	16,139	6,907	2,340
1965 definition of region (31 counties)	17,624	12,748	1,381

Source: New York Regional Plan Association, *The Region's Growth* (New York: NYRPA, 1967), pp. 81–82. Reproduced by permission.
  *Persons per square mile.
  †1960.

one or more large central cities surrounded by a multitude of independent, middle, and small suburbs. For example, the city of Los Angeles had a population of 3,175,800 million in 1970, but the central city was surrounded by more than forty-six suburban cities whose residents made regular trips all over the metropolitan area. The total population of the city of Los Angeles and its forty-six adjacent cities was 7,032,000 in 1970. Just listing the names and populations of California cities would give an erroneous picture of how L.A. County cities fit together in a regional whole. To take account of this problem, Census Bureau statisticians developed two concepts in 1950: *Urbanized Area* and *Standard Metropolitan Statistical Area* (SMSA). These names have since recurred in official publications and now constitute the standard methods of representing the complexity of metropolitan regions in the United States.

Urbanized Areas are the built-up, heavily populated urban and suburban territories surrounding a central city. Urbanized Areas include only urbanized territory and exclude everything else; hence Urbanized Area is a tailored measure of a metropolitan region and its population. However, the boundaries of the Urbanized Area change every ten years in response to changing population, so the concept has been unwieldy for trend comparisons that require intercensal data. The SMSA meets this need (at the cost of exactitude) and has, for this reason, become the more popular measure of metropolitan regions. SMSAs consist of a central city or twin cities of 50,000 or more population *plus* the surrounding "socially and economically integrated" countries (U.S. Census 1978: xvii–xxiii). If any portion of the county is socially and economically integrated with the central city, the whole county is included in the SMSA. As a result, SMSAs include within their boundaries whole areas of desert, farms, or orchards. This inclusion is an obvious inexactitude. Figure 8-5 shows SMSAs in 1974. The most extreme distortion is Washoe County, Nev., the SMSA for Reno. This immense rectangle is mostly desert, but the occupation of a northern corner by Reno, a city of 50,000 or more, compels the U.S. Census to declare the desert

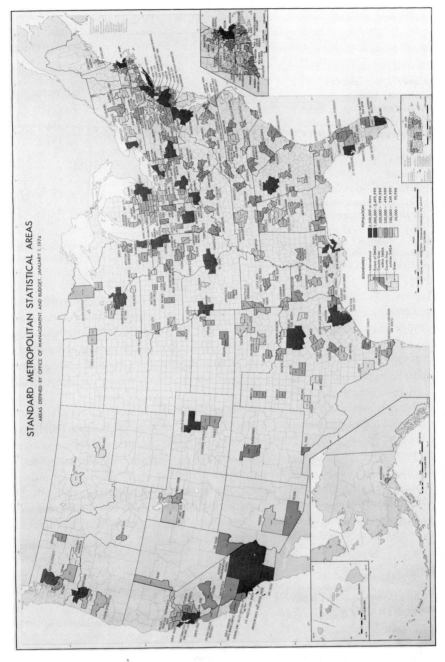

Figure 8-5. U.S. Standard Metropolitan Statistical Areas in 1974. (Source: U.S. Bureau of Census.)

Table 8-4. Number, Population, and Area of Standard Metropolitan Statistical Areas and of Urbanized Areas, in the United States, 1950 and 1970

	1950	1970	Percentage Change (1970/1950)
Standard Metropolitan Statistical Areas			
Number	168	243	145
Total population (millions)	89.2	139.4	156
Total area (square miles)	207,583	387,616	187
Persons per square mile	429.7	359.6	84
Urbanized Areas			
Number	157	248	158
Total population (millions)	69.2	118.4	171
Total area (square miles)	12,805	35,081	274
Persons per square mile	5406.3	3373.2	62

Source: Marion Clawson and Peter Hall, *Planning and Urban Growth: An Anglo-American Comparison* (Baltimore: Resources for the Future published by the Johns Hopkins University Press, 1973), p. 12. Reproduced by permission.

county a "metropolitan" area. Despite the inexactitude, the SMSA has become the preferred measure of metropolitan regions because county boundaries do not change from one census to another and it does not exclude population and organizations that regularly participate in the urban system merely because they are not located in the built-up area. This fixity permits intercensal comparisons, and researchers have on balance preferred the baseline safety of the SMSA to the accuracy of the urbanized area.

The two methods yield different but similar estimates of urban size. Table 8-4 compares SMSAs and Urbanized Areas in respect to population and areal change between 1950 and 1970. The SMSA definition gives the total big city population in 1970 as 139.4 million and the area as 378,616 square miles. These estimates are much bigger than the Urbanized Area definition for 1970. The difference is especially large in areal measurement: the Urbanized Area is less than a tenth the SMSA. However, both measures show that between 1950 and 1970 total area increased more rapidly than total population. The inevitable result was decreasing urban density, and both measures record that decline.

ECOLOGICAL ANALYSIS OF METROPOLITAN DECENTRALIZATION

The master trend of nineteenth-century urbanism was centripetal; the master trend of twentieth-century urbanism is centrifugal. What caused this reversal of master trend? Urban ecologists have emphasized changes in transportation technology at the local, regional, and international level (Hawley 1978: 4; McKenzie 1933: 173). In this view, the nineteenth century was a period of technological imbalances: long-distance transportation was already industrial whereas local transportation was still preindustrial. The industrial technology of long-distance transport depended on the steam engine. Railroads and steamboats were technological advances that shaped the nineteenth century. Reductions in shipping costs and increased rapidity of service expanded international markets. Products made in London or New York could be economically shipped to Australia and vice versa so people on one continent were able routinely to consume goods produced on another. The expansion of international markets permitted economies of scale in manufacturing, capital-intensive production, and international specialization. Since heavy industry promoted the growth of large cities, steam transportation was a prerequisite to industrial urbanization.

On the other hand, local transportation did not equivalently improve in the nineteenth century. People mainly walked. As the populations of these cities grew in response to industrialization, cities expanded their surface area but bumped against limits to radial expansion imposed by dependence on pedestrian transportation. Cities could grow no wider than a person could walk in an hour's time: about 3 miles. Therefore nineteenth-century cities could not expand their boundaries much beyond the three-mile radius. This radius opened for settlement a maximum of 28.5 square miles. This narrow compass did not permit radial expansion to keep pace with rapid population growth. Hence residential densities unavoidably increased during the nineteenth century.

The other side of this persuasive argument is the reduction of population density in twentieth-century cities in response to improvements in local transportation (Duncan 1974: 193–194). Transportation improvements really began in the nineteenth century, the first big one being the horse-drawn trolley in the 1840s. It permitted riders to travel twelve miles an hour, thus extending the radius of settlement beyond the three-mile pedestrian limit. In the 1880s, electric trolley cars appeared. The New York City subway system was completed in 1904. Trolley cars and subways permitted riders to travel twenty-five miles in an hour's commutation. Thus the transportation technology of the twentieth century extended yet further the radius of settlement already extended by horse-drawn trolley. In this manner, fixed rail transportation opened 1,935 square miles of suburban territory beyond the 28.5 square miles of pedestrian core. However, the cost of commutation and single-family housing necessarily restricted suburban access to the wealthier classes who could afford the expenditures. Therefore trolley service could only reduce, not reverse, the centripetal trend toward high-density cities that early industrialization set in motion.

Turn-of-the-century systems moved passengers as rapidly as any contemporary ground transportation, but trolley or subway service depended on fixed rails with stations at regular intervals. Passengers had first to reach the station in order to board the train. Getting to the station still depended on pedestrian transportation. This requirement restricted suburban settlement to a corridor running alongside the track. The corridor could not be wide because total transportation time now included the foot journey from home to the station. This journey had to be conducted at three mph even if the remainder proceeded at twenty-five. Settlement of fixed-rail corridors in the late nineteenth century created the star-shaped city in which corridors formed around transportation lines. This star-shape was the characteristic form of big cities at the turn of this century (Mallach 1979: 13). Smaller cities lacked public transportation and were therefore immune to the formation of suburban corridors along fixed-rail corridors.

The passenger automobile was the next technological innovation to reshape urban morphology. In the United States, passenger automobiles came into mass production in 1915. Their population has continuously increased since then at a rate much higher than that of the human population (Table 8-5). Passenger automobiles permitted urbanites to build a single-family home in suburban areas outside the trolley corridor. As more and more families did so, unsettled territory near the city gradually filled with population. Settlement of interstitial areas first reduced, then eliminated the density contrast between transportation corridors and other suburban localities. Big cities thus lost their distinct star shapes. Instead, twentieth-century cities sprawled across the landscape in an amorphous, low-density blob. When the blob expanded, new areas acquired low suburban densities. However, the boundary between metropolitan suburbia and rural countryside blurred and was replaced by the rural-urban fringe of noncity, nonrural land use.

Motor trucks were a technological innovation too. They came into general industrial use around 1920, and their vehicular population has increased much

Table 8-5. Motor Vehicle Registrations and Motor Fuel Usage, 1900–1970.

| | Motor Vehicle Registrations (000) | | Motor Fuel Usage (million gallons) |
	Automobiles	Trucks	
1970	89,279	18,748	96,331
1960	61,682	11,914	63,210
1950	40,339	8,598	39,830
1940	27,465	4,886	24,038
1930	23,034	3,674	15,777
1920	8,131	1,107	3,448
1910	458	10	
1900	8		

Source: U.S. Bureau of the Census, *Historical Statistics of the United States, Colonial Times to 1970, Bicentennial Edition* (Washington, D.C.: U.S. Government Printing Office, 1975), Part II, p. 716.

faster than the human population. Trucking proved an alternative to railroad transportation of bulk goods that had some economic advantages. (But see Snell 1974: 39–40; Sloan 1963: 398–413). It reduced the repetitive loading, unloading, and reloading of cargoes that rail transport required. Trucks were simply loaded at their point of origin and unloaded at their destination. Trucking also eliminated dependence on railroad terminals or sidings in plant site selection. Manufacturers could locate wherever land was cheapest, rather than in densely settled industrial districts where plant space was at a premium (Weber 1904: 40). Table 8-6 illustrates the reduction in railroad sidings in plants located in the New York metropolitan area. Prior to 1920, when manufacturers relied on railroad transport, 63 percent of plants in the region were connected to railroad lines by sidings. As truck transportation became competitive, plant sidings declined. Suburban manufacturing plants relied on trucks to haul raw materials and finished products. Suburban plants also escaped the traffic congestion of downtown areas, thus avoiding expensive delays in delivery.

Trucking accelerated manufacturing decentralization but obviously did not singly cause it because the decentralization had already begun two decades before motor trucks became carriers. Other technological and economic considerations made suburban plant location attractive even without the convenience of truck transportation. One such consideration was cheap labor (Gordon 1978: 49–50). In the early period of manufacturing decentralization, relocating plants were moving from core zones where labor was dear to ring zones where labor was cheap (Table 8-7). This situation had been reversed by 1954, when central city labor had become cheaper than suburban labor. Another factor was rural electrification, which made power for machinery as available in suburbs as in city cores. These considerations antedated motorized trucking and independently encouraged relocation of manufacturing plants in metropolitan suburbs. Nonetheless, the process could not have gone forward so rapidly nor so extensively had not motor trucks extended the tether that had hitched manufacturing plants to core locations.

In summary, the joint effect of passenger automobiles and motor trucks was to accelerate prior trends toward suburbanization of population and manufactur-

Table 8-6. Percentage of Plant Sites Having Railroad Sidings, New York Metropolitan Region, 1956

Year Site Aquired	Entire Region	New Jersey Counties	Rest of Region
Before 1920	63	71	50
1920–1945	50	59	39
1946–1956	40	42	36

Source: Edgar M. Hoover and Raymond Vernon, *Anatomy of a Metropolis* (Cambridge: Harvard University Press, 1959), p. 37. Reprinted by permission.

Table 8-7. Average Annual Earnings of Manufacturing Production Workers in Zones of New York Metropolitan Region as Percentage of Wages in Manhattan, Selected Years, 1899–1954 (Manhattan = 100)

	1899	1929	1954
Core (except Manhattan)	93	88	105
Inner ring	89	83	121
Outer ring	84	78	117

Source: Edgar M. Hoover and Raymond Vernon, *Anatomy of a Metropolis* (Cambridge: Harvard University Press, 1959), p. 45. Reprinted by permission.

ing (McKenzie 1933: 69-71). Growing suburbs surrounded the city core, a heritage of the nineteenth century, and were reached by road transport, a twentieth-century innovation. In response to this adjustment of population, retail trade also withdrew from central city stores and settled in suburbs, notably in shopping centers surrounded by parking lots. Some suburbs were strictly residential, others emphasized manufacturing, still others were commercial. In most cases, North American suburbs contained mixtures of retail trade, manufacturing, and residences. Mixed uses are to some extent incompatible because retail business attracts traffic to quiet residential streets and heavy manufacturing plants are noisy and blight-inducing. On the other hand, retail shopping centers and manufacturing plants pay property taxes but require few city services. Therefore suburban cities typically want to attract business in order to reduce the tax burden on home owners. For this reason, only affluent suburbs entirely exclude retail business or manufacturing plants because only these suburbs have home owners wealthy enough to pay the high taxes that exclusion of business imposes.

THE POLITICAL ECONOMY OF SUBURBANIZATION

Suburbanization is the master trend of twentieth-century cities in North America. The orthodox explanation of this trend has long emphasized transportation technology in the manner sketched above (Ogburn 1937: 51). However, transportation orthodoxy has encountered increasing skepticism. No one doubts that transportation technology did have the suburbanizing impact claimed; hence the transportation argument is correct as far as it goes (Ashton 1978: 71). But critics observe that the technological argument overlooks political, ideological, ethnic, and class influences that were of at least equal importance in suburbanization. Moreover, technology itself is only an aspect of political economy to which one must look for a complete explanation of suburbanization (Gordon

1978: 26). The momentum of this critical wave is still building, and ambiguities remain, but the revisionist critique has already compelled such far-reaching reappraisal that transportation technology alone no longer is a complete, convincing, or up-to-date explanation of North American suburbanization in the twentieth century.

One issue addresses the type of competition between passenger automobile and public transportation on the one hand, and motor truck and railroad on the other. The existence and outcome of this competition is unambiguous. Passenger automobiles provided a private alternative to public transportation on motor buses, suburban railroads, trolley lines, or subways. Passenger mileage aboard public transportation increased until 1950, its peak year (Table 8-8). Since then, passenger mileage on board public transportation has continuously declined, despite the growth in population of metropolitan areas whose inhabitants are the principal users of public transportation. The absolute decline in passenger mileage aboard public transportation contrasts with the continuous increase in number and fuel use of private passenger automobiles (Table 8-5). Obviously the two trends are related in that the public's acquisition of passenger automobiles reduced ridership on all forms of public transportation. Moreover, as the balance tipped against public transportation and ridership declined, transit lines reduced service and raised fares in response. Then more people decided to buy private automobiles, thus initiating another round of deterioration of public transportation. In many U.S. cities today, public transportation is so dirty, unsafe, expensive, and unreliable that only the poor, the handicapped, the aged, or juveniles now ride it. In the middle of the 1970s, 80 percent of journeys to work in U.S. cities were aboard private automobiles, and 84 percent of automobiles carried only the driver. Conversely, 20 percent of the journeys to work were aboard public transporation. However, the proportion aboard public transportation varied widely from city to city. The leader in American public transportation is New York City, where 67 percent of journeys to work were by subway or bus.

Table 8-8. Revenue and Nonrevenue Passengers on Public Transportation by Type for the United States, 1922–1970 (millions of passengers)

	Railroad	Trolley Coach	Motor Bus	Total
1970	2,116	182	5,034	7,332
1960	2,313	657	6,425	9,395
1950	6,168	1,658	9,420	17,246
1940	8,325	534	4,239	13,098
1930	13,072	16	2,479	15,567
1922	15,331		404	15,735

Source: U.S. Bureau of the Census, *Historical Statistics of the United States, Colonial Times to 1970, Bicentennial Edition* (Washington, D.C.: U.S. Government Printing Office, 1975), Part II, p. 721.

Trucks and railroads have engaged in competition for freight business. It is true that ton-miles of total haulage increase in response to population increases, and thus created more business for railroads and trucking companies to share. However, the trucking industry has increased much faster than ton-mileage and in so doing has tended to take up business that would otherwise have accrued to the railroads. This decline has threatened the solvency of American railroads [2]. In 1972, the Penn Central line went bankrupt because of chronic losses. The formation of Amtrak in 1975 likewise represented the federal merger and subsidy of bankrupt railroads.

Competition among alternative modes of transportation is neither improper, avoidable, nor undesirable, but there is evidence that the business competition exceeded the strictly technological. One issue is clandestine sabotage of public transportation in major American cities by motor vehicle interests in the period 1929–1956. Testimony before the U.S. Senate Committee of the Judiciary (Snell 1974) revealed that General Motors Corporation, Firestone Tire Company, Standard Oil of California, and other large business interests formed the National City Lines (NCL), a holding company, in 1930 to acquire shares in municipal trolley lines in major American cities. National City Lines compelled electric trolley managements to switch to diesel-powered buses, thus enriching the conspirators. In 1949 a federal jury in Chicago convicted Firestone Tire, General Motors, and Standard Oil of California of criminal conspiracy to acquire, motorize, and resell electric streetcar lines. However, the conspirators had already been involved in replacement of electric transit systems with GM buses in forty-five cities including New York, Philadelphia, Baltimore, St. Louis, Oakland, Salt Lake City, and Los Angeles.

The destruction of public transporation in Los Angeles illustrates the conspirators' *modus operandi.* In 1938, General Motors and Standard Oil organized Pacific City Lines, an NCL affiliate, to acquire, motorize, and resell electric railroads in California. In Los Angeles, Pacific City Lines acquired control of the Pacific Electric Railway, worlds's largest trolley system serving fifty-six cities and eight million passengers yearly. Pacific City Lines replaced trolley service with diesel buses and pulled up the railroad tracks. Loss of tracked right-of-ways compelled buses to compete on equal terms with private automobiles, so buses proved less effective in heavy traffic than trollies (Snell 1974: 38). Therefore dieselization reduced the attractiveness of mass transit, set in motion the spiral of destruction, and reduced the people of Los Angeles County to dependence upon private automobiles and freeways.

Snell claimed that actions of the conspirators constituted monopolistic "restraint of trade" under the Sherman Anti-Trust Act. However, the legal issue is not critical here (Mintz 1974). What is significant is mobilization of economic power to sabotage competitors, thus profoundly influencing metropolitan transportation arrangements and therewith suburbanization. Obviously, this conspiratorial intervention tended to tilt the balance in favor of automobiles. Therefore the outcome of the competition between trollies and cars reflected the collusion of vested interests as well as any purely technological advantages of automotive transport.

The Highway Lobby

Another place in which vested interests have tilted the balance in favor of automotive transport is federal and state highway construction. Highway construction has been an indispensable prerequisite of suburbanization in this century. Automobiles and trucks are worthless without roads on which to drive them, and vehicle utility to an owner increases in direct proportion to highway mileage and condition (Mallach 1979: 8). In the same sense, automobile-dependent suburbs require highway service without which residents must stay within the densely settled transporation corridors obtruding from the center city. Governments build highways. The more highways governments build, the greater the public encouragement of private trucks and automobiles. Table 8-9 details the cumulative mileage and cost of federally aided highway transport between 1923 and 1970. The statistics show the big increase in costs after the Federal Highway Act of 1956 and the increasing proportion of total cost carried by the federal treasury.

An alliance of special interests (now aptly called the "highway lobby") has been for more than half a century the organizer of political campaigns to expand state and federal highway construction [3]. Such political intervention is not new. Nineteenth-century business interests combined to obtain public subsidies for canal building and railroad rights-of-way [4]. In this sense, political intervention on behalf of one's transportation special interest is as American as apple pie. Moreover, the practice is, in principle, entirely defensible because government has the authority and arguably the duty to intervene in the economy to benefit the public. Nonetheless, government intervention in transportation unavoidably politicizes purely "technological" issues. Because politics are involved, transportation outcomes are not simply reflections of technological imperatives but also reflections of the political influence of their backers.

The highway lobby consists of giant automobile and truck manufacturing firms, construction industries, oil companies, construction and trucking labor unions, officials of the federal and state highway departments, the American Automobile Association, and financial institutions. Each of these has a pecuniary interest in road building and supports the political agitation for highway construction in order to increase its earnings. Manufacturing firms want highways built to stimulate truck and automobile purchases. Oil companies want gasoline-buying customers. Unions want jobs for their members. Highway officials want big budgets and corresponding salaries. The Automobile Association wants dues-paying members, and savings institutions want to sell mortgages to automobile-owning home owners. The support of highway construction by this panoply of special interests does not prove that road construction was not also in the public interest; and there is at least the presumption, widely shared, that the consuming public went along with highway construction because it was passively in favor (Clawson and Hall 1973: 267). On the other hand, the political intervention of special interests on behalf of highway construction has been too continuous and transparent to permit the naïve conclusion that only selfless concern for the public interest motivated it.

Government Housing Policy

Federal and state housing policy has been a second source of public subsidies for suburbanization since 1940 (Friedland 1981: Ch. 1). This intervention in the marketplace has taken five principal forms. First, federal and state governments exempt home mortgage interest from income taxation. This exemption costs governments billions of dollars in lost tax revenue every year. The tax exemption reduces the costs of home ownership and thus encourages economically marginal people to buy single-family homes in suburbs. This tax exemption is not universal. For example, Canada does not exempt home mortgage payments from income taxation, and in Britain, the rental value of an owner-occupied home is fully taxable as income (Clawson and Hall 1973: 15).

Another federal and state subsidy of suburbanization is the home finance industry (Table 15-6). Regulations permit savings and loan associations to pay more savings interest than banks but restrict the investments of these associations to home mortgages. This government policy channels money into the home mortgage market, thereby augmenting mortgage accessibility to home

Table 8-9. Mileage and Cost of Federal Aid Highway Systems, 1923-1970

	Cumulative Federal Mileage	Cost Total ($ millions)	Percent Federal
1970	895,208	4,625	76.0
1960	866,841	3,264	69.6
1950	643,939	753	51.8
1940	235,482	269	55.8
1930	193,652	237	42.2
1923	169,007	130	43.8

Source: U.S. Bureau of the Census, *Historical Statistics of the United States, Colonial Times to 1970, Bicentennial Edition* (Washington, D.C.: U.S. Government Printing Office, 1975), Part II, p. 711.

buyers. The Federal Housing Authority and the Veterans Administration also underwrite mortgages for qualified families (Stone 1978: 185, 197). These federally underwritten mortgages amounted to one-third of the total mortgage debt in the middle of the 1970s. Federal underwriting makes suburban mortgages accessible to families who would not otherwise be able to secure a home mortgage (Harvey 1977: 125–126). Finally, the Federal National Mortgage Administration buys mortgages. In 1970 this federal agency held 6 percent of outstanding nonfarm residential mortgages. Were all these political interventions cancelled, the price of home mortgages on the free market would rise, and fewer people would be able to buy single-family dwellings. The upshot of cancellation over a generation would have been less suburbanization.

The highway lobby has been the most vigorous champion of federal and state support of home ownership (Ashton 1978: 72). Home ownership, automobile ownership, and road construction are mutually reinforcing constituents of suburbanization such that augmentation of any one increases the other two. Thus when home ownership is encouraged, new home owners in suburbia need automobiles and roads on which to drive them (Clawson and Hall 1973: 22). Conversely, when roads are built, car ownership is encouraged and car-owning households can build single-family homes in hitherto inaccessible locations within a metropolitan region. Understanding this relationship, the highway lobby's separate constituents have thrown their political weight behind federal intervention in the mortgage market to create the demand that would subsequently enrich them.

It would be a distortion to suppose that only the power of the highway lobby created the political impetus for federal and state support of home ownership. From the very beginning of the automobile age (1895–1910) it was already clear that Americans liked automobiles and desired to own them, even at great expense, for reasons of social prestige as well as utility. Second, there is no doubt that most Americans wanted to live in suburban homes and welcomed whatever public policies that made this life-style more accessible to them (Berry and Gillard 1977: 8). This preference reflects a widely shared social value with roots in the American past. In the twentieth century, a declining proportion of Americans have been able to live in the open countryside engaging in agriculture. However, automobile transportation did make it possible for nonagricultural workers to live in single-family dwellings surrounded by a plot of land. At its best the suburb offered a compromise within the city: a semirustic home environment and access to nonagricultural work. This option was expensive but Americans have been willing to pay the price because they regarded this car- and home-owning life-style as an ultimate good for which other sacrifices were acceptable. Therefore Americans did not resist federal and state interventions to promote home ownership; indeed, most supported these interventions at the polls even though the actual work of lining up legislators and mobilizing political power was left to the highway lobby.

Third, the timing of road construction tends also to suggest that government spending was responding to public pressure rather than encouraging automobiles. In the period 1923-1940, vehicle registrations increased 215 percent, but federal highway mileage increased only 139 percent (Table 8-10). Only after 1940 did the growth of highway mileage exceed the growth of vehicle registration, but this reversal may be interpreted as catching up with public demand for roads. Over the whole period 1923-1970 vehicle registrations increased faster than federal road building, so highways were more crowded in 1970 then they had been in 1923.

Fourth, public transportation was a mess in 1900. The streetcar entrepreneurs were public figures with unsavory reputations. "As often as not" they bribed legislators to obtain franchises, sold watered stock to the public, and robbed the tills of the street railroads they managed (Mallach 1979: 1-3). For many railroad builders, the main business was buying real estate cheaply in unserved localities, then reselling the land at huge profits once the street railroad franchise had been obtained and the first track laid. Providing good streetcar service was a secondary concern. Users complained that street railroads were overcrowded, unheated, dangerous, inconveniently routed, expensive, and uncomfortable. A combination of rider dissatisfaction and mismanagement was causing street railroad bankruptcies long before the automobile's competition became a contributor. In the years 1909-1915, 114 railroad companies went broke while many others were forced to consolidate (Mallach 1979: 5). When automobile transportation became a realistic possibility, America's urban residents were ready to buy cars to avoid public transportation they already had reason to dislike. The intervention of federal, state, and local governments on behalf of the private automobile was one response to long-standing rider discontent.

Finally, the intellectual heritage of the nineteenth century emphasized the social evils resulting from high-density living in rented dwellings. Revulsion against the industrial slum led many nineteenth- and turn-of-the-century reformers to emphasize the debilitating consequences of living in a slum. For example, Danish reformer Jacob Riis (1892, 1902) wrote books denouncing slums and claiming that numerous social evils (drunkenness, crime, prostitution, child abuse) arose because people lived in filthy, overcrowded slums. Urban

Table 8-10. Percentage Increase in Vehicle Registration and Federal Highway Mileage, 1923-1970

	Percentage Increase		
	1940/1923	1970/1940	1970/1923
Federal highway mileage	139	380	530
Vehicle registrations	215	334	718

Source: U.S. Bureau of the Census, *Historical Statistics of the United States, Colonial Times to 1970, Bicentennial Edition* (Washington, D.C.: U.S. Government Printing Office, 1975), Part II, pp. 711, 716.

visionary Ebeneezer Howard (1902) conjured up images of "garden cities of tomorrow" in which people lived in small cottages surrounded by greenery and healthful outdoor recreation. The best-informed opinion of this transitional period believed that high-density living should and could be replaced by single-family dwellings in rural or semirural environments in order to maximize happiness and eliminate the environmentally induced depravity and degradation of industrial slums. Thus Adna Weber (1904: 41) pointed out that even the largest cities in America could "now be made as healthful as the country, because cheap rapid transit [not automobiles!] enables city workers to live many miles away from their work places." This line of thought tended to justify government intervention on behalf of home ownership in suburbs. Indeed, public officials who encouraged suburbanization did so for the most part in the sincere belief that government intervention was creating a better environment for human development and was, therefore, in the public interest.

Marxist interpretation (Gordon 1978: 49-50) has emphasized the big-volume employer's financial interest in a conservative, stable working class. It is true that this employer interest existed. Confronting labor unrest and socialistic agitation in central cities, employers concluded workers would be less strike-prone in a semirural environment where they owned their own home. Home ownership conferred a stake in the property system as well as the obligations of meeting regular mortgage payments, a deterrent to striking. Exactly these considerations encouraged corporations to establish suburban company towns in Pullman, Ill.; Hershey, Pa.; Gary, Ind.; and elsewhere. Taken alone, this critique implies that suburbanization was an employer plot to pacify the rebellious working class. That view is too simple. Admittedly, employers consulted their own interests, but they also regarded suburbanization as a noble ideal. This ideal they shared with the best informed minds of their time. Even radicals like Henry George (1883: 316) decried the "unhealthiness" of urban congestion and looked forward to a utopian future in which each family should have "its healthful house, set in its garden." The origin of this ideal and its congruence with class relationships and the means of production is a complex and still unresolved issue. What is crucial here is only the acknowledgment of the web of technology, social scientific ideas, visionary idealism, and greed that seconded political intervention on behalf of home ownership in suburbs.

The Continuing Capitalist Crisis

Road building and mortgage market support were public activities directly benefiting the business and labor interests represented in the highway lobby. However, these federal interventions in the economy also supported employment, investment, and commerce in general, and in this manner stimulated the economy. The specific origins of these interventionist measures are President Franklin D. Roosevelt's New Deal. Their New Deal purpose was to stimulate aggregate demand and thus help pull the nation out of the Great Depression (Clawson and Hall 1973: 15). Federal and state administrations since Roosevelt have continued his policy of road building and mortgage support to keep down unemployment and stimulate business (Ashton 1978: 71-74; Harvey 1977: 125-126, 133, 137). In this sense, therefore, federal intervention to promote suburbanization was a response to the crisis of capitalism in the Great Depression and it has been continued since then in order to prevent a recurrence of that crisis. Admittedly, other measures would have served this countercyclical purpose. For example, the federal government might have stimulated employment by building public housing rather than by encouraging single-family homes in suburban tracts (Stone 1978: 185). Hence the crisis of capitalism is not a sufficient explanation for why the federal government chose to encourage suburbanization. Additionally, the trend toward suburbanization was already visible in 1890—almost a half century before the Great Depression; the crisis of capitalism in the 1930s cannot be assigned responsibility for this earlier trend. Nevertheless the crisis of American capitalism provided the economic context within which the march toward suburbanization accelerated since 1933. In that sense, the economic crisis compelled political intervention that accelerated suburbanization (O'Connor: Ch. 5).

SUMMARY

Urban morphology is the physical structure of cities. In the nineteenth century American cities were compact and densely settled. The prevailing trend in the twentieth century has been the formation of metropolitan regions. This process has gone forward because of deconcentration of industry, retail trade, and residence formerly located in the city core. The three-sided movement has created the typical structure of American cities today: a densely settled central city surrounded by low-density residential, industrial, or mixed suburbs. Transportation technology has been a determinant of urban morphology since the nineteenth century, when local transport was preindustrial and long-haul transport was industrial. This imbalance necessitated concentration of growing population in densely settled core cities. Truck and automobile transportation have revolutionized local transport in the twentieth century. As a result of these new technologies, industries and residences are able to locate in suburban rings rather than in densely settled urban cores.

Yet transportation technology has never been the only determinant of urban morphology in the United States. The political and economic power of the highway lobby has been a powerful, nontechnological influence favoring suburbanization. The historic values of the American people also encouraged relocation in semirural suburban environments. Recoiling from densely packed nineteenth-century slums, scientific thought and visionary idealism also advanced the desirability of single-family dwellings in low-density suburbs. The mercenary interest of private employers seconded these considerations. In the 1930s the world crisis of capitalism compelled the federal government to seek ways of creating employment. Suburbanization was adopted as one countercyclical technique, and this adoption accelerated suburbanization. Since the New Deal, massive state and federal intervention in road construction and mortgage finance has subsidized and encouraged suburbanization. In all, these values plus ideological, economic, and political influences were at least as important as transportation technology in producing suburbanization.

NOTES

1. This is a general problem of sociology. See the methodological debate between Robert Nisbet and Gerhard Lenski. Robert A. Nisbet, *Social Change and History.* New York: Oxford, 1969, especially parts II and III. For a functionalist rebuttal, see Gerhard Lenski, "History and Social Change," *American Journal of Sociology* 82 (1976): 548-564.
2. Heavy trucks cause more road damage than they pay for in highway user taxes. The California Department of Transportation estimates that trucks cause 99 percent of pavement damage on highways. The worst offenders are the 80,000-pound behemoths that Congress permitted to use interstate highways in the wake of the gasoline shortage of 1974. The United States Department of Transportation estimates that maintenance of the nation's existing interstate highway system will cost $104 billion between 1980 and 2000—as much as the system cost to construct. Deterioration of highways has been much more rapid than anticipated and heavy trucks are apparently to blame. The deteriorated road system is an unpaid bill—amounting to a subsidy by taxpayers—that has tilted the balance of freight haulage in favor of trucks and away from railroads. See Fred W. Frailey, "America's Highways: Going to Pot," *U.S. News and World Report,* July 24, 1978, pp. 36-38; Robert Sherrill, "Raising Hell on the Highways," *The New York Times Magazine,* Nov. 27, 1977, p. 95.
3. The highway lobby is an informal coalition, not a membership group. The coalition forms and reforms behind variegated and often ephemeral organizations. For example, the Automobility Foundation is a tax-exempt trust whose purpose is to educate the American public about the social desirability of automobiles. Most of those making tax-deductible contributions are members of the National Automobile Dealers Association. See *Los Angeles Times,* February 22, 1981, pt. V, p. 5. Similarly, in the Los Angeles County election

of November 4, 1980, the Southern California Transportation Action Committee submitted ballot arguments against mass transit. This ad hoc body had formed just before the election to coordinate the antitransit campaign, and the contributors represented a cross-section of vested industrial interests with a stake in highways, automobiles, and suburbs.

4. For a muckraking novelist's account of corruption in the turn-of-the-century street railroad industry, see Theodore Dreiser, *The Financier*, rev. ed. New York: Boni and Liveright, 1927.

REFERENCES

Ashton, Patrick J. 1978. "The Political Economy of Suburban Development," pp. 64–89, in William Tabb and Larry Sawers, eds. *Marxism and the Metropolis.* New York: Oxford University Press.

Berry, Brian J. L., and Quentin Gillard. 1977. *The Changing Shape of Metropolitan America.* Cambridge Mass.: Ballinger, 1977.

Blair, Thomas L. 1974. *The International Urban Crisis.* London: Hart-Davis, MacGibbon.

Castells, Manuel. 1977. "Towards a Political Urban Sociology," pp. 60–78 in Michael Harloe, ed. *Captive Cities.* London: Wiley.

Clawson, Marion, and Peter Hall. 1973. *Planning and Urban Growth: An Anglo-American Comparison.* Baltimore: Johns Hopkins University Press.

Duncan, Otis Dudley. 1974 [1957]. "Population Structure and Community Structure," pp. 190–216 in Charles Tilly, ed. *An Urban World.* Boston: Little, Brown.

Engels, Friedrich. 1958 [1844]. *The Condition of the Working Class in England.* Trans. and ed. W. O. Henderson and W. H. Chaloner. Oxford: Basil Blackwell.

Friedland, Roger. 1981. *Power and Crisis in the Central City.* London: Macmillan.

George, Henry. 1883. *Social Problems.* Chicago: Belford, Clarke & Co.

Geruson, Richard T., and Dennis McGrath. 1977. *Cities and Urbanization.* New York: Praeger.

Glaab, Charles N., and A. Theodore Brown. 1976. *A History of Urban America,* 2nd ed. New York: Macmillan.

Gordon, David M. 1978. "Capitalist Development and the History of American Cities," pp. 25–63, in William Tabb and Larry Sawers, eds. *Marxism and the Metropolis.* New York: Oxford University Press.

Harvey, David. 1977. "Government Policies, Financial Institutions, and Neighborhood Change in United States Cities," pp. 123–139, in Michael Harloe, ed. *Captive Cities.* London: John Wiley.

Hawley, Amos H. 1978. "Urbanization as Process," pp. 3–26, in David Street, ed. *Handbook of Contemporary Urban Life.* San Francisco: Jossey-Bass.

——. 1981. *Urban Society,* 2d Ed. New York: John Wiley.

Howard, Ebeneezer. 1902. *Garden Cities of Tomorrow.* London: S. Sonnenschein.

Kasarda, John D. 1978. "Industry, Community, and the Metropolitan Problem," pp. 27–57, in David Street, ed., *Handbook of Contemporary Urban Life*. San Francisco: Jossey-Bass.

Lang, James. 1975. *Conquest and Commerce: Spain and England in the Americas*. New York: Academic Press.

Loomis, W. F. 1973. "Rickets," pp. 113–122 in Kingsley Davis, ed. *Cities: Their Origin and Human Impact*. San Francisco: W. H. Freeman.

McKelvey, Blake. 1963. *The Urbanization of America, 1860–1915*. New Brunswick N.J.: Rutgers University Press.

——. 1968. *The Emergence of Metropolitan America, 1915–1966*. New Brunswick, N.J.: Rutgers University Press.

McKenzie, R. D. 1933. *The Metropolitan Community*. New York: McGraw-Hill.

Mallach, Stanley. 1979. "The Origins of the Decline of Urban Mass Transportation in the United States, 1890–1930." *Urbanism Past and Present* 8: 1–17.

Mintz, Morton. 1974. "GM, Ford Units Criticized on WWII Role." *Washington Post* (February 27): pt. A, 4.

O'Connor, James. 1973. *The Fiscal Crisis of the State*. (New York: St. Martin's Press).

Ogburn, William F. 1937. *Social Characteristics of Cities*. Chicago: International City Managers' Association.

Riis, Jacob. 1902. *The Battle with the Slum*. New York: Macmillan.

——. 1892. *How the Other Half Lives*. New York: Scribner's.

Sloan, Alfred P. 1963. *My Years with General Motors*. Garden City, N.Y.: Doubleday.

Snell, Bradford C. 1974. "American Ground Transport," U.S. Congress, Senate 93rd Congress 2nd Sess., Committee on the Judiciary, Subcommittee on Antitrust and Monopoly. Committee Print. Washington, D.C.: U.S. Government Printing Office.

Sternleib, George and James W. Hughes. 1980. "The Changing Demography of the Central City." *Scientific American* 243: 48–53.

Stone, Michael E. 1978. "Housing, Mortgage Lending and the Contradictions of Capitalism," pp. 179–207, in William Tabb and Larry Sawers, eds. *Marxism and the Metropolis*. New York: Oxford University Press.

U.S. Bureau of the Census. 1978. *County and City Data Book, 1977*. Washington, D.C.: U.S. Government Printing Office.

Warner, Sam Bass, Jr. 1968. *The Private City*. Philadelphia: University of Pennsylvania Press.

——. 1972. The Urban Wilderness. New York: Harper & Row.

Weber, Adna F. 1904. "The Significance of Recent City Growth: The Era of Small Industrial Centers." *Annals of the American Academy of Political and Social Science* 23: 223–236.

Weber, Max. 1961. *General Economic History*. New York: Collier Books.

Westcott, Diane N. 1979. "Employment and Commuting Patterns: A Residential Analysis." *Monthly Labor Review* 102: 3–9.

Zorbaugh, Harvey. 1929. *The Gold Coast and the Slum*. Chicago: University of Chicago Press.

CHAPTER 9

World Metropolitan Areas

International comparisons are essential to a proper perspective on urban morphology. First, international comparisons create a world metric against which local size and shape can be evaluated in any region or nation. The significance of a fact or statistic always depends upon context, and the world context is the final. Second, the world context controls parochialisms, which otherwise color national or regional analysis of urban morphology. Thus the growth of metropolitan areas has been the dominant trend in the United States in the last half century, and transportation technology has been advanced as the explanation. Is that explanation wholly correct? To the extent that identical patterns recur in all countries and regions of the world, the United States is not unique. The first issue is whether and to what extent world urban trends resemble those of the United States in outward form. This question concerns results. The second issue is whether and to what extent resemblances of external form result everywhere from the same causes. This question concerns processes. If all the countries of the world are changing in the same way for the same reasons, then a universal level of explanation has been achieved.

Issues involve forms and processes. The issue of form is the extent to which suburbanization has been the master trend in big cities outside of North America. The issue of process is the extent to which automobile and truck transportation has been the cause of parallels in metropolitan form. If the improvements in local transportation technology produced suburbanization in the United States, the same technology ought to have produced suburbanization everywhere else. Conversely, transportation technology cannot explain gross discrepancies in metropolitan form or process between the United States and comparable countries because a universal cannot explain a difference. Much hangs on the issue of international "comparability." International disparities in economic development reduce comparability because rich nations and poor nations are massively different (Renaud, 1981: 36-37). Hence, the most useful comparisons juxtapose the United States with other developed nations, thus ensuring rough comparability in national wealth. This procedure highlights the contribution of technology independent of national wealth.

METROPOLITAN AREAS OF THE WORLD

International comparisons are easier to contemplate than to execute because nations have different standards for measuring urbanization and metropolitan population (Gibbs and Davis 1958). However, the University of California's International Urban Research Center (1959) developed a technique analogous to the Standard Metropolitan Statistical Area (SMSA) but capable of worldwide application. IUR's method was to list all the world's cities of 50,000 or more population, then to consider administrative territorial units surrounding each principal city. Those administrative units, variously defined, were added to the city's metropolitan population provided (1) they abutted the principal city, (2) their work force was at least 65 percent nonagricultural, (3) they were close enough to the central city to permit daily commutation, and (4) the total metropolitan area thereby created contained at least 100,000 persons. Central cities whose adjoining areas did not satisfy all four criteria were dropped from IUR's list of world metropolitan areas. IUR estimated "a probable total of 1,046 metropolitan areas" in the world in 1954. However, they were able to recover data on only 720. Nonetheless, the metropolitan areas covered contained an estimated 84 to 88 percent of the world's metropolitan population (Gibbs and Schnore 1960).

The IUR data are compelling evidence that a generation ago metropolitan areas were already a worldwide phenomenon, not merely a North American or United States phenomenon. Accepting this conclusion, Hall (1977: 24) declared: "the phenomenon of [metropolitan] growth is universal," and his view now enjoys overwhelming support. These metropolitan areas consist of densely settled central cities and a socially and economically integrated periphery in which settlement is lighter. The metropolitanization of the world's cities did not, however, reflect an identical relationship to industrialization everywhere. In fact, Gibbs and Schnore (1960: 166) reported a "clear tendency toward an inverse relationship between level of industrialization and rate of metropolitan growth" in the less developed world between 1940 and 1950. This overurbanization clearly distinguishes the process of urbanization in the developed and less developed regions, even if the form is similar. Therefore the world's tendency toward metropolitanization might be a similarity of form only, and not of process too.

URBAN MORPHOLOGY IN WESTERN EUROPE

An obvious and confounding difference between the metropolitan areas of North America and Europe is the age of European cities. Major European cities were old and large in population long before the Industrial Revolution. In 1700, the population of Philadelphia was 5,000 whereas the population of London was 674,500. Indeed, the population of London was 50,000 in Roman times (Tickner, 1935: 46). With the Industrial Revolution, North American cities closed the gap with Europe in less than a century and took the form of the industrial city described in the previous chapter. European cities were also undergoing industrialization in the last half of the eighteenth century and in the nineteenth century, but their industrialization built upon the social and physical heritage of the preindustrial past whose residues lay lightly upon North America.

This historic contrast has particularly affected central cities near the historic core of the preindustrial city. But there is no strong basis for claiming that preindustrial cores of European cities essentially deflected or dislodged the processes of urban morphology in the industrial era. Many compelling analogies between European and North American cities suggest, on the contrary, that common imperatives of industrial urbanization overrode discrepancies in preindustrial heritage. As in North America, capitalist industrialization in nineteenth century Europe promoted the growth of densely settled cities much greater in total population than before (Dickinson 1961: 447). In fact, crowding was worse in European cities than in North American cities. Comparing the two continents, Weber (1904: 30) reported that in 1890 the top twenty-eight U.S. cities housed 9.7 million persons on 638,000 acres, a density of 15 people per acre. In Britain, the largest 22 cities housed 8.8 million on only 231,000 acres, a density of 38 per acre. Germany's largest 15 cities contained population densities of 25 per acre. This discrepancy initially implies a quantitative difference between North American and European industrial cities, but the discrepancy was an illusion. As Weber (1904) himself observed, the chief source of the contrast was the widespread use in the United States of horse-car and electric trolley car, thus permitting "detached homes" on the periphery. European cities lagged in public transportation and for this reason, Weber explained, their populations had to reside in the core at higher densities than those prevailing in North America. Thus the major contrast between Europe and the United States turns out on close inspection to hang upon transportation technology as early as 1890.

As in North America, European cities have become decentralized in the twentieth century. The result has been the formation of metropolitan areas surrounding a central core city. Dickinson (1961: 449) identified fifty metropolitan regions in Europe, excluding the Soviet Union. Of these the largest was Greater London with a population of 10,491,000 and the smallest the twin cities of Marseilles-Aix. Three concentric zones described these European metropolitan regions. The central zone was the historic town, densely settled with narrow streets, residues of preindustrial society. The first ring is a compactly built-up zone surrounding the historic city. Constructed in the nineteenth century, this ring was the scene of industrial urbanization. By the middle of the twentieth century, the first ring had typically became a zone of high-density residence with mixed commercial and industrial uses. The historic city and its first ring constitute the urban core analogous to the industrial city in nineteenth-century North America. The second ring is suburban. Developed since 1900 in the period of decentralization, the suburban ring "includes many old villages and small towns that have been urbanized and transformed to become the nuclei of sprawling urban areas." These suburban rings also contain "really large industrial plants" that once concentrated in the first ring (Dickinson 1961: 519).

Metropolitan Paris

The Paris metropolitan region is the largest of continental Europe and fairly representative of trends generally shared by nations belonging to the European Economic Community. The city's origin was ca. A.D. 900 when the beleaguered inhabitants of the locality built a fortress for protection against marauding Vikings. The Île de la Cité is a tiny island on which was located the original settlement. This island still constitutes the city's center. Here is located the Cathedral of Notre Dame. The first city wall, built between 1180 and 1210, enclosed 675 acres. These walls still enclosed the city until 1600. Thereafter the city grew beyond the walls despite efforts to restrain it. By 1860, with the Industrial Revolution well underway, the population of the city was one million in ten central *arrondissements* (precincts). Napoleon III extended the city walls to encompass ten additional arrondissements that with the older ten now constitute the core of Paris. Construction of the Paris subway (Métro) in 1900 brought public transportation to this terminus. Population growth outside the twenty central arrondissements in this century has been extensive but mostly independent of subway service. In 1974, the historic center of Paris contained 3 million persons on sixty-six square miles, a density of 45,454 per square mile. The Paris agglomeration, including the next ring, contained 7.3 million persons on 463 square miles, a density of 15,667 per square mile. Finally, the Paris region contained 8.5 million persons on 5,000 square miles, a density of 1,700 per square mile (Blair 1974: 32–33).

Suburban growth began about 1880 when the middle class progressively deserted the densely settled historic city. Between 1881 and 1911, the suburban ring added more people than central Paris, and after 1911 the population of central Paris actually began to decline. These trends have continued. Between 1968 and 1975, central Paris lost 300,000 residents, a decline of 11.6 percent. In the same period, suburban growth continued, with the ring of maximum growth twenty to thirty miles from the center of Paris (Hall 1977: 57). The decline of population of central cities is typical of Western European metropolitan regions, and Paris is in this respect very representative of Europe. Suburbanization in this century has tended to reduce population densities in metropolitan Paris, but densities remain high by world standards. In 1975 metropolitan Paris still contained a population density of 25 per acre, still 1.7 times higher than New York City in 1890 (Hall 1977: 60). Despite actual declines of population, density of settlement in central Paris was ninety-nine per acre in 1975. In contrast, central London's population density was only 37 per acre in 1971.

As in North America, suburbanization of residence has been accompanied by suburbanization of heavy industry. Two thirds of the Paris region's industrial jobs were outside the central city in 1975. Since 1960, this industrial decentralization has gone ahead with the full support and encouragement of planning authorities whose principal objective has been to reduce congestion in the core. However, the process of industrial decentralization was visibly underway between the wars (1918–1939), well before regional plans began to affect industrial locations. Industrial decentralization has been neither even nor extreme. The very first suburban ring contains the bulk of the Paris region's heavy industrial plants (Castells 1977: 37), and most of these plants cluster in the northwest sector. There industrial parks such as Boulogne-Billancourt concentrate heavy industry in close proximity to high-density dwellings. These apartment houses are the residential quarters of the industrial workers of the nearby factories. Many are public housing projects called HLMs, a French acronym for "low-rent dwellings."

If industrial and commercial deconcentration had progressed fully, every ring of the Paris region would contain its representative share of jobs and people. But Castells (1977: 32–33) proves this balance has by no means been achieved. The ratio of jobs to working population shows that the Paris center had more jobs than workers in 1968, whereas the rings had more workers than jobs. The result of this imbalance is daily commutation from the residential periphery to the city center. In 1968 fully 46 percent of workers in central Paris commuted to their jobs from suburban areas. Most of the commuters were white-collar workers (Hall 1977: 58). Mass commutation underlines the specialization of the Paris center in office jobs at the same time that office workers are heavily located in suburban residences. Interestingly, the jobs : population ratio declines until the third ring, then rises at the fourth. This U-shaped distribution indicates that there are relatively more jobs at the perimeter of the region from which daily commutation to the Paris core has become excessively burdensome.

Worker commutation to central Paris depends heavily on private automobiles, the numerical growth of which has been continuous since 1945. The Paris region has one of the highest rates of car ownership in Western Europe: one car for 3.9 residents. However, the Paris subway system continues to attract ridership, thus reducing public dependence on automobile transportation. The attraction of the Paris subway is evident in Table 9-1, which compares public and private transportation. Public transportation's superiority in Paris is strictly the result of subway use; other French cities do not have subways. Relatively speaking, of course, all French cities relied less upon private passenger automobiles than did twenty American cities in 1976 (Table 9-1). Heavy use of bicycles and motorcycles in French cities supplemented the public transit alternative to driving a private passenger automobile. In Paris 65 percent of commuters reached their work place without utilizing a private passenger automobile. However, the ease of automotive commutation to a central city depends on the number and extensiveness of freeway linkages between core and suburbs as well as on central city parking facilities. In these preparations Paris is deficient compared with North American cities. Therefore automotive traffic in Paris is already everything the city can bear. Traffic congestion is infuriatingly severe, parking places in scant supply, and etiquette, normally a French specialty, is a Gallic pageant of oaths and obscene gestures (Kessler, 1981). Unable to stem traffic growth, Parisian planners have accepted "the fact that car ownership will grow" in the future and are attempting to reduce traffic congestion by increasing the supply

Table 9-1. Commutation by Mode of Transport in Five French Cities (1965), and Comparison with the USA in 1976 (percentages)

	Private Vehicles	Public Transport	Cycle	Other	Total
Paris area	35	51	13	1	100
Marseilles	57	28	11	4	100
Toulouse	50	22	25	3	100
Caen	58	9	32	1	100
Bordeaux	64	6	30	0	100
20 US Cities, 1976	80	19		1	100

Sources: U.S. Bureau of the Census, *Selected Characteristics of Travel to Work in 20 Metropolitan Cities, 1976.* Current Population Reports, Series P. 23, number 72 (Washington, D.C.: U.S. Government Printing Office, 1978); M. Michel Barbier and M. François Mellet, *Determination of Elasticities of Demand for the Various Means of Urban Passenger Transport,* Report of the 13th Round Table on Transport Economics, European Conference of Ministers of Transport, 1971, p. 9.

of freeways linking periphery and core, as well as a major circular road system on the periphery (Blair 1974: 76).

The suburbanization of Paris in the last half century has depended heavily on the automobile, and the prospect of the future is road building to permit and facilitate a regional transportation system containing a still higher population of private automobiles. Since 1949 government planning authorities have been struggling to restrain the growth of the Paris metropolitan region, to channel development away from the congested core, and to ameliorate automobile traffic (Coppa 1976: 183-184). Successive plans have had some effect especially in the creation of a polycentric region in which heavy industry subcenters are linked to the center by fixed-rail transit. Nonetheless, planning's influence has been defensive in character and modest in impact. Economic forces of the free market have been the ascendant decision makers in the Paris region. Unsurprisingly, the direction of change in the Paris region is analogous to Los Angeles and other American cities, as is the propelling force of automotive traffic. Thus the same causes are producing the same changes.

Other European Countries

The dominance of central Paris is possibly more extreme than elsewhere in Europe. This dominance is itself an anachronistic residue of the preautomobile city. But Paris has developed automotive-dependent residential, commercial, and industrial suburbs, and this trend is typical of trends in Europe generally. For example, Tables 9-2A and B show the process of metropolitan regionalization in England and Wales from 1900, with projections to 2001. Urban populations have grown, but urban acreage has grown faster, and the inevitable result has been overall reduction in density of urban areas. This is suburbanization, and the

Table 9-2A. Urban Acreage. England and Wales, 1900-2001

Year	Urban Population (000's)	Urban Acreage (000's)	Urban Acreage Per Thousand Urban Population	Urban Area as Percentage of Total Land Area
1900	32,500	2,000	61.5	5.4
1939	41,500	3,200	77.1	8.6
1980–81*	53,800	4,900	91.1	13.2
2000–01*	63,700	6,000	94.2	16.2

Source: Robin Best, *The Major Land Uses of Great Britain* (Wye: Wye College, 1959): 30, 32. Reprinted by permission.
  *projected.

Table 9-2B. Urban Growth in England and Wales, 1901–2001

Year	Urban Population in Millions	Urban Area in Hectares		Urban Land Provision: Hectares per 1000 Population
		Area (000s)	Percent England and Wales	
1901	32.5	674	4.5	20.7
1939	41.5	1206	8.0	29.1
1951	43.8	1339	8.9	30.6
1971	48.8	1646	11.0	33.7
2001*	51.3	2117	14.1	41.3

Source: Robin B. Best, *Land Use and Living Space* (London: Methuen, 1981), p. 76. Reprinted by permission of author and publisher.

*estimated.

trend is unambiguously the result of automotive traffic. In 1920, the automobile population in Britain was 187,000; by 1970, this population had increased to 12,000,000, a gain of 1,069 percent in fifty years. Car ownership in Britain has by no means caught up with the rate in the United States, but international differences are ever smaller. In 1960, Britain contained 110 automobiles per thousand population; this was the U.S. ratio in 1923, so the British ownership rate lagged thirty-five years behind the United States. In 1969, however, the British rate had increased to 200 per thousand. This was the U.S. ratio in 1946, a lag of just over twenty years (Clawson and Hall 1973: 85–86).

However, automotive-dependent suburbanization in Britain has not eliminated the journey to work aboard public transport. Suburban automobile owners in Britain prefer to leave their cars at home and commute to work aboard a train, bus, or subway. Table 9-3 shows that 87.9 percent of commuters to central London in 1971 reached their work place via public transportation. Only 11.4 percent utilized a private passenger automobile. Naturally the British public's transportation choices have been constrained by existing facilities. The Greater London Council has completed three concentric rings of freeways around the city's perimeter, but the GLC has not constructed high-speed freeways from the perimeter to central London. Therefore automotive commuters seeking access to the central city must proceed at a snail's pace along surface streets to their central city destination—and hope that by some miracle they will find a parking space once the aggravating ride is over. Public transportation is more rapid than automotive transportation in London. However, London's bus and subway fares are the world's highest. In 1981, the fare for a six-mile trip on the London Underground was US$1.93. To make matters worse, automated ticket vending machines could not change paper money. Therefore Underground riders had to wait up to one-half hour in line to obtain change from an agent. To avoid this delay, some Underground riders learned to carry sacks of change, clanking their way through a day's activities rather than wait in dreary subway lines.

Table 9-3. London Commuter Traffic, 1971

	Persons (000)	Percent of Total
Public transport	989	87.9
Railroad	454	40.3
Subway	389	34.6
Bus	146	12.9
Private transport	137	12.1
Automobile	128	11.4
Motorcycle/cycle	9	0.7
Total	1,126	100

Source: Central Statistical Office, *Social Trends No. 3.* (London: HMSO, 1972), p. 147. Reprinted by permission of the Controller of Her Britannic Majesty's Stationery Office.

As in Britain, the spread of automobile ownership among the nations of continental Europe has eliminated the previous necessity for living within walking distance from public transportation. Planners attribute the spread of towns and suburban development to growing public utilization of the automobile. However, certain disparities of European and American suburbanization emerge. First, suburban Europeans are more likely to travel to work aboard public transportation than are suburban Americans. Second, British and European suburbs consist of semidetached, two-family homes on small lots. In contrast, North American residential suburbs characteristically contain single-family homes on large lots. Because land prices are higher in Europe than in America, families must double up on lots. This choice doubles the density of European suburbs, but these remain as low in density compared with their own central cities as are North American city centers compared with densities in theirs.

European governments have expressed misgivings about the social and economic hazards of overdependence on automobile transportation (Meise and Wegener 1972: 68). To restrain automotive usage, Social Democratic governments tried to resist the political pressure in favor of highway construction. However, conservative European governments have embarked on ambitious road construction projects, until chronic gasoline shortages after 1974 created additional arguments for public transportation. It is a measure of the still great discrepancy in automobile usage on the continent that highway mileage per capita was only one tenth as high in Western Europe as in the United States in 1972 (Blair 1974: 77). As a result principally of this intercontinental contrast, European societies utilize much less energy per capita than do Canada or the United States. In 1975 the United States consumed fifty-five barrels of crude oil equivalent per capita and Canada consumed fifty-one. In the same year Sweden and Switzerland consumed thirty and sixteen, respectively, and West Germany twenty-six. Yet the per capita incomes of these Western European societies equal or surpass the North American standard.

Of course, European distances are shorter too than those in North America. Therefore trips and highways are shorter and oil consumption proportionately reduced (Renaud, 1981: 36). Yet until the chronic oil shortages of the middle 1970s, interregional differences in highway mileage were declining because European nations were building highways more rapidly than the United States. This highway construction was a political response to the expansion of automobile ownership in European societies and of the contingent demand of automobile owners for highways on which to drive their cars. Even so, at rates prevailing before 1974, Europe will not catch up with the United States in highway mileage until the twenty-first century, if then. But escalating oil costs have much reduced the enthusiasm of European governments for ambitious programs of highway construction. In 1977 the United States spent $44 billion on oil imports but imported only half its total oil consumption. With the exception of Britain, Norway, and the Soviet Union, European societies produce no oil and are compelled to import every drop. Therefore they are exceedingly price-conscious and the future of European highway construction is in doubt.

Obviously Europe's dependence on the private automobile has been significantly less than that of North America. Nonetheless, as in North America, the growth of Europe's automobile population has harmed intercity rail transportation. According to Blair (1974: 77), Europe's road building precipitated "a momentous postwar decline in rail transport." This deterioration occurred in every Western European society, but West Germany's railroads have deteriorated the most. Admittedly "uneconomic state monopolies" bear some of the blame for this decline in volume and quality of railroad freight and passenger service. However, European transport ministers agree that the motor vehicle is the principal cause (Aberle and Hamm 1978: 9).

METROPOLITAN REGIONS IN JAPAN

According to the United Nations (1908: 58) the Tokyo—Yokohama metropolitan region will become the world's largest between 1975 and 1990. Tokyo's 1960 population was 9.6 million, but the Tokyo metropolitan area encompassed 21 million, fully 21.3 percent of the entire Japanese population. Japanese geographers (Kishimoto 1970: 32) treat Tokyo as the largest node of the "Tokaido megalopolis" created by the sprawling interpenetration of six big cities: Tokyo, Yokohama, Nagoya, Kyoto, Osaka, and Kobe. These six contained 47 percent of Japan's population in 1965. A decade later, Tokyo, Yokohama, and Nagoya ("the big three") contained 50 million residents, 45 percent of the Japanese population. More generally, Japanese government statisticians have established criteria of "densely inhabited districts" (DIDs). These are contiguous enumeration districts with population density of 4,000 or more persons per square kilometer, a very high density indicative of urbanization. In 1960, statisticians enumerated 970 DIDs in Japan; these had grown to 1,087 in 1965.

Suburbanization in Japan is partially indicated by the incorporation of smaller towns within expanding metropolitan regions. In 1920, for example, the "Tokyo region" contained only fourteen subcenters of 10,000 or more population. By 1965, the expanded Tokyo region contained sixty-seven such subcenters. Nagoya, Osaka, and other big Japanese cities recorded similar expansions. Table 9-4 shows the suburbanization of Tokyo between 1950 and 1965. In 1950, the rate of expansion in Tokyo's core was higher than in its suburbs. But the core's rate of expansion continuously declined whereas suburban expansion continuously increased. By 1965 suburbs were already growing twice as fast as the core.

Density gradients provide additional evidence of suburbanization in Japan. *Density gradients* measure the decline in density with every additional kilometer of distance from the city's center. Mills and Ohta (1976: 690-691) computed density gradients for population, employment, and manufacturing employment in twenty-two Japanese cities betwen 1965 and 1972. They compared these gradients with comparable data from twenty urbanized areas of the United States in the period 1960-1970. In both countries they found that unit density of population, employment, and manufacturing employment tended to decline with distance from the center. Additionally, even in the brief periods surveyed, Mills and Ohta found that density gradients were leveling in both countries. This shift indicated more tapered, less abrupt declines in density with each unit of distance from the center. The only exception was manufacturing employment in Japan, which tended to increase rather than decrease its density gradient in the period 1969-1972.

Table 9-4. Suburbanization of Tokyo Metropolitan Region, 1950-1965

	Population (000)		Percentage Increase		
	1950	1965	1950/55	1955/60	1960/65
Tokyo Core	6,278	10,869	28.0	20.5	12.2
Tokyo Suburbs					
Kanagawa	2,488	4,431	17.4	17.9	28.7
Saitama	2,146	3,015	5.4	7.4	24.0
Chiba	2,139	2,702	3.1	4.6	17.2

Source: Seiji Yamaga, "Urbanization in the Northern Suburbs of Tokyo," in Association of Japanese Geographers, eds., *Japanese Cities* (Tokyo: Association of Japanese Geographers, 1970), p. 72. Reproduced by permission of the Association.

Evaluating these comparisons would lead one to conclude that Japan is experiencing a suburbanization quite analogous to that of the United States. However, density gradients in Japan were between two and eight times greater than in the United States. This difference shows that Japanese cities do not sprawl over the landscapes as widely as do U.S. cities. Japanese cities are much more densely settled, particularly in manufacturing employment. Although a tendency toward suburbanization is present in Japan, this tendency has by no means produced so extreme a suburban decentralization as it has in the United States.

In 1980 Japan became the world's leading manufacturer of automobiles. Most of these automobiles are exported; the rate of vehicle ownership in Japan was only one third the U.S. rate in 1972 (Mills and Ohta 1976: 721). Although Japanese cities have a higher density gradient of employment than do American cities, the Japanese cities rely much more heavily than do American cities upon public transportation. In 1970, 46 percent of commuters in Japanese cities reached their work place aboard public transportation, and only 14.5 percent utilized a private passenger automobile; the others mostly walked. In the same year, 78.3 percent of commuters in U.S. cities reached their job in a private automobile, and only 12.1 percent aboard public transportation. Public transportation in Japanese cities is notoriously crowded. "Pushers" are employed on Tokyo subways to squeeze riders into cars so the doors can close. People who have traveled on the Tokyo subway at rush hour compare the experience favorably to Dante's Inferno. But statistics show Japanese commuters still prefer public transportation to private automobiles. One reason is rush hour traffic congestion, which is so severe that a crowded (but rapid) subway is preferable. Of course, traffic congestion exists because public authorities have declined to build roads to relieve it. Japanese governments have regarded public transportation as a more efficient solution to urban transportation needs than private automobiles.

As these examples of Japan and Europe indicate, suburbanization is not a uniquely American phenomenon. "Careful research makes it clear that urban areas have been decentralizing all over the industrialized world throughout the twentieth century" (Mills and Song 1979: 82). Since the Second World War, suburbanization has even become a worldwide phenomenon because the population of cars and trucks is rising faster than the population of human beings in every region of the globe. The result is more or less the same everywhere. Where fixed rail systems tended to locate population along radial arteries in a star-shaped city, buses and motor cars "fill in the spaces where single, semi-detached houses are spread out at low densities" (Blair 1974: 51). However, ownership of private motor vehicles is everywhere associated with high real wages. As a result, the population of private motor vehicles per capita is higher in the more developed than in the less developed countries. Therefore the suburbanizing impact of automotive transportation is more obvious in developed nations even though the identical process is already underway in less developed countries.

THE SOVIET UNION

Surveys of world urbanization inescapably establish the world trend toward metropolitanization based on automotive transport. Thus Castells (1977: 21) concludes that "the role played by technology in the transformation of urban forms is indisputable." In particular, he adds, "the motor car has contributed to urban dispersion. . . . " These concessions do not, however, establish the sufficiency of technological determinism as a total explanation of world metropolitanization. As Castells (1977: 22) also observed, "the metropolitan region is not the necessary result of mere technological progress." Transportation technology is a force, but human societies have restrained or channeled this force in a variety of ways to yield a variety of morphological solutions. This variability proves that transportation technology does not simply impose itself upon societies, dictating one-to-one correspondences between drawing boards and regions. Instead, technology advances a class of solutions, and societies pick among the alternatives.

Transportation in the Soviet Union illustrates this potential for diversity within shared technology. On the one hand, the Soviet Union has become an advanced industrial society, participating in whatever technological imperatives shape such societies. On the other, the Soviet Union continues to display divergences in the technology of transportation, housing, and urban morphology from equivalently developed capitalist societies. Soviet divergences appear to result from the quite different economic and political system of that society (Renaud, 1981: 39). Regardless of the wisdom or desirability of Soviet divergences from the West, these divergences do establish the possibility of controlling and channeling transportation, housing, and urban morphology in ways that developed capitalist societies, especially the United States, do not control them. If technology were the only determinant of these processes the Soviet Union could *not* diverge from the capitalist West because the technology of transportation is universal, and a universal cannot produce a difference.

The deviant characteristics of the Soviet case have long been apparent. Gibbs and Schnore (1960: 165) observed that metropolitanization in the Soviet Union in the period 1940–1950 was notably less than expected on the basis of some indicators and more than expected on the basis of others. This disparity they attributed in part to "centralized control of industry and population." The major issue is the relative underdevelopment of huge metropolitan regions in the Soviet Union. The nation's biggest cities are not as big as they "ought" to be on the basis of Western experience. This departure reflects the Soviets' extensive control of regional growth and their long-standing prejudice against big cities on both economic and qualitative grounds.

These deviations are only partial, not total. Metropolitanization has been an indisputable force in the Soviet Union as elsewhere in the world. Signs of this metropolitanization are growth of urban population, spread of urbanization over whole regions, integration of central cities and satellite cities in metropolitan systems, transportation growth and change, and declining overall densities of settlement in metropolitan regions. Moscow is a central example. Hall (1977: 150) avers that "The communist world has its giant metropolitan cities too; and no better example exists than . . . the city of Moscow." In 1970, the city of Moscow had a population of over 7 million. It was the center of a 5,666 square mile metropolitan region containing numerous satellite cities and towns. The population of the Moscow region was 10.7 million people. The population of Moscow reached these levels despite determined efforts of the government to curb the city's growth. The 1939 plan called for a maximum population of 4 million, and this figure had been exceeded by 1959 (Hall 1977: 160). Furthermore, the city's political limits were extended in 1960 to incorporate outlying areas that had grown up in previous generations.

To integrate satellite cities and central Moscow, authorities created a series of ring highways and radial avenues. The first is the Sadovy ring, five miles from downtown Moscow. Two others follow at farther removes from central Moscow. The belt boulevards accompany green belts that are six to eight miles wide, with which Soviet planning authorities early girded the city in order to prevent unwanted occupation of undeveloped land (Blair 1974: 33-34). Under Stalin, Gorky Street and Leningrad Avenue were developed as monumental radial boulevards for automotive traffic between satellites and central Moscow (Hall 1977: 163). Although these are not freeways, they do carry four to six lanes of traffic and thus bear a distinct resemblance to like constructions around Houston, Los Angeles, or Paris, all centers of capitalist society.

In all these respects, the development of metropolitan Moscow, showplace of Communism, bears distinct resemblances to metropolitanization in capitalist societies, and there is no escaping the shared technological imperatives that produce this convergence. On the other hand, numerous disparities also distinguish Moscow and other Soviet cities from their Western counterparts. One is the underdevelopment, compared with industrial capacity, of automobile use in them. In 1970, the ratio of automobiles to population in the Soviet Union was five automobiles per thousand people. In the same year, the car-population ratio in the United States was 439 per thousand. Thus the rate of car ownership in the United States was eighty-nine times greater than in the Soviet Union in 1970, but the industrial output of the United States was only 1.5 times greater than the gross industrial output of the Soviet economy. In Soviet cities rates of automobile ownership are much lower than in the country as a whole. The most prosperous Soviet city, Moscow, contained only 1.4 automobiles for every one thousand residents in 1969 (Hall 1977: 151). In 1990 Moscow authorities project ownership rates of seventy automobiles for every thousand residents—less than 16 percent of the U.S. rate in 1970. Especially in urban areas, Soviet rates of automobile ownership are too much below Western norms to admit an explanation in terms of comparative national wealth, technological determinism, or both.

Private automobile ownership in the Soviet Union has admittedly rocketed upward since World War II. Between 1946 and 1971, the total motor vehicle population of the Soviet Union increased almost ninefold, but the population of automobiles increased eighty-fourfold (Clarke 1972: 72–73). However, the automobile population of the Soviet Union in 1971 was still only 529,000, whereas in 1970 the population of automobiles in the United States was 89,279,000. On the other hand, the population of trucks was 564,000 in the Soviet Union compared with 18,748,000 in the United States. Obviously the Soviets were grossly short of both cars and trucks in 1970 compared with the United States, but the shortage of cars was much greater than the shortage of trucks. In the United States the population of trucks in 1970 was 21 percent of the car population. In the Soviet Union, the truck population was 107 percent of the automobile population.

Available data on mass transit and railroad traffic in the Soviet Union are equally incompatible with the supposition that technological universals of industrial development simply determine transportation modalities. In 1979, the Soviet Union produced almost twice as many diesel locomotives as did the United States. Measured in passenger-kilometers, the volume of railroad traffic in the Soviet Union and Japan increased 142 and 125 percent, respectively, between 1966 and 1975. In the same period, passenger-kilometers on United States and Canadian railroads *decreased* to 70 and 57 percent, respectively, of the 1966 volume (Table 9-5). The international contradictions in direction of change are the first startling finding. Second is the absolute discrepancy in volume. Both the Soviet Union and Japan moved twenty times more passengers by rail in 1975 that did the United States. Admittedly, the shortage of automobiles in the Soviet Union compels people there to ride railroads. Moreover, Soviet railroad service is slow, overcrowded, and unreliable. Soviet citizens ride trains because they have no alternatives. But noncompetitive conditions do not also prevail in Japan, whose passenger train ridership per capita exceeds that of the Soviet Union. A supremely capitalist economy, Japan produced more passenger automobiles for domestic and export sale in 1980 than any other nation. Even so, the Japanese people flock aboard intercity railroad lines to an unparalleled extent. Indeed, the explanation of this consumer preference is the technological superiority of the trains! Japanese "bullet" trains shuttle passengers between Tokyo and neighboring cities at speeds of 125 mph, and private automobiles cannot match this speed [1]. Obviously, the technology for high-speed intercity rail traffic already exists. If technologies imposed themselves on societies, the United States and Canada would be already making use of high-speed railroad technology, whereas they do not. Moreover, the Japanese

Table 9-5. Railroad Traffic in Passenger-Kilometers for Selected Countries, 1966 and 1975 (millions)*

	1966	1975	Percentage Change
United States	27,620	15,715	−56.9
Canada	4,166	2,930	−70.3
Japan	258,277	323,192	+125.1
USSR	219,404	312,517	+142.4

Source: United Nations Department of Economic and Social Affairs, *United Nations Statistical Yearbook, 1976* (New York: United Nations, 1977), pp. 482–485. Reproduced by permission.
*Figures relate to domestic and international traffic on all railroad lines except those entirely within an urban unit and plantation, industrial mining, and funicular and cable railways. Passenger-kilometers include all passengers except military, government, and railroad personnel where carried without revenue.

case reverses the claim of technological superiority recklessly attributed to the automobile: in Japan trains are faster, therefore, superior.

Passenger mass transit in the Soviet Union provides more evidence of international divergence. Soviet authorities have long endorsed "generous investment in cheap and efficient public transport systems" whose model is the Moscow city subway. "Most observers agree that . . . the Moscow city transport system justifies the claims made for it" (Hall 1977: 167). In 1977 the country's seventh subway system opened in Tashkent, a Kazakhstan city of 1.6 million residents. New subway systems are under construction in Gorky, Minsk, Novosibirsk, Sverdlovsk, Kuibyshev, and Riga. Soviet subways are "fast, clean, and cheap." "The stations are large, architecturally distinctive, and free of graffiti" [2]. Streetcar, trolley bus, and motor bus lines have also increased in number within and on the perimeter of Soviet cities. Feeder service is excellent. Passenger mileage aboard all forms of public transportation has continuously increased since 1940. Hall (1977: 168) declares that regional transportation systems in the Soviet Union are "serious contenders for the title of the world's best commuter service."

The flourishing state of public transportation in the Soviet Union contrasts with Western Europe and especially the United States. In nations of the European Economic Community, public transit volume has generally "managed to hold its own" despite rising rates of automobile ownership and usage (van Witsen 1978: 9). On the other hand, public transportation usage in the United States peaked around 1950, and its absolute volume since then has declined to 50 percent of the 1950 amount. Because of deferred maintenace, breakdowns and interruptions of service had become common in the public transit systems of major American cities by the middle 1970s. In New York City 567 subway cars were thirty years old in 1981. In Philadelphia some cars were fifty-seven years old. The ancient subway cars are covered with graffiti and vandalized daily. Stations are dark, filthy, and unsafe. To restore the subway system, New York

City transit authorities estimated the city needed to spend one billion dollars a year for the whole decade of the 1980s. Other American cities have public transportation problems almost as severe as New York's, but big cities lack the money to maintain, much less repair, their public transportation systems [3]. The financial plight of American public transportation arises because governments are unprepared to subsidize public transportation as do Soviet authorities. The rightness of the American choice is not at issue here, but a political choice—not a technological imperative—is plainly at work (Neyer, 1981). If technologies simply imposed themselves on societies, public transit in the Soviety Union would also be declining in service and usage.

Another technology relevant to suburbanization is home building. In the United States new residential housing construction has been overwhelmingly single-family detached homes. This type of housing has been the pivot of metropolitan growth everywhere in the United States. In Britain, two-family detached homes replace single-family homes as the typical form of suburban residence. Elsewhere in Europe two-family homes in automobile-dependent suburbs are also the epitome of an affluent life-style. However, multifamily apartment units are found in continental European suburban locations to a much greater extent than in Britain or the United States. Until recently site-built housing has completely predominated in North America and Europe. Currently, factory-made mobile homes are selling well in the United States to low-income persons priced out of the site-built market. Suburban tracts of mobile homes offer detached dwellings to the metropolitan working class, the aged, and, ocasionally to students.

Virtually no single-family site-built housing is constructed in the Soviet Union. Instead of detached homes for one or two families, Soviet housing authorities construct "high density suburbs of five-story housing" (Blair 1974: 63). Thus suburban growth is almost exclusively in public housing projects rather than single-family, privately owned dwellings. Additionally, Soviet housing projects are thown up in seventy-five-acre micro-districts each of which aims to represent a planned residential-recreational-employment environment for 15,000 to 20,000 persons. Therefore Soviet metropolitan growth adds rail- or bus-linked housing globules rather than, as in the United States, vast swatches of automotive-dependent space at low residential densities. In August 1954, the Council of Ministers of the Soviet Union called for emphasis upon prefabricated construction using reinforced concrete. The Soviet housing industry thereafter abandoned site-built housing in favor of "standardised designs and industrialised methods" (Zhukov and Fyodorov 1974: 17). The purpose of this change was a reduction of the time and cost of building. Currently, the Soviety Union leads the world in volume of housing construction, chiefly because of its extensive prefabricated housing. The notion of prefabricating housing projects has circulated in the West for some decades but has thus far attracted few takers. Yet prefabricated housing is a technology that is employed extensively in Soviet society but not in the West. Factory-constructed housing in the Soviet Union has been much criticized for drabness, boring uniformity, poor quality, and rapid deterioration. In one micro-district, 10 percent of newly constructed apartments were officially declared "uninhabitable" because of inferior workmanship. Nonetheless, the Soviet deviation indicates that housing technologies do not impose themselves upon societies (Frolic 1970: 681).

POLITICAL AND ECONOMIC DETERMINANTS
OF METROPOLITANIZATION

Why do Soviet metropolitan regions differ from Western ones? The political and economic institutions of the Soviet Union provide the answer. Unlike the mixed, but still predominantly private enterprise economies prevailing in Western Europe, North America, and Japan, the economy of the Soviet Union is centrally planned and socialist. In such an economy, state planners decide what shall be produced in what quantity and at what prices. These decisions flow from the top down to the production level, where they are translated into goods available for consumption or investment. Since the first Five-Year Plan (1927–1932) Soviet economic planners have favored investment in heavy industry over production of consumer goods. Their purpose has been the rapid industrialization of their country. Post-Stalin reforms have favored the augmentation of consumers' share of national product, but concessions to consumer production are invariably regarded as slowing the rate of basic industrial growth, and Soviet planners have been sparing about increasing consumers' share.

Soviet planning philosophy has consistently preferred collective dwellings to individual homes and public transportation to private automobiles (Hall 1977: 162). The simplest explanation of Soviet choices in the fields of housing and transportation is cheapness. Soviet law demands that rents be low so that every family, no matter what its income, can have a minimum standard of shelter [4]. To implement this policy Soviet authorities set rents that are below the cost of provision, typically only 4 percent of the average worker's wage (Doroshinskaya 1977: 27). This subsidy gives the government a direct stake in reducing the national housing bill by squeezing the most housing space out of each ruble allocated. Prefabricated housing tracts are cheaper to build than detached homes. In fact, prefabricated housing projects and detached single-family homes are at opposite ends of the cost spectrum. Prefabricated housing offers rock-bottom prices whereas the endlessly sprawling American suburbs are "perhaps the most wasteful settlement ever devised" (Coppa 1976: 175). Therefore, when the population is housed (or ill-housed) in prefabricated housing projects, more of the national product is left over for investment in heavy industrial development and, of course, armaments. Upper-income Soviet consumers would possibly prefer single- or two-family detached housing, but the state command economy does not offer them the choice.

Soviet authorities believe mass transportation is cheaper than private automobiles. Cheapness is a powerful desideratum for many reasons. One is Soviet social policy, which requires that transportation prices be low in order to make service accessible to low-income citizens. To secure equal access, Soviet authorities subsidize public transportation, whose fares are actually below the cost of providing the service. These subsidized fares reduce consumer demand for automobiles and also guarantee high ridership on public lines. Given this reliable army of transit riders, Soviet authorities have a motive to minimize the subsidy by underserving the population. Underserving takes the form of overcrowded, dirty, and uncomfortable conveyances in which the passengers of Soviet public transportation have occasionally to ride (Taubman 1973: 90–93). When better conditions are provided, the cost of transit subsidies increases and therewith metropolitan transport's burden on the Soviet economy. The authorities support Moscow's transit system more generously than the other Soviet cities' systems, whose standard of service falls correspondingly below what the world sees in Moscow.

There is more to the cheapness of mass transit than merely the rich possibilities for underserving the ridership that the Soviet economy affords. Simply on a cost per passenger-kilometer basis, bus, trolley, and subway transportation is everywhere one third or less the cost of automobile transportation. The great advantage of the automobile is individual convenience, not cost per passenger-kilometer. In a market economy, consumers have the option of deciding how much transportation convenience they want to buy, and they typically value their time more highly than do state planning authorities. The Soviet economy does not permit this choice. To minimize the national transportation bill, national planners have declared that everyone (except bigshots!) shall ride public transportation, thus committing the nation to saving money [5]. They money saved becomes available for other national purposes (education, defense, industrialization), and Soviet officials would rather have these than transportation convenience for the masses.

Although the economic institutions of Soviet society do the daily work of restricting private automobile ownership in favor of mass transit, the political institutions of Soviet society must take the political heat. Official hostility to the private automobile encounters vigorous and increasing political opposition from persons who want to buy one but cannot because state policy favors mass transit [6]. Every year the number of these dissenters increases. As matters stand, hopeful automobile buyers must sign up in advance, then wait five years for their turn. Automobile prices are three times North American prices for 4-cylinder vehicles of comparable quality. All sales are cash only; no installment purchase is allowed. Because Soviet take-home pay is only a third of North American and automobile prices are three times higher, the economic deterrent to automobile ownership is obvious. Nonetheless, Soviet consumers are clamoring for more private automobiles, and this clamor is chiefly responsible for the dramatic upsurge of automobile production in the Soviet Union since 1946.

These concessions contradict people who naïvely regard the political system of the Soviet Union as wholly unresponsive to public opnion (Taubman 1973: 4-6). Limited concessions do not represent a capitulation to consumer demand. Soviet authorities still keep a tight lid on automobile construction and in the process provoke the exasperation of persons who want more consumer durables. Soviet authorities fight back at the ideological as well as the institutional level. Newspaper campaigns against "consumerism" criticize citizens whose conception of life's purpose revolves around acquisition of consumer goods (among which automobiles rank highest) in apparent emulation of bourgeois society. Authorities ask Soviet citizens to deemphasize consumer acquisition and seek life satisfaction in work, adult education, sports, culture, military service, and patriotism. The conflict of goals thus manifested is a social conflict. However, the political system of the Soviet Union gives authorities broad (but not infinite) leeway to suppress rather than capitulate to consumerism. A multiparty political system in a capitalist democracy does not have the capacity to shape or suppress consumer demand in peacetime. As one result, the automobile interest bloc is politically preponderant in Western Europe, North America, and Japan—but suppressed politically in the Soviet Union. Political liberalization of the Soviet state would permit those who favor automobile production to change policies presently inhibiting it, and these changes would have profound long-run changes in the morphological structure of metropolitan regions of the Soviet Union.

SUMMARY

Metropolitan regions are universal developments in the twentieth century. In Western Europe, Japan, and especially North America, metropolitan regionalization has taken the form of automobile-dependent suburbs consisting of detached homes at low population densities. These examples give the impression that automobile technology simply imposed itself upon society, creating as an offspring the suburban life-style. This orthodox view has some validity because automotive technology is a prerequisite of the metropolitan regionalization created in this century.

Yet the strictly technological explanation has ignored the political and economic institutions of developed societies. In the West and Japan, free markets prevail in the economy and parliamentary democracy in the polity. These institutions encourage automobile-dependent suburbanization, but they are not universal. In the Soviet Union, the economy depends on state planning and command. The polity reflects the dictatorship of the Communist Party. The institutions of the Soviet polity and economy have been able to restrain the suburbanization of metropolitan regions.

The desirability or undesirability of Western or Soviet institutions is complex and not at issue here. The point is that political and economic institutions are preponderant shapers of metropolitan regions in this century (Renaud, 1981: 38). These institutions regulate and control technology; indeed, the meaning of technological "efficiency" is hard to determine outside of a political-economic context.

NOTES

1. In 1967 the average trip to work aboard public transportation in a U.S. city took twice as long as the same trip by car. Edgar W. Butler, *Urban Sociology.* New York: Harper & Row, 1976, p. 179.
2. Dan Fisher, "Tashkent Is Latest Proud Owner of Soviet Subway System," *Los Angeles Times,* December 25, 1977, pt. I, p. 10.
3. John J. Goldman, "Major Transit Systems Losing Battles with Decay," *Los Angeles Times,* March 9, 1981, pt. I, p. 1.
4. "Citizens of the USSR shall have the right to housing. This right shall be ensured by the development and protection of state and public housing, assistance to co-operative and individual house building, fair distribution under public control of housing, allotted with reference to the implementation of the housing programme, and likewise by low rent." Article 44, Revised Constitution of the USSR.
5. Communist Party and industrial officials are the ones who own cars. A sad joke going around Moscow asks for a definition of an automobile. The answer: a four-wheeled vehicle driven by the whole working class through its vanguard representatives. Leslie Symons and Colin White, *Russian Transport.* London: G. Bell & Co., 1975.
6. Dan Fisher, "Still Not Enough Cars for Russians," *Los Angeles Times,* October 17, 1977, pt. I, p. 1.

REFERENCES

Aberle, G., and W. Hamm. 1978. "Economic Prospects for Railways," *Report of the 39th Round Table on Transport Economics.* Paris: European Conference of Ministers of Transport.

Blair, Thomas L. 1974. *The International Urban Crisis.* London: Hart-Davis, MacGibbon.

Castells, Manuel. 1977a. *The Urban Question.* Trans. Alan Sheridan. Cambridge: MIT

Clarke, Roger A. 1972. *Soviet Economic Facts, 1917-1970.* New York: Wiley.

Clawson, Marion, and Peter Hall. 1973. *Planning and Urban Growth: An Anglo-American Comparison.* Baltimore: Johns Hopkins University Press.

Coppa, Frank J. 1976. "Cities and Suburbs in Europe and the United States," pp. 167-191, in Philip C. Dolce, ed. *Suburbia: The American Dream and Dilemma.* Garden City, N.Y.: Anchor Press/Doubleday.

Dickinson, Robert E. 1961. *The West European City.* London: Routledge and Kegan Paul.

Doroshinskaya, Yelena. 1977. "Leningrad's Budget." *Soviet Union 325:* 27 ff.

Frolic, B. Michael. 1970. "The Soviet Study of Soviet Cities." *Journal of Politics* 32: 675-695.

Gibbs, Jack P., and Kingsley Davis. 1958. "Conventional versus Metropolitan Data in the International Study of Urbanization." *American Sociological Review* 23: 504-514.

——. and Leo Schnore. 1960. "Metropolitan Growth: An International Study." *American Journal of Sociology* 66: 160-170.

Hall, Peter. 1977. *The World Cities,* 2nd ed. New York: McGraw-Hill.

International Urban Research. 1959. *The World's Metropolitan Areas.* Berkeley and Los Angeles: University of California Press.

Kessler, Felix. 1981. "Parisians Battle the City's Traffic in Tiny Plastic Cars Made for Two." *Wall Street Journal* Nov. 17: II, p. 1.

Kishimoto, Minoru. 1970. "Characteristics of Japanese Urbanization and Metropolitanization," pp. 31-38, in *Japanese Cities.* Tokyo: Association of Japanese Geographers.

Meise, J., and M. Wegener. 1972. "Influence of the Existing Transport Infrastructure on the Choice of Techniques to Provide Modern Urban and Suburban Transport Lines." *Report of the 17th Round Table on Transport Economics.* Paris: European Conference of Ministers of Transport.

Mills, Edwin S., and Katsutoshi Ohta. 1976. "Urbanization and Urban Problems," pp. 673-751, in Hugh Patrick and H. Rosovsky, eds. *Asia's New Giant: How the Japanese Economy Works.* Washington, D.C.: Brookings Institution.

Mills, Edwin S., and Byung-Nak Song. 1979. *Urbanization and Urban Problems: Studies in the Modernization of the Republic of Korea, 1945-1975.* Cambridge: Council on East Asian Studies of Harvard University.

Neyev, Valerie. 1981. "Private Cars or Public Transport?" *Soviet Life* 12: 16.

Renaud, Bertrand. 1981. *National Urbanization Policy in Developing Countries.* New York: Published for the World Bank by Oxford University Press.

Tickner, F. W. 1935. *London Through the Ages.* London: Thomas Nelson & Sons.

Taubman, William. 1973. *Governing Soviet Cities.* New York: Praeger.

United Nations, Department of International Economic and Social Affairs. 1980. Population Studies No. 68. *Patterns of Urban and Rural Population Growth.* New York: United Nations.

van Witsen, Ir. M. 1978. "Scope for the Use of Certain Old-Established Urban Transport Techniques: Trams and Trolley Buses." *Report of the 38th Round Table on Transport Economics.* Paris: European Conference of Ministers of Transport.

Weber, Adna F. 1904. "The Significance of Recent City Growth: The Era of Small Industrial Centers." *Annals of the American Academy of Political and Social Science* 23: 223-236.

Zhukov, K., and V. Fyodorov. 1974. *Housing Construction in the Soviet Union.* Moscow: Progress.

CHAPTER 10

Human Ecology

Ecology is the study of relationships between organisms and their environment. Human ecology is a derivative approach that conceives of urbanization as an adaptive response of human populations to changing environmental conditions. According to Hawley (1981: 363), the theory's leading exponent, *human ecology* is the study of "the organization and functioning of territorially based systems including communities, cities, metropolitan areas, and nations." Cities and metropolitan regions are adaptive when they improve the survival chances of human populations through division of labor. Cities' specific shapes are explainable, under this rubric, by the functional imperatives of population survival. For example, each of the 16 million residents of the New York metropolitan region could decide to engage in hunting and gathering rather than his or her present nine-to-five occupation. This romantic mass reversion to a "natural" life-style would miscarry because the New York metropolitan region cannot support 16 million hunters and gatherers. Each hunter or gatherer in this fantastic experiment would go to bed hungry that night, and each would then read in the grumbling of his or her tummy nature's warning that personal survival requires social and spatial division of labor within a population. In this sense, each unsuccessful hunter or gatherer would have bumped up against the functional imperatives of population survival and have been compelled by these imperatives to return to the division of social labor (Gibbs and Martin 1962: 142-143).

The conceptual linkage with biological theories of species survival, competition, and symbiosis is obvious, and the framers of human ecology have acknowledged and welcomed the parallelisms. Important changes in ecological thinking have developed in the last half century (see Aldrich, 1979: 31-33). Traditional

242

human ecologists believed that competition was the social mechanism that governed population adaptation. Thus McKenzie (1933: 159) described the city and metropolitan region as "natural products of economic competition under present conditions of transportation and communication." His view equated economic competition in metropolitan regions with the competitive struggle for existence among animal species in a jungle. Berry and Kasarda (1977: 4, 12) observe that contemporary human ecology has backed away from a simple biotic analogy, stressing instead the interdependence of human populations. Interdependence arises in two forms: social division of labor and voluntary grouping of like individuals. Adjustments in these two modalities of interdependence provide a basic mechanism whereby a population adjusts to a "constantly changing yet restricting environment." Here the metaphor of an ant hill replaces the old-fashioned metaphor of a jungle [1]. Nevertheless, in every formulation of human ecology, the population is understood to adjust itself to a changing environment in the overriding interest of survival. Cities improve the survival chances of human populations; therefore cities exist. At this basic level, the perspective of human ecology remains very much as it was a half century ago.

Duncan's (1959) seminal formulation defined four parameters of the *ecological complex:* population, social organization, environment, and technology. The acronym POET permits easy recall of these parameters. Here population refers to an internally structured human group of a given (usually large) size and demographic composition. Although human populations are composed of individuals, the ecological approach treats the population as a whole as its unit of analysis. A population seeks to survive and adapts its social organization and technology to that end. In this sense, the population of Boston or any other great city is a single acting and reacting unit. In Duncan's (1959) formulation, social organization meant only the division of labor in society as measured by the number of industries and occupations. In simple societies of the past, the division of labor was only into mens' work and womens' work: two industries. Modern societies have butchers, bakers, candlestick makers, and thousands of other specialized occupations and industries. To the industrial division of labor Berry and Kasarda (1977: 12) add commensalistic interdependence as an independent dimension of social organization. *Commensalistic interdependence* is the grouping of like people in labor unions, clubs, and "common interest groups." Environment includes the natural order as well as all other social systems that are external to and impinge upon a population under study. Technology refers to tools, techniques, and, in some formulations, to the knowledge basis upon which a population relies to extract sustenance from its environment. Obviously tractors and computers belong in the technological repertoire of modern societies, but ecologists have been uncertain whether science, religion, and even poetry belong there as well.

The four variables of the ecological complex are interdependent because change in one produces changes in the others (Berry and Kasarda 1977: 15). Suppose, for example, the population of Boston tripled tomorrow, the other elements of the ecological complex remaining the same. Confronting this abrupt change in population, Bostonians' wanted routines, reflective of yesterday's equilibrium, would collapse because incapable of supporting the augmented population. For example, an abrupt tripling of the population would produce shortages of housing, food, clothing, fuel, and sanitary facilities—making survival impossible unless Bostonians changed their behavior. A lengthy and unpleasant period of adjustment to population growth would then occur in social organization, environment, and technology. If these were unable to adjust, the final result would be the emigration of surplus population, reduction of surplus population by attrition, or both, until at last the metropolitan area population reached a size capable of being supported. This would be a point of momentary equilibrium awaiting only another autonomous change in any constituent to trigger another unpleasant readjustment.

Human ecologists regard the distribution of urban populations in space as reflective of the population's ongoing adjustment to ecological imperatives. Aware of the necessity to frame a general theory of urban morphology, rather than only a model of twentieth-century metropolitanization, ecologists have advanced a number of abstractions. These abstractions permit human ecologists to describe spatial adjustments in any population in the entire historical experience of urban society. Concentration of population is centripetal adjustment of formerly dispersed population. Deconcentration is centrifugal movement of population away from a center toward a periphery. Concentration and deconcentration are in balance. As people come together and densities rise, competition for land occupancy becomes severe. Ultimately, competition becomes so severe that people find they can advantageously move toward the periphery. This discovery signals a level of concentration that was suboptimal and triggers a reactive phase of deconcentration. As deconcentration builds up, the population's spatial location shifts toward optimality, defined as a situation in which no one can benefit by moving without harming another person. So long as anyone can beneficially move without harming anyone else, population distribution is disequilibrated. Just where that optimal distribution will be depends on the ecological balance. Primitive hunters and gatherers found an equilibrium that was deconcentrated; industrial cities of the nineteenth and early twentieth centuries reached a concentrated (dense) solution. Any human population can be described in terms of its concentration or deconcentration and these characteristics related to the population's adjustment to ecological imperatives.

URBAN LAND USE DECISION MAKING

Urban land use is how people use land in cities. Typical uses include residence, streets, manufacturing, commerce and so on. A map showing land uses (Figure

10-1) is a close description of urban morphology. The difference is that morphology is a description of the whole; land use refers to individual parcels. Nonetheless, the whole is the sum of its parcels in this case, so an explanation of urban land use quickly becomes an explanation of urban morphology.

Urban land use is the visible outcome of prior processes of decision making and allocation. Land use decision making involves three hierarchical levels. The first is rule making. Legislatures enact laws governing land use. Sometimes these laws

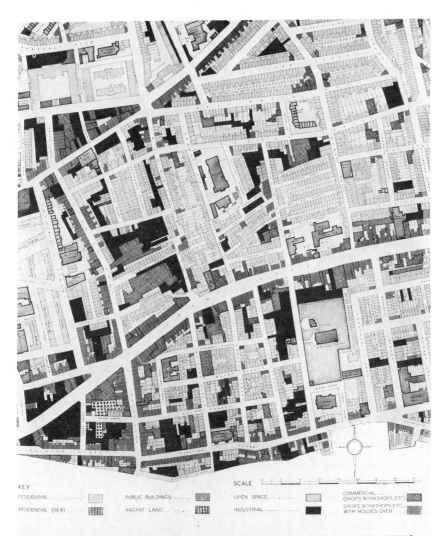

KEY

RESIDENTIAL	PUBLIC BUILDINGS	OPEN SPACE	COMMERCIAL (SHOPS, WORKSHOPS, ETC)
RESIDENTIAL (NEW)	VACANT LAND	INDUSTRIAL	SHOPS, WORKSHOPS, ETC. WITH HOUSES OVER

SCALE

TYPICAL AREA IN THE EAST END, SHOWING THE EXISTING INTERMIXTURE OF INDUSTRY, HOUSING ETC

Figure 10-1. Land Use in East London 1943

are direct as when states set aside areas for public parks. Sometimes these laws are indirect as in taxation or escrow policies (George, 1954). Either way law making is a basic part of land use decision making in any society. Second, rule interpretation and enforcement convert laws into effective constraints upon actual land use. In every society courts and police have responsibility for interpreting and enforcing laws affecting land use. People can live in parks unless the police drive them out so the effectiveness of laws prohibiting residence in parks depends, in the last analysis, upon police vigilance. The third level of land use decision making is user expediency. User expediency is doing whatever seems most satisfactory, as for example, selecting a residence close to one's work place. Expedient decision makers may be households or institutions, but each decision maker's expediency is shaped by law, law enforcement, and the personal expediency of other land users. Thus, college students desire to reside close to campus but students at New York University cannot choose to reside in Washington Square Park convenient as that location would be. Law forbids anyone to live in the public parks and New York City police enforce this law. Similarly, students at UCLA would like to live in Westwood, but housing prices are so high there that students choose to live in cheaper neighborhoods farther from campus. Either way land users made their expedient choices in socially conditioned and restricted contexts.

Rule making, rule enforcement, and user expediency are always the proximate causes of land use decision making in societies. That is, these three provide channels through which changes in population, organization, environment, and technology (POET variables) affect land use. Urban ecologists have, however, stressed the direct effect of POET variables upon user expediency in a minimalist state, free market context. Correct as far as it goes, this ecological treatment produces an "apolitical" model of land use decision making (Shlay and Rossi, 1981: 703). In an apolitical model of land use decision making the rule making and rule enforcement services of the state all but disappear from view, and attention shifts exclusively to the level of user expediency. Increasingly unrealistic in modern societies, the apolitical character of urban ecology has attracted theoretical criticism on this ground, and a lively debate currently centers about whether it is possible to salvage urban ecology.

SALOON KEEPERS VS. CLERGYMEN: A LAND USE COMPETITION

Competition among land users is a central idea of urban ecology, and a thorough understanding of this process is necessary. A simple illustration posits an evenly populated terrain (Figure 10-2). *A* and *B* are saloons located on opposite sides of the periphery. We assume that prices, services, go-go dancers, and

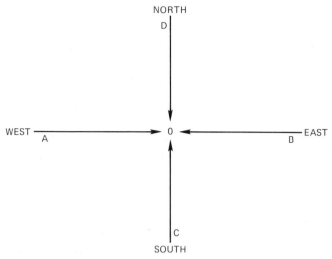

Figure 10-2. Saloons vs. Clergymen.

ambience are identical so *A* and *B* compete only in terms of proximity to drinkers who always choose the nearest saloon. Therefore *A* has been obtaining the business of drinkers located west of the center and *B* the business of drinkers located east of the center. To increase business volume *A* moves into the center of the terrain. Now Saloon *A* receives the patronage of all those located west of the center for whom this saloon is still the closer. But Saloon *A* also obtains the patronage of those drinkers located east of the center for whom this new location in the center is now closer than Saloon *B*. In retaliation, the proprietor of *B* moves his saloon into the central area, locating the new premises right next door to Saloon *A*. A saloon district now exists in town. Being adjacent in the population center, Saloon *A* and *B* each receives one half of the city's liquor business. Neither saloon can relocate without reducing its volume. A spatial equilibrium temporarily exists.

Now assume that *C* and *D* are churches seeking to bring sinners to salvation. As before, Church *C* obtains congregants south of the population center and Church *D* obtains those north of the center. For increased effectiveness, the pastor of *C* decides to relocate the church to the center of town, hoping thereby to obtain the attendance of some of those congregants who previously attended Church *D* while retaining all the original flock. Divining this intention, the pastor of church *D* begins to look for a more central location too. Both pastors arrive in the center of town only to find that honky-tonk saloons already occupy the most desirable corners. However, the landlord promises to evict the saloon keepers provided the pastors can pay a higher rental for the properties. Which can afford higher rent, churches or saloons? That depends on which institutions the population more generously supports, an issue closely related to the character of the population. In Calico, Calif., a silver mining boom town of the nineteenth century, a population of 4,600 miners supported twenty-two saloons and one church, the latter mainly used for burying the losers of gunfights.

Churches and saloons are alternative and competing land users: each competes with others like itself as well as with alternative land users. Since the saloon keepers already controlled the most desirable land parcels, the pastors have to wrest the land away from them, thus changing the land use. If they succeed, an invasion-succession sequence (described below in more detail) has transpired. The winner of the competition will be the more affluent user. This user has first choice of location and therefore of land use. As a result of competition for desirable central land, however, the cost of land in the center rises. As new users are added (e.g., banks, department stores) this illustration increases in complexity as well as realism. But the process of competitive land use persists, as does the social mechanism for land use decision making: the free market. Superficial reflection on this example would lead to the conclusion that user expediency in the free market is the *only* mechanism governing the location of churches, saloons, and possibly other urban institutions [2]. The case of Salt Lake City, Utah, immediately dispels this misapprehension. Salt Lake City is the world capital of Mormonism, a religion that disapproves of drinking booze. Salt Lake City has numerous churches and no saloons, and its most desirable central square is occupied by the Mormon Tabernacle. This land use did not arise because saloons are so unprofitable that this Utah city of 170,000 population cannot support even one. Saloons are absent in Salt Lake City because they are illegal in Utah. Having made this decision, Utah's legislature and courts have implicitly declared that saloons may occupy no Utah land. Therefore there are no saloons in Utah cities. These observations are elementary, but they remind the unwary that a free maket in urban land exists only where prior political decisions have been made to permit it. In this sense, the free market in urban land is only the visible tip of the decision-making iceberg, and the visible portion should not be confused with the much larger whole.

THE DESIRABILITY OF CENTRAL PLACES

In general, urban ecologists have taught that centrally located land is the most desirable metropolitan land because it is the most accessible (Berry and Kasarda 1977: 5). Hawley (1981: 91) states that the "commanding position" of the central business district in nineteenth-century cities derived "in no small degree from the superior access afforded by central location." Central business districts also offered "advantages of proximity" to "like units having similar location requirements." The obvious anomaly posed by deconcentration of industry and population in the twentieth centruy has been deflected because ecologists have been able to calim the deconcentration resulted from improvements in local transportation technology, a principal variable of ecological theory (Duncan 1974: 193). Moreover, given deconcentrated metropolitan populations, the desirability of central places has tended to reappear in the rise of satellite centers and administrative growth in the core (Kasarda 1972). Finally, "the deconcentration of urban functions has not yet eliminated the gradient variation in land use intensity" (Hawley 1981: 185).

A gradient of land values and intensity signals the existence of desirable central places. Competition causes land prices to rise as parcels approach the center. The result is land values that decline toward the periphery and rise toward the center (Duncan 1974: 193). To offset very high land values in the desirable center, high-intensity land use is necessary. This usage implies high-rise structures that pile users on top of one another, thus reducting each user's cost. High-density residence takes the form of multifamily dwellings, especially apartment houses. High-density commercial use takes the form of towering skyscrapers. The familiar upshot is the metropolitan skyline whose buildings reflect by their height the underlying price gradient of land values.

CLASSICAL MODELS OF URBAN MORPHOLOGY

In the period 1922–1945, the study of urban land use was a strictly American interest, reflecting American data and social conditions and linked at the periphery to real estate speculation. Obviously, the ability to predict the direction and type of metropolitan growth would confer the ability to earn speculative profits in real estate by purchasing cheap land in the confident expectation of future price increases (Weiner and Hoyt 1960; Hoyt 1933). Hence the formulation of predictive models of metropolitan growth became an applied social science of enormous interest beyond the frontiers of the academic community.

Early studies drew upon ecological theory to formulate dynamic models of metropolitan land use. Three models were particularly important: concentric zone, sector, and multiple nuclei. Although they drew upon the same storehouses of ecological theory, each model yielded a different prediction of city form. Contemporaries compared these predictions with real cities in order to determine goodness of fit, and that activity continues today. However, the orientation of contemporary debate is no longer over which model is the true one. On the contrary, there is nearly universal agreement that all three are useful but none wholly or simply correct. Also the models are not mutually exclusive, and metropolitan regions sometimes display complex mixtures. "Most cities exhibit . . . aspects of the three generalizations of the land-use pattern" in the authoritative opinion of Harris and Ullman (1945: 16). Current discussion questions the validity of the whole ecological approach to urban land use. Some contemporary authors such as Castells deny even the possibility of framing reliable models of urban morphology. Others are dubious that North American evidence is sufficient proof of universality, and this issue has compelled internationalization of research interest.

Concentric Zone Model

The details of classical models of metropolitan land use now concern only specialists and historians, but a brief discussion of each is in order because these

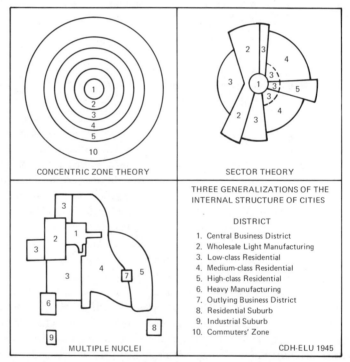

Figure 10-3. Three Models of Urban Morphology. (Reprinted from "The Nature of Cities" by Chauncey D. Harris and Edward L. Ullman in volume no. 242 of THE ANNALS of the American Academy of Political and Social Science. © 1945 by the American Academy of Political and Social Science. All Rights Reserved. Reproduced by permission.)

models reflect sophisticated appraisals of what the free market in land tends to produce when socially permitted to operate without restriction. Figure 10-3 offers a visual comparison of the three models' predictions. The concentric zone model (Burgess 1928) was the earliest of the three, and it has always been the most influential. Deriving his model from close study of Chicago, Burgess claimed all cities spread radially from the center to produce expanding circles. Each circle enclosed a homogeneous zone, not a gradient. Burgess observed that distance from the center of the city was associated with the increasing socioeconomic status of residents. Around the central business district, the metropolitan core, was the "zone of transition" in which resided the indigent, the derelict, the bohemian, the unmarried, and victims of racial discrimination. These people occupied high-density dwellings in advanced deterioration. In the next ring lived working-class people in modest homes or apartments. Beyond the working-class districts emerged a middle-class residential district of aging but sound detached homes on small lots. The exterior zone consisted of commuters, mostly high-status and white-collar. Their homes were detached, new, and on large lots. Here density of population per acre was lowest. Beyond the commuters undisturbed land awaited the expansion of the growing city.

Sector Model

Hoyt's (1933) sector model also assumes a city expanding radially from the periphery into developed land on the fringe. This land is cheap whereas central land is dear. However, Hoyt's version emphasized continuity of development along transportation lines. In Hoyt's view, functions migrate from sites nearer the core toward the periphery along existing transportation lines. As they do, they create pie-shaped wedges of homogeneous land use. For example, a high-class residential area in the east would expand toward the east; a low-class residential sector in the south would expand toward the south. Hoyt also took special account of terrain (ignored by Burgess), noting that migration of high-class residence tended toward high ground, open country, and rapid access transit lines.

Multiple Nuclei Model

Land use need not be built around a single downtown center, and in many cities multiple centers exist. For example, metropolitan London began as the contiguous cities of Westminster and the "City of London," and metropolitan Los Angeles began as the contiguous cities of Santa Monica, Pasadena, Long Beach, and Los Angeles. Where multiple centers exist, cities grow up in districts each of which is a growth pole for its sector. The resultant metropolitan form then depends on the growing together of the independent districts whose existence is not a derivative of some common center. Some districts are symbiotic, some compatible, and some incompatible. Thus central business district and wholesale district are symbiotic, and both are compatible with low-class residential use in a neighboring district. On the other hand, high-class residential use is incompatible with the districts described above and tends to back away from all three.

INVASION-SUCCESSION

Any map of city form is unavoidably misleading because forms are always changing. Therefore ecological models of city shape needed to provide an explanation of how change occurred. This explanation ecologists (Park 1936) borrowed from biological models of invasion and succession of compatible and incompatible plant species. In the urban setting, a land use invasion begins when a new land user encroaches upon an established user's territory. Gibbard (1941) described invasion-succession as "a cycle of change that occurs when one population type, or ecological order, displaces the immediately preceding one in a functionally delimited area." "Residential succession" is one type, which refers to displacement and replacement of one residential population by another. This type is most common. The second type is functional succession when one type of land user displaces another type. An example is commercial use displacing residential.

Invasion is the competitive intrusion of a new land user; succession is the consolidation of the newcomer's hegemony. Park (1936: 176) declared that the function of invasive competition was to produce succession, "a division of labor which has diminished competition." Some authors described invasion-succession as multistaged processes. For example, Burgess (1928: 112; see also Riemer 1952: 129-135) described four phases: invasion, reaction, influx, and climax. In the invasion phase, newcomers appear, initiating competition with established land users. In the reaction phase, established users become consciously and collectively aware of the challenge and react defensively against it. In the influx phase, new users tilt the balance in their favor, and resistance falters. In the climax phase, new users establish their hegemony, the previous users having departed.

The causes of metropolitan invasion-succession are various. Sometimes the changing balance of population requires an expanding group to occupy land pre-

viously used by a static group or group decreasing in number. Similarly, pros-
pering groups or industries may invade territory occupied by declining industries
or groups. Burgess emphasized the radial expansion of the city from its center
and the consequent necessity for lower-income groups to push outward into
residential neighborhoods already occupied by higher-income groups toward the
periphery. Hoyt stressed the vacuum created by the departure of the highest-
income groups for new and expensive housing on the metropolitan perimeter
(see Berry and Gillard 1977: 10). This vacuum was filled by lower-income
groups escaping from the center, but the process of departure and replacement
created mixed land uses in the phases of invasion, reaction, and influx. Hoyt's
model also made room for lateral invasion and succession as pie-shaped wedges
emanating from the center measured their economic muscle against one another
at the periphery.

CRITICISMS OF URBAN ECOLOGY

In the literature of urban ecology the process of land use change is always
invasion-succession and the mechanism economic competition. In the American
context, these assumptions are more realistic than in many others because metropolitan land has always been for sale to the highest bidder in America (Masotti
and Walton 1976: 2, 60). Indeed, Berry and Gillard (1977: 14) state that "the
physical forms of American cities . . . have been the outcome of a real estate
market of profit-seeking builders, land speculators, and investors." Any player of
Parker Brothers' board game *Monopoly* has a working sense of how these
entrepreneurs operate and what their motives are. Still the assumption that only
money counts in land use decision making has been completely discarded.
Hauser (1968: 216), for example, has noted that ecological models "assume that
land-use patterns are the result of the free play of economic forces. Such a degree of *laissez-faire* has never existed in America or anywhere else."
One objection has emphasized social values (Kolb 1954-1955: 31-32). An
exemplary study is Firey (1945), who analyzed land use in central Boston.
Downtown Boston's most valuable land is occupied by old churches, cemeteries,
historic buildings, and duck-infested parks. Indeed, high rises and historic buildings exist side by side. The survival of historic land uses into the present depends
upon sentiment and value rather than economic calculation. Yet the uneconomic
uses persist, and this persistence proves that values and sentiment can override
the law of supply and demand in the determination of parcel use.
Another sentimental force is neighborhood cohesion. Some working-class and
ethnic neighborhoods in American cities have displayed high levels of neighborhood consciousness and solidarity (Gusfield 1975). Cohesive neighborhoods have

the capacity to mobilize political and economic power to resist a land use invasion. When ethnic neighborhoods resist obtrusive bureaucrats or gouging landlords, their solidarity achieves heroic stature. Some community studies (Gans 1962: Fried 1973) have tended to romanticize the solidarity of ethnic neighborhoods, picturing them as islands of human warmth and fellow feeling in a cold, impersonal society. The truth of this capsulization ought not to obscure the nasty side of neighborhood solidarity. Gibbard (1941: 836) long ago noted that "resort to riot action to check invasion" does occasionally occur in working class and ethnic communities. Burning crosses and brickbats have been vigilant, unofficial guardians of established land uses in American cities. Illegal violence expresses the solidarity of rival tribes, but there is no grounds for romanticizing that solidarity. Yet illegal violence does affect land use, and ecological theory has been unable to incorporate it into explanatory models of metropolitan growth.

Urban politics have also affected land use in American metropolitan regions, and urban ecology has been silent about this reality. A dramatic example is rent control in New York City. This wartime emergency measure has survived as law into the present, despite the agonized opposition of landlord interests, because voters favor it. The wisdom of its retention is not at issue here. There are grounds for arguing the law aggravated the housing situation of renters by wastefully inducing premature destruction of still sound older housing (Fishman 1978). Nonetheless, rent control laws in New York City have for forty years controlled market forces and thus affected the physical structure of the great city. The obtrusion of rent control laws into the competitive market is a massive anomaly in ecological theory.

Zoning and urban renewal offer additional examples of political displacement of market decision making (Shlay and Rossi, 1981). Zoning first appeared in 1913, when the legislatures of three Midwestern states empowered cities to establish residential districts from which manufacturing and commercial establishments would be banned (Scott 1971: 152). Property owners challenged the constitutionality of zoning laws on the grounds that restrictions deprived them of property rights without compensation. The legality of zoning was uncertain until 1916, when the New York City Board of Estimate drafted a zoning regulation that proved invulnerable to legal challenges. New York's code justified zoning as regulation in the public interest analogous to fire, police, and sanitary protection. Sustained in the courts, this interpretation of zoning permitted municipalities to control the use of privately owned land without invoking the power of eminent domain or paying compensation. New York City's zoning resolution became the model for other cities, which rapidly adopted the practice of restricting land uses by law. By 1927, 527 American cities had adopted zoning ordinances (Scott 1971: 249).

After the Second World War, suburban cities adopted zoning ordinances to control growth. To a substantial extent, suburban cities utilized large-lot zoning ordinances to exclude low-income, high-density, and minority-occupied housing as well as heavy industry. According to Davidoff and Brooks (1976: 145) zoning ordinances accomplished this de facto exclusion in three principal ways. First, zoning ordinances often restricted the type of dwelling units permitted. These restrictions commonly excluded multifamily units. Second, suburban zoning ordinances added to the cost of new housing by imposing standards of construction and spaciousness in excess of what was required to protect the health, safety, and welfare of the population. Excessively stringent standards raised the price of housing, thus excluding low-income households. Third, zoning ordinances excluded mobile homes and factory-built housing. Because mobile homes provide inexpensive housing for the poor, suburban restrictions on their introduction prevented low-income households from obtaining residence in the community. All these practices were arguably contrary to the greater public interest, and in a 1971 decision, the Supreme Court of New Jersey declared that Mount Laurel Township could not exclude low-income households in disregard of the general welfare of the state's population. Nonetheless, zoning ordinances have exerted and continue to exert an enormous impact upon suburbanization in the United States (Shlay and Rossi, 1981: 717).

Urban renewal offers another example of political displacement of market decision making. Under the provisions of the 1949 Housing Act, the federal government launched a program of urban renewal in the 1950s (Anderson 1964). Two thirds of total costs were borne by the federal government, the rest by local taxpayers. Urban renewal transformed entirely the downtown areas of Boston, Newark, Baltimore, Los Angeles, and large sectors of nearly every big city's center. Under the political authority of eminent domain, urban renewal agencies and highway planners evicted 250,000 families every year, and paid the evictees an average of $80 in compensation. New housing for the evicted families was not provided, so people whose deteriorated housing had been torn down (at a cost to the taxpayer of $30 billion in direct outlays and bonded debt) just moved to another deteriorated dwelling somewhere else. Planners regarded welfare workers as "unduly concerned" with the problems of the poor (Scott 1971: 255, 463, 607). In many cities federal bulldozers razed lively neighborhoods, replacing them with sterile compounds devoid of interest and unsafe to visit after dark (Jacobs 1961). In the 1950s and 1960s, neighborhood groups led many successful movements of resistance against federal renewal projects and the "pro-growth coalition" of business and labor that supported them (Mollenkopf 1978: 118). On the other hand, urban renewal did revive deteriorating central city retail districts, retrieve blighted neighborhoods around major universities in big cities, and delay the further deterioration of central city fiscal affairs. (Castells 1977: 394) [3]. These were noteworthy consequences of public sector intrusion into the private market in urban land. The concentric zone, the sector, and the multiple nuclei models are understandably silent on how such intrusions can occur. They reflect here the inability of prewar ecological theory to explain the postwar obtrusion of the public sector. As the public sector has become more prominent in metropolitan affairs, the inadequacies of urban ecology have likewise become more obvious [4].

A WORKING MODEL OF THE NORTH AMERICAN METROPOLIS

The three classical models have fused into a working model of the North American metropolis. This working model, which incorporates the strong points of each earlier constituent, has four assumptions. First, North American cities typically consist of a large central city, or twin cities. These dominate the metropolitan region in which, however, numerous place-named subcenters abound. Second, the central city (or cities) are encapsulated by surrounding residential and industrial suburbs. Third, metropolitan population growth involves the continuous expansion of the periphery into undeveloped land on the outlying fringe. Fourth, central cities contain more than their share of poor people, nonwhites, the aged, unemployed workers, welfare recipients, deteriorated housing, and high-density occupancy. Encapsulating suburbs have less than their equal share of the above (but many of each!), and more than their share of white-collar employees, skilled workers, husband-wife families, and new, low-density housing.

This contrast is overstated in the interests of typicality, but just how accurate is it? Most evidence indicates that the first three assumptions have been and remain widely applicable. Admittedly, in the 1970s signs of central city revitalization led some observers to conclude suburbanization had ended. Beale (1978: 376) called attention to the return of young, single white professionals to ailing central cities. This kind of central city revitalization acquired the name "gentrification." *Gentrification* is "the refurbishing of central city neighborhoods . . . by people who are well educated and well-to-do" (Sternleib and Hughes 1980: 48). Prominent examples include the rejuvenation of Brooklyn Heights in New York City and Georgetown in Washington, D.C. There suburban whites returned to downtown areas, purchased deteriorated properties, refurbished them, and took up residence in what had been declining neighborhoods. Other examples were not hard to find and, in the absence of conclusive statistics, many observers speculated about the end of suburbanization and the return of the middle class to central cities. Such a trend would invalidate the "hole-in-the-doughnut" model of the American metropolis, which had come into prevailing usage over four decades.

The existence of some counterflow is indisputable and its potential for dramatic change great. However, 1980 census returns indicated that the earlier trend toward suburbanization was by no means reversed in the 1970s. In the fifty-seven SMSAs of 650,000 or more residents, twenty-three showed increases in central city populations and thirty-four showed absolute population declines between 1970 and 1980. On the other hand, suburban population increased in fifty-two SMSAs and declined in only five. The proportion of Americans residing in suburbs increased from 41 to 43 percent in the 1970s. Assessing such evidence, Sternleib and Hughes (1980: 48) appropriately conclude that gentrification is a "minuscule trend compared with other forces affecting cities."

The Central City

Gentrification returns educated, higher-status persons to central cities, thus reducing the status disparity between suburban and central city populations. But this contrast was already somewhat blurred in 1960. Schnore (1972: 71–92) examined 200 SMSAs and 163 smaller U.S. cities in order to determine whether and to what extent suburban rings were gaining high-status population at the expense of central cities. His measure of social status was educational attainment. Schnore found that in the decade 1950–1960 rings increased their share of highly educated adult residents compared with central cities while decreasing their share of less educated adults in 60 percent of the cities studied. In an additional 31 percent of cities, central cities were increasing their share of less educated residents compared with suburban rings, but the rings were not gaining highly educated adults compared with central cities. In 91 percent of the cities studied, however, central cities were increasing their share of less educated adult residents compared with suburban rings. In only 9 percent of the cases were suburban rings increasing their share of less educated adults compared with central cities whole losing or failing to gain highly educated adult residents. Schnore's results showed that ring to central city status contrasts were increasing in 91 percent of American cities in the expected manner. However, in only 60 percent of the cases studied were suburban rings *also* gaining highly educated residents compared with central cities. In sum, the hole-in-the-doughnut momentum was obviously dominant in the decade 1950–1960, but the speed of change in the predicted direction was unequal, and in a tenth of the cases reversals of direction occurred. In this tenth of all cities, a subdominant pattern of gentrification already existed in the decade 1950–1960.

Gentrification in the 1950s, however, was almost exclusively found in smaller and younger cities located in the South and West. Among cities with populations of 250,000 or more, Schnore (1972: 89) found that 83 percent had suburban rings gaining highly educated populations and central cities gaining less educated populations. Similarly, among cities established in the period 1780–1830, 87 percent were increasing the status contrast of suburban and central city population in the manner noted above. The big old cities more closely approximated the hole-in-the-doughnut growth pattern than did smaller, newer cities where signs of gentrification were already apparent in the 1950s. For example, in Tucson, Ariz., the central city population was already of higher status than the ring population in 1960.

Annexations explain some of these regional contrasts in ring to central city status contrasts. When central cities annex suburban territories, they almost always increase their share of highly educated population compared with unannexed suburban territory. In fact, Schnore (1972: 96) found that in every one of the twenty-nine SMSAs of 250,000 or more in which annexations occurred, the median income of central city residents was raised in consequence. Because high-growth Southern and Western cities have been annexing ring territory, they have tended to bring back high-status suburbanites into the central city. The net effect of annexations has thus been to reduce the apparent status contrast of central city to ring populations, but the reduction has been more apparent than real. Exactly how much more is uncertain, but it seems likely that when the effects of annexations are discounted, gentrification in the 1950s was less pronounced than one might otherwise conclude. Schnore attributed the regional contrast in morphology to preindustrial residuals as well as the pervasive influence of automotive transport. Automobiles reduce the density gradient of metropolitan regions, and the shaping influence of automobiles has been more pervasive in the cities of the South and West, whose whole growth period has occurred in the automotive age. In the Northeast and Midwest, preautomotive morphology and transportation arrangements have exerted a lingering and retarding effect on suburbanization.

PREINDUSTRIAL AND INTERNATIONAL COMPARISONS

Contemporary cities of the Third World do not fit the North American models. Third World cities typically locate their high-status residents in the densely settled central cities (Ginsburg 1965; Schnore 1965). The suburban rings are sites of shantytowns in which the migratory poor reside. There are innercity slums too, and some accounts discern a process of suburbanization in the movement of new migrants from innercity slums of first settlement to delapidated shanties on the periphery. But the center of gravity in Third World cities plainly locates the high-status elites in the heart of town. Analysts agree that Third World cities reverse the usual distribution of wealthy and poor in relation to their North American counterparts. Third World cities commonly have two central poles: an old town and a colonialist town. The old town is the precolonial center. In Algiers, this is the *kasbah* ("fortress"), which, even during the heyday of colonialism, Europeans dared not enter. In Jerusalem, it is the walled city containing the historic market. Cairo, Jaffa, Delhi, and Shanghai (Tilly 1974: 47) are other precolonial cities in which the old city survives as a distinct settlement pole. European colonialists often founded their commercial cities next to the old towns. These European cities attracted capitalistic enterprise and European settlement, thus creating a little Paris or London cheek by jowl to the native towns. Since ecological theory posits a unitary center of dominance in every region, the dualism actually observed in Third World cities today poses an embarrassing theoretical anomaly.

Sjoberg (1960, 1965) produced a particularly influential critique of ecological theory. His international and comparative study revealed that preindustrial cities do not conform to the working model of North American metropolitan regions. On the contrary, in preindustrial cities, the rich, powerful, and prestigious classes occupy the center of town, and the poor and downtrodden occupy the outlying suburbs. Furthermore, the most desirable central land is given over to religious and government buildings rather than to a central business district. Also in most Third World cities, influential native groups prefer precapitalist traditions to newer urban forms associated with modernization. "Urban sociologists should not overlook the forces that impede" the profanation of precapitalist patterns of land use (Sjoberg 1965: 221). Sjoberg disputed the generalizability of ecological theory on the basis of this evidence.

A defender of ecological tradition, Hawley (1968) accepted Sjoberg's evidence but claimed that this evidence was compatible with ecological theory. Hawley claimed that dominant "functions" occupy central places. Since the dominant functions ("basic industries") of preindustrial cities are religion and government, Hawley argued, these functions would be expected to claim the most desirable central sites. Hawley claimed further that pedestrians or animal-drawn transportation made central residences desirable and produced a settlement by the dominant classes in the city center. By reducing the burdens of commutation, automotive transportation and electronic communications have, in Hawley's judgment, rendered the periphery more desirable for residence and thus produced the affluent suburb of the twentieth-century metropolitan region. Hawley found, therefore, no contradiction between ecological theory and Sjoberg's preindustrial city.

Responding subsequently to additional negative evidence from around the world, Hawley (1981: 315) claimed that modern cities everywhere are "converging" around the North American working model in which the poor occupy the metropolitan core and the more affluent the enveloping suburbs. According to this revised view, any residual differences between North American and other regional urban morphology are unimportant so long as all world regions are moving toward ultimate convergence around a common "industrial" model. The cause of the convergence, according to Hawley, is the revolution in local transportation and communication technology in this century. Wherever and insofar as this technological revolution has penetrated, the tendency toward convergence around a North American model can be expected there.

Research necessary to test this sophisticated revision is still incomplete and awaiting "another generation of scholars" (Meadows and Mizruchi 1976: 60). However, London and Flanagan (1976) have completed a thorough inventory of existing literature bearing on the convergence hypothesis. They approached their huge task on a continent-by-continent basis. In Latin America and South and Southeast Asia, London and Flanagan discerned evidence of convergence around the North American model. In Europe and Africa, they found no evidence of convergence. "One might conclude that there is no uniform pattern to be observed anywhere and . . . this would be correct."

However, London and Flanagan (1976: 57) insist that ecological principles and results are distinguishable, and only the former really count. They conclude that world evidence confirms the universal applicability of ecological principles even though occasional "resistances" have prohibited the coming to fruition of the North American metropolitan results. For example, in Europe they found a preindustrial "ecological foundation which . . . resists changes in the direction of the United States industrial city's pattern." Even in growing cities of Europe—London, Paris, Vienna, Stockholm, Budapest—they found the middle and upper classes tending to "remain centralized" while industry moved toward the "working class areas" on the periphery. The major contributor to this "resistance" in the United States is the relatively free play of market forces in contrast to "European emphasis on government urban planning." In tropical Africa, London and Flanagan (1976: 50) also discerned that "command interference with the market mechanism" was "obscuring" an underlying tendency for cities to converge around the North American model.

This mixed conclusion underscores the continued tendency of ecological theory to regard as illegitimate the obtrusion of the public sector into the process of land use decision making. Yet this obtrusion is increasingly prominent in the United States and has completely overwhelmed the private sector in the communist nations. Whether public sector obtrusion is desirable or undesirable in its consequences need not concern us here. The point is that the public sector is capable of taking over all or some of the process of land use decision making previously assigned to the free market. Moreover, when the public sector does obtrude, as increasingly it does (Rodwin 1970), glaring divergences from the North American model result. In the opinion of Berry and Kasarda (1977: 413), successful public interventions have already produced "urban social and spatial structures that differ markedly from those evolving in the context of spontaneous ('natural') ecological forces." A sociological explanation of urban morphology must be capable of explaining why the balance between the public and private sectors' shares of land use decision making is shifting toward the former, and what difference the shift makes. Treating the public sector as a "resistance" to private enterprise ignores this central question, and much criticism of ecological theory centers around this point.

LAND USE IN BRITAIN

Metropolitan land use decision making in Britain provides a case study of this question. Britain, Canada, and the United States share a cultural, linguistic, and legal heritage and also a roughly analogous level of industrialization. Yet metropolitan land use in the three nations is not identical, and close study indicates that the expansion of the public sector's authority in Britain after World War II has been the immediate cause of British-North American differences. Of course, differences are neither immense nor diametrical. Metropolitanization has been underway in Britain during this century for exactly the reasons it has been underway in North America. Results have been analogous to North America in many respects: road building, mass automobile ownership, low-density suburbs, urban sprawl, migration of middle-income population to suburbs, and isolation of depressed central cities. Indeed, in the industrially stagnant North and West of Britain, central city deterioration has advanced nearly as far as in the Northeast of the United States and much further than elsewhere in Europe. The existence of extensive parallelism between Britain and the United States is, therefore, indisputable, and the parallelisms in the case even outweigh the divergences (Clawson and Hall 1973: 45).

Before World War II, Britain permitted private enterprise to make land use decisions in metropolitan areas. Since then, the private sector's role has been substantially reduced and the public sector's enhanced. The shifting balance is the immediate cause of numerous points of divergence between Britain and North America. The origins of British legislation was a series of government reports issued between 1937 and 1944. Of these, the most notable was the Abercrombie Plan of 1944, which called for comprehensive legal controls over industrial location to curb the economic growth of London. Abercombie's plan also favored the formation of a green belt or forest preserve five miles wide all around London to forestall urban sprawl. Beyond the green belt, the Abercrombie Plan called for the establishment of new towns to take up the population overspill, as well as the expansion of existing small towns within a 100-mile radius for the same purpose. The Abercrombie Plan and other government reports called on the government "to nationalize development rights on all land that was not already built upon" (Clawson and Hall: 1973). The means were radical, but the conservative end was to support by law the "existing distribution" of regional population by preventing the excessive growth of London and the South by migration from the stagnating North and East. Best (1976) concludes that planning controls have had a significant impact in controlling and directing the process of urbanization in Britain since World War II.

In 1945 the Labour Party came to power in Britain in what contemporaries called a socialist revolution by electoral consent (Laski 1943). Clement Attlee's Labour government laid down the legislative basis for a system of comprehensive land use planning derived from the earlier reports. Three acts were crucial: Distribution of Industry Act, 1945; New Towns Act, 1946; and Town and Country Planning Act, 1947. The Town and Country Planning Act was the cornerstone of the system. This act nationalized development rights on all land. Authorities were required by law to prepare regional and local development plans and to review land use applications to assure conformity to government plan. Nonconforming uses were prohibited by law, which thus deprived private owners of the previously enjoyed right to make any use they desired of privately held real property. This act has been the basic law framing metropolitan land use in Britain since World War II. The effects have probably disappointed the law's supporters and have, in any case, left unchanged the stagnation of the North and West that triggered the controls. But the laws were basically successful in containing urban sprawl in Britain. During the 1930s, the average acreage lost to urbanization every year was 60,000. Since 1947 this loss has been reduced to 40,000 acres annually. "This is the result of policies of urban containment which have been generated by the local planning authorities set up under the 1947 Planning Act" (Clawson and Hall 1973: 43).

New Towns Act, 1946

The New Towns Act required the central government to create new cities as catchments for population overspill prevented from settling in London and the overpopulated cities of the South. British new towns are strictly defined as towns built under the provisions of the New Towns Act of 1946 by a development corporation (Clawson and Hall 1973: 199). In this sense, the British new towns are not, as commonly alleged, legal counterparts to North American new towns (for example, Reston, Va.) created by private enterprise [5]. By 1971, Britain had constructed twenty-eight new towns, which housed 1.7 percent of the total population, or 1,450,000 people. "All these new towns were deliberately created . . . by a decision of the central government after careful consideration of the planning problems of the region in which they were located" (Clawson and Hall 1973: 200).

The new towns were intended as self-contained and socially balanced communities, not suburbs of a central city. Self-containment meant an economic basis capable of supporting the resident population without commutation. Social balance meant a cross section of the British population. Economic self-containment of the new towns has been achieved, but the goal of social balance has fallen short. As in North America, new towns have attracted many professional and skilled workers but have had few jobs for the unskilled. The result has been social imbalance in new towns' population. Data show that the population of new towns underrepresents "the old, the poor, and the colored" who continue to reside in deteriorated central cities. Still, the imbalance observed in social composition is less extreme than in North American suburbs.

The causes of this shortfall in social balance are instructive. To survive, fledgling new towns needed to attract industry and build good housing. This requirement compelled new town corporations to permit market forces to affect their decision making. This pragmatic adjustment resulted in industrial decentralization emphasizing skilled and managerial jobs. "So the problems of the urban poor" were forgotten by new towns' authorities, who assigned this issue to their central city counterparts. The result proves that new towns' planners were not free to make plans in defiance of market forces. Alternatively, market forces compelled new towns' planners to behave like private developers to some degree. For this reason, new towns fell short of their projected goals of social balance, but not as far short of these goals as wholly private developments in the United States.

The Labour government intended a drastic reduction of private enterprise in housing. Subsequent governments modified the radical objectives of the original legislation, but public housing has still been much more prominent in Britain than in the United States. Between 1945 and 1970, public housing contributed 54 percent of new construction in Britain; private enterprise built only 46 percent. In the United States, all public housing starts amounted to less than 4 percent of total housing in 1980. As a result of the public housing predominance in Britain, the government has been more successful in coping with unfair and racially discriminatory housing practices. A comprehensive review of segregated housing in Britain finds "there is no ghetto in the American sense" (Peach et al. 1975: 413). The causes are complex but they include the predominance of the public sector, access to which is on the basis of universal qualification "rather than money market and income." Public housing is thus identified as a powerful tool of "social engineering" in Britain.

COMPARISON OF BRITAIN AND NORTH AMERICA

What is the source of these British-North American differences in the balance between private enterprise and public sector? Clawson and Hall (1973: 217) mention the American public's "faith in the ability of private enterprise" and "philosophical opposition to government action." In addition, private developers in America have lobbied actively to make certain that land values increased by urbanization accrue to them rather than to the public. There is a temptation to lay the British-North American difference to the existence in Britain of a social-ist labor movement capable of gaining political power. Berry and Kasarda (1977: 358) stress Labour's "enthusiastic commitment to planning" and its "ideological opposition to profit-seeking development." It is surely true that Attlee's Labour government owed its electoral constituency to the working class, the lower-salaried employees, and the unions. The Labour program also conceived of town and country planning as the spatial equivalent of economic planning and na-tionalization to which, as a socialist party, they were committed. Conservative opponents attacked the planning program in the name of private enterprise and derived disproportionate political support from corporate enterprise, banks, and monied individuals. In this sense, the class conflicts in British political life were the prerequisites of "nationalization of land development rights" under the Labour government.

However, a simple class formulation does some injustice to the British case. First, Labour's town and country planning was, of all its programs, the least controversial. The Labour Party passed this legislation in a context of informed agreement among rational men of good will rather than class partisanship. Second, the radical measures in land use decision making were by no means leading political issues to an electorate more interested in issues of nationaliza-tion of industry and full employment. In the United States there has never been this consensus on the desirability of restricting urban sprawl or the appropriate-ness of government intervention to this end (Warner 1968: especially Ch. 10). Therefore Depression-spawned government reports about the plight of cities and the desirability of "arriving at a rational urban land policy" to curb "specula-tion" never mobilized a political constituency capable of making laws (U.S. National Resources 1937: 14).

SUMMARY

Urban ecology developed in the era of unrestricted private predominance in land use decision making. This theory still conceives of metropolitan shape as the result of private competition in free markets. The theory has provided a valuable baseline of comparison for postwar developments, and it still stands as the most parsimonious explanation of how North American cities were shaped. However, there is criticism of the inability of ecology to explain public obtru-sion in the process of land use decision making and allocation. The best in-formed human ecologists are uncomfortably aware that "political power is . . . becoming a major element of the urbanization process" (Berry and Kasarda

1977: 402). When the public sector takes over this power, market competition ceases to be the mechanism for land use decision making. Adherents view urban ecology as a general theory of urban land use. Critics regard it at best as a model of land use decision making in capitalist societies. Such a model does not offer a satisfactory explanation for land uses in socialist or communist societies or in mixed private-public economies. To explain the predominance of public or private sectors in metropolitan land use, one must first explain the nation's or region's balance of class forces as expressed in the comparative political power of capitalist and working classes.

NOTES

1. For a critique of metaphorical organicism in sociology, see Robert Nisbet, *Social Change and History*. New York: Oxford, 1969.
2. This illustration draws upon Harold Hotelling, "Stability in Competition," *The Economic Journal* 39 (1929): 41–57. See also August Loesch, *The Economics of Location*. New Haven: Yale University Press, 1954.
3. "It may be that new programs of slum clearance and urban redevelopment will change the conventional pattern of American cities. But up to now most cities display deterioration at the center, centrifugal flight, absorption of suburbs and, in general, growth near the periphery of the metropolitan area." Stuart Queen and David Carpenter, *The American City*. New York: McGraw-Hill, 1953, p. 107. Urban renewal did not reverse this trend, but it did tend to brake it.
4. For annotated bibliographies reviewing zoning and urban renewal in the United States, see Dennis J. Palumbo and George A. Taylor, eds. *Urban Policy*. Detroit: Gale Research, 1979, pp. 68–84; Joseph Zikmund and Deborah Ellis Dennis, eds., *Suburbia*. Detroit: Gale Research, 1979, pp. 105–117.
5. In 1968 the U.S. Congress passed the New Communities Act to provide financial support for privately developed new towns. Burby and Weiss have provided a comparative study of thirteen privately financed new towns in the United States including two (Jonathan, Minn., and Park Forest South, Ill.) developed with federal support. See Raymond J. Burby and Shirley F. Weiss, *New Communities U.S.A.* Lexington, Mass.: D.C. Heath, 1976. On the history of new towns in the United States, see Clarence S. Stein, *Toward New Towns for America*. Cambridge: MIT Press, 1957.

REFERENCES

Aldrich, Howard. 1979. *Organizations and Environments*. Englewood Cliffs, N.J.: Prentice-Hall.

Anderson, Martin. 1964. *The Federal Bulldozer*. Cambridge: MIT Press.

Babcock, Richard F., and Fred P. Basselman. 1973. *Exclusionary Zoning*. New York: Praeger.

Beale, Calvin L. 1978. "Internal Migration in the United States Since 1970," pp. 37–89 in U.S. Congress, House of Representatives, 95th Congress, 2nd Sess., Select Committee on Population. *World Population: A Global Perspective*. Washington, D.C.: U.S. Government Printing Office.

Berry, Brian J. L., and Quentin Gillard. 1977. *The Changing Shape of Metropolitan America*. Cambridge Mass.: Ballinger.

——., and John D. Kasarda. 1977. *Contemporary Human Ecology*. New York: Macmillan.

Best, Robin. 1976. "The Changing Land-Use Structure of Britain." *Town and Country Planning* 44: n.p.

Burgess, Ernest W. 1928. "Residential Segregation in American Cities." *Annals of the American Academy of Political and Social Science* 140: 105-115.

Castells, Manuel. 1977. *The Urban Question*. Trans. Alan Sheridan. Cambridge: MIT.

Clawson, Marion, and Peter Hall. 1973. *Planning and Urban Growth: An Anglo-American Comparison*. Baltimore: Johns Hopkins University Press.

Davidoff, Paul, and Mary E. Brooks. 1976. "Zoning Out the Poor," pp. 135-166, in Philip C. Dolce, ed. *Suburbia: The American Dream and Dilemma* Garden City, N.Y.: Anchor Press/Doubleday.

Duncan, Otis Dudley. 1959. "Human Ecology and Population Studies," pp. 678-716, in Philip M. Hauser and Otis Dudley Duncan, eds. *The Study of Population*. Chicago: University of Chicago Press.

——. 1974. "Population Structure and Community Structure," pp. 190-216, in Charles Tilly, ed. *An Urban World* Boston: Little, Brown.

Firey, Walter. 1947. *Land Use in Central Boston*. Cambridge: Harvard University.

Fishman, Richard P. 1978. *Housing for All Under Law*. Cambridge Mass.: Ballinger Publishing.

Fried, Marc. 1973. *The World of the Urban Working Class*. Cambridge: Harvard University Press.

Gans, Herbert. 1962. *The Urban Villagers*. New York: Free Press.

George, Henry. 1954. *Progress And Poverty*. New York: Robert Shalkenbach Foundation.

Gibbard, Harold A. 1941. "The Status Factor in Residential Successions." *American Journal of Sociology* 46: 835-842.

Gibbs, Jack, and Walter T. Martin. 1962. "Urbanization, Technology, and the Division of Labor: International Patterns." *American Sociological Review* 27: 667-677.

Ginsburg, Norton S. 1965. "Urban Geography and 'Non-Western' Areas," pp. 311-360, in Philip Hauser and Leo F. Schnore, eds. *The Study of Urbanization* New York: Wiley.

Greer, Scott A. 1965. *Urban Renewal and American Cities*. Indianapolis: Bobbs-Merrill.

Gusfield, Joseph. 1975. *Community: A Critical Response*. New York: Harper & Row.

Harris, Chauncey D., and Edward L. Ullman. 1945. "The Nature of Cities." *Annals of the American Academy of Political and Social Science* 242: 7–17.

Hauser, Francis L. 1968. "Ecological Patterns of European Cities." pp. 193–216, in Sylvia Fava, ed. *Urbanism in World Perspective.* New York: Thomas Y. Crowell.

Hawley, Amos. 1950. Human Ecology. New York: Ronald.

——. 1968. "Human Ecology." *International Encyclopedia of the Social Sciences.* Vol. 4 pp. 328–337. New York: Macmillan.

——. 1981. *Urban Society,* 2nd ed. New York: Wiley.

Hoyt, Homer. 1933. *One Hundred Years of Land Values in Chicago.* Chicago: University of Chicago Press.

Jacobs, Jane. 1961. *The Death and Life of Great American Cities.* New York: Vintage.

Kasarda, John D. 1972. "The Theory of Ecological Expansion: An Empirical Test." *Social Forces* 51: 165–175.

Kolb, William. 1954–1955. "The Social Structure and Functions of Cities." *Economic Development and Cultural Change* 3: 30–46.

Laski, Harold J. 1943. *Reflections on the Revolution of Our Times.* New York: Viking.

London, Bruce, and William G. Flanagan. 1976. "Comparative Urban Ecology: A Summary of the Field," pp. 41–66, in John Walton and Louis Masotti, eds. *The City in Comparative Perspective.* New York: Wiley.

Masotti, Louis, and John Walton. 1976. "Comparative Urban Research: The Logic of the Comparisons and the Nature of Urbanization," pp. 1–16, in John Walton and Louis Masotti, eds. *The City in Comparative Perspective.* New York: Wiley.

McKenzie, R. D. 1933. *The Metropolitan Community.* New York: McGraw-Hill.

Meadows, Paul, and Ephraim Mizruchi, eds. 1976. *Urbanism, Urbanization and Change: Comparative Perspectives.* 2nd ed. Reading, Mass.: Addison-Wesley.

Mollenkopf, John. 1978. "The Postwar Politics of Urban Development," pp. 117–152, in William Tabb and Larry Sawers, eds. *Marxism and the Metropolis* New York: Oxford University Press.

Park, Robert. 1936. "Succession: An Ecological Concept." *American Sociological Review* 1: 171–179.

Peach, Ceri, Stuart Winchester, and Robert Woods. 1975. "The Distribution of Coloured Immigrants in Britain," pp. 395–419, in Gary Gappert and Harold M. Rose, eds. *The Social Economy of Cities,* Vol. IX, *Urban Affairs Annual Reviews.* Beverly Hills: Sage.

Riemer, Svend. 1952. *The Modern City.* Englewood Cliffs, N.J.: Prentice-Hall.

Rodwin, Lloyd. 1970. *Nations and Cities.* New York: Houghton Mifflin.

Schnore, Leo F. 1965. "On the Spatial Structure of Cities in the Two Americas," pp. 347–398, in Philip M. Hauser and Leo F. Schnore, eds. *The Study of Urbanization.* New York: Wiley.

——. 1972. *Class and Race in Cities and Suburbs.* Chicago: Markham.

Scott, Mel. 1971. *American City Planning Since 1890.* Berkeley and Los Angeles: University of California Press.

Shlay, Anne B., and Peter H. Rossi. 1981. "Keeping Up the Neighborhood:

Estimating Net Effects of Zoning." *American Sociological Review* 46: 703–719.

Sjoberg, Gideon. 1960. *The Preindustrial City*. New York: Free Press.

——. 1965. "Cities in Developing and in Industrial Societies: A Cross-Cultural Analysis," pp. 213–263, in Philip Hauser and Leo F. Schnore, eds. *The Study of Urbanization*. New York: Wiley.

Sternlieb, George and James W. Hughes. 1980. "The Changing Demography of the Central City." *Scientific American* 243: 48–53.

Tilly, Charles. 1974. "Chaos of the Living City," pp. 86–108, in Charles Tilly, ed. *An Urban World*. Boston: Little, Brown.

U.S. National Resources Committee. 1937. *Our Cities*. Washington, D.C.: U.S. Government Printing Office.

Warner, Sam Bass, Jr. 1968. *The Private City*. Philadelphia: University of Pennsylvania Press.

Weiner, Arthur, and Homer Hoyt. 1960. *Real Estate,* 5th ed. New York: Ronald.

PART FOUR

Communities

World
Urbanism

Migration, Neighborhood, and Association

Cities have only three methods for recruiting population: natural increase, net migration, and boundary revision (Tilly 1974: 41). *Natural increase* is an excess of births over deaths. When natural increase is positive, cities gain population; when births and deaths are equal, no change results; and when deaths outnumber births, city populations decline. Natural increase always encourages city growth, but natural increase produces urbanization only when urban populations are growing more rapidly than rural ones. If urban population is growing but rural population is growing faster, cities gain in size but decline as a proportion of the society's population. Since urbanization is an increase in the urban proportion of society's population, natural increase produces urbanization only when more rapid in city than in urban areas.

The second method of recruitment is net migration. *Net migration* is the number of people who moved into a city minus the number of people who moved out. When these numbers are equal, migration produces no change in city population except for turnover. In an extreme case, if every resident left and was replaced by a newcomer, city population would remain the same but all the people would be new. This turnover would have a tremendous impact upon city life; for example people would not know their neighbors. However, the size of every city's population would be unaffected. So long as more people are moving into cities than are moving out, cities are gaining population from migration. Net migration produces urbanization only when cities are gaining population by migration faster than rural areas. We can imagine a situation in which people are moving to cities from rural areas, but even more people are born in the rural areas. Under this circumstance, cities would be gaining new residents by migration but losing population in relation to rural areas. Hence urbanization would be negative.

Boundary revision is the third method of population recruitment. Boundary revisions increase population by incorporating new territories previously beyond the city's perimeter. Because cities do expand radially from a center, some rural people find themselves within city limits even though they have not changed residence. Boundary revision is sometimes deceptive in sociological consequence. If the city limits of Milwaukee were redrawn to include the whole population of Wisconsin, the urbanization of the state would attain 100 percent, the theoretical limit. However, millions of new Milwaukee residents would still engage in dairy farming and these millions would be urban in name but not in life-style. Thus simple declaration by government statisticians can create the illusion of urbanization while leaving realities untouched. On the other hand, when city limits are redrawn to reflect prior growth of populations engaged in nonfarm occupations and urban in life-style, boundaries are only catching up with sociological realities.

These three sources of population recruitment are not equally important. Migration is the most important, especially when viewed in historical context. Because natural increase in cities has always been slower than in rural districts, it alone would never have produced urbanization. On the contrary, natural increase alone would have resulted in a constantly declining proportion of urban population in the world's societies. Although cities would grow in absolute population, they would fall behind in their proportion of total population. Urbanization depended on transferring population from rural districts to cities. The mechanism of this transfer was rural-urban migration, the movement of people previously living in rural districts to cities.

Rural-urban migration has been the greatest source of urban population growth, but cities also recruit population from other cities. These are interurban migrants. In societies beginning industrial urbanization, rural-urban migration is much larger than interurban migration. In heavily urbanized societies, however, interurban migration normally exceeds rural-urban migration. Between 1970 and 1975, for example, 13 percent of moved households in the United States had shifted from one SMSA to another; these were interurban migrants. Only 5 percent of moved households entered SMSAs from nonmetropolitan counties (Morrison and Wheeler 1976: 8). Interurban migration in the United States has accelerated the urbanization of Sunbelt states in the last generation. The consequences of this regional shift have been profound, but they have not included the urbanization of the United States. People who move from one city to another increase the urban population in one place and decrease it in another; they do not increase the urban proportion of society's population. In Third World countries, where urbanization is so rapid, rural-urban migration is most extensive. In the industrial countries, where urbanization is already approaching its limit, rural-urban migration has tapered off. However, the urban history of the world is essentially a history of rural-urban migration. Some of this migration was international, some internal. The migration of European peasants to North American cities was international because the migrants crossed national boundaries. The migration of rural blacks from the South to Northern cities was internal because the rural migrants crossed no international boundaries.

Migration, natural increase, and boundary revision are in principle independent of one another. Any one might be positive and the others negative. Net population change is the sum of positives minus negatives. One can find every possible combination of these three sources in the population histories of individual cities. However, if we consider whole systems of cities, the typical cases are only two. In the preindustrial epoch, death rates in cities exceeded birthrates owing to a combination of imbalanced sex ratios, unhealthful living conditions, poor diet, and inadequate public health. The result was dependence of preindustrial cities on continuous migration from the countryside just to replenish the urban population [1]. Natural increase was negative but migration was positive, so stability of city population resulted.

Industrial urbanization abolished this balance. For the first time, cities began to experience natural increase. This increase resulted mostly from declining death rates in cities as a result of improvements in sanitation, public health, diet, and neonatal care. Everywhere in the world urbanization is associated with lowered birthrates because small families are part of the urban life-style. Nonetheless, cities have acquired the capability of augmenting population by natural increase because infant mortality is low. This was never possible before. Therefore natural increase has become a modest force for population growth in cities instead of a net destroyer of urban population.

Net migration and boundary revision have also encouraged the growth of city populations in the nineteenth and twentieth centuries. Rates of rural-urban migration accelerated as a result of industrialization, and new migrants augmented city populations already reproduced by natural increase. The overall result was continuous, unidirectional growth of urban population. As these populations grew, cities expanded radially toward their periphery, incorporating previously nonurban territories. Therefore boundary revision became a reliable source of population gain in industrial urbanization.

MIGRATION TYPOLOGY

Petersen (1968: 268) has defined migration as "relatively permanent movement of persons over a significant distance." His definition excludes temporary relocations (such as vacationing), but it leaves to each observer the problem of deciding what constitutes an appropriate threshold of permanence and distance.

Nevertheless, given a true migration, one may also distinguish various types. Tilly (1978: 48–49) has identified four types of migration: local, circular, chain, and career. Local migration "shifts an individual or household within a geographically contiguous market." Distances moved are small by prevailing standards, and movers are familiar with the cultural context of their destination before they leave. Most migration is of this sort and always has been. Moving from city to suburb is an example of local migration. Another example is moving into a nearby city from a marginal rural area or contiguous small town.

Circular migration involves moving households or individuals "to a destination through a set of arrangements which return the migrants to the origin after a well-defined interval" (Tilly 1978: 52). This type of migration is also called sojourning, and those who practice it are sojourners (Siu 1952). An example is seasonal harvest labor that begins when a crop ripens and migrants take to the road, and ends when, the crop having been harvested, field hands return home. Sojourning has been common in cities too, but has never contributed to urbanization because sojourners always return to their point of origin (McGee 1973: 136).

Chain migration is the third type (Graves and Graves 1974: 123). *Migration chains* move "sets of related individuals or households from one place to another" by means of social arrangements "in which people at the destination provide aid, information, and encouragement to the new migrants" (Tilly 1978: 53). Chain migrations involve pioneers and settlers (MacDonald and MacDonald 1974). Pioneers arrive first; there is no kin to provide them with aid, information, or encouragement. Once established, the pioneers are in a position to assist others to make the migration. Those assisted are typically the kin of the pioneers. Since most kin share a locality of origin, migrants assisted by pioneers are, in most cases, both kin and hometown associates, a doubly strong social connection. Chain migration has been and continues to be the basic mechanism of urbanization (Tilly and Brown 1967: 111).

Career migration occurs when individuals or households move in response to bureaucratic employment opportunities. Business or government transfers of personnel take this form. Thus when the Air Force transfers personnel from one base to another, the movers are career migrants. Sometimes career migrants change employers as they move along a regularized career hierarchy. Either way, the migrants move into employment that has been prearranged and their encouragement depends mainly on the new employer, not their kin.

These four types do not exclude one another. There has never been a city of any magnitude whose migrant population did not contain representatives of each type. Still, urban history indicates that local and circular migration were more prominent in the preindustrial period than now. Conversely, chain migration and career migration are typical forms of migration to modern cities.

Modern cities have experienced a relative shift of emphasis in migration, but this shift has not eliminated earlier types. Table 11-1 illustrates this association. The reasons are straightforward. In the preindustrial world, travel was slow,

Table 11-1. Typology of Urban Migrations

	Local	Circular	Chain	Career
Origin/destination				
Rural-urban	x	x	x	
Interurban	x			x
Historical era				
Preindustrial	x	x		
Industrial			x	x
Status of migrants				
High	x			x
Low	x	x	x	

dangerous, and expensive. Therefore distances traveled were usually short. Local migrations predominated because ordinary folk could not make ocean voyages. In the industrial world that has emerged since 1750, travel has become increasingly fast, safe, and cheap. This improvement has permitted masses to relocate over great distances (Petersen 1978). As a result, local migration has declined in relative prominence. Its principal form in urbanized societies is suburbanization, a form of interurban migration. Moreover, preindustrial cities depended on circular or sojourning migrants to replace their population. Sojourning is incompatible with industrial urbanization. Industrial urbanization means people are permanently relocating because rural areas are surrendering population to cities. Therefore urbanization has imposed a change from circular to chain migration upon rural-urban migrants (Table 11-1).

Career migration occurred in bureaucratic empires but chiefly among elites. Career migration is still associated with high status. People who migrate to known jobs along a career line are educated and affluent. Rural-urban migration involves career discontinuity: agricultural occupations are abandoned and urban ones assumed. But career migration always occurs in a context of occupational continuity. For this reason, career migrants to cities are usually urban in origin so their migration is interurban rather than rural-urban (Table 11-1). Interurban migration is most prominent in developed industrial societies whose urbanization approaches the limit. These societies are no longer transferring indigenous population from country to city because there are few people left on farms.

CHAIN MIGRATION AND NEIGHBORHOOD FORMATION

Circular and chain migrations become urban neighborhoods (MacDonald and MacDonald 1974). Pioneers from a rural locality go to a city and inform people they left behind about the employment and housing they find. Just being in a city, pioneers are able to learn what industries and occupations are thriving and to make contacts more successfully than people who must operate from a distance. Therefore pioneers locate housing and employment and pass on the information to people they know. The people whom the pioneers know are located in the rural locality from which the pioneers emigrated and are the recipients of housing and employment information from the pioneers. In this manner, migrants establish an information network that links those already in the city with those left behind (Graves and Graves 1974: 124).

Those information networks channel migrants from place to place. A rural locality might be equidistant between two major cities, but all its rural-urban migrants go to one city rather than the other because the migration network has provided the rural people with information about that city but not about the other. Moreover, those who go to cities in which their friends and kin already reside can expect assistance in securing housing and employment, whereas those who go elsewhere must fend for themselves (Siu 1952). Naturally, people prefer to go where friends and kin can help them, and this preference creates correspondences between particular villages and particular cities [2]. Cities and countryside in general are loosely linked in official statistics. What is humanly linked are specific villages and specific cities. The linkage is the information and assistance network provided by the migration chain.

When newcomers arrive in a city, their first stop is often the home of friends or neighbors from home (Li 1978; Rogg 1971). Often this sponsor actually provides room and board for a protégé while the newcomer finds housing and employment, learns the language, and makes other adjustments to the new city. The housing the newcomer finds will probably be near the sponsor's housing, often next door; this is partly by preference (Lloyd 1979: 129). But opportunity matters too. Of Americans who changed residences in 1969-1970, 61 percent remained in the same county. This sizable proportion illustrates the tendency to locate housing close to one's current residence. This tendency results from the ease with which people learn about local housing and the difficulty of learning about housing at a greater distance.

As newcomers locate housing and work, they become sponsors of other rural-urban migrants. Uncle sponsors nephew who sponsors brother who sponsors cousin and so on (Lloyd 1979: 121-129). As each newcomer settles in the sponsor's vicinity, there grows up a whole neighborhood of people from the same rural locality. This is also an ethnic neighborhood, and its residents are connected by marriage and kinship as well as by dialect and hometown memories. As the process repeats itself in other parts of the city, other ethnic neighborhoods emerge. The overall result is the creation of an urban mosaic of ethnic neighborhoods (Agocs 1977: 10). Each neighborhood was formed on the basis of nearby settlement of people known to one another already. There was often no intention of forming an ethnic neighborhood, nor was ethnicity the specific principle at work. The principle was kinship and friendship. However, the kin of migrants are almost always coethnics, as are their friends from home. The friends of their friends and the kin of their kin turn out to be coethnics too. The net result of consecutive residential choices made on the basis of kinship and friendship is an ethnic neighborhood.

INSIDER/OUTSIDER ETHNIC AWARENESS

Outsiders regard a neighborhood as ethnic rather than network-based. Outsiders also assume coethnics cluster together because they are excluded everywhere else rather than because they simply like to live near friends. Outsiders choose an ethnic label that is broad and unitary. Coethnic insiders appreciate the network connections that structure their own neighborhood and think of it as a plurality of interconnecting networks rather than a unitary bloc. For example, in Toronto, Passache and Jansen (1969: 17) found that Italian or German churches, newspapers, businesses, and so forth were available to "people of Italian and German ethnic origin only *in the eyes of outsiders*" (their italics). In reality, the various institutions actually serviced selective networks based on kinship, friendship, and political affiliation. Some Italians patronized this butcher, some that. Some Germans used this baker, some another. Neighborhood institutions were "not available to all members of the Italian or German ethnic groups" (Passache and Jansen, 1969: 17). Insiders knew which newspaper to read and which business to patronize, but outsiders did not understand the internal life of the neighborhoods and wrongly assumed they housed a homogeneous population.

Figures 11-1 and 11-2 are turn-of-the century maps that illustrate an outsider's neighborhood consciousness. For example, these maps show "Southern Italian" neighborhoods in Cleveland and Boston, yet there were no such neighborhoods in either city. Italians were among the most parochial of peasant immigrants to North America (Glazer and Moynihan 1970: 186), and major American and Canadian cities actually contained several Italian neighborhoods, sometimes adjoining, sometimes separate. Each one catered to people from a village or province of Italy (Lopreato 1970: 41-42). "Each regional group regarded those from other regions with their strange dialects and customs, not as fellow Italians, but as distinct and inferior ethnic types" (Vecoli 1963: 413). Within these regionally distinct neighborhoods, the various streets—even the apartment houses—acquired reputations for heavy representation of people from particular Italian villages [3].

People from the same village or province treated one another as coethnics. The term *paisano* applied to someone from the same village or province, and such a person could claim privileges of solidarity denied Italians from other places.

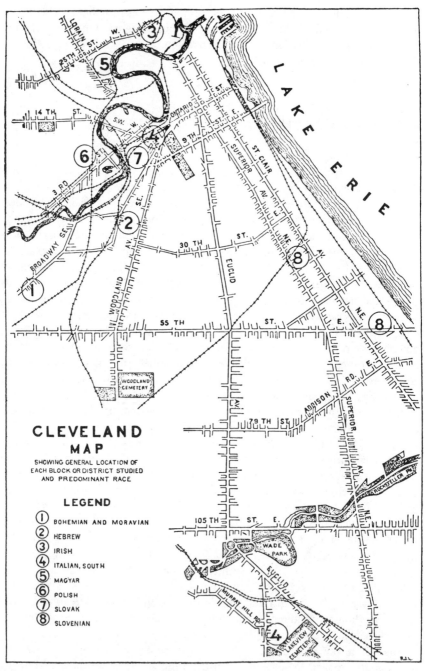

Figure 11-1. Ethnic Neighborhoods in Cleveland, 1911. (Source: Report of the Immigration Commission, 1911.)

278

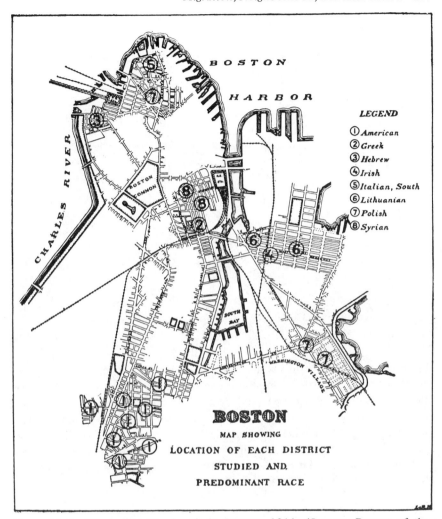

Figure 11-2. Ethnic Neighborhoods in Boston, 1911. (Source: Report of the Immigration Commission, 1911.)

Paisani were regarded as possessing modal personalities, and endogamy was preferred. The relationships among Italian immigrants from different provinces were competitive and often antagonistic. This pluralistic confusion can be described as ethnic groups within ethnic groups.

Figure 11-3 represents this recurrent process. *A*-land is an ethnic homeland with five villages, but only the residents of villages 1, 2, and 3 migrate to The Big City. As a result of chain migration, people from these three villages make connections with friends and kin in The Big City. The result is homogeneous settlements of people from each village. This three-village cluster gains the name

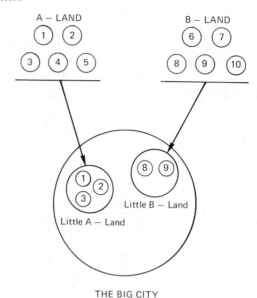

Figure 11-3. Neighborhood Formation in Urbanization

Little *A*-land and its residents are called *A*-landers by outsiders. However, the people who live in Little *A*-land know one another as village-one people, village-two people, or village-three people. These villagers quarrel with one another and form denigrating ethnic stereotypes about their *A*-land neighbors. Little *B*-land was formed in the same manner from residents of villages 8 and 9. The basis for neighborhood formation was kinship and friendship, not ethnicity. But outsiders perceive the result as Little *A*-land or *B*-land and suppose that this identity was the one around which the neighborhood formed.

CHAIN MIGRATIONS AND CIRCULAR MIGRATIONS CONTRASTED

In circular migrations, newcomers replace people who died or returned to the rural homeland. Therefore the ethnic enclave does not grow in size. In chain migrations, rural-urban migrants do not return. The result is depopulation of the countryside. The theoretical limit of this depopulation is reached when the whole population of the countryside has emigrated to The Big City. In effect, whole villages have then relocated their populations in the city. Depopulating migrations result in ever increasing populations of urban ethnic enclaves.

Circular migrations replace deceased or departed sojourners with newcomers fresh from the rural hinterland. Newcomers expect to return to the hinterland after completing a sojourn and have, therefore, little motive to acculturate (Wong 1979: 16). After all, a person who adopts the ways of The Big City becomes a misfit in *A*-land or *B*-land. Forgetting the home dialect is a basic example. One who has forgotten the *A*-land dialect cannot comfortably return to *A*-land, and Big City speech is no use in *A*-land. On the other hand, chain migrations bring people to the city who have no expectation of returning to their homeland and have a motive to learn the language of The Big City. In time, they are likely to forget the home dialect and to lower the cultural barriers that originally divided them from other city residents. As barriers drop, ethnic groups form that have broader referents. For example, Sicilians, Neapolitans, and Calabrians eventually merged into a unitary Italo-American group (Barton 1975). In sum, chain migrations imply acculturation, whereas circular migrations imply cultural diversity.

A sharp contrast between chain migrations and circular ones is useful but slightly overdrawn. We cannot suppose rural-urban migrants are students of sociology! They are rarely aware that macrosocietal forces are transferring the redundant population of the countryside to cities. Many rural-urban migrants who live their whole lives in The Big City originally expected only to sojourn. After initial debarkation, personal circumstances produced a change of mind. Of course, these circumstances were not random. Sociologists can see macrosocietal influences that produced individual circumstances. Nonetheless, the result of uncertainty among rural-urban migrants is a blend of sojourning and permanent orientations: some people are sojourning, some settling, some uncertain.

European migration to the United States in the period 1880–1924 illustrates this complexity. Approximately 85 percent of these Europeans were rural-urban migrants. Their movement to cities of North America was clearly a manifestation of world urbanization involving permanent reduction of rural population. However, the immigrants were unaware of this macrosocietal process. Approximately 40 percent of those who debarked in North America ultimately repatriated (Axelrod 1972: 32–49). Repatriation was the intention of an even larger proportion of those initially debarking, possibly 80 percent. However, half of the sojourners changed their minds and decided to stay. The net effect of European migration was thus a relocation of rural population from Europe to big cities in North America, urbanizing both continents. While this shift was in progress, however, a majority of the immigrants in North American cities continued to regard themselves as sojourners, not settlers. In reality, sojourning and chain migrations were occurring simultaneously in the same population, and only the balance of comings and goings permits the conclusion that the final result of this complex movement was a net transfer of human population to cities and away from rural villages.

CAREER MIGRATION AND NEIGHBORHOOD

Career migration has weaker links to neighborhood formation than do chain or circular migrations, although there are occasional parellels. For example, military officers live on the base, a kind of neighborhood; doctors cluster around hospitals, professors around universities, and civil servants around government buildings. But when large, bureaucratic employers provide the auspices for migration, newcomers look to bosses—not kin—for relocation assistance. Employees go wherever the boss sends them, and the boss is likely to select destinations in which they have no kin or friends.

As a result, career migrants in a city are independent of kin and provenance. Proximity to work imposes an expedient constraint on neighborhood choice: other things being equal, people prefer to live close to their jobs. The residential decisions of career migrants also depend on income and social status. Cosmopolitan neighborhoods recruit residents on the basis of education, occupation, and income rather than kinship or provenance. The result is metropolitan neighborhoods whose composition is determined by socioeconomic status more than provenance. Since career migrants are heavily upper status, suburban neighborhoods of contemporary North American cities typically have this character.

Neighborhoods thus created rarely develop much solidarity among residents. If residents look to their work place for community, they ignore the neighborhood. Career migration reduces neighborhood identification because careerists have strong commitment to occupational community and often anticipate recurrent changes of residence in the course of a work life (Wilensky 1960). High rates of neighborhood turnover, expectations of transience, and occupational communities obstruct neighborhood solidarity (Hesslink 1970). On the other hand, even careerists sometimes experience dissatisfaction with occupational community and turn to neighbors for social contacts. "Neighbors become important," Keller writes (1968: 34) "when relatives are not available or where people lack the skills or opportunities to make friends." Having settled where their career directed, career migrants have few if any relatives in their new neighborhood so they turn to neighbors instead. Moreover, one-earner families are more common at high-income levels. Nonemployed wives of career workers often spend much time around the neighborhood. Hence a female network is likely to arise in the suburban neighborhood even when husbands limit their own social associations to the work place.

What happens to first-settlement neighborhoods when children of the immigrants grow up and find careers of their own? Insofar as adult children become interurban career migrants, one would expect reductions of central city ethnic neighborhoods and the growth of income-linked neighborhoods in suburbs. That is, the children of immigrants go wherever their employers send them and obtain housing in the best neighborhood they can afford. Evidence on this point is mixed. Lieberson (1963) compared residential segregation among foreign stock and native stock Americans in U.S. cities and found that levels of ethnic segregation were declining in every decade, just as one would expect if interurban career migration replaced chain migration. Roof (1980) found a similar decline in residential segregation among Southern-born whites and blacks when he compared 1940 and 1970. Among whites and blacks alike, segregation levels decreased with the growth in the Northern-born component of the population but increased with the growth in the Southern-born component, thus tending to confirm Lieberson (1963: 355). But Kantrowitz (1973: 78) found that ethnic segregation was *not* declining in residential areas of New York City, and he disputed the assimilationist conclusions of Lieberson on methodological grounds. Darroch and Marston (1971) also found that segregation was as high among white-collar as among blue-collar residents of Toronto. Comparing residential segregation in Boston, Seattle, and Cleveland, Guest and Weed (1976) found no tendency for reduction. "The continued existence of ethnic segregation in American cities is clear from these results. There is no evidence that it will disappear in the near future" (1976: 1109).

The apparent persistence of residential segregation in high-status suburbs is compatible with a sector model of urban ecology. Agocs (1977: 11; 1979) concludes that ethnic residential clusters in North American cities have tended to expand outward from center to periphery as the residents' socioeconomic status improved. Thus an immigrant community on the west side would tend to move successively farther into the western suburbs without losing ethnic homogeneity in the process. As cities expand, suburbs change their socioeconomic and ethnic character as well (Logan and Semyonov 1980). Similar sectoral dispersions have occurred in Third World shantytowns, many of whose residents moved there from residences in central city slums (Skeldon 1977: 508). Existing social networks structure these intrametropolitan relocations: people moving to suburbs settle where others from their central city neighborhood previously moved. Therefore the most typical form of suburbanization is short-distance chain migration. Such a process recreates in suburban, middle-class environments ethnic neighborhoods formed a half century earlier in central city slums.

Acculturation and bureaucratic employment do impede the perpetuation of first-settlement networks in suburbs. As a result of acculturation, central city people have acquired friends beyond the circle of their kin, coethnics, and neighborhood. Bureaucratic employers also post workers where they have no kin or friends. Over decades, these twin processes undermine reproduction of first-settlement neighborhood networks. The predictable result is heterogeneous suburbs of second settlement surrounding ethnically homogeneous central city neighborhoods. At present, evidence does not permit rejection of this conventional expectation, firmly rooted in Robert Park's (1950) assimilationism.

However, any tendency in this direction is *slower* than sociologists of Park's generation had expected, and at least temporary reversals of direction (counter-assimilationist) occur.

WARREN'S NEIGHBORHOOD TYPOLOGY

"Neighborhood" is hard to define. Some residential areas are communities; others just places to sleep. Warren (1977) distinguishes six types of urban neighborhood: integral, parochial, diffuse, stepping-stone, transitory, and anomic. These six types reflect the possible combinations of only three variables: attitude of residents toward their neighborhood, organization of the neighborhood, and the neighborhood's connections to the larger community. In the integral neighborhood neighbors like and approve of their neighborhood, are well organized in formal and informal associations, and have numerous links to outside organizations. At the opposite extreme is the anomic neighborhood, in which neighbors dislike their neighborhood, have few associations with one another, and have no organizational links to outside organizations. Warren's other types are alternative combinations of these binary variables.

Of Warren's three variables, the first and most important is whether or not a residential neighborhood is a "positive reference group" for the people who live there. A *positive reference group* is a neighborhood with which people are pleased to identify themselves. At one extreme are neighborhoods whose residents are glad to identify themselves with it and take pride in its reputation. "I'm from Park Avenue" implies the informant is upper-class, an impression people are normally pleased to convey because of the deference that rich people receive. At the other extreme are neighborhoods whose residents wish they lived somewhere else and are ashamed to admit they live in a rundown part of town. "I live in the Project" indicates the informant is probably an unemployed welfare recipient who does not command high deference in society. Most neighborhoods contain people with contrasting attitudes. Some people are ashamed to live on Park Avenue, and some people are proud to live in the South Bronx. However, the predominance of negative or positive attitude is the most critical determinant of neighborhood character. High-status, exclusive neighborhoods provide residents with prestige, whereas slums stigmatize the unfortunates who live in them. The attitude of people toward their neighborhood is solidly connected to social stratification in society, but it would be a mistake to suppose social stratification wholly explains the attitudes of neighborhood residents. Many low-income neighborhoods have a public spirit and pride that eclipses the smug satisfactions of wealthy households in their prestigious addresses.

People in ethnic and immigrant neighborhoods are often aware of their cultural difference from the rest of the community and take pride in this difference. Although a neighborhood may be poor, its residents are proud to identify themselves with it and the place from which its people earlier emigrated. Artist and bohemian colonies in great cities also bring together people who have little money, often existing on the slenderest of resources. New York's Greenwich Village (Ware 1935; Light 1974) once attracted bohemians whose outrageous, intellectual life-style set them apart from "solid citizens" as clearly as did the cultural differences in ethnic communities. The bohemian identity provided many Villagers with personal satisfaction, and they accordingly took considerable pride in residing in a neighborhood known to contain a high proportion of socially rebellious individuals. At the opposite extreme, public housing projects in the United States typically acquire an unsavory reputation for crime, squalor, subtance abuse, and delapidation. Residents are ashamed to admit they live there and thus reflect a negative identification with their neighborhood. Some people who live in exclusive suburbs (like Scarsdale or Grosse Pointe) are ashamed to admit this provenance because of the smug, bourgeois identities these suburban cities imply.

Neighborhoods may be well or poorly organized. Organization is the extent of participation in formal and informal social groups. Formal groups are named bodies with identified leadership and objectives. Informal groups are neighbors who communicate frequently, like each other, and spend time together. When formal and informal organizations in a neighborhood are numerous and all or nearly all its neighbors participate, that neighborhood is well organized. When, on the other hand, organizations are few and participation minimal, a neighborhood is poorly organized. Coping with local problems (such as crime, vandalism, substance abuse) is much easier in well-organized neighborhoods, and such places readily maintain an attractive environment with which residents are proud to identify. When neighborhood organization breaks down, neighbors cannot combine to control social problems, and problems run amok, thus contributing to the residents' unhappiness with their neighborhood. In general, working-class neighborhoods depend more on informal social groups for neighborhood organization whereas middle- and upper-status neighborhoods more heavily utilize formal voluntary associations.

Warren observes that, however organized, neighborhoods may or may not have links to the outside community. Linkages to outside bodies, formal and informal, are means for mobilizing and exerting influence. If the neighborhood needs more police, fire, or santitation service, the neighbors' ability to obtain augmented service really depends on influencing city hall. This influence depends, in turn, on the kind and number of linkages the neighbors have to powerful external groups such as political parties, unions, churches, banks, and so forth. Working-class neighborhoods have fewer and less influential outside connections. In part, this inequality results from the low economic and social status of working-class people. However, it also reflects the preponderance of informal social groups in working-class neighborhoods. Informal groups do not have so many linkages to outside bodies. For example, Whyte (1955) described a street corner gang in New Haven, the Nortons. This gang had no affiliates outside the neighborhood [4]. On the other hand, a Catholic parish can turn to the mother church, and a Democratic club can turn to the Democratic Party when local people need to exert influence upon outside agencies. For this reason, formal voluntary associations are politically more effective than informal social groups.

AUSPICES OF MIGRATION

Auspices of migration are "social structures which establish relationships between the migrant and the receiving community before he moves" (Tilly and Brown 1967: 111). Work, friends, and kin are the auspices that most frequently organize migrations. Of these three, kin and friends prevail in circular and chain migrations, and work auspices prevail in career migrations. Migrants who enter cities under auspices of kin, friends, or work are assisted migrants. Those who come under no auspices are unassisted migrants. Although most migrants enter cities under some auspices, some are unassisted. The ratio of assisted to unassisted varies and depends on ethnic origins and social structure.

Barton (1975: 48–63) compared the auspices of migration among Italians, Slovaks, and Romanians in Cleveland between 1890 and 1950 and distinguished major and minor migration chains and no-auspices migrations. Major migration chains eventuated in large aggregations of persons from the same village or region. Minor chains eventuated in smaller groups. Among Italians, 81 percent emigrated in major or minor migration chains, and only 19 percent came as solitary individuals from districts of sparse migration. The Slovaks were at the opposite extreme. Among them, 34 percent were solitary migrants, and 66 percent arrived in migration chains. Both the Romanians and the Slovaks utilized minor village chains (six to twenty persons) more extensively than did Italians, among whom 51 percent arrived in major village chains of twenty-one or more persons.

Cornelius (1975) examined migration auspices in Mexico City. Twenty-five percent of rural-urban migrants indicated their decision to migrate had been influenced by kin already in Mexico City at the time they migrated. Nearly half of all migrants and two thirds of first-time migrants reported their best source of information about jobs was relatives in Mexico City. On arrival in the city, approximately three quarters received some form of assistance from relatives already living there. More than half found permanent housing with these relatives. Residential location of the rural-urban migrants depended heavily on where relatives were already living. "Most migration to large cities in Mexico has been mediated by kinship ties" (1975: 22) [5].

A study of internal migration to Wilmington, Del., also gathered data bearing on auspices. Tilly and Brown (1961) asked 190 migrants who, if anyone, had assisted them or encouraged them to come to Wilmington. Eighty-four percent indicated that kin, friends, or "other" agents had provided migration auspices. Only 16 percent were unassisted. Work auspices were more common among white-collar than blue-collar workers, and auspices of kinship more common among the blue-collar workers. Unassisted migration was 24 percent among white-collar workers and only 12 percent among blue-collar workers (1961: 118). Unassisted migration was 20 percent of white migration and 10 percent of non-white. All others were assisted.

Auspices of migration affected the kinds of help migrants received. Employers provided information about jobs but little information about housing or living conditions. Therefore people who migrated to Wilmington under work auspices were unassisted in finding housing. On the other hand, kin provided more information about jobs than did employers and also provided information about housing and living conditions. Friends provided nearly as much information about jobs as did employers and more information about living conditions. These results indicate that kin and friends were not only more important sources of information about jobs than were work auspices, but they were the *only* sources that helped with housing and living conditions. This discrepancy reflects the impersonality of work auspices and the consequent necessity of depending on one's personal resources for effecting a migration.

American results give the impression that kin and friends auspices are more important than work auspices. The same conclusion accords with evidence gathered in other developed market societies as well as in Third World countries. In East European communist societies, however, work auspices are possibly of greater importance in assisted migrations. Two institutional features of communist societies produce these discrepancies. First, communist cities have chronic and severe housing shortages. Second, the state subsidizes public sector rents. This subsidy is ostensibly in the interest of social equality because low rents eliminate interfamily housing disparities based on ability to pay. On the other hand, rents in public housing are so low they really constitute a state gift to those lucky enough to obtain an apartment. The unlucky scramble for high-priced, dilapidated apartments in the private sector. In Yugoslavia, public housing projects have waiting lists of five or more years and no one is permitted to stay in a city who cannot provide the police with a permanent address. Given this housing situation, unassisted migrants to cities are disadvantaged. In principle, anyone may apply to the authorities for housing and wait his or her turn. In reality, employers have informal connections with housing authorities and are able to provide a "state gift" apartment as well as a job to anyone hired (Simic 1973: 94–95). Under these circumstances, employer auspices are indispensable to migration because others simply cannot obtain housing. Unassisted migration is virtually eliminated and the role of kinship and friendship auspices decreased. Yet auspices of kin and friends are still effective in locating housing in the private sector and also in obtaining jobs in public enterprises. That is, a kinsman's friend may know someone who can find a job for someone's brother in return for a bribe or favor. After a job is obtained, an employer can obtain a state-gift apartment for the brother, and in this manner kinship of friendship auspices in work carry over to housing (Simic 1973: 99).

Case histories (Simic: 101–104) offer a more detailed account of how new migrants find work and housing in Belgrade, Yugoslavia. Consider the case of Rade, a twenty-six-year-old mechanic. He arrived in Belgrade with little education at age fifteen and was fortunate to find two acquaintances from a neighboring village who lent him money and a place to sleep for a week. Then he found a job as an unskilled worker on a construction crew, and the enterprise obtained a bed for him in a workers' dormitory in the Karaburma District. By studying at night he completed elementary school, and after two years of military service, he returned to Belgrade and obtained a better job with the construction company. With further study, he was promoted to master mechanic, and the company found him a better place to live in a worker's hotel. In the hotel he had a private room for the equivalent of $3.20 monthly, but the hotel did not allow families or women in the rooms.

Todor moved to Belgrade alone, leaving his wife and children in their village. He found an unskilled job and obtained company housing in a single workers' dormitory. After a year, his wife and two children joined him, but the only housing they could find was in a peasant village outside Belgrade. They lived there two years, and Todor commuted to work by bus. Finally, they found a single room in central Belgrade and the whole family moved in. Meanwhile, Todor completed his technical training and was invited to join the Communist Party. He accepted, and the family's living standards immediately improved. His enterprise found his family a state-owned one-bedroom apartment with a private bath.

LANDSMANNSCHAFTEN

Landsmann is a German word meaning a person from one's place of origin. *Landsmannschaften* are social organizations whose members are *Landsmen*, people who share a place of origin. The German word has achieved international recognition among sociologists and anthropologists. Landsmannschaften are recurrent, nearly universal social associations in urban areas [6].

Landsmannschaften perform a variety of services: political representation, social welfare, economic mutual aid, religion, and sociability. A Landsmannschaft bears the name of its provenance and declares a multipurpose service objective. For instance, Japanese immigrants in the United States before World

War II formed Landsmannschaften on the basis of provincial (ken) origins. These were called *kenjinkai,* and those from Hiroshima affiliated with the Hiroshima Kenjinkai, whereas those from Wakayama were members of the Wakayama Kenjinkai, and so forth. The kenjinkais published newspapers, offered legal advice, sponsored savings clubs, served as employment agencies, and offered assistance in business and politics. They also sponsored annual picnics and other social events (Light 1972: 63). Little describes the numerous tribal unions in West African cities in similar terms. Their purpose was "fostering and keeping alive" tribal culture and thus "maintaining a person's attachment to his native town or village and to his lineage there" (1965a: 329). To this end, tribal unions provided members with mutual aid, including financial support when unemployed, money when ill, and funerals for deceased members. Doughty (1970: 34) counted 1,050 provincial and hamlet associations in Lima, Peru. In size, these Landsmannschaften ranged from 5 to 1,000 members, and their average size was 64. Maintaining a clubhouse, each association organized Sunday soccer games, dances, social occasions, political lobbying, and philanthropic drives to benefit their native village. Doughty found the clubs' identification with provenance did not disappear, even after "decades of existence." Migrants held onto their provincial identities "no matter what" their socioeconomic status subsequently became.

Landsmannschaften play their greatest role when sex ratios are unbalanced, typically when there is a preponderance of males (Lyman 1968). Imbalance creates a large class of single persons who turn to Landsmen for sociability and assistance.

VOLUNTARY ASSOCIATIONS

Landsmannschaften and kinship groups are ascriptive because they confer membership or eligibility for membership on the basis of an unchangeable, unchosen identity assigned in the past (Hsu 1963: 207, 224, 225). In contrast to this technique of placement, voluntary associations bring together people of like interest only (Smith and Freedman 1972: 17-18). Voluntary associations introduce unrelated persons who must interact on a universalistic basis. The basis of their interaction is stipulated in rules that set down the rights and duties of membership, and anyone fulfilling the duties of membership obtains the right to the benefits (Light 1972: 171). An insurance company is an example: anyone may join, and so long as members pay premiums they are entitled to benefits in exact proportion to the premium paid and risk imposed. However, a political party, a sports club, a parents' association, a veterans of fraternal lodge are also voluntary associations in which the qualified may come together in enjoyment of the benefits of membership so long as they fulfill the obligations of members. No one qualifies for association membership just because of provenance, clanship, or family.

Mixed associations combine voluntary and ascriptive membership principles, usually by restricting eligibility to a subclass while admitting to active membership only those eligibles who voluntarily join. For example, a womens' club limits eligibility to women, but only those women who join are members of the club. The limitation of eligibility to women is ascriptive. The requirement of joining is voluntary. Therefore the womens' club is an association that mixes voluntary and ascriptive principles. Many mixed associations give the external appearance of purely voluntary groupings. For example, a neighborhood tavern is supposedly a place to drink, and anyone is free to walk in and order a beer. But it commonly happens that a tavern's customers share some ascriptive identity such as ethnicity. In London, the Irish congregate in pubs on the basis of provenance. "Cork men will meet in one pub, and Connemara men in another, and so forth" (Jackson 1964: 31). For these Irishmen their pub is a Landsmannschaft even though the sign over the swinging doors does not proclaim it to be. Youth clubs in Ibadan, Nigeria, are equally deceptive. Ninety-five percent of the people in Ibadan are Yoruba, and the West African city's youth clubs are in principle open to any young person. In reality, the clubs have acquired a clientele based upon regional origin and subtribal homogeneity. One club caters to Oyo, another to Egbe, a third to Ijesha, and so forth (Bogdan 1976: 205). Religious institutions are the most striking examples of disguised Landsmannschaften. Many are supposedly open to any coreligionist, but locality connections everywhere obtrude [7]. In Freetown, Sierra Leone, Banton (1957: 37) found most Muslim tribesmen had "their own mosques or praying rooms," so unpleasant did the tribesmen find worship in the presence of ethnically unrelated coreligionists. Irish and Italian Catholics in North American cities have worshipped separately in the same spirit as have Freetown Muslims. In all these instances, what appear to be purely voluntary associations actually impose ascriptive tests that exclude some of the formally qualified from membership.

SOCIAL DISORGANIZATION

Cities contain a bewildering variety of ascriptive, voluntary, and mixed social associations. Let us consider the club situation among Filipino immigrants in Los Angeles. These newcomers join interethnic voluntary groups such as the Democratic Party, parent-teacher associations, the League of Women Voters, the Rotary Club, and so forth. In all these the Filipino members associate with non-Filipinos. But there are also eighty ethnic voluntary associations "associated with various groups" of Filipino ancestry. Morales (1974: 63) mentions Anak Ti Batak, Filipino-American Community of Los Angeles, Laoagenians, Sons of Panoy, Philippine Junior Women's Club, and numerous others. In addition, there is the Filipino Christian Church and the St. Columban Catholic Church, predominantly Filipino in composition. Only Filipinos are qualified for membership in these ethnic voluntary associations, but just being Filipino does not confer membership either: everyone must join first and fulfill the obligations of membership to retain current status. In contrast, the Filipino community also contains an uncounted but very large number of nuclear and extended families and informal Landsmannschaften, all of which bulk very large in members' lives. No one has to join these; a person automatically becomes a member at birth and retains membership until death. These ascriptive bodies perform social services for their members just as do the ethnic voluntary and interethnic voluntary associations. For example, if Filipinos need a job, their kin will help them find one. This is a social service for the needy individual. The social structure of the Filipino community in Los Angeles actually consists of all three levels (ascriptive, mixed, voluntary), each of which makes a distinct contribution to the community's welfare.

In a pioneering study of Polish immigration to North American cities, Thomas and Znaniecki (1920: 86) distinguished between social organization based on Old World institutions and social reorganization around Polish-American voluntary associations such as fraternal orders, churches, and clubs. The Old World associations were ineffectual in America, but new Polish-American voluntary associations helped to confer identity, organization, and cohesion on the immigrant colonies. However, some Polish immigrants did not join or participate in Polish community life, so social disorganization arose. Thomas and Znaniecki argued that community disorganization was a temporary, interstitial phase reflecting the still incomplete transition from Old World ascription to Polish-American voluntary associational life. In a related formulation Robert Park concluded that the division of labor in cities tended to "break down or modify" an older social structure based on ascription and to introduce social association based on voluntary adherence. "It is in the cities that the old clan and kinship groups are broken up and replaced by social organization based on rational interests and temperamental predilections" (Park 1950: 353).

A decade later, Louis Wirth (1938) developed a bleaker view. According to Wirth, the great size, density of population, and ethnic heterogeneity of big cities tended to undermine ascriptive solidarities—without replacing them with voluntary associations. First, simple country people moved to great cities. Then the experience of living in cities tore apart their ascriptive (tribe, kin, ethnic) social groupings, leaving them isolated and uncertain about basic values. This psychological uncertainty is called *anomia,* and its prevalence in society is *anomie.* Wirth acknowledged that government agencies and voluntary associations arose to provide some services that neighborhoods and kinship lineages could no longer accomplish. For example, instead of controlling juvenile delinquents by appealing to shared moral values, neighbors called the police (Fischer 1976: 33). However, Wirth did not believe that voluntary associations or government agencies fully replaced the moral solidarities upon which urban society at bottom depended. Thus the police help to reduce crime in urban neighborhoods, but they are less effective in this regard then shared moral values, a city's first line of defense against crime. If urban living destroys the moral values that inhibit deviance, as Wirth believed, then police, prisons, and electric chairs only reduce disorganization and anomie; they cannot reverse deterioration, nor can they restore preurban moral solidarity.

Wirth's ideas were plausible and stimulated research in many countries. Contrary to expectation, the results were disconfirming (Gutkind 1962: 152-153). "Most of the critical sociological research does not support the theory of urban anomie" (Fischer 1976: 236). A lengthening parade of ethnographic studies (Gans 1962; Suttles 1968; Liebow 1967; Whyte 1955) produced evidence that people in slums were neither disorganized nor anomic. Even slum dwellers belonged to groups that imposed moral values to which members tried to adhere in their daily lives. These groups were more often informal cliques than voluntary associations. Also the moral standards that these informal cliques inculcated were opposed at many points to prevailing standards in the middle class. For example, Whyte (1955) studied an informal clique of young men ("the Nortons") who hung around a corner in New Haven. These young men stole, loafed, fought, gambled, bribed officials, told dirty stories, and consorted with disreputable women. They were not church goers. In all these respects, the corner boys behaved in a manner disapproved by prevailing social standard of the American middle class. But they had a code of honor to which they adhered. This code required each corner boy to help his friends and refrain from hurting them in business or personal life (Whyte 1955: 256). The code of honor also told the corner boys which laws they could violate without dishonor (gambling laws) and which they could not (selling narcotics). It also prescribed the girls with whom they could trifle and the girls ("nice girls") they had to marry. In sum, these tough young men were neither disorganized nor anomic.

Wirth's anomie theory made three errors. First, he overlooked the manner in which chain migration recreated rural communities in big cities. Second, he underestimated the social effectiveness of informal groupings (such as corner cliques) in working-class neighborhoods. Third, he overestimated the rate at which ascriptive ties would deteriorate in urban environments. Informed opinion on this point has completely changed. Assessing North American research results, Wellman (1979) even concludes that ascriptive solidarities do not decline *at all* in urban environments. A "new orthodoxy" holds that ascriptive solidarities continue to flourish because of their "continued efficacity" in economics, politics, and sociability. This new orthodoxy rests on "the sheer empirical demonstration of the continued vitality" of ascriptive solidarities in urban areas (Wellman, 1979). Few urban people are isolated and anomic, and those are chiefly the disabled and aged.

Wellman (1979) reported that 98 percent of people in East York, a Toronto suburb, had at least one intimate tie and 61 percent had five or more. About half the intimates named were kin; the remainder were nonkin, but mainly friends other than neighbors or coworkers. Nineteen percent of East Yorkers had only kin for intimate social association; 18 percent had only nonkin. All the others had intimate social associations with kin and nonkin. East Yorkers had primary social associations all over metropolitan Toronto and were not bound to their neighborhood. Only one quarter reported intimate associations outside Toronto (Wellman 1979: 1215).

Third World urban research also proceeded on the expectation that rural-urban migrants would collide with an urban environment that undermined their ascriptive solidarities. No evidence turned up, and researchers were initially surprised. For instance, Marwick (1958: 153) noted that rural Africans in cities of South Africa were "still in the grip of a kinship system that imposes on them a clannishness quite out of keeping with urban living." Subsequent studies replicated the clannishness but concluded that ascriptive solidarities are compatible with urban living (Aldous 1962; Meillassoux 1968: 62–63). At the same time, voluntary associations in West Africa facilitate the adjustment of rural-urban migrants "by substituting for the extended group of kinsmen a grouping based upon common interest which is capable of serving many of the same needs as the traditional family or lineage" (Little 1965b: 342). Some urban Africans participate simultaneously in "modern" voluntary organizations as well as old-fashioned tribal, lineage, or provenance groupings (Banton 1957: 19–20, 181). Sojourning Africans also move without apparent strain into traditional tribal associations as soon as they return to the countryside and then revert to urban styles when again in a city environment (Mayer 1962: 579).

African voluntary associations provide their members with many of the social services also provided by tribes and Landsmannschaften (Little 1965b: 329). This duplication of social services sets up competition among voluntary, mixed, and ascriptive types of association, but competition does not preclude coexistence of alternative forms. A combination of voluntary and ascriptive groups maximizes the likelihood that every urban African can locate membership groups providing social services. If one form or the other completely disappeared, a proportion of the African urban population would lack social moorings, and these people might turn into the atomized, disorganized mass that Wirth expected.

Often vocabulary associations impose membership qualifications that exclude lower-status persons. For example a university womens' club excludes women who have not completed college. The rules of the club and the scandal of violating them are important social sanctions regulating the normative behavior of members (Little 1965a: 98, 115). Ascriptive social groupings link people from different class levels. In West Africa, members of a tribal union share a common identity independent of class level. Similarly, the Sons of Italy is predominantly working and lower middle class, but the fraternity legitimizes the participation of both working-class and upper-class persons of Italian descent in New Haven (Whyte 1955: 207-208). Chinese clans simply ascribe membership to people who do not have to join, and ascriptive bodies of this sort automatically create a membership corps that completely reflects the group's spectrum of class levels (Hsu 1963: 224-225). Therefore ascriptive bodies tend to introduce a principle of vertical differentiation in city life, knitting together people of diverse class levels, whereas voluntary associations tend to introduce a horizontal division, bringing together people of common class level.

FUNCTIONS OF SOCIAL ASSOCIATIONS

In preindustrial cities, municipal services were few, and private associations had to fill this vacuum for members. Even in the most underdeveloped societies, municipalities now offer social services that complement what voluntary and ascriptive social associations have long offered their members. For example, municipalities hire police to protect citizens, but neighborhoods, families, and clubs also offer protection. Suttles (1972: 21-43) calls this a "defended neighborhood." The violent reaction to forced busing by residents of South Boston in the middle 1970s illustrated the manner in which those defending a neighborhood easily exceed the boundaries of strict legality (Buell 1980). In Italian neighborhoods of New York City, neighborhood men once assumed responsibility for detecting and punishing petty criminals. The police rarely interfered. Yet the streets of Italian communities were remarkably free of petty crime (Light 1974: 8-17). In general, neighbors who know one another's business and watch the streets are able to deter burglary and violent crime, whereas unintegrated neighborhoods are easy prey to criminals [8].

Social welfare is another sphere of public-private dualism. In preindustrial cities, private bodies were the only agencies caring for the social welfare of the disabled, unemployed, or orphaned (Sjoberg 1960). The welfare state now makes transfer payments to the needy and their dependent children, thus rendering the interventions of private bodies less critical. However, some private bodies have continued to perform social welfare work now usually left to welfare state agencies. Japanese and Chinese communities in North America long took the principal responsibility for looking after coethnics. Asian elites also discouraged coethnics from seeking public welfare assistance (Light 1972; Light and Wong 1975).

Institutional completeness of a neighborhood is the extent to which private bodies offer services paralleling in scope and quality what people could obtain outside the neighborhood. Breton (1964) found that institutional completeness of immigrant communities in Montreal was variable: some immigrant communities displayed high completeness; others low. When institutional completeness was high, immigrants tended to restrict social contacts to coethnics; when completeness was low, immigrants had many social contacts with outsiders. Elites of immigrant organizations had a "vested interest" in strengthening ethnic solidarity in order to bolster their clientele's preference for in-group services they provided.

Small businesses contribute to the institutional completeness of an urban neighborhood. Small businesses permit consumers to obtain goods and services locally from a coethnic. The extensiveness of an ethnic small business sector depends on social networks, which provide business services such as capital, information, labor, and cooperation (Cummings 1980). Networks also motivate entrepreneurs and provide role models for young persons (Light 1972). Small businessmen are a voice for law and order in big cities because their economic survival depends on the free access of customers to local stores. (Light 1967; Conklin 1975: 73) [9]. Locked into an ethnic marketplace by big business competition on the outside, small business owners must confront and reduce local lawlessness—or go broke.

Government services tend to create a homogeneous environment in cities insofar as each neighborhood receives identical police and fire protection, social welfare provision, schools, hospitals, sewerage, street cleaning, and so on. However, public authorities are never the *only* agencies providing services. Families, clans, lineages, Landsmannschaften, voluntary associations, cliques, and small businesses also provide citizen services, sometimes in profusion and sometimes sparsely. Sometimes these private bodies provide services directly, as when Landsmen pay the funeral expenses of deceased members. Sometimes private bodies intervene politically to obtain a bigger share of public services, as when neighborhood merchants demand more police protection. Either way, the unevenness of private activity makes for unevenness in the quality of urban life. Where private interventions are many, varied, and effective, the quality of urban life is higher (Cummings 1980: 26-29).

SUMMARY

Cities recruit population by natural increase, net migration, and boundary changes. Of these, net migration has been the major source of urbanization. In preindustrial societies, migration only replaced population lost through an excess of deaths over births. Migrations are local, circular, chain, or career in character. Local and circular migrations predominated in preindustrial cities, whereas chain and career migrations are more typical of cities in the modern world.

Migration patterns are the major influence on neighborhood formation. Circular and chain migrations create ethnically homogeneous enclaves on the basis of kinship and friendship. This produces a confusion of internal and external ethnic consciousness in which enclave residents perceive many more ethnic differences than outgroup members. Career migrations have weaker links with neighborhood. Their effect is chiefly imposed through the status and income of the migrants who pick housing on this basis. The result of career migration is ethnically heterogeneous neighborhoods that are economically and socially segregated.

Landsmannschaften and kinship are the two principal forms of ascriptive social organization in migrant neighborhoods. Voluntary associations enroll anyone qualified who sustains the obligations of membership. Voluntary associations also provide services to neighborhoods, but the coexistence of voluntary and ascriptive associations maximizes delivery of services to urban populations. Private bodies supplement the public delivery of services so that the quality of life in neighborhoods really depends upon a combination of public and private services, not public ones only.

NOTES

1. "Everywhere, whether in the early Middle Ages or in Antiquity, in the Near or Far East, the city arose from a confluence and settling together of outsiders, and because of the poor sanitary conditions of the lower classes, it was able to maintain itself only through continuous new immigration from the countryside" (Weber II, 1968: 1237). See also Russell (1972: 31).

2. This was even true in the Middle Ages, long before industrial urbanization: "A man equipped with particular skills went to a city where relatives existed who spoke his language and were employed in the same type of work" (Russell 1972: 33).

3. "From the various towns of western Sicily they have come, settling down with the kin and townspeople here [Chicago], until the colony is a mosaic of Sicilian towns. Larabee Street is a Little Altavilla; the people along Cambridge [Avenue] have come from Alimena and Chiusa Sclafani; the people on Townsend [Street] from Bagheria; and the people on Milton [Street] from Sambucazambut. The entire colony has been settled in like fashion" (Zorbaugh 1929: 164).

4. But the Nortons were not powerless. "In Cornerville, there are a number of

political clubs, each one started by a politician and built around him. . . . The political club is made up of a number of corner gangs" (Whyte 1955: 206).

5. "Of Cuba's six provinces, Havana and Las Villas have been the birthplace and childhood home of over two-thirds of the Cubans living in West New York. . . . Almost all respondents credited Cuban family and friends with helping them come to the United States or giving them aid once they were in the United States" (Rogg 1971: 480–481).

6. "A common trait of all cities in the world is that they were to a large extent settlements of people previously alien to the given location. . . . The urban population often retains its tribal identity with connubial segregation or, where this is not the case, it at least retains membership in its former local and clan associations" (Weber III, 1968: 1244–1255).

7. "The vast majority of the 316 permanent congregations which existed on the Lower East Side [of New York City] in 1907 were landsmannschaft synagogues. . . . The landsmannschaft principle carried well beyond the synagogue. The mutual aid associations . . . were essentially associations of fellow townsmen." Arthur A. Goren, *New York Jews and the Quest for Community.* New York: Columbia University Press, 1970, p. 20.

8. "If there is intense social interaction on an intimate face-to-face basis, if there is normative consensus and if there is surveillance of the behavior of members of the community, social control will be strong, to the extent that legal or formal controls may be unnecessary" (Conklin 1975: 140).

9. "*Pasadena*—plagued by shootings, purse and wallet snatchings, vandalism, theft, and harassment of customers, the Boys Market in this city's northwest has closed." Bert Mann, "Neighborhood Crime Closes Supermarket," *Los Angeles Times,* September 11, 1980, pt. IX, p. 1. See also "Crime and Black Business: The Noose Tightens on Inner-city Commerce," *Black Enterprise* 3(1973): 17ff. "The fear of crime in some [inner city] areas has minimized the hours a shopkeeper can safely remain open, and driven commercial insurance rates skyward or made such insurance altogether unavailable." "Crime insurance," *Black Enterprise* 3(1973): 33.

REFERENCES

Agocs, Carol. 1977. "Ethnic Neighborhoods in City and Suburbs: Metropolitan Detroit, 1940–1970." Ph.D. dissertation, Wayne State University.
——. 1979. "Ethnic Groups in the Ecology of North American Cities." *Canadian Ethnic Studies.* 11: 1-18.
Aldous, Joan. 1962. "Urbanization, the Extended Family, and Kinship Ties in West Africa." *Social Forces* 41: 6-12.
Axelrod, Bernard. 1972. "Historical Studies of Emigration from the United States." *International Migration Review* 6: 32-49.

Babchuk, Nicholas, and Alan Booth. 1969. "Voluntary Association Membership: A Longitudinal Analysis." *American Sociological Review* 34: 31–45.

Banton, Michael. 1957. *West African City*. London: Oxford University Press.

———. 1965. "Social Alignment and Identity in a West African City," pp. 131–147, in Hilda Kuper, ed. *Urbanization and Migration in West Africa*. Berkeley and Los Angeles: University of California.

Barton, Josef J. 1975. *Peasants and Strangers: Italians, Rumanians, and Slovaks in an American City, 1890–1950*. Cambridge: Harvard University Press.

Bell, Wendell, and Maryanne T. Force. 1956. "Urban Neighborhood Types and Participation in Formal Associations." *American Sociological Review* 21: 25–34.

———, and Marion Boat. 1957. "Urban Neighborhoods and Informal Social Relations." *American Journal of Sociology* 62: 391–398.

Bogdan, Robert. 1976. "Youth Clubs in a West African City," pp. 204–221, in Paul Meadows and Ephraim Mizruchi, eds. *Urbanism, Urbanization and Change: Comparative Perspectives,* 2nd ed. Reading, Mass.: Addison-Wesley.

Breton, Raymond. 1964. "Institutional Completeness of Ethnic Communities and the Personal Relations of Immigrants." *American Journal of Sociology* 70: 193–205.

Buell, Emmett H., Jr. 1980. "Busing and the Defended Neighborhood." *Urban Affairs Quarterly* 16: 161–188.

Conklin, John E. 1975. *The Impact of Crime*. New York: Macmillan.

Cornelius, Wayne A. 1975. *Politics and the Migrant Poor in Mexico City*. Stanford: Stanford University Press.

Cummings, Scott. 1980. "Collectivism: The Unique Legacy of Immigrant Economic Development," pp. 5–32 in Scott Cummings, ed. *Self-Help in Urban America*. Pt. Washington, N.Y.: Kennikat Press.

Darroch, A. Gordon, and Wilfred G. Marston. 1971. "The Social Class Basis of Ethnic Residential Segregation: the Canadian Case." *American Journal of Sociology* 77: 491–510.

Doughty, Paul L. 1970. "Behind the Back of the City: 'Provincial' Life in Lima, Peru," pp. 30–46, in William Mangin, ed. *Peasant in Cities*. Boston: Houghton Mifflin.

Fischer, Claude S. 1976. *The Urban Experience*. New York: Harcourt.

Gans, Herbert J. 1962. *The Urban Villagers*. New York: Free Press.

Glazer, Nathan, and Daniel Patrick Moynihan. 1970. *Beyond the Melting Pot*. 2nd ed. Cambridge: MIT Press.

Graves, Nancy B., and Theodore D. Graves. 1974. "Adaptive Strategies in Urban Migration." *Annual Review of Anthropology* 3: 117–151.

Guest, Avery M., and James A. Weed. 1976. "Ethnic Residential Segregation: Patterns of Change." *American Journal of Sociology* 81: 1088–1111.

Gutkind, Peter C. W. 1962. "African Urban Family Life." *Cahiers d'Etudes Africaines* 3: 149–217.

———. 1966. "African Urban Family Life and the Urban System." *Journal of Asian and African Studies* 1: 35–42.

Hesslink, George K. 1970. "The Functions of Neighborhood in Ecological Stratification." *Sociology and Social Research* 54: 441–459.

Hsu, Francis L. K. 1963. *Clan, Caste, and Club*. Princeton: D. Van Nostrand.

Jackson, John A. 1964. "The Irish," pp. 293–308, in Ruth Glass, ed. London: Prospects of Change. London: Macgibbon and Kee.

Kantrowitz, Nathan. 1973. *Ethnic and Racial Segregation in the New York Metropolis: Residential Patterns among White Ethnic Groups, Blacks, and Puerto Ricans*. New York: Praeger.

Keller, Suzanne. 1968. *The Urban Neighborhood*. New York: Random House.

Li, Peter S. 1978. *Occupational Mobility and Kinship Assistance: A Study of Chinese Immigrants in Chicago*. San Francisco: R and E Associates.

Lieberson, Stanley. 1963. *Ethnic Patterns in American Cities*. New York: Free Press.

Liebow, Elliot. 1967. *Tally's Corner*. Boston: Little, Brown.

Light, Ivan H. 1967. "Ghetto Violence and the Growth of Negro Business." *Berkeley Journal of Sociology* 12: 130–142.

——. 1972. *Ethnic Enterprise in America*. Berkely and Los Angeles: University of California Press.

——. ed. 1974. *Greenwich Village, 1919–1972: Guide to Periodical Literature*. Monticello, Ill.: Council of Planning Librarians.

——., and Charles Wong. "Protest or Work: Dilemmas of the Tourist Industry in American Chinatowns." *American Journal of Sociology* 80: 1342–1368.

Little, Kenneth. 1965a. *West African Urbanization*. Cambridge: Cambridge University Press.

——. 1965b. "The Role of Voluntary Associations in West African Urbanization," pp. 325–345, in Pierre L. van den Berghe, ed. *Africa: Social Problems of Change and Conflict*. San Francisco: Chandler.

Litwak, Eugene. 1960. "Geographic Mobility and Extended Family Cohesion." *American Sociological Review* 25: 385–394.

Lloyd, Peter. 1979. *Slums of Hope? Shanty Towns of the Third World*. New York: St. Martin's Press.

Logan, John R., and Moshe Semyonov. 1980. "Growth and Succession in Suburban Communities." *The Sociological Quarterly* 21: 93–105.

Lopreato, Joseph. 1970. *Italian Americans*. New York: Random House.

Lyman, Stanford M. 1968. "Contrasts in the Community Organization of Chinese and Japanese in North America." *Canadian Review of Sociology and Anthropology* 5: 51–67.

MacDonald, John S., and Leatrice D. Macdonald. 1974. "Chain Migration, Ethnic Neighborhood Formation, and Social Networks," pp. 226–236, in Charles Tilly, ed. *An Urban World*. Boston: Little, Brown.

Marwick, M. G. 1958. "The Modern Family in Social Anthropological Perspective." *African Studies* 17: 137–158.

Mayer, Philip. 1961. *Townsmen or Tribesmen*. Capetown; Oxford University Press.

McGee, T. C. 1973. "Peasants in the Cities." *Human Organization* 32: 135–142.

Meillassoux, Claude. 1968. *Urbanization of an African Community*. Seattle: University of Washington Press.

Morales, Royal F. 1974. *Makibaka: The Pilipino American Struggle*. Los Angeles: Mountain View Publishers.

Morrison, Peter A., and Judith P. Wheeler. 1976. "Rural Renaissance in America?" *Population Bulletin* 31: 3–26.

Park, Robert Erza, 1950. "Human Migration and the Marginal Man," pp. 345–356, in Robert Erza Park, ed. *Race and Culture.* New York: Free Press.

Passache, J. Gottfried, and Clifford J. Jansen. 1969. "Unity and Disunity in Two Ethnic Groups in Toronto." Paper presented, Annual Meeting of the Canadian Sociology and Anthropology Association, York University, June 6, 1969.

Petersen, William. 1968. "Migration, I: Social Aspects." *International Encyclopedia of the Social Sciences* 10: 286–292.

——. 1978. "International Migration." *Annual Review of Sociology* 4: 533–575.

Rogg, Eleanor. 1971. "The Influence of a Strong Refugee Community on the Economic Adjustment of its Members." *International Migration Review* 16: 474–481.

Roof, Wade Clark. 1980. "Southern Birth and Racial Residential Stratification: the Case of Northern Cities." *American Journal of Sociology* 86: 350–358.

Russell, Josiah Cox. 1972. *Medieval Regions and Their Cities.* Bloomington: Indiana University Press.

Simic, Andre. 1973. *The Peasant Urbanities: A Study of Rural-Urban Mobility in Serbia.* New York: Seminar Press.

Siu, Paul C. P. 1952. "The Sojourner." *American Journal of Sociology* 58: 34–44.

Sjoberg, Gideon. 1960. *The Preindustrial City.* New York: Free Press.

Skeldon, Ronald. 1977. "Regional Associations: A Note on Opposed Interpretations." *Comparative Studies in Society and History* 19: 506–510.

Smith, Constance, and Anne Freedman. 1972. *Voluntary Associations.* Cambridge: Harvard University Press.

Suttles, Gerald. 1968. *The Social Order of the Slum.* Chicago: University of Chicago Press.

Thomas, William I., and Florian Znaniecki. 1920. *The Polish Peasant in Europe and America.* Vol. IV. Boston: Richard C. Badger.

Tilly, Charles. 1974. "Urbanization," pp. 37–54, in Charles Tilly, ed. *An Urban World.* Boston: Little, Brown.

——. 1978. "Migration in Modern European History," pp. 48–72, in William H. McNeil and Ruth S. Adams, eds. *Human Migration.* Bloomington: Indiana University.

——., and C. H. Brown. 1967. "On Uprooting, Kinship, and the Auspices of Migration." *International Journal of Comparative Sociology* 8: 139–164.

Vecoli, Rudolph J. 1963. "Chicago's Italians Prior to World War I: A Study of their Economic Adjustment." Ph.D. dissertation, University of Wisconsin.

Ware, Carolyn. 1935. *Greenwich Village, 1920–1930.* Boston: Houghton Mifflin.

Warren, Donald I. 1977. "Neighborhoods in Urban Areas," pp. 224–237, in Roland L. Warren, ed. *New Perspectives on the American Community.* 3rd ed. Chicago: Rand McNally.

Weber, Max. 1968. *Economy and Society*, 3 Vols. New York: Bedminster Press.

Wellman, Barry. 1979. "The Community Question: The Intimate Networks of East Yorkers." *American Journal of Sociology* 84: 1201–1231.

Whyte, William Foote. 1955. *Street Corner Society*. Chicago: University of Chicago.

Wilensky, Harold J. 1960. "Work, Careers, and Social Integration." *International Social Science Journal* 12: 543–560.

Wirth, Louis. 1938. "Urbanism as a Way of Life." *American Sociological Review* 44: 1–24.

Wong, Sui-Lun. 1979. "Industrial Entrepreneurship and Ethnicity: A Study of the Shanghainese Cotton Spinners in Hong Kong." Ph.D. dissertation, Wolfson College of the University of Oxford.

Zorbaugh, Harvey W. 1929. *The Gold Coast and the Slum*. Chicago: University of Chicago Press.

_____

CHAPTER 12

Ethnic Niches

The city is a common center to which people converge from diverse homelands. As a result, cities are places where peoples mix and meet. This process creates a cosmopolitan atmosphere because the world exists in microcosm within the city limits. Sometimes peoples of diverse origins blend together to form a culturally new urban population, the melted down product of its constituent groups. Sometimes urban ethnic groups settle propinquitously, but do not intermingle. This separate togetherness results in an urban mosaic of distinct neighborhoods. Most commonly, urban life is a complex of minglings and separations rather than simply one or the other. Viewed historically, the process of mingling and separating begins with original migration but continues ever after. In this process, ethnic boundaries are drawn and redrawn, and ethnic interests aligned and realigned. Ethnic groups find economic niches within cities and cease to depend on sentimentality as the sole basis of group feeling.

ETHNICITY IN PREINDUSTRIAL CITIES

Many ancient cities originated in the propinquitous settlement and federation of ethnically diverse peoples. For example, the population of ancient Athens consisted originally of distinct Attic tribes and their constituent phraties. Karl Marx (1965: 76-77) distinguished kinship tribes and locality tribes, the latter formed on the basis of residence rather than blood relationship. Tribal identities are ethnic identities, and whan people from one village in Attica went elsewhere, they retained this ethnic identity in the place of destination. Every Attic group traced its origin from a god and directed its pieties to this divinity. As a result, Athenian ethnic groups were religious solidarities as well as kinship and locality solidarities.

These ethnically and religiously divergent lineages confederated from political expediency. Their confederation created Athens (Engels 1962: 271). As Fustel de Coulanges (1864: 127) long ago demonstrated, the federation required symbols of solidarity around which Athenians could create a moral order. These symbols were produced by the common adoration of Pallas Athene in which all Athenians, whatever their tribal origin, were required to participate. However, constituent tribes retained their separate identities and religions, and when the archon sacrificed to Pallas, each tribe provided one assistant. Similarly, the seven hills of Rome were originally occupied by seven ethnic groups. On the Palatine hill was the Latin city; on the Capitoline hill the Sabine city; on the Coelian hill the Etruscan, and so forth (Fustel de Coulanges 1864: 361). "Rome did not seem to be a single city; it appeared like a confederation of several cities." This confederation of tribes produced the Roman city-state (Hammond 1972: 242). The constitution of Rome perpetuated ancient tribal distinctions long after cultural assimilation had obliterated them. Thus votes in the Senate were by tribes and clans, and each tribe provided two Vestal priestesses to tend the sacred fire. The Bible (Numbers, 1:4) also records that the Jewish people originated as a federation of twelve tribes united around the Yahweh cult. King David's Jerusalem was the capital of this tribal federation, but the capital city's "Jewish" majority consisted then of coreligionists who still regarded one another as ethnically distinct because tribally divided (Weber, 1952: 51–57).

Noncitizens of ancient cities were also divided into ethnic groups. Classical Athens is an example. By the fourth century B.C. the city's political empire and flourishing commerce had produced large noncitizen populations of *metics* and slaves. *Metics* were resident foreigners who practiced a trade in Athens. They were of "mixed origin" but "generally Greeks" in the fifth century B.C. A century later, metics were mostly non-Greek (Austin and Vidal-Naquet 1973: 104). A census taken in the late fourth century B.C. indicated a population of 21,000 citizens and 10,000 metics. In addition to metics, the numerous slaves were also of diverse ethnic origins. Some slaves were Greek, but barbarian slaves predominated. Slaves confiscated from the metic Kephisodoros in 414 B.C. consisted of three Thracians, two Syrians, three Carians, one Scythian, one Melitene, one Colchian, and one Illyrian (Austin and Vidal-Naquet 1973: 284). Since slaves and metics combined were at least as numerous as the free citizens of Athens, we can conclude that approximately 50 percent of Athenians were non-Greeks, born abroad.

This example illustrates the extent of ethnic diversity in great cities of preindustrial antiquity, thus disconfirming the thoughtless view that founders and residents of Rome were ethnically the same because "all Romans," the founders and residents of Athens "all Athenians," and so forth. Of course, the Athens of antiquity did not contain representatives of every world region as does New York City. There were no Koreans, Indonesians, or Japanese. In this sense, the diversity of ethnic groups in ancient Athens was narrower than in industrial cities today. Yet relative to the times, the diversity of ethnic populations in ancient Athens was as great as New York City's now. In preindustrial societies, transportation was slow, and people traveled short distances compared with today. In this perspective, places that are by contemporary standards nearly adjacent now were long journeys distant from each other then. Therefore city people built ethnic identities around tribal and locality differences that seem parochial by contemporary standards.

SOJOURNING AND ETHNIC IDENTITY

In ancient times no less than now, cultural assimilation everywhere reduced the ethnic diversity of city populations. Writing in the thirteenth century, Moorish scholar Ibn Khaldun called attention to the "existence of group feeling in cities" and the tendency of conquered peoples to adopt Arabic as their language (1958: 302, 306). The peoples of Attica eventually developed an Athenian ethnic identity, Latin tribes became Romans, and Hebrew tribes became Jews over the course of centuries. However, the perpetuation of ethnic differences in preindustrial cities did not depend wholly upon the intergenerational perpetuation of the original cultural differences among the founders. On the contrary, preindustrial cities derived their perpetually ethnic character from rural-urban sojourning. Because urban deaths exceeded urban births, preindustrial cities required continuous in-migration from rural districts just to maintain a given population. As a result, most adult residents of ancient cities were born in country districts. Country-born sojourners spoke the rural dialect and cherished rural lifestyles. Tendencies toward cultural assimilation among the city-born were forestalled by high death rates in the city and the continuous migration of country people.

By choice, and often by law, sojourning people from the same rural locality resided in the same urban neighborhood. Sjoberg (1960: 100) also describes "well-defined neighborhoods with relatively homogenous propulations." These neighborhoods arose from rural-urban sojourning. As might be expected, this residential settlement accentuated and perpetuated the ethnic mosaic. Quite commonly, these neighborhoods were fenced off by internal walls (Sjoberg 1960: 92) whose gates were closed at night for security. These internal walls gave the preindustrial city the character of a honeycomb in each cell of which resided a separate ethnic group.

THE CULTURAL DIVISION OF LABOR

Coethnics inhabiting neighborhoods of the urban honeycomb also dominated certain trades. People of one group were butchers, of another bakers, and of a third candlestick makers. Hechter (1976, 1978) has termed this specialization "cultural division of labor." Since preindustrial tradesmen and artisans lived behind or over their shops, ethnic trades were practiced in ethnic neighborhoods. Therefore the streets of preindustrial cities commonly bore the name of the trade principally practiced there or, alternatively, the predominant family's name was bestowed upon the street "as evidenced in some European and Latin American cities today" (Sjoberg 1960: 102). To a substantial extent, people who lived on the same street practiced the same occupation, hailed from the same rural district, were related by blood and marriage, spoke the same dialect, practiced the same religion, and regarded the other inhabitants of the preindustrial city as aliens (Sjoberg 1960: 101).

Coethnics residing in the same neighborhood wanted to monopolize industries and occupations by excluding outsiders from their practice. To this end, the most characteristic institution was the nepotistic trade guild (Sjoberg 1960: 188). The headquarters of the guild was in the residential neighborhood where its craft was practiced. Guild membership was a "prerequisite to the practice of any occupation," and kinship was the "paramount" qualification for guild membership. A hiring preference for kinsmen is nepotism, and the trade guilds of preindustrial cities were nepotistic [1]. Since most of the people living on the street were kin hailing from the same district, this nepotistic guild policy completed the insulation of the ethnic neighborhood (Sjoberg 1960: 191). When kin arrived from the country, sponsors taught them the group's trade, and the nepotistic guild licensed them to practice it. Any outsider who tried to practice the trade would have to confront the guild's vigilant monopoly, which was often legal as well as practical. Therefore unauthorized practice of a protected occupation risked imprisonment as well as a gamut of private penalties, even homicide.

Guilds of coethnics are exceedingly ancient. Even in Sumer, some clans held title to agricultural land and other clans were occupational. Occupational clans may have been residentially centered in various quarters of the city. These occupational associations "bear comparison with guilds" (Adams 1966: 83), "in that their recruitment and internal structure must have followed kin lines." Analogous kinship-linked occupational bodies also existed in pre-Hispanic Mexico. Aztec *capullis* were kinship groups that "frequently specialized in crafts and professions, providing a characteristic 'guild-like' aspect to craft production." An Aztec historian tells of "more than 30 crafts" practiced by the inhabitants of Tenochtitlan, and each craft was practiced in the residential center of its guild (Adams 1966: 94).

Le Tourneau (1956; see also Lapidus 1967: 97) has provided a detailed account of ethnicity, guild, and nepotism in Muslim cities. The most obvious ethnic neighborhoods belonged to Jews and Christians, the principal minorities. However, Muslims also formed ethnic neighborhoods on the basis of village of origin (Le Tourneau, 1956: 19). In Fez, Morocco, people from Touat resided inside a walled ghetto until the seventeenth century, yet this minority was Muslim and Arabic-speaking. "The individuals of the same group often practice the same occupation" (Le Tourneau 1956: 29). For example, Berbers of Haut-Guir served as porters at Fez; the Jbala mountaineers were Koranic instructors and swordsmiths; Sus people were merchants of olive oil, coal and butter. At Tunis, those from Ghumrassen were short-order cooks; Suf people were water carriers; Ouargla people served as domestic servants. The only fully heterogeneous people Le Tourneau found were black slaves whose places of origin had been obscured by abduction and sale. Yet even slaves formed guilds of cooks and domestic servants.

Chinese cities recruited labor from villages [2]. These villages depended on the remittances of sojourning members. Villages specialized in occupations that their men practiced while sojourning in cities. Wealthy villages specialized in high-prestige occupations such as public administration. Poor villages had to specialize in "disparaged occupations" in obscure towns (Skinner 1976: 355). Sojourners resided in propinquity to others of their native place, and all practiced the same occupation. The result was a "pattern of economic specialization by native place" that, Skinner (1977: 544) concludes, can "profitably be analyzed in terms of an ethnic division of labor." Of course, the sojourner groups were Chinese-speaking and mostly of Great Han physical type. Nonetheless, dialects differed, and the sojourners plainly regarded one another as cultural aliens. Guilds regulated most industries and occupations, attempting to recruit their membership from all people "engaged in a single economic activity." Often, but not always, guild members were restricted to those from a particular native place. Native-place guilds thus constituted apparently lasted for long periods. For example, Peking's Leather Box Guild, established in 1689, was still conducted in 1942 by people who originated in Shanghai (Golas 1977: 563).

These divisions into ethnic neighborhoods were usually voluntary but sometimes involuntary. In medieval and Renaissance Europe, cities sometimes required people from the same rural locality or province "to organize as 'nations' sharing well-defined privileges and bearing collective responsibility" for social welfare and public order. These ethnic enclaves also established a "quasi-monopoly of some particular trade" and tried, with much success, to obtain legal protection for this monopoly (Tilly 1978: 53). European guilds of the Middle Ages were less successful than elsewhere in imposing their control on city economies. Most European guilds had little direct influence in regulating prices, internal competition, hours of work, and methods of work. But their key restrictions bore on nepotistic recruitment: only the kin of members could be admitted to practice the craft. From the thirteenth century, opponents of the European guilds accused them of abusing their power to regulate apprenticeship, and "there is no doubt" European guilds restricted apprenticeship (Thrupp 1963: 264).

The segregation of Jews in a walled ghetto continued this medieval policy into the nineteenth century in cities of eastern Europe. All Jews were required to live in the ghetto and were restricted to "typically Jewish" occupations, especially tailoring. Popular hatred of Jews explains why their walled ghettos survived in eastern Europe long after Napoleon Bonaparte ordered their ghettos' destruction in the West. But the walled ghettos of Poland ought not be misunderstood as only monuments to Polish anti-Semitism (Andreski 1963: 100). Segregated neighborhoods were typical of the Middle Ages, and only their persistence distinguishes the Jewish ghettos from those that had earlier divided the Christian population into mutually mistrustful ethnic groups.

INDUSTRIAL URBANIZATION IN EUROPE

Industrial urbanization reduced but did not eliminate the ethnic division of labor in European cities. In the middle of the eighteenth century, France still contained a multiplicity of local cultures. People who lived only fifty miles from Paris were "a hundred years removed from it in thought and action" (Weber 1977: 97). Tilly (1978: 53; see also Braudel, 1973: 380) described the rural-urban migration of Limousin sojourners to Paris in the nineteenth century in terms that might equally well have suited the twelfth. That is, the Limousins hailed from Limousin Province and lived in a Limousin neighborhood when in Paris, where they formed a residential group known as "Limousins." Anyone could identify a Limousin by his dialect. Limousins were stonemasons to the extent that Limousin and mason were nearly synonymous in Paris. Yet Limousins were completely French. Other provincials in Paris were almost as parochial. "All sources show the masons, stonecutters, and the setters from Marche or Creuse keeping to themselves in Paris," where they spoke their own dialect and maintained "traditional solidarities" (Weber 1977: 281). As late as 1914, Paris still contained ghettos formed by clusterings of provincial people from the same rural localities. Thus Auvergnats clustered in Rue de la Roquette; Bretons in Montparnasse; Alsatians around La Vilette, and, like the Limousins, all looked forward to returning to their rural localities of origin as soon as economically possible.

This return was becoming ever more difficult because modernization of agriculture permitted increased output with fewer workers. Ultimately, the Limousins, the Bretons, the Alsatians, and the Auvergnats had to become permanent Parisians with no farm to cushion the swings of the business cycle. As this change transpired, peasant sojourners relaxed their regional chauvinism and acquired a class identity. Major French industrial cities thus acquired an industrial working class consisting of dispossessed ruralites whose regional identities no longer obstructed joint political or industrial action. This industrial working class could not exist in the Middle Ages because sojourning (rather than chain migration) was the method of rural-urban migration, and sojourning consistently reinvigorated the regional-ethnic diversity of urban populations.

Tsarist Russia in the Twentieth Century

In late Tsarist Russia too, industrial urbanization brought sojourning peasants to the cities to serve as factory hands. Their sojourns were temporary, lasting only as long as factories had work; when the business cycle turned down, peasants returned to their farms and helped with the chores. Johnson (1979) has closely analyzed the employment of factory hands in Moscow at the turn of this century and found that 93 percent of factory operatives were peasants, all Russian-speaking adherents of the Orthodox faith. Most of the peasants came from the Moscow region. These workers could be roughly described as identical in regional origin, religion, and language, but they behaved as though differentiated into numerous ethnic communities. The basis of ethnic awareness among Moscow proletarians was *zemliachestvo,* the association of *zemliaks.* Zemliaks were "follow villagers." In Moscow, zemliaks stayed together, residing in the same neighborhood, offering and receiving mutual assistance.

Zemliaks clustered in identifiable industries and occupations. They "tended to develop regional specialties" merely by following trades their fathers and grandfathers had practiced. Factories were nepotistic and awarded priority in hiring to persons who were the kin of zemliaks already employed (Johnson 1979: 62). In one cotton mill more than 50 percent of the workers in 1899 came from Riazan province, and 23 percent were from a single county of that province. Migrants from different places even clustered in different divisions of the factory (Johnson 1979: 69).

The role of zemliachestvo in political and social action is unclear, but Johnson (1979: 75–79) finds evidence that unrest was greatest where zemliaks clustered. The leadership of worker protest was usually recruited from among zemliaks. In one case, thirty-seven of forty-one workers fired from a factory hailed from a single township of Nizhnii-Novgorod province (Johnson 1979: 77). Of course, the principal revolutionary institutions were the political parties, organized on class rather than ethnic lines even though the trade unions were ethnically linked. This situation is paradoxical. Johnson (1979: 159) concludes that Moscow workers were not really class-conscious. The obligations these Moscow workers felt were to zemliaks rather than to the proletariat. This is possible though unproven, but there is no doubt the Bolsheviks depended on unions, and unions depended on zemliachestvo.

Britain

In Britain, industrial urbanization involved, as elsewhere in Europe, the rural-urban migration of native-born country people, but there was in addition a significant influx of foreign labor as well (Kiernan 1978). Of these, the Irish were the largest group and also the first to immigrate to Britain (Engels 1958: 104). The Irish were ethnically distinct, Catholic, and, in the nineteenth century, Gaelic-speaking. In industrial cities of Britain, the Irish banded together in slum neighborhoods usually called Irish Town or Little Ireland. These neighborhoods formed on the basis of chain migration, one kinsman joining another. Among themselves the Irish also formed associations on the basis of county origins, and those from Cork or Connemara found separate places of congregation and fellowship. The Irish performed low-wage manual labor in railroad construction, stevedores, garbage collection, and domestic service.

Most of those who streamed into British cities after 1750, however, were born in Britain rather than abroad. In 1881 34 percent of London residents had been born in other parts of the United Kingdom (Smith 1892: 61). Most internal migrants came from rural counties and had, for the most part, been "driven off the land." Although born in Britain, these dislocated countrymen formed ethnic enclaves in London. Their method of relocation was a chain migration. Once a nucleus of countrymen had been formed in any London district, that nucleus grew "by the importation of friends and relatives." Ultimately the nucleus became an ethnic neighborhood consisting of rural Britons hailing from one or another agricultural county.

We find one village sending . . . its youth to Finsbury [district], another to Hornsey, a third to a big establishment in Cheapside. So, if an employer is Welsh he may find a Welsh colony near his works; if from Devon a colony of Devonshire men (Smith 1892: 124).

Figure 12-1 shows the residential clustering of British countrymen in East London and Hacney in 1881. Some counties show high concentrations of migrants, others low. The British migrants were not randomly distributed in the East End, where foreign-born workers chiefly clustered. The occupations of the countrymen in London also indicate ethnic clustering (Smith 1892: 96). On the West India dock most of the stevedores were native Londoners; on the

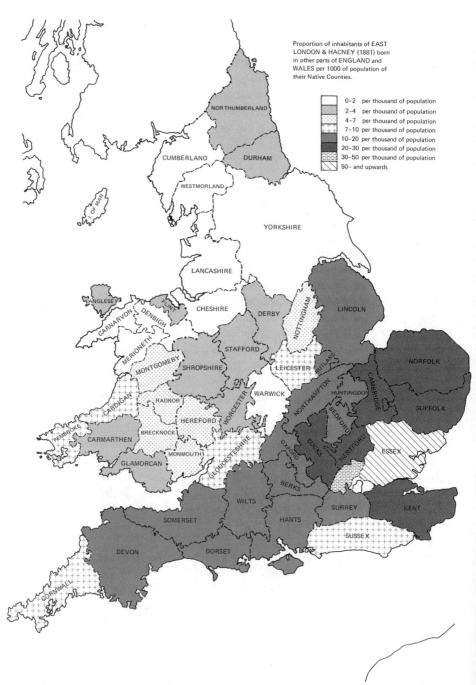

Figure 12-1. County of Origin of East Londoners, 1881. (Source: H. Llewellyn Smith, "Influx of Population." In Charles Booth, ed. *Life and Labour of the People in London*. London: Macmillan & Co., 1892).

310

Millwall dock, most were country-born. Other important occupations of the country-born were police, building trades (except plasterers), printing, iron works, boot and show manufacturing, railroads, and metropolitan transport. Many country workers in the building trades were seasonal. They entered London in the spring, then returned to their rural counties in the fall when the slack season arrived.

ETHNIC GROUPS IN U.S. CITIES

Unlike Europe, industrial urbanization in the United States had no internal labor reservoirs from which to recruit the industrial work force of growing cities. As a result, U.S. urbanization relied for most of its history on the immigration of foreign laborers. The major exception was the migration of rural, Southern blacks to industrial North and Midwest cities in the period 1917-1965. In this period, war and restrictive immigration laws closed the United States to foreign labor, and Southern blacks became an internal labor reservoir from which big cities could recruit needed labor.

To satisfy the requirements of an expanding industrial economy, American business ransacked the earth for cheap labor. The result was a convergence in American industrial cities of peoples from every continent. The ethnic mosaic thus formed was much more variegated than Europe's or Britain's because immigrants did not share common languages, histories, religions, or nationality. Moreover, they were recruited from the most benighted regions ("the wretched refuse of your teeming shore") of Europe and Asia. Figure 12-2 partially illustrates this observation. The map indicates the areas of Europe from which U.S. immigrants were drawn in 1900. Immigration to the United States (and to Canada) originated in identifiable regions of Europe. The three heaviest regions of emigration were western Ireland, Poland, and southern Italy. Each of these contained a distressed population. Western Ireland was the most impoverished, backward section of Ireland; Poland and western Russia contained urban Jews subject to official intolerance; southern Italy was and remains an impoverished, overpopulated rural region.

The cultural division of labor among America's immigrants is still reflected in lingering stereotypes. The Irish policeman, Italian barber, French chef, Jewish tailor, Chinese laundryman, Japanese gardener, Negro domestic, and German brewmaster are familiar examples. These roles have become so stereotyped through overuse that people are often surprised to discover how accurate the stereotypes once were. Lieberson's (1980: 316-319) analysis of sixty-six non-Southern cities closely examined the ethnic component of occupations in 1900. After standardizing group size to eliminate compositional effects, Lieberson pre-

Figure 12-2. European emigration to the United States, contributing districts, collecting points, and routes followed, 1900. (Source: U.S. Industrial Commission, 1901.)

sented data that tended to confirm many traditional stereotypes. Thus blacks constituted 74 percent of all domestic servants in the sixty-six cities, Germans constituted 72 percent of all brewers, and Irish 26 percent of all policemen. As Lieberson's data make clear, specialization occasionally produced a virtual monopoly of an occupation by people from a single immigrant minority. For example, this extreme was approached among brewers and domestic servants in 1900. In the same manner, 82 percent of Boston's laborers and 74 percent of its domestic servants were Irish-born in 1850 (Handlin 1969: 253). However, monopolistic occupations were exceptional. More commonly, coethnics were merely overrepresented in an occupation or industry that they shared with other groups. Census manuscripts from Boston in 1850 show that 9 percent of artisans were Germans, a percentage four times greater than the Germans' proportion of the city's labor force. On the other hand, 92 percent of artisans were non-Germans, so Germans clearly did not monopolize this occupation, although they were overrepresented in it.

Handlin (Table 12-1) lists the actual number of occupations performed in 1850 by Bostonians born outside Boston. If place of birth had been altogether unconnected with occupation, one would expect people from a particular place to have been randomly scattered among occupations, but they were clustered

Table 12-1. Cultural Division of Labor in Boston, 1850

Birthplace/Color	Number Employed	Number of Occupations	Index of Clustering (100 = unclustered)
Massachusetts	13,553	660	66
New England	7,986	564	57
Other USA	997	203	20
Negro	575	46	8
Canada	1,381	189	19
Latin America	60	23	38
England	1,369	255	26
Ireland	14,595	362	36
Scotland	433	117	27
Wales	23	16	70
Germany	929	153	17
Switzerland	10	9	90
Netherlands	36	19	53
France	143	68	48
Italy	105	33	31
Spain and Portugal	67	26	39
Scandinavia	172	46	27
Russia and Poland	46	19	41
All Groups	43,567	993	100

Source: Oscar Handlin, *Boston's Immigrants*, 2d ed. (Cambridge: Harvard University Press, 1969). Table XIV. Reproduced by permission.

instead. People born in Massachusetts practiced only 660 of Boston's 993 occupations. A rough index of clustering shows what percentage of its maximum occupational diversity each immigrant group practiced. The most restricted were blacks. Black workers clustered in only 45 occupations of the 993 practiced in Boston. These 45 occupations are 8 percent of the 575 occupations in which blacks might have been employed had perfect dispersion of black workers prevailed. On the other hand, among the Swiss, nearly perfect dispersion did, in fact, prevail as ten workers engaged in nine occupations. The largest immigrant minority, the Irish, were represented in only 362 occupations and were wholly unrepresented in 631.

The immediate cause of immigrant clustering in occupation or industry has always been formal and informal labor-channeling. The principal informal channel is word of mouth [3]. Immigrants learn about occupations their associates have entered, and they can enter only occupations about which they have learned. Therefore information chains slot immigrants into particular industries or occupations—ignoring others that might have been as good or better. In Third World cities, the dependence on informal channels is so extreme that job seekers rarely apply where they have no kin or friends already employed (Hart 1973: 77). The research of Hurh, Kim, and Kim, (1978: 22) in Chicago has shown how important information still is. They found that 90 percent of Korean factory workers in Chicago learned about their job from other Koreans. Only 10 percent obtained job information from public employment agencies, American newspapers, or other non-Korean sources.

Formal labor-channeling institutions of two basic types also exist. The first is indenture. Here the employer advances passage money to an immigrant in return for agreement to work for a stipulated term. In this case, an immigrant's choice of occupation is made by the lender. Since the lender recruits workers from his own village, all the workers from that village flow into a particular industry, creating a cultural division of labor. In the colonial period and through the early nineteenth century, much immigration to the United States took place under indenture agreements.

A related institution is labor contracting. In the late nineteenth century, labor contractors of various nationalities would meet arriving vessels and greet debarking immigrants in their native language, attempting to sign them up for jobs. Labor contractors tended to channel their compatriots into particular occupations. Thus Goren (1970: 21) explains that Jewish labor contractors recruited workers "from the old town" as they arrived in New York City. "Whole branches of the apparel trades were identified with particular towns of Eastern Europe." Among Italians, the "padrone system" of labor contracting was even more extensive. Padroni were also *paesani,* fellow villagers whom debarking immigrants thought they could trust. The padroni rounded up workers from the villages of their region, then took over the responsibility for supplying, disciplining, and paying them out of funds supplied by an employer

(Vecoli 1963: 412). Koren (1897: 122) estimated that two thirds of the Italian male population was "subject in some degree to the padrone system."

ETHNIC NICHES

Ethnic niches in cities are the industries and neighborhoods in which coethnics predominate and with whose fortunes the welfare of the group is accordingly connected. When the niche flourishes, its occupants thrive; when the niche languishes, its occupants suffer. The more specialized the niche, the more accentuated this effect (Hechter 1978: 300). In Ibadan, Nigeria, Cohen (1969) observed a highly specialized niche among the Hausa minority. These Hausa had for many generations sojourned in Ibadan while conducting the cattle business there. The cattle were driven down from Hausaland to Ibadan, where Hausa merchants were in charge of storing, feeding, and selling them. Although urban Hausa practiced several occupations, most Hausa in Ibadan depended on the cattle industry for their livelihood. Therefore, the welfare of the cattle industry became the touchstone against which every aspect of Hausa life had to be measured. The Hausa had little choice but to adjust their group's life-style, politics, and even their religion to the exigencies of the cattle trade.

A second illustration is the tourist industry in American Chinatowns in the middle 1970s (Light and Wong 1975). This specialized niche occupied approximately 50 percent of Chinatown workers. Chinatown people were compelled to adjust their way of life and their social and political expression to the tourist industry. One adjustment was tolerating non-Chinese on the streets of their residential community. The toleration was burdensome because no one enjoys living in a zoo. On the other hand, Chinatown residents accepted the unwelcome necessity in the interest of propping up the tourist industry on which so many Chinese livelihoods depended. However, the Chinese did not depend wholly on one industry. Some were employed in Chinatown's garment factories; others worked for non-Chinese employers outside of Chinatown. Some were unemployed; and a few were welfare recipients. Diversification within the occupational niche supported a diversification of social and political expression that was absent among the Hausa of Nigeria. The Chinese-Hausa comparison illustrates the close connection between diversification of niche and diversification of belief.

The term "niche" is borrowed from ecology, where it refers to the interdependence of organisms in a community of plants and animals (Barth 1956; Hannan 1979: 260). Species are interdependent because the number and activities of each depend on the number and activities of others. In periods of stability, a balance exists among the interdependent species; in periods of instability, changes in behavior and population of one compel adjustments in the behavior and population of others. In an analogous manner, the cultural division of labor eventuates in niches that can support symbiotic, noncompetitive relationships among ethnic groups (Williams 1977) [4]. These relationships are symbiotic because butcher, baker, and candlestick maker are ethnically different, but all exchange their product for those of other ethnics. As a result, each ethnic niche benefits from production conducted in other niches. The relationships are non-competitive because stable niches permit each ethnic group to concentrate on its own product or service while leaving the others to do likewise: so long as the butcher cuts meat and the baker kneads bread, they need not compete.

Destabilized niches, however, encourage intergroup competition. Population change and technological change are two important sources of destabilization. When the population of one group abruptly expands in relation to others, the enlarged group exceeds the carrying capacity of its niche. Under these circum-stances, the superfluous population of the growing group may flow into niches previously monopolized by others. As alien workers flow into its once stable niche, coethnic defenders mobilize for their exclusion. Their motive is protec-tion of their own livelihoods, whose short-run security depends on preventing aliens from ruining the trade by lowering wages or worsening working condi-tions. The formation of the Anti-Jap Laundry League of San Francisco in 1908 illustrates this familiar process. This league was the political organization of white proprietors of steam laundries and French laundry owners and workers. Its purpose was to conduct a two-pronged campaign against Japanese competitors in the laundry business. The league engaged in boycott, personal soliciting of white patrons, and anti-Japanese billboard advertising. It also pressured San Francisco politicians to refuse permits to Japanese steam laundries, and in this effort the league was wholly successful (Light 1972: 71-72). When in 1919 a Japanese opened a steam laundry without a permit in defiance of the authorities, the police closed his laundry. This was the end of Japanese competition in steam laundries in San Francisco.

The outcome of this industrial conflict is of little interest now, but its causes are. Had the Japanese stayed out of the laundry trade, they would have stirred up no animosity on the part of those already practicing it. Why did the Japanese invade a French niche? A significant cause was the increase in the Japanese population of San Francisco as a result of immigration. The enlarged Japa-nese population had outgrown its earlier niche; and the enlarged group over-flowed into adjacent niches already occupied by other groups. This overflow destabilized the cultural division of labor, causing competition and intergroup conflict.

Technological change can also destabilize ethnic niches, thus producing inter-group competition and conflict. An example is the longshore industry in Port-land, Ore. This industry was long operated by men of Scandinavian and German descent. Nepotistic hiring and a strong union always turned back the overflow of outgroups (Pilcher 1972). However, the next threat was containerization of cargoes, a technological improvement that reduced the need for longshore workers. Having failed in their attempt to substitute cheap labor, longshore employers now turned to labor-saving technology, and were successful. The longshore union finally agreed to permit containerization and nonreplacement of retiring workers so long as no layoffs of existing workers resulted. This policy cushioned the shock of technological change for existing longshore workers, but it deprived them of the ability to pass on their jobs to younger kinfolk. As a result, the sons of German or Scandinavian longshoremen had to look to other industries for employment.

These examples cannot do justice to the complex ways in which technical and population change can destabilize a cultural division of labor, but they do indicate how destabilization promotes intergroup competition. This competition tends to intensify ethnic feeling (Bonacich and Modell 1981: Ch. 23). Indeed, Cohen (1969: 4) defines ethnicity as an emergent from intergroup strife "in the course of which people stress their identity and exclusiveness." The purpose of stressing ethnicity is to prevent outgroups from successfully impinging on one's niche, or when the situation is reversed, to enhance the predation of the ingroup. Therefore people's sense of ethnicity decreases in periods of intergroup accommodation and increases when niches are destabilized (Light 1981).

This generalization explains why urban settings often accentuate ethnic solidarity (Cohen 1974: xi): Cities bring many groups into close propinquity, the balance of ethnic niches is precarious, and destabilization of anyone's niche destabilizes the whole system, thus subjecting every group to stress. Destabilization in industrial cities is continuous because change is continuous. Of course, peaks and troughs occur, but a day never passes without technological and population changes that tend, however slowly, to change the status quo. The result is production of ethnicity among people who need the solidarity ethnicity provides to obtain or protect their niches (van den Berghe 1976: 251; Taylor 1979; Nielsen 1980).

ETHNIC SUCCESSION

In principle, peasant migrants could establish ethnic niches in exclusive neighborhoods and highly paid occupations. In reality, the niches thus established center in the least attractive neighborhoods and occupations. Rural-urban immigrants become slaughterhouse workers, not mortgage bankers; and they live in slums, not the Ritz. Two reasons obtrude everywhere. First, rural-urban migrants are skilled only in agriculture, and agricultural skills are useless in urban labor markets. Second, new migrants must compete in the labor market with groups who have already been living in the cities to which they have migrated. Even if these established old-ethnic groups had no urban-related occupational skills or contacts initially, after a generation's residence they have acquired some. Because of acquired contacts and skills, old-ethnics have first access to the job supply. Naturally they take the better jobs in the more attractive industries, leaving new migrants to accept whatever unpreferred work is still available (Hodge 1973; Lieberson 1980: 294–295). Insofar as newcomer groups only fill vacated niches at the bottom of the occupational ladder, they do not compete with predecessor groups. Therefore reoccupation of vacant niches commonly occurs without intergroup conflict.

In the course of industrial urbanization this process repeats itself as successive waves of rural migrants land in big cities. The result of successive migration is successive niche formation with each group that arrives later ranking lower in socioeconomic status than each predecessor group. This is the rank-sequence rule of ethnic succession: earlier immigrants rank above later ones (Light 1981: 58). The occupational niches of the successive groups form a ladder of prestige, income, and attractiveness. Since occupations also pay for housing, the residential neighborhoods of the successive groups also tend to form along a ladder of prestige, cost, and attractiveness, with the newest arrivals having the cheapest, least attractive housing (Warner and Srole 1945: 98).

As urban populations increase, metropolitan economies expand. Their expansion creates opportunities in high-ranking occupations and industries. Those already residing in the expanding cities grab the higher-ranking vacancies created by the expansion of the economy. As groups move up, vacancies develop in abandoned niches at the bottom of the occupational ladder. These vacant niches permit new rural-urban migrants to find jobs and housing in growing cities. The sequential pyramids in Figure 12-3 illustrate this. At time one, group 1 is all alone, and its members occupy upper-, middle-, and lower-status occupations, industries, and neighborhoods. At time two, group 2 people arrive. They take the lower positions so that group 1 people now occupy only middle- and upper-status positions. Group 1 has been upwardly mobile in terms of the average socioeconomic status of its households. At time three, group 3 people appear. They take over the lowest level positions in the occupational, industrial, and housing hierarchy. Now group 2 people move up to middle-status level, and group 1 becomes homogeneously upper status. The urban system grows in overall size mainly because of rural-urban migration; the expansion of the metropolitan system creates room at the top; old-ethnics move upward in social rank as newcomers arrive.

This process is called *ethnic succession* (Light 1981: 58). The succession model has obvious appeal because cities in Australia, North America, and Europe

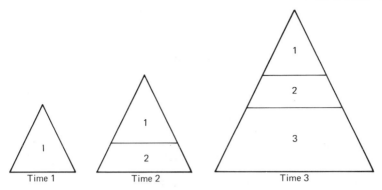

Figure 12-3. Ethnic succession.

do show a rough empirical correspondence to it. Over successive generations, white American and Canadian ethnic groups have moved up the social ladder from starting places near the bottom. As predecessors moved upward, new-comers did occupy their abandoned jobs and housing. This process has given rise to a rough correspondence in industrial regions between the social rank of a white minority and its time of arrival. Apparently this situation has always existed, for even in 1900 the socioeconomic status of urban ethnic groups in-creased with length of residence in the United States (Lieberson 1980: 339).

Ethnic succession also describes the process of immigration, niche formation, and status attainment in Australia (Inglis 1975; Shibutani and Kwan 1965: 121), Britain, and Western Europe. In Western Europe today "guest workers" occupy the worst jobs and housing. Guest workers are chiefly Turks, Italians, Portuguese, and North Africans who have migrated to industrial cities in France, Belgium, Switzerland, West Germany, and Sweden (Table 12-2). As a result of this postwar migration, hardly any Swedes still work on Volvo production lines. These jobs belong now to Turks and Greeks. The Swedes have moved up to managerial positions. A similar situation exists in Switzerland, where Clinard (1978: 138) found that Italians had taken over the lowest levels in the Swiss occupational ladder, thus "automatically elevating large segments of the native Swiss population in the social structure." Evaluating the situation in Europe, Freeman (1979: 218) declares that the arrival of immigrant workers has every-where "promoted a portion of the national work force into nonmanual and supervisory positions."

In Britian, the newest immigrants are citizens, not guests. These are "Com-monwealth immigrants," most of whom are nonwhite. To a substantial extent, the Commonwealth immigrants have piled up in the least desirable occupations and neighborhoods. Smith (1974: 39) found that 67 percent of minority men in Britain were engaged in unskilled manual occupations, whereas only 37 percent

Table 12-2. Foreign Workers in Main Labor Receiving Countries of Western Europe, 1976 and 1979

	Foreign Workers		Percentage of Total Labor Force, 1979
	1976	1979	
Germany	2,027,100	2,025,100	9.3
Austria	171,000	175,200	6.4
Belgium	306,300	310,100	8.0
Denmark	39,400	42,867	1.5
France	1,642,800	1,642,800	7.5
Luxembourg (1977)	49,000	50,400	33.4
Netherlands	180,500	196,400	4.0
United Kingdom	1,665,000	n.a.	3.0
Sweden	235,500	231,999	5.3
Switzerland	516,000	490,700	17.3

Source: Saskia Sassen-Koob, "Towards a Conceptualization of Immigrant Labor," *Social Problems* 29 (1981): 75. Reproduced by permission of author and publisher.

of all men were so engaged. At the other end of the occupational ladder, only 14 percent of minority men worked in nonmanual occupations, compared with 42 percent of all men.

A major controversy today concerns the ethnic succession of nonwhites in the United States. Succession theorists have claimed that blacks and Hispanics in large cities are the "newest immigrants" whose low socioeconomic status is completely explained by the timing of their arrival in urban labor markets. White old-ethnics (Irish, Italian, Jewish) outrank nonwhites because whites entered the industrial cities earlier, just as the white old-ethnics rank below their own Yankee predecessors for the same reason. The succession framework organizes the orthodox explanation for criminality among urban minorities. For example, in his national television series, "The Age of Uncertainty," John Kenneth Galbraith told Americans in 1977 that misbehaving blacks and Puerto Ricans in the slums are no worse than had been their now respectable white predecessors. Galbraith's succession model identifies the stage of rapine and riot as the natural precursor of respectability attendant upon social ascent in due and inevitable course. The most fervent affirmation of succession theory appears in Banfield (1974), a conservative polemic. Banfield portrayed rural-urban migration as a process of resocialization in which improvident and ignorant peasants acquire middle-class social foresight, thus earning a higher rank in urban labor markets. A Marxist version is Szymanski (1976), who understands ethnic succession as a process in which capitalists import docile labor to replace seasoned workers who have learned how to organize unions. Szymanski's data show that blacks are no longer on the bottom: Latin American immigrants now have lower incomes than blacks. Currently, the lowest-ranking worker in North American society is the undocumented Mexican, and this worker is also the most recent rural-urban migrant.

Radicals have rejected the succession framework for nonwhites without disputing its applicability to whites. Split labor force (Bonacich 1972, 1976) and dual labor market writers (Gordon 1972: 43-52; Flanagan 1973: 253-273) have emphasized the institutional barriers that have prevented nonwhites from moving upward in the social hierarchy as rapidly as one would expect on the basis of succession. The reaction against the succession framework is sharpest in Blauner (1972: 51-81), who argues that color prejudice locked nonwhites into ghettos. "Therefore their social realities cannot be understood in the framework of immigration and assimilation that is applied to European ethnic groups." Research has lent this view mixed support. On the one hand, Lieberson (1980: 307-320) and Thernstrom (1973: 176-191) independently compared the social mobility of blacks and foreign-born whites in American cities around 1900. "There was a continuing cycle of migration and social mobility in which the bottom rungs of the class ladder were occupied by successive waves of relatively uneducated and unskilled newcomers to the community" (Thernstrom 1973: 241-242). Both reported, however, that by the turn of this century there was already evidence that blacks were more encapsulated in residential ghettos, more subject to hostile discrimination, and less rewarded for educational achievement than foreign whites. This evidence suggests that the ladder of ethnic succession has not carried nonwhites upward at the same rate as whites. On the other hand, Lieberson (1980: 335-336) also found that the socioeconomic gap between whites and blacks in sixty-six cities greatly increased after 1914. Prior to that date, socioeconomic differences between immigrant whites and blacks had been modest and the immigrant whites were also regarded as racially inferior to Yankees. Thus Roberts (1912: 53) declared that "white people" had left slaughterhouse work to Poles and Italians. After 1914, foreign-born whites increased the socioeconomic gap between themselves and blacks. Lieberson attributes the growing intergroup status disparity to mass migration of poor blacks from the rural South between 1917 and 1965.

Lieberson's balanced conclusions acknowledge that ethnic succession and institutional obstructions to succession are compatible rather than, as earlier supposed, mutually exclusive. That is, earlier debates asked whether the socioeconomic position of urban blacks, Hispanics, and white ethnic groups could be wholly explained on the basis of ethnic succession on the one hand or of institutionalized barriers to mobility on the other. This dichotomy was false because succession has affected the rank order of urban ethnic groups at the same time that nonsuccession influences (racism) have affected this rank order as well. Nonsuccession influences are mechanisms of acceleration or retardation that cause ethnic groups to surge above or fall behind their expected rank in a succession sequence (Light 1981: 60-61). Acceleration influences include previous urban experience, white skin, English language facility, cultural compatibility with the majority, and serendipitous initial location in expanding industrial niches and cities. Retardation influences include the opposite of all the above as well as the actual historical timing of immigration.

Leapfrog Migration

Leapfrog migration occurs when newcomer groups occupy middle- or high-status niches in a city, rather than low-ranking vacancies. Leapfrog migration violates the rank-sequence rule of ethnic succession, thus reducing the correspondence between time of arrival in the urban labor market and socioeconomic rank. Leapfrog migration and ethnic succession are nonetheless compatible processes. In the county of Los Angeles, both processes of urban recruitment are visible. As rural Mexicans pile up in low-ranking niches reflecting their status as most recent arrivals, intercity migrants move into middle- and high-ranking niches in violation of rank-sequence. The niches thus occupied cause leapfrogging newcomers to rank higher than some native Angelenos. Intercity migrants are both domestic and international. The domestic component consists of white professionals relocating from the East and Midwest in response to urbanization of the Sunbelt. The international component consists of Asian and Latin American professionals seeking economic opportunities in the United States. These intercity migrants have graduate degrees that qualify them for high-ranking jobs in preference to locally raised but less educated whites, blacks, and Hispanics. A phenomenon of developed urban systems, leapfrog migration has been increasing in the United States since approximately 1930.

Studying Boston's immigration history, Thernstrom (1973: 43-44) found that prior to 1930 in-migrants were predominantly working class. Thereafter the proportion of middle- and upper-middle-class immigrants increased steadily, and these new arrivals entered the city's labor market at middling levels of the socioeconomic ladder, not at the bottom. More generally, the socioeconomic level of legal immigrants to the United States has shifted sharply upward since the Immigration and Naturalization Act of 1965 (Fortney 1970). This act awards priority of admission to skilled and professional workers. These workers and the overseas families of American citizens now account for virtually the whole annual quota of international immigrants, leaving starving peasants no lawful way to obtain entry into the United States. The now predominantly Latin American and Asian immigrants (Table 12-3) are no longer the "wretched refuse" of their countries of origin. Very commonly the new immigrants have college degrees, money in the bank, and sophisticated occupational and business skills. This new trend has been much in evidence in Miami, whose Cuban population, a third of the city's total, is largely bourgeois in social origin whereas the city's migrant black population consists chiefly of former agricultural workers (Ramirez 1980).

Table 12-3. Immigrants to the United States by Country of Last Permanent Residence, 1820-1978 (percentage)

Last Residence	1820-1978	1961-1970	1971-1978
Europe	74.4	33.8	19.0
Asia	5.9	12.9	33.4
Americas	18.6	51.7	45.1
Africa	0.3	0.9	1.6
Oceania	0.2	0.6	0.5
All Others	0.6	0.2	0.4
Total	100	100	100
	(48,664,000)	(3,321,700)	(664,000)

Source: U.S. Bureau of the Census, *Statistical Abstract of the United States: 1980* (Washington, D.C.: U.S. Government Printing Office, 1980), p. 93.

ETHNICITY IN INDUSTRIAL AND PREINDUSTRIAL CITIES: A COMPARISON

Ranging over the history of cities from earliest beginnings to the present, we have recurrent evidence of the centrality of ethnic groups, who enter the city by migration and then find industrial niches. In this respect preindustrial and industrial cities have been identical, and one can accordingly identify the sequence of migration-niche formation–social accommodation as an invariant regularity of world urbanism. A point of industrial-preindustrial discrepancy is institutional control over the ethnic niches. In preindustrial cities, guilds regulated access to niches; no guilds exist in industrial cities, and niche regulation has accordingly been informal rather than formal. Of course, this contrast is somewhat overdrawn for purposes of analysis. Some crafts and professions still control recruitment, remuneration, and methods in their industry. In the cases of the legal and medical professions, this control is a legal right, not just a capability. Conversely, the guilds of preindustrial cities were not always successful in exercising control over the trades they claimed (Thrupp 1963), and some trades of lower status were wholly unregulated by guilds. On the whole, however, modern societies vest control over employment in employers or in state officials, who are bureaucratic, impersonal authorities.

Furthermore, these authorities are expected to hire on the basis of merit rather than kinship. This norm does not prevent abuses: workers are supposed to be hired and promoted on the basis of merit, but much hiring and promotion still depends on nepotism and ethnic or racial discrimination. The latter is an extension of the former and is frequently confused with it because a consistent policy of nepotism yields an ethnically and racially homogeneous work force. In this respect industrial cities contrast dramatically with their preindustrial counterparts in which nepotism was the approved, expected, and often the only lawful practice.

Social disapproval of particularism has weakened the control of ethnic groups over urban niches. On its face, this change results from and encourages flexible adjustment to industrialization. Industrial cities must make room for rural-urban migrants. Nepotistic trade guilds hindered this adjustment; when new groups entered a city, they encountered a tightly organized economy whose guilds successfully excluded them. Therefore the disappearance of guilds and of particularism have made it easier for industrial cities to integrate rural migrants into urban economies, thus increasing the flexibility of societal adjustment to urbanization.

The opposite is also true. In Third World cities the spirit of ethnic particularism is more pronounced than in large cities of the world system's core. According to McGee (1971: 151) this "consolidation of ethnic groups within particular occupational niches" has posed and continues to pose "a major barrier to occupational mobility" in Third World cities, frustrating the process of economic development. Efforts to dislodge ethnic niches in the course of modernization in Africa have often caused the people affected to intensify their ethnic feelings and ethnic political activity, thus frustrating modernization.

Industrialization also requires technological change, but that change threatens ethnic niches. The guilds always attempted to prevent technological innovation in order to safeguard the livelihood of their members. At this juncture, the foot-dragging attitude of the guilds was in contradiction to the imperatives of industrialization. Wherever ethnic niches persist in industrial cities today, they persist under the threat that new immigration or technological innovation will eliminate them. Social disapproval of ethnic particularism is another part of this struggle. Because particularism is disapproved, the security of ethnic niches is no longer a shared value to which successful appeal can be made in a crisis. Therefore, excluding the Japanese from the laundry business would be much harder today than it was in 1908, when French workers could successfully appeal to the solidarity of the white caste. Industrial societies are prepared to break up ethnic niches in cities whenever these form obstacles to labor absorption.

ACCULTURATION AND ASSIMILATION

A generation ago, sociologists endorsed the view that racial and ethnic contacts passed through recurrent cycles of contact, competition, conflict, and accommodation. After each cycle was completed, minority groups had moved closer to assimilation (Park 1950: 150). Assimilationism depended upon the assumption that that the economies of industrial cities were incompatible with ethnicity and would gradually drive it out. Ware (1931: 612) explained that "economic pressure is constantly at work" to tear apart ethnic communities. First, economic pressures decreased the cultural and physical isolation of ethnic communities by means of urbanization, public education, and mass communication. Second, economic success encouraged moving around in response to opportunities, thus tearing apart the families and ethnic communities of origin. Finally, the marketplace rewarded those "successful at the economic game with scant regard for the group from which they came."

Current thinking (Lyman 1968) has backed away from these early views for three reasons. First, research has demonstrated that even when people move away from hometowns in response to job opportunities, they retain social contact with their place of origin. One way is by visiting. Recently uprooted peasants make regular trips to their hometowns for extensive visits. As a result, even urban-born people of the third generation often have more friends and social contacts in their grandparents' hometown than in their own urban birthplace (Simic 1973). Those who cannot travel visit by telephone. Here technology supports the maintenance of distant social ties that connect people to their past.

Second, ethnic niches provide economic benefits (Bonacich 1975: 111; Reitz, 1980). In New York City Glazer and Moynihan (1970) found that native-born Jews, Irish, and Italians still clustered around traditional occupations whose welfare and defense constituted a shared material interest of all those also sharing an ethnic heritage. Defending these long-standing niches keeps the spirit of ethnicity alive. The modern acknowledgment that material interests support ethnicity (Bonacich and Modell 1981) contradicts Ware's old-fashioned belief that ethnicity was a sentimental tie in which people persisted despite its unprofitability. Granted, substantial evidence (Ianni 1957; Falk 1973) indicates that cultural assimilation accompanies upward social mobility in American society. Still, this finding only confirms the view that niches encourage ethnicity, because the people who move out of the niche cease to be ethnic. Because in modern, industrial societies some individuals do break away from the "ethnic economy" (Bonacich and Modell 1981) into the mainstream, the ethnic core is continuously reduced in size by desertion unless renewed through immigration. In the dwindling core, the concentration of coethnics in a niche produces a material interest in support of ethnic solidarity.

Third, the modern tendency is to understand ethnicity as a multilevel continuum of nested identities, such that people can readjust their definition of ethnicity to correspond to changed life circumstances. When people moved into urban economies, they reduced the salience of their narrow ethnic identities and increased the salience of wider identities. Thus the immigrant generation thought in terms of a particular village; now they are Italo-Americans or Irish Americans, for example.

The cause of this widening of ethnic identity is uncertain. The prevailing explanation interprets it as a result of intergroup competition for urban niches. In this competition, small groups are at a disadvantage because big groups win. Therefore people whose ethnic identities are narrow are losers because they cannot form groups large enough to overpower competitors. This situation encourages groups to expand their boundary of ethnicity in order to embrace compatible neighbors, thus obtaining a larger and more powerful bloc (Kornblum 1974: 159; Light 1981).

SUMMARY

Ethnic groups have always been cornerstones of urban social structure. Ethnic groups enter cities as migrants and then find their way into more or less homogeneous neighborhoods and industries. Ethnic niches provide security, and so long as neighborhoods and livelihoods are secure, social accommodation prevails. However, population growth, and technical change destablize social accommodation, break up ethnic niches, and promote intergroup conflict. Intergroup competition around destablized niches revives ethnicity.

Ethnic succession is sequential movement of ethnic groups up a ladder of hierarchically arranged niches such that earlier groups outrank later ones. Because ethnic succession involves linked upward movement of groups at varying levels of the socioeconomic hierarchy, ethnic succession is not competitive. On the contrary, ethnic succession gives vested groups a stake in the expansion of the economic system through the introduction of lower-ranking newcomers needed to occupy inferior vacancies. Ethnic succession is characteristic of industrial urbanization, and its auspices have greatly reduced the intergroup tensions that arise when niches are destabilized in urbanization.

Nonetheless, urban settings often accentuate ethnic solidarity. First, cities bring many groups into propinquity. Second, the balance of ethnic niches is precarious. Third, destabilization of any niche destabilizes the whole system, thus subjecting every group to stress. Fourth, destabilization in industrial cities is continuous because change is continuous. The result is production of ethnicity among people who need the solidarity ethnicity provides to protect their niches.

NOTES

1. John Stuart Mill (1920: 480–481) wrote about this issue: "So complete, indeed, has hitherto been the separation . . . between the different grades of

laborers, as to be almost equivalent to an hereditary distinction of caste; each employment being chiefly recruited from the children of those already employed in it, or in employment of the same rank with it in social estimation, or from the children of persons who, if originally of lower rank, have succeeded in raising themselves by their exertions."

2. Chinese immigrants in foreign countries have organized themselves in an identical manner with extensive overlap of occupation and locality origins. See Chuen-Yan David Lai, "The Demographic Structure of a Canadian Chinatown in the Mid-Twentieth Century," *Canadian Ethnic Studies* 11 (1979): 61; Stanford M. Lyman, *Chinese Americans.* New York: Random House, 1974, Chs. 2, 3; James L. Watson, *Emigration and the Chinese Lineage.* Berkeley and Los Angeles: University of California Press, 1975, Chs. 5–8.

3. "The help of friends is important. These often hear of vacancies . . . and pass on the knowledge to those out of employment. There is much camaraderie that helps . . . to show a man who is in need of it the ways to a berth." Ernest Aves, "The Building Trades," in Charles Booth, ed. *Life and Labour of the People in London,* Vol. 5. London: Macmillan, 1859, p. 114.

4. Although there are analogies between ecological balance of nonhuman species and ethnic niches, the firmness of this analogy is still controversial. See Hannan and Freedman (1979); Aldrich (1979).

REFERENCES

Adams, Robert M. C. 1966. *The Evolution of Urban Society.* Chicago: Aldine.

Aldrich, Howard. 1979. *Organizations and Environments.* Englewood Cliffs, N.J.: Prentice-Hall

Andreski, Stanislav. 1963. "An Economic Interpretation of Anti-Semitism in Eastern Europe." *Jewish Journal of Sociology* 5: 201–213.

Austin, M. M., and P. Vidal-Naquet. 1977. *Economic and Social History of Ancient Greece.* Trans. and rev. M. M. Austin. Berkeley and Los Angeles: University of California Press.

Axelrod, Bernard. 1972. "Historical Studies of Emigration from the United States." *International Migration Rev.* 6:32–49.

Banfield, Edward C. 1974. *The Unheavenly City Revisited.* Boston: Little, Brown.

Banton, Michael. 1967. *Race Relations.* New York: Basic Books.

Barth, Fredrik. 1956. "Ecological Relationships of Ethnic Groups in Swat, North Pakistan." *American Anthropologist* 58: 1079–1089.

Barton, Josef J. 1975. *Peasants and Strangers: Italians, Rumanians, and Slovaks in an American City, 1890–1950.* Cambridge: Harvard University Press.

Blauner, Robert. 1972. *Racial Oppression in America.* New York: Harper & Row.

Braudel, Fernand. 1973. *Capitalism and Material Life, 1400–1800*. Translated by Miriam Kochan. New York: Harper and Row.

Bonacich, Edna. 1972. "A Theory of Ethnic Antagonism: The Split Labor Market." *American Sociological Review* 37: 547–559.

——. 1975. "Small Businesses and Japanese American Ethnic Solidarity." *Amerasia Journal* 3: 96–112.

——. 1976. "Advanced Capitalism and Black/White Race Relations in the United States: A Split Labor Market Interpretation." *American Sociological Review* 41: 34–51.

Bonacich, Edna, Ivan H. Light, and Charles Choy Wong. 1977. "Koreans in Business." *Society* 14: 54–59.

Bonacich, Edna, and John Modell. 1981. *The Economic Basis of Ethnic Solidarity: A Study of Japanese Americans*. Berkeley and Los Angeles: University of California Press.

Brinkley-Carter, Christina. 1980. "The Economic Impact of the New Immigration on 'Native Minorities,'" pp. 211–221, in Roy Bryce-Laporte, ed. *Sourcebook on the New Immigration*. Washington, D.C.: Smithsonian Institution.

Clinard, Marshall B. 1978. *Cities with Little Crime: The Case of Switzerland*. Cambridge: Cambridge University Press.

Cohen, Abner. 1969. *Custom and Politics in Urban Africa*. Berkeley and Los Angeles: University of California Press.

——. 1974. "Introduction: The Lesson of Ethnicity," pp. ix–xxiv in Abner Cohen, ed. *Urban Ethnicity*. London: Tavistock.

Engels, Friedrich. 1958. [1844]. *The Condition of the Working Class in England*. Trans. and ed. W. O. Henderson and W. H. Chaloner. Oxford: Basil Blackwell.

——. 1962. "The Origin of the Family, Private Property, and the State," pp. 185–359, in Karl Marx and Frederick Engels. *Selected Works*, Vol. II. Moscow: Foreign Languages Publishing House.

Falk, Gerhard. 1973. "Assimilation Process in America." *International Behavioral Scientist* 5: 70–80.

Flanagan, Robert J. 1973. "Segmented Market Theories and Racial Discrimination." *Industrial Relations* 12: 253–272.

Fortney, Judith. 1970. "International Migration of Professionals." *Population Studies* 24: 217–232.

Freeman, Gary P. 1979. *Immigrant Labor and Racial Conflict in Industrial Societies: The French and British Experience, 1945–1975*. Princeton: Princeton University Press.

Fustel de Coulanges, N. D. 1864. *The Ancient City*. Garden City, N.Y.: Doubleday Anchor Editions, n.d.

Glazer, Nathan, and Daniel Patrick Moynihan. 1970. *Beyond the Melting Pot*. 2nd ed. Cambridge: MIT Press.

Golas, Peter. 1977. "Early Ch'ing Guilds," pp. 555–580, in G. William Skinner, ed. *The City in Late Imperial China*. Stanford: Stanford University Press.

Gordon, David M. 1972. *Theories of Poverty and Underemployment*. Lexington, Mass.: D.C. Heath.

Goren, Arthur A. 1970. *New York Jews and the Quest for Community*. New York: Columbia University Press.

Hammond, Mason. 1972. *The City in the Ancient World*. Cambridge: Harvard University.

Handlin, Oscar. 1959. *The Newcomers: Negroes and Puerto Ricans in a Changing Society*. Cambridge: Harvard University Press.

——. 1969. *Boston's Immigrants*. 2nd ed. Cambridge: Harvard University Press.

Hannan, Michael T. 1979. "The Dynamics of Ethnic Boundaries in Modern States," pp. 253–275, in John W. Meyer and Michael T. Hannan, eds. *National Development and the World System: Educational, Economic, and Political Change, 1950–1970*. Chicago: University of Chicago Press.

—— and John Freeman. 1977. "The Population Ecology of Organizations." *American Journal of Sociology* 82: 929–964.

Hannerz, Ulf. 1974. "Ethnicity and Opportunity in Urban America," pp. 37–76, in Abner Cohen, ed. *Urban Ethnicity*. London: Tavistock.

Hart, Keith. 1973. "Informal Income Opportunities and Urban Employment in Ghana." *The Journal of Modern African Studies* 11: 61–89.

Hechter, Michael. 1976. "Ethnicity and Industrialization: On the Proliferation of the Cultural Division of Labor." *Ethnicity* 3: 214–224.

——. 1978. "Group Formation and the Cultural Division of Labor." *American Journal of Sociology* 84: 293–318.

Hechter, Michael. 1979. "The Position of Eastern European Immigrants to the United States in the Cultural Division of Labor: Some Trends and Prospects," pp. 111–130 in Walter L. Goldfrank, ed. *The World System of Capitalism: Past and Present*. Beverly Hills: Sage.

Hodge, Robert W. 1973. "Toward a Theory of Racial Differences in Employment." *Social Forces* 52: 16–30.

Hurh, Won-Moo, Hei-Chu Kim, and Kwang-Chung Kim. 1978. *Assimilation Patterns of Immigrants in the United States: A Case Study of Korean Immigrants in the Chicago Area*. Washington, D.C.: University Press of America.

Ianni, Francis. 1957. "Residential and Occupational Mobility as Indices of Acculturation of an Ethnic Group." *Social Forces* 36: 65–72.

Inglis, Christine. 1975. "Some Recent Australian Writing on Immigration and Assimilation." *International Migration Review* 9: 335–344.

Johnson, Robert Eugene. 1979. *Peasant and Proletarian: The Working Class of Moscow in the Late Nineteenth Century*. New Brunswick, N.J.: Rutgers University Press.

Khaldun, Ibn. 1958. *The Muqaddimah: An Introduction to History*. Translated by Franz Rosenthal. London: Routledge and Kegan Paul.

Kiernan, V. G. 1978. "Britons Old and New," pp. 23–59, in Colin Holmes, ed. *Immigrants and Minorities in British Society*. London: George Allen and Unwin.

Koenig, Samuel. 1943. "Ethnic Factors in the Economic Life of Urban Connecticut." *American Sociological Review* 8: 193–197.

Koren, John. 1897. "The Padrone System and Padrone Banks." *U.S. Department of Labor Bulletin* 9: 113–129.

Kornblum, William. 1974. *Blue Collar Community*. Chicago: University of Press.

Kristol, Irving. 1970. "The Negro Today is Like the Immigrant Yesterday," pp. 139–157, in Nathan Glazer, ed. *Cities in Trouble*. Chicago: Quadrangle.

Lapidus, Ira M. 1967. *Muslim Cities in the Late Middle Ages.* Cambridge: Harvard University Press.

Le Tourneau, Roger. 1957. *Les Villes Musulmanes de l'Afrique du Nord.* Algiers: La Maison des Livres.

Lieberson, Stanley. 1980. *A Piece of the Pie: Blacks and White Immigrants Since 1880.* Berkeley and Los Angeles: University of California Press.

Light, Ivan. 1972. *Ethnic Enterprise in America.* Berkeley and Los Angeles: University of California Press.

——. 1981. "Ethnic Succession," pp. 53–86, in Charles Keyes, ed. *Ethnic Change.* Seattle: University of Washington Press.

——, and Charles Choy Wong. 1975, "Protest or Work: Dilemmas of the Tourist Industry in American Chinatowns." *American Journal of Sociology* 80: 1342–1368.

Lopreato, Joseph. 1970. *Italian Americans.* New York: Random House.

Lyman, Stanford M. 1968. "The Race Relations Cycle of Robert E. Park." *Pacific Sociological Review.* 11: 16–22.

Marx, Karl. 1965. [1887]. *Capital.* Vol. I. Moscow: Progress Publishers.

McGee, T. C. 1971. *The Urbanization Process in the Third World.* London: G. Bell and Sons.

Mill, John Stuart. 1920. *Principles of Political Economy,* Vol. I. New York: D. Appleton and Company.

Nahirny, Vladimir, and Joshua A. Fishman, 1965. "American Immigrant Groups: Ethnic Identification and the Problem of Generations." *Sociological Review* 13: 311–326.

Ng, Wing Chung. 1977. "An Evaluation of the Labor Market Status of Chinese Americans." *Amerasia* 4: 101–122.

Neilsen, François. 1980. "The Flemish Movement in Belgium after World War II: A Dynamic Analysis." *American Sociological Review* 45: 76–94.

O'Kane, James M. 1975. "The Ethnic Factor in American Urban Civil Disorders." *Ethnicity* 2: 230–43.

Park, Robert Ezra. 1950. *Race and Culture.* New York: Free Press, 1950.

Pilcher, William. 1972. *The Portland Longshoremen.* New York: Holt, Rinehart and Winston.

Ramirez, Anthony. 1980. "Cubans and Blacks in Miami." *Wall Street Journal:* May 29.

Reitz, Jeffery G. 1980. *The Survival of Ethnic Groups.* Toronto: McGraw-Hill.

Roberts, Peter. 1912. *The New Immigration.* New York: Macmillan.

Schermerhorn, R. A. 1970. *Comparative Ethnic Relations: A Framework for Theory and Research.* New York: Random House.

Shibutani, Tamotsu, and Kian M. Kwan. 1965. *Ethnic Stratification.* New York: Macmillan.

Simic, Andre. 1973. *The Peasant Urbanites: A Study of Rural-Urban Mobility in Serbia.* New York: Seminar Press.

Sjoberg, Gideon. 1960. *The Preindustrial City.* New York: Free Press.

Skinner, G. William. 1976. "Mobility Strategies in Late Imperial China: A Regional Systems Analysis," pp. 327–364, in Carol A. Smith, ed. *Regional Analysis,* Vol. I. *Economic Systems.* New York: Academic Press.

——. 1977. "Regional Urbanization in Nineteenth Century China," pp. 211–249, in G. William Skinner, ed. *The City in Late Imperial China*. Stanford: Stanford University Press.

Smith, David J. 1974. *Racial Disadvantage in Employment*. London: PEP.

Smith, H. Lewellyn. 1892. "Influx of Population," pts. I, II. pp. 58–165, in Charles Booth, ed. *In Life and Labour of the People in London*, Vol. III. London: Macmillan.

Szymanski, Albert. 1976. "Latin Workers in the United States" Paper presented, Annual Meeting of the Pacific Sociological Association, March 26.

Taylor, Ronald L. 1979. "Black Ethnicity and The Persistence of Ethnogenesis." *American Journal of Sociology* 84: 1401–1423.

Thernstrom, Stephan. 1973. *The Other Bostonians*. Cambridge: Harvard University.

Thrupp, Sylvia. 1963. "The Guilds," pp. 230–280, in M. M. Postan, E. E. Rich, and Edward Miller, eds. *The Cambridge Economic History of Europe*, Vol. III. Cambridge: Cambridge University Press.

Tilly, Charles. 1978. "Migration in Modern European History," pp. 48–72, in William H. McNeill, and Ruth S. Adams, eds. *Human Migration*. Bloomington: Indiana University Press.

van den Berghe, Pierre L. 1971. "Ethnicity: The African Experience." *International Social Science Journal* 23: 507–518.

——. "Ethnic Pluralism in Industrial Societies: A Special Case." *Ethnicity* 3: 242–255.

Vecoli, Rudolph J. 1963. "Chicago's Italians Prior to World War I: A Study of Their Economic Adjustment." Ph.D dissertation, University of Wisconsin.

Ware, Caroline F. 1931. "Ethnic Communities." *Encyclopedia of the Social Sciences*, 5: 607–613.

Warner, W. Lloyd, and Leo Srole. 1945. *The Social Systems of American Ethnic Groups*. New Haven: Yale University.

Weber, Eugen. 1977. *Peasants into Frenchman*. Stanford: Stanford University Press.

Weber, Max. 1952. *Ancient Judaism*. New York: Free Press.

Williams, Robin M., Jr. 1977. *Mutual Accomodation: Ethnic Conflict and Co-operation*. Minneapolis: University of Minnesota Press.

Wilson, Kenneth L., and Alejandro Portes. 1980. "Immigrant Enclaves: An Analysis of the Labor Market Experiences of Cubans in Miami." *American Journal of Sociology* 86: 295–319.

Wirth, Louis. 1939. "Urbanism as a Way of Life." *American Journal of Sociology* 44: 3–24.

Zorbaugh, Harvey. 1929. *The Gold Coast and the Slum*. Chicago: University of Chicago Press.

PART FIVE

Political Economy

CHAPTER 13

Labor Absorption

The growth of metropolitan populations raises the problem of finding work for new city dwellers. Labor absorption is easiest when labor force growth arises from natural increase. Under this condition a city has ten to twenty years after the birth of a child before he or she enters the labor market. But urbanization poses a sterner challenge by introducing rural-urban migrants. Their arrival is abrupt and their need for work immediate. One day they arrive; the next they need a job. Moreover, the source of the immigrant laborers is outside the political boundaries of the metropolitan recipient, and rules governing immigration are national rather than local. Cities do not make urbanization policy; nations do. For example, Miami does not make U.S. migration policy; Congress does. Nonetheless Miami has had the real responsibility for employing Cuban and Haitian immigrants to the United States. Miami authorities could hardly have anticipated this responsibility twenty years ago, nor could they have refused to accept it [1].

Labor absorption incapacity arises when cities attract so many new workers that the local job supply cannot keep pace. Unemployment and underemployment then result. In this situation one is tempted to blame urban unemployment on excessive migration, and migration on excessive population growth in the countryside. In a world context this argument has appeal because the abrupt growth of world population obviously requires massive economic growth in cities just to keep pace. In a national or local context, however, the issues are always more complex. First, national governments have responsibility for managing population growth and must accept a judgment of political failure when population growth proceeds more rapidly than economic development. Second, who is to say whether people are arriving too rapidly or jobs are not being created fast enough?

Labor absorption has external and internal aspects. The external aspect is the objective size of the absorption problem. The appropriate measures of size are the number and rate of increase in the population of job seekers. A large, rapidly increasing population of job seekers poses a big problem of labor absorption. The internal aspect is the absorptive capacity of each metropolitan area. This internal aspect is an obvious function of metropolitan size such that large, growing metropolitan areas have more labor absorption capacity than small, stagnant ones. But there is a qualitative dimension too. Even though they may be the same size, metropolitan areas differ in their ability to find jobs for newcomers. Swabbing up a kitchen mess provides a useful analogy to the labor absorption function of cities. Ability to clean up a soggy mess depends on the size and growth rate of the mess on the one hand, and the size and absorptive capacity of towels on the other. Some towels are more absorbent than others and, as television commercials have relentlessly demonstrated, the more absorbent ones just take up spill better than the bargain brands.

LABOR ABSORPTION IN CITIES

When the economy of a metropolitan area is expanding and labor is scarce, the absorption of migrant labor poses few social or economic difficulties. Newcomers take vacant jobs and no one objects. Housing starts are strong, and the newcomers earn the money to buy housing. The newcomers also fill in low-ranking vacancies in neighborhoods and industries, thus permitting the long-resident population to move up the social hierarchy in the familiar patterns of ethnic succession. When economic clouds appear on the horizon, however, and this is most of the time, resident city workers become fearful of their own economic future and develop a reactive motive to protect their neighborhoods, industries, and occupations against the real or potential competition of newcomers. This scenario is very familiar in urban history. In late medieval Europe, guildsmen of Flanders and northern Italy would not permit any day laborers to work until every guild member had work at the prevailing wage (Van Der Wee 1975-1976). In Elizabethan England residents rioted against the foreigners who crowded into industrial towns and alleged that the newcomers undercut the prevailing wage rate, taking work away from those already employed (Clark and Slack 1976: 94). In the United States, Canada, and Western Europe today, many workers are afraid that foreigners will take their job from them or, because of the pressure of their competition, lower prevailing wage rates, reduce the capital intensity of production, overburden the urban infrastructure, and thus reduce the living standard of the established work force.

A split labor market arises whenever cheap and distressed labor enters metropolitan labor markets (Bonacich 1972, 1979). *Distressed labor* consists of workers who, lacking resources of their own, are desperately in need of work. *Cheap labor* is workers prepared to accept what are by local standards very low wages. Normally, distressed workers are cheap labor too. Rural-urban immigrants are the most prominent class of cheap and distressed labor. Lacking savings and accustomed to rural poverty, migrants are prepared to accept any job, however revolting, at wages considerably below what town people demand.

Whenever split labor markets exist or come into existence, metropolitan workers fear the effects of cheap labor influx [2]. The intensity of fearfulness depends on the local scarcity or surplus of labor. In periods of labor surplus (high unemployment), a big influx of cheap labor is likely to produce a severe reaction. Conversely, when a labor shortage exists, unions waive their usual objections to cheap labor influx in the interest of economic growth. Metropolitan workers are fearful of the real and potential competition of cheap labor newcomers as well as the effects of these newcomers on urban infrastructure, the general wage rate, and capital intensiveness of production. Real competition arises when newcomer workers get jobs away from job holders by underbidding the prevailing wage. Potential competition arises when existing job holders perceive a possibility that real competition may arise in the future. Decline in the general wage rate occurs when, as a result of increased supply of labor, employers pay lower wages and still obtain hands. Urban infrastructure deteriorates when, as a result of augmented population, public use of schools, parks, hospitals, beaches, street cars, and roads increases without an increase in the supply of facilities. Reductions in capital intensiveness arise when, as a result of plentiful cheap labor, employers prefer to hire cheap workers rather than invest in productivity-improving technology. Since these decisions spell increasing demand for cheap labor migrants and reduced demand for existing job holders, a decline in the capital intensiveness of production actually displaces high-wage with low-wage labor and is a disguised form of real labor competition [3].

To protect themselves against cheap labor competition, job holders devise economic *shelters* (Freedman 1976) that regulate and impede the flow of labor into urban labor markets. Some of these shelters have the force of law; others have only the economic power of the job holders to defend them. Guilds no longer exist but other sheltering devices do. Among them are labor certification requirements, seniority systems, nepotistic hiring practices, minimum wage laws, wages and hours regulations, craft unionism, child and woman labor restrictions, compulsory education laws, and racial, ethnic, or religious discrimination. Whatever their proclaimed intent, all these restrict the size of the eligible work force, excluding low-wage workers. For instance, minimum wage laws stipulate the lowest legal wage that employers may pay. In 1981 this federal minimum wage was $3.35 hourly. However, many women, children, and immigrants were prepared to work for less than this amount. In this circumstance, the legal minimum tended to prevent cheap and distressed workers from underbidding the labor market, thus preventing them, in some cases, from finding a job at all.

As labor market shelters proliferate, the result is segmented or dual labor markets in major cities. *Dual labor markets* consist of distinct labor markets within which unequal conditions prevail (Tolbert, Horan, and Beck 1980). Mobility from one labor market to the other is infrequent and difficult (Kalleberg and Sorenson 1979: 356). "Sociologists . . . have long argued that workers do not compete in a single labor market" (Bibb and Form 1977: 976). In the favored, primary labor market wages are high, jobs secure, working conditions pleasant, union protection common, career hierarchies exist, and work is capital-intensive. In the less favored, secondary labor market, the opposite conditions prevail. Wages are low, sometimes below the legal minimum wage. Working conditions are harsh, sometimes unlawfully dirty or dangerous (Briggs 1975: 480). Unions are weak and few; employer union busting is easy and common. Jobs are dead ends and work involves large crews of poorly equipped workers rather than expensive technology managed by a few well-paid workers. Most important, unemployment is high among workers in the secondary sector who are more numerous than the unattractive jobs for which they compete (Doeringer and Piore 1975).

To a large extent, workers in the slowly growing, sheltered, high-wage labor market segment have been whites, whereas those in the rapidly growing, un-sheltered, low-wage segment have been nonwhites (Bibb and Form 1977: 992; Beck 1980). The most distressed workers were illegal workers from Mexico, but blacks, Asians, and Native Americans were also more than usually prominent (Briggs 1975). Workers in the low-wage segment prefer to break into the high-wage segment with its careers, union protection, and pleasant working conditions, but institutional barriers prevent them from fully exploiting their only competitive advantage: a desperate willingness to work long hours for low wages. For example, nepotistic hiring practices prevent nonwhites from obtaining access to sheltered industries because nonwhites do not have white relatives employed in these trades.

O'Connor (1973: 127) finds the segmented labor market in the United States coincides with the area distinction between central cities and suburbs. The low-wage, competitive sector jobs have clustered in the central cities, whereas high-wage jobs in the monopoly sector of the private economy cluster in the suburbs. Friedland (1981: Ch. 10) has echoed this claim, interpreting the downtown "office economy" as the only dynamic feature of central cities' economies. The exception is not as sharp as it seems for, as Ginzberg (1977) has observed, lower white-collar occupations in finance, insurance, and real estate have lower than average wages so this segment of the downtown office economy is really a reservation for low-wage whites. Nonetheless, there is much evidence that whites, blacks, and Hispanics participate in propinquitous but disjunctive labor markets. Table 13-1 shows the percentage of civilian labor force in central cities and suburbs by race and Hispanic origin in 1978. Nearly two thirds of the whites worked in the

Table 13-1. Labor Force Status of Persons Sixteen Years and Over by Sex, Race, Hispanic Origin, and Area, 1978 Annual Average

	White	Black	Hispanic Origin
Civilian labor force			
Central cities	36.5	72.1	56.9
Suburbs	63.5	27.9	43.1
Total	100	100	100
Unemployment rate			
Central cities	5.7	13.9	9.6
Suburbs	4.9	10.5	8.4
Number (000)	59,566	7,803	3,986

Source: Diane N. Westcott, "Employment and Commuting Patterns: A Residential Analysis," *Monthly Labor Review* 102 (July 1979): 4.

suburbs, whereas 72.1 percent of blacks and 56.9 percent of Hispanics worked in central cities. Unemployment rates are higher among nonwhites than among whites and higher in central cities than in suburbs. In effect, two thirds of whites participated in the lowest unemployment sector, whereas the bulk of blacks and Hispanics participated in the highest unemployment sector.

Since World War II the economy of the United States has produced more jobs in low-wage than in high-wage industries. Ginzberg (1977) found that between 1950 and 1976 three out of five new jobs in the private sector emerged in retail trade and service industries. These have always been low-wage and labor-intensive industries. For example, fast-food outlets like McDonald's employ teenagers at low wages, and in the 1970s fast-food outlets were the most rapidly growing American industry. The trend toward low-wage jobs has encouraged (and been encouraged by) the immigration of distressed workers from Mexico, Latin America, and Asia. Sassen-Koob (1980: 20-22) estimates that between 1972 and 1985, immigrant workers will account for only 13.3 percent of total labor force growth but 33.4 percent of labor force growth in semiskilled manual occupations and 23.9 percent of growth in all blue-collar occupations. Few immigrant workers have jobs in the high-wage monopoly sector (Bonacich and Hirata 1981: 55).

The trend toward low-wage jobs has supported the emergence of a dual economy, but the causes of this trend are complex, poorly understood, and subject to continuing debate [4]. Dual labor market economists have claimed that industry characteristics are basic. According to this view, monopolistic industries permit big business corporations to pay high wages in exchange for labor peace. Thus Stone (1975) has shown that U.S. Steel Corporation introduced and supported career hierarchies, job security, pension rights, and welfare fringe benefits in order to maintain the lifetime loyalty of its work force. From the point of view of a giant corporation, worker loyalty is worth the extra labor cost. However, in competitive industries, even reluctant employers must seek out cheap labor in order to meet competition. For this reason, O'Connor (1973) argues, high-wage/low-wage dualism in labor markets reflects the prior and more basic distinction between the monopoly and competitive sectors of the business population.

On the other hand, Bonacich (1979, 1980) has argued that dualism in labor markets results from loopholes in protective legislation enacted at the behest of the domestic working class. The federal Labor Standards Act of 1938 introduced minimum wage, overtime pay, equal pay, and child labor provisions. This legislation compels employers to pay high wages and provide safe and sanitary working conditions, but this protective legislation excluded many industries, notably agriculture, wholesale trade, retail trade, insurance, finance, real estate, and services. Hence employers in these industries have been permitted to hire cheap labor under inferior working conditions. Accordingly, these industries became low-wage enclaves whose distressed workers are disproportionately recruited among youths, women, and nonwhites.

Another legal irony is the contradiction between welfare legislation and immigrant labor. The Social Security Act of 1935 is the cornerstone of U.S. welfare legislation, whose major programs are Old Age, Survivors, Disability and Health Insurance, Supplemental Security Income (aged, blind, disabled), and Aid to Families with Dependent Children. Other federally supported welfare programs include food stamps, railroad retirement, veterans' benefits, black lung disease (for coal miners), unemployment insurance, and workmens' compensation. The effect of welfare legislation was to exempt the disadvantaged from having to enter the labor market as distressed, cheap labor. The lame, halt, blind, and unemployed have had the option of refusing low-wage jobs because the welfare system provided them an alternative livelihood.

Welfare and protective legislation do little to help distressed immigrants. Because foreign workers are noncitizens, poorly informed, and often illegally in the United States, they cannot obtain welfare benefits. Therefore they must accept low-wage work because they perceive no option of relief. Additionally, immigrants congregate in the least protected industries such as restaurants, hotels, and garment factories. In these industries many employers do not meet minimal legal standards of safety or hygiene nor pay the minimum wage. Immigrants sometimes know their employers are violating the U.S. labor laws, but because unlawfully in the United States, and/or unlawfully at work, exploited foreigners cannot complain to the police without risk of deportation. Therefore their wages and working conditions remain below the legal standard in many industries (Sassen-Koob 1980: 13).

A generation ago, most employer violations of labor law occurred in agriculture, and undocumented (illegal) Mexican workers were the chief victims. However, this pattern changed as rural Mexicans immigrated to U.S. cities in search of work. In 1970, fully 85 percent of Mexican-origin workers were urban (Solache 1981: 2). In 1980, about two thirds of illegal workers of all nationalities lived and worked in urban areas (Portes 1977: 38; Sassen-Koob 1981). Since the subject is illegal employment, exact estimates of its extent are impossible to obtain, but it seems a safe guess that in 1981 about 5 percent of job holders in the United States were illegally in the country, illegally at work, or both [5]. In the ten biggest cities of the United States, the percentage of illegally employed workers in the metropolitan labor force was possibly twice the national average and may have reached 12 to 15 percent in selected localities.

Immigrants concentrate in the biggest cities. In 1980 approximately 40 percent of immigrants resided in the ten largest U.S. cities, although these cities together accounted for less than 10 percent of the total U.S. population. In the period 1966–1976, New York City alone received one quarter of all immigration to the United States. One tenth of the 1960 population of the Dominican Republic was residing in New York City in 1980 (Sassen-Koob 1980: 7–11). Similarly, in 1980 approximately one third of Miami's population was Cuban-born. One third of the population of Los Angeles county was Spanish-speaking, mostly Mexican. In metropolitan regions, immigrant workers concentrate in central cities and in the low-wage, labor-intensive industries that still cluster in central cities (Wilson and Portes 1980: 298).

The existence of low-ranking central city enclaves has generated controversy about the extent to which immigrant workers actually compete with native-born workers. On the one hand, the American labor movement has denounced the toleration of illegal workers on the grounds that these foreigners take jobs away from Americans [6]. Evaluating the evidence, Bonacich and Hirata (1981: 58) have flatly declared: "the local working class is potentially threatened by the introduction of immigrant workers." Conversely, available cheap labor benefits all employers, even those who do not directly employ it. According to this view, the introduction of immigrant cheap labor is a class stratagem of the bourgeoisie, whose purpose is to increase profits at the expense of labor.

Employers retort that foreigners take only low-paying jobs that Americans refuse (Berman 1978) [7]. Therefore Americans and foreigners do not compete in the labor market. This argument has some force. Even Marxists concede that distressed immigrants take low-paying jobs that the native-born poor, having the option of welfare, refuse to do. Direct competition is absent. However, one does not have to choose between the view that all immigrants are in job competition with all natives or that no immigrants offer any job competition to any native-born Americans. Sassen-Koob (1981: 21) has taken a sensible intermediate position:

It seems unlikely that a majority of immigrants are gaining access to primary market jobs and thereby displacing natives. It is rather in the secondary labor market that the arena for competition between immigrant and [native-born] minorities is located.

According to her view, *some* immigrants, not all, do take jobs that poor Americans would otherwise take. This is direct competition. Additionally, the mere presence of distressed immigrant labor gives employers the luxury of refusing to upgrade menial jobs in order to make them attractive to poor Americans (Sassen-Koob 1981: 28). This is indirect competition. In the short run, central city poor are the only group to suffer an adverse competitive impact from the immigration of distressed foreigners. These poor are heavily, but not exclusively, nonwhites. In the long run, it is possible, the presence of distressed labor slackens demand for skilled workers in capital-intensive, heavy industries, thus undermining the position of the primary sector workers. Portes (1977: 35) also claims that immigrant workers help "retard the upward trend of wages," thus reducing the paycheck of primary sector workers. But any such effects are long-term. In the short run, primary sector workers in suburbs are unaffected by the labor competition of distressed foreigners in central cities.

PREJUDICE OR LABOR COMPETITION?

To what extent does labor market segmentation reflect ethnic or race prejudice rather than labor competition? This question is complex and controversial. The prejudice theory (Allport 1958) stresses the priority of overgeneralized attitudes of disfavor toward minorities. These unfavorable attitudes then cause intergroup conflicts. Prejudiced people exclude the victims of their prejudice from jobs, labor markets, neighborhoods, cities, and even their country because of their prejudices. Thus prejudice explains discrimination, labor market segmentation, minority unemployment, and xenophobia. For instance, blacks in America have long suffered rates of unemployment twice as high as whites, and it is plausible to suppose prejudice is the cause of this lamentable situation. However, the old-fashioned prejudice theory is much disputed now. The existence of prejudice is still undisputed, but what is disputed is the explanatory sufficiency of prejudice in real and concrete situations of intergroup conflict. As Varaday (1979: 34) has observed, prejudice often exists without discrimination and discrimination without prejudice. Therefore, prejudice cannot cause discrimination.

Americans have unfavorable attitudes toward immigrants. In 1980 a Roper poll reported that 80 percent of Americans believed immigration was too high and its volume should be reduced (Chaze 1980). Prejudice is a convenient explanation for this public attitude, but that explanation quite overlooks the distinct possibility that self-interest (not prejudice) explains the public's disfavor. The Roper poll found that many Americans feared cheap labor immigrants might get their jobs away from them [8]. Whether right or wrong, this perception was widespread.

Admittedly the prejudice theory fits some cases better than others. In the case of blacks, a substantial body of evidence (Meeker and Kau 1977; Thernstrom, 1973; Lieberson 1980) suggests that racism has obstructed their economic and social integration even in Northern cities of the United States. But even in the best-fitting case of blacks, the prejudice theory falls short of complete adequacy. For example, Bonacich (1976) has pointed out that rates of unemployment among urban blacks were lower than unemployment rates among urban whites until 1940, yet public opinion surveys indicate that conscious attitudinal racism among whites has much declined since World War II. Why should black unemployment be higher now that white racism is lower? The finding is incompatible with the view that prejudice causes unemployment but compatible with the view that white prejudice against blacks receded as blacks ceased to threaten whites with cheap labor competition. "The antagonism toward black workers," Bonacich (1976) continues, "was not simply race prejudice." Similarly, in his survey of fifteen U.S. cities in 1968, Cummings (1980) found that whites in job competition with blacks were more intolerant of blacks than whites not in competition with them. Cummings's findings suggest that intergroup competition is a cause of prejudice, not the mere result of prejudice. This conclusion is compatible with a split labor market interpretation of black unemployment and white racism.

The split labor market theory (Bonacich, 1972, 1976, 1979) reverses the prejudice theory. Split labor markets arise when high-priced labor fears cheap labor. Under these circumstances, high-priced labor seeks to exclude low-priced labor because it is in the short-run, parochial interest of high-priced labor to do so. The confrontation of divergent interests in a three-cornered competition (capitalists and cheap labor vs. high-priced labor) exacerbates ethnic tension. Prejudice and hostile stereotyping are symptoms of intergroup tension—not the cause.

Split labor market (SLM) theory has clarified the intergroup processes in urbanization of market societies. First, SLM theory explains prejudice whereas the prejudice theory has no contextual explanation for the existence of prejudice and must assume it was transmitted by primary socialization from an earlier generation. Second, SLM theory explains why intergroup tensions (and prejudice, their symptom) rise and fall in predictable relationship to labor surplus or shortage in cities. The prejudice theory cannot explain short-term up and down variation in intensity of prejudice because a constant cannot explain a change. Third, SLM theory is parsimonious because it identifes prejudice as a superstructural ideology reflecting contradictions in the economic sphere of capitalist society. The prejudice theory has no firm anchorage in any general theory of social change. Fourth, SLM theory explains all kinds of segmentation of labor markets (for example, youth unemployment) whereas the prejudice theory encompasses only ethnic or racial segmentation. Finally, to the extent that policy is based on the presumption that prejudice is only a personal moral problem, public policy is unable to recognize or cope with institutionalized conflict arising from "the economic function and situation" of despised minorities (Freeman 1979: 148).

Events in Miami, Fla., illustrate the theoretical controversy. In 1980, an abrupt influx of Cubans and Haitians into Miami occurred in response to political uncertainty in the Caribbean. This influx followed twenty years of more gradual emigration of Cubans into Miami. In May 1980, a two-day riot erupted in Miami's Liberty district, a solidly black residential neighborhood. Black-Cuban competition for jobs and housing was identified as a background precipitant of this violent outburst, yet there was little evidence of long-term ethnic or racial prejudice. American Blacks have no tradition of hating Cubans, and Cubans come from a society in which interracial amity is more valued and common than in the United States. In this instance, therefore, real intergroup competition appears to account for Miami's intergroup tension. Prejudice is an unsatisfactory explanation of why Miami blacks chose May 1980 to have a violent demonstration. On the other hand, SLM theory is compatible with events, although there is no claim here that SLM processes provide a complete explanation of this complex event.

SPLIT LABOR MARKETS IN WESTERN EUROPE

It would be surprising if split labor markets existed only in the United States for as Hechter (1978: 311) has observed, "every developing industrial economy" occasionally experiences "shortages of unskilled labor." Immigration relieves labor shortages. A severe shortage of labor did, in fact, arise in Western Europe in the 1950s and 1960s. According to Kindleberger (1967) the importation of foreign workers was the key to Europe's rapid industrial recovery in the postwar decades. However, the foreign workers in Europe were never immigrants conceded rights of naturalization. In law foreign workers were temporary guests of the labor-importing countries, and their legal right to remain in the host country was precarious.

Guest workers in continental Europe are a pot pourri of nationalities from southern Europe, Eastern Europe, North Africa, and the Middle East. Their immigration destinations have been Belgium, France, Switzerland, West Germany, Sweden, and Britain with the expected specialization of migration streams developing. Table 12–2 displays the unequal composition of migrant workers in the labor force of various European countries in 1976 and 1979. The immigration of guest workers began in 1948 and peaked in 1974 when about 7.5 million foreign workers had jobs in Britain and the countries of the European Economic Community. In Britain, the immigration was slower to get underway, and Freeman (1979: 179) judges that the sluggishness of British economic development in the 1950s reflected labor shortages unrelieved by immigration. Unlike Western Europe's guest workers, colored immigrants in Britain enjoy civic rights because most come from Commonwealth nations and carry British passports. West Indians, Pakistanis, and Indians were the principal newcomers in Britain, the bulk of their immigration taking place in the 1960s.

Before European countries began importing foreign workers, employers could not find takers for undesirable, low-wage jobs. In France, Freeman (1979: 204-205) writes, the native-born workers were "simply no longer willing to perform mean, unpleasant, and poorly compensated tasks." In the United States, the expansion of the welfare system had created a similar situation by offering the option of nonwork for the poor. However, in Europe native-born workers declined low-wage jobs because they had better job opportunities in a labor-short economy. Guest workers took the vacated, low-wage, undesirable jobs without initiating competition with European workers. European governments admitted the foreign workers in the expectation that when unemployment increased, the guest workers would return to their countries of origin, vacating their jobs and housing for reoccupancy by native-born workers. The European countries wanted sojourning labor power, not immigrants. Therefore labor-importing countries of Europe were reluctant to grant the guest workers civil, social, or political rights. Guest workers' children did not acquire citizenship because, under the *jus sanguinis*, citizenship is transferred by the parent's nationality. European governments strictly regulated the employment of foreign workers requiring passes and permission to change jobs, while resisting the workers' requests for family reunification in the host country. European governments preferred to import single men who could live in dormitories, supporting their families with remittances to the home country.

The analysis of labor market dualism has advanced farthest in the United States, and there remains uncertainly about the extent to which European societies have experienced the same dualism. Nonetheless, there are obvious parallels between labor market dualism in the United States and what currently exists in Western Europe. Rex (1979: 15) has observed that the tendency toward "the formation of a dual labour market or a split labour market" is not only pronounced in Europe but "may be inevitable in a successful capitalist industrial society." Reviewing the situation in Britain, Bosanquet and Doeringer (1973) found extensive similarity with the United States. Admittedly, lines between immigrant and native worker segments were more blurred than in the United States. Still, "many of the same symptoms of labour market duality are present, and a basic distinction can usefully be made, in Britain as well as the United States, between the primary and secondary sectors" (1973: 432). Evaluating their conclusion, Donnison (1980: 126-127; Townsend 1979: 646-647) regrets the tendency for dual labor market research in Britain to focus on the national level rather than "the inner city level" where immigrant-native boundaries are most pronounced.

As in North America, foreign workers in Britain and Europe have tended to concentrate in the largest cities, but these have been industrial cities. In West

Germany, for example, foreign workers accounted for 6.6 percent of persons in 1975, but in heavily urbanized regions their percentage of population was three to five times higher than this national average (Rist 1975: 10, 69; Schmitter 1979: 165, 211-212). Reiman and Reiman (1979: 79) also have noted "the concentration of the alien population in certain large cities" where, despite severe legal restrictions, approximately 10 percent are illegal aliens. In the continental cities where they concentrate, foreigners tend to occupy distinct innercity neighborhoods. Thus in Augsburg, an industrial city of West Germany, the foreign population is twice as high as in the country as a whole and most foreigners live in identifiable districts. In the Kreuzberg district of West Berlin a Turkish enclave developed and successfully resisted the efforts of municipal authorities to renew the neighborhood.

Commonwealth immigrants in Britain "are concentrated largely in urban industrial areas such as London, Birmingham, and Bradford" (Studlar 1979: 88). Table 13-2 shows that migrants from the Irish Republic, the Commonwealth, and foreign countries (mostly E.E.C. member-states) were overrepresented in conurbations, but Britain's internal migrants were not. Thus, 64 percent of migrants from the Irish Republic resided in conurbations in 1971, whereas only 32 percent of all Britons did so. On the other hand, only 31.3 percent of internal migrants (from Great Britain) resided in conurbations, a negligible divergence from Britain's general proportion. However, the migration of foreign workers to Britain was also selective of specific conurbations. Migrants avoided depressed conurbations, (Tyneside, Central Clydeside). In Greater London, however, migrants showed a distinct clustering, choosing this metropolitan region two to three times more frequently than did other Britons. The result is localization of the problem of labor absorption in London. Parliament made the laws governing immigration, but London absorbed much of the burden of finding jobs for immigrants. Within London and the Midlands industrial cities, Commonwealth immigrants also tend to cluster in identifiable inner-city wards (United Kingdom, Department of the Environment 1973: 140-141; Freeman 1979: 45).

In the cities they inhabit, foreign workers concentrate in less desirable occupations and industries where they experience higher than average unemployment. For instance, in Stuttgart, guest workers constituted only 10 percent of the labor force in 1974, but they made up 22 percent of the recipients of unemployment benefits (Schmitter 1979: 165). In the popular view, foreigners accept the dirty work that Europeans refuse. However, when dirty work is well paid, Europeans are still glad to perform it (Godschalk 1979). In Britain, Commonwealth immigrants are most visible as street cleaners and transit employees; but they also work in heavy industry. Rex and Tomlinson (1979: 107) found that between a third and a half of Commonwealth immigrants in Birmingham worked "in hot, dirty industries marked by shift work." Unemployment among Commonwealth immigrants was twice as high as among other Birmingham workers. Similar situations existed in immigrant-congested boroughs of central London,

Table 13-2. Migrants Within Five Years Preceding United Kingdom Census of 1971 Residing in Conurbations (percentage)

	Migrants: Area of Origin				
Conurbations	UK: All Persons	Irish Republic	Commonwealth	Foreign Country	Great Britain
Tyneside	1.45	0.3	0.5	0.6	1.53
W. Yorkshire	3.11	2.6	4.2	1.2	0.33
Merseyside	2.3	2.8	1.1	1.1	2.1
S.E. Lancashire	4.3	6.9	4.2	2.2	4.3
W. Midlands	4.3	7.5	6.5	1.3	4.1
Greater London	13.4	41.9	28.5	27.7	12.9
Central Clydeside	3.1	2.0	1.4	1.3	3.2
All Conurbations	32.0	64.0	46.4	35.4	31.3

Source: Office of Population Censuses and Surveys, London General Office, Edinburgh. Census of 1971, *Great Britain Migration Tables*, Part I *(10%) Sample*. (London: HMSO, 1974), Table IB, pp. 4–5. Reproduced by permission.

where unemployment was much higher than elsewhere in the city (United Kingdom Department of the Environment 1973: 140-141). Three quarters of migrant workers in France and West Germany are employed in low-paid manual jobs. The most visible such jobs are street cleaning and construction labor, but many guest workers have jobs in heavy industry too. Their preponderance on assembly lines in striking (Table 13-3) and distinguishes the European situation from the American. In the United States, assembly line jobs in heavy industry are unionized and well paid. They belong in the primary sector so few immigrants get them.

So long as labor shortages prevailed, foreign workers did not compete with

Table 13-3. Percentage Distribution of Migrant Workers, Selected European Countries, by Industry

	France, 1971	Federal Republic of Germany, 1973	Switzerland, 1973
Total migrant workers	100	100	100
Agriculture	6	1	2
Mining	3	3	1
Construction	31	16	11
Manufacturing	33	60	52
Commerce	10	6	9
Services	17	14	25

Source: United Nations Department of Economic and Social Affairs, Population Studies, No. 62. *World Population Trends and Policies* Volume I *Population Trends* [Sales No. E.78.XIII.3] (New York: United Nations, 1979), Table 151, p. 260. Reproduced by permission.

European workers. Additionally, the foreign workers eliminated industrial bottlenecks, thus permitting the general expansion of the economy. This noncompeting phase ended in 1974 when petroleum shortages, inflation, and unemployment began to trouble the labor-importing countries of Western Europe. Unemployed European workers then began to covet jobs held by immigrants at the same time that immigrants were breaking out of the low-wage enclaves in which they had theretofore been encapsulated. The result was augmented job competition between immigrant and European workers. European workers demanded shelter, and to provide it, European governments curtailed recruitment of foreign workers and made "zealous efforts to persuade unemployed migrants . . . to return home" (Böhning 1979: 402). Repatriation policies reduced the immigrant labor force in Europe by approximately 2 million, or 26 percent. However, most foreign workers did not repatriate, and the foreign worker population in 1980 was still three quarters as large as in 1974.

As unemployment in Europe increased, protests against foreign workers mounted. In France, Belgium, Britain, and West Germany, protest demonstrations accused immigrant workers of taking jobs away from nationals. In the summer of 1973 anti-immigrant violence broke out in France, and eleven Algerians were killed (Freeman 1979: 110). In 1974 France suspended idenfinitely any new arrivals of foreign workers "to prevent growing ethnic tension between the French and foreigners, especially North Africans, and to relieve unemployment" (Koelstra and Simon 1979: 242). In January 1981, French Communists led a demonstration against North African immigration in a Paris suburb. In the same year West Germany strengthened border controls even though economists insisted that foreign workers were performing only low-paid work that Germans refused to accept. In Switzerland aliens were accused of clannishness, indifference to naturalization, and welfare dependency. Complaints of "over foreignization" prompted six anti-immigrant ballot initiatives between 1965 and 1978 (Hoffman-Nowotny and Killias, 1979). In Britain, immigrants were blamed for depressing wages (Allen, Bentley, and Bornat 1977: 64). Spectacular riots reflected the "widespread hostility" of the British public to Commonwealth immigrants. In 1976, 600 persons were injured in a club-wielding battle in London's Notting Hill section between immigrants and British (Studlar 1979). Stereotyped as "disease carrying criminals who would rape and plunder" Britain, the immigrants became explicit targets of working-class hostility (Freeman 1979: 50). In July, 1981 nine days of rioting racked Birmingham, Manchester, Liverpool, London, and other major cities of Britain as youthful blacks (and some whites) looted and burned retail stores in inner city neighborhoods.

Because immigrant workers were noncitizens and lacked political rights, European governments ignored their interests, responding instead to anti-immigrant sentiment among voters. In West Germany guest workers have been expelled as soon as unemployed. France achieved the same objective by tolerating illegal workers then deporting them as needed (Rex 1979: 11). British policy was more complex because Commonwealth immigrants had legal rights to enter, reside, and vote in Britain. However, the 1968 and 1971 Commonwealth Immigration Acts created legal barriers to the job-seeking rights of Commonwealth immigrants as well as aliens (Rex 1979: 22). As elsewhere in Europe, British immigration policy has been steadily moving toward increased restrictive and "more overtly racist" immigration policies (Freeman 1979: 45). On the European continent, only Sweden has granted voting rights to foreign workers.

The increasingly restrictive policies of European governments lagged behind but followed the anti-immigrant direction of public opinion. The causes of this anti-immigrant sentiment were xenophobic and racist in at least some part. First, European workers disliked immigrants even when no issues of labor competition were at stake (Walliman 1974). Second, as Castles and Kosack (1973: 443) observed, antiforeign prejudice is "not of the same intensity toward the various immigrant groups in each country." Colored immigrants are most unpopular in Britain, whereas in France blacks are preferred to Algerians, although both are disliked. Germany has not permitted black workers to enter and reserves its greatest hostility for Italians and Spaniards, preferring Turks. This patchwork of prejudice is inexplicable in terms of resource competition, for there ought to be on that basis no antipathy to any save competitors and equal antipathy to all of those. Finally, there is no evidence of any linear relationship between number of immigrants and intensity of public hostility (Freeman 1979: 278). Indeed, Studlar (1977) found "no strong correlations" between job or housing competition and British opinion about immigrants. British opinion was overwhelmingly negative, but resource competition models would expect that real competition (not merely preceived competition) would produce higher than average anti-immigrant sentiments.

Evidence of a situational reaction to immigration is also strong. First, some research (Rasmussen 1973, Rose 1969, Rex and Moore 1967) has found that resource competition with immigrants produced higher than average anti-immigrant sentiment among those affected. The ethnic minorities preferred in a European city have generally been those who do not live there. Second, the working class is most exposed to job and housing competition with immigrants, and the working class has been the principal source of anti-immigrant sentiment in Europe (Freeman 1979: 189). Third, it is difficult for trade unions to organize immigrants, and in Belgium, France, and Germany immigrants are less likely to join unions than are native workers. This reluctance causes "concern among the trade unions since it could have repercussions on the bargaining strength of the workers as a whole" (Minet 1978). Finally, as unemployment and intergroup competition increased in Europe, governments everywhere responded by increased restrictions on immigrants. These measures are a frank acknowledgment that anti-immigrant sentiment increases with augmented resource competition. Reviewing the evidence, Castles and Kosach (1973: 452) concede a limited applicability of the prejudice theory to anti-immigrant senti-ment in Europe, but they also note resource competition offers "a more signif-icant reason why the working class should be prejudiced against immigrants."

Two interpretations of foreign workers in Europe have appeared. According to Castells (1975: 49) guest workers compose a "reserve army of the unem-ployed" in the Marxist sense. Their function in a capitalist society is to depress wages and enhance profits. They accomplish this function by accepting lower wages than European workers and threatening the organized workers of Europe with scab labor. Politically excluded and distressed, the immigrant workers are tools of the bourgeoisie in its class struggle with organized labor. Schmitter (1979: 39) disputes Castells' view on the familiar grounds that "native and migrant workers do not and have not competed for the same positions in the labor market." Guest workers were permitted "precisely because certain un-skilled and unpleasant and badly paid jobs could no longer be filled by native workers." On the other hand, she acknowledges that the political and legal re-strictions that have *thus far* inhibited the guest workers from initiating real com-petition with natives are slowly weakening. Guest workers have acquired some civil and social rights in every country, and utilizing these rights they may pry open the door of political rights in the future. Political and legal equality will then allow the foreign workers to compete as equals with natives, thus permit-ting them at last to play the role of industrial reserve army.

LABOR ABSORPTION IN COMMUNIST CITIES

Some evidence suggests that communist cities encounter problems of labor absorption that are sometimes subtly, sometimes obviously akin to those en-countered in market societies. Communist authorities inhibit resource competi-tion in cities by regulating the influx of labor. Internal pass regulations prevent more workers from going to cities than cities can employ. Those denied passes must stay where they are or request permission to migrate to some less popular locality whose quota is unfilled (Shelley 1980: 114). In the Soviet Union, the period of forced urbanization (1926-1931) is long over, and there is often ac-knowledgment that labor absorption has proceeded too far. For example, in the Byelorussian SSR urbanization contributed to labor shortages in agriculture (Kondratiev 1978). To counter this shortage, the republic has adopted a policy of encouraging childbirth, improvement in labor productivity by mechanization—and restriction of urbanization. Of course, this policy implies refusal of permis-sion to emigrate from rural districts, and this refusal is effective because of the police power of the state, but disgruntled individuals compelled to stay in agri-culture have motives to complain.

A similar situation exists in the People's Republic of China. To brake urban growth, Chinese authorities have employed "a system of travel permits and location-specific grain rations" (Rawski 1979: 126). Only those can obtain food in cities who can prove they are legally entitled to live there. Additionally, Chinese authorities have required urban students to work on collective farms ostensibly to stimulate socialist consciousness, but the requirement had the additional benefit of reducing youth unemployment in cities. Agricultural employment in China involves long hours of labor-intensive work. As a result, some people have illegally quit agriculture and migrated to cities. Rawski (1979: 126) concludes that "the only sizeable" group of urban unemployed in China consists of young people who have illegally left rural work assignments. Some engage in black marketeering and others in predatory crime. But it seems clear that Chinese cities would have more unemployment and more obvious difficulties of labor absorption if they relaxed the controls that now prevent many workers from leaving agriculture.

Cheng's (1980) fieldwork in a south China farm machinery repair plant turned up complaints of corruption in administration of the pass system. Urban workers assigned to this rural factory complained that their legal residences had been arbitrarily transferred to the countryside, thus depriving them of the housing, health, matrimonial, and educational amenities of urban workers. There was no formal way for them to find a city job, "and even if they managed to do so, the factory administration could compel them to stay" in the country. Conversely, some town-bred youth had succeeded in obtaining temporary assignments in the factory rather than an undesirable assignment to "work as peasants in the production teams" of agricultural communes (Cheng 1980: 110). These town youths retained their legal residence in the city with all its privileges. Regular workers complained that these youths were children of big shots who had the informal power to negotiate privileged treatment for them.

We don't have such connections, and our fathers are not "big enough" so we're stuck here until we are sixty. If you come back then, you will still find us. (Laughter).

We've got to work here for life, but their sons and daughters can be transferred. That is what we mean by "bureaucrats connect with one another."

Even marriage to a legally domiciled townsperson did not provide an escape. Peasants who married a townsperson could not live with their urban spouse without permission of their rural employer and this permission was not routinely granted. Because marrying well was an important avenue of social mobility for young women, denial of a town domicile effectively closed this avenue to them and their offspring. In effect, rural domicile (domicile = legal residence) amounted to a legal stigma inherited by children. Children of townspeople inherited the right to reside in town and children of peasants inherited the obligation to reside on farms.

East European Communist societies have stressed industrial urbanization but skimped on urban housing. The resulting imbalance caused labor absorption problems quite different from those characteristically encountered in capitalist cities: communist cities have jobs for more people than they can house. People employed in major industries, educational institutions, and public administration have access to state-subsidized housing that is by prevailing standards excellent in quality as well as virtually free. Unskilled and semiskilled workers are typically younger people who have left agricultural villages. Because metropolitan housing is unavailable for them, these younger workers must reside in suburban villages. To reach their jobs, they make long commutations aboard trains where public drunkeness is a problem on the after-hours return trip (Shelley 1980: 121).

Because communist states regulate rural-urban migration as well as metropolitan wages, newcomers do not threaten the employment or wage level of established city residents. There is also no evidence of ethnic antagonism over these issues even though ethnic diversity in cities is much greater than in the surrounding republics (Kozlov 1978: 27). However, urbanization in Soviet Asia has apparently produced ethnic tensions in an unusual manner. Russians migrate to big cities of central and Asian republics "to provide trained personnel" in their industries "since the training of local personnel in these republics did not keep pace" with economic growth (Kozlov 1978: 30). As a result, urbanization in Soviet Asia has involved "an influx of Russian groups . . . into many large towns in non-Russian areas." Bennigsen and Wimbush (1978: 173) claim Asian natives resent leapfrogging Russians who hold 50 percent of the highest-paying jobs in Asian cities. The Asians want these high-paying jobs for themselves and "in recent years ethnic tensions have risen sharply" (1978: 185). Moreover, Russians and Asians live in separate neighborhoods with "little social mixing." The linguistic dominance of Russian in towns is an additional sore point despite the obvious utility of a common national language in a polyethnic society (Volkova 1965).

Evidence of ethnic tension is indirect but persuasive. Kozlov (1978: 44) acknowledges that the influx of Russians in Asian cities has "definitely inhibited" the rural-urban migration of natives: that is, the Russian influx has prevented some rural Asians from obtaining urban domicile. In effect, Russians have occupied employment vacancies in cities, thus locking rural Asians out of their own republic's major cities. The Soviet situation resembles in this respect the competition of native blacks and foreign-born whites for jobs in U.S. cities in the period 1870-1914. Thomas (1972: 143-148) found that urban migration of blacks in this period was inversely related to urban migration of foreign whites: the more foreign whites came, the fewer blacks came. This situation resulted from the "strong competition of white workers from abroad" with native blacks so that the number of blacks who could "obtain employment in the booming urban areas of the North and West" was in this manner inhibited. Rural blacks found opportunities only when foreign whites were unavailable for urban migration. The tensions between native blacks and foreign whites in American cities are well understood, and there is ground for inferring that similar tensions affect Russian-Asian relations in big cities of Soviet Asia.

SOUTH AFRICA

The Republic of South Africa is a capitalist society in which influx controls govern the absorption of labor in cities (Bonacich 1981: 239). Under the separation of the races (apartheid) policy enforced since World War II, blacks have legal domiciles on native reservations called Bantustans. Here only are they permitted to acquire real property and practice self-government. The economic viability of Bantustans is declining as soil erosion and overpopulation make livelihoods harder to gain (Burawoy 1976: 1059) The Bantustans depend upon the remittances of urban workers to make up the inadequacy of local subsistence agriculture. In an unregulated market economy, black workers from the Bantustans would flock into big cities where they would form a pool of distressed labor available to undercut the prevailing wage (Bonacich 1981: 259). This situation would give town employers an incentive to fire high-wage white workers and replace them with cheap black workers. Low-wage black workers would return at night to urban slums in which they would reside with their families. In fact, Bonacich (1979: 44) declares that "typical split labor market dynamics" have been a "perennial feature of South African history, from the original Cape settlement to the present day."

However, since 1948 apartheid laws have prevented the development of open labor market competition in South African cities, where the laws prohibit the employment of nonwhites in white-only jobs, a current list of which is maintained by the police. This list entirely prevents employers from replacing whites with nonwhites, however cheap the latters' wage. The white-only jobs are superior in every respect to nonwhite-only jobs. Furthermore, pass laws prevent unemployed blacks from obtaining urban domiciles. "The apartheid system of South Africa is the prime example of the effective use of police powers, force, and regulations to compel [black] people to return to their rural homes" (Riddle 1978: 249). South African police maintain close surveillance of African workers in cities, and any unemployed, undocumented blacks are immediately "repatriated" to their Bantustan. This policy prevents the formation of a reserve army of unemployed blacks in the slums and, Bonacich (1979: 45) argues, benefits the white working class. Burawoy (1976) also calls attention to the exclusion of black workers' families from cities under the pass laws. This exclusion compels the wives and children of black workers to remain on Bantustans, thus relieving big business of the cost of supporting them in urban slums. This monetary savings gives big business an economic stake in apartheid.

SUMMARY

Everywhere in the world cities have the task of absorbing newcomers into the employed labor force. When labor is in short supply, and newcomers occupy bottom-ranking vacancies, this absorption proceeds without difficulty. However, labor surplus or the threat of it in the future gives established workers a motive for resisting the influx of newcomers. This motive is only accentuated when newcomers enter the metropolitan labor market as distressed labor willing to undercut the prevailing wage rate. Under these circumstances, intergroup relations become antagonistic. Established workers reach for shelters to protect themselves against low-wage competition.

In the childrens' games of musical chairs nursery school toddlers circle around grouped chairs, then scramble for seats when the music stops. Those who find no seat are the losers. So long as there is a chair for everyone, there is no conflict. But conflict quickly appears when the number of chairs is decreased while the number of competing toddlers increases. Jobs in cities are analogous to chairs in this children' game. In periods of migratory influx, the number of competitors increases. In periods of unemployment, the number of chairs decreases. The joint effect of labor influx and increasing unemployment is intensified competition. When, as so commonly happens, the newcomers are of one ethnic or racial group and the oldtimers of another, competition for jobs deteriorates into racial and ethnic hostility. The alternative to this scenario is for all the workers to get together and restructure the game so that enough jobs are provided for everyone.

Emphasis in this chapter on the situational causes of intergroup tension accurately reflects the trend of research in this area. But it would be unsound to pose a choice between prejudice and resource competition. The two are not incompatible, and there are grounds for accepting the existence of an ideational element in race or ethnic prejudice unrelated in the historical short run to resource competition. When immigrant workers enter metropolitan labor markets, they confront attitudinal as well as economic barriers to absorption. These barriers may be high or low, but they are always ideational reflections of the past. An ideational legacy of disliking is compatible with present toleration unless intergroup resource competition emerges. In periods of labor shortage even disliked groups are tolerated. Table 13–4 expresses this relationship in a fourfold scheme where prior attitudes and present economic competition reinforce or contradict one another. Intergroup antagonism is most severe when unfavorable

Table 13-4. Labor Absorption in Metropolitan Areas

Resource Competition	Initial Public Attitudes Toward Immigrants	
	Favorable	Unfavorable
None	No intergroup tension; labor absorption rapid and complete	Latent intergroup tension; labor absorption unobstructed
Severe	Deteriorating intergroup relations; barriers to labor absorption developing	Manifest intergroup antagonism; labor absorption inhibited

attitudes and resource competition coincide, and least severe when attitudes are favorable and resource competition is nil.

Communist societies have suspended the "laws" of the free market, thus suspending the conditions that cause split labor markets in cities. First, East European communist societies have eliminated observable unemployment. Second, administrative regulations govern the size of the urban labor force, thus inhibiting the tendency for impoverished ruralites to congregate in urban slums. Third, administrative regulations determine the level of wages in every industry and occupation so local supply and demand of labor are defused of this significance. Communist societies thus prevent groups from coming into open labor competition in the marketplace, but there is behind-the-scenes competition for political influence, corruption in bureaucracy, and interregional political tension. In this circumstance, it is a temptation to conclude that capitalist societies encourage open labor competition and therewith intergroup conflict and prejudice. However, the case of South Africa shows that capitalist societies can also suspend the laws of the labor market but the resulting political tension supports racial antagonism even in the absence of economic competition.

NOTES

1. Recognizing this situation, ports of entry complain to national governments about the unfair burden that immigration places on cities. The comments of San Francisco Supervisor John Molinari on Indo-Chinese refugees in the Bay City reflect this common concern of metropolitan politicians: "It's up to the federal government to assimilate them throughout the country. Just because this is a port of entry and we have a large Asian population doesn't mean they [Indo-Chinese] all have to settle here. We have a housing crisis." "Molinari on the Issues," *East/West,* October 3, 1979, p. 6.

2. "The chief question which is usually raised regarding the advantages and disadvantages of immigration . . . has to do with its effect upon industry and especially upon native labor. It is claimed by many, especially among the working classes themselves, that the large immigration of laborers, accustomed to a lower wage and an inferior standard of living, tends to drive out American-born labor from various occupations, or at any rate to force down the general level of wages. It is claimed on the other hand that, so far as American labor is displaced by the lower grade of foreign labor, it finds occupations in higher forms of industry. The result is . . . that the severest and most unpleasant work is done for us by immigrants while the level of American labor is continually raised" (John R. Commons 1901: Ch. 1, p. 295).

3. Bonacich (1979: 25–29) has listed five ways that cheap labor can *indirectly* displace high-price labor. These are dilution of jobs to require less skill; displacement of small business by big business utilizing cheap labor; displacement by a low-wage petite bourgeoisie; displacement by imports from cheap labor countries; displacement by runaway shops.

4. Bonacich (1980: 35) distinguishes split labor market and dual labor market theories. Basically the distinction hangs upon the technological determinism presumed in dual labor market theory, whereas split labor market theory stresses the priority of labor cost. However, both approaches are trying to explain the puzzling reality of high- and low-priced labor markets in close proximity. In neoclassical economic theory, this juxtaposition could not occur because employers would introduce the cheaper labor until any disparity in price of labor evaporated and a single price for labor prevailed in the whole market.

5. Sassen-Koob (1980: 11) distinguishes three types of undocumented workers (illegal aliens): entries without inspections, visa abusers, and fraudulent documents. EWIs sneak across the border and melt into the general population. They are the largest group of undocumented workers, numbering from 3 to 6 million in 1980. Visa abusers enter the United States legally, but they overstay their permission, melting into the general population to escape detection. Fraudulent documents are utilized by another group to obtain entry illegally—but with the appearance of legality. When the fraud is discovered, the perpetrators have vanished into the general population. Estimates of the number of undocumented persons are derived from the number of deportable aliens located. In 1967, this number was 86,597; in 1977 it was 1,060,129.

6. "Illegal immigrants have for years been taking jobs from American citizens. . . . [They] often work for substandard wages and accept substandard working and living conditions, are easy targets for blackmail and intimidation by unscrupulous employers, and are all too frequently a drain on the welfare resources of the communities where they live." Andrew Biemiller, President, AFL-CIO, in the U.S. Congress, Senate Committee on the Judiciary, 94th Congress, 2nd Session, *Immigration, 1976*. Washington, D.C.: U.S. Government Printing Office, 1976.

7. "Seasonal workers often are not available from the domestic work force, in part because welfare and other governmental programs . . . discourage the unemployed from seeking seasonal work. Unreasonable government restrictions

on the employment of young people also prevent our youth from seeking gainful employment in agriculture during their vacation." "We continue to oppose legislation that would put the burden of proof on employers as to whether a person is an illegal alien." Statement of John C. Datt, Director, American Farm Bureau Federation in U.S. Congress, *op. cit.,* pp. 174–175. In this volume see p. 23ff. for the views of expert witnesses regarding the extent and impact of illegal immigration in the United States.

8. "Already illegal immigrants are blamed for keeping wages depressed by taking grubby jobs that are usually shunned by legal residents with ready access to welfare. Businesses such as hotel and restaurants are accused of secretly encouraging the influx to guarantee a supply of cheap labor." *U.S. News and World Report,* May 5, 1976, p. 26. See also: William L. Chaze, "Will the U.S. Shut the Door on Immigrants?" *U.S. News and World Report* April 12, 1982: 47–50.

REFERENCES

Allen, Sheila, Stuart Bently, and Joanna Bornat. 1977. *Work, Race and Immigration.* Bradford: University of Bradford Press.

Allport, Gordon W. 1958. *The Nature of Prejudice.* Boston: Beacon.

Beck, E. M. 1980. "Labor Unionism and Racial Income Inequality: A Time-Series Analysis of the Post World War II Period." *American Journal of Sociology* 85: 791–814.

——, Patrick M. Horan, and Charles M. Tolbert, II. 1978. "Stratification in a Dual Economy: a Sectoral Model of Earnings Determination." *American Sociological Review* 43: 704–720.

Benningsen, Alexandre A., and S. Enders Wimbush. 1978. "Migration and Political Control: Soviet Europeans in Soviet Central Asia," p. 173–187, in William H. McNeill and Ruth S. Adams, eds. *Human Migration.* Bloomington: Indiana University Press.

Berman, Phyliss. 1978. "Does the Melting Pot Still Meld?" *Forbes* (October 30): 63–75.

Bibb, Robert, and William H. Form. 1977. "The Effects of Industrial, Occupational, and Sex Statification in Blue-Collar Markets." *Social Forces* 55: 974–996.

Böhning, W. R. 1979. "International Migration in Western Europe: Reflections on the Past Five Years." *International Labour Review* 118: 401–414.

Bonacich, Edna. 1972. "A Theory of Ethnic Antagonism: The Split Labor Market." *American Sociological Review* 37: 547–559.

——. 1976. "Advanced Capitalism and Black/White Race Relations in the United States: A Split Labor Market Interpretation." *American Sociological Review* 41: 34–51.

——. 1979. "The Past, Present, and Future of Split Labor Market Theory." *Research in Race and Ethnic Relations* 1: 17–64.

——. 1980. "The Creation of Dual Labor Markets." Paper presented, Structure of Labor Markets Conference, Athens, Ga.

——, 1981. "Capitalism and Race Relations in South Africa: A Split Labor Market Analysis." p. 239–277, in Maurice Zeitlin, ed. *Political Power and Social Theory*. JAI Press.

——, and Lucie Hirata. 1981. "International Labor Migration: A Theoretical Orientation." Paper presented, Center for International Studies, Duke University, May 15, 1981.

Bosanquet, Nicholas, and Peter B. Doeringer. 1973. "Is There a Dual Labour Market in Great Britain?" *Economic Journal* 83: 421–435.

Briggs, Vernon M. 1975. "Illegal Aliens: The Need for a More Restrictive Border Policy." *Social Science Quarterly* 3: 477–484.

Burawoy, Michael. 1976. "The Functions and Reproduction of Migrant Labor: Comparative Materials from South Africa and the United States." *American Journal of Sociology* 81: 1050–1087.

Castells, Manuel. 1975. "Immigrant Workers and Class Struggles in Advanced Capitalism: the Western European Experience." *Politics and Society* 5: 33–66.

Castles, Stephen, and Godula Kosach. 1973. *Immigrant Workers and Class Structure in Western Europe*. London: Oxford University Press.

Chaze, William L. 1980. "Refugees Stung by Backlash." *U.S. News and World Report* (October 13): 60–64.

Cheng, Man-Tsun. 1980. "An Exploratory Case Study of the Management Systems and Work Attitudes in the Farm Machinery Manufacturing and Repairing Factory at the Huan-Cheng Commune." M.A. thesis, Chinese University of Hong Kong.

Clark, Peter, and Paul Slack. 1976. *English Towns in Transition*. London: Oxford University Press.

Commons, John R. 1901. "Immigration and its Economic Effects," pp. 293–743 in *U.S. Industrial Commission Reports*. Washington, D.C.: U.S. Government Printing Office.

Cummings, Scott. 1980. "White Ethnics, Racial Prejudice, and Labor Market Segmentation." *American Journal of Sociology* 85: 938–950.

Doeringer, Peter B., and Michael J. Piore. 1975. "Unemployment and the 'Dual Labor Market.' " *The Public Interest* 38: 67–79.

Donnison, David, with Paul Soto. 1980. *The Good City: A Study of Urban Development in Britain*. London: Heinemann.

Freedman, Marcia. 1976. *Labor Markets: Segments and Shelters*. Montclair, N.J.: Allanheid Osmun.

Freeman, Gary P. 1979. *Immigrant Labor and Racial Conflict in Industrial Societies: The French and British Experience, 1945–1975*. Princeton: Princeton University Press.

Friedland, Roger. 1981. *Power and Crisis in the Central City*. London: Macmillan.

Ginzberg, Eli. 1977. "The Job Problem." *Scientific American* 237: 43–51.

Godschalk, J. J. 1979. "Foreign Labour and Dirty Work." *The Netherlands Journal of Sociology* 15: 1–11.

Hechter, Michael. 1978. "Group Formation and the Cultural Division of Labor." *American Journal of Sociology* 84: 293–318.

Hoffman-Nowotny, J. J., and Martin Killias. 1979. "Switzerland," pp. 45–62 in Ronald E. Krane, ed. *International Labor Migration in Europe.* New York: Praeger.

Kalleberg, Arne L., and Aage B. Sorenson. 1979. "The Sociology of Labor Markets." *Annual Review of Sociology* 5: 351–379.

Kindleberger, Charles P. 1967. *Europe's Post-War Growth: The Role of Labor Supply.* Cambridge: Harvard University Press.

Koelstra, Rein W. and Gildas Simon. 1979. "France," pp. 133–143, in Ronald E. Krane, ed. *International Labor Migration in Europe.* New York: Praeger.

Kondratiev, Vladimir. 1978. "Employment Patterns and Prospects in European Socialist Countries." *International Labour Review* 117: 355–368.

Kozlov, V. I. 1978. "Changes in the Settlement and Urbanization of the Peoples of the USSR as Conditions and Factors of Ethnic Processes." *Soviet Sociology* 17: 26–53.

Lieberson, Stanley. 1980. *A Piece of the Pie: Blacks and White Immigrants Since 1880.* Berkeley and Los Angeles: University of California Press.

Meeker, Edward, and James Kau. 1977. "Racial Discrimination and Occupational Attainment at the Turn of the Century." *Explorations in Economic History* 14: 250–276.

Minet, Georges. 1978. "Spectators or Participants? Immigrants and Industrial Relations in Western Europe." *International Labour Review* 117: 21–35

O'Connor, James. 1973. *The Fiscal Crisis of the State.* New York: St. Martin's Press.

Piore, Michael J. 1979. *Birds of Passage: Migrant Labor and Industrial Societies.* Cambridge: Cambridge University Press.

Portes, Alejandro. 1977. "Labor Functions of Illegal Aliens." *Society* 14: 31–38.

Power, Jonathan, and Anna Hardman. 1976. *Western Europe's Migrant Workers* London: Minority Rights Group.

Rasmussen, Jorgen. 1973. "The Impact of Constituency Structural Characteristics upon Political Preferences in Britain." *Comparative Politics* 6: 123–145.

Rawski, Thomas G. 1979. *Economic Growth and Employment in China.* New York, Oxford University Press.

Rex, John, and Sally Tomlinson. 1979. *Colonial Immigrants in a British City.* London: Routledge and Kegan Paul.

Rex, John. 1979. "Race Relations Theory and the Study of Migration to Advanced Industrial Societies," pp. 11–21, in Jan Berting, Felix Geyer, and Ray Jurkovich, eds. *Problems in International Comparative Research in the Social Sciences.* Oxford: Pergamon.

——., and Robert Moore. 1967. *Race, Community, and Conflict.* London: Oxford University Press.

Riddell, J. Barry. 1978. "The Migration to the Cities of West Africa: Some Policy Considerations." *The Journal of Modern African Studies* 16: 241–260.

Reiman, Horst, and Helga Reiman. 1979. "Federal Republic of Germany." Pp. 63–87 in Ronald E. Krane, ed. *International Migration in Europe.* New York: Praeger.

Rist, Ray G. 1978. *Guestworkers in Germany: The Prospects for Pluralism.* New York: Praeger.

Rose, Eliot J. B., et al. 1969. *Colour and Citizenship*. London: Oxford University Press.

Rukavishnikov, V. O. 1978. "Ethnosocial Aspects of Population Distribution in Cities of Tataria." *Soviet Sociology* 17: 59–79.

Sassen-Koob, Saskia. 1980. "Immigrant and Minority Workers in the Organization of the Labor Process." *Journal of Ethnic Studies* 8: 2–34.

———. 1981. "Towards a Conceptualization of Immigrant Labor." *Social Problems*.

Schmitter, Barbara Epple. 1979. "Immigration and Citizenship in West Germany and Switzerland." Ph.D. dissertation. University of Chicago.

Shelley, Louise. 1980. "The Geography of Soviet Criminality." *American Sociological Review* 45: 111–122.

Solache, Saul. 1981. "Urban Growth Patterns and Mexican Immigration to the United States, 1790–1970." Ph.D. dissertation. University of California at Los Angeles.

Stone, Katharine. 1975. "The Origins of Job Structures in the Steel Industry," pp. 27–84, in Richard C. Edwards, Michael Reich, and David M. Gordon, eds. *Labor Market Segmentation*. Lexington, Mass.: D. C. Heath.

Studlar, Donley T. 1977. "Social Context and Attitudes toward Coloured Immigrants." *British Journal of Sociology* 28: 168–184.

———. 1979, "Great Britain." pp. 88–117, in Ronald E. Krane, ed. *International Labor Migration in Europe*. New York: Praeger.

Thernstrom, Stephan. 1973. *The Other Bostonians*. Cambridge: Harvard University.

Thomas, Brinley. 1972. *Migration and Urban Development: A Reappraisal of British and American Long Cycles*. London: Methuen.

Tolbert, Charles, Patrick M. Horan, and E. M. Beck. 1980. "The Structure of Economic Segmentation: A Dual Economy Approach." *American Journal of Sociology* 84: 1095–1116.

Townsend, Peter. 1979. *Poverty in the United Kingdom*. London: Allen Lane

United Kingdom Department of the Environment. 1973. "Greater London Development Plan." *Report of the Panel of Inquiry*, Vol I. London: Her Majesty's Stationery Office.

Van Der Wee, Harman. 1975–1976. "Reflections on the Development of the Urban Economy in Western Europe During the Late Middle Ages and Early Modern Times." *Urbanism Past and Present*. Winter: 9–14.

Varaday, David P. 1979. *Ethnic Minorities in Urban Areas*. Boston: Martinus Nijhoff.

Volkova, N. G. 1965. "Changes in the Ethnic Composition of the Urban Population of the North Caucasus During the Soviet Period." *Soviet Sociology* 4: 17–33.

Walliman, Isidor. 1974. "Toward a Theoretical Understanding of Ethnic Antagonism: the Case of Foreign Workers in Switzerland." Zeitschrift für Sociologie 3: 84–94.

Wilson, Kenneth L., and Alejandro Portes. 1980. "Immigrant Enclaves: An Analysis of the Labor Market Experiences of Cubans in Miami." *American Journal of Sociology* 86: 295–319.

CHAPTER 14

Marginality

In a tidy world, city people unemployed too long would go elsewhere, leaving only the employed in the city. However, the world is not so tidy. Some city residents have learned how to survive on small, irregular incomes; others get by with no money. Therefore a distinction between the employed and the unemployed is too crude a description of the ways city people make a living. A continuum is more realistic. At one extreme are the permanently employed at full-time work that they reasonably expect to perform without interruption for the balance of their working life (Townsend 1979: 589). At the other extreme are the long-term unemployed who have given up all hope of ever finding a job and have stopped looking for one. Between these extremes are workers who drift in and out of employment, whose working years consist of alternating bouts of employment and unemployment. Sometimes these workers have full-time work, defined in the United States as at least forty hours weekly. Sometimes they have part-time work, which is any employment occupying fewer than forty hours weekly. Part-time workers are neither unemployed nor fully employed. The term *underemployed* refers to part-time workers who want or would accept full-time work were it offered.

Underemployment and unemployment are symptoms of unabsorbed or partially absorbed labor. Of course, most city workers experience some underemployment or unemployment in the course of their working lives, and occasional unemployment or underemployment is compatible with economic integration. When however, the balance tilts in the other direction, and employment becomes a brief, infrequent interlude between protracted periods of unemployment, then integration in the urban labor market is incomplete. In Figure 14-1 the solid line is the boundary between the employed and unemployed sections

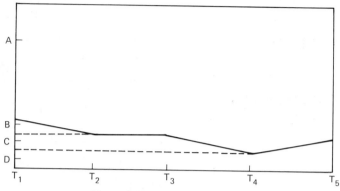

Figure 14-1. Urban Marginality.

of the working age population. The area above the solid line indicates the employed; the area below the solid line indicates the unemployed. Stratum A workers are always employed. Stratum B workers are unemployed from T_1 until T_2 but are fully employed thereafter. Stratum C workers are employed only between T_3 and T_5—and then only partially. Stratum D workers are always unemployed.

In Figure 14-1 the two topmost layers describe the boundary of the mainstream economy. People in the two bottommost layers (C and D) are unabsorbed and marginal.

Marginality is a tricky word. Perlman (1976: 243) has distinguished several inappropriate uses of this word. She concludes marginality should designate "underemployed people who are not wage earners," and the proper problem of urban marginality is how such people are integrated into the urban economy. Following her lead, *marginality* refers only to households of permanent city residents who have no members in the absorbed labor force. Certain groups usually fall in this category. Among them are the physically disabled, the aged, and the long-term unwell. None of these is able to work and every city has marginal households whose usual earner or earners have been incapacitated. In addition, some households are marginal even though able-bodied adults reside in them. These households are of two classes: marginal households receiving public welfare assistance, and those not receiving any. Of the former, the largest category in the United States is families headed by an able-bodied mother who cannot work because needed at home to care for young children.

MARGINALITY AND POVERTY

Marginality should be distinguished from poverty, with which it does, however, overlap significantly. *Poverty* is a state of deprivation below some minimal social standard. Townsend (1979: 88) defines poverty as "lack of resources" necessary to permit socially approved diet, activities, or customs. Governments have measures of just what constitutes poverty-level minimums. The United States government has a "poverty index" that measures the adequacy of a household's money income in terms of the household's size, number of children under eighteen, the local cost of living, farm vs. nonfarm residence, and so forth. Households whose money incomes fall beneath the appropriate minimum are declared "below the poverty line" (Table 14-1). In 1979, the Current Population Survey of the United States Census found that 24.5 million Americans resided in households with incomes below the poverty line. These persons amounted to 11.4 percent of all Americans. Utilizing a similar measure, the International Labour Office of the United Nations has estimated that 12 percent of the total population of the Western European countries in the Organization for Economic Cooperation and Development (OECD) were poor in 1973 (Van Ginneken, Join-Lambert, and Lecaillon 1979).

Marginal households are disposed to poverty because they have no regularly employed earner. However, marginal households need not be poor nor poor households marginal. For example, when welfare allowances are sufficient, marginal households of the aged or disabled have a low income that is, nonetheless, above the poverty line. In 1980, the U.S. Bureau of the Census enumerated 7.1 million working age adults unable to work by reason of disability. These disabled adults constituted 5.7 percent of the population of persons aged eighteen to sixty-four. However, of these 7.1 million disabled adults, only 1.8 million had money incomes below the official poverty level.

Conversely, people who work full time (and are not marginal) can be poor provided their pay is low and their families are large. In fact, the households of low-paid workers are the largest single bloc of poor people and have been for as long as information has been available. In 1899, Rowntree found that 77 percent of those in poverty in York, England, were low-paid workers, and in 1936 the

Table 14-1. Poverty Thresholds for the United States, 1976

Family Size	Annual Money Income	
	Nonfarm	Farm
1 Person	$2,884	$2,438
2 Persons	3,711	3,128
3 Persons	4,540	3,858
4 Persons	5,815	4,950
5 Persons	6,876	5,870
6 Persons	7,760	6,585

Source: Employment and Training Report of the President. Transmitted to Congress 1978. (Washington, D.C.: U.S. Government Printing Office 1978), p. 95.

low-paid were still 43 percent of York's poor. Subsequent analyses have recurrently found that the poor of European and North American cities most typically reside in households whose earner works in a low-paid job (Townsend 1979: 588). In 1978 the U.S. poverty level was $6,662 for a nonfarm family of four. To earn this much money, the average woman worker had to obtain forty-nine weeks of full-time employment and the average man worker had to obtain thirty-nine weeks of full-time employment. Because of unemployment, however, one third of women and one fifth of men actually failed to obtain the requisite weeks of full-time employment. Even at average wages, these workers were threatened with poverty as a result of unemployment. Workers earning the statutory minimum wage ($2.65 hourly in 1978) earned only $5,512 in fifty-two weeks of full-time employment. This sum amounted to 83 percent of the poverty minimum in that year. Assuming these low-wage workers sustained the average unemployment of six weeks in 1978, they earned only $4,240, or 64 percent, of the poverty minimum. It is therefore easy to understand how low wages and unemployment singly or in combination cause full-time workers to earn less than the statutory poverty level.

Poverty arises when resources are inadequate but money income is only one of several resources that together constitute wealth. Resources other than cash incomes are in the aggregate nearly as important. To illustrate this observation, Townsend (1979: 89) divided total resources of a sample of U.K. households into five sources: net disposable income in cash, assets, employer welfare benefits, social service benefits, and private income in kind. Net disposable income in cash is wages and salaries. Assets consist of cash earnings on life insurance, savings accounts, bonds, and the like as well as the rental value of owner-occupied housing. Employer welfare benefits include fringes such as money value of employer-paid health insurance, life insurance, or automobile. Social service benefits are the cash values of free services people receive from the state. These may include medical care, housing, police and fire protection, education, and so on. Private income in kind means goods and services that people receive as gifts or, more commonly, because they reciprocate goods and services. No money changes hands. An example is a babysitting cooperative whose members exchange this service. Townsend estimated the money value of goods and services received in kind, then added them to the general tally.

Townsend (1979: 229) compared the distribution of resources among U.K. households in different income quintiles. In all quintiles, money income was the largest single source of wealth, accounting for 60.9 percent of total wealth in the highest quintile and 55.1 percent in the lowest. However, 40 percent of wealth derived from nonwage sources. The rental value of an owner-occupied home was a second-ranking source of wealth for all income groups. Employer welfare benefits were big contributors to the wealth of the highest quintile group but contributed virtually nothing to the bottom quintile. Employer welfare benefits were also the least egalitarian form of wealth because the topmost quintile received thirty-three times more of this wealth than did the bottom quintile. Conversely,

private income in kind was the most egalitarian source of wealth: the top quintile received only twice as much of this kind of wealth as did the lowest quintile.

Townsend's figures suggest that if a person's wage income stopped because of
unemployment, average Britons would still have 40 percent of their usual resources. This might be enough to permit survival. For example, owner-occupiers
still enjoy the rental value of their homes when unemployed. The cessation of
employer welfare benefits has little effect on the lowest-income people since
such people receive virtually none even when employed. In most societies, social
service benefits to a household increase when unemployment affects the breadwinner. Finally, an unemployed breadwinner has plenty of leisure to engage in
home production of food by gardening as well as exchange of goods and services
with others, scavenging in garbage dumps, streetcorner peddling, carwashing,
bargain hunting, contest entering, sewing, and other informal economic activities.

THE EXTENT OF MARGINALITY IN THE WORLD'S CITIES

Every city in the world contains marginal households, but their number and
visibility is variable. Number of disabled depends on prior social conditions, such
as diet, public health, and housing. Their visibility depends importantly on the
extent to which institutions (such as welfare agencies) provide income and housing to marginal households. Where they do, the visibility of marginal households
is low. Where they do not, marginal households exist in poverty and their
members' efforts to survive make them visible. For example, in preindustrial
cities, needy persons frequented public thoroughfares and begged from passersby.
To stimulate charity, they displayed and exaggerated their infirmities. This
presence no longer troubles industrial cities because institutional welfare permits
the disabled to live without begging. But whenever public resources fall short,
marginal households still emerge from the background and claim a position at
the center of metropolitan visibility.

Cities also contain marginal households headed by able-bodied adults. In cities
of the Third World marginality has reached extraordinary proportions as a result
of "influx of migrants from rural areas in search of jobs" (Lubell 1978: 747).
This influx vastly exceeded the absorptive capability of growing cities, and the
surplus households stayed on even though they lacked employment (Riddell
1978). The marginals are visible because public welfare assistance is scanty and
in many cases deliberately excludes migrant households in the hope of driving
them back to the countryside. As a result, marginal households have been compelled to provide their own housing and employment. The housing of Third
World marginals has often taken the form of self-built shanties made of scrap
materials (Perlman 1976).

In cities and towns of developed market societies, able-bodied marginals exist but are much less numerous and visible than in Third World cities. First, the rate of urbanization has been slower and unabsorbed labor accordingly less. Second, public welfare arrangements are more generous, thus permitting a higher proportion of marginal households to obtain social invisibility. Nonetheless, it is possible to identify population segments among whom underemployment and unemployment is so chronic that marginality exists. Among urban blacks in the United States, for example, rates of unemployment are generally high and among black youth often exceed 40 percent. About one fifth of able-bodied black adults must exist outside the mainstream economy and a corresponding segment of urban black households is marginal. In Europe, marginal households cluster among immigrant workers, but repatriation of these noncitizen workers has reduced the volume of urban marginality in European cities.

Metropolitan regions differ in the extent of marginality in work age populations. Table 14-2 compares Dallas, the District of Columbia, and Philadelphia with the metropolitan United States in 1976 in respect to labor force participation and unemployment. In the metropolitan United States as a whole, labor force participation (employment to population ratio) was higher among whites than blacks and others in both central cities and suburbs. Additionally, blacks and other nonwhites had higher rates of unemployment than whites in both central cities and suburbs. But these are national averages, and there was much intercity variation. For instance, in Dallas the labor force participation rate among central city blacks (66.9 percent) was higher than among Dallas whites

Table 14-2. Employment and Unemployment in Selected Large Metropolitan Areas, 1976

	Employment/Population Ratio*		Unemployment Rate	
	Central Cities	Suburbs	Central Cities	Suburbs
United States: Metropolitan Areas				
White	55.4	59.6	7.9	6.8
Black & other nonwhites	50.5	57.8	13.1	11.8
Dallas				
White	63.7	65.3	4.3	4.2
Black & other nonwhites	66.9	56.6	6.6	8.0
District of Columbia				
White	56.8	65.9	5.5	3.9
Black & other nonwhites	56.9	73.1	10.4	4.2
Philadelphia				
White	47.8	58.3	7.9	7.1
Black & other nonwhites	38.1	48.8	19.2	13.7

Source: U.S. Department of Labor, Bureau of Labor Statistics, News Release 77-867, October 5, 1977, Table 5.
*Percentage of total population employed.

and higher even than among central city whites in general (55.4 percent). Similarly, the rate of unemployment among central city blacks in Dallas (6.6 percent) was lower than among central city whites in general (7.9 percent). In sum, blacks were better off in Dallas in 1976 than were whites in other American cities. In contrast, Philadelphia was a metropolitan region in which worse than average economic conditions existed. Among whites and minorities in general, labor force participation rates in Philadelphia were appreciably lower than in metropolitan areas of the United States. Unemployment rates were appreciably higher among minorities.

In all metropolitan regions, the labor force participation rates varied inversely with unemployment among minorities and white workers alike. This inverse relationship arises from discouragement of workers who, unable to find work, stop looking, and thus cease to be unemployed in the opinion of the Department of Labor. The marginal population in every metropolitan region consisted of the unemployed and those out of the labor force who would have been at work if unemployment rates were zero. Obviously, the number of marginal adults was appreciable in every metropolitan region, but lower in some than in others.

THE INFORMAL SECTOR

How is urban marginality possible? One might naively suppose city people cannot survive without jobs or money. Millions of cases prove the opposite, and confronting an uncertain employment future, many students are delighted to have this reassurance. The secret of marginal survival is want satisfaction without wages. Marginal workers satisfy material wants by eliminating superfluous ones and participating in the urban informal sector. The urban *informal sector* consists basically of petty self-employment for cash, but it also includes other ways of satisfying material needs such as production and exchange of goods and services in kind, bargain hunting at stores, salvage, and even entering contests. For example, someone who sells souvenirs or pencils on a street corner raises cash from petty self-employment. Someone who tends a garden eats some of the produce, sells some for cash, and exchanges some for a neighbor's home-brewed beer. In fact, most persons self-employed in the urban informal sector do operate more than one small business because the proceeds of each business are so slim; hence only a battery of petty enterprises raises enough to live on. Thus a person might sell souvenirs on weekends and holidays, work in a garden on clear days, and peddle vegetables door-to-door as a supply was harvested. Underemployed people commonly moonlight in self-employment to fill out their meager income, so these marginal workers combine wage income and self-employment income. In most American cities supermarkets throw out much salvageable produce, and needy people have learned to pick through refuse cans in search of a free dinner.

Hart (1973) distinguishes the legitimate and illegitimate subsectors of the informal sector. In the legitimate subsector are all legal forms of self-employment. Growing and selling carrots is a legal form of self-employment that a marginal household might undertake. Growing and selling cannabis, on the other hand, is an illegal form of self-employment that the very same household might operate in tandem with its legitimate carrot business. Similarly, a taxi service is a legal form of self-employment whereas pimping and prostitution are illegal services. Again, the legal and illegal businesses might be operated by different people in different households, by different people in the same household, or by the same person—as, for example, a taxi driver who "procures" when passengers so request.

The case of Mr. A. shows how migrant workers supplement their wages in the informal sector (Hart 1973: 66). Mr. A. is a member of the Frafra ethnic minority, and he emigrated to Accra, Ghana, from the rural interior twenty years ago. Now forty-five years of age, he works as a street cleaner for the municipality in the mornings and earns seven pounds monthly for this work. Mr. A. is underemployed in this formal sector job whose wage buys him only his food. To supplement this wage, Mr. A. spends his afternoons tending a garden, the proceeds of which bring in six additional pounds a month as well as nutritious food for him to eat. Gardening is still not enough to make ends meet. To make more money, Mr. A. also works as a night watchman and earns a few pounds a month in this manner. During his two-week annual vacation, Mr. A. intensifies his gardening. Although he has not visited Frafra in twenty years, he is saving money toward his "big plan" of retirement in his native village.

The hallmark of informal sector self-employment is simplicity. Informal businesses are small, usually one-person affairs that require little capital and can be operated part time on a flexible schedule. Sethuraman (1977a) has listed nine criteria that indicate an informal sector business. First, they are small, employing ten persons or fewer, including part-time and casual help. Second, they often violate civil law in the course of normal business. This violation need not involve criminal law but may pertain only to sanitary, wage, or tax legislation: for example, accepting payment in cash and not paying tax on the income. Third, family members are the nucleus of the firm. Fourth, the informal sector businesses typically have no fixed hours or days of operation. Fifth, business premises are temporary or mobile. Sixth, businesses use no inanimate energy being typically dependent on proprietor elbow grease. Seventh, businesses do not depend on or obtain capital loans from banks or other formal sector financial institutions. Eighth, output is sold directly to the consumer. Ninth, those employed have fewer years of formal education than are usually required for wage employment in the formal sector.

EXTENT OF THE INFORMAL SECTOR: WORLD COMPARISONS

The extent of the urban informal sector is hard to estimate. Government statistics do not record it (Light 1980). This oversight arises for several reasons. First, informal sector businesses are so small and ephemeral that officials cannot locate them to count them. Second, their proprietors are often in violation of civil or criminal law so they have a motive to remain invisible to the government. Third, bureaus of statistics have been operating in the comfortable belief that "economic activity" consists only of wage-earning in the formal sector. Finally, governments have a motive to ignore the informal sector since its existence reflects poorly upon the government's management of the economy.

One indirect approach to measurement is through unemployment rates. Rates of marginal business enterprise rise when business conditions deteriorate, thus indicating a turn toward self-employment among the urban unemployed. The outstanding illustration is the street corner apple vendor of the Great Depression. These vendors became very visible as bread lines lengthened, and nearly all of them were unemployed workers who had turned to informal sector self-employment to supplement their earnings. U.S. statistics record this trend (Table 14-3). Between 1929 and 1935 retail grocery sales declined, but the number of "single-store" independents increased as business volume declined.

Unemployment statistics underestimate the amount of unemployment and above all of underemployment (Kritz and Ramos 1976). Especially in the Third World, unemployment is a luxury the poor cannot afford. In Third World countries the informal sector is very big and highly visible. Downtown streets are thronged with peddlers hawking every conceivable item to passersby while evading the police. The peddlers employ intelligent if antisocial stratagems to snag customers. For example, in Ife, Nigeria, peddlers disconnect the traffic lights in

Table 14-3. Retail Trade in the United States for Independents and Chains, 1929 and 1935

	Stores		Sales ($000)	
	1929	1935	1929	1935
Independents	1,375,509	1,474,149	38,081	24,246
Chains	148,037	127,482	9,834	7,550
All stores	1,543,158	1,653,961	49,114	33,161

Source: U.S. Bureau of the Census, *Census of Business: 1935. Retail Distribution*, Vol. IV, *Types of Operation* (Washington, D.C.: U.S. Government Printing Office, 1937), p. 6.

order to stall traffic. Stalled drivers then become targets for a sales pitch from waiting peddlers.

This situation has produced many independent studies of informal sector size in Third World cities. The results have uniformly indicated that the informal sector is vast. Koo (1976) reported that 35 percent of Seoul's working age people were self-employed in that city's huge informal sector. This is one million people. Lubell's (1978) review indicated that the informal sector included between 30 and 58 percent of the labor force in six Third World cities. Sethuraman (1977b: 344) also found that the informal sector in African cities "provides work for some 60-70 percent of all employed persons." However, a few African cities apparently do not have large informal sectors. Oberai (1977) claims that Khartoum, Sudan, draws migrants to its full-employment economy where they are quickly absorbed into formal sector employment "rather than relegated into irregular, low-status activities on the fringe of the urban economy."

An informal sector exists in some cities of developed market societies, but its size is relatively and absolutely smaller than in cities of developing societies. There being no official statistics, the most direct evidence is visual. In cities of the developing world, informal sector workers are visible everywhere. They also reside in self-built shantytowns whose dilapidated structures bestrew the landscape. These conditions are much less visible in cities of the developed market societies. However, some European cities offer visual evidence of informal sector workers. In southern Europe, conditions of economic underdevelopment prevail, and informal economic activity is highly visible in self-built slums. But in the economically developed European societies, informal economic activity is virtually invisible except in France [2].

How much informal sector economic activity exists in North American cities? An exact answer is impossible to offer, but some statistical evidence indirectly suggests the existence in American slums of much informal economic activity resulting from economic marginality. First, there is the geographic and ethnic concentration of officially defined poverty. Table 14-4 shows that among whites more than half of impoverished persons resided in metropolitan areas in 1978. Of these approximately equal components resided in central cities and suburbs. On the other hand, among blacks nearly three quarters of impoverished persons resided in cities, and of these 80 percent resided in central cities. Nearly 60 percent of impoverished blacks resided in central cities, whereas less than one quarter of impoverished whites did so. The extent of poverty among urban blacks is also startling. Nearly one third of blacks in central cities were members of households with money incomes below the official poverty level.

Second, there are the extraordinarily high rates of central city unemployment, especially among minorities. Third, labor force participation is lower in slum areas than in nonslum metropolitan areas (Manpower Report 1974). Labor force participation means a person is employed or looking for work. When the rate of labor force nonparticipation edges up in low-income populations, statisticians

Table 14-4. Persons Below Poverty Level by Residence and Race, United States, 1978

| | Persons Below Poverty Level by Race, 1978 | | | |
| | Number (000) | | Percentage | |
	White	Black	White	Black
Metropolitan areas				
Central cities	4,590	4,417	10.2	31.5
Suburbs	4,632	1,006	5.9	20.1
Nonmetropolitan areas	7,036	2,202	11.2	37.2

Source: U.S. Bureau of the Census, *Statistical Abstract of the United States: 1980* (Washington, D.C.: U.S. Government Printing Office, 1980), p. 464.

conclude that slum dwellers have given up looking for a job and are getting by without one. Table 14-5 shows that labor force participation was lower among black and Hispanic teenagers than among white teenagers, and the unemployment rate was higher. On the other hand, among women twenty years of age and older, intergroup differences recede. Among adult black males, labor force participation remained below the white level, whereas Hispanic males recorded a higher rate of labor force participation than did white males.

The concentrations of poverty, unemployment, and labor force nonparticipation among central city minorities index their economic marginality. Economically marginal teenagers and adults engage in informal sector economic activity to supplement irregular wage income, as ethnographic accounts of life in big city slums (Whyte 1955; Liebow 1967; Hannerz 1969) have long reported. Accord-

Table 14-5. Employment Statistics by Color and Ethnicity, United States, 1980

| Labor Force Participation Rate* | Color or Ethnicity | | |
	Black	Hispanic	White
Women			
16-19	32.4	38.2	52.5
20 and over	54.9	48.8	50.8
Men			
16-19	35.8	55.9	59.6
20 and over	74.4	85.5	79.7
*Unemployment Rate**	13.0	9.6	6.0
Unemployment: median			
duration in weeks	7.2	5.8	6.2

Source: U.S. Department of Labor, Bureau of Labor Statistics. Report 602, *Employment in Perspective: Minority Workers,* May 1980, pp. 1, 2.
   *Rate per 100 persons.

ing to Valentine (1978), marginal urban blacks survive by combining work, welfare, and hustling. None of these activities individually is capable of supporting a household, but when all are combined the marginal family can survive [3]. Work means low-wage jobs in the secondary sector. Because of unemployment and low wages, work alone is not enough to support poor families. Federal, state, and local welfare authorities provide additional resources which supplement wages. But welfare and wages are still not enough, so central city blacks add "hustling" to the package. As its name implies, hustling is "hard work" requiring many hours of weekly effort and continuous mental attention. Hustling is the name black Americans have given to their urban informal sector. Hustling involves stringing together a battery of petty economic activities none of which alone is capable of supporting an individual and his or her dependents. Male and female hustlers use different methods. A hustling man often brings together three activities: sponging off girlfriends, petty commerce, and victimless crime. Sponging off girlfriends is accomplished in defiance of "man in the house" laws that deny welfare relief to able-bodied men. Accordingly, economically marginal men cannot obtain direct access to social welfare so they charm their way into the kitchen of a woman who can.

Mothers can obtain welfare. Obtaining it is a mainstay industry of women in slums. Welfare dependency of able-bodied women usually involves public support of fatherless children. As a result of complex changes in American society, the number and proportion of female-headed households in all classes has markedly increased since 1940, but such households are still much more numerous in low-income and nonwhite populations. These mothers have children to feed, no access to free child care, and scant possibility of getting a job anyway. "The only option for many of these women is welfare" (*Employment and Training Report* 1979: 121).

Welfare dependency of mothers become fraudulent when able-bodied men secretly reside in their homes. This situation is common in American slums, whose welfare-dependent mothers have, after all, never taken vows of chastity. Other developed countries experience similar problems in providing relief to fatherless children. In the depressed Lambeth borough of central London, the United Kingdom Department of the Environment (1977) conducted a study of "temporary unions" among single-parent families. Their results indicated that 15 percent of white and 22 percent of black families in this ward conformed to this unstable pattern. "The women remain single and largely independent, though at any particular time she [sic] is likely to have a sexual relationship—including currently cohabiting—with 'her man' who may or may not be one of the fathers."

In addition to welfare dependency and fraud, marginal people engage in petty commerce and sometimes in illegal enterprise too (Ferman and Ferman 1973). All the unemployed people whom Maurer (1979: 6) interviewed supplemented their income by petty commerce. Petty commerce involves the provision and exchange of goods and services in kind as well as in cash. Welfare recipients take jobs in defiance of the law, the proceeds helping to supplement their relief checks. Additionally, marginal women and men buy and resell goods in small quantities from door to door, on streetcorners, and at sports events where big crowds gather. For example, a man can purchase cigarettes and beer in the supermarket, then hawk them to people leaving their cars for a major sporting event. Women sell greeting cards and cosmetics to neighbors. In urban slums, this kind of petty self-employment is visible everywhere. In New York's Harlem neighborhood, for example, anyone walking down 125th Street will be besieged by peddlers. This situation became so severe in 1974 that the neighborhood's storekeepers complained to the police that street peddlers were interfering with their business (Light 1979: 38).

ILLEGAL ENTERPRISE

Illegal enterprise is traffic in unlawful goods and services. Examples include prostitution, gambling, drugs, and, during the Prohibition era (1919–1933), alcohol (Light 1977a). Illegal enterprise is a deviant form of business because it involves the sale of a product or service to a willing customer. In this respect illegal enterprise differs from predatory crime. Additionally, the victims of predatory crime form a class potentially able and willing to complain against an accused person in court. Thus, a vendor of pornographic pictures provides a commodity for which customers willingly pay. On the other hand, a purse-snatcher has enriched only himself at the expense of a victim.

A substantial consumer demand has always existed for many illegal goods and services. This consumer demand makes it profitable to provide the illicit commodities, but those who do so must bear the risks that illegal industries impose. Mortgage bankers have no motive to peddle dirty pictures or carry numbers bets because they can earn more money legally, and the immorality of dispossessing orphans does not deter them. Economically marginal urban groups form a reserve of needy workers many of whom are prepared to risk jail in order to earn money in illegal enterprise. In many cases, their choice is made easier by cultural norms that endorse the morality of some illegal business. Gambling is the best example. Although illegal in some states, gambling does not strike everyone as immoral. Sports, track, and numbers gambling are working-class preoccupations in which many marginal people find part-time and even full-time employment at reasonable wages. In 1970 New York's Bedford-Stuyvesant slum contained 1,345 numbers runners and 76 higher-ranking comptrollers whose job was administering the numbers gambling in their area. Numbers gambling syndicates were the biggest employers in the slum, second only to the federal government

(Light 1977b). Drug dealing is also a big business in the slums. Friedlander (1972) found more young men marketing heroin in New York City than the city's total youth unemployment. In Los Angeles Bullock (1973: 100) called the illegal subeconomy the "greatest single source" of income for young black and Mexican men in the inner city. Street dealers in pills and marijuana viewed their activity as a "business" whose product intensified the consumer's pleasure in sex, music, and eating. In a good month, a slum teenager earned as much as $3,000 dealing in pills, substantially more than he would have earned in the federal government's CETA program (Valentine 1972).

The ethnic vice industry offers another illustration of the manner in which marginal urban groups have been drawn into illegal enterprise (Light 1977a). In the period 1880-1944, black and Chinese neighborhoods in American cities were centers of prostitution, gambling, and drug traffic, forming a vice district to which whites went when they desired to purchase an illegal or disreputable commodity. Contemporaries blamed this noteworthy localization of vice on the depravity of Chinese and blacks, whose presence, it was argued, tended to undermine the morality of whites. This view overlooked the demographic effect of urbanization on the one hand and the effect of economic marginality on the other. Owing to the presence of sojourning immigrants, American cities contained large surpluses of able-bodied white men in the prime of life. These bachelors wanted to buy sexual contacts. On the other hand, blacks and Chinese needed jobs. Disadvantaged in the general labor market and economically marginal, these nonwhites had a motive to perform all the occupational roles that the vice industry provided. American consumers were prepared to pay economically marginal people handsomely for doing just that.

PREDATORY CRIME

The association of predatory crime and big cities is long-standing. Table 14-6 shows that the rate of property and violent crime known to the police varied directly with size of city in 1979. Because these were crimes *known* to the police, the question arises whether the indicated rates fairly reflect true rates. Victimization surveys ask people to report instances of personal victimization, thus tapping true rates of occurrence. Victimization surveys (Table 14-7) also show relationships between crime rates and city size, with larger cities having higher rates of property crime and violent crime. Furthermore, victimization surveys indicate crime rates are reliably higher in central cities than in suburbs.

The association of crime and delinquency with big cities is a worldwide phenomenon. In every country of the world, crime and delinquency rates are lower in rural than in urban areas (Clinard and Abbott 1973: 81-82). Moreover, delin-

Table 14-6. Crime Rates* by Type for City-Size Groups: United States, 1979

Population of Cities	Crime Rates	
	Violent Crime Total	Property Crime Total
250,000 or more	8,456	7,218
100,000–249,999	7,827	7,125
50,000–99,999	6,661	6,135
25,000–49,999	5,963	5,543
10,000–24,999	4,990	4,674
Fewer than 10,000	4,504	4,225
Rural areas	2,270	2,076

Source: U.S. Bureau of the Census, *Statistical Abstract of the United States: 1980* (Washington, D.C.: U.S. Government Printing Office, 1980), p. 184.
*Offenses known to the police per 100,000 population.

quency and crime rates increase with city size so the bigger cities in any country have more crime and delinquency than smaller cities. Finally, the majority of reported crimes in all countries occur in big city slums (Clinard and Abbott 1973: 139). In countries of the Third World, where urbanization has proceeded so rapidly in this century (see Chapter 6), crime rates have skyrocketed too. Because predatory crime rates concentrate in slums (Braithwaite 1981), cities with large slums have extraordinarily high crime rates. Therefore crime rates are particularly high in primate cities of the Third World in which a very high proportion of city residents are economic marginals residing in slums.

The worldwide association of crime and delinquency rates with big cities is so marked that some criminologists have regarded it as a law of nature. Admittedly, this phenomenon is remarkable for its uniformity, but explaining it is more difficult than initially appears. For instance, much research has proceeded on the hypothesis that high-density settlement produces anomie, which in turn causes crime and delinquency. This plausible view is a special case of Wirth's (1938) anomie theory of urbanism. However, reviewing two generations of research on this hypothesis, Choldin (1978: 109) concludes: "the density-pathology hypothesis, fails to be confirmed within urban areas."

The density-pathology hypothesis fares badly in the international comparisons. The world contains many big cities that have crime rates lower than those prevailing in their American counterparts. Serious crimes in New York City are three times more frequent per capita than all crimes in Tokyo, but forty-five cities of the United States had crime rates higher than New York City's in 1975 (Bayley 1976: 56). Clinard (1978: 1) has likewise observed that Switzerland's cities are exceptions to the general rule that urbanization promotes crime. "Even in the largest Swiss cities crime is not a major problem."

Clinard and Abbott (1973: 139-164) compared crime rates in two slums of

Table 14-7. Personal Crimes: Victimization Rates by Type of Crime and Type of Locality of Residence of Victims, United States, 1977.

Metropolitan Areas	Victims per 1,000 Resident Population Age 12 and Over	
	Violent Crimes	Property Crimes
1,000,000 or more		
Central cities	50.4	103.3
Suburbs	37.0	108.7
500,000–999,999		
Central cities	50.9	123.8
Suburbs	36.2	115.1
250,000–499,999		
Central cities	47.5	116.0
Suburbs	32.8	115.0
50,000–249,999		
Central cities	41.4	112.9
Suburbs	29.5	93.7
Nonmetropolitan areas	22.1	70.9

Source: U.S. Department of Justice, Law Enforcement Assistance Administration, National Criminal Justice Information and Statistics Service, *Criminal Victimization in the United States, 1977* (Washington, D.C.: U.S. Government Printing Office, 1977), p. 31.

Kampala, Uganda. In Kisenyi, crime and delinquency rates were high and people feared to walk the streets in daylight. In Nauwongo, crime rates were low. But Kisenyi and Nauwongo did not differ in density of residential or household population, economic welfare, age or condition of built structures, municipal services, age, or ethnic composition of population. Why, then, were Nauwongo's crime rates lower than Kisenyi's? Clinard and Abbott identified several features of the social structure in Nauwongo that contributed to that slum's lower crime rates: more interhousehold visiting, less changing of residences, greater social participation, including religious participation, and more stable family relationships. These characteristics of Nauwongo added up to a social climate in which slum dwellers shared norms and values and had access to informal mechanisms of social control. This kind of local environment is any society's basic resource for controlling predatory crime.

This conclusion is compatible with extensive literature bearing on crime rates and economic conditions. The superficial case for an association is obvious: marginal people concentrate in slums where, lacking jobs, they have an economic motive to steal. Therefore marginality causes predatory crime. The idea is plausible, but two major limitations obtrude. First, crimes of violence (such as rape, assault, or murder) are sometimes motivated by gain, but more often they are not. A rational motive cannot explain an irrational crime—and a need for money cannot explain senseless violence. An economic explanation of urban crime rates applies better to crimes against property than to crimes of violence, yet both types of crime are more common in slums than elsewhere.

Second, the empirical evidence connecting unemployment and crime rates is shaky. Reviewing three generations of research on this recurrent issue, Glasser (1978: 708) declared: "Research has repeatedly found a direct correlation between unemployment rates and crime rates, but not so powerful and consistent a relationship as to exclude other factors in crime causation." Gillespie (1978: 615) reached a similar conclusion in his impressive review of 123 research articles and books bearing on this issue. Finding "substantial if not overwhelming support" for an empirical connection between unemployment and crime, Gillespie stopped short of asserting a causal connection. Negative evidence exists, and only a preponderance of findings supports the hypothesized relationship.

This ambiguity is unsurprising. People disapprove of intimidation, stealing, and violence, and even in slums the unemployed object to this conduct. In a simple sense, neither poverty, marginality, nor unemployment *causes* urban crime. On the other hand, there is no denying the worldwide association of each with high rates of crime and delinquency in urban slums. Conversely, these unwholesome social conditions make it more difficult to sustain the kind of community integration that supported low crime rates in Nauwongo. It is well to remember that Abraham Lincoln learned to read by candlelight and walked ten miles a day to school. Lincoln's example proved that socioeconomic handicaps could be overcome and has served for this reason as an inspiration to generations of school children. However, no one would claim that bad lighting and poor transport were anything but handicaps against which Lincoln had to struggle. In the same sense, poverty and marginality can be and in exceptional cases are overcome, but these adverse social conditions are plainly obstacles on the path to a crime-free society.

IMMIGRANT ENCLAVES

The marginal self-employment of metropolitan slum dwellers constitutes, by and large, a desperate last resort of those whose alternative is penury. However, research has undercut the traditional view that informal sector self-employment never generates significant income or viable business enterprises. In fact, the marginal self-employment of metropolitan slum dwellers does offer satisfactory income in many cases and even the prospect of social mobility via business enterprise as well (Nihan and Jourdan 1978; Nihan, Demol, and Jondoh 1979). What began as a one-man operation with no fixed place of business or invested capital can turn into a substantial business with a work place, employees, capital equipment, and a bank account. In South Korea, for example, large marginal populations exist on the periphery of growing cities, and the marginal workers eke out a living in petty commerce. But as Koo and Hong (1980: 624) have observed: "Many small property owners in the peripheral sector seem to be doing remarkably well economically." Holding education constant, Koo and Hong found that informal sector self-employed earned "more money than white collar workers." Gerry and Birkbeck (1981: 146) present the example of Ndjouga Kebe, a Senegalese millionaire. At an early age the impoverished Kebe left his farm, emigrated to Zaire, opened a marginal enterprise, and made a fortune. Returning to Dakar, Kebe bought hotels, luxury apartments, and banks. Kebe's story is known all over Africa, where it helps to convince the poor in urban shantytowns that some miracle might prosper their marginal self-employment. The lure of wealth in self-employment smacks of the Horatio Alger tradition, the hope of rising in the world through one's own efforts. Therefore, Lloyd (1979: 162) has characterized the work ethic of Third World slum dwellers as "entrepreneurial petit bourgeois" rather than proletarian and socialist.

Marxists understand this hope as an ideological "illusion." They also regard the informal sector as a catchment for unabsorbed labor on the one hand and an outpost of capitalist exploitation on the other. For example, Gerry and Birkbeck (1981) showed that 1,500 "self-employed" ragpickers in Cali, Columbia, sell their junk to agents who pass it up the line to factories linked to the capitalist world economy. In this view (see also Portes 1979) the ragpickers are disguised employees of the factories they serve, but as "self-employed workers" the factories can buy their labor for less than the cost of subsistence. Other pessimists emphasize the futility of informal sector business. "Shoe shine boys, sellers of ticky-tacky, cigarette vendors, tourist touts, porters, all eke out a living without contributing anything to economic development" (Power and Hardman 1976).

The lure of self-employment is not limited, however, to the marginal unemployed of capitalist or developing societies. Even in Communist cities, a significant segment of the working class *prefers* marginal self-employment to factory labor, and many who undertake informal sector self-employment are surprised to learn how well it pays. In Belgrade, Simic (1973: 68) reports, there are numerous "marginally rewarding occupations" practiced on the city's streets. Examples include musicians, knife and scissors sharpeners, umbrella repairmen, shoeshine agents, garbage can pickers, lottery ticket dealers, patent medicine sellers, postcard vendors, and cigarette and snack vendors. Shady self-employment includes black marketeers specializing in money changing, short-supply goods, resale of socialist property, and the like. In Poland and Hungary, much private business activity also occurs in cities. As in Yugoslavia, this activity consists of legal and illegal enterprise. In Poland the number of self-employed grew from 147,000 in 1960 to 188,000 in 1976 (Misztal 1981: 97). Three quarters of the Polish people approve of unlimited free enterprise in handicrafts and small-scale trade, and two thirds approve of it in small industrial enterprises (Nowak 1981:

51). In the early years, communist governments maintained that the petty commerce of peasants and urbanites only reflected the cultural heritage of precommunist society. However, analysts of communist societies (Korbonski 1978: 106) have pointed out that this private economic activity is remarkably lucrative and has served in many ways to rectify failures of the communist economy, especially in distribution.

ENCLAVES IN AMERICA

In the United States several noteworthy cases of immigrant success came to public attention in the 1970s: Cubans in Miami, Koreans in Los Angeles, and Arabs in Chicago. In all these cases, foreigners arrived in American cities and developed small business networks of remarkable size. In Chicago, Arab small businessmen took over inner-city grocery stores abandoned by whites in the wake of inner-city riots of the 1960s. Blackistone (1981) found 356 Arab-owned grocery stores in Chicago, and of these 195 were in neighborhoods with 50 percent or higher black population. Koreans in Los Angeles numbered 1 percent of the county population in 1980, but they operated 5 percent of the city's retail and service businesses (Bonacich, Light, and Wong 1977). According to the *Los Angeles Times* (April 13, 1980), Koreans and Taiwanese represent a "new middle class" in the inner city. Cuban-owned enterprises in Miami increased from 919 in 1967 to more than 8,000 in 1976. Most are small, but a few employ hundreds of workers. Cubans concentrate in textiles, leather, cigar-making, construction, and finance. They control 40 percent of Miami's construction industry and 20 percent of the city's banks (Wilson and Portes 1980: 304). More surprisingly, Wilson and Portes found that the money return on education in the Cuban-owned subeconomy was as good as the return in the primary sector, and much better than in the secondary sector of Miami's dual labor market.

Reflecting on these instances, Wilson and Portes concluded that ethnic enclaves really amount to a third method of labor absorption in cities. That is, cities can absorb new workers in their primary labor market, their secondary labor market, and/or in the economic enclave that the immigrants fashion for themselves. In the vast preponderance of cases, immigrants do not get the opportunity to work in the preferred primary sector, so their real choice is between self-employment and dead-end jobs in the secondary sector. Many prefer legal and illegal self-employment, and those who prosper can employ coethnics and kin. In short, the ethnic small business sector creates jobs and these jobs help solve the immigrants' problem of economic integration. When the ethnic small business sector is large, then the economic burden of absorbing immigrants is actually carried by the small businesses that immigrants themselves have opened.

Among Los Angeles Koreans, for example, 45 percent of adult men were self-employed in 1978, and 80 percent of Korean workers were either self-employed or employed by fellow Koreans. Only 20 percent of Koreans worked for wages or salary in non-Korean enterprises. Because of self-employment, the absorption of Koreans placed only the slightest burden on the Los Angeles economy, whereas Koreans' consumption actually *created* jobs for non-Koreans. The Korean case is possibly more extreme than others, but the self-employment solution to labor absorption of marginals is by no means novel in America. Equivalent rates of self-employment existed at the turn of this century among foreign whites and Asians in major American cities.

MIDDLEMAN MINORITIES

The economic success of Cubans in Miami naturally raised the question why other marginal groups had been unable to accomplish as much. "If the Cubans could better themselves, why not the blacks?" (Ramirez 1980). The answer requires distinguishing among types of self-employment. In particular the marginal self-employment of metropolitan slum dwellers must be distinguished from the self-employment of middleman minorities and of an ethnic bourgeoisie. Specifically, Miami's informal sector contains thousands of marginal blacks who are self-employed in legal and illegal enterprises. Unfortunately, these people cannot be statistically enumerated, but if they were it would be evident that Miami's blacks and urban blacks in general are not underrepresented in informal sector self-employment. Their underrepresentation occurs only in small business enterprise—not in marginal self-employment.

Economic marginality is a successful explanation of informal sector self-employment, but economic marginality does not confer the ability to make an informal sector business grow any more than hunger confers the ability to run a farm. The ability to develop a small business depends on resources, which are threefold: class resources, class cultural resources, and ethnic resources (Light 1980). Class resources are chiefly money and education. People with money to invest can buy a viable small business, whereas the destitute have to work as ragpickers, street musicians, or the like. Additionally, people with higher educational training are able to solve business problems more successfully than are the uneducated. Class cultural resources are the business-related information, skills, and attitudes acquired in childhood in the course of primary socialization. In bourgeois families, children acquire information, skills, and attitudes that encourage and support their subsequent choice of and success in business. In the specific case of Cubans in Miami and Koreans in Los Angeles, class resources and class cultural resources importantly seconded their economic accomplishments

[4]. Koreans brought money into the United States, an estimated $25,000 to $100,000 in nearly every case. Moreover, approximately 70 percent of Korean men had completed college in South Korea, whereas only 15 percent of all residents of Los Angeles had this much education. Cuban émigrés were also to an important extent of the anti-communist bourgeoisie who, if they arrived penniless at least brought with them educational background and class culture that encouraged their enterprise in Miami.

Middleman minorities are marginal trading peoples who have long histories of heavy representation in business. The world has many commercial peoples. Jews, Chinese, Armenians, Parsees, and Hausa are prominent examples (Bonacich and Modell, 1981: 13–33). These commercial minorities have always displayed a tendency to prefer cities. Admittedly, marginal trading peoples had learned to favor business self-employment because this field offered them protection from the disadvantages in the labor market they otherwise encountered. In this respect, they too turned to urban self-employment because they could not get jobs or, at least, not good ones.

However, long histories of self-employment endowed middleman minorities with cultural resources unknown to the uprooted peasantry of the world's slums. In the course of primary socialization, the children of middleman minorities acquired the values, skills, and information they would subsequently need to become successfully self-employed. Family structures also adapted to the exigencies of business management. On the one hand, the middleman culture produced solidaristic families whose unpaid labor would support the family business (Wong, 1979). On the other hand, middleman minorities stressed extended kinship networks whose members provided one another a variety of services on a basis of long-term reciprocity. In the case of these middleman minorities, the ethnic culture of the group has evolved to support an independent business sector. This is an ethnic, not a class culture. Gypsies are a case in point. Wherever they exist, Sway (1982) has shown, Gypsies engage in typical forms of self-employment, especially fortune-telling, metalwork, and automotive sales. But the Gypsy culture that supports these forms of self-employment is an ethnic rather than a bourgeois culture. Sharing this ethnic culture, all Gypsies have been well prepared to make a living in self-employment, and it is unsurprising that they are able to outperform *gajos* (non-Gypsies) in business.

Confronted with labor force marginality, the bulk of the world's slum dwellers have not been able to draw upon cultural traditions of entrepreneurship that middleman minorities elaborated over generations. As a result, informal sector self-employment has abounded, but this proliferation has been individualistic and ephemeral. This departure accounts for a remarkable paradox in central city slums of the United States: the slums are teeming with marginal workers self-employed in informal sector businesses, but there are few locally owned retail or service proprietorships with fixed business premises (Sexton 1978). Instead, such retail and service storefronts as one sees along the street tend to be owned by middleman minorities and middle-class foreigners.

THE CULTURE OF POVERTY

What causes chronic poverty? Drawing on a series of ethnographic studies in Latin America, Oscar Lewis (1968) blamed the "culture of poverty," meaning "a way of life that develops among some of the poor" under conditions of wage labor, underemployment, and low wages. Originating as a "reaction" to their "marginal position" in capitalist society, the culture of poverty later turned into an intergenerationally transmitted cluster of poverty-perpetuating behavior traits. Lewis itemized seventy traits that he held interrelated, self-defeating, and typical of chronically poor households in market societies. For example, Lewis found poor people were unsophisticated shoppers, easily gyped by usurious lenders who offered easy credit or "no money down" terms. Instead of buying large economy sizes in low-priced supermarkets, poor people bought smaller sizes of higher-priced brand-name goods in expensive corner stores. Impoverished women engaged in serial sex with men who did not stay around to help support their numerous offspring, themselves the result of nonutilization of money-saving contraceptives. In this sense, the life-style of the chronically poor contributed to their own poverty and the poverty of their children, who grew up knowing no better.

The culture of poverty theory embroiled Lewis in a scholarly controversy that has not wholly subsided. Some critics called attention to the scanty evidence— a handful of nonrandomly selected families—from which Lewis framed sweeping generalizations. The issue of serial sexuality came in for empirical attack on the grounds that Lewis and Moynihan (see Rainwater 1967) had overstated the frequency of this pattern. Valentine (1968) claimed the so-called culture of poverty was spurious. Since poor people of every ethnic background behaved this way, there could be nothing specifically cultural about poverty because culture refers to the distinctive way of life of a group. Valentine also observed that many behavior patterns of the poor were situational, not cultural, in origin. For example, poor people buy small quantities of food in corner stores because they have insufficient money to buy the giant economy size and no car to take them to the distant supermarket where it is sold. Finally, Valentine accused Lewis of blaming the poverty of poor people on the poor people rather than on the institutions oppressing and exploiting them.

This final point was really a question of emphasis, for Lewis (1968: 199) in response objected that nothing in his concept "put the onus of poverty on the poor." He also conceded that social institutions were the "main reason" for the persistence of mass poverty in the modern world, insisting only that they were not "the only reason" because the life-style of the poor contributed to impoverishment too. Assessing this controversy, one concludes the culture of poverty was pretty much exploded as a cultural theory: each group has its own culture, and a world culture of poverty does not exist. It is also clear that history, social institutions, and worldwide relationships of economic dependency must be invoked to explain why poverty is so much more pervasive in developing nations than in the developed. If a universal culture of poverty were alone at work, one would expect no international differences here.

ROTATING CREDIT ASSOCIATIONS

Rotating credit associations are clubs whose members lend one another money. Although the details of these clubs differ from one country to the next, Geertz (1963: 213) has shown that a basic model can be extracted from the diverse customs of many peoples. This basic model he has appropriately labeled the "rotating credit association." In a comprehensive review of rotating credit throughout the world, Ardener (1964: 201) defines it as "an association formed upon a core of participants who agree to make regular contributions to a fund which is given in whole or in part to each contributor in rotation." This definition is illustrated in Figure 14-2, which shows a rotating credit association of eight members, each of whom contributes $10 at a meeting held every ten days. At the first meeting, member one takes the whole pot amounting to $80. He becomes a debtor to the club. At the second meeting, the members again pool

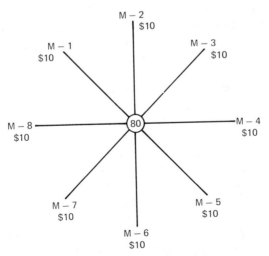

Figure 14-2. Rotating Credit Association with Eight Members.

their funds, but member two takes the whole sum, becoming a debtor to the club. And so it goes until the eighth meeting, at which member eight finally receives his lum sum of $80. Of course, the people who utilize rotating credit associations never call them by this generic name. They use the local name. In Mexico, people call them *cundina* or *tanda;* in China, *hui;* in Japan, *tanomoshi* or *mujin;* in West Africa *esusu;* in Jamaica, *partners,* and so forth. But insofar as each of these local clubs conforms to the basic rotating credit scheme (Figure 14-2), each represents an ethnic variation on a general theme.

Rotating credit associations (RCAs) are widespread in Africa, Asia, and Central America. Most of the people who utilize them are economically marginal. Lomnitz (1977) found RCAs widespread among residents of Cerrada del Condor, a shantytown adjoining Mexico City. She described the tanda as an "important system of economic cooperation" that involved most households. The tanda performed many useful services for these marginal households. It encouraged saving by providing a secure, congenial environment in which to save. It permitted households to acquire large sums of money without having to pay usurious interest. It reinforced social solidarity among the membership, enabling them to cooperate in other matters of mutual concern. These services are valuable to economically marginal people who do not use banks because of lack of familiarity and mistrust. More basic is the unprofitability of servicing people without money. Banks need customers with money, and poor people lack money. Therefore their accounts are unprofitable for banks, which avoid slums for this reason. As a result, economically marginal people are deprived of the usual financial institutions that encourage thrift among the employed. Lacking them, the economically marginal must improvise informal savings institutions of their own. RCAs fill this need.

Most members use RCA funds to buy consumer goods. Thus employed, RCAs are effective agencies of consumer credit among people who cannot obtain loans from banks. RCAs are also more cost-effective than numbers gambling banks. These racketeer-dominated banks capitalize on the financial insecurity of the poor, providing a financial service that, superficial appearances to the contrary, really has much in common with a savings bank Christmas Club (Light 1977b). However, the racketeers charge a big fee for this service, whereas RCAs are free and offer in addition numerous side benefits. Of these probably the most effective is their stimulus to saving. RCA participants believe that they save more than they would if they utilized a solitary method. This increase arises from "the discipline of having to regularly meet with the rest of the group and make a deposit" (Miracle, Miracle, and Cohen 1980: 707). There is a point of similarity here with the Weight Watchers' technique for inducing obese people to diet: every week the club puts its members on a scale, and each one's loss or gain is shouted out to general approval or disapproval. This fanfare encourages members to diet more strenuously than they would if responsible only to themselves. Of course, starving people have no problem with obesity, but they do have trouble saving money and, facilitating this, RCAs provide a valuable service for low-income households.

Increasing evidence indicates that the poor are not, as previously supposed, the only users of RCAs nor is consumption the sole purpose of fund takers. Miracle, Miracle, and Cohen (1980: 701) report the RCAs "commonly serve a broad spectrum of the African population, not just the poorer segments." Similarly, Velez (1982) found professional men and women forming tandas in Mexico City. In most cases, their purpose was social, the enhancement of *confianza* among participants. But merchants and traders have also utilized RCA funds for business purposes. Class culture and resources are probably the major influence on participants' decision to consume or invest the proceeds of their RCA. However, investment of the money has potentially dynamic effects on the credit-starved slum. Most marginal business is doomed to smallness because proprietors have no access to credit and cannot invest in their own business. RCA funds make it possible to sidestep the capital shortage that typically inhibits the upgrading of marginal sector self-employment.

The main case in evidence derives from the contrast of Chinese, Japanese, West Indian black, and black American economic history in the United States before World War II (Light 1972: Ch. 2, 3; Bonnett 1976). Asians and foreign blacks utilized RCAs to support their business enterprise and real estate purchase. Because RCAs were available, Asians and foreign blacks were able to circumvent the financial obstacle posed by the inadequate service of mainstream banks. The upshot was rates of small business ownership higher than those of native-born whites, despite the economic marginality of the Asians and native blacks.

On the other hand, RCAs had dropped out of the cultural repertoire of American blacks in the South. Therefore this useful folk institution was unavailable for retrieval when the descendants of enslaved Africans moved to big cities. Lacking RCAs, Southern-born black Americans lacked the means to raise capital for business and real estate investment. When mainstream institutions denied them loans, as they usually did, the black Americans had no RCA on which to fall back. In effect, denial of capital stymied black American business enterprise, causing native black participation to fall behind the rate of native whites and much behind that of Asians and foreign blacks.

RCAs are uninsured and when defalcations occur, depositors simply lose their money. Defalcations occur when a debtor to the fund absconds or just goes broke. Sometimes defalcations are spectacular. In 1979, a Hawaiian Japanese defaulted on a tanomoshi of 1,100 persons, leaving an unsecured debt of $16 million. Two weeks later Korean American newspapers covered a Korean RCA defalcation in San Francisco. In this case, a woman organizer declared insolvency while $500,000 in debt [5]. These cases are spectacular because of the large sums of money involved, but there is no doubt defalcations occur in RCAs involving more modest sums and in which economically marginal people—not millionaires—are the participants. On the other hand, Cope and Kurtz (1980: 215) point out that the entire membership of an RCA has a "vested interest" in the dependability of all recruits, and untrustworthy people are routinely excluded. Unless participants believe their funds are safe they refuse to join, so the existence of an RCA is proof that the members had been satisfied on this critical point. Moreover defaults are in actuality rare. Velez (1982: 98) asked sixty Mexican participants whether they had experienced a default in a tanda, and only four acknowledged one. Two knew about a fraud, but restitution was made in this case so participants did not lose. Velez declared the frequency of dishonesty to be "extremely low."

SUMMARY

The urban informal sector consists of petty self-employment in legal and illegal activities as well as welfare dependency, reciprocity in the exchange of goods and services, and household self-sufficiency. The informal sector is very much larger in cities of the developing world than in the cities of developed market societies. However, an informal sector does exist even there. It employs people who will not or cannot obtain employment in the secondary or primary labor market. The informal sector is the last resort of people who cannot find work in the mainstream or who refuse to accept the discipline and conformity that mainstream employment imposes. Such people are often able to make a surprisingly adequate living by means of informal sector activity, and many who do so prefer it to wage employment. Middleman minorities have a history of adaptation to marginality, and their ethnic culture provides resources for successful self-employment.

NOTES

1. "There is very little refusal to work" in the inner-city black slums, writes Valentine (1978: 19). "The one important exception is young men and women who decline to accept the demeaning and minimally paid jobs that are typically available." Teenage employment is accordingly high but "it seems possible that some part of this may now be voluntary."
2. An informal economy and ethnic small business sector are missing in Switzerland and Germany. Schmitter (1979: 44) attributes their absence to "legal regulations" that prevent guest workers from undertaking self-employment.

3. Gardening is uncommon in American cities, but popular in Britain: "A large proportion of urban families have gardens and this can make a significant difference to some families' chance of maintaining their standard of living in adversity" (Townsend 1979: 223).
4. Wilson and Portes (1980: 315) stress the ethnic dimension in Cuban enterprise: "Immigrant entrepreneurs make use of language and cultural barriers and of ethnic affinities to gain privileged access to markets and sources of labor. . . . The necessary counterpart to these ethnic ties of solidarity is the principle of ethnic preference in hiring and of support of other immigrants in their economic ventures."
5. These stories are reported in the *Joong-gang Daily News,* February 2 and 20, 1979. This newspaper appears in the Korean language and serves the Korean community in Los Angeles. The author thanks Terry Chang for her translation.

REFERENCES

Ardener, Shirley. 1964. "The Comparative Study of Rotating Credit Associations." *Journal of the Royal Anthropological Institute,* Vol. 94 pt. 2: 201–229.

Bayley, David H. 1976. "Learning About Crime: The Japanese Experience." *The Public Interest* 44: 55–68.

Blackistone, Kevin B. 1981. "Arab Entrepreneurs Take Over Inner City Grocery Stores." *Chicago Reporter* 10 (May): 1–5.

Blaustein, Arthur I., and Geoffrey Faux. 1972. *The Star-Spangled Hustle.* New York: Doubleday and Co.

Bonacich, Edna. 1973. "A Theory of Middleman Minorities." *American Sociological Review* 38: 583–594.

——., Ivan H. Light, and Charles Choy Wong. 1977. "Koreans in Business." *Society* 14: 54–59.

Bonacich, Edna, and John Modell. 1981. *The Economic Basis of Ethnic Solidarity.* Berkeley and Los Angeles: University of California.

Bonnett, Aubrey W. 1976. "Rotating Credit Associations among Black West Indian Immigrants in Brooklyn: An Exploratory Study." Ph.D. dissertation, City University of New York.

Braithwaite, John. 1981. "The Myth of Social Class and Criminality Reconsidered." *American Sociological Review* 46: 36–57.

Bullock, Paul. 1973. *Aspiration vs. Opportunity: 'Careers' in the Inner City.* Ann Arbor: Institute of Labor and Industrial Relations of the University of Michigan and Wayne State University.

Choldin, Harvey M. 1978. "Urban Density and Pathology." *Annual Review of Sociology* 4: 91–113.

Clinard, Marshall B., and Daniel J. Abbott. 1973. *Crime in Developing Countries.* New York: Wiley.

Clinard, Marshall B. 1978. *Cities with Little Crime: The Case of Switzerland.* Cambridge: Cambridge University Press.

Cope, Thomas, and Donald V. Kurtz. 1980. "Default and the Tanda: A Model Regarding Recruitment for Rotating Credit Associations." *Ethnology* 19: 213–231.

Cummings, Scott, ed. 1980. *Self-Help in Urban America.* Pt. Washington, N.Y.: Kennikat Press.

Employment and Training Report of the President. 1979. "Women Who Head Families: Employment Problems and Perspectives." Pp. 95–112. Washington, D.C.: U.S. Government Printing Office.

Ferman, Patricia R., and Louis A. Ferman. 1973. "The Structural Underpinnings of the Irregular Economy." *Poverty and Human Resources Abstracts* 8: 3–17.

Friedlander, Stanley. 1972. *Unemployment in the Urban Core: An Analysis of 30 Cities with Policy Recommendations.* New York: Praeger.

Geertz, Clifford. 1963. "The Rotating Credit Association: A 'Middle Rung' in Development." *Economic Development and Cultural Change* 10: 241–263.

Gerry, Chris, and Chris Birkbeck. 1981. "The Petty Commodity Producer in Third World Cities: Petit-Bourgeois or 'Disguised' Proletarian?" pp. 121–154, in Frank Bechofer and Brian Elliott, eds. *The Petite Bourgeoisie.* New York: St. Martin's Press.

Gillespie, Robert W. 1978. "Economic Factors in Crime and Delinquency: A Critical Review of the Empirical Evidence," pp. 601–626, in U.S. Congress, House of Representatives, 95th Congress, 1st and 2nd Sess., Committee on the Judiciary, Subcommittee on Crime. *Unemployment and Crime.* Washington, D.C.: U.S. Government Printing Office.

Ginzberg, Eli. 1978. "Summary of Remarks by Eli Ginzberg," pp. 136–139, in U.S. Congress, House of Representatives, 95th Congress, 2nd Sess., Committee on the Judiciary, Subcommittee on Crime. *Unemployment and Crime.* Washington, D.C.: U.S. Government Printing Office.

Glaser, Daniel. 1978. "Economic and Sociocultural Variables Affecting Rates of Youth Unemployment, Delinquency, and Crime," pp. 708–740, in U.S. Congress, House of Representatives, 95th Congress, 2nd Sess., Committee on the Judiciary, Subcommittee on Crime. *Unemployment and Crime.* Washington, D.C.: U.S. Government Printing Office.

Graves, Nancy B., and Theodore D. Graves. 1974. "Adaptive Strategies in Urban Migration." *Annual Review of Anthropology* 3: 177–151.

Hannerz, Ulf. 1969. *Soulside.* New York: Columbia University Press.

Hart, Keith. 1973. "Informal Income Opportunities and Urban Employment in Ghana." *The Journal of Modern African Studies* 11: 61–89.

Hraba, Joseph. 1979. *American Ethnicity.* Itasca, Ill.: F. E. Peacock.

Koo, Hagen, and Doo-Seng Hong. 1980. "Class and Income Inequality in Korea." *American Sociological Review* 45: 610–626.

Koo, Hagen. 1976. "Small Entrepreneurship in a Developing Society: Patterns of Labor Absorption and Social Mobility." *Social Forces* 54: 775–787.

Korbonski, Andrzej. 1978. "Social Deviance in Poland: The Case of the Private Economy," pp. 89–112, in Ivan Volges, ed. *Social Deviance in Eastern Europe.* Boulder, Col.: Westview Press.

Kritz, Ernesto, and Joseph Ramos. 1976. "The Measurement of Urban Unemployment." *International Labour Review* 223: 115–127.

Kurtz, Donald F. 1973. "The Rotating Credit Association: An Adaptation to Poverty." *Human Organization* 32: 49–58.

Lewis, Oscar. 1968. "The Culture of Poverty," pp. 187–200, in Daniel P. Moynihan, ed. *On Understanding Poverty*. New York: Basic Books.

Liebow, Elliott. 1967. *Tally's Corner*. Boston: Little, Brown.

Light, Ivan. 1972. *Ethnic Enterprise in America*. Berkeley and Los Angeles: University of California.

——., 1977a. "The Ethnic Vice District." *American Sociological Review* 42: 464–479.

——., 1977b. "Numbers Gambling among Blacks: A Financial Institution." *American Sociological Review* 42: 892–904.

——. 1979. "Disadvantaged Minorities in Self-Employment." *International Journal of Comparative Sociology* 20: 31–45.

——. 1980. "Asian Enterprise in America," pp. 33–57, in Scott Cummings, ed. *Self-Help in Urban America: Patterns of Minority Economic Development*. Pt. Washington, N.Y.: Kennikat Press.

Lloyd, Peter. 1979. *Slums of Hope? Shanty Towns of the Third World*. New York: St. Martin's Press.

Lomnitz, Larissa. 1977. *Networks and Marginality*. Trans. Cinna Lomnitz. New York: Academic Press.

Lubbell, Harold. 1978. "Urban Development and Employment: the Third World Metropolis." *International Labor Review* 117: 747–756.

Manpower Report of the President. 1974. "The New Geography of Employment: Migration and the American Worker," pp. 69–99. Washington, D.C.: U.S. Government Printing Office.

Maurer, Henry. 1979. *Not Working*. New York: Holt, Rinehart and Winston.

Miracle, Marvin P., Diane S. Miracle, and Laurie Cohen. 1980. "Informal Savings Mobilization in Africa." *Economic Development and Cultural Change* 28: 701–724.

Misztal, Bronislaw. 1981. "The Petite Bourgeoisie in Socialist Society," pp. 90–104, in Frank Bechofer and Brian Elliott, eds. *The Petite Bourgeoisie*. New York: St. Martin's Press.

Modell, John. 1977. *The Economics and Politics of Racial Accommodation: The Japanese of Los Angeles, 1900–1942*. Urbana: University of Illinois Press.

Nihan, Georges, and Robert Jourdain. 1978. "The Modern Informal Sector in Nouakchott." *International Labour Review* 117: 709–719.

——., Erik Demol, and Comlavi Jondoh. 1979. "The Modern Informal Sector in Lomé." *International Labor Review* 118: 631–644.

Nowak, Stefan. 1981. "Values and Attitudes of the Polish People." *Scientific American* 245: 45–53.

Oberai, A. S. 1977. "Migration, Unemployment, and the Urban Labour Market." *International Labour Review* 115: 211–223.

Perlman, Janice E. 1976. *The Myth of Marginality*. Berkeley and Los Angeles: University of California Press.

Portes, Alejandro. 1979. "Unequal Exchange and the Urban Informal Sector." NP, Duke University.

Power, Jonathan, and Anna Hardman. 1976. *Western Europe's Migrant Workers.* London: Minority Rights Group.

Rainwater, Lee. 1967. *The Moynihan Report and the Politics of Controversy.* Cambridge, Mass.: MIT Press.

Ramirez, Anthony. 1980. "Cubans and Blacks in Miami." *Wall Street Journal* May 29.

Riddell, J. Barry. 1978. "The Migration to the Cities of West Africa: Some Policy Considerations." *The Journal of Modern African Studies* 16: 241–260.

Schmitter, Barbara Epple. 1979. "Immigration and Citizenship in West Germany and Switzerland." Ph.D. dissertation, University of Chicago.

Scott, Mel. 1971. *American City Planning Since 1890.* Berkeley and Los Angeles: University of California Press.

Sethuraman, S. V. 1977a. "The Urban Informal Sector: Concept, Measurement, and Policy." *International Labour Review* 114: 69–81.

——. 1977b. "The Urban Informal Sector in Africa." *International Labour Review* 116: 343–352.

Sexton, Donald E., Jr. 1978. *Groceries in the Ghetto.* Lexington, Mass.: D.C. Heath.

Simic, Andre. 1973. *The Peasant Urbanites: A Study of Rural-Urban Mobility in Serbia.* New York: Seminar Press.

Sway, Marlene. 1982. "Gypsies as a Middleman Minority." Ph.D. dissertation, University of California, Los Angeles.

Townsend, Peter. 1979. *Poverty in the United Kingdom.* London: Allen Lane.

United Kingdom Department of the Environment. 1977. *Inner London: Policies for Dispersal and Balance.* London: Her Majesty's Stationery Office.

Valentine, Charles A. 1968. *Culture and Poverty.* Chicago: University of Chicago Press.

Valentine, Paul W. 1972. "Crime a Vital Prop to Ghetto's Economy." *Washington Post* (March) 5: pt. A, 1.

Valentine, Bettylou. 1978 *Hustling and Other Hard Work.* New York: Macmillan.

Van Ginneken W., L. Join-Lambert, and J. Lecaillon. 1979. "Persistent Poverty in the Industrial Market Economies." *International Labour Review* 118: 699–711.

Velez, Carlos G. 1982. *Bonds of Mutual Trust: The Cultural Systems of Rotating Credit Associations among Mexicans and Chicanos.* New Brunswick: Rutgers University Press.

Volges, Ivan. 1978. "Social Deviance in Hungary: The Case of the Private Economy," pp. 65–88, in Ivan Volges, ed. *Social Deviance in Eastern Europe.* Boulder, Col.: Westview Press.

Whyte, William Foote. 1955. *Street Corner Society,* 2nd ed. Chicago: University of Chicago Press.

Wilson, Kenneth, and Alejandro Portes. 1980. "Immigrant Enclaves: An Analysis of the Labor Market Experiences of Cubans in Miami." *American Journal of Sociology* 86: 295–319.

Wirth, Louis. 1938. "Urbanism as a Way of Life." *American Journal of Sociology* 44: 3–24.

Wong, Charles Choy. 1977. "Black and Chinese Grocery Stores in Los Angeles' Black Ghetto." *Urban Life* 5: 439–464.

CHAPTER 15

Housing

The power to design a housing system in a major city is the power to influence life in that city. This is a planner's dream—and a nightmare of Orwellian tyranny for other people. Of course, no individual ever wields such enormous power. But housing systems do come into existence, and their existence is mute evidence that economic and political forces have made housing commitments that will affect urban life for generations. Market and political forces may reach housing decisions in tandem or in isolation. When in tandem, housing stock is the result of mixed public and private interventions. This mixed situation prevails in Britain, Israel, and Sweden, as well as in other developed Western societies. When market forces prevail, the housing stock is built by private enterprise, as in the United States. When political considerations are paramount, the housing stock results from government intervention. This situation prevails in cities of Communist societies.

HOUSING IN THE UNITED STATES

The sociological study of urban housing originated in Chicago in the 1920s. Chicago sociologists and their numerous intellectual descendants have provided accurate portraits of how housing decisions have been made in great cities of the United States in this century. Chicago sociologists found that groups competed for metropolitan housing, and the basis of competition was ability to pay. High-income groups bought the most desirable housing in the most desirable neighborhoods. Basically, these were single-family dwellings on large suburban lots. Middle-income groups then bought used housing vacated by the higher-income former owners. Lower-income groups moved into used dwellings vacated by middle-income movers, and so on. In this manner, the metropolitan housing supply expanded when the affluent moved into newly constructed dwellings. The rest of the movement in housing simply involved filling in the vacancies left behind when more affluent households vacated their homes. This process is called *filtering*. Filtering benefited everyone and provided housing for the poor, even though the intention of the affluent was only to improve their own accommodations.

Filtering is still the central housing process at work in cities of the United States. The experience of Chicago is exemplary. Between 1960 and 1970, 481,553 new housing units were constructed in Chicago. Of this total, 129,496 were located in the city's center and 352,057 in the larger metropolitan area (Berry and Kasarda 1977: 23). Suburban construction actually produced a housing surplus in the Chicago metropolitan area, and this surplus triggered a "massive chain of successive housing moves" as families all over the city moved to more desirable housing. Minorities were important beneficiaries of this filtering process. Blacks actually took over more than 128,000 units vacated by whites, and this residential succession released for demolition many thousand of the city's oldest, inner-city housing units. Berry and Kasarda (1977: 24) describe this Chicago case as "a classic example of filtering mechanisms at work."

Residential Succession

Residential succession refers to the "displacement and replacement of one population type by another in a built-up residential area" (Gibbard 1941: 836). Residential succession resembles filtering because new groups take over housing vacated by predecessors who have moved away. Broadly interpreted, residential succession is a special case of filtering. Long and Spain (1978: 1) call residential succession "the primary process through which massive alterations have occurred in the racial composition of many American cities since World War II." By this, they mean that the movement of blacks into previously white housing has been the largest force affecting the housing supply and distribution. However, in Gibbard's more narrow usage, residential succession involves displacing others— pushing them out—whereas filtering creates vacancies that pull newcomers into a more desirable neighborhood.

In the classic case, residential successions begin when central city residents pile up at high densities as a result of rural-urban migration. As central city densities increase, overcrowded residents begin to look for housing in fancier neighborhoods slightly farther from the center of town. This search brings these persons into housing competition with higher-income neighbors who need not be aware of yet higher-status vacancies into which they might, in turn, relocate. This competition for housing is analogous to intergroup competition for occupational and industrial niches (see Chapter 13). Indeed, the ecological niche of any urban group consists equally of its principal industries and occupations on the one hand and its residential neighborhoods on the other. In periods of stability, a group has firm control of "its" neighborhood and "its" industries, and challenges to either destabilize the whole metropolitan community.

Residential successions succeed when newcomers outbid predecessors for housing. At first glance, this result is mysterious because in the preponderance of cases, it requires the poor to outbid the rich. Yet this puzzling result does occur for three reasons. First, those who invade a neighborhood are typically the most affluent of a generally lower-income group. These people commonly rank as high or higher than the least affluent of their generally more affluent predecessors (Varaday 1979: 25). Thus Long and Spain (1978: 16) found that black families who replaced white families in central city neighborhoods had incomes higher than nonmover blacks and incomes as high as or higher than the whites they replaced. Second, residential successions succeed because lower-income groups typically use housing more intensively than do higher-income groups. In many neighborhoods, this usage requires converting single-family homes into multi-family dwellings. Two or three poor families are able to outbid a single more affluent family—and thus acquire their housing. Finally, poor households may be willing to pay a higher proportion of their income for housing than more affluent families. This is generally true of blacks who, as a result of housing discrimination, pay a larger percentage of their total income for housing than do whites (Schietinger 1951: 834). As a result, blacks pay as much for housing as whites even though black incomes are generally lower.

Incumbents resent and resist displacement from their housing, fearing that an influx of low-income households will have undesirable consequences—especially reduction of property values, increase in crime rates, disruption of friendship patterns, reduction of attendance in ethnic churches, and depersonalization of familiar landscape and shopping areas. Research indicates that reduction of property values does not occur in racial succession, so this fear is groundless (Varaday 1979: 29). Slum property is valuable even though slums are undesirable places in which to live. However, objections based on quality of life are reasonable and compatible with evidence. Racial succession is "often accompanied by declines in the quality of housing," even when its price stays the same or increases (Varday 1979: 4). Violent street crime is another serious concern of residents of racially changing communities, and there is much evidence that the influx of low-income nonwhites does accompany increases in street crime (Varaday 1979: 30). Moreover, blacks and Mexicans do not patronize synagogues or Greek Orthodox churches, so the congregations of such places do dwindle when blacks and Mexicans take over a neighborhood. From the point of view of the congregants this decline is undesirable. Because quality of life objections are solidly grounded, they should not be automatically declared coverups for white racism. Racism exists, but it is not the only reason people resist displacement from their homes.

In central cities most efforts to resist racial succession end in failure. Whites give up and find homes elsewhere. Infrequently racial transition brings riots. Riots occur when economic, political, and legal avenues of redress have failed to forestall an impending, unwanted succession in residential housing (Gibbard 1941: 841). Such outbreaks occur chiefly in working-class neighborhoods whose residents are handier with fists than lawsuits. Admittedly, big riots are few, though dramatic. But historic race riots are only visible swirls in a violent undercurrent. Suttles (1968) has described techniques of intergroup boundary maintenance in low-income areas where walking on the wrong side of a street can bring a beating. Intimidation is a technique of boundary maintenance. Certain areas of most American cities are simply unsafe for those of the wrong color or ethnic background. Daily intimidations create a climate of mobilization in which breech of a territorial line can produce a riot, but it is the daily condition of fear—rather than the occasional riot—against which the measure of violence should be taken. When street violence is a daily threat, some people will be afraid to move into a neighborhood, even if the courts and police protect their right to do so. Under this circumstance, intimidation is affecting residential choice, and there is no escaping the subordinate but persistent role that intimidation has played in the determination of who shall occupy which housing in American cities (Berry and Kasarda 1977: 23-36).

Filtering and succession are complementary processes in that both are usually at work. However, at least since 1960, neighborhood change in U.S. cities has arisen more from filtering of vacancies than from displacement. For one thing, the rural-urban migration of blacks tapered off in this period, thus relieving the pressure of density in central cities. For another, housing construction in peripheral suburbs was rapid. Marshall (1979) studied suburbanization in 112 U.S. metropolitan areas in the period 1965-1975, a time of acute racial unrest when inner-city riots had presumably created a climate of fear among central city whites, and "white flight" was a plausible explanation of suburbanization. But Marshall (1979) found that rates of white suburbanization were basically the same in cities whether or not they had inner-city riots. "The most general summary is that whites are drawn to the suburbs rather than pushed to them" (Marshall, 1979: 991). Similarly, Frey (1979) found that racial composition of a central city was only a weak predictor of white suburbanization. Much stronger were various measures of central city economic decline, thus suggesting whites left for suburban jobs rather than from fear of blacks. Of course, from the point of view of residential succession, the effect was the same whatever the cause:

vacated neighborhoods became available for residential occupancy by new-comers. In this manner, the creation of new housing on the suburban periphery opened up used housing in central cities, and the housing stock of metropolitan areas was enlarged and redistributed.

Institutional Influences on American Housing

Chicago sociologists taught that neighborhood change was a "natural" process. Institutions merely existed to transmit and implement housing decisions that originated in independent households. That is, a household first decided to buy some housing, then a contractor built it, a banker financed it, and the police protected it. The aggregate of individual household decisions ultimately became a metropolitan housing stock. This analysis is partially valid now, and may have been wholly valid in the 1920s. The housing stock of U.S. cities favors owner-occupied dwellings in relation to other developed societies (Table 15-1), but it is no longer believed that this U.S. housing stock arose as a *natural* process. As William Form (1954) long ago observed, the "image of an unorganized market" ignores and overlooks the independent influence of various institutional actors such as realtors, home builders, business, local and federal government, banks, and public utilities. These institutions exercise independent power in the housing process and thus tend to impose their choices on households rather than pas-sively serving whatever purposes households assign them.

The major institutional influences directly affecting housing in the United States are local and national government and mortgage-lending financial institu-tions. Table 15-2 lists the major housing agencies of the federal government and

Table 15-1. Housing: International Comparisons of Tenure*

Country	Year	Owner-Occupied	Rented
West Germany	1972	33.5	66.5
France	1968	43.3	44.4
Denmark	1970	45.7	49.9
United Kingdom	1971	48.2	51.8
Italy	1971	50.9	44.1
Belgium	1970	53.6	41.3
Japan	1973	58.8	40.5
United States	1970	62.9	37.1

Source: United Kingdom Central Statistical Office. *Social Trends No. 8, 1977* (London: HMSO, 1977), Table 9.4, p. 151. Reproduced by permission.

*Excludes households in rent-free or work contract accommodation; percentages may not, therefore, add to 100.

Table 15-2. Major Housing Agencies of the Federal Government

Department of Housing and Urban Development (HUD)	Created by the Department of Housing and Urban Development Act of 1968, HUD oversees a variety of housing assistance programs. Among the major program responsibilities are rent supplements, the National Housing Act, low-rent public housing, college housing, and fair housing. HUD is really an umbrella agency that coordinates the work of numerous subsidiaries.
Federal Housing Administration (FHA)	Created in 1934, the FHA insures residential mortgages to improve their marketability. Between 1934 and 1970, the FHA insured $130 billion in mortgages, assisted 9.5 million families to become home owners, and helped finance 1.4 million rental apartment units. Some insurance functions of the FHA were transferred to HUD in 1968.
Federal National Mortgage Association (FNMA)	"Fannie Mae" is a private corporation under government sponsorship. It provides supplementary assistance to the home mortgage market by purchasing acceptable mortgages when and wherever local investment funds are in short supply. Eligible mortgages are only those insured by the FHA, the VA, or the Farmers' Home Administration. Between 1954 and 1968, FNMA purchased $11.4 billion in home mortgages.
Veterans' Administration (VA)	The VA's home loan guarantee program provides credit to eligible veterans for purchase or construction of homes. The VA underwrites the mortgage loan, pledging the faith and credit of the federal government to the lender as collateral. Between 1944 and 1968 the VA underwrote more than $72 billion in home loans.
Federal Insurance Administration (FIA)	The FIA has two underwriting programs: flood insurance and riot insurance. These provisions reinsure private insurance companies against the risks of lending in perilous localities.
Government National Mortgage Association (GNMA)	"Ginnie Mae" was split from the FNMA under Title VIII of the Housing and Urban Development Act of 1968. The GNMA is a government corporation that supports mortgages for military and aerospace workers as well as low- and medium-priced housing. The GNMA purchases mortgages insured by the FHA under Title VIII of the National Housing Act.
Federal Home Loan Bank Board (FHLBB)	An independent agency operating in the executive branch, the FHLBB supervises the federal home loan bank system, the Federal Savings and Loan Insurance Corp., and the Federal Savings and Loan system. In 1968, member institutions of the FHLBB included 2,063 federally chartered savings and loan associations, 2786 state-chartered S&Ls, 51 mutual savings banks, and one insurance company.

explains each one's functions. The active intervention of the federal government in housing began in the 1930s. An official report (U.S. National Resources 1937: 5) indicated that cities were suffering heavy unemployment and relief at the same time that "in the larger cities especially the percentage of home ownership has reached its peak or is going down." To stimulate employment and encourage home ownership, the Roosevelt administration inaugurated the Federal Housing Administration (FHA). The FHA insured home mortgages against default, thus stimulating investment in single-family home construction while promoting home ownership. The framers of this legislation conceived of home ownership as a "device for achieving social stability" by endowing working people with property to protect and mortgage payments to meet (Harvey 1977: 125). Another federal agency promoting this objective is the Federal National Mortgage Association (FNMA), which packages and sells to financial institutions the government-insured mortgages. Housing and Urban Development officials and some Congress members claim that the FNMA should allocate more of its mortgage funds to inner-city housing in order to undo the credit starvation caused by private redlining. Federal deposit insurance strengthens the solvency of savings and loan associations while interest regulations long permitted the associations to pay higher deposit interest than banks, assuring them preferential access to public savings. All these federal interventions encouraged home construction in automobile-dependent suburbs, setting in motion processes of residential succession in central cities whose more affluent residents moved away to purchase new suburban housing.

Urban renewal is a second, quite dramatic political influence that the federal government has exerted on the metropolitan housing stock. Using the state's power of eminent domain, government can compel property owners in a renewal area to sell their property to a renewal agency. Having acquired all the property in a targeted area, the renewal agency then constructs the planned improvements, and in most cases sells properties in improved areas back to private owners. As the text of the law shows (Table 15-3), Congress was aware of the employment-generating effect that urban renewal would have. Urban renewal produces "an almost immediate politicization of the whole urban proble-

Table 15-3. Excerpt from the Housing Act of 1949 (Public Law 171, 81st Congress; 63 Stat. 413; 42 U.S.C. 1441)

Sec. 2. The Congress hereby declares that the general welfare and security of the Nation and the health and living standards of its people require housing production and related community development sufficient to remedy the serious housing shortage, the elimination of substandard . . . housing through the clearance of slums and blighted areas and the realization as soon as possible of the goal of a decent home and suitable living environment for every American family. . . . The Congress further declares that such production is necessary to enable the housing industry to make its full contribution toward an economy of maximum employment, production, and purchasing power.

matic . . . " (Castells 1977: 463). Its effect in the United States, as apparently in France, has been to wipe out blighted neighborhoods populated by working-class and ethnic minority groups. These people are relocated in housing no better in most cases than what was bulldozed away (Hartman and Kesler 1978: 171) [1]. The renewal area then becomes a fashionable business, educational, or residential environment. For this reason, studies of urban renewal have treated the process as political displacement of the poor by a "pro-growth" alliance of business, labor, and government housing agencies (Mollenkopf 1978).

Zoning is the major influence that local government imposes on housing in the United States (Mollenkopf 1978). Suburban municipalities pass and enforce zoning ordinances that restrict the type of housing a builder can erect in their city. Some ordinances impose density limits, some specify housing type, some demand lots of particular size. In general, suburban zoning tends to restrict the building of low- and medium-priced housing. Suburbs favor single-family dwellings on large lots, and this housing is so expensive only the affluent can afford it. Such zoning does, in candor, support the economic interests of suburban home owners whose property investment is enhanced by social exclusivity and shortage of supply. Zoning requirements also support housing filtration because new buildings must find high-income buyers. As these buyers leave their previous premises, vacancies appear and lower-income people fill in, thus completing the process of neighborhood succession. But this result is by no means so "natural" as urban sociologists of the Chicago tradition once supposed. On the contrary, suburban zoning requirements appear as an exogenous political force that independently shapes the formally free housing choices of households.

Private financial institutions exercise another independent influence on housing in American cities (Stone 1978). These lending institutions prefer big mortgages because they are the most profitable after servicing costs have been met. They also prefer socially homogeneous neighborhoods of single-family houses because they offer the safest investment climate. Financial institutions have exerted independent leverage to steer housing construction into the types and localities they prefer. Their method of intervention is known as redlining [2]. *Redlining* consists of a battery of techniques, but the central one, as the name implies, involves map making. On these maps mortgage bankers have outlined agreed upon zones in which they will lend and zones in which they will not lend. Inner-city ghettos are redlined. Redlined zones become financial lepers, and a person desiring to borrow money for construction or remodeling in such a zone finds mortgage bankers unwilling to lend. In this sense, a household's residential freedom is illusory because households are not free to do what mortgage bankers disapprove.

Accumulating evidence indicates that redlining has been and remains a pervasive influence on housing in every U.S. metropolitan area (Tomer, 1980). Laws regulating the banking industry have been remarkably lax, and public agencies collected no data on where mortgages were taken. However, hearings before the

Table 15-4. Conventional and Home Improvement Loans of Major Private Lenders in Three Cities, 1975 (percentages)

Property Location	Chicago*	Philadelphia	Hartford†
City	22.6	23.4	4.9
Suburbs	74.9	39.8	77.5
Outside	2.5	36.8	17.6
Total	100	100	100
Number of Loans	13,962	12,503	4,477

Source: Statement of Gale Cinotta, Chair, National Peoples' Action, pp. 140-146 in U.S. Congress, Senate Committee on Banking, Housing, and Urban Affairs. 95th Congress, 1st Sess. *Community Credit Needs* (Washington, D.C.: U.S. Government Printing Office, 1977).

*Chicago First National Bank, one of six lenders studied, was the only institution from which deposit information was available. Of all deposits, 76 percent came from Chicago and 24 percent from the suburbs.

†Among five lending institutions studied, 67 percent of deposits came from the city and one third from the suburbs.

U.S. Senate Banking Committee (1978) produced a succession of witnesses who described redlining practices in their city. The Center for New Corporate Priorities' report on Los Angeles (Pt. II: 1064-1113) documented lending patterns for each of 1,565 census tracts in Los Angeles County. They found that 14 percent of the population lived in neighborhoods that received less than one percent of loans. "People in East Los Angeles saw only $1 in mortgage lending per capita ... while Beverly Hills residents received $617 per capita." Harvey (1977: 131) found that central Balitmore's heavily black neighborhoods evidenced "scarcely any institutional involvement of any sort," and such housing transactions as occurred in this environment were for cash or by privately held (usually seller) mortgage. Table 15-4 reproduces data introduced by National People's Action in testimony before the Senate Committee on Banking, Housing, and Urban Affairs. It shows that in Chicago, Philadelphia, and Hartford central cities received much less than their expected share of mortgage loans from private lenders. Mortgage redlining is really a special case of the general boycott of central city areas in which mainstream financial institutions have engaged for a generation, but the Mafia does not take up the slack in mortgages as it does in consumer lending (Light 1977).

Public Housing in the United States

Housing has always been expensive. In 1890-1900 an average home cost ten years average income. This cost was successively reduced until in 1970 Americans were paying only 2.3 times their annual income for homes. Cost reduction permitted many more families to achieve home ownership than would otherwise have been able to do so. However, after 1972 home costs rose again and were approaching four times annual income in 1980. Many factors contributed to the abrupt reversal of the trend. Zoning restrictions have contributed to shortages of land for building, thus producing price increases for lots. Additionally, costs of labor and construction materials have outpaced the cost of living. High interest rates, increasing property taxes, and utility charges added to the housing bill. As a result also of more two-earner families, the ability of households to pay for homes increased in the decade and sellers took what the traffic would bear. Demand for rental housing increased too because divorce and delayed marriage reduced the average size of households and therewith increased the number of households seeking accommodation in the rental housing market (Gonder and Gordon 1980; Foley 1980: 462).

As housing costs rose in relation to incomes, people had to cut corners to afford it. Some people are too poor to afford decent housing. According to Stone (1978), 25 percent of Americans have incomes too low to permit them to buy decent housing with an expenditure of no more than one quarter of net income. Such people are shelter poor because if they buy adequate shelter, they cannot buy other necessities, and vice versa. Slums provide substandard housing that the poor can afford. For this reason, slums are essential components of any housing stock that relies wholly upon the private sector. On the average, housing in the United States is newer, bigger, and better equipped than anywhere else in the world. However, the slums in American cities contain housing that is worse than the worst housing found in countries with less than half the gross national product of the United States. These countries subsidize the housing of their low-income population from tax funds in order to bring shelter above a minimal level of decency (Warner 1972: 27).

Public housing consists of government-owned apartments in blocks or projects, sometimes large and sometimes small. In the United States, public housing tenants are renters. Public housing is a negligible component of America's housing stock. Until 1968, only 2 percent of U.S. housing units were public, and even after a decade of accelerated building, only 4 percent of housing units were public in 1980. The modest size of public housing creates an environment in which private markets make a lot of housing decisions. As the public housing sector increases its absolute and relative size, approaching 100 percent of all units at the limit, the private sector declines. Therefore a negligible public housing sector is really a condition for the applicability of an ecological analysis emphasizing filtering and residential succession. Because the public sector is so small in the United States, ecologists (Berry and Kasarda 1977: Pt. 3) can accurately describe housing distribution and production as filtering.

A complete analysis of American housing, however, must explain why the public sector is so much smaller in the United States than in other industrially developed Western societies (Warner 1972: 27) [3]. Ecology cannot explain this.

The answer is inevitably complex, but the central theme is overpowering political resistance. Public housing's enemies are, first of all, "stable working-class or middle-class neighborhoods" whose residents oppose the construction of public housing projects in their locality because of fears, not altogether unjustified, that project tenants will increase crime, vandalism, addiction, and drive down property values in the area (Whelton 1971; Wolman 1975: 35). For example, in Chicago Berry and Kasarda (1977: 23-52) described efforts by the Chicago Housing Authority (CHA) to obtain building authorization in white neighborhoods. Two white suburbs were willing to accept their "fair share" of scattered site public housing units, but most suburbs pursued "a policy of containment" so successful that the CHA could find no sites on which to build. Therefore no public housing was built. More generally, the leading scholar in the area of public housing in the United States, J. S. Fuerst (1974: 141) has concluded that the opposition of suburban interests on the one hand, and of building, financial, and realtor interests on the other has produced a politically preponderant opposition that has stunted the growth of public housing. The desirability of this outcome is not as issue here [4]. The point is, institutional actors have intervened in the political process to support an environment in which private sector housing overwhelmingly predominates. This intervention precluded what institutions did not want (public housing) as their other interventions supported what they did want (suburban homes). In this sense, institutional interventions have already shaped the U.S. housing stock, which cannot therefore be understood as the natural resultant of unhampered market processes.

HOUSING IN BRITAIN

Housing in metropolitan areas of Britain bears many points of similarity to housing in metropolitan areas of the United States. In both societies, the quality of a household's housing depends crucially on its income, occupational level, and color. Table 15-5 shows how access to housing amenities (bath, toilet, central heating) depends on household characteristics. In both societies, metropolitan areas tend to consist of affluent suburbs sourrounding deteriorating inner cities. These inner cities increasingly house the society's aged, ethnic minorities, unemployed, chronically poor, and socially deviant households (U.K. Home Office 1977: 5). Points of similarity in this respect are sufficiently plain that, in a well-publicized report, the United Kingdom Department of the Environment has wondered publicly whether "the inner areas of London, Glasgow, Liverpool, Manchester, and Birmingham are to go the same way as those of the USA?" [5].

But this broad similarity coexists with sharply different housing construction and access in the two societies. The greatest point of dissimilarity is the very

Table 15-5. Housing Amenities and Tenure by Color and Socioeconomic Level* of Head of Household, United Kingdom, 1975-1976 (percentages)

	White	Colored	Professional and Managers	Skilled Manual	Unskilled Manual
Bath or shower					
Sole Use	92	76	97	93	86
Shared or none	8	24	3	7	14
Inside toilet					
Sole use	91	75	97	86	85
Shared or none	9	25	3	14	15
Central heating					
With	48	39	72	34	28
Without	52	61	28	66	72

Source: United Kingdom Central Statistical Office, *Social Trends No. 8, 1977* (London: HMSO, 1977), Table 9.10, p. 153. Reproduced by permission.
*Excluding armed forces, full-time students, and those who have never worked.

large and still growing public housing sector in Britain. In 1975, public housing (called "council housing" in Britain) accounted for more than one third of the housing stock (Peach, Winchester, and Woods 1975). This public housing consisted of units of varying ages and design located in the suburban periphery as well as in the central city. In general, the newer public housing units in British cities have sites on the periphery and the older units in the central city. This locational and age diversity resulted from the antiquity of public housing in Britain. The first units were built in the period 1918-1922, and these are by now among the older housing of the nation as well as being centrally sited as a result of suburbanization since their construction.

When the First World War ended in 1918, Britain confronted an urgent housing shortage. Fearing politically destabilizing increases in housing costs, the Liberal government authorized tax-supported grants to municipalities for housing the working class (Merrett 1979: 34). The Housing and Town Planning Act of 1919 required local authorities to survey housing needs and provide the housing needed at controlled prices. The immediate beneficiaries were the urban working class. This act provided the legal basis for successor legislation that has always maintained the obligation of local authorities to regulate housing conditions and to intervene when necessary. Public housing in Britain is still a politically partisan issue (Bryant and White 1976). The Labour Party has laid more stress than the Conservative Party on government's social responsibility to provide housing. Indeed, in 1978 the Conservative Thatcher government initiated a policy of selling existing public housing to vested tenants, thus converting public sector renters into property owners (Wolman 1975: 21). About 50,000 public housing units were sold yearly. In November 1980, the Conservatives introduced a bill for higher rents in public housing, and during the debate, a row approaching fisticuffs erupted on the floor of Parliament. However, in comparison with the United States, British society—and the major political parties—have verbally embraced a social service philosophy of housing: government has the final responsibility for adequately housing the workers (Wolman 1975: 17).

As a percentage of all housing, the private rental sector in Britain has consistently declined since 1919. In that year 90 percent of housing units were private rentals, but by 1972 only 13 percent of all units were still private rentals (Wolman 1975: 47). Table 15-6 shows how much the owner-occupied and public housing sectors have expanded in Britain since 1951 while the private rental sector has shrunk. The decline of the private rental sector has also occurred in the United States, where 54 percent of all housing units were private rentals in 1910 but only 35 percent in 1970 (Wolman 1975: 48). In the United States as in Britain, the trend toward owner-occupancy is partially the result of rising real incomes and suburbanization. But the decline of private rentals has been more abrupt and extreme in Britain, which had initially a larger private rental sector but now has a smaller one than does the United States.

Rent control, tax laws, and public housing are the most plausible explanation for the more abrupt and more extreme decline of private rental housing in Britain. Britain's rent control policy came into effect for the first time in 1915 as a wartime emergency measure. Subsequently, politicians accepted rent control as a necessary evil in periods of housing shortage, and since the housing shortage never disappeared, rent control has been a permanent feature of British life ever since 1915 (Wolman 1975: 42). Rent control laws kept rents down, but they also discouraged new housing investment and adequate maintenance of existing housing. As a result, the private rental sector tended to diminish in size and deteriorate in physical quality [6]. Second, British tax laws have not permitted the generous depreciation allowances that U.S. laws award owners of private rental property. Indeed, British law has permitted no depreciation at all, treating the rental units as though they would last forever. This unrealistic taxation discouraged investment in private rental housing. Finally, public housing itself has encouraged the decline of the private rental sector in Britain. Public housing starts have in-

Table 15-6. Stock of Dwellings: Change and Tenure in the United Kingdom, 1951-1976 (000)

	1951-1961	1961-1970	1976
Owner-occupied	6,967	9,567	10,957
Rented from local authorities or New Town corporations	4,400	5,848	6,557
Rented from private owners and all other	5,233	3,768	3,093

Source: United Kingdom Central Statistical Office, *Social Trends No. 8, 1977* (London: HMSO, 1977), Table 9.1, p. 149. Reproduced by permission.

creased the housing supply, thus reducing upward pressure on rents and dis-
couraging investment in the private sector.

As a result of protracted decline, the private rental sector now comprises the
"poorest quality housing in the united Kingdom." The next step up is public
(council) housing. Owner-occupied housing is most desirable, but access requires
ability to pay whereas council housing is cheaper as well as better than private
rental housing (Wolman 1975: 17-18) [7]. Demand for council housing "far
exceeds" supply, and council housing authorities ration access by waiting lists,
eligibility rules, and transfer rules (Bassett and Short 1980: 113). Waiting lists
are long. As of February 1980, 12,246 households were waiting for council
housing vacancies in one inner London borough. These were 13 percent of all
households in the borough [8].

The popularity of public housing in Britain is a startling contrast to its un-
popularity in the United States, where "projects" are dreaded reservations for
underclass blacks. Fuerst and Petty (1977: 497-499) maintain that stigmatization of public housing in America has been the unfortunate result of judicial
decisions and management policy that have prevented projects from excluding
problem families while compelling them to exclude the upwardly mobile. No
one is willing to live in such housing unless desperate, and no one wants these
housing projects in his or her residential neighborhood. To undo this evil, Fuerst
and Petty argue, public housing managers should have authority to evict problem
families.

This demand is easy to belittle from a safe distance while piously affirming the
duty of others to tolerate the foibles of their neighbors. However, those who live
in housing projects cannot afford so charitable a view because they must raise
families and lead difficult, penny-pinching lives in these surroundings. Table
15-7 provides three illustrative cases of problem families in public housing
drawn from the files of the Chicago Housing Authority. When public housing
projects draw problem families like magnets, the lives of other tenants are dis-
rupted by violence, vandalism, arson, drugs, noise, dirt, and fear. If neighbors
move out and are replaced by more problem families, the public housing project
has moved another step toward pariah status.

Public housing in Britain has not altogether escaped these problems. Outer
boroughs of British cities have tried to prevent the siting of council housing
nearby and have been successful more often than not. As a result, "the majority
of the ill-housed in London and other major conurbations are in the inner city,"
while space to house them goes unoccupied in the suburbs (Wolman 1975: 36).
However, council housing in Britain has avoided stigmatization and has been
able, as a result, to attract and hold a broad cross-section of socioeconomic
levels. One reason is the greater physical attractiveness and low rents of public
housing in Britain in relation to private rentals. A second reason is the general
shortage of housing. But two administrative policies seem to have helped as well.
Local council authorities in Britain have more authority to evict problem fami-

Table 15-7. Case Histories of Three Problem Families from Files of Chicago Housing Authority

---

Family 1: A mother and eight children. Father currently in Illinois State Prison for raping step-daughter, age fourteen. Girl at reformatory because of history of sexual delinquency. Semiliterate mother is alone with seven children whom she can hardly control. One child has a record of sex offenses. Children frequently miss school. Mother recently found sleeping on grass with boyfriend.

Family 2: Mother and nine children; father deserted. Eldest son convicted of armed robbery and now in prison. Mother has encouraged small children to steal milk from neighbors. Mother fights neighbors, and police have been called on four occasions. The two eldest daughters associate with motorcycle gang members who have made the family apartment their club house.

Family 3: Father, mother, and seven children. Father suffering syphilitic paresis. Mother has a boyfriend half her age, possibly the father of youngest child. Boyfriend lives with family. Boyfriend has sex with eldest daughter as does father. Children are in constant trouble in neighborhood. Apartment is unkempt and insanitary. Neighbors complain this family endangers welfare of their own children.

Source: Adapted from J. S. Fuerst, "Public Housing in Chicago," in J. S. Fuerst, ed., *Public Housing in Europe and America* (London: Croom Helm, 1974), pp. 163–164.

lies than do their counterparts in U. S. projects. Problem families wind up in problem projects. Problem projects are public housing estates in which all tenants are problem families. This segregation denies no one shelter, while simultaneously protecting the rights of ordinary families to decent environments and safeguarding the reputation of public housing in general.

Homelessness

Housing is scarce in Britain, especially in major conurbations. Homelessness is the most dramatic expression of housing shortage. Homelessness comes periodically to public attention when homeless people squat on temporarily vacant or condemned premises and defy orders to vacate, demanding instead that local authorities give them public accommodation (Bryant and White 1976: 81). The Housing (Homeless Persons) Act of 1977 awarded the homeless priority access to public (council) housing in the hope of reducing homelessness, but the new law has occasioned complaints that debarking immigrants who cannot find housing in British cities now declare themselves homeless. Council housing authorities must thereupon award the immigrants first priority for council vacancies, bypassing ill-housed Britons who may have been waiting for better housing for years. Because so many British households are waiting for council housing vacancies, the Conservatives have attracted votes by appealing to the resentments of whites disadvantaged in housing competition with Commonwealth immigrants. First, reduction of immigration would reduce the growth in demand for housing, thus reducing the shortage. Some segments of the working class undeniably perceive the immigrants as unwanted competitors for housing as well as jobs (Rex and Moore 1967: 20, 280). A second course of shortage relief would be to increase the construction of new housing. In principle, either the public or private sector could increase [9]. The Labour Party prefers the former option, and the Conservatives stress the latter. Because public sector housing depends on tax subsidies, increases in council housing starts would necessitate tax increases whose burden would, in all probability, fall on home owners. On the other hand, stimulating the private sector would require Britain to end public sector housing starts in order to permit rents to rise and therewith construction incentives. The result would be further disparities between the already privileged inhabitants of existing council housing and those paying high prices for inferior private rentals.

Urban Managerialism

Confronting this tangle, Rex and Moore (1967: 273) concluded that housing in British cities was no longer "allocated simply by a process of competition in the market." They found instead that "there is a primary problem of allocation of resources between the public welfare sector and the private house owner," and also that "a class struggle over the use of houses" was the actual mechanism for allocating housing among the groups. This class struggle in housing is "the central process of the city as a social unit" (p: 272). As subsequently enlarged by Pahl (1975: Chs. 9-14; 1977), this viewpoint has come to be known as urban managerialism because of its emphasis upon the role of gatekeepers in housing allocation. A continuing and unsettled issue is how much autonomy the bureaucratic gatekeepers actually have, but there is wide agreement that laws and market forces do not dangle the gatekeepers like helpless puppets on a string (Bassett and Short 1980: 52). Gatekeepers exert "an independent influence" on housing, and their influence may reinforce or contradict the inequalities of income that emerge from the economic system (Pahl 1977: 50).

Rex and Moore (1967: 39, 274) distinguished six "housing classes" in Britain: outright owner of an entire house, owner of a mortgaged house, council housing renters, renters of an entire house let by private landlords, home owner letting rooms to meet mortgage payments, and tenant of furnished rooms. These six classes almost reduce to three simpler tenures: owner-occupiers, council renters, and private renters. These three tenures correspond imperfectly with white collar, blue collar, and immigrants, respectively. Table 15-8 exposes some of this correspondence. Colored persons are underrepresented in outright ownership but

Table 15-8. Tenure Profile of Heads of Households, Great Britain, 1976 (percentages)

	Outright Owners	Mort-gagors	Local Authority	Unfur-nished Private	Furnished Private	All Tenures
Color of head of household						
White	99	97	98	98	88	98
Colored	1	3	2	2	12	2
Socioeconomic level						
Professional and managerial	25	33	5	15	15	19
White collar	26	23	14	24	39	21
Skilled manual	28	33	39	29	20	33
Semiskilled	16	10	29	25	20	20
Unskilled	5	1	13	7	5	7
Weekly Income						
Up to £25	37	3	36	36	28	27
£25-50	30	17	31	31	37	27
£51-70	17	36	24	20	21	25
£71 and over	16	44	9	13	14	21
Education						
Any degree	45	65	25	38	63	45
No degree	55	35	75	62	37	55

Source: United Kingdom Central Statistical Office, *Social Trends No. 8, 1977* (London: HMSO, 1977), Table 9.12, p. 154. Reproduced by permission.

dramatically overrepresented in furnished private rentals or "lodging houses." This tenure they share with lower white-collar workers. Manual workers are heavily overrepresented in council housing. Professionals and managers are overrepresented in owner-occupied housing. Private renters would prefer council housing, but access requires more housing to be built, and owner-occupiers are unenthusiastic about paying the subsidy. Expanding the private sector requires higher rents which would only increase the distinction between the blue-collar workers who enjoy subsidized housing and those on the outside, notably immigrants, who must pay high rents.

Managers of public sector housing have working control of access to its privileged shelter. Their means of control are the bureaucratic rules that determine eligibility and priority. Of these, Rex and Moore (1967) found the "principal barrier" to rehousing immigrants in Birmingham was a requirement of five years of prior residence. Excluded by this requirement from public housing, immigrants turned of necessity to the private rental and owner-occupied sectors. In private rentals, immigrants congregated in furnished rooms ("lodging houses"). Others turned to home ownership but here they encountered brokered housing markets that confined them to inner-city properties purchased by "unorthodox forms of finance" (Rex and Tomlinson 1979: 130). Private sector redlining occurs in British conurbations too, although the evidence of its extensiveness is less persuasive than in the USA (Elliott and McCrone 1980). In the "zones of transition," residential succession in the private sector occasioned race riots and tension parallel to succession in American cities (Rex and Moore 1967: 223, 284).

HOUSING IN COMMUNIST SOCIETIES

Communist societies of Eastern Europe do not prohibit private ownership of owner-occupied dwellings, nor have they eliminated a private sector in housing. Even in the Soviet Union, the revised constitution of 1977 guarantees the right of home ownership. New private sector housing is still under construction, but its proportion of total housing starts has declined since 1940. The predominance of public sector housing is massive, and this situation reverses that of the United States, where a gigantic private sector dwarfs a midget public sector (Table 15-9).

Communist cities have severe shortages of housing. As a result, residents live at high densities in tiny apartments. In 1970 state housing in the Soviet Union provided 11.2 square meters per person (Table 15-10). Most families shared kitchens. A universal measure of density is occupants per room. In 1978, renter-occupied units in U. S. SMSAs had 0.39 persons per room. Owner-occupied units had a density of 0.53 persons per room. In 1961 average density per room in the Soviet Union was 2.7 persons (Abrams 1964: 278). The density of occupation in Soviet apartments is being reduced but levels are still very high. Newer flats

Table 15-9. Housing Construction in the Soviet Union, 1946–1975 (millions of square meters of useful floor space)

	State and Cooperative	Private*	Collective Farms
1946–1950	72.4	44.7	83.8
1951–1955	113.0	65.1	62.4
1956–1960	224.0	113.8	136.3
1961–1965	300.4	94.0	96.5
1966–1970	352.5	72.8	93.2
1971–1975	407.3	64.3	73.2
Percentage Change	563	144	87

Source: Central Statistical Board of the Council of Ministers of the USSR, *The USSR in Figures for 1977* (Moscow: Statistika, 1978), pp. 194–195. Reproduced by permission.
*Employees at own expense and with state credits.

Table 15-10. Housing Stock in Towns and Urban-Type Settlement of the Soviet Union, 1940–1970 (millions of square meters of useful floor space)

	1940	1950	1960	1970
Total housing stock in towns	421	513	958	1529
Public	267	340	583	1072
Private	154	173	375	457
Square meters of floor space for every urban person, average	6.7	7.0	9.6	11.2

Source: K. Zhukov and V. Fyodorov, *Housing Construction in the Soviet Union* (Moscow: Progress Publishers, 1974), p. 67.

under construction in the Soviet Union are currently projecting a density of one person per room (Fomin 1977). Even if achieved, this goal would give the best Soviet housing an average density higher than all but 13 percent of London housing, yet London has a severe housing shortage by Western standards. In 1978 only 6 percent of low-income American families had densities greater than 1.01 persons per room in renter-occupied units.

Soviet authorities point out that half the housing stock in Nazi-occupied territories was destroyed during the Second World War. This destruction left a fearful legacy of housing shortage to overcome. More than 70 percent of Soviet housing has, in fact, been constructed since 1945. Moreover, Soviet authorities call attention to very high rates of new housing construction (Fomin 1977). "Between 1956 and 1970 more housing was erected in the USSR than in any other country in the world, whether one measures in absolute figures or per capita ones" (Taubman 1973: 109). These objections are fair and put housing issues in historical perspective. But a closer examination reveals other objections. First, the housing shortage in the Soviet Union existed before the Second World War, so the war cannot have caused the shortage, although it certainly aggravated it [10]. Second, a tenth of Soviet population died in the Second World War, and these tragic deaths reduced the severity of the postwar housing shortage. Third, the high rates of housing construction in the Soviet Union were not high enough. When market societies experience a housing shortage, their rate of housing construction increases until it ends the shortage. The postwar housing shortage in the Soviet Union has dragged on for three decades, and if we project present trends, we see it will not disappear until 2000.

Social Effects of Overcrowding

Societies have the right to allocate their productive resources however they wish. Communist societies are at liberty to stress heavy industry at the expense of civilian housing. This choice involves a trade-off of costs and benefits: on the one hand, the benefits of accelerated industrialization and military power; on the other, the social costs of inferior housing. Just what are the social costs of inferior housing? They could be severe if Communist societies permitted slums and mass homelessness. But they do not. Housing in the Soviet Union is admittedly drab (Herman 1971: 218). In the opinion of Gennady Fomin (1977: 20), Chairman of the USSR State Committee for Civilian Construction and Architecture, "it is no secret" that mass construction of prefabricated housing "has resulted in monotonous architecture in several places." Yet Soviet cities do provide spartan but decent accommodation for even the poorest residents. Slums do not exist there, and the worst housing in the major cities of the United States is worse than the worst in Soviet cities (Davidow 1978).

Soviet authorities do not believe a housing shortage is wholly undesirable. From 1930 until at least the middle 1960s Soviet planners actually maintained that small, crowded apartments produced *desirable* social consequences (Frolic 1964: 286-287). In their view, small, uncomfortable housing encouraged married women to work for wages rather than to perform housework. Womens' labor force participation helped solve the country's labor problem and "the woman question," while undermining the bourgeois family, reeducating the population to socialist labor, and ending "man's present enslavement by his possessions" (Miliutin 1978: 81). Therefore Miliutin called for "the minimum necessary equipment" in new residential housing and calculated this minimum was 8.4 square meters per room. Three decades later Soviet planners (Abrams 1964: 284) still repeated his arguments:

The question arises whether there is any need for such an abundance of rooms in an apartment. After all, not many rooms are required for sleeping, rest, and some kind of home occupation during one's free time. Is there any need to preserve in the future all the household functions which we now have? We do not think so.

In effect, Soviets concluded the cheaper course of action (housing shortage) was also the more socially desirable one.

Soviet planners rejected the counterargument that high densities per room would have pernicious social effects. In this conclusion they were probably correct because Western research has come independently to the same conclusion. Reviewing the literature on residential crowding in America, Baldassare (1977, 1978) examined the validity of hypothetical parallels between overcrowding and pathology in rats and humans [11]. He found no evidence that overcrowding as such produced pathological behavior in humans, and he concluded that social structures can produce pathology at low densities or eliminate it at high densities. Similarly, Booth (1976) examined all the literature bearing on the social effects of crowding. He found residential crowding had no effects on adult health, reproduction, child health, child development, family relations, community life, and political activity. This view is confirmed by Choldin (1978), who also found no confirmation of the density-pathology hypothesis in his extensive review of the literature.

This negative conclusion is less surprising than it initially seems. After all, the meaning of high density per room depends importantly on how much time occupants spend in the rooms. When public facilities are lacking (no playgrounds, no libraries, no cinemas, and so on) people stay home, and high densities per room affect them. Also, when street crime is endemic, people stay home in fear, and high densities per room affect them. Soviet urban planning has permitted high densities per room while taking care to provide collective facilities in neighborhoods. Obligatory standards require planners to provide trees, cinemas, playgrounds, game courts, gardens, shopping, and other amenities within each neighborhood (Fomin 1977). When these are adequate, high densities per room need not produce pathological behavior even though crowded rooms are uncomfortable, disagreeable, and undesired. On the other hand, Soviet experience with *microrayons* has disappointed their naïve expectations that a healthy, enthusiastic neighborhood life would spring up wherever physical facilities were provided. Soviet sociologists report that urban dwellers reject assigned residential communities, preferring the nonlocal company of work mates and kin (Frolic 1970: 682).

However, Baldassare (1981) did find that American women's dissatisfaction with high density was greater in households with small children. This finding is compatible with fragmentary evidence that suggests low birth rates and high divorce rates may be unanticipated consequences of overcrowded housing in the Soviet Union (Berent 1970). About 20 percent of Soviet divorces occur because marriage partners staged a legal separation in order to obtain two one-room flats. After a search, they locate a divorced family and "exchange their two small flats for a spacious two-room apartment." Remarried, their short divorce was only a "device to obtain a better flat" (Binyon 1980b). This subterfuge is a droll illustration of how overcrowded housing undermines the Soviet family. A lowered birthrate is a more serious consequence. Of course, overcrowded housing is at most a contributory cause, and Western countries have also experienced low birthrates in the last generation. Nonetheless, some Soviet authorities believe overcrowded families decide to restrict births because they cannot obtain enlarged housing for a larger family. The Soviet Union, Bulgaria, and the German Democratic Republic have acknowledged that low birthrates are inhibiting the growth of their labor force and thus curtailing their economic development. These countries have also intervened to support higher birthrates, as have Czechoslovakia and Romania (Heitlinger 1976; Moskoff 1980; Frenkel 1976). Improved housing for big families is one means of increasing the birthrate, and this argument may prove more persuasive in communist planning circles than any other purely social argument (Kondratiev 1978).

Political Protests

Inadequately housed residents of Soviet cities have complained about this deprivation, and their complaints have reached communist officials who responded by allocating additional resources to housing. In principle, this process could end the housing shortage. However, popular clamor has to compete with the demands of industry and the military for greater resource allocations. As already stated, Communist parties in power have favored industry at the expense of housing and allocated to housing only the irreducible minimum of resources required for public order. Public political pressure has therefore proved unable to eliminate the housing shortage, although political protest has produced some improvement.

Because a free market in metropolitan housing does not exist, unmet public demand for more and better housing has not produced enough new starts in the private sector. But the private sector has responded. Since the 1960s, cooperative housing has permitted families to club together and buy apartments in new housing they design. These cooperatives save the state the expense of financing the dwelling and supporting its maintenance from public funds (Herman 1971: 212-213). Those able to buy cooperative housing have, however, turned out to be the most affluent stratum of the industrial and political elite (Wesolowski and Slomczynski 1968: 191). In this manner, market-originated inequalities in housing provision have appeared in big cities of the communist world. In Talinn, Estonia, the cooperative sector accounted for 25 percent of the housing stock in 1980, but this segment was larger than elsewhere in the Soviet Union. According to Pozdnyakov (1979) the cooperative sector accounted for 15 percent of all new residential housing under construction in 1979.

The chronic shortage of housing in communist societies is a fact to which localities must adjust because they lack the resources to increase the local stock of housing. Intense competition for existing housing is the unavoidable result. One manifestation of competition is a "certain hostility" between townsmen and municipal officials on one side and newcomer immigrants on the other [12]. Townsmen perceive newcomers as competitors for an already scanty housing supply. Municipal officials glumly view newcomers as legal claimants for public housing they cannot provide. They resort to administratve measures to prevent newcomers from settling in their city (Gaspar 1974: 132-134). In Warsaw "people from outside" cannot be allocated a flat, cannot buy one, and must have employer's certification that they are essential workers even to register a domicile there (Konrad and Szelenyi 1977: 169). Sometimes resistance to newcomers has an ethnic undertone. For example, Estonia's population was 12 percent non-Estonian in 1949 but as a result of migration, the non-Estonian component had become 40 percent by 1980. Estonians now compete for housing in short supply with non-Estonians, mostly Russians, and Estonian officials have politely suggested that Russian migrants are "more needed" in Siberia than in Estonian cities (Binyon 1980a).

As in Britain, competition for public sector housing has given rise to managerialism. Public housing managers make rules that determine who gets good housing and who is housed at all. Essential workers receive housing priorities, and these workers turn out to be well connected with a town's basic industries. Matthews (1978: 112) claims that "like occupational groups" are housed near one another and that "social segregation" of neighborhoods undoubtedly exists. If so, this phenomenon must come about through manipulations of rules governing housing allocations because managers—not markets—make these decisions. Because of administrative regulations, upper- and middle-strata workers have obtained state-gift housing from metropolitan authorities, whereas lower-status workers have been "compelled to build or buy a small house of their own" in the suburbs (Konrad and Szelenyi 1977: 1681; Shelley 1980: 121).

SUMMARY

Groups compete for metropolitan housing: social classes compete with one another; migrants compete with natives; and the public sector competes with the private. The terms of this competition are political and economic power. Economic power reflects unequal rewards in the occupational sphere and generally favors high-status groups. Having more money, high-status groups prevail when intergroup competition for housing depends on money. Conversely, low-status groups normally have more political than economic power. Private housing permits the more affluent to buy superior housing. This is economic power. Public housing taxes the rich to house the masses. This is political power.

In the United States, intergroup competition for metropolitan housing takes place in a framework of limited government and private enterprise. The public sector is negligible, but political influence is constantly at work to maintain a climate in which private housing flourishes. The result has been the twin processes of filtering and residential succession through which nearly everyone obtains housing. The obvious predominance of the private sector in U. S. housing gave rise to the erroneous impression that the sociology of housing was a natural process.

In Britain, intergroup competition for housing is more obviously political because a mixed public-private housing stock exists. As in the United States, filtering and residential succession determine the distribution and type of housing in the private sector. But financial institutions intervene to shape household choices, and the private sector is in competition with the public sector, a re-distributive agency. The terms of this competition are political because outcomes depend on election results. Within the public sector, groups compete for housing by influencing the bureaucratic rules and regulations that govern allotments. The newest migrants have the worst housing.

Communist cities have large public sectors and small private ones, but even here the contrast between economic and political power occurs. Political power predominates, and its origin is the five-year plan. This plan completed, localities have only minor flexibility of decision making. As in Britain, the bureaucracy concentrates political power in its ability to frame rules and regulations governing housing allocations. As matters stand, these rules benefit higher-status and long-term residents while disadvantaging lower-status and new migrants. The cooperative sector permits the more affluent long-term residents to purchase housing superior to that of the public sector. The newest migrants have no housing at all in the city and must commute to urban work places.

NOTES

1. This is the classic indictment of capitalism. Frederick Engels (1962: 610) pointed out that slum clearance under capitalism does not abolish slums, but merely shifts them elsewhere. "The same economic necessity which produced them in the first place produces them in the next place also."
2. The U.S. Department of Justice brought suit against the American Institute of Real Estate Appraisers, alleging violations of the Fair Housing Act of 1968 by "establishing standards that required or encouraged appraisers and lenders to treat race as a negative factor in determining the value of houses and in evaluating the soundness of home loans." See *East/West* [San Francisco], November 23, 1977, p. 1.
3. Anthony Downs lists five housing objectives that the filtering cannot effect and public housing can: expansion of total housing supply to keep prices down; deconcentration of central city poverty; construction of housing of type needed but not already in inventory; stimulation of building industry; upgrading deteriorated areas. Cited from Fuerst (1974: 136).
4. "Numerous surveys have shown that most Americans prefer single-family detached houses for family life and child rearing" (Choldin 1978: 462). Given this popular preference, one could argue that institutional interventions tended to give households the housing they wanted—and what would be wrong with that? Such are presumably the terms in which a political defense of U.S. housing institutions could be raised.
5. Before urban renewal, the city of Glasgow had the worst slums in Britain, perhaps in Western Europe, and unemployment rates are still twice the average in England. See Cameron (1971: 315).

6. "The present problem is that the private rental sector in the United Kingdom has simply ceased . . . to yield a reasonable return on investment and has become economically non-viable" (Wolman 1975: 41).

7. This is also true in Japan, where public housing accounts for 9 percent of total housing stock. See Hoshino (1973: 130).

8. "Camden's housing problem," *New Society* 53 (July 10, 1980): 70.

9. The housing shortage has tended to increase the proportion of incomes spent for shelter. But this proportion remains surprisingly low by American standards. In the United States people expect to pay 25 percent of their income on housing, a percentage that may have increased in the last decade. However, in Britain people spend between 11 and 15 percent on shelter. Since disposable incomes in Britain are only half as great as in the United States, it is apparent that the British housing shortage results in part from unwillingness or inability to spend enough money on shelter.

10. In fairness, one should note that poor housing antedates the Communist government in the Soviet Union. Hamm (1976: 196) found "severe crowding" in St. Petersburg in 1900. Four persons per room was common, and rents were the highest in Europe. The "private sector" was wholly responsible for this housing shortage in Russia.

11. "Population density and pathological behavior are definitely linked. This is a well-known fact" (Blair 1974: 47). Well-known, yes, but not a fact. Blair cites no evidence to support this fact, for there is none.

12. "Where housing is scarce or substandard, migrants to cities are seen as exacerbating housing problems with two results: further pressure on the existing housing stock and the 'ghettoization' of migrant groups unwilling or unable to command higher standard housing" (Green 1977: 242).

REFERENCES

Abrams, Charles. 1964. *Man's Struggle for Shelter in an Urbanizing World.* Cambridge: MIT.

Baldassare, Mark. 1977. *Residential Crowding in Urban America.* Berkeley and Los Angeles: University of California Press.

——. 1978. "Human Spatial Behavior." *Annual Review of Sociology* 4: 29–56.

——. 1981. "The Effect of Household Density on Subgroups." *American Sociological Review* 46: 110–118.

Bassett, Keith, and John R. Short. 1980. *Housing and Residential Structure: Alternative Approaches.* London: Routledge and Kegan Paul.

Berent, Jerzy. 1970. "Causes of Fertility Decline in Eastern Europe and the Soviet Union." *Population Studies* 24: 35–38, 247–292;

Berry, Brian J. L., and John D. Kasarda. 1977. *Contemporary Human Ecology.* New York: Macmillan.

Binyon, Michael. 1980a. "Low Birthrate and Influx of Russians Make Estonians Fear for Future," *London Times* (July 15): 7.

——. 1980b. "Divorce in Russia is a Way of Making Up." *London Times* (August 13): 1.

Blair, Thomas L. 1974. *The International Urban Crisis.* London: Hart-Davis Mac-Gibbon.

Booth, Alan. 1976. *Urban Crowding and Its Consequences.* New York: Praeger.

Bryant, Coralie, and Louise G. White. 1976. "Housing Policies and Comparative Urban Politics," pp. 81-95, in John Walton and Louis H. Masotti, eds. *The City in Comparative Perspective.* New York: Wiley.

Cameron, Gordon C. 1971. "Economic Analysis for a Declining Urban Economy." *Scottish Journal of Political Economy* 18: 315-344.

Castells, Manuel. 1977. *The Urban Question.* Trans. Alan Sheridan. Cambridge: MIT Press.

Choldin, Harvey M. 1978. "Urban Density and Pathology." *Annual Review of Sociology* 4: 91-113.

Davidow, Mike. 1978. *Cities Without Crisis.* New York: International.

Elliott, Brian and David McCrone. 1980. "Urban Development in Edinburgh: A Contribution to the Political Economy of Place." *Scottish Journal of Sociology* 4: 1-26.

Engels, Frederick. 1962[1887]. "The Housing Question," pp. 545-635, in Karl Marx and Frederick Engels. *Selected Works.* Vol. I. Moscow: Foreign Languages Publishing House.

Foley, Donald C. 1980. "The Sociology of Housing." *Annual Review of Sociology* 6: 457-478.

Fomin, Gennady. 1977. "Housing." *Soviet Union* 332 (November): 21-30.

Form, William H. 1954. "The Place of Social Structure in the Determination of Land Use." *Social Forces* 32: 317-323.

Frenkel, Izaslaw. 1976. "Attitudes Toward Family Size in Some East European Countries." *Population Studies* 30: 35-57.

Frey, William H. 1979. "Central City White Flight: Racial and Nonracial Causes." *American Sociological Review,* 44: 425-448.

Frolic, B. Michael. 1964. "The Soviet City." *Town Planning Review* 34: 285-306.

——. 1970. "The Soviet Study of Soviet Cities." *Journal of Politics* 32: 675-695.

Fuerst, J. S. 1974. "Public Housing in the United States," pp. 134-152, in J. S. Fuerst, ed. *Public Housing in Europe and America.* London: Croom Helm.

Fuerst, J. S., and Roy Petty. 1977. "Public Housing in the Courts: Pyrrhic Victories for the Poor." *The Urban Lawyer* 9: 496-513.

Gaspar, Tibor. 1974. "Housing in Hungary," pp. 126-133, in J. S. Fuerst, ed. *Public Housing in Europe and America.* London: Croom Helm.

Gibbard, Harold A. 1941. "The Status Factor in Residential Successions." *American Journal of Sociology* 46: 835-842.

Gonder, John, and Steve Gordon. 1980. "The Housing Needs of 'Non-Traditional' Households," pp. 12-76, in U.S. Congress, Senate, 96th Congress 2nd Sess., Committee on Banking, Housing, and Urban Affairs. Subcommittee on Housing and Urban Affairs. *Rental Housing.* Washington, D.C.: U.S. Government Printing Office.

Green, Sarah Clark. 1977. "Dimensions of Migrant Adjustment in Seoul, Korea." Ph. D. dissertation Brown University.

Hamm, Michael F. 1976. "The Breakdown of Urban Modernization: A Prelude to the Revolutions of 1917," pp. 182–200, in Michael F. Hamm, ed. *The City in Russian History*. Lexington: University Press of Kentucky.

Hartman, Chester, and Rob Kessler. 1978. "The Illusion and Reality of Urban Renewal: San Francisco's Yerba Buena Center," pp. 153–178, in William Tabb and Larry Sawers, eds. *Marxism and the Metropolis*. New York: Oxford University Press.

Harvey, David. 1973. *Social Justice and the City*. Baltimore: Johns Hopkins University Press.

——. 1977. "Government Policies, Financial Institutions and Neighborhood Change in United States Cities," pp. 123–140, in Michael Harloe, ed. *Captive Cities*. London: Wiley.

Heitlinger, Alena. 1976. "Pro-Natalist Policies in Czechoslovakia." *Population Studies* 30: 123–135.

Herman, Leon M. 1971. "Urbanization and New Housing Construction in the Soviet Union." *American Journal of Economics and Sociology* 30: 203–219.

Hoshino, Shinya. 1973. "Comparative Studies on Housing Policies in Three Metropolitan Cities: New York, Greater London, and Tokyo." Ph.D. dissertation, Brandeis University.

Kondratiev, Vladimir. 1978. "Employment Patterns and Prospects in European Socialist Countries." *International Labour Review* 117: 355–368.

Konrad, Gyoergy, and Ivan Szelenyi. 1977. "Social Conflicts of Underurbanization," pp. 157–174, in Michael Harloe, ed., *Captive Cities*. London: Wiley.

Light, Ivan H. 1977. "Numbers Gambling: a Financial Institution." *American Sociological Review* 42: 892–904.

——. 1981. "Ethnic Succession," pp. 53–86, in Charles Keyes, ed. *Ethnic Change*. Seattle: University of Washington Press.

Long, Larry H., and Daphne Spain. 1978. "Racial Succession in Individual Housing Units." *Current Population Reports, Special Studies: Series P 23, No. 71*. Washington, D.C.: U.S. Government Printing Office.

Marshall, Harvey. 1979. "White Movement to the Suburbs: A Comparison of Explanations. *American Sociological Review* 44: 975–994.

Massey, Douglas S. 1979. "Effects of Socioeconomic Factors on the Residential Segregation of Blacks and Spanish Americans in U.S. Urbanized Areas." *American Sociological Review* 44: 1015; 1022.

Matthews, Mervyn. 1978. *Privilege in the Soviet Union*. London: George Allen and Unwin.

Merrett, Stephen. 1979. *State Housing in Britain*. London: Routledge and Kegan Paul.

Miliutin, N. A. 1978 [1930]. *Sotsgorod: The Problem of Building Socialist Cities*. Trans. Arthur Sprague. Cambridge: MIT Press.

Mollenkopf, John H. 1978. "The Postwar Politics of Urban Development," pp. 117–152, in William Tabb and Larry Sawers, eds. *Marxism and the Metropolis*. New York: Oxford University Press.

Moskoff, William. 1980. "Pronatalist Policies in Romania." *Economic Development and Cultural Change* 28: 597–614.

Pahl, R. E. 1975. *Whose City?*, 2nd ed. Harmondsworth: Penguin.

——. 1977. "Managers, Technical Experts, and the State: Forms of Mediation, Manipulation and Dominance in Urban and Regional Development," pp. 49–60, in Michael Harloe, ed. *Captive Cities*. London: Wiley.

Peach, Ceri, Stuart Winchester, and Robert Woods. 1975. "The Distribution of Coloured Immigrants in Britain," pp. 395–419, in Gary Gappert and Harold M. Rose, eds. *The Social Economy of Cities* Vol. IX, Urban Affairs Annual Reviews. Beverly Hills: Sage.

Pozdynyakov, Yevgeni. 1979. "The Right to Good Housing." *Soviet Life* (October): 51–52.

Rex, John, and Robert Moore. 1967. *Race, Community and Conflict*. London: Oxford University Press.

Rex, John, and Sally Tomlinson. 1979. *Colonial Immigrants in a British City*. London: Routledge and Kegan Paul.

Schietinger, E. F. 1951. "Racial Succession and Value of Small Residential Properties." *American Sociological Review* 16: 832–835.

Shelley, Louise. 1980. "The Geography of Soviet Criminality." *American Sociological Review* 45: 111–122.

Stone, Michael E. 1978. "Housing, Mortgage Lending, and the Contradictions of Capitalism," pp. 179–207, in William Tabb and Larry Sawers, eds. *Marxism and the Metropolis*. New York: Oxford Press.

Suttles, Gerald. 1968. *The Social Order of the Slum*. Chicago: University of Chicago Press.

Taubman, William. 1973. *Governing Soviet Cities*. New York: Praeger.

Tomer, John. 1980. "The Mounting Evidence on Redlining." *Urban Affairs Quarterly* 5: 488–504.

United Nations Department of Economic and Social Affairs, Population Studies No. 62, *1979 World Population Trends and Policies*, Vol. II: Population Policies. New York: United Nations.

United Kingdom Home Office. 1977. *Urban Deprivation, Racial Inequality, and Social Policy*. London: Her Majesty's Stationery Office.

U.S. National Resources Committee. 1937. *Our Cities*. Washington, D.C.: U.S. Government Printing Office.

U.S. Congress, Senate. 1975. 94th Congress, 1st Sess., Committee on Banking, Housing, and Urban Affairs. *Home Mortgage Disclosure Act of 1975*. pts. 1 and 2. Washington, D.C.: U.S. Government Printing Office.

Varady, David P. 1979. *Ethnic Minorities in Urban Areas*. Boston: Martinus Nijhoff.

Warner, Sam Bass, Jr. 1972. *The Urban Wilderness*. New York: Harper & Row.

Wesolowski, W., and K. Slomczynski. 1968. "Social Stratification in Polish Cities," pp. 175–211, in J. A. Jackson, ed. *Social Stratification*. Cambridge: Cambridge University Press.

Whelton, Clark. 1971. "Battle of Forest Hills," *Village Voice* (November 25): 1.

Whyte, William Foote. 1955. *Street Corner Society*. 2nd ed. Chicago: University of Chicago Press.

Wolman, Harold L. 1975. *Housing and Housing Policy in the U.S. and the U.K.* Lexington, Mass.: D.C. Heath.

CHAPTER 16

Politics

Politics are contested social interventions intended to affect the framing and implementation of government policies. In the urban context, critical policies govern the productive organization of a population on a terrain and the infrastructure serving that population. The productive organization of a population is how many and what kinds of goods and services its terrain contains and where these facilities are located. Basic industries are the core of the population's productive organization. The metropolitan *infrastructure* includes population-serving facilities such as highways, housing, schools, hospitals, sewers, public services, and retail trade. Although nonbasic in the technical sense (see Chapter 2), the infrastructure is an essential support of any metropolitan economy in that the labor force cannot produce basic goods or services without infrastructure. Conversely, an infrastructure is useless without basic industry by means of which the metropolitan region can earn its living.

Population, productive organization, and infrastructure are interdependent. First, basic industry needs to be sufficiently productive to support the whole population of a locality, and tensions arise when people are too many or too few for basic industry. Second, infrastructure needs to be sufficiently developed to support basic industry's working force on the one hand, and the whole population on the other. Tensions arise when infrastructures do not meet both tests. Finally, industry and infrastructure need to be compatible in quality. Qualitative compatibility means an infrastructure that provides the kind of support an industrial plant requires. For example, housing workers in Florida requires construction and heating incompatible with the climate of Alaska. Affecting the size and quality of infrastructure as well as of basic industry, government policies af-

420

fect all inhabitants. Everyone in a metropolitan area feels the favorable or unfavorable impact of government policies upon his or her surroundings and life chances. Therefore, all have a stake in intervening to affect government policies affecting themselves. This intervention is urban politics.

Any issue on the political agenda of a metropolitan area is an urban issue in a general sense. But distinctively urban political issues center on government policies to affect the balance and compatibility of industry and infrastructure in a locality. These policies achieve their objective by influencing industry, infrastructure, or both. Some groups want infrastructural or industrial growth. Their political activity accordingly comes down on the side of government policies expected to yield the increases they want. Other groups benefit from smallness or stability of population. Their political activity supports policies yielding these outcomes. But urban politics are not really about things. Ultimately, the relationships among groups is at issue in urban politics.

BIG CITY BANKRUPTCY IN THE UNITED STATES

Fiscal crisis arises because central cities are unable to pay their debts, default on loans, and turn to the federal government for "bail out" assistance. New York City's bond defalcation in 1975-1976 provides a striking example, but insolvency troubles many Northeastern cities, and the problem is by no means recent. The U.S. National Resources Committee (1937: 16-17) declared that urban finance was an "emerging problem" of vast proportions. In the Great Depression, "urban areas . . . were forced to pass the hat, begging for financial support." The Depression era problem of big city finance arose because unemployment in big cities was much higher than elsewhere and thus imposed a giant bill for social welfare while reducing the residents' ability to meet even ordinary expenses of government such as schools, fire and police protection, and sanitation. In effect, the Depression produced increased expenses of infrastructure and reduced the capacity to pay for it. Municipal infrastructures became too big for municipal industry to support, and cities turned for financial assistance to state and federal government.

The fiscal crisis of the Great Depression was temporary, and the restoration of prosperity ended it. However, since the Second World War a chronic imbalance of industry and infrastructure has arisen in central cities. This imbalance reflects the emergence of a chronically unemployed population of marginal workers in central cities and the suburbanization of basic industry. Loss of industry to the suburbs and to the Sunbelt has adversely affected the ability of some central city governments to raise money by taxation. Tabb (1978: 246) has estimated that between 1969 and 1976 New York City lost 542,000 jobs as a result of industrial flight. Each job lost cost the city between $651 and $1,035 annually in taxes. If the jobs had not been lost, New York City's revenues would have been $1.5 billion higher in 1976 than they actually were and there would have been no bankruptcy.

Job loss also increases the proportion of marginal people in the central city population, thus imposing additional costs on central city government. Augmented marginality means central cities contain more indigents receiving welfare assistance in one form or another. These indigents impose on central city governments a heavy burden of tax-supported expenditure for medical care, housing, police and fire protection, schools, sanitation, sewerage, and other services. Indigents receive these services but pay no share of their cost in taxes to local government. In addition, social alienation in depressed central cities creates a heavy burden of crime, arson, vandalism, and substance abuse. Relieving these evils requires extra expenditures for police, fire service, welfare and health, construction, and maintenance. As a result, the per capita general expenditure in big cities is higher than in smaller cities, and the outstanding debt per capita is also higher (Table 16-1). With remarkable uniformity big cities have higher taxes than their surrounding suburbs despite the generally lower personal income in central cities (Table 16-2). The cities also have higher property taxes, higher general expenditures, and higher debt outstanding per capita than do their states (Table 16-3).

Suburban cities are not confronting insolvency as are the big central cities they ring. Suburban cities produce enough income to pay for their infrastructure. On the one hand, suburban cities have thriving industries and fully employed citizens capable of paying taxes. This is their *tax base*. Because the tax base is strong, suburban cities can support local government from taxes and do not require any or as much extralocal assistance for the infrastructural services they supply. On the other hand, the costs of suburban government (excluding education) are relatively light. Suburban government is inexpensive because suburban

Table 16-1. Local Government Finance by Size of County, 1967

	Local Government	
Size of County	Direct General Expenditure per Capita ($)	Debt Outstanding per Capita ($)
10,000– 24,999	232	178
25,000– 49,999	233	195
50,000– 99,999	246	236
100,000–249,999	273	295
250,000 or more	351	421

Source: U.S. Bureau of the Census. *Statistical Abstract of the United States: 1970* (Washington, D.C.: U.S. Government Printing Office, 1970), p. 422. See also Dahl 1978.

Table 16-2. Central City and Suburb per Capita Nonselect Tax Collections in 1977, Selected SMSAs* (dollars per capita)

SMSA	Central City Taxes	Suburban Taxes	CC Taxes/ Suburban Taxes
Boston	487	306	1.59
New York	616	374	1.65
Chicago	237	155	1.53
Detroit	288	147	1.96
Cleveland	213	154	1.38
Miami	302	202	1.50
Atlanta	361	171	2.11
Dallas	254	132	1.92
Albuquerque	133	33	4.03
Los Angeles	400	296	1.35

Source: Office of Policy Development and Research, U.S. Department of Housing and Urban Development for the Interagency Task Force on Urban Data, *Changing Conditions in Large Metropolitan Areas* (Washington, D.C.: U.S. Government Printing Office, 1980), Table 34.

*Of eighty-eight SMSAs for which data were reported, central city per capita tax collection exceeded suburban in *every* case.

cities (and favored central cities) have light burdens of unemployment and welfare. As a result, they do not have to buy medical care, groceries, housing, and infrastructural services for a numerous class of indigent residents (Zech 1980). In addition, suburban cities have low social expenses for public order because robbery, violence, arson, substance abuse, and vandalism are less frequent than in central cities.

Metropolitan politics in the United States prevasively reflect the unwelcome costs of central city poverty, alienation, and social control. One manifestation is the fragmentation of local governments. This fragmentation ringed the average American central city with eighty-six local governments in 1972. These local governments include cities, school districts, and special districts such as the Port of New York Authority. Table 16-4 shows the extent of metropolitan fragmentation in some leading American cities. New York had 554 local governments in its SMSA, 1 special district, and 1 other government. The Chicago SMSA had 72 local governments (mostly suburban cities), 1 county government, 1 school district, 9 special districts, and 11 other governments. Each of these governments had legal authority over some territory or function within the designated metropolitan areas.

Admittedly, governmental fragmentation began in the 1920s, and transportation technology was an initiating condition (McKenzie 1933: 195). But the flight from taxation was a consideration even in the early period and has by now become the "ultimate impetus" to governmental fragmentation of metropolitan areas (Markusen 1978: 98). Suburbs provide a tax haven where home owners

Table 16-3. Taxation, Expenditure, and Debt per Capita for Selected States and Cities, 1974–1975 (dollars)

State/City	Property Tax per Capita	General Expenditure per Capita	Debt Outstanding per Capita
Georgia	58	166	459
Atlanta	100	286	1,237
New Jersey	175	318	232
Newark	234	801	422
New York State	266	932	1,361
New York City	348	1,330	1,934
Ohio	29	196	328
Cleveland	54	301	596
Pennsylvania	43	194	259
Philadelphia	57	421	700
Texas	57	124	392
Dallas	121	196	586

Source: U.S. Bureau of the Census, *County and City Data Book, 1977* (Washington, D.C.: U.S. Government Printing Office, 1978).

and industry can escape the costs of central city unemployment, poverty, crime, and social alienation.

The assured fiscal independence of suburbs explains their otherwise puzzling reluctance to merge with central cities in a unitary metropolitan area government (Newton 1978). Such an arrangement would reduce governmental duplication, introduce economies of scale, and augment control. Instead of merger, suburban governments enter special districts with central cities on those issues for which a unified metropolitan authority is in their interest. Therefore American cities have ad hoc special districts with authority over metropolitan transportation, pollution, public recreation, or waste disposal. Special districts and suburban municipalities make up about 60 percent of government units in metropolitan regions. These special districts increase government fragmentation, but they are the only basis on which suburban governments and central cities can coordinate action on common problems. Suburban municipalities resist political mergers with big, central cities because they do not wish to share the taxpayer cost of central city poverty, unemployment, crime, vandalism, and substance abuse (Berry and Kasarda 1977: 226). In addition, suburban municipalities often maintain high-quality, high-cost school programs that would deteriorate under fiscal merger with central cities. Harris and Ullman (1945: 17) long ago chided the suburbs for "lack of civic responsibility" toward the metropolitan areas in which they exist. As a moralistic evaluation, their complaint is

Table 16-4. Underlying or Overlying Local Governments with Jurisdiction in Central Cities, 1977; Selected SMSAs

City	County Govern-ment	School Districts	Special Districts	Other Govern-ments	Local Govern-ments in SMSA
New York	0	0	1	1	554
Boston	0	0	3	3	190
Chicago	1	1	9	11	72
Cleveland	1	3	6	10	211
Miami	1	County	1	2	33
Atlanta	2	2	4	8	90
Dallas	1	7	4	12	223
Los Angeles	1	8	7	16	232

Source: Office of Policy Development and Research, U.S. Department of Housing and Urban Development for the Interagency Task Force on Urban Data, *Changing Conditions in Large Metropolitan Areas* (Washington, D.C.: U.S. Government Printing Office, 1980), Table 31.

arguably valid today, but the narrow economic and social interests of American suburbs are, in all candor, incompatible with metropolitan integration [1].

URBAN RENEWAL AND MUNICIPAL BANKRUPTCY

Confronting the flight of business corporations, many central cities turned to urban renewal in the 1950s and the early 1960s in the expectation that renewal would revivify the downtown, encourage business to stay, restore the tax base, and maintain local prosperity. But some evidence suggests that urban renewal only accelerated the decline of central cities, thus encouraging the municipal bankruptcies of the middle 1970s. Friedland (1981: Ch. 9) found that in the largest 130 central cities, total taxes, property taxes, and short-term municipal debt were positively associated with extent of urban renewal on the one hand and the number of corporate office headquarters on the other. The more urban renewal, the greater the debt and therewith fiscal vulnerability of the central city.

According to Friedland, municipal governments went into debt to support urban renewal programs whose beneficiaries were big business corporations with headquarters in central cities. The municipal debt rose when cities acquired and cleared slum land on which high-rise office structures were later erected. Partially funded by federal aid, slum clearance was accomplished in the expectation business enterprise would open jobs to city residents, thus strengthening the local tax base and relieving local unemployment. If the plan had worked, central cities would have received back in taxes more than their investment in land clearance. But according to Friedland, the plan did not work because downtown corporations were employers of white-collar workers residing in suburbs. Inner-city minorities did not qualify for white-collar jobs in downtown high-rises, but these people had paid the taxes that cleared the land on which office buildings were erected under government subsidy. Thus central cities spent taxpayers' money to subsidize business corporations that did not provide jobs for local workers. The debt thus contracted only aggravated the financial problems of central cities, accelerating their plunge into bankruptcy a decade later.

MUNICIPAL MISMANAGEMENT AND GOVERNMENT WASTE

Big city fiscal complaints encounter the rejoinder that "excessive wages and exorbitant welfare payments" are the real causes of municipal insolvency. Insolvent cities are urged to "put their house in order" before turning for bail out assistance to state legislature and Congress (Tabb 1978: 342). The fiscal rebound of New York City offers a persuasive illustration. Bankrupt in 1975, New York City was successfully floating B-rated municipal bonds in 1980. How was the bankrupt city's credit reestablished? The major step was formation of a bankers' advisory committee known as the Municipal Assistance Corporation for New York. The bankers' advisory committee masterminded the fiscal reorganization of the bankrupt city (Rohatyn 1980). First, bankers ordered politicians to declare a wage freeze for municipal employees with deferrals of past increases until the city's fiscal position improved. Second, the municipality ordered a 20 percent cut in its work force with corresponding reductions in municipal services. Third, the municipality introduced increases in transit fares while deferring maintenance on the subway system. Fourth, the municipality increased tuition at the City University of New York. Fifth, the city reduced pension benefits of municipal employees. Finally, the city increased sales taxes while reducing taxes on business (Rohatyn 1980: 20). In return for these concessions, banks agreed to reduce the interest paid them by the city and to extend the city's repayment period. In the resulting phase of austerity, 1975-1980, New York City's municipal expenditures grew less than 10 percent, whereas expenditures of New York State increased 35 percent and federal expenditures increased 80 percent. In 1980, New York City declared a balanced budget, the first in two generations.

New York City's example proves that bankers' austerity measures can restore solvency by decreasing expenditures, increasing taxes, and providing a low-cost, attractive environment for business. In effect, this strategy achieves municipal solvency by tilting the local balance of infrastructure and industry in favor of industry. However, the restored solvency of New York City does not neutralize the claim that municipal insolvencies reflect the high cost of servicing unemployed people. Obviously when the unemployed are not serviced, no costs are incurred. When reducing the number of municipal employees reduces municipal services, government obtains economies at the expense of public welfare. For instance, the reduction of the sanitation work force left garbage on New York City streets for two weeks before collection, and increases in transit fares reduced ridership. In all such cases, the solvency of government was restored by not servicing the population, and the lack of service reduced public welfare. Reduction of public welfare is an unfunded, nonmonetarized social cost. This cost particularly affects low-income people among whom a high proportion of total wealth (see Chapter 14) consists of government services—not wage income.

Mismanagement and circumstances are not alternatives between which one must choose in evaluating the causes of municipal insolvency. It is possible both contribute, in which case improved management might restore solvency without remedying long-term adverse trends in employment and population. Bahl (1978) found that the fiscal problems of American big cities resulted more from adverse trends than from municipal mismanagement. In the specific case of New York City, Tabb (1978: 242-243) points out that almost 10 percent of the city's population were receiving Medicaid assistance at an average cost of $2,000 per recipient yearly. Naturally, New York's government costs more than suburban Scarsdale's because the indigent cannot afford Scarsdale. Hence the inter-city discrepancy in welfare cost is no proof that New York's cost of government was really "excessive." Moreover, in the year of insolvency, New York's per capita welfare benefits were actually lower than those of Chicago, Detroit, Philadelphia, or Milwaukee, where insolvency did not occur. These lower benefits that suggest that runaway costs were not the cause of New York's insolvency—but it is, of course, no proof that cost of government was not high in each of these cities (Cohen 1976).

Most older cities do have a history of corruption in local government. In the nineteenth century and through the first half of this century, Chicago, Boston, Kansas City, New Orleans, New York, Memphis, Philadelphia, and San Francisco contained powerful, racketeer-connected political machines (Wald 1980). Political machines lined up working-class votes for cooperative politicians prepared to take bribes and find jobs for machine supporters. Immigrant ethnic groups, notably the Irish, made spectacular use of the polls to obtain jobs and contracts from city hall (Clark 1980). Lineberry and Sharkansky (1978: 116-122) conclude that old-fashioned political machines no longer exist. Lowi (1976: 537) argues that swollen municipal bureaucracies are the "new machines" in big cities (Cohen 1976: 499). Suburban and Sunbelt cities tend to have lower-cost government than do older central cities of the Northeast and North Central regions—but they also provide a narrower range of services to the public (Liebert 1976). Before its bankruptcy, New York City did much for its citizens, Los Angeles did little, and the cost of government in each varied accordingly.

Sunbelt-Frostbelt differences in level of public service arose in several ways.

The cities of the Northeast and North Central regions had to absorb European immigration in the nineteenth and early twentieth century. In those days, municipal machines performed many welfare services for the immigrants. On Thanksgiving and Christmas, machine politicians delivered free turkeys to constituents and expected voters to show their gratitude at the polls. Federal food stamps accomplish the same relief purposes today—and much more—so there is no welfare need for municipal machines now (Merton 1957: 193-194). Having grown in size since the New Deal, Sunbelt cities came of age in an era when welfare-oriented machine politics had been largely superceded so machines did not arise in them. Second, with the major exception of Mexicans, Sunbelt cities have attracted internal migrants of the middle class rather than the potpourri of ethnic minorities which created the social context of urban machine politics in the nineteenth and early twentieth centuries. Third, Sunbelt cities have continued to elect conservative slates pledged to limited government. The prevailing philosophy of limited government has inhibited the assumption of welfare functions, and thus contained the cost pressures which have contributed to municipal bankruptcy in Northeastern and Northcentral cities. Finally, Sunbelt states are low wage areas inhospitable to labor unions. Sunbelt cities have been able to hire cheap, non-union labor, thus reducing the cost of municipal government. Fifth, many Sunbelt cities are dominated by business elites who successfully resist political concessions to their municipal working class.

This Sunbelt-Frostbelt contrast highlights the political significance of urban poverty in a context of interlocal and interregional competition for growth. A capitalist economy rewards cities that ignore their indigent, undercut labor unions, and restrict municipal services. Such localities and regions are attractive to capital because taxes are low, labor cheap, and unions few. On the other hand, localities that provide a higher than prevailing standard of welfare for the indigent, acknowledge the legitimacy of municipal employee unions, and extend the range of government services for citizens are unattractive to capital because taxes are high and labor dear. When these conditions exist, businesses leave town and a city's tax base deteriorates. Ultimately, municipalities confront bankruptcy—the final signal that infrastructural expenses exceed revenues. At this point politicians must have the permission of bankers to govern, and this permission bankers grant only when municipal services are reduced, welfare programs slashed, and municipal unions restricted.

So long as fiscal issues remain local, insolvent municipal governments have little choice but to accept the political program imposed by bankers. A national urban policy is a political alternative, but the United States remains virtually unique among the world's industrial societies in lacking a positive urban policy (Fainstein and Fainstein 1978: 127-128). Yet some legal groundwork does already exist. The Demonstration Cities and Metropolitan Development Act of 1966 declares that "cities . . . do not have adequate resources to deal effectively with the critical problems facing them." Therefore, "Federal assistance is essential." But when bankruptcies occur, the federal government has no legislative basis for rendering assistance. In effect, federal urban policy is to permit bankers to ride herd on local governments, setting limits on how generously they may treat the indigent, how many public services they may offer, and how much municipal unionism they shall tolerate.

SOVIET URBAN POLITICS

Urban politics in the Soviet Union offer valuable points of comparison with the United States. In general, capitalist societies grant more political autonomy to cities than do communist societies. This discrepancy arises because local autonomy is a condition of market autonomy, and capitalist societies rely on a national market to allocate population and industries among competing cities. Of capitalist societies, the United States is the most extreme in the autonomy accorded municipalities (Markusen 1978: 93). Communist societies allocate population and resources by central plan rather than by free market, so they generally accord localities less autonomy than do capitalist societies. Among Communist societies, the Soviet Union is the most centralized. Its five-year plans (*Gosplans*) stipulate how many people each locality shall accommodate with required services, thus leaving very little for municipal authorities to decide. Admittedly, the Soviet Union is decentralizing its urban and regional planning and now accords municipalities responsibilities for construction, allocation, and administration of housing. Still, the Soviet Union is "highly centralized" and cities there have much less autonomy than they do in the United States (Frolic 1970: 689).

Western observers once regarded Soviet cities as totalitarian administrations under the rigid control of a local Communist Party [2]. Stalin described local governments as "transmission belts" linking the party and the masses, and his view of local government obviously did not assign much policymaking autonomy to local government. The role of local government in Stalin's vision was only to administer political decisions made in Moscow. No independent politics occurred at the municipal level. Current Western thinking about Soviet local government changed, partially because Soviet local government has changed since Stalin died. Urban politics does exist in the contemporary Soviet Union, but its bureaucratic forms are different from those in U.S. cities. Soviet urban politics are a "bureaucratic arena" in which municipal officeholders, the Communist Party, industrial managers, and municipal bureaucracy compete for power within the framework of a comprehensive national plan (Taubman 1973: 6). Bankruptcy is not a problem, but money is the central issue.

City soviets (city governments) consist of two branches: a large city council of deputies and an executive committee (*ispolkom*). A municipal ispolkom typically includes twenty-five persons some of whom are heads of municipal departments, some Communist Party officials, some delegates at large from the council of deputies. The ispolkom reports to its council of delegates, but it also reports to its executive counterpart at the highest level of government, usually a Soviet republic. This principle of "dual subordination" is intended to "blend central coordination with local initiative," and, to some extent, it succeeds (Taubman, 1973: 37).

Unlike U.S. cities, Soviet cities have few sources of local revenue and rely on money that the Gosplan allocates. In 1962 city soviets derived approximately 37 percent of total revenue from local sources, chiefly profits of municipal enterprises, taxes on automobiles, unions, and clubs, and fees for administrative services to citizens. Taxes on local sales and properties contributed less than 10 percent of municipal budgets in the Soviet Union, whereas New York City raised almost two thirds of its operating revenue from these taxes (Frolic 1976: 151–152). Soviet mayors contrast the reliability of their centrally authorized revenue with the uncertainty of municipal funding in the United States (Doroshinskaya 1977). Soviet cities are not bankrupt, so what, they ask, is the value of American municipal autonomy? (Frolic 1976: 151).

The fiscal soundness of Soviet cities is more apparent than real, however, because Moscow recurrently shortchanges most cities in order to strengthen heavy industry [3]. As a result, cities are chronically short of operating money, unable to provide adequate citizen services, and compelled to beg for donations from local industries. These industries are bureaucratically independent of the cities in which they locate and report to agencies of the Soviet government, thus rendering local coordination of city and industries extraordinarily difficult. The case of Magnitogorsk is admittedly extreme, but its problems exemplify those experienced with less severity by nearly all Soviet cities. Created in the 1930s as an industrial new town in the Urals, Magnitogorsk had become a medium-sized city by 1960, but the municipality controlled very little of the city's infrastructure. The Magnitogorsk Metallurgical Combine owned 52 percent of all housing in the locality and operated most municipal services, including electricity and mass transit. The Magnitogorsk Construction Trust owned another 24 percent of city housing, and a machine parts factory owned 8 percent. The remaining 16 percent of housing belonged to a variety of organizations including the Magnitogorsk city soviet, which owned 2 percent. Owning the electrical company, the Metallurgical Combine provided the city only its surplus power and routinely cut off city power when in need of electricity for production. When the city ispolkom approached the combine manager on behalf of Magnitogorsk, requesting more authority over housing, utilities, and transport, the manager jokingly disputed the existence of Magnitogorsk (Taubman 1973: 59). Only the combine really existed he jibed.

A decade of reform reduced this town-industry imbalance. The municipal ispolkom employed its political leverage to compel local industries to divest themselves of controlling authority over municipal infrastructure while donating new, industry-built facilities to the municipality. This success required effort because industries had motives to resist municipalization of their resources. However, the ispolkom convinced the local Communist Party that the municipality required control of its infrastructure in order to coordinate a rational distribution of services in the public interest. With party assistance, the municipality was able to obtain political concessions from economic notables operating in the city. Negotiations between municipality and big industry have been central issues of local politics in Magnitogorsk as in most Soviet municipalities. The city's ability to secure concessions is proof of the effectiveness as well as the existence of local politics. Nonetheless, in 1970 Magnitogorsk was still a "company town" where four heavy industries owned 65 percent of the housing supply, operated an inadequate water supply, and routinely ignored citizen complaints of inadequate service (Taubman 1973: 60).

The urban hierarchy sets up another set of political issues: cities of one size class compete for funding with cities of bigger and smaller classes; within size classes, individual cities compete for funds. Soviet cities receive central revenue in proportion to their perceived importance to national goals. Moscow and Leningrad are favored cities that the central government regards as showplaces of Communism (Sternheimer 1979: 408). Their infrastructures are adequately supported at national expense. But province capitals complain they receive less support than Moscow and Leningrad, and large cities complain they receive less than province capitals. Medium-sized cities are discontent with their share in relation to large cities, and small cities regard themselves as deprived in relation to medium-sized cities (Taubman 1973: 73). At the bottom of the heap, the district level towns obtain the scantiest allocations. The result of underfunding is inadequate infrastructure, and little can be done about it. Taubman (1973: 77) mentions the case of Aiaguz, a Kazakhstan city of 35,000 founded in 1939. The railroad administration owned its water supply, and service was inadequate. The railroad refused to improve service: too expensive. The municipal electricity system was also inadequate, so the Aiaguz city soviet appealed to the Kazakhstan council of ministers for appropriations to expand service. The republic ministry denied the city's petition, remarking that the needs of industry must come first. Having no independent resources, Aiaguz could not improve infrastructural services without higher authorization. When this authorization proved impossible to obtain, nothing more could be done locally. Those who did not wish to live in Aiaguz under these circumstances were, of course, free to leave, but permission to settle in well-serviced cities (such as Moscow or Leningrad) is virtually impossible to obtain. Realistically speaking, the choice of disgruntled citizens was Aiaguz or some other equally underserviced small town in the provinces.

Although Soviet cities are fiscally sound, spending no more than they take in as revenue, they achieve fiscal health by underproviding services for citizens:

housing, utilities, transportation, and so forth. One result is the impoverishment of daily life, and sotto voce grumbling among the citizenry. More serious is distorted urbanization of the whole country. Five-year plans have persistently imposed curbs on big city growth in favor of small- and medium-sized cities. These curbs have, indeed, restricted the growth of the largest cities to some extent (see Chapter 7), but the restrictions have been less effective than projected, and the largest cities have displayed a persistent tendency to grow larger than desired more rapidly than anticipated. Accordingly, the central plan's directives have been of little use in Soviet cities. By 1960 half of Soviet cities operated like capitalist cities independently of any national plan, and some big cities such as Kiev and Sverdlovsk even lacked urban plans. "Cities with plans found them more or less useless" (Taubman 1973: 22).

The reason was industries' preference for big cities . This preference arose from infrastructural starvation of smaller centers so new industries locating in them had to provide their own housing, utilities, transportation, and so on in order to have any. Providing municipal services in smaller cities required industries to allocate facilities to infrastructure, reducing their capacity to fulfill production quotas and thus to earn a bonus. By locating in big cities, industries could mask the infrastructural costs of production, leaving the city soviet to foot the bill for housing, educating, transporting, and otherwise servicing their workers. In this manner, ignored infrastructural costs produced distortions in Soviet urban planning to the extent that plans became useless. Only local politics provided some mechanism for dealing with the imbalances of industry and infrastructure in Soviet cities, but local politics had no formal role in Soviet government and often required illegal dealing to achieve local coordination.

COMMUNITY POWER STRUCTURES

Community power structures are decision-making networks in cities (Galaskiewicz 1979). A community power structure includes those who pull strings behind the scenes as well as the politicians they control. Therefore a community power structure may be wider than local government, although personnel from local government typically belong to it. An extensive literature on community power structures exists. By the middle 1970s, there were over 300 articles and books dealing with community power. Most treated community power in the United States, but a few international studies also exist. For the most part, community power studies are case studies of decision making in middle-sized cities "outside the direct influence of metropolitan centers" (Hawley and Svara 1972: 5).

Community power studies have attempted to penetrate the clichés of government in order to learn how decisions are really made. Two methods emerged: (1) the reputational method first advanced in a case study of Atlanta by Floyd Hunter (1953) and (2) its principal rival, the decisional method introduced in New Haven by Robert Dahl (1961). Reputational studies are concerned with latent power, the potential influence over a decision. Decisional studies concerned actual influence in a decision. The distinction proved important in theory and practice. Reputational studies exposed a core of leaders and key leaders by asking a panel of knowledgeable people, who are the community's most generally accepted leaders, and then asking the leaders to identify their leaders. Surprising unanimity of opinion appeared in response. Informants and leaders appeared to agree on a clique of upper-class men to whom all looked for decision making. Few leaders were government officials. In Atlanta, Hunter (1953) identified forty reputational leaders but only four of these were public officials. Most reputational leaders were bankers, attorneys, manufacturers, or other businessmen in the private sector.

Decisional studies tried to learn who was actually making decisions rather than who had a reputation for influence. To this end, they first identified key issues in the locality, then tried to learn who had been influential in reaching a decision in each. In New Haven, Dahl (1961) selected three local issues: education, urban renewal, and political nominations. He found that decision makers in one area were rarely influential in the other two. The major exceptions were public officials, especially the mayor, who was influential in all three decisions. Moreover, the various influentials did not emerge from a Yankee upper class but reflected instead a variety of status levels. Distinguishing economic and social notables, Dahl found neither group had much "direct influence" on government policy-making.

Reputational studies following Dahl tended to confirm his results, and the image of community power emerging from such studies obtained the label pluralism in acknowledgment of the plurality of interest leaders who actually affected decisions. In contrast, the reputational studies suggested an elitist image of community decision making by businessmen operating in the shadows. Sociologists studying community power typically employed reputational methods and obtained elitist results, whereas political scientists studying the same phenomenon employed decisional methods and obtained pluralist results.

Pluralist and elitist studies yielded divergent pictures of how municipalities in America are ruled. Bonjean and Olson (1964) have distinguished four points of systematic difference in this respect. First, elitists claimed the decision makers were illegitimate because they lacked public or associational office. Pluralists stressed the primacy of elected officials in decision making and found no improprieties in this situation. Second, elitists claimed that those actually making decisions were backroom cliques unknown to the general public. Pluralists found that the real decision makers were also well known to the general public. Third, elitists asserted the illegitimate and invisible decision-making network was also a cohesive unit of intermarrying, socially acquainted upper-class families. Pluralists found, in contrast, that the real decision makers sprang from a variety of status levels, and religious and ethnic backgrounds, and these leaders did not engage in purely social interactions with one another. Fourth, elitists depicted an influence network whose members exerted power over every important issue. On the other hand, pluralists found that, except for key elected officials, those influential in one area were rarely influential in others.

How can one reconcile these divergent results? Conceivably, reputational and decisional methodologies yield different conclusions. This possibility attracted considerable discussion as pluralists and elitists attempted to demonstrate that the other's methodologies were faulty. Pluralists won the first round. Wolfinger (1960) proposed that reputational methods substituted side-of-the-mouth low down based on folklore for solid evidence. Another pluralist, Polsby (1960a, 1960b) reexamined the Lynds' *Middletown,* an elitist classic, and concluded their evidence did not support an elitist conclusion. Elitists have returned the methodological criticism. Reexamining data from Dahl's New Haven study, a pluralist classic, Domhoff (1978) located an upper-class elite manipulating politicians. Utilizing documentary sources unavailable to Dahl, Domhoff developed evidence that an upper-class network linking Yale University, the Chamber of Commerce, and the Manufacturers' Association had secretly controlled the politicians who formally made urban renewal decisions. This document encouraged the elitist conclusion that New Haven politicians were really lackeys of behind-the-scenes business interests. Domhoff also disputed Dahl's distinction between social and business elites on the grounds that Dahl had derived his social elite from too narrow a group. Specifically, Dahl had identified the social elite with invitation lists to debutante cotillions and found these lists overlapped little with top business leadership. However, when Domhoff examined membership lists of exclusive clubs in New Haven, he found social elite and business elite converged and overlapped at this level [4].

Conceivably, pluralist-elitist divergences of result have arisen because cities differ: some cities have elites who dictate everything; others have pluralistic participation. Although methodological issues are still unsettled, this eclectic possibility is safer than the alternative supposition that all cities everywhere are equally pluralist or equally elitist. For example, Boston, Philadelphia, and Charleston do have patrician upper classes based on old wealth and social register listings. In contrast, Houston and Los Angeles have self-made millionaires who struck it rich in movies, pizza, oil, or automobile dealerships. Some Western business tycoons sport gold teeth, cowboy hats, and Ozark accents; it is no wonder their cities do not publish a social register. Substantial research has, in fact, assumed that local power structures differ, and sought to "identify community characteristics" determining pluralist or elitist power systems. A number of empirical generalizations have emerged. Clark's (1975) secondary analysis of decision making in fifty-one cities found a consistent relationship between size

Table 16-5. Power Structure and Community Characteristics

Community Characteristic	Pluralist	Elitist
Population		
Big	X	
Small		X
Economy		
One industry		X
Diversified	X	
Voluntary associations		
Few		X
Many	X	
Labor unions		
Few		X
Many	X	
Elite attitudes		
Favor pluralism	X	
Favor elitism		X
Political structure		
Partisan elections	X	
Nonpartisan elections		X
Social composition		
Heterogeneous	X	
Homogeneous		X

of city and power structure: smaller communities tended toward elitism and larger ones toward pluralism. Industrial diversification is another influence. In general, one-industry towns are elitist and multi-industry towns pluralist. This relationship extends to ethnic minorities, which tend to be pluralist when their industrial bases are diversified and elitist when they rely on a single industry (Light and Wong 1975). A well-developed associational life, labor unions, partisan elections, heterogeneous social composition, and nonexclusive elite attitudes are additional factors tending to encourage pluralism in community power structure. Table 16-5 summarizes these empirical relationships.

COMMUNITY POWER IN INTERNATIONAL PERSPECTIVE

Most of the research on community power structures has provided case studies of North American cities in the mid-twentieth century. The historical and comparative limitations of this perspective are obvious. How do North American results compare with what exists currently elsewhere in the world and with what once existed in North America? Miller (1970) has provided what remains the most systematic effort to obtain results for the comparative side of this question. He conducted community power research using conventional methodologies in four cities: Lima, Peru; Cordoba, Argentina; Bristol, United Kingdom; and Seattle, United States. In each city he utilized decisional and reputational methods to isolate a "top" leadership and a "key" leadership consisting of leaders' leaders. The results of this comparative analysis showed much international variation but generally indicated the preeminence of business leaders in a pluralist framework.

Miller found "no single solitary elite structure" and no institutional hegemony in any city. In all four cities, the community power structure included leaders from a variety of institutional spheres who vied for influence on local issues. Table 16-6 ranks the five most influential institutional spheres in the four cities. The plurality of spheres represented in this list tends to support a pluralist model of local power structures, and Miller's analysis of Seattle, read in isolation, would also warrant this interpretation. On the other hand, private business enterprise ranked first, second, or third in influence in every city. Its average rank was second, and only local government slightly exceeded this average rank. The average rank of labor unions was fourth, significantly below business and local government. This was even true in Bristol, where the Labour Party had controlled municipal government since 1926. The universal preponderance of business class leadership was further indicated in Miller's comparison of top and key leaders, the latter a superelite consisting of leaders' leaders. In every city except Lima, business class leaders were more influential in key leadership than in top leadership, and business class leaders were the largest single key leadership bloc in every city except Lima (Miller 1970: 220, 222), As one might expect, the predominance of business leaders in key leadership was great-

Table 16-6. Relative Power Rankings of the Five Most Influential Institutions in Seattle, Bristol, Cordoba, and Lima

Rank	Seattle, USA	Bristol, U.K.	Cordoba, Argentina	Lima, Peru
1	Business and finance	Local government	Catholic church	Local government
2	Local government	Business and finance	Business and finance	Political parties
3	Labor unions	Political parties	Local government	Business and finance
4	Mass communication	Labor unions	Labor unions	Military
5	Education	Education	Military	Labor unions

Source: Delbert C. Miller, *International Community Power Structures* (Bloomington: Indiana University Press, 1970), p. 205. Copyright 1970: Indiana University Press. Reproduced by permission.

est in Seattle, where two thirds of key leaders (but only one third of top leaders) were engaged in business or finance. Organized labor and its political party was the largest countervailing force to "economic power" in all four cities, but this countervailing force always ranked lower than business.

Taubman's (1973) analysis of Soviet urban government reached conclusions surprisingly similar to those of Miller. The prevailing interpretation of Soviet local government has emphasized the power monopoly of the local Communist Party, a self-proclaimed representative of all the people that tolerates no electoral opposition. However, the realities of local politics involved interbureau competition among ispolkom, municipal departments, industry, and the Communist Party. The conflict of reds and experts has been as prominent in Soviet local government as in other areas of Soviet life (Sternheimer 1975; Lane 1976: Ch. 5). The Communist Party did not, in fact, exercise dictatorial control over Soviet local government. Goldfarb (1978) has also observed that independent political expression in communist societies persists in veiled forms despite the suppression of interparty competition for power. Three sources support this independent political power: the high culture of prerevolutionary Russia (of whom Alexander Solzhenitsyn may be taken as fairly representative); internal contradictions of communist societies; and the cultural institutions of the communist societies, especially universities and the media. Are Soviet cities pluralistic or elitist in power arrangements? The answer depends on what test is employed. American pluralists have declared that an elitist power structure exists when any small, well-defined group always gets its way on contested issues. On this basis, Dahl and Polsby have rejected the claim that an elite of businessmen surreptitiously controls city government in American cities. But applied to Soviet cities, the same test (Taubman 1973: 111-112) indicates there is no elite in Soviet urban politics either. On the other hand, in most Soviet cities (excluding Moscow and Leningrad) the single greatest influence on local government is top management of industrial organizations. Organized labor has next to no influence. Of course, these Soviet managers are not representatives of capitalism, but they do represent an exogenous and preponderant economic source of political influence in the communist world.

POLICY OUTPUTS

Policy outputs are government directives, the products of prior processing through a pluralist or elitist power system (Smith 1979). Alford (1967: 266) has distinguished long-range and short-range influences upon policy outputs. The long-range influences are social structure and culture of a locality. Short-range influences are situations arising in response to events. In his comprehensive review, Clark (1975: 283) distinguishes "incrementalist" and "external" approaches to policy output. External approaches have deemphasized local leadership on the assumption that community characteristics and/or societal pressures leave local leaders little leeway for independence. According to this assumption, pluralism or elitism of power system affects output little because policy outputs depend closely on contingencies external and prior to leadership action. A version of externalism is the observation that a capitalist economy pressures municipal officials to reduce public welfare expenditures, narrow the range of public services, and restrict municipal employee labor unions. In this example, a capitalist economy is an external cause and local welfare policy its presumptive effect. Given this capitalist economic context, one might argue, the elitist or pluralist character of local government would have no policy effect since any government must adjust welfare policy to market pressures.

Efforts to demonstrate a political effect on local policy output have shown how relatively unimportant local politics is. Of course, the importance of local politics depends on how much autonomy national urban policy awards municipalities. In extreme cases, localities have no autonomy at all, and local politics are only national politics in microcosm (Clark 1975: 290). Nevertheless, there is international and comparative evidence of local political effects even in centrally planned societies. Without challenging the primacy of external constraints and community characteristics, incrementalists have shown that under certain conditions local politics can make an independent contribution to policy outcomes. Regional differences in policy output tend to support the incrementalist view. For example, New York City's general expenditures per capita were nearly seven times greater than those of Dallas in 1974–1975 (Table 16-3). Yet these two cities operate in the same national political environment and the same capitalist economy. Therefore, intercity budget differences presumably reflect municipal characteristics, and there is presumptive grounds for supposing that municipal government is an important contributor.

Aiken and Alford (1974) examined community characteristics bearing on policy output of 676 U.S. cities of 25,000 population or more. The policy outputs they studied were participation-nonparticipation, speed of participation, and the extent of participation of local governments in federally supported public housing, urban renewal, and War on Poverty programs. They found "dramatic differences" in regional participation. They also learned that local community characteristics of cities affected policy output independently of regional location. In general, program participation was greatest in big old cities with low-income, poorly educated citizens, Democratic voting habits, small governments, high unemployment, and low in-migration. City government form made little difference, but Aiken and Alford did conclude that "level of deprivation" was not the only influence on these policy outputs. Decentralized, pluralistic communities with stable interorganizational relationships appeared most capable of program innovation, and these determinants of policy output were independent of demographic characteristics of the cities. The role that Aiken and Alford accord to local government is modest, but more than negligible.

POLICY IMPACTS AND URBAN PROTEST

Policy impacts are effects of policy outputs on citizen awareness. These impacts begin with fiscal authorizations as, for example, a municipal decision to spend tax money on garbage collection, education, police and fire protection, sewers, or social welfare. The next step is government performance. Performance translates authorized budget into services delivered (e.g., tons of refuse collected per $1,000 expended). Performances may be objectively effective or ineffective, but the policy impact of a performance is how citizens evaluate it. One can imagine objectively effective municipal government performance that does not satisfy the citizens, and objectively inadequate performance that does. Citizen evaluation is the issue.

In the aftermath of ghetto disorders of 1967, the National Advisory Commission on Civil Disorders compared citizen satisfaction with municipal services in fifteen major U.S. cities. The commission divided the fifteen cities into big-riot, small-riot, and no-riot cities in the expectation that intercity differences in services would explain rioting. Police, welfare, education, hiring, and retail trade were the sectors in which investigators expected to find intercity differences in treatment of blacks. As expected, the research did expose intercity differences in treatment of blacks. The police forces of some cities brutally violated the civil rights of black citizens. In other cities the police were sympathetic to black protests and respectful of civil liberties. Blacks were also aware of these intercity differences and praised or blamed local institutions accordingly. In general, the treatment of blacks in American cities depended on the proportion of blacks in the local electorate. Cities with large black electorates treated blacks well, whereas cities with small proportions of black voters were indifferent to black demands (Rossi et al. 1974: 8).

These intercity differences, however, were "simply not related" to rioting in 1967 and 1968. In all the evidence gathered, "no differences could be shown" in the treatment of local blacks among cities whether or not they had civil disorders (Rossi et al. 1974: 6). These results suggested the riots resulted from dissatisfactions, such as unemployment, independent of and not subject to the control of local government. Banfield (1974) argued that riots resulted from the preponderance of riot-prone individuals in the black population, a population characteristic. This preponderance reflected the rural-urban migration of Southern blacks as a result of which, Banfield argued, a volatile, violent, lower-class culture prevailed in the ghetto. Banfield expected the experience of city life to pacify lower-class blacks as it had pacified lower-class Irish, rural-urban migrants of a preceding generation. A related view held that riot-prone blacks were socially disorganized rural-urban migrants suffering anomic shock from the experience of city living. The social disorganization theory was situational rather than cultural but agreed with Banfield that rural-urban migrants ought to be more riot-prone than urban-born blacks.

However, this expectation suffered successive disconfirmations in research [5]. Contrary to expectation, blacks most likely to riot were urban-born. Rural-born blacks were less likely than urban-born blacks to riot and more likely to have steady jobs. In this sense, evidence exposed a connection between riot-proneness and employment, and between migration and riot-proneness. But the connections were complex and counterintuitive. In general, rural-born blacks were more willing than urban-born blacks to accept low-grade manual work at low wages. A higher proportion of urban-born blacks were unwilling to perform low-wage work but unable to obtain any other kind of employment. Urban-born blacks were more prepared than rural-born blacks to engage in violent political protests against their economic alternatives (*Manpower Report* 1974: 97-98). Marginal workers were riot-prone, but economic marginality reflected the *unwillingness* to perform low-wage manual labor rather than a shortage of low-wage jobs. This surprising situation was compatible with the view that socialization in a big city taught urban-born blacks to reject low-wage manual work while registering their rejection with violent political protests that the country-born eschewed.

FRANCE, 1830-1957

These U.S. results correspond well with what Tilly (1974) discovered about municipal riots in France between 1830 and 1957. To test the theory of social disorganization and anomie, Tilly compiled a list of collective disorders in France over more than one century. If these disorders resulted from urbanization, he reasoned, then rates of disorder in a locality ought to increase with urbanization. Tilly's data showed that riots did center in big cities. He also found a roller-coaster pattern of variation in rioting over time. In some years many riots occurred, in others none. However, his data did not indicate any correspondence between urbanization and riot frequency. The "swings of collective violence" did not correspond with rate of urban population growth. Tilly (1974: 99) also found "no relationship at all" between the volume of in-migration in a city and the frequency of rioting there. Arrest records of the Paris police also showed no overrepresentation of migrants among those jailed in the rioting of 1848. These results suggested that riots did not reflect social disorganization attendant upon rural-urban migration. The strongest correlate of local rioting in France was national political crisis. Many local riots occurred in the revolutionary years of 1830 and 1848. Summarizing his data, Tilly concluded that urban rioting in France depended on a coincidence of national and local circumstances. A national political crisis was a triggering event, but riots in a city depended on the existence of a seasoned proletariat sufficiently organized to raise a collective response to the political crisis. In this sense, city life contributed organization (not disorganization) to the resident working class, and this organization facilitated instrumental use of disorder to register political protest.

THIRD WORLD CITIES

When riots erupted in cities of France and the United States in the period 1967-1970, political elites in Third World cities feared their slums would quickly follow suit. After all, cities of the Third World contained and still contain much larger proportions of indigent migrants than do cities of the developed world. In the 1960s, approximately one quarter of the population of Mexico City, Manila, and Djakarta, and one half of the population of Ankara and Lima resided in self-built shantytowns on the periphery of the city. An additional proportion resided in central city slum tenements. Twenty to 40 percent of the metropolitan labor force in these cities also consisted of the unemployed or the marginal self-employed. Metropolitan indigents of the Third World live in squalor indescribably worse than in the developed world and also encounter in their daily rounds conditions of upper-class existence as good as the best in Paris or Chicago. If rural-urban migration and slums produced violent political protest, then Third World cities ought to experience more extensive protests than European or U.S. cities.

However, revolutionary protests have not arisen in the slums of Third World cities. In the aftermath of these predicted nonevents, researchers have concluded that earlier depictions of insurrectionary slums were romantic misperceptions. True, the urban poor still express cynicism and disgruntlement about local politics, but they have not challenged the political system they mistrust. The explanation of this incongruity has centered on a distinction between slums of hope and slums of despair (Lloyd 1979: 1). Slums of despair arise when slum residents have lost faith in their ability to improve their future. Slums of hope contain slum dwellers who, rightly or wrongly, believe that the future will adequately reward their economic striving. In slums of hope, the residents attend to the daily work of making a living and improving their homes, with only occasional reformist ventures into politics. In the 1970s, social science accounts of slum life in the Third World stressed their "vitality, achievement, and petit bourgeois conservatism" (Lloyd 1979: 32). These were slums of hope. In reflection of this reality, Third World political elites changed their attitude toward shantytowns once viewed as dangerous nodules of plebeian revolt. Instead of bulldozing away these shantytowns and sending riot police to disperse the wretched inhabitants, Third World politicians increasingly acknowledged the shantytown's right to exist and established liaisons with local leaders.

Land tenure rights and infrastructural services are key political issues in Third World shantytowns. Shantytown residents have built their shacks on private or public land to which they have no legal title. As their city expands, this land increases in value. Shantytown residents want local politicians to recognize that they have legal title to the land they occupy, and local politicians utilize this desire as a lever to control the political behavior of shantytown residents. Residents who cause trouble have their homes bulldozed away by police riot squads. Those who vote for the local boss can hope to receive recognition of their land titles and therewith property rights over a piece of valuable urban real estate. The same reciprocation governs municipal services. Shantytown residents pay no taxes and receive no services. However, the residents very much wish to acquire paved streets, police and fire protection, sewers, piped water, garbage collection, and electricity. Slums that support local politicians receive some infrastructural services in return. The politicians thus acquire the political support of the slum dwellers. As infrastructural services improve and title recognition looms, shantytown dwellers acquire an incentive to improve their shanties (Lloyd 1979: 26). In Lima, Peru, for example, some twenty-year-old shantytowns have become established neighborhoods "with good quality houses" and regular municipal services. This transformation is the slum dwellers' aspiration: beginning with only a self-made shanty on an illegally occupied site, they have acquired in a generation legal title to a decent home in a regularly serviced neighborhood.

Yet daily life in slums of hope has a violent side too. Cornelius (1975) has provided a clear picture of grass roots politics in six slums of Mexico City. The pivotal relationship is a paternalistic link between the neighborhood's *cacique* (boss) and a municipal politician in the Institutional Revolutionary Party (PRI), Mexico's dominant party. The local cacique is a self-proclaimed leader whose authority depends on thugs. Caciques negotiate with PRI politicians for municipal services and normalization of land titles. In return for these services, they "tax" slum residents, and their thugs oversee the collection. Any who resist are beaten, killed, or their homes are burned. The private terrorism seems incredible, but shantytowns do not receive regular municipal services—including police protection. Caciques are notoriously crooked, and slum dwellers make cynical references to their shameless greed. However, Cornelius (1975: 153) observes that the authority of caciques depends in the long run on their ability to obtain real benefits for the slum dwellers they tax. Caciques are permitted to steal so long as they "get things done."

URBAN SOCIAL MOVEMENTS

Urban social movements can be classified according to system effects, manifest content, or intergroup alliances. Castells (1977a: 263) has chosen system effects, defining an urban social movement as social practices tending toward "structural transformation" of an urban system or "substantial change" in the balance of class power. Thus defined, an urban social movement creates a revolutionary change. Therefore Castells identifies protest movements and participation movements to accommodate less dramatic changes. Reform movements obtain an independent change in one element of an urban system (say, housing or police protection) without changes in other elements. Participation movements create an appearance of popular involvement in order to perpetuate a political status quo. Participation movements are commonplace trappings of political parties that need legitimation. Requiring "maximal feasible participation" of the poor, Lyndon Johnson's War on Poverty is a familiar example (Alford and Friedland 1975: 455). In the opinion of Castells, single-issue local movements are reform movements unless they begin to link their local problem with "contradictions" in other spheres of capitalist society. For example, a movement of the homeless to demand housing aims at a social reform until the homeless people begin to link their homelessness with other class-linked contradictions of the capitalist system such as unemployment. When contradictions are linked, what began as a local movement of municipal reform can become a revolutionary social movement.

Walton (1979) has classified urban social movements on the basis of intergroup alliances, not effects. In his lexicon, an urban protest movement is locally based on a marginal population. Such a movement is small and weak and cannot achieve much. A reform movement unites the marginal population and the local working class. Such an alliance has the power to achieve reforms. A revolutionary movement unites marginals, urban workers, and peasants against the society's ruling class. Such a movement has the capability of overthrowing a government and installing a wholly new social system. Walton does not clarify the issues around which such alliances might coalesce, but it is clear that on a scale of difficulty a revolutionary movement is the most difficult to achieve and a protest the easiest.

Borja (1977) classified urban social movements on the basis of objectives, of which he distinguished five basic types: environmental defense, rejection of redevelopment, housing movements, facilities-demanding movements, and movements of resistance to public works. Environmental defense is local efforts to prevent degradation of air, water, or soil. The local protest against the Three

Mile Island nuclear power plant is exemplary. Movements of redevelopment rejection arise when neighborhoods attempt to prevent urban renewal. Housing movements bring together people who need improved housing to demand public intervention on their behalf. Resistance to public works produces a local political movement whose members share a common interest in preventing a disruptive highway, airport, or other big project slated for their neighborhood. In terms of personnel, all such movements typically bring together coalitions of working- and middle-class people with "occasional support from advanced capitalist groups." They are generally of "a democratic nature," but Borja (1977: 210) does not suppose they must advance beyond the reformist phase. On his account, movement life cycle begins with mobilization, proceeds to permanency, then to legal recognition of associative identity, and ends with a vested interest in the political order. Hence, reform movements do not beget revolutionary movements.

Castells (1976) has argued that urban social movements are the only source of political change in cities. This argument depends, Pickvance (1976: 207) has noted, on the assumption that municipal authorities never grant concessions, even minor ones, unless they confront a revolutionary movement. Additionally, Marxist scholars stress the efficacy of noninstitutional political actions. These are illegal political actions such as violent demonstrations, sit-ins, or armed insurrection.

"Participation through normal institutionalized channels has little impact on the substance of government policies" (Alford and Friedland 1975: 472). The futility of institutional politics in bourgeois societies reflects, in this view, the systemic power of the capitalist class. *Systemic power* exists where economic actors control government policy simply by virtue of the economic resources they control (1975: 473). As the case of New York City shows, bankers and industrialists are the final arbiters of metropolitan policies, and they have this systemic power by virtue of their economic resources rather than because of elective office [6].

Admittedly violence is politically effective, and according to Gamson (1975), it always has been. But it is, for all that, unclear that noninstitutional social movements are the only sources of urban political change or that political change occurs only when noninstitutional social movements compel concessions. Referring to Olives's (1976) analysis of sixteen urban social movements in Paris, Pickvance (1976: 209) observes that only nine were successful. Of these, all but two involved local mobilization utilizing noninstitutional political action. However, two movements produced political effects without mobilizing the base population for noninstitutional direct action. These concessions were admittedly reforms, but their efficacy belies the claim that noninstitutional social movements are the only way to produce urban political changes. Even in France, a centralized, bureaucratic state, urban systems display some flexibility and are sometimes able to assimilate citizen protests.

Conversely, violent social movements do not invariably produce meaningful urban change. For example, the spectacular ghetto disorders of the late 1960s in the United States constituted a noninstitutional social movement of the black underclass. But this social movement did not effect "a structural transformation" of the American urban system in Castells' terminology. Social conditions in American inner cities are no better if not worse now than they were in 1967. It is even arguable that the violent protests alienated the white working class and thus precluded a reform coalition that might have been capable of effecting a meaningful reduction of unemployment, crime, pollution, welfare dependency, and other serious problems of American inner cities (Fainstein and Fainstein 1974: 233-234).

European Marxists have contributed most of the recent literature on urban social movements (Castells 1976). Drawing on European experience, these scholars have given the impression that the working class sponsors such movements. However, the middle class has provided the mobilized base for urban social movements in the United States in the last decade. One such movement is the antibusing movement (Useem 1980). This middle-class social movement has been highly successful despite the principally institutional politics in which supporters engaged. Tax limitation movements also mobilize middle-class taxpayers, not slum dwellers. In 1978 California voters overwhelmingly approved an initiative measure (proposition 13) drastically reducing property taxes on single-family homes. This campaign was financed by big business and real estate dealers, its chief beneficiaries, but the popular basis was the home-owning middle class, representing 64 percent of California's population and about 80 percent of its voters. This middle-class social movement was quite successful in its political objective, even though it utilized only institutional tactics.

SUMMARY

In the United States, the Soviet Union, Europe, Mexico, and most Third World countries, urban politics center upon balancing population, infrastructure, and industry. Underserviced city residents want expensive municipal services, but cities do not always have the capability to pay for these services. In noncommunist societies, economically marginal people typically want municipal services whose cost falls on their employed neighbors. City governments have to balance the needs of different groups, and they reach out to national governments for the financial wherewithal when local solutions are impossible. National governments have to balance the claims of cities against competing interests. As a result municipal politics are not really local. Solutions to the most chronic and serious problems of cities (unemployment, for example) require cities to affect national policy. Therefore changes are hard to obtain at the local level, and those who protest a single issue locally are likely to encounter big obstacles.

City problems thus require urban social movements for effective action in most cases. One reason is the primacy of economic notables in local power structures. This primacy is not invariant or monolithic, but it is the usual situation, and where it exists an obstacle is interposed between popular demands and their political satisfaction at the local level. Urban social movements link people in different cities who share a particular kind of problem. When mobilized in a supralocal social movement, these people are more likely to overcome vested interests opposing them at the local and national level. However, in attempting to effect modest changes in local conditions, the participants in a social movement may become aware of the extent to which the specific reform they seek requires a reshuffling of national political alignments. For example, protests against pollution of the Niagara Falls region runs up against the political representation of the needs of industry, and solving the regional problems of Niagara Falls requires reconsideration of fundamental national policies affecting cities in the United States. In this scenario what began as a pragmatic effort to resolve a local problem proceeds to the mobilization of a supralocal social movement whose participants experience enhancement of political consciousness in the course of their protest.

NOTES

1. Many leftist attacks on suburbia make it sound very attractive: "Its small scale and political independence has [sic] offered suburban residents a measure of control over their social and economic environment which was impossible to achieve in the city." Patrick J. Ashton, "The Political Economy of Suburban Development," pp. 64-69, in William Tabb and Larry Sawers, *Marxism and the Metropolis.* New York: Oxford, 1978. What's wrong with control over one's environment? Would anyone who had it want to give it up?
2. The orthodox view: "The USSR is a one-party state in which the Communist Party of the Soviet Union holds a monopoly position and directs the operations of government at all levels." Arthur S. Banks, ed., "Union of Soviet Socialist Republics," in *Political Handbook of the World: 1977.* New York. McGraw-Hill, 1977.
3. This problem receives attention at the highest party levels: "Some time ago the Political Bureau of the CPSU served a strict warning to ministers who allowed a serious lag between housing construction and the construction of industrial facilities." Address of Leonid Brezhnev, Plenary Meeting of the Central Committee of the CPSU, on October 21, 1980. See *Soviet Life* November 1980.

4. Charles Bonjean's review of Domhoff offers a valuable critique of the entire community power literature: *Contemporary Sociology* 8(1979): 199–201.
5. For a review of the literature on urban riots in the 1960s, see Alford and Friedland (1975: 464–471).
6. See the remarks of Cleveland's Mayor Dennis Kucinich in a newspaper interview: Robert Scheer, "Kucinich Sees His Role as Cleveland's Protector," *Los Angeles Times,* February 12, 1979, pt. I, P. 1. Subsequently Kucinich was defeated in his reelection effort, and a banker-approved candidate came to power in the insolvent city.

REFERENCES

Aiken, Michael, and Robert R. Alford. 1974. "Community Structure and Innovation: Public Housing, Urban Renewal, and the War on Poverty," pp. 231–287, in Terry N. Clark, ed. *Comparative Community Politics.* New York: Wiley.

Alford, Robert R. 1967. "The Comparative Study of Local Politics," pp. 263–302, in Leo F. Schnore, ed. *Social Science and the City.* New York: Praeger.

Alford, Robert R., and Roger Friedland. 1975. "Political Participation and Public Policy." *Annual Review of Sociology* 1: 429–479.

Bahl, Roy. 1978. "The Fiscal Problems of Declining Areas," pp. 268–280, in U.S. Congress, House of Representatives, 95th Congress, 2nd Sess, Select Committee on Population. *Consequences of Changing U.S. Population,* No. 11. Washington, D.C.: U.S. Government Printing Office.

Banfield, Edward C. 1974. *The Unheavenly City Revisited.* Boston: Little, Brown.

Berry, Brian J. L., and John D. Kasarda. 1977. *Contemporary Human Ecology.* New York: Macmillan.

Bonjean, Charles, and David M. Olson. 1964. "Community Leadership: Directions of Research." *Administrative Science Quarterly* 8: 291–300.

Borja, Jordi. 1977. "Urban Movements in Spain," pp. 187–211, in Michael Harloe, ed. *Captive Cities.* London: Wiley.

Castells, Manuel. 1976. "Theoretical Propositions for an Experimental Study of Urban Movements." Ch. 6 in C. G. Pickvance, ed. Urban Sociology: Critical Essays. New York: St. Martin's Press.

——. 1977a. *The Urban Question.* Trans. Alan Sheridan. Cambridge: MIT Press.

——. 1977b. "Toward a Political Urban Sociology," pp. 61–77, in Michael Harloe, ed. *Captive Cities.* New York: Wiley.

Clark, Dennis. 1980. "The Expansion of the Public Sector and Irish Economic Development," pp. 177–190, in Scott Cummings, ed. *Self-Help in Urban America.* Pt. Washington, N.Y.: Kennikat Press.

Clark, Terry N. 1975. "Community Power." *Annual Review of Sociology* 1: 271–295.

Cohen, Henry. 1976. "Governing Megacentropolis: The Constraints," pp. 497–507, in Paul Meadows and Ephraim Mizruchi, eds. *Urbanism, Urbanization, and Change: Comparative Perspectives.* 2nd ed. Reading, Mass.: Addison Wesley.

Cornelius, Wayne A. 1975. *Politics and the Migrant Poor in Mexico City.* Stanford: Stanford University Press.

Dahl, Robert A. 1961. *Who Governs? Democracy and Power in an American City.* New Haven: Yale University Press.

Domhoff, G. William. 1978. *Who Really Rules? New Haven Community Power Reexamined.* Santa Monica, Calif.: Goodyear.

Doroshinskaya, Yelena. 1977. "Leningrad's Budget." *Soviet Union* No. 325: 27ff.

Fainstein, Norman I., and Susan S. Fainstein. 1974. *Urban Political Movements.* Englewood Cliffs, N.J.: Prentice-Hall.

Fainstein, Susan S., and Norman I. Fainstein. 1978. "National Policy and Urban Development." *Social Problems* 26: 125–146.

Friedland, Roger. 1981. *Power and Crisis in the Central City.* London: Macmillan.

Frolic, B. Michael. 1970. "The Soviet Study of Soviet Cities." *Journal of Politics* 32: 675–695.

——. 1976. "Noncomparative Communism: Chinese and Soviet Urbanization," pp. 149–161, in Mark G. Field, ed. *Social Consequences of Modernization in Communist Societies.* Baltimore: John Hopkins University Press.

Galaskiewicz, Joseph. 1979. "The Structure of Community Organization Networks." *Social Forces* 57: 1346–1364.

Gamson, William A. 1975. *The Strategy of Social Protest.* Homewood, Ill.: Dorsey Press.

Goldfarb, Jeffrey C. 1978. "Social Bases of Independent Public Expression in Communist Societies." *American Journal of Sociology* 83: 920–930.

Harris, Chauncey D., and Edward L. Ulman. 1945. "The Nature of Cities." *Annals of the American Academy of Political and Social Sciences* 242: 7–17.

Hawley, William D., and James H. Svara. 1972. *The Study of Community Power: A Bibliographic Review.* Santa Barbara Calif.: ABC–Clio.

Hunter, Floyd. 1953. *Community Power Structure.* Chapel Hill: University of North Carolina.

Lane, David. 1976. *The Socialist Industrial State.* Boulder Col.: Westview Press.

Liebert, Roland J. 1976. *Disintegration and Political Action: The Changing Functions of City Governments in America.* New York: Academic Press.

Light, Ivan H. and Charles Choy Wong. 1975. "Protest or Work: Dilemmas of the Tourist Industry in American Chinatowns." *American Journal of Sociology* 80: 1342–1368.

Lineberry, Robert L., and Ira Sharkansky. 1978. *Urban Politics and Public Policy.* 3rd ed. New York: Harper & Row.

Lloyd, Peter. 1979. *Slums of Hope? Shanty Towns of the Third World.* New York: St. Martins Press.

Logan, John R. 1978. "Growth, Politics, and the Stratification of Places." *American Journal of Sociology* 84: 404–416.

Lojkine, Jean. 1977. "Big Firms' Strategies, Urban Policy, and Urban Social Movements," pp. 141-156, in Michael Harloe, ed. *Captive Cities*. London: Wiley.

Lowi, Theodore. 1976. "Machine Politics and the Legacy of Reform," pp. 535-542, in Paul Meadows and Ephraim Mizruchi, eds. *Urbanism, Urbanization, and Change: Comparative Perspectives,* 2nd ed. Reading, Mass.: Addison-Wesley.

Lynd, Robert S., and Helen M. 1929. *Middletown*. New York: Harcourt.

———. 1937. *Middletown in Transition*. New York: Harcourt.

Manpower Report of the President. 1974. "The New Geography of Employment: Migration and the American Worker," pp 69-99. Washington, D.C.: U.S. Government Printing Office.

Markusen, Ann R. 1978. "Class and Urban Social Expenditure: A Marxist Theory of Metropolitan Government," pp. 90-111, in Willam Tabb and Larry Sawers, eds. *Marxism and the Metropolis*. New York: Oxford University Press.

McKenzie, R. D. 1933. *The Metropolitan Community*. New York: McGraw Hill.

Merton, Robert K. 1957. *Social Theory and Social Structure,* rev. ed. New York: Free Press.

Miller, Delbert C. 1970. *International Community Power Structure*. Bloomington: Indiana University Press.

Newton, Kenneth. 1978. "Conflict Avoidance and Conflict Suppression: The Case of Urban Politics in the United States," pp. 76-93, in Kevin Cox, ed. *Urbanization and Conflict in Market Societies*. Chicago: Maaroofa Press.

O'Connor, James. 1973. *The Fiscal Crisis of the State*. New York: St. Martin's Press.

Olives, Jose. 1976. "The Struggle Against Urban Renewal in the 'Cité d' Aliarte (Paris),' " pp. 174-197, in C. G. Pickvance, ed. *Urban Sociology: Critical Essays*. New York: St. Martin's Press.

Pickvance, C. G. 1976. "On the Study of Urban Social Movements," pp. 198-218, in C. G. Pickvance, ed. *Urban Sociology: Critical Essays*. New York: St. Martin's Press.

Polsby, Nelson W. 1960a. "How to Study Community Power: The Pluralist Alternative." *Journal of Politics* 22: 474-484.

———. 1960b. "Power in Middletown: Fact and Value in Community Research." *Canadian Journal of Economic and Political Science* 26: 592-603.

Portes, Alejandro, and John Walton. 1976. *Urban Latin America: The Political Condition from Above and Below*. Austin: University of Texas Press.

Report of the National Advisory Commission on Civil Disorders. 1968. Washington, D.C.: U.S. Government Printing Office.

Rohatyn, Felix. 1980. "The Coming Emergency and What Can Be Done About It." *New York Review of Books* (December 4): 20-26.

Rossi, Peter H., Richard a Berk, and Bettye K. Eidson. 1974. *The Roots of Urban Discontent*. New York: Wiley.

Smith, Richard A. 1979. "Decision-Making and Non-Decision Making in Cities: Some Implications for Community Structural Research." *American Sociological Review* 44: 147-161.

Sternheimer, Stephen. 1979. "Modernizing Administrative Elites: The Making of Managers for Soviet Cities." *Comparative Politics* 11: 403-423.

Tabb, William K. 1978. "The New York City Fiscal Crisis," pp. 241–266, in William Tabb and Larry Sawers, eds. *Marxism and the Metropolis.* New York: Oxford University.

Taubman, William. 1973. *Governing Soviet Cities.* New York: Praeger.

Tilly, Charles. 1974. "The Chaos of the Living City," pp. 86–107, in Charles Tilly, ed. *An Urban World.* Boston: Little, Brown.

U.S. National Resources Committee. 1937. *Our Cities.* Washington, D.C.: U.S. Government Printing Office.

Useem, Bert. 1980. "The Boston Anti-Busing Movement." *American Sociological Review* 45: 357–369.

Wald, Kenneth D. 1980. "The Electoral Base of Political Machines." *Urban Affairs Quarterly* 16: 3–30.

Walton, John. 1979. "Urban Political Movements and Revolutionary Change in the Third World." *Urban Affairs Quarterly* 15: 3–22.

Wolfinger, Raymond E. 1960. "Reputation and Reality in the Study of Community Power." *American Sociological Review* 25: 636–644.

Zech, Charles E. 1980. "Fiscal Effects of Urban Zoning." *Urban Affairs Quarterly* 16: 49–58.

Name Index

Subject Index